POLITICAL ACTION FOLLOWS POLITICAL PHILOSOPHY

★

MORE DISPATCHES FROM

THE HISTORY OF THE FUTURE

DR. ROBERT OWENS

WESTPHALIA PRESS
An imprint of Policy Studies Organization

Also from Westphalia Press

westphaliapress.org

POLITICAL ACTION FOLLOWS POLITICAL PHILOSOPHY

★

MORE DISPATCHES FROM
THE HISTORY OF THE FUTURE

Political Action Follows Political Philosophy
Dr. Robert Owens
All Rights Reserved © 2015 by Policy Studies Organization

Westphalia Press
An imprint of Policy Studies Organization
1527 New Hampshire Ave., NW
Washington, D.C. 20036
info@ipsonet.org

ISBN-13: 978-1-63391-230-4
ISBN-10: 1633912302

Cover and Interior design by Taillefer Long at Illuminated Stories:
www.illuminatedstories.com

Daniel Gutierrez-Sandoval, Executive Director
PSO and Westphalia Press

Updated material and comments on this edition
can be found at the Westphalia Press website:

www.westphaliapress.org

CONTENTS

★ INTRODUCTION ★

Political Action Follows Political Philosophy

The vast majority of human action reflects the thoughts, beliefs, and feelings of the actor. There have always been and there will always be those whose actions are erratic or divorced from reality. The actions of this small minority are best ascribed to pathology not philosophy. For the rest of us, we think therefore we are. What we think about today, we act upon tomorrow.

In the realm of political action this holds true. The philosophies propagated today may not bear fruit or even appear to germinate during the lifetime of those who share them. However, if they resonate with the thoughts, beliefs, and natures of others they will bring forth a harvest in due time.

The time and effort involved in producing a coherent and logical body of work in the field of political philosophy may feel like a fool's errand or wasted effort to the authors working away often without recognition, in seclusion, and never seeing the validity of their thoughts acknowledged by their peers or their intended audience. However, anyone involved in such an effort needs to have a long view and the fortitude to plant so that others may harvest.

Having prefaced my thoughts and illuminated my actions let me plant some seeds:

For my entire life, I have had Progressive instructors, politicians, friends, and relatives admonish me that the reason for subverting the greatest experiment in personal liberty, individual freedom, and economic opportunity in the History of humanity is that we need to provide for the less fortunate. They often refer to providing some type of economic security for those who cannot provide for themselves. They often mean the leveling of society so that there is a minimum level of economic security.

The problem with "economic security" is that the term is so vague. How do we know when it has been achieved? Much like a war on terror it is open ended and can be interpreted in many ways. What is considered economic security to one may not be to another.

If by economic security we mean security with regard to physical needs and a minimum amount of food that is one thing. If by economic security we mean the guarantee of a certain standard of living or a pre-assigned social status, we are speaking of something else altogether.

It seems clear that any society which has achieved the levels of sophistication and civilization that we have should be able to provide for the basic needs of our citizens who cannot take care of themselves without endangering the freedom of all. There will be debates as to the levels of help which should be provided; however, as to the belief that we should not allow our fellow citizens to starve or freeze, I believe we are all agreed.

These questions will undoubtedly cause political debate, and they may even cause tempers to flare; however, that there is some minimum standard all will agree. These minimum standards of economic security can be provided to those who cannot provide for themselves without endangering the wider economy and without unduly infringing upon the liberty of the productive members of society.

However, any attempt to guarantee the pre-assigned social status of anyone, or any group, the attempt to provide for those who can provide for themselves and choose not to do so will inevitably cause so many dislocations in the economy and require so many regulations wherein both personal freedom and economic opportunity will be severely restricted.

This is where the debate heats up. We have those who believe our society can and should protect and provide for those who cannot protect and provide for themselves and those who wish to use social welfare for social engineering.

The levels of taxation and regulation needed to support the minimalist approach can easily be borne by our society and our economy without compromising our freedom if they are applied evenly and fairly. A flat tax without loopholes, subsidies, or any of the other trappings of crony capitalism does nothing to inhibit innovation, enterprise, or competition. Regulations requiring the equal treatment of individuals or the setting of safety or access levels likewise do not detract from opportunity as long as they are universally applied.

However, to attain the maximized levels of central planning required to impose a Utopian vision of equality of outcome on any society requires so many regulations and such high levels of taxation that they effectively strangle innovation, enterprise, and competition.

Why couldn't that gigantic prison house of nations, the USSR, compete with the United States?

Because they professed to seek a society wherein everyone was equal at all times. Did they accomplish it? No, the ruling Communists simply replaced the ruling hereditary aristocracy. They killed millions to improve life. They destroyed the incentive and creativity of their people in an effort to produce a more productive economy by fiat instead of freedom. They eventually made working for the collective so meaningless that a common saying was, "They pretend to pay us, so we pretend to work." Citizens ended up with worthless money, empty stores, and services such as healthcare that only worked for the privileged government workers. In any society that robs Peter to pay Paul, eventually everyone changes their name to Paul.

As dire as the results have always been for Utopian experiments, it is the morality of attempting to level society that needs to be questioned. I contend that competition is a fundamental quality of humanity. Striving to improve and to provide for our self and our families are basic instincts, and when governments interfere with these in an effort to ensure the success of some they have to limit the success of others.

This has a butterfly effect where a regulation for a positive action here about this affects something else negatively over there about that. Multiply this many thousands of times and we have a cascading effect that restricts opportunity except for those who direct the effort to achieve the equality of all. Or as the last remaining commandment at Orwell's *Animal Farm* eventually said, "All animals are equal, but some animals are more equal than others." [1]

No one is as smart as everyone. No set of central planners seeking the improvement of some can substitute their decisions for the millions of decisions made by free individuals seeking their own improvement. It just won't work. It never has, and it never will. Therefore, I contend that if it is inherently detrimental to society as a whole and since it is impossible to achieve it is immoral to attempt.

Man was created with free choice. This is fundamental to our nature. Therefore, what goes against that nature is contrary to the truth of who man is or is meant to be.

That the darker side needs to be restrained is generally agreed. Every society condemns murder. Even thieves have a code; at home they know theft is wrong. Children should be protected and provided for as should those who cannot protect or provide for themselves. No people have prospered or advanced by leaving their poor to starve or their sick to die.

Likewise, no people have ever successfully built a society on the pipe-dream of equality of outcome. All that has ever produced is the fever dream of a socially engineered stagnant society where the government picks winners and everyone except the choosers and the chosen few end up as losers.

The idea that man is meant to be free, birthed this country. No matter how far we fall beneath the Progressive avalanche of regulation, taxation, and corruption, this idea will one day once again take flight. As long as there are those who will propagate the philosophy, the action will one day follow. Just as sure as a sunrise always follows the darkest night, someday a free America will rise from the ash heap of History to which socialism inevitably leads.

The following Dispatches from the History of the Future convey the basic political philosophy which I believe will one day re-inspire our nation to stride upon the stage of History with another round of liberating political action.

Keep the faith. Keep the peace. We shall overcome.

Dr. Robert R. Owens

DISPATCH ONE

A Declaration of Independence

It has happened just as foretold. The Progressive Republicans have joined with their Democrat fellow-travelers and once again sold our inheritance for a bowl of promises. We voted for an end to the out of control spending and what did we get? Three and a half trillion[1] steps closer to the abyss. It's time to admit that when you fall off a cliff it doesn't matter much if you were pushed or if you walked. The fall might not be so bad but that sudden stop at the end isn't so good.

Maybe it's just me but I'm tired of the same old same old in our politics. The big-box monopoly parties have morphed into two sides of the same coin. Today we choose between the Conservative Progressives' policies of tax and spend, infringe personal liberty, and outsource our sovereignty or the Liberal Progressives' policies of tax and spend, in-fringe personal liberty, and outsource our sovereignty. We've been caught on the horns of a dilemma trying to choose between Tweedledee and Tweedledum, and since we don't want to throw our vote away we must vote for one of the big boys after which the campaign promises dissolve and we're hung out to dry.

As a voter I've had my Damascus Road Experience. The scales have fallen from my eyes. I've reached the point where I would rather vote for someone who might actually try finding another way to operate our government besides taxing like the Sun King and spending like a drunken sailor whose credit card limit is constantly raised and who can print his own money.

It's time to stop talking. It's time to take action. The Founders of our nation dedicated their lives, their fortunes, and their sacred honor to birth our state and this noble experiment. It's time for us to do the same. This nation was conceived as a representative republic designed to operate on democratic principles. For over 100 years the Progressives have worked to transform the land of the free and the home of the brave into a People's Democratic Republic. What's the difference? The difference between a Democracy and a People's Democracy is "the difference between a jacket and a straightjacket."[2]

How did we arrive at the current situation?

James Madison our fourth president and the chief architect of the U.S. Constitution said, "There are more instances of the abridgement of the freedom of the people by the gradual and silent encroachment of those in power, than by violent and sudden usurpation."[3] We didn't get here all in one jump. First the camel said, "Can I just stick my nose in your tent to stay warm?" and finally the generous man found himself out in the cold as the camel settled down for a nice warm nap, one inch at a time.

The compassion of our people built a safety net for those who needed help and the greed of the lazy turned it into a hammock. America, the Land of the Free is being transformed[4] into an America that is dedicated to the unsustainable achievement of, from each according to their abilities to each according to their need.[5] When you rob Peter to pay Paul eventually Peter changes his name to Paul and the house of cards[6] tumbles down.

The willingness to share our heritage led America to welcome more immigrants each year than the rest of the world combined,[7] and the abuse of our generosity turned into a migration invasion that threatens to overwhelm us and destroy the future of our children. Taxes imposed to meet the ever-swelling demands of government have turned into a blatant, wealth re-distribution[8] program that makes most pyramid schemes look fair. It's as if our predatory government looks at a productive citizen as merely a source of residual income. Or as the ads promise, our Progressive leaders lay on the beach of self-importance and our checks just keep pouring in. We're no longer respected as Citizens. Instead, we're coveted as consumers or human capital.

It's time for action.

We as citizens who love our country must break the logjam caused by an imperial presidency, an abdicating legislature, an activist court, a suffocating bureaucracy, and the strangulation of regulation. The constant growth of government destroys freedom for "as government expands liberty contracts."[9]

It's time to actively work for America's acceptance of a different way.

And what might this different way be?

Something radical, something that almost strains the bounds of the imagination, something that would immediately unleash the bent-up energy of a free people: a return to constitutionally limited government!

But how do we get there from here? We need to build a new party to win the reins of government from the two-headed bird of prey which has assumed perpetual power through perpetual re-election. What we need now are citizens willing to sacrifice their repose and enter the arena. We need non-professionals to clean up the mess and right the ship of state.

What we don't need is one more election where the Conservative Progressives replace the Liberal Conservatives because as Albert Einstein said, "Insanity is doing the same thing over and over again and expecting different results."[10]

We need a new party. We must work to unite the Tea Party Movement with the many splinter parties which hold the same basic values. We must reclaim our liberty from the professional politicians and professional radicals who have manipulated the system to achieve unlimited power which they use to spend us into insolvency, tax us into poverty,[11] and regulate[12] us into serfdom.

This new party must siphon off all the conservatives who are members of the twin party out of habit or family tradition. This new party must rise fast and work hard. It must capture the center and the right declaring boldly that it will defend what America stands for but not necessarily all that stands for America. The time has come to fight for the right before we are swallowed by the wrong.

Winston Churchill said, "If you will not fight for the right when you can easily win without bloodshed, if you will not fight when your victory will be sure and not so costly, you may come to the moment when you will have to fight with all the odds against you and only a precarious chance for survival. There may be a worse case. You may have to fight when there is no hope of victory, because it is better to perish than to live as slaves."[13]

We can't let divisions divide us or else they will bury us. United we stand, divided we fall. None of us can do this alone but together we can.

Keep the faith. Keep the peace. We shall overcome.

DISPATCH TWO ✪

"A NICKEL ISN'T WORTH A DIME TODAY"[1]

On September 22, 2011 in a speech to business executives Navy Adm. Mike Mullen, Chairman of the Joint Chiefs of Staff said, "Debt is the biggest threat to U.S. national security."[2] When the leader of the people famous for $800[3] hammers and $640[4] toilet seats has to lecture business leaders about the perils of deficit spending we know capitalism in America has jumped the track.

After World War I the world's monetary system was in disarray. The victorious allies sought to revive the gold standard. However the structure which had been put in place after 1918 collapsed during the Great Depression. Some economists believe that the world's attempt to remain on the gold standard prevented central banks from expanding the money supply enough to revive the world's economies.

After World War II, representatives of the once again victorious allies met at Bretton Woods, New Hampshire to create a new international monetary system. At that time the United States accounted for more than 50% of the world's manufacturing capacity and also held most of the world's gold. Since America was the uncontested economic Superpower these leaders decided to tie world currencies to the dollar. The value of the dollar would in turn be controlled and supported by the fact that the dollar would be tied to gold at $35 per ounce.

While the Bretton Woods System[5] was in force the central banks were given the task of maintaining fixed exchange rates. This was accomplished by massive and continuous intervention in foreign exchange markets. When a country's currency became too expensive in relation to the dollar, that country's central bank would sell its currency for dollars thus driving down the value of its currency. But if the value of a country's money became too low, that country would then aggressively buy its own currency to drive the price up.

This Bretton Woods System worked well until 1971. By then, due to the "Guns and Butter"[6] economic policies of the Johnson and Nixon administrations, inflation in the United States and America's rapidly expanding trade deficit undermined the value of the dollar. As a result America urged the now recovered and economically powerful Germany and Japan to increase the value of their currencies. Both nations did not want to do this. Raising the value of their currencies hurt their exports by increasing the prices for their goods in the United States which was their largest market.

United States and the other major economic powers agreed to a new system known as Managed Float.[8] This Managed or Dirty Float meant that central banks would still intervene with the buying and selling of their own currencies to eliminate any changes that might be perceived as too dramatic.

How long will this system of floating money, fiat currency, and systemic debt last?

Since I started with a quote from my favorite American philosopher, Yogi Berra I will frame my comments about the end result of America's love affair with monopoly money and ever growing debt[9] with another nugget from this source of double think profundity, "It's tough to make predictions, especially about the future."[9]

You know, I know and anyone who has enough economic awareness to realize you can't spend more than you make forever knows that our present governmental financial framework is unsustainable. Why? Apparently our leaders believe you can spend more than you make forever.

If you have ever tried to manage your Visa payments by charging them to MasterCard you know the end of that game. Our leaders have pawned our grandchildren's future for the votes they buy with social programs, tax giveaways, and bail-outs. However it is hard to lay all the blame on the shoulders of the perpetually re-elected. The government is the people writ large. Almost every household in America is in debt. Almost every business in America is in debt.

Debt is not a bad thing in and of itself. Actually it is one of the most liberating inventions in the world. It allows economic activity to grow based upon future activity instead of just on current holdings. This provides a multiplier effect that has given rise to the modern world.

However, when we spend more of the future than the present can service we have inverted the pyramid and are inviting a correction. Even if the Corporations Once Known as the Mainstream Media are blathering on about how good the stock market is doing, that the pretend unemployment rate is falling, that there is no inflation, and that the President says everything is getting better, the alternative media knows the present course is unsustainable. Unsustainable! That word is spoken day after day on Fox and printed multiple times every day online from thousands of blogs, magazines, and newspapers. All it means is it can't last forever, or as an alarmist might say, "A crash is coming!"

Sure the stock market is flying high. With the Fed pumping multiple billions a month into the banking system and with interest rates near 0 why wouldn't it? With that kind of money coming in why not play the Lotto? Sure the unemployment rate is falling as long as you don't count the people who have quit looking for a job. Sure there's no inflation as long as you don't count energy or food. And of course the President says everything is getting better all the time which is what his teleprompter tells him to say.

So, how long will this system of floating money, fiat currency, and systemic debt last?

None of us gets to live in the world we grew up in because the world moves too fast. Things change. What was science fiction yesterday is your cell phone today. One thing we can know for sure is that it isn't over till it's over.[10] Yet from a realistic evaluation of the deep hole, we have spent ourselves into the future isn't what it used to be[11] and if the world were perfect it wouldn't be.[12]

Is there any way to stop this train wreck before we hit the wall? Can we reign in Washington and stop the 6.85 million per minute that the best and the brightest are spending? What do you think? The great Tea Party victory of 2010 affirmed Boehner as the leader of the co-opted opposition who promptly voted for multiple debt ceiling increases, and renewed the Patriot Act. Do you think another Progressive Republican has a chance to beat Hillary or would make any difference if they did? I wish I had an answer to that because I'm tired of answering the question.[13] What do you think?

★ DISPATCH THREE ★

A WORD TO THE WISE

The most insidious result that central planning and the overabundance of government control that it requires is not the maladjustments that it inevitably creates in the economy. It is not the crony capitalism and bureaucratic nepotism that it always fosters. It is not the smothering blanket of nanny-state regulations that strangle creativity. It is not even the tendency to one-party rule even when camouflaged behind a two party system that is in reality two heads of the same bird of prey. It is not a system which may actually contain only two parties if you believe there is a court party and a country party.[1]

No, none of these missteps on the way to an illusionary utopia are the most insidious result of any system no matter what it is called that is some variation on the socialist theme of "From each according to their ability and to each according to their need."[2] Instead the most insidious result of the effort by some to control all is a change in the character of the people.

When government regulation becomes an all-embracing web of minutia that requires lawyers, accountants, and other translators of government-speak to comprehend, when safety-nets become hammocks, and when the do-gooders believe that they know what is best for everyone reaches a tipping point people begin to expect others to do for them what they used to do for themselves. A nation of self-reliant, go-getters can be changed into a sea of slugs on the dole constantly crying and voting for more.

The descendants of the pilgrims and the pioneers are content to wait for their government check[3] and their food stamps[4] as long as there is a game on their flat screen and minutes left on their obamaphone.[5] Militant apathy has ossified the sinews of a once great people. So many people don't care about anything beyond their creature comforts, the most basic of which are guaranteed, that the will to succeed has been squashed.

When you guarantee success and everyone gets a trophy just for showing up few will strive to do more than is required. When success is punished by the ridicule of the media and the inequality of government policies such as a progressive income tax that says, "The more you make the more we take" few will strive to do more than is required. When college entrance quotas and set-asides say, "We don't seek the best and the brightest we look at race and gender to pick the winners and losers" few will strive to do more than is required. When government subsidies and tax-breaks say, "If you have connections the government will hold back the crushing reality of the market at tax-payers' expense" few will strive to do more than is required.

Today in America we are surrounded by low-information voters who either don't pay any attention to affairs beyond their life or who get their news exclusively from the Progressive-controlled Corporations Once Known as the Mainstream Media. Their opinions are scripted for them by the Progressive group-think of corporate hacks constantly building a narrative to advance their Utopian agenda. If it doesn't fit it doesn't print. If they don't like what you say it will never play. America's once dynamic free press transformed into a one-sided monologue reciting over and over, "Government knows best."

Our government-controlled and increasingly standardized education system works hard to say as some of my students have; "a 'D' is good enough." Or, "At our school we receive an attendance diploma it just means we were there it don't mean we learned anything." Assignments such as I witnessed in a 12th grade Political Science class, "Watch Michael Moore's film, 'Fahrenheit 9/11' and then write an essay on how many ways Bush lied to trick us into invading Iraq" show indoctrination has in many places swallowed education. Circumstances such as these tend to stifle those who would drive innovation and promote those who are just along for the ride, and pass the mediocre while holding back the brilliant.

We have moved from a capitalist system to a mixed economy[6] and now under a president who promised to fundamentally transform America[7] we are lurching into a socialist system in all but name that seeks to ensure equality of result instead of the equal opportunity which has traditionally been the seedbed of America's meritocracy. We have transitioned from a small limited government, a representative republic that operates on democratic principles into an all-powerful central government that operates through a massive bureaucracy. Executive orders[8] are used to make end-runs around Congress and the Constitution. Unconstitutional and illegal recess appointments are used to avoid[9] the scrutiny of a Senate confirmation. Our borders are for all intents and purposes open[10] like an automatic door at Wal-Mart. Forgetting what Ronald Reagan told us, "A nation without borders is not a nation."[11]

Norman Thomas, an early Socialist candidate for President said, "The American people will never knowingly adopt socialism. But, under the name of 'liberalism' they will adopt every fragment of the socialist program, until one day America will be a socialist nation, without knowing how it happened."[12] And as Lenin said, "Socialized Medicine is the Keystone to the Arch of the Socialist State."[13]

Step-by-step we have journeyed from being a people birthed in rebellion against tyranny, a people who founded the world's first experiment in a government of the people, by the people and for the people. Until a nation founded upon a written constitution which guaranteed limited government, personal liberty, and economic freedom has become just another failed utopia that is spending itself into oblivion as the band plays, "let the good times roll."

At a time like this it is good to remember some of the wisdom of those who have gone before:

Noah Webster said, "There is no nation on earth powerful enough to accomplish our overthrow. Our destruction, should it come at all, will be from the inattention of the people to the concerns of their government."[14]

Alexis de Tocqueville said, "The American Republic will endure, until politicians realize they can bribe the people with their own money."[15]

Benjamin Franklin said, "When the people find that they can vote themselves money that will herald the end of the republic."[16]

Barry Goldwater said, "A government that is big enough to give you all you want is big enough to take it all away."[17]

AND

Alexander Tyler said, "A democracy is always temporary in nature; it simply cannot exist as a permanent form of government. A democracy will continue to exist up until the time that voters discover that they can vote themselves generous gifts from the public treasury. From that moment on, the majority always votes for the candidates who promise the most benefits from the public treasury, with the result that every democracy will finally collapse due to loose fiscal policy, which is always followed by a dictatorship."[18]

A word to the wise they say is sufficient.

DISPATCH FOUR

ARE THE STATES OUT OF DATE?

The people of the founding generation did not think of Americans as Americans. They did not see them as one people but instead as citizens of the various states. Even as late as the Civil War, people such as Robert E. Lee, who disagreed with secession and wanted a united United States, left because his State seceded and not because he suddenly wanted Virginia to be another country. Another example of the feelings of many in the founding generation was the fact that the term "We the People of the United States" that opens the Preamble to the Constitution[1] caused great controversy during the ratification debates. It was pointed out as a blatant attempt to make the States irrelevant.

The Constitution was meant to improve the federation of the various States as created under the Articles of Confederation.[2] It was not meant to create anything new. This was stressed over and over by the supporters of the Constitution in the ratification debates. The Framers voted by State, and, though some of the Framers wouldn't sign the completed document, since it was adopted by all the States it was called unanimous. The ratification votes of the various conventions voted by State not as individuals. As provided in the original document the members of the Senate were not elected by the people at large. They were instead selected by the State legislatures. The House was designed to represent the people, and the Senate was designed to represent the States.

The Constitution never would have been ratified without this provision designed to protect the States from losing their integrity as sovereign republics which had voluntarily joined together. This was essential and this was generally understood.

So when was our social contract[3] revised? How can a contract be unilaterally revised?

When did we agree to surrender our liberty in exchange for security? When did we agree to move from a voluntary federal republic to a centrally planned democracy? When did our freedom from warrantless searches morph into 360° surveillance? When and how were the guarantees found in the Bill of Rights turned inside out and upside down?

The scariest thing I see about all this as I travel around the country is not that our totalitarian wanabes will use any excuse and any subterfuge to undermine limited government for the benefit of their power and their crony capitalist's profit. No, that doesn't scare me or surprise me at all. What catches my attention is that as I speak to more and more people about this creeping corporatism the majority of them say things like, "I'm glad the government is watching out for terrorists" or "If you're not saying or doing anything wrong why should you care if the government listens in?"

Not only have Americans been dumbed down to the point where the majority of college freshmen need remedial studies, but these descendants of the pioneers have lost sight of the American Dream. Asked "What is the American Dream?" most citizens today will recite the pabulum spooned out by the Federal Reserve Bubble Machine, the political hacks who gave them power, and the Wall Street Casino that profits by the game: "The American Dream is to own your own Home."

That is not the American Dream! The American dream is limited government, personal liberty, and economic opportunity.

At what point do unilateral changes to a contract render it null and void?

It will still be called the United States of America. The stars and stripes will still wave, there will still be elections, and we will still hear that this is the freest most prosperous nation on earth as our freedom slips away and our opportunities shrink.

During the ratification debates it became clear that the Constitution would not be ratified unless there was a promise that the first order of business for the new government was going to be to amend the document to state some things that a majority of people thought were missing. The promise was made and the first 10 amendments were added. Today we call this our Bill of Rights. While some people can recite all of them and many more can recite a few almost every American knows they exist. The Bill of Rights has a treasured place in the American heart.

Few if any know what was said in the Preamble to the Bill of Rights,[4] which is neither mentioned nor studied today. This sets out their purpose and is enlightening as a starting off point for understanding what they are and what we are losing.

"THE Conventions of a number of the States, having at the time of their adopting the Constitution, expressed a desire, in order to prevent misconstruction or abuse of its powers, that further declaratory and restrictive clauses should be added: And as extending the ground of public confidence in the Government, will best ensure the beneficent ends of its institution." The Bill of Rights was added in order to prevent misconstruction of the words of the document or the abuse of its power by the government to be established under the Constitution. This could not be possible unless the words of these amendments were supposed to mean what they say, not what black-robed partisans can interpret them to say.

The Bill of Rights was not written nor adopted in their order of precedence. The number 1 amendment requested by the States was set as the 10[th5] or capstone. "The powers not delegated to the United States by the Constitution, nor prohibited by it to the States, are reserved to the

States respectively, or to the people." In other words, all the citizens of the various States were concerned most that the central government does not run roughshod over the States which were the home republics closest to and controlled by the people. They feared that the central government would become a Leviathan, crushing dissent and smothering freedom.

And they never heard of the Internal Revenue Service (IRS) the National Security Agency (NSA) or the Environmental Protection Agency (EPA). They never imagined an unelected, appointed for life Supreme Court that would cancel amendments to State constitutions that were legally adopted according to the processes within those constitutions. Not since they had overthrown King George had they lived under the suffocating tyranny of a Patriot Act or rule by decree such as executive orders.

According to the amendment process[6] in the Constitution, the States can offer amendments to the Constitution by calling for a convention to propose such amendments. Many people are afraid of a convention believing that those who advocate for a limited government, personal liberty, and economic freedom could not carry the day and the Constitution would be altered in a negative way.

It is time to admit to ourselves that the Progressives have been and are changing their "Living Document" every day in countless ways: executive orders, regulations (from the EPA for example) and legislation (the 4th Amendment bending Patriot Act for example). We must face the fact the dam has broken and the foxes are guarding the hen house. The ship has sailed and the fix is in. We need a reset button before we slide completely into the abyss of totalitarianism. The flag will still fly, the national anthem still play, yet the land of the free and the home of the brave will be fundamentally transformed[7] into a centrally planned, regimented, surveillance state.

Once the scales have fallen from our eyes and we see that just because they call themselves liberals, people who want to control every aspect of everyone's lives are no more liberal than any of the other statists who have sought total control to impose their idea of utopia on anyone at any time in any place.

What we need is an American Spring. We need Americans to act like Americans and demand the freedom which is their birthright. Freedom is not just another word for nothing left to lose. We the people who believe in limited government, personal liberty and economic freedom have got to unite or we might end up joining a worldwide chorus singing, "And freedom, oh freedom well, that's just some people talkin' your prison is walking through this world all alone."

The center no longer holds. We must all work to influence our States, our home republics, to reign in the runaway Washington-centered bureaucracy machine before we are strangled in the red tape and buried in regulations.

The States must prove their relevance or perhaps the States are out of date.

DISPATCH FIVE

BRING THE MONSTER OUT

When taxes become destructive they surpass the consent of the governed bending to the will of tyranny. When regulations strangle competition instead of securing it from evil combinations they become counterproductive and defeat the very purpose for which they were proposed. When foreign entanglements bleed the nation but do not secure the peace or defeat the enemy they become interventionist vehicles for vested interests. When spending becomes a hemorrhaging of assets leading to national bankruptcy those who continue to pile debt upon debt seek not the good of the nation but instead its destruction. When leaders selected to unite instead do all they can to divide they no longer advance the interest of the whole and are instead partisan leaders in a factional fight.

A social contract[1] is the one made between a people and their government. It is an agreement whereby the people surrender certain aspects of their independence for the guarantee of corporate security and the enjoyment of a general welfare. In the case of most countries this is an unwritten and unconscious arrangement built upon tradition and precedent as in the case of England. However in the United States we have an actual contract: the Constitution. This was ratified by the original States, and the subsequent state was formed under it and each State after ratification joined as full and equal partners in the greatest experiment in human freedom in History. Each subsequent State was also recognized and admitted as a full partner. There are no junior States, all are equally sovereign within their own territory and all are equal in their relationship to the federal government.

All contracts may be legitimately changed over time as long as there are mechanisms either within the document or established by the document to do so. Within our Constitution there is an amendment process,[2] and it has been amended 27 times so far. Whether we agree with those amendments or not they have been legally ratified and accepted becoming part of the document. However, over the years our government structure has been changed, and our manner of life transformed more by the informal changes of passing generations and subsequent precedent than by the formal amendment process.

Nowhere in the Constitution is the central government given the power to wage unending undeclared war. Nowhere is the central government given the right to ignore the requirement to protect the states from invasion. Nowhere is there found any basis for executive orders, signing statements, or bureaucratic regulations having the force of law without legislative action by Congress.

Well-connected rabble rousers now say equality will not be achieved until everything is equal in everybody's house.[3] Leveling the playing field has finally thrown off its cloak of deceit and exposed itself as "from each according to their ability to each according to their need."[4] The professional civil rights entrepreneurs who've extorted vast amounts of personal wealth with threats of boycotts and demonstrations have been unmasked as the true purveyors of prejudice seeking to keep race and gender differences alive for their own benefit. Union bosses build political empires using the legally forced dues of members with more money spent on political activity than on member service. The union bosses ride in limousine comfort from board meetings to political rallies while their members lose jobs. The pensions of the bosses are golden parachutes while the pensions of the members are underfunded.

The Land of the Free is held captive, locked in a two-party system where both parties are merely two heads on the same bird of prey. Both parties are dedicated to more spending and bigger government. Both parties exploit gerrymandering of districts and overwhelming corporate donations to ensure a hierarchy of the perpetually re-elected using a seniority system to enhance their power. Legal barriers exist at every turn to stop any new parties from gaining access that might deflect the central government from its ever-increasing growth towards totalitarianism.[5]

When will enough be enough? When will citizens rise in their righteous indignation and demand not a New Deal[6] not a Great Society[7] a New Frontier[8] or a Fundamentally Transformed America[9] but instead their original deal. The one we wrested from the hands of the tyrant King George. The one we've fought to establish and defend from Yorktown to Kandahar, and the right of a free people to live as they choose, to work for their own benefit, and choose their own destiny. Free from the smothering governmental control which has been the lot of most people in most places since the beginning of time. When will the yoke of tyranny become too heavy to be borne? What will be the spark that lights the torches and brings the incensed villagers to the gate of the castle demanding, "Bring the monster out!" so that a stake can be driven through the heart of tyranny and freedom can return to the land?

When that day comes what will we the people do? Will we try to resurrect the government of old that ultimately brought us full circle, or will we be bold enough to forge anew the social contract and design better ways to ensure the beast of tyranny doesn't once again break the chains of restraint?

DISPATCH SIX

Bringing a Knife to a Gun Fight

Why isn't it pointed out by the pontificating talking heads that every recent mass murder in recent memory has occurred in a legally declared "Gun-Free"[1] zone? We might as well put signs in front of our schools, malls, army cafeterias and hospitals that say, "If you're a crazy person no one here is armed." Perhaps if we put a sign in front of these establishments that said, "Protected by Smith and Wesson" we would get better results?

How does anyone believe that disarming lawful citizens actually make lawful citizens safer?

Our fearless leaders are following the Progressive playbook to the letter. First and foremost "Never let a serious crisis go to waste."[2] Capitalizing on the tragedy caused by a sick person with a stolen gun these wannabe totalitarians see an opportunity to disarm their victims and are preparing to make a move. They realize they won't be able to outlaw the private ownership of guns in America all in one fell swoop. However, their strategy is always two steps forward one step back. This is the same strategy that has worked so well for them in capturing the education system, the media, and the two major political parties.

Now they bring their previous conquests to bear to help them achieve a long cherished goal of a defenseless America that they can shape into the shabby and dismal centrally-planned highly regimented socialist nightmare they portray as Utopia.

The education wing has given them a dumbed down populace who have never studied the Federalist Papers enough to know the Second Amendment wasn't written to protect hunters. It was written to ensure the American public could stand up to any tyrants who would ever attempt to step on the throat of freedom.

The Corporations Once Known as the Mainstream Media beat the drum everyday calling for gun control, bullet control, an end to the freedom to buy and sell legal firearms or anything else they can dream up that moves their Progressive heroes closer to their goal: a gun free zone around every lawful citizen. In the meantime their entertainment wing churns out the vilest filth filled with violence and mayhem in movies and games. At the same time these pious hypocrites make money providing examples of chainsaw massacres and other scenes of slaughter, walk around with private security and send their children to private schools with armed guards.

This has been accomplished in other lands. The Germans and the Russians were disarmed. Did that enhance their security? The Australians and the British have been disarmed. Has that enhanced their security? Does anyone seriously believe that criminals will not break gun laws? They are criminals. Breaking laws is what they do. Just as locks are only for honest people gun laws only disarm lawful citizens.

Should people who own guns keep them secure? Certainly! Should people with guns know how to safely use them? Certainly! Should we surrender our constitutionally guaranteed right to keep and bear arms?[3] Absolutely not. These rights have already been infringed upon to the point where in most places it is not legal for most citizens to keep let alone bear arms.

Instead of meekly sitting still while our rights suffer further erosion we the people need to let our representatives know that we will not suffer any more incremental subversion of our liberty. We must let them know in every way that we will not go gently into the long dark night. We will not stand as sheep to be sheared of the rights given to us by our creator, recognized in our Declaration of Independence, and carved into the stone of our Constitution.

The masses of sheeple who have been bred by generations of government paternalism and educational propaganda are clamoring to be shorn of yet more of their heritage. Their cheerleaders from the anchor desk to the late night variety shows and their idols on stage and CD are herding them to the shearing pens. If we stand still for executive orders that contradict the plain intent of the Constitution we will deserve whatever we receive.

Now is the time for all good men to come to the aid of their country. Now is the time for the patriot to say, "We have gone this far and no further." Freedom isn't free. It never has been and it never will be. If we want to preserve this land of liberty the time is coming when we will have to do whatever has to be done. And it might be time to live out some of the clichés we have used for so long:

Realize God created man, but it was Samuel Colt who made them equal as you keep your powder dry, locked, loaded, and determined not to bring a knife to a gun fight.

Keep the faith. Keep the peace. We shall overcome.

★ DISPATCH SEVEN ★

Can Learning the Truth Unlearn the Lie?

I have witnessed a teacher of Political Science in America require a class to watch Fahrenheit 911 by Michael Moore and then write an essay outlining how many ways President Bush lied to trick America into invading Iraq. If you don't find this assignment offensive you've already had you quota of Kool-Aid and you should step away from this article and dial 911. Tell them someone is about to tell you the truth and you aren't prepared for what that might do to your world-view.

Conversely when I say we should have listened to the Anti-Federalists, echoing the message of my book *The Constitution Failed*[1] I'm sure many who often turn to these dispatches from the History of the Future are ready to call the headquarters of the Vast Rightwing Conspiracy and report that poor old Dr. Owens has veered off the reservation.

I was once hired to teach history in a high school devoted to promoting the Socratic learning style using the works of the Enlightenment in the hopes of molding another generation akin to the Founders, critical thinkers dedicated to the proposition that liberty is the fountainhead of achievement. I was fired before the semester started because I did not hold the Founders in enough reverence believing as I do that they were mere men and not demigods infallible and universally inspired.

Don't get me wrong. I do believe that the Founders of American independence and the Framers of the Constitution were a unique collection of political geniuses who did their best to craft the vehicle for their posterity's benefit and for this nation's greatness. The limited government they founded allowed the forever pent-up abilities and longings of man to burst forth into the flowering of American Exceptionalism, the brilliance of the American experiment.

However, that experiment crashed upon the shoals when Abraham Lincoln and the newly birthed Republican Party decided to interpret the Constitution which had been freely entered into by sovereign States to say that no State could ever voluntarily leave even though this is not stated anywhere in the document. Having made that determination this minority government used the overwhelming majority they had in what was left of the Congress to shackle the power of the Industrial North to crush the seceding Agricultural South.

Slavery, which cannot be divorced from its evil nor defended in any way, provided the spark, the rallying cry, and the effective explanation for a war which shattered the myth of a federal republic composed of sovereign states.

Since that war between brothers our nation has inexorably grown from the vision expressed by Jefferson in the Declaration of Independence of a commonwealth of freemen into what is rapidly becoming a statist express highballing its way to the gulag of collectivist uniformity and shabby mediocrity. Gone is the meritocracy of the young republic. Gone is the equality of opportunity smothered in the cold dead grasp of the equality of outcome. Gone is the blind justice of a nation of laws devoured by the politically correct insanity of social justice. The Progressives and their coalition of mega-state lobbies have turned the protections of a Constitution written to limit government into a suicide pact wherein the nationalist federal government chooses open borders in contravention of federal law and States are condemned for passing laws which requires police to enforce the law.

It is time to think the unthinkable and to embrace the abhorrent conclusion that the Constitution has failed. It was meant to limit government. This is proven conclusively by the 10th Amendment which states, "The powers not delegated to the United States by the Constitution, nor prohibited by it to the States, are reserved to the States respectively, or to the people."[2] Without the promise of the immediate adoption of the first 10 amendments, the Bill of Rights, the Constitution would never have been ratified by a majority of the States. This important though neglected amendment says, and means that only those powers expressly delegated to the central government are legitimate not the endless multiplication of powers which allows that government to intrude into every aspect of our lives as it does today.

The very reason for a written Constitution was and is to limit the government created by that document to the powers expressly delegated not to open the door for interpretation and precedent to expand infinitely until all limits are gone. If that wasn't the intent why have a Constitution at all?

Though many trace the diversion from Republican purity to Theodore Roosevelt and the Progressives the truth is Hamilton set the stage for a big government. He fathered the movement away from a decentralized federation of free people agreeing to disagree so that compromise would leave enough space for liberty to bloom. John Marshall the second Chief Justice of the Supreme Court manufactured the power of judicial review by exploiting political factions clearing the path for the rule of unelected black robed aristocrats with the power to turn a country of laws into a country of men.

This history lesson may not make my fellow Patriots glow with the satisfaction derived from accepting the Constitution as inviolable scripture received from on high. However, our current decent into the Progressive's transformed America[3] should make every lover of liberty ready to embrace the truth. The only question remaining: Can learning the truth unlearn the lie?

DISPATCH EIGHT

Choose This Day Who You Will Serve

In our current confrontation with Radical Islam the battle lines are portrayed as those between a secular society, us and a religious society, them. I reject this portrayal as a betrayal of the faith of our Founders and of those patriotic Americans who still hold fast to Jesus as God and Savior, we too are a religious people.

America was founded as a Christian country. Anyone who denies that has not studied enough History or has been sadly misled. Columbus accentuated his desire to spread the Christian faith[1] to his patrons the King and Queen of Spain and in his log.[2] The first thing that the English did upon landing at Jamestown was to set up a cross to dedicate their endeavor to Jesus their Savior. Were these early explorers and colonists always true to their faith? Did they always operate under principles derived from God's Word? Sadly they did not. However, to say that the Christian faith was not an integral part of their motivation and worldview is simply not true.

In the latter part of the twentieth century Progressive leaders pushing a collectivist agenda decided to declare us a pluralistic society.[3] They sought to detach the heavily Bible influenced Constitution into the dustbin of History by substituting what they call a living constitution for the rock-solid one the Framers bequeathed us. Mr. Obama, the quintessential Progressive in his speech to the Muslims of Egypt, Turkey, and many places spices up his apology tours[4] by asserting that America is not a Christian country.[5] This statement of his belief and goal does not make it true.

Keeping all of these recent changes aside, most Americans still believe in God[6] and the majority[7] consider themselves Christians. As a Christian, an Historian, and a Political Scientist in response to numerous questions I would like to share my beliefs concerning government, economies, and the rights of man.

As far as a government goes the only Biblically correct one is that God is God and we are His people. He is the King and we are the sheep of His pasture. As concerning an economic system God's economy knows no lack and is exceedingly abundantly provisioned by the owner of the cattle on a thousand hills.

This being true I do not believe that God mandates any type of human government or economic system as pre-ordained, sanctified, or holy. However, I do believe that humanity as God has created it does require certain governmental and economic conditions to develop and thrive as God intended.

God created us in His own image. He gave us the power to create and to choose. He gave us a mind open to learning and ever eager to improvise. He also gave us what I believe is the most crucial aspect of our make-up: our free will or the power to choose. We can choose to follow Him and do what He desires, or we can choose to follow the leadings not only of our thoughts but of our emotions also. In other words we can dwell within the Kingdom of God wherein He is our King and we are His people or we can choose to live in the Kingdom of man and become the subjects of either our own designs or of whoever manages to gain control of the physical world around us.

If God wanted slaves or robots He could have created slaves or robots. Instead He created us and gave us a mind to think and a will to choose because He wanted us to decide to love Him and follow Him freely without compulsion. Therefore I believe that since free thought and free choice are the foundation of man's nature freedom is necessary if man is to live as God designed. This being the case I believe that any governmental or economic system that denies man's freedom interferes with and attempts to supplant God's plan, the definition of evil.

There are of course limits to freedom as expressed in the Ten Commandments. Beyond this we should be free to choose our own way. Will we follow God or will we follow man. Within these limits and building on the moral framework the Bible provides I believe that a republic based upon the commitment to life, liberty, and the pursuit of happiness using democratic principles is the governmental structure which most closely matches man's God-given nature. I also believe that free market capitalism is the economic system which best allows man to develop and live as God intended. Conversely, when man rejects God and seeks to create his own utopia he builds some sort of centrally planned command economy and the intrusive government needed to impose it upon others.

A free economy and the free government it requires allows the independent choices of many to produce the greatest prosperity for all as everyone seeks to do the best they can because they reap the rewards. In a socialist or any type of hybrid economy between capitalism and socialism bureaucrats make the decisions and stagnation is the inevitable result. As Gary North, a Christian economist expresses it, "The essence of Democratic Socialism is this re-written version of God's commandment: 'Thou shalt not steal, except by majority vote.'"[8] Or as Winston Churchill observed, "Socialism is a philosophy of failure, the creed of ignorance, and the gospel of envy, its inherent virtue is the equal sharing of misery."[9] And that is not life as God intended.

If we look at History it is an outworking of the initial fall of man. In the beginning God created the world including man and it was all good. Then at the dawn of our existence we choose to go our own way instead of following God. We chose to follow the siren song of "You shall be like God" and ever since we have attempted to create heaven on earth. All we have succeeded in doing is to open the gates of Hell instead. A case in point would be the age-old question, if God is good why is there evil in the world followed by the age-old answer God gave us free choice and we chose evil.

With the help and guidance of those who seek to play god themselves humanity has often been convinced to surrender their freedom for security, to bargain away their God-given nature and assume the subservient nature of slaves.

In America the purveyors of socialism cloak their designs in the language of populism. They loudly proclaim that they seek a fair deal for everyone, except of course for the people they intend to loot. They want fair elections as long as nothing is done to stop fraudulent voting. They want equality enforced by unequal treatment. In other words they seek to build the kingdom of man where they can be king.

We have a mind to think and the capacity to make a free choice. As the day of reckoning draws near all I can recommend is, think and choose. We can choose to follow the path of redistribution, class warfare, and collectivist dependency or we can choose to at least attempt a return to limited government, personal liberty, and economic freedom. Don't be fooled by the progressive media and their obvious bias. To be free is God's design. For us to be a slave to dependency is man's.

One of America's most beloved troubadours told us, "The words of the prophets are written on the subway walls and tenement halls"[10] and one of those secular prophets he was referring to reminded us "You're gonna have to serve somebody, yes indeed You're gonna have to serve somebody, Well, it may be the devil or it may be the Lord But you're gonna have to serve somebody."[11]

Or as my favorite book says it, "And if it seems evil to you to serve the LORD, CHOOSE FOR YOURSELVES THIS DAY WHOM YOU WILL SERVE, WHETHER THE GODS WHICH YOUR FATHERS SERVED THAT *were* on the other side of the River, or the gods of the Amorites, in whose land you dwell. But as for me and my house, we will serve the LORD."[12]

Did You Do Anything to Keep Liberty Alive?

One day our grandchildren may ask us this question. Will we have an answer that will make us and them proud or will we have to sit silent knowing we stood silent when it was time to speak or remained passive when it was time for action? Now is the time for all believers in limited government to stand up and be counted. Now is the time for all who believe, "that all men are created equal, that they are endowed by their Creator with certain unalienable rights that among these are life, liberty and the pursuit of happiness"[1] to remember "That to secure these rights, governments are instituted among men, deriving their just powers from the consent of the governed."

The 2014 mid-term elections may well be the most important in our lifetime. America faces a crisis as profound as the Revolution and as divisive as the Civil War. This has been brought on by the Progressives who seek to fundamentally transform[2] America through evolutionary means. Incrementally, one entitlement program, one regulation, and one tax rate increase at a time, these Evolutionaries have used class warfare, activist judges, a politically-correct education system, and a complicit media to create a dependent constituency. They've constructed a matrix of sports addiction, celebrity worship, and recreational prescription medicine that makes the bread and circuses of Rome appear as crude as they were effective. Welcome to the Brave New World.

In 2008 the Progressives achieved what the media called a "Veto Proof" majority in both houses. This was typical of the Progressive-controlled media's spin. With a fellow Progressive holding court in the

White House there was no chance the long-cherished dreams of national healthcare, massive interference in the economy, and expansion of the bureaucracy would be vetoed. The description of the majorities should have been "Filibuster-proof" meaning there was no way for the minority party to thwart the will of the majority. Even when the Democrats lost their 60th seat in the Senate with the addition of a Progressive Republican taking Teddy Kennedy's seat, they still had a filibuster-proof majority. The only reason they did not achieve more of their agenda such as amnesty for illegal immigrants is that members of their own party balked at a complete surrender of our heritage.

Fast forward and after several years of the 2010 Tea Party led re-capture of the House Nancy Pelosi and her troops are chomping at the bit to finish their Evolution and drive the final nails in the coffin of limited government.

Those who wish to stop the mad rush into the arms of an all-embracing federal government must register! They must vote! They must do all they can to influence anyone and everyone to elect a true veto-proof majority with the power and the will to reverse the slide into insolvency, which will trigger either a default upon our overwhelming debt or a collapse of our economy. Either of which opens the door for the current administration to impose their statist solutions irrevocably altering the nature of the United States. The name will remain the same but let no illusions of normalcy cloud your sight; this will be a new nation, the Obamanation.

In the coming mid-term elections it is imperative that those who wish to reverse course send a veto-proof majority in both the House and the Senate to Washington or President Obama will block every attempt to return to the traditional American model of limited government. And even if this happens the newly awakened Patriots must realize their victory will energize the portion of the country desiring a European-style welfare state. They must realize just as Truman in 1948 ran against the

"Do-nothing Congress"[3] more than against Tom Dewey and Clinton in 1996 ran against the "Mean-spirited"[4] Congress more than against Bob Dole, in 2014 Mr. Obama and his surrogates will run against the "Obstructionist"[5] Congress more than against any individual opponents the Republicans might nominate.

The Town Hall meltdowns of 2009 and the Tea Party phenomenon of 2010 have surged across America as no spontaneous movement has in many years. The energy and enthusiasm of this grassroots explosion has rocked primaries from Coast-to-Coast. The political establishment in both parties were bracing for a tsunami of popular indignation at the ballot-box in 2012. Instead the Republicans nominated another Progressive which left the conservative base sitting on the sidelines.

The Republicans managed to hold the House leaving the Democratic Senate Majority Leader to lead well-disciplined troops in blocking every move the Conservatives make, and the media will hang the ensuing deadlock squarely around the neck of the Tea Party.

In 2014 to make sure that the rising Tea Party Samson successfully pulls down both the House and the Senate pillars of the Temple of Progressivism, the novice Conservative political activists need to understand voting is not enough. We need to exert every ounce of influence among friends, neighbors, and family to bring out an historic vote. We should stand ready to drive people to the polls, work the polls, do anything we can to plant the flag of Liberty once again in the capital of the Land of the Free and the Home of the Brave.

Turning to the Word of God we're counseled, "If My people who are called by My name will humble themselves, and pray and seek My face, and turn from their wicked ways, then I will hear from heaven, and will forgive their sin and heal their land."[6] Our Founders declared, when tyranny raises its head and when a government founded to ensure the rights of citizens begins to trample upon those rights their descendants should remember, "That whenever any form of government becomes destructive to these ends, it is the right of the people to alter or to abolish it, and to institute new government, laying its foundation on such principles and organizing its powers in such form, as to them shall seem most likely to affect their safety and happiness."[7]

As peaceful citizens let those who love Liberty use their guaranteed rights to write, speak, assemble, and vote to preserve what we've been given for our children and our grandchildren. Let every politician know, whether they wish us well or ill, that "we shall pay any price, bear any burden, meet any hardship, support any friend, oppose any foe, in order to assure the survival and the success of liberty."[8] If we will do this, then it's our time upon the stage we'll take a stand beside the Founders, the Framers, and the Greatest Generation when our children or grandchildren ask us, "Did you do anything to keep liberty alive?" we will be able to say more than, "I didn't notice what was going on," or "I couldn't find the remote."

DISPATCH TEN

Does Equality Mean We are All the Same?

In the Declaration of Independence[1] a new thing entered the world, a country founded upon the idea of equality. The Old World consisted of societies built upon hereditary class and entrenched privilege. Beginning with words that still burn within the breast of Patriots, this great document proclaims two types of equality.

Based upon the first clause, "We hold these truths to be self-evident, that all men are created equal," the first type is equality before the law.[2] We all stand before the bar of justice on the same footing. There aren't different laws for different classes. The definition of murder is the same for the homeless person, the mechanic and the billionaire. This equality, a natural part of our creation proclaims that neither classes nor other artificial divisions will ever be recognized in law or enshrined through legislation.

Based upon the second clause, "that they are endowed by their Creator with certain unalienable rights that among these are Life, Liberty and the pursuit of Happiness," the second type is equality of opportunity.[3] Everyone is entitled to their life and the fruits of it. Each of us has an equal right to the liberty of action, the freedom to choose our life's path and to make our own decisions. And each of us has the right to pursue happiness. In almost all other lists such as this from the period, many of them written into state constitutions by the same people who wrote the Declaration, this is the right to own property and the happiness here is assumed to mean the right to use our own talents and the things they gain for us for our own benefit as long as we do not injure nor hinder others.

These rights and the equality they express were later protected by the

Constitution. Congress shall not confer titles of nobility.[4]Congress shall not pass bills[5] of attainder[6] convicting groups or individuals without a trial. Through the use of these and other negatives the Framers sought to secure Americans the possession of the equality proclaimed by the Declaration. The Bill of Rights[7] went even further in declaring what Congress could not do in the attempt to guarantee the continued exercise of the equality granted by our Creator. The mechanism the Framers used to keep freedom alive was limiting government for they knew governments gain power by subtracting freedom from individuals.

However, it needs to be noted that the limitations placed upon government as a means of securing the equal rights of citizens in no way states that there should be a leveling of all people or that there will not continue to be distinctions and differences among them. This was never stated and never intended for the belief in or vision of a population with standardized talents, inclinations and goals does not match reality. There are as many different sets of these as there are people. In each individual, life should be open to choice. The only boundaries being that we do no harm nor proscribe the choice of others. This is the level playing field of creation, a pure equality of opportunity to be harvested in proportion to the Creator's gift of talents and our investment of time and effort.

As long as the role of government is limited, and as long as people are free to operate within the informal social arrangements of a non-regimented, non-stratified society there's no tension between equality of opportunity and liberty. This quest for equality of outcome has become a social goal adopted as a reason for destroying society as it is in the name of society as a small cadre of radicals thinks it should be. In the aftermath of economic or societal collapse, revolutionaries, or in the case of the American Progressives "Evolutionaries," will seek to erect in the place of popular government a bureaucratic tyranny devoted to leveling all to the lowest common denominator. Except of course for the levelers themselves who rise by deciding who gets what, and it's the deciders who always seem to get the most. For, some perceive that equality of all is not the same as the equality of some, or as the ruling pigs in George Orwell's novel, *Animal Farm* declare, "All animals are equal, but some animals are more equal than others."[8] This reflects the subversion of equality of opportunity into equality of outcome[9] or as it's termed by Progressives equal opportunity.

To build this monument to mediocrity the philosophers of progressivism subtly change the meaning of equality. Instead of the opportunity for all to succeed it becomes the certainty of everyone getting a trophy for showing up, a diploma for attendance or a check for not working. Built upon the premise that if all are created equal all should end up equal thus denying the goal of equality the chance to go as far and as fast as talent and hard work can lead.

★ DISPATCH ELEVEN ★

ECONOMICS 102

People avoid silence because they're afraid of what they might hear. Although we value our freedom of speech, polite conversation in America is subject to one crushing rule, "Don't talk about religion or politics!" Most of us were raised with this stifling warning in our ears. The purpose was to avoid arguments at the dinner table but the result is a population unconcerned in the two subjects affecting life the most. I can only talk about the weather for so long which displays the wisdom of memorizing sports stats and watching American Idol. With the two biggest topics off the table we're faced with either trivial pursuit or silence. Bored with the weather and having neglected my memorization and viewing options I propose a topic to stimulate vigorous conversation without causing any bickering: economics.

Barry, Harry, and Nancy knew they had to take us through-the-looking-glass while their iron grip on inside-the-beltway power was unchallenged. With no effective break on their power for the first two years, Congress moved so fast their yesterday became our tomorrow. That tomorrow is now today. The ruling party rammed their agenda through without one opposition vote. Every revolution needs an emergency to justify radical surgery and the economy was the emergency available. Consequently, these descendants of Franklin D. Roosevelt (FDR) and Lyndon B. Johnson (LBJ) shoved a raw deal down the throat of a great society.

Almost everyone is in agreement that the first stimulus failed. According to MSNBC, "In January, Obama's economic team predicted unemployment would rise no higher than 8% with the help of $787 billion in new government spending."[1] The President may see glimmers of hope[2] however the administration which ran on the slogan, "The worst economy since the Great Depression"[3] misread how bad the economy was.[4] How bad is it? What's worse than the Great Depression? What's their answer to this baddest of bad economies? What's their Plan B? Try Plan A again, and again, and again? I think what our leaders need as they drive the largest economy the world has ever known over the cliff is Economics 102, Macroeconomics or how an economy works.

Most people, including the best-government-money-can-buy, look at the economy as if it were controlled by magic having no idea where the rabbit goes or where the doves come from, and since I doubt I'll convince any of our all-knowing leaders to enroll in freshman macroeconomics I want to offer a crash course in Economic Reality.

1. Government regulations distort markets and inflate bubbles.
2. Every generation experiences at least one bubble and at least one bust.
3. Every bubble bursts.
4. Every burst bubble is followed by a panic.
5. Panics inspire economic regulations.
6. Economic regulations reflect political ideologies not economic realities.
7. Economic regulations always regulate the excesses of the last bubble.
8. Economic regulations are always blind to the excesses of the next bubble.
9. Since consumption is the purpose for production any economic regulation that ignores this fact always leads to the misapplication of resources and the misdirection of effort.
10. Depressions are recessions with government help.
11. It is impossible to spend yourself into prosperity.
12. It is impossible to tax yourself into prosperity.
13. Higher taxes lead to smaller government revenue and black-markets.

The New Economy leads straight to the Second World, from freedom to conformity from capitalism to Obamanomics. Instead of a fair race with the rapidly transforming economies of Asia, America runs hobbled like a child in a three-legged race strapped to the stiff-legged ideas of collectivism.

Why would our leaders want us economically hobbled? What would they gain if we fall into the swamp of poverty engulfing most of the world? Wouldn't they be right there with us? Go to any Second or Third World country and you'll see the rich and powerful behind walls in gated-communities where they live in the First World while everyone else sits in the dust eating leaves. In America, we avoided this fate with the growth of a massive middleclass. Under assault with stagnant wages, rising prices, and disappearing jobs the middleclass is being outsourced. How is this being accomplished?

Remember the mantra of the Clintons? "It's the economy stupid!"[5] That's has always been the Progressive's strategy,[6] riding like a flea on a rat is cradle-to-grave social engineering in the guise of economic policy. The Progressives drive the economy into the ditch all the while saying it is someone else's fault and shrieking that we need more of what is causing the problem: bloated government and runaway spending. A lack of basic economic understanding is destroying the greatest economy ever forged. A zero-sum game causes divisions and arguments about who gets what when we all used to strive for the same thing: success by growing the pie.

America is splintering as the melting pot becomes a smelting pot. What is its cause? The divisiveness of class-warfare encouraged by the only people who win through America's split between red and blue, rich and poor, us and them. Who are they? If it isn't us I guess it's them.

DISPATCH TWELVE ★

★

EDUCATION IS THE FOUNDATION OF THE FUTURE

Have you ever asked yourself, "How can Progressives hate America? How can anyone who was raised in the most free and prosperous society in the History of the world believe America is an imperialistic power and the source of evil?"

If we can't understand our adversary we may defeat them, but we will never know what it is that motivated them. This lack of understanding leaves us open to assault by the same forces in the future. If we wish not only to defeat the forces of Progressivism but also set America on the path to restoration we must understand the root cause of the Progressive delusion and modern Liberalism which Michael Savage has correctly labeled a mental illness[1] and I consider a Socially Transmitted Disease.

If you want to understand something it is necessary to learn where it came from and how it came to be. Even if President Obama was educated partially in his adopted country of Indonesia he is a prime example of the assembly-line progressive education that has become the norm in America today: bash America at every chance and cram the idea of a living constitution and the necessity for government intervention in every aspect of daily life.

We've all heard horror stories of the anti-American bilge being pumped into our youth in today's schools, so the following personal experiences shouldn't shock anyone too much.

As an educator I participated in a program that combined college and high school classes so that students could earn credit towards their high school diploma and at the same time work on an Associate Degree. I was happy to work in this program, and I helped many hardworking students earn their Associates

Degree at the same time they earned their high school diploma giving them a decided advantage when they went on for their Bachelor degree.

During the course of my years in the trenches of blended education I was in control of the college side of the class; however, I had no authority to stop the blatant dissemination of Progressive propaganda that made up the totality of some teachers' curriculum. While in the classroom I strive to present material in such a way as to lead students in the direction of critical thinking. I would present both sides and urge students to evaluate and come to their own conclusions. Many times after a semester of teaching Political Science students would come up and ask, "Now that the class is over tell us, which are you a conservative or a liberal?"

Many of my high school teacher colleagues were not so subtle. Here are two examples that were more the rule than the exception in many classes:

1. One Political Science class had the following assignment; watch Fahrenheit 9/11[3] by Michael Moore and then write an essay on how many ways President Bush lied to trick America into an unjust war.
2. In a History class the students were assigned to read Upton Sinclair's *The Jungle* and then write an essay on the dehumanizing effects of capitalism.[3]

The list of such blatant and crude attempts to mold our children into good little Progressives that I witnessed would fill a book on how not to teach, but this is nothing new. I am 66 years old and though not as out-in-the-open or in-your-face I was subjected to the same type of illiberal liberalism when I was a youngster in school.

In grade school I did encounter one History teacher who had been in the profession since before my father was born. She still thought that it was a good thing to teach American History as an objective subject instead of a vehicle for her own agenda. She inspired students to look at the evidence and think. She however was the exception. From Math to English and from Geography to

History teachers were constantly extolling the benefits of government social programs and depicting America as a world-class bully marching around imposing its will on poor little nations that couldn't protect themselves.

In high school I was suspended for accusing a Social Studies teacher of being a communist. Years later he admitted that he in fact had been a communist since the 40s. Another teacher rejected any History paper that he felt was too patriotic which he dismissed as jingoism. A teacher of Russian spent more time in class extolling the virtues of the USSR than teaching the language. When I complained about this 45 minute daily propaganda session I was again suspended. All of this took place back in the 1960s. This isn't a new problem.

The Progressives realized long ago that if they could take over the nation's education system they could raise up generations of Americans with no conception of the uniqueness of America as the world's bastion of freedom and liberty. Today we see the fruit of this campaign: legions of voters ready to throw away our heritage for a government check. The descendants of the Founders are willing to surrender their freedom to strive for the best in exchange for the security of just enough to get by.

So as the wisest woman I have ever known, my wife asks me, "What can we do now?"

Back in the early 1990s we decided that what we needed to do was go to school so that we could become teachers. Neither of us wants to impose our ideas on others, but we do want to present the materials in an objective manner and help our students acquire the critical thinking skills necessary to be informed citizens. Whenever a student asks me to figure out what their grade is during a semester I tell them, "If you give a man a fish he will eat for a day. If you teach him to fish he can eat forever." I then proceed to teach them how to find an average and how to translate that into a letter grade.

What can we do now? All can't become teachers but we can all become involved in our local school boards. We can all do our due diligence and find out what is being taught at our local schools, and we can follow the procedures to correct what is wrong and implement what is right. One thing is for sure that if we do not regain control of our schools we will lose the future.

Our leaders are leading us down the primrose path to collectivism. Our education establishment is conditioning America to accept it. Step-by-step, inch-by-inch we have strayed from a federal republic operating on democratic principles with liberty and justice for all to a centralized bureaucracy dispensing cradle-to-grave loot taken from producers and redistributed to non-producers. We may have gotten here step-by-step but we are not too many steps away from one step too many. Barack Obama has stated that his goal is to fundamentally transform[4] America. From stimulus slush finds, a shadow government of Czars, and imperial edicts he is systematically remaking us into a centralized state based on social democracy[6] and wealth redistribution.

In 1962 the leader of the socialist slave camp we knew as the USSR, Nikita Khrushchev, said "The United States will eventually fly the Communist red flag…The American people will raise it themselves. We can't expect the American People to jump from Capitalism to Communism, but we can assist their elected leaders in giving them small doses of Socialism, until they awaken one day to find that they have Communism."[7]

Education has led the way to this precipice and only education can lead our way back. If we don't learn from our mistakes and once again begin building up America through education we may learn that Khrushchev was right.

Did we win the Cold War defeating an enemy dedicated to our destruction to end up proving the wisdom of a cartoon character, "We have met the enemy and he is us."[7]

DISPATCH THIRTEEN

EVERYBODY WANTS TO GO TO HEAVEN

Everybody wants an "A" but nobody wants to study. Everybody wants to be rich but nobody wants to save. Everybody wants to lose weight but nobody wants to exercise. Everybody wants to go to heaven but nobody wants to die. No matter how you say it, the desire for something without the willingness to do the hard things required to achieve it, will always lead to disappointment. This is the cadence of the conundrum, the drumbeat of the do-nothing dreamer, the national anthem of the nihilist; the perennial I want but I will not work formula for failure.

The signature phrase for the conservatives of this generation of Americans should be, "We all want a sound economy but we aren't willing to endure the life-style changes it would take to get there."

Case in point: the coming Fiscal Cliff,[1] the looming disaster of sequestration that every talking head on every network blathers about endlessly, "It will happen" "It won't happen." Pick a side and it will be argued back and forth hour after hour, "The President won't let it happen. The President wants it to happen." Over and over we are barraged by the same few people who constitute the pundocracy of America debate what will happen. There is only one thing they are all agreed upon. If we go over this cliff, created by a vote of Congress and a signature by the President it will be terrible for our country. Why stop there? It will be terrible for the entire world.

Just think if we Americans raise our taxes and reign in our drunken sailor spending binge it will be a disaster for us and for everyone who draws breath on this planet. Not to worry we, the poor unwashed in fly-over country, don't have to scratch our pumpkin heads and wonder why it would be a disaster if our country took the steps necessary to save our economy the network appointed chatter chiefs are quick to tell us.

One side says raising taxes on anyone in a weak economy may push us over into a recession. This of course comes from the people who evidently don't buy their own bread, pump their own gas, or know any of the millions who are now permanently out of work; in other words personally prosperous people who believe the Great Recession actually ended. The other side says raising taxes on anyone they don't consider rich would be a disaster.

Both sides agree that at least half of the spending cuts would be a disaster. One side points at defense spending as a surrender of national security. While the other side points at cuts in entitlements as throwing grandma off the cliff.

The answers they propose are as predictable as a Hallmark Christmas movie. The Progressive Democrats say raise the taxes on the evil rich and cut spending to the defense department. The Progressive Republicans say raise revenues by closing loop holes and cut spending on entitlements. The problem with this is that just like Representative Paul Ryan's draconian budget it still never gets us to a balanced budget let alone paying down the principle on the National Debt. Both sides favor plans that keep on borrowing even if it might be at lower levels than at present. Maybe we will only borrow 36 cents of every dollar instead of 46. Wow! That should really make our arrival at the ash heap of History a few moments later.

And that is the heart of the problem. Or as another old saying tells us nobody wants their own ox gored. It is the "Not in my backyard syndrome" applied by everyone to something. We all want cuts in spending but not in our spending. We all agree that wasteful programs should die but every program has its supporters. This is where reality takes a bite out of dreams. Unless we balance our budget and reverse the slide into bankruptcy our days as a great power, let alone our days as the world's only super power, are numbered, and everyone knows China is counting off the numbers.[2]

Looking around in the cloistered world of self-appointed opinion writers I hate to have to be the one to tell my fellow Americans this but we have to do the work to get the "A," save the money to get rich, do the exercises to lose the weight, and we most assuredly will have to die to go to heaven.

We, through our elected representatives, have spent like there was no tomorrow until tomorrow is mortgaged to pay for today without asking the question, "How are we going to pay for tomorrow?" I guess we have always figured we could use the day after tomorrow for collateral. That may work for a while or at least until our children and grandchildren have been sold into slavery to the highest bidder.

Unfortunately my generation, the Boomers who proudly offered Bill Clinton and George Bush the Younger as our contribution to the pantheon of American Presidents, has kicked the can down the road while paraphrasing Louis XV on the eve of the French Revolution, "After me the flood." Or as many fellow boomers have phrased it to me, "It won't crash in my lifetime."

Now the handwriting is on the wall, the torches and pitchforks are seen on the horizon, and it is becoming obvious though the end may not come on December 21, 2012 but it isn't too far off. Anyone who isn't comatose in the cultural soma of social media and the game can see you can't continue to spend more than you bring in forever. The interest on the National Debt is going to eat us alive. Our creditors won't keep lending us more and more once they realize our only answer is to print our way out of debt.[3] Ask any scam artist trying to live by charging their Visa to the MasterCard when the shop keepers start cutting up the cards the happy days aren't here anymore.

What we need to do is go over the fiscal cliff, and instead of using the ensuing economic contraction as an opportunity[5] to re-launch the United

States in a fundamentally new direction tighten our belts.[6] We have to go through a period of austerity to return to reality.

Endlessly printing money always leads to money that isn't worth anything. Even if our current leaders think they have figured out a soft landing for this lead balloon they haven't, and when that bubble pops the economy stops.

Our fiscal conservatives who want to return to a gold standard should tell everyone that doing that will cause a contraction[7] in the value of money that will resemble a train going 100 miles an hour hitting a brick wall. There just isn't enough gold in the world to value every American dollar at one dollar. A return to gold would give us an economy based on real money, and that would be a good thing. However the proponents of this course need to be honest about the transition from funny money to real money: there will be a great deal of pain on the way back to reality.

There are plans to do something from the right. There is the plan to cut off Social Security at 55.[8] Everyone younger having paid into the world's greatest Ponzi scheme all their lives get another deal. Even if it is a better deal they will still feel like they are getting ripped off because they are. There is also the plan to cut all the wasteful spending out of Medicare but leave it all over at the Pentagon. These plans won't fly because they only have one wing.

The left has a plan too. Raise taxes on the rich, and keep on spending. This may eventually pass due to the President's perceived strength and the Republican leadership's Progressive inclinations and acceptance of defeat but it will only continue our progress towards national suicide.

The fact is we can either choose to cut the spending, raise revenues, and save the future or we can continue to stagger like drunken sailors spending our children's as yet unearned money until our creditors pull in the leash. I know calling for higher tax revenues is heresy to most conservatives, and I am not in favor of the government taking one more cent than necessary for constitutional purposes. Saving the country from ruin is the ultimate constitutional purpose.

Like any household that is buried in debt we need more money and less spending; the trick is getting both. The slight-of-hand artists in Washington are great at striking Grand Bargains for taxes now and spending cuts that never materialize. That never has worked and it certainly won't work now. We could do it without tax increases. Without taxes the spending cuts would have to be much deeper and more painful, and we can't get anyone to sign on for the pain of cuts with taxes.

Here's the secret of raising revenues with taxes. We can't raise rates which merely increases tax avoidance. A flat tax would bring in increased revenues by growing the economy and would indeed be fair. In contrast raising rates in a progressive tax system is merely punitive and is a populist trick to buy the votes of those who earn less.

If we don't endure the pain now, if we don't endure the necessary radical fiscal surgery despite years on life support, decades of refusing to take our medicine will finally cause our economy, and with it our dreams of a brighter future, to die. However, we won't get to go to heaven. Instead we will go into debtor's prison as our beloved nation sinks beneath mountains of debt into the second or third rank. We will watch as a tomorrow which could have been ours becomes someone else's.

When our children and grandchildren ask us, "Where's my inheritance?" we will have to say, "We spent it yesterday." When they ask, "Where's our future?" we will have to say, "We spent that too."

Instead of being pushed over the cliff, let's dive over and then resist any attempt to restore the spending. Let's take the pain so that our children can gain.

★ DISPATCH FOURTEEN ★

EXECUTIVE ORDERS

The problem with social engineering is that the engineers don't know how to drive the train. More like a complicated machine than a single-celled organism society is a collection of individuals. Human nature decrees that freedom of choice which is an inherent part of our social DNA therefore a healthy society is one built upon the choices and decisions freely arrived upon by the individuals who make up the whole. It is the self-interest and self-direction of these choices which build into the productive life of a free society.

Adam Smith addresses the contributions of societies individuals when, "he intends only his own security; and by directing that industry in such a manner as its produce may be of the greatest value, he intends only his own gain, and he is in this, as in many other cases, led by an invisible hand[1] to promote an end which was no part of his intention."

Conversely, Friedrich Hayek warns us "To act on the belief that we possess the knowledge and the power which enable us to shape the processes of society entirely to our liking, knowledge which in fact we do not possess, is likely to make us do much harm."[2] Unfortunately politically motivated social engineers short circuit this process by replacing the countless choices and decisions of free people with the corrosive and stifling mandates of central planning.

Our nation was not founded to be a centrally planned socially straight-jacketed empire ruled by the decrees of a sovereign. We were founded upon the revolutionary principles born of our colonial heritage and the thinking of the Enlightenment. Having fought our way free from the crushing embrace of an overbearing king, our Founders were determined to establish a representative republic of the people, by the people, and for the people.

We are a Constitutional Republic. We are a Nation of Laws. As Thomas Paine said in the Rights of Man, "The government of a free country ... is not in the persons but in the laws."[3] Paine also remarked that if someone should ask, "Where is the King of America?"[4] let us answer, "In America Law is King!"

Having studied the writings of Montesquieu and other Enlightenment thinkers, having established and maintained the separate branches of the various state governments, the Framers of our Constitution enshrined the principle of the separation of powers. This separation of powers is expressly stated in our Constitution. Article I, Section 1 states, "All legislative Powers herein granted shall be vested in a Congress of the United States, which shall consist of a Senate and House of Representatives." Article II, Section 1 states "The executive power shall be vested in a President of the United States of America." Article III, Section 1 states "The judicial Power of the United States, shall be vested in one Supreme Court, and in such inferior Courts as the Congress may from time to time ordain and establish." These passages separate the three functions, legislative, executive, and judicial into three distinct spheres and it is the dynamic relationship between the three that restrains the government from becoming repressive and allows freedom to bloom.

Montesquieu said, "There can be no liberty where the legislative and executive powers are united in the same person."[5] James Madison, the Father of the Constitution said, "The accumulation of all power, legislative, executive, and judiciary in the same hands...may justly be pronounced the very definition of tyranny."[6]

Executive Orders have been used by presidents since George Washington. They are nothing new. Yet they have always been controversial.

Washington issued the first one instructing the heads of departments to make a "clear account" of matters in their departments. His next one called for a national day of thanks giving. He also issued the first one to cause controversy when he issued an order in 1793 stating that the United States would be "friendly and impartial toward the belligerent powers" of Britain and France. In this "Neutrality Proclamation," Washington justified his power to issue such a statement based on the "law of nations."

Perhaps a constitutional justification could have been found in the powers of the President over foreign affairs but these were not referenced. Washington did not convene the Congress to debate the proclamation before issuing it. Immediately James Madison criticized Washington's order as an overextension of executive authority and an infringement on Congress's authority to decide issues of war and peace.

Although they have been stirring controversy since the dawn of the Republic originally Executive Orders were just what the name implies, orders from the executive and they were only binding upon the departments which made up the executive department. Most were never published and were only seen by the federal agencies involved. Some were of historical note such as when Lincoln suspended the writ of habeas corpus[7] and issued the Emancipation Proclamation or when Wilson segregated the military.[8]

The Presidency of FDR marked a major turning point in the use of Executive Orders, as in many other things. Roosevelt confronted the Great Depression as the moral equivalent of war and fought an undeclared war in the Atlantic and crippled Japan through trade sanctions. Truman desegregated the military. Eisenhower ended wage and price controls imposed by his predecessor. Kennedy and Johnson ended discrimination in housing and education. Nixon declared a war on drugs. Presidents used executive orders to steer the ship of state.

Then starting with the Clinton Administration a sea change took place in the use of Executive Orders. President Clinton used his executive power to achieve results he failed to achieve legislatively.[9]

Over time though technically applying only to executive agencies, Executive Orders have taken on a wider interpretation until today they have become legally binding mandates issued by presidents who rule by decree.

With President Obama, seconded and supported by his Attorney General Holder, deciding not to enforce laws they disagree with, the rule of law has ended in the United States. We can date our passage from a nation of laws to a nation of men not with this momentous decision but more effectively from the moment our elected representatives declined to declare this action to be unconstitutional and illegal.

Today we have a government that is careening out of control and those we have elected to protect our rights by upholding the Constitution are abusing our rights and subverting the Constitution. Thomas Paine made it clear which was the cart and which was the horse when he said, "A constitution is a thing antecedent to a government, and a government is only a creature of a constitution. The constitution of a country is not the act of its government, but of the people constituting a government."[10]

We have clearly reversed the order. The cart is before the horse and the tail is wagging the dog. The use and abuse of executive orders have changed us from a nation of laws to a nation of men, from a federal republic with a limited government to a centrally-planned bureaucracy with leaders attempting to rule by decree. We know where they want to lead us. The question before us now is: Will we go quietly into that dark night?

★ DISPATCH FIFTEEN ★

FEDERAL RESERVE: CONSTITUTIONAL OR MERELY LEGAL?

The Federal Reserve is the Central Bank of the United States. It is in charge of printing money issuing bonds and setting interest rates for those bonds. Article I, Section 8 of the Constitution says, "The Congress shall have Power ... to coin Money, regulate the Value thereof." The Federal Reserve is never mentioned. Has it always been this way? Does any other country do this? How did the Federal Reserve get its power over our currency and our economy? And the issue that so many are interested in today: Is the Federal Reserve constitutional?

Has it always been this way?

At the dawn of the Republic our first Secretary of the Treasury Alexander Hamilton issued several reports which in many ways set the tone and pointed the way for the development of America in the economic sphere. His first report on the public credit recommended that the new central government not only honor the debts contracted under the original government as established under the Articles of Confederation but that it also assume the war debts of the States. This recommendation was followed by Congress and the Washington administration created what has evolved into a permanent national debt.[1]

In 1790 Hamilton submitted his second report[2] which asked Congress to charter the Bank of the United States. Several aspects of the bank Hamilton proposed will sound familiar and it can be seen that they provided the mold for the Federal Reserve. His plan was closely modeled after that used by Great Britain's Bank of England.

According to Hamilton's vision the Bank of the United States would be a public/private hybrid. It would have an exclusive charter for 20 years. Its initial capitalization would be 10 million dollars consisting of 8 million from private investors and 2 million from the government. Congress would give the Bank the right to print paper money up to the 10 million held in deposit.

Most importantly the central government would declare that the notes issued by the Bank would be the only notes which would be accepted in payment for taxes. This would give the notes of the Bank of the United States credibility and value, which none of its state chartered competitors could match. This was Hamilton's proposal. Now all he had to do was get it passed into law.

The report was introduced to Congress in 1790 and by February 1791 it passed both the House and the Senate and arrived on the desk of President Washington. This is when the battle of the Titans really began. Leading Anti-Federalists and strict constructionists[3] such as James Madison, Thomas Jefferson, and Edmund Randolph, argued that the Constitution did not grant the government the power to incorporate a bank. According to their line of reasoning it was not an enumerated power[4] and therefore it was reserved to the States or the people. Those arguing for a strict interpretation of the newly minted Constitution, which Madison and Randolph had helped write, urged Washington in a written report not to sign the bill.

Ever the fulcrum between his philosophically divided advisors Washington presented Hamilton with the argument opposing his plan and asked him to present his argument in favor. Hamilton using his excellent reasoning and communication skills presented President Washington with the original argument for the implied powers[5] granted to the central government by the Constitution. This report appealed to what is now known as the "Necessary and Proper" clause.[6] He argued that the government was inherently empowered to do whatever was necessary to implement the laws required to use the enumerated powers. President Washington accepted Hamilton's argument, signed the bill, and the first Bank of the United States was born.

Beginning on July 4, 1791 the first thing the new Bank did was inflate a financial bubble by offering the largest initial stock offering the nation had ever seen. Investors showed their confidence in Hamilton's plan by quickly buying the options on the first issue of stock. Many of these initial investors were members of Congress. The initial price for the options was $25. This was soon bid up to over $300. It soon crashed to $150. Thus within days of its first action this original central bank inflated a bubble that soon burst. However, Secretary Hamilton setting the example for the central bankers to follow, stepped into the breach and averted a general financial panic by purchasing government securities with public funds thus stabilizing the markets and rewarding those who had initially speculated and "Too big to fail" was born.

The bank opened for business in December 1791. All manner of people, landowners, manufacturers, merchants, politicians, and most important of all, the government of the United States lined up to deposit money and to obtain the new Bank script. Within months the Bank was the single largest economic enterprise in the nation.

Beginning a pattern that would be repeated over and over the bank which had been created to ensure a firm foundation for the American economy inflated another bubble and caused another crash.

First the Bank flooded the market with easy loans and a massive issue of paper dollars. This move added liquidity pushing the new securities market into a sharp rise. However, then the Bank reversed course and began calling in many loans. Investors and speculators were especially affected as they were forced to sell securities to pay the loans. When the largest of the speculators William Duer[7] was forced to declare bankruptcy the markets collapsed. This in turn caused the financial markets to freeze up putting a stop to much of the nation's credit and commerce. This is known as the Panic of 1792.[8] The crash didn't last long, because Secretary Hamilton once again stepped in and bought government securities with public funds injecting much needed capital into the economy.

Over its 20 year life the first Bank of the United States functioned as the central bank. It worked to regulate state banks, closing those that issued too much paper. It attempted to guide the entire economy through its monetary and interest policies. It coordinated all its branches up and down the east coast to project a united front in its economic policy by either tightening or loosening credit.

By the time it came for a renewal of the bank's charter the Federalists were no longer in the seats of power and the newly ascendant Democratic-Republicans, led by Thomas Jefferson, defeated its bid for another 20 years, and the first Bank of the United States, America's initial experiment with central banking, was over.

Does any other country do this?

Yes, many other countries have central banks. Today it is considered a hallmark of an advanced economy.

How did the Federal Reserve get its power over our currency and our economy?

There were subsequent attempts to re-establish central banking in the United States. There was a Second Bank of the United States[9] chartered in 1816, but after being blamed for a series of bubbles and crashes its charter was not renewed and it ceased operations in 1836. In 1863 in the depths of the Civil War Congress passed the National Banking Act which chartered numerous Federal Banks. This law also taxed paper money issued by State banks but not paper money issued by the Federal Banks giving them a decided advantage.

In 1913 the Federal Reserve System[10] was born. It established what is known as a decentralized central bank in that it has semi-autonomous branches. It was given the power to control the currency, issue bonds, and set interest rates for those bonds. It was established as a public/private concern and was actually owned by stock holders. Who are these stock holders? They are private banks[11] and ownership of stock is required to participate in the system. The system was instituted to provide the foundation for a stable banking industry and an elastic currency that could be used to smooth the rough edges of the business cycle.[12] Whether this latest experiment in American central banking has fulfilled its mission each citizen should judge for themselves.

Is the Federal Reserve constitutional or merely legal?

The first Bank of the United States was never challenged in court as to whether or not the government had the power to create a central bank. But the second Bank was. The Supreme Court in 1819 ruled in Mc-Culloch v. Marylan[13] that it was in fact constitutional due to the implied powers clause. Thus looking to precedent, and unless the Supreme Court reverses itself, the Federal Reserve is considered to be authorized within the confines of the broadly interpreted Constitution.

There was an important constitutional issue born with the creation of America's first Central Bank. With the birth of the First Bank of the United States the acceptance and use of implied powers became the central government's method to expand its powers beyond those expressly delegated in the Constitution. This in turn paved the way for our acceptance of things that are clearly unconstitutional just because they are legal.

The argument of Madison, Jefferson, and Randolph upholding a strict constructionist view would be codified and added to the Constitution in the same year the Bank was charted, and perhaps in response to it, in the 10th Amendment[14] but this did not end the appeal to implied powers as a means to the government's ends. In theory this sounds good. In practice it has turned our limited government into an out of control leviathan crushing the free out of our free market and sucking the liberty out of the American experiment.

As my favorite American philosopher, Yogi Berra once said, "In theory there is no difference between theory and practice. In practice there is."[15]

★ DISPATCH SIXTEEN ★

FREEDOM IS AS FREEDOM DOES

Is there any one political or economic system that God wants everyone to follow? I do not believe God has ordained any one type of government or economy as the divinely ordained path.

The only government he ever instituted was a kingdom with himself as the King and that was rejected by His own people when they instead wanted to be like the people who surrounded them. And even though God had His prophets warned them that this earthly king would take their lands, their children, their goods and their freedom they persisted in rejecting a divine King for kings who would claim divine rights.

The only economy God has instituted is the divine economy where there is never a lack and always abundance. With the cattle on a thousand hills God does not participate in recessions and He has promised many times that those in His hands cannot be plucked out. He promises that though a thousand fall on one side and ten thousand on the other destruction shall not consume those who trust in Him. And though in the eyes of this world it may appear that the evil often triumphs and the good are forsaken He tells us, "Those who wait on the Lord shall renew their strength; they shall mount up with wings like eagles, they shall run and not be weary, they shall walk and not faint."

Free choice is a major part of God's plan. As a matter of fact that is His plan. He could have just as easily created humans who had no free choice, could not disobey, never fall and always remain just as he designed them. But instead He desired the loving family that can only come about from love freely given and freely received.

Individually God has given each of us free choice. Therefore, I believe freedom to make choices unencumbered by outside interference is a fundamental building block of human nature and thus a required element of any society which matches the reality of the human condition. Each of us gets to decide which we are going to believe, our eyes of flesh or our eyes of faith. Is the world true or is God true? As for me and my house, we will serve the Lord. That is my free choice and you are free to make yours.

I believe that God desires us to make free choices with regard to faith and lifestyle. Therefore, personal freedom is necessary for life as God intended. And this has a great impact upon the first half of our question, is there any one political system that God wants everyone to follow?

It is apparent that the only form of government ever devised by man that requires personal free choice as a prime component is democracy. All other forms of government are some variation of the divine right of somebody to tell everybody else what to do. By the way, that's democracy as in one-citizen-one-vote not as in Democratic People's Republic. And since all forms of direct democracy eventually devolve into a tyranny of the majority the only thing that works over time is a representative republic which operates on democratic principles. Meaning a system wherein the people have the opportunity to select their own representatives as long as those representatives actually represent the people and do not become the pawns of powerful special interests.

Also based upon the fact that personal freedom is a fundamental component of life as God desires for humanity which brings us to the second half of our question: Is there any one economic system that God wants everyone to follow? It is apparent to even a casual observer that free market capitalism is the only economic system ever devised by man that requires personal freedom to operate. All other economic systems ultimately translate into some variation of a command economy. Some bureaucrat somewhere decides how many widgets to make and that's how many widgets are produced regardless of need or demand. Command economies foster disequilibrium and maladjustments. There are always either too many widgets or not enough. In a fee market capitalist system demand always dictates production and inherently guides supply.

America was originally launched as a representative republic based upon democratic principles with a free economy which based upon the above exemplifies the ideal for a nation-state. This is what we have known. If the Progressives continue to succeed in their efforts to fundamentally transform America then what can we expect? [1]

Look at the areas of American life so far transformed, massive government take-overs either through outright purchase or indirectly through regulation of industry, insurance, and finance. Taking this as a guide we should expect further intrusion of the central government into the economy thus transforming America into a command economy with all the problems inherent in that type of system.

The healthcare take-over which is scheduled to phase in like boiling water phases in for a frog, feeling so comforting until it's too late to jump out. Using the need to modify our behavior to cut healthcare costs we should expect the central planners to inch-by-inch transform our daily routines of eating and exercise until they are telling us when to jump and how high. It is often the unintended consequences which have the greatest effects as a result of the Progressive impulse to create a Utopia.

The only way Utopians ever try to create a heaven on earth is to build nanny-states to protect us from ourselves with no thought of how the unintended consequences actually harm the people and the intention was to help. Eventually there is also no limit to the amount of force it takes to compel compliance once the bureaucracy has decreed something is good for the collective. An example from Obamacare is the provision forcing insurance companies to accept pre-existing conditions for all children insured. This sounds great. And it will surely protect the kids. But what it really does is prompt many insurance companies to quit insuring children[2] because they realize this government-mandated provision will cause them to lose money, and despite the Progressives belief that people should open and maintain private businesses as non-tax supported social agencies people who own businesses do so to make money.

Another example is businesses either dropping insurance for their employees because the fines imposed will be cheaper than the insurance or seeking an exemption.[2] It is projected that 30%[3] of employers will drop their employee healthcare once Obamacare is fully instituted. So much for "If you have your plan and you like it,… or you have a doctor and you like your doctor, that you don't have to change plans."[4,5] Which has since proven itself to be the lie of the year in 2013.[6]

The financial take-over through regulation has not been unwrapped yet and even the politicians most involved in writing it say they don't know what's in it so its long-term impact can only be imagined.[7] Does anyone imagine it will be good for free-enterprise, competition, and capitalism? As the Progressives continue to experiment looking for some way to accomplish the impossible, heaven on earth, the uncertainty keeps people from investing, businesses from growing and the economy from recovering. After one term and now another it should be apparent that the current administration has successfully turned a recession into a new normal of lower expectations and a loss of hope.

But then again my hope was never in the government to begin with, and since they didn't give it to me they can't take it away. My hope is in Jesus and He never fails.

★ DISPATCH SEVENTEEN ★

Grow the Economy Not the Bureaucracy

Business is like water. It follows the path of least resistance. A fact that should birth shame in the hearts of all Americans is that for the last decade American Businesses have been in a mad rush for the door. They've left America, once the epitome of free enterprise, choosing instead to establish themselves in Communist China. Today Federal red tape and taxes are strangling American free enterprise.

Innovation is like lightning. It comes in a flash, burns white hot, and is impossible to bottle. When free enterprise is stifled by government interference in the marketplace the incentive to develop and produce are stunted. Americans have always been the can-do people. We've always been the leaders in invention and innovation. Our entrepreneurs have traditionally led the world in new patents and processes. In 2011 many sources predicted China would take the lead in high-tech patents applied for and new industrial processes pioneered.[1] It takes thinking outside the box to find the new and provide the best. In America today the Federal Government has set to work making the box stronger, to weaving a mesh of regulations and taxes, and turning the box into a cage.

The grand gesture, voting to repeal Obamacare presented by the House Republicans as proof that they've become true fiscal conservatives, is a hat-trick meant to beguile the newly awakened and lull them back to sleep. The smoke screen of denying funding as a way to stop the implementation is a hollow argument offered by people who know better to people who should know better. The aspects of the national health plan that began taking effect in 2011 and continue today do not require any funding. They come in the form of regulations, fees and taxes.[2]

Grid lock is the best we have to hope for from the 112th Congress. The very idea that any repeals or rollbacks of the omnibus thousand-page take-over bills will pass in Harry Reid's Senate and be signed by Mr. Obama is laughable. Not only will the Senate not validate the results of November 2010, it is working diligently to stack the deck with new rules to prevent the enlarged minority from interfering with the evolutionary changes the Progressives constantly seek to enact as they attempt to evolve past the Constitution.[3] The invocation of the Nuclear Option ending the filibuster of judicial and other executive appointments is a case in point. What we need now is the party of "Hell no!" acting as a roadblock to the Progressives long march to the corporate state. Reading the Constitution at the beginning of the session is a great act of showmanship. Demanding that every piece of legislation contain a clause citing the constitutional empowerment for its enactment is long overdue.

However, what we need is a House that remembers that according to the Constitution all tax bills must originate in the chamber of the people. What we need is more than showmanship and more than doing what should have been done since 1789. What we need is a House that's willing to call out the other branches of the Federal Government when they exceed their constitutional powers. The House has the power to investigate, subpoena, the power to impeach, and the power to bring suit in Federal Court. They have the power to expose the Progressive juggernaut for what it is: an express train on the road to serfdom.[4]

Their economic plan is merely inflating the next bubble and praying that the rest of the world considers America too big to fail. America is fast approaching the tipping point[5] as a global manufacturing power. Manufacturing made-up 53% of the economy in 1965, it only accounted for 39% by 1988, it accounted for merely 9% in 2004, and the decline continues. The warning signs[6] are everywhere: a loss of a staggering 32%[7] of manufacturing jobs since the year 2000, employment in the computer industry is lower in 2010 than it was in 1975,[8] and we've lost approximately 42,400 factories[9] since 2001. We are turning into merely a source of raw materials and a market for manufactured goods from China, which is the textbook description of a colony.

No matter what the rhetoric and the stated intentions; it appears the consequences of the last 10 years work by the best government that money can buy are the unintended consequences. These political savants are so clueless that their answer[10] to the problem of too much government and too much regulation is to appoint new committees, commissions, and expand the bureaucracy to study the old and recommend solutions that entail new regulations and more government.

This isn't rocket science. We aren't trying to figure out the orbit perimeters of a sling-shot around the Moon to reach Saturn. This is Political Science and Economics: the arcane arts of who gets what, when, and how.

If we want manufacturing and innovation to grow reduce taxes to the lowest in the world and take the steel boot of regulation off the throat of free enterprise and watch our manufacturing base and our industrial output soar. If you want more jobs stop stifling small business with uncertainty and watch the unemployment rate fall. If we want more consumer spending instead of the next round of bail-outs and stimulus pay-offs to campaign contributors give the American people a one-year federal tax holiday and watch consumer activity go through the roof. In other words grow the economy not the bureaucracy.

★ DISPATCH EIGHTEEN ★

HISTORY DOESN'T REPEAT ITSELF BUT IT DOES RHYME

When I was studying to become a Historian I ran afoul of the professors tasked with helping me arrive at my destination. When you study for advanced degrees in History you are required to choose an area of specialization and if you are particularly ambitious you might choose two separate areas. Being an over achiever who has always been blessed with an inquiring mind I choose four and proceeded to complete the necessary classwork for all of them. Near the end of my career as a professional History student the professor in charge of the program told me I had to pick one field that would be my overarching area of study.

By this time I was writing opinion columns for the school newspaper much along the lines of the weekly columns I churn out today. In each article I would examine an event or situation from current events and place it in a historical and constitutional context. I called these articles the "History of the Future" which is what current events are. So, when asked to declare a comprehensive Historical Interest I told my professor that I had decided to specialize in the History of the Future, and if he was interested he could ask me in 10 minutes and I would tell him what his last statement meant. He didn't think it was nearly as clever as I did.

Although it was unknown to me at the time my professor was well aware of my writing and was therefore not dazzled by my answer. He was bemused, he was shocked, and he was angered. He thought I was irreverent in my approach to History and mocking in my tone toward

Historians. Then, as now, I believed that if History doesn't help us to live in the present it is merely curiosity or voyeurism that compels us to gaze upon the past. I believe I might have said that or its equivalent along the way, and this had not earned me the heartfelt appreciation of those whom I hoped to one day call my peers.

Once I successfully navigated the shoals and received my professional Historian's badge I continued seeing History as a useful lens for the interpretation of current events presented in my weekly articles which I continue to call the History of the Future. However, as I continue to relate the present to the past in an attempt to discern the future I have noted my divergence from common knowledge and accepted wisdom when it comes to the relation of knowledge of History to actions in the present.

Everyone knows and many people say, "Those who fail to learn from History are doomed to repeat it."[1] I believe that a historical context is necessary for any understanding of the present. I also believe that a lack of historical context is one of the major contributing factors to the current state of affairs in America. I do not however believe that historical events repeat. Yes one war seems to inevitably follow another, but they are always different wars. World War II followed World War I and in many ways completed one war in two acts but it was a war as different in strategy as it was in tactics. They were two different wars. Just as the current Great Recession follows the Great Depression and although they bear many similar aspects such as government complicity in their depth and duration they are most decidedly two separate catastrophes.

All of which leads me to my heretical belief, echoing Mark Twain that "History doesn't repeat itself but it does rhyme."[2] Take for instance the current spate of sweetheart deals and cronyism that has led us down the road to the crash of 2008, the downgrade of 2011, and the ongoing inflation default as we attempt to print our way to solvency. Although this is unprecedented in size and scope, though it is the first economic crisis that threatens to cause America to spiral down from the first rank of nations, this is not the first time craven politicians and their crony capitalist supporters have sought to turn the public treasury into a personal ATM.

In 1863 the principle stockholders and executive officers of the Union Pacific Railroad Company launched a new venture Crédit Mobilier of America.[3] The venture also had the support and protection of high-level political leaders. This construction company officially sought to build and maintain the first railroad to span the continent. Unofficially the company looted the federal treasury of as much money as it could while doing as little actual construction as possible. The venture made enormous profits for some before causing a panic that ruined the fortunes of many innocent people resulting in a loss of faith in the practices of both business and government.

Crédit Mobilier was initially founded by Thomas C. Durant who was the Vice President of Union Pacific. Within a short time the actual control of the company was assumed by two well-connected brothers from Massachusetts: Congressman Oakes Ames and his brother, Oliver.

Here's how the scheme worked: The men who owned Crédit Mobilier controlled the Union Pacific Railroad which was at the time racing the Central Pacific Railroad to meet in the middle of the country and unite a nation mired deep in the Civil War. These men used their positions at the railroad to award no-bid contracts to Crédit Mobilier to complete the construction. They awarded contracts totaling $94,000,000 when the actual costs were less than $54,000,000.

A large percentage of the money had been provided to the Union Pacific from Congress in the form of low-interest loans and enormous land grants. As the sums involved became larger and the Railroad plunged into unsustainable debt Congressman Ames sought to avoid oversight by selling stock to leading politicians for prices well below their perceived value. Like all pyramid schemes this one eventually ran out of enough new investors to keep the perpetual motion going. As in all pyramid schemes first ones in and first ones out made fortunes while last ones in and last ones out lost their shirts.

In 1872 public indignation and economic ruin finally moved Congress to investigate. The resulting scandal ruined the reputations of numerous high officials including the Vice President, leading Senators, and Congressman. The crony capitalists were also exposed as grafters, and were the first in a long line of Robber Baron looters who have used political connection and government preference to walk off with the public's money. After a thorough investigation which left not one stone unturned although the principle actors were revealed no politician was thrown out of office, no one was ever prosecuted, and those who built the pyramid got to keep the cash. In 1897, the Union Pacific was completely reorganized and the present Union Pacific has no relationship to a scandal that rocked the nation and impacted millions.

Today these crony capitalists and the politicians who advance and protect them have brought our economy to the brink of disaster. Once again after brutal investigations and maximum exposure no one has been expelled from the corridors of power and no one has been prosecuted. These same politicians who have spent the income of unborn generations are walking away with pensions and benefits, their crony capitalist pals are laughing all the way to the bank, and the citizens are left holding the bag. Day-by-day, hour by hour, minute by minute the headlines continue to reinforce my belief that History doesn't repeat itself but it does rhyme.

★ DISPATCH NINETEEN ★

How Do We Re-Industrialize America

Manufacturing in America peaked in 1979[1] when 19.5 million Americans actually produced durable goods. In the last 30 years our manufacturing sector has declined by 40%[2] losing almost 8 million jobs. Nearly 6 million jobs have been lost since 2000[3] and since the Great Recession began we have lost an average 89,000 manufacturing jobs every month[4] for the last two years. Due to this dramatic constriction America has fallen below 12 million workers employed in manufacturing for the first time since 1946[5] and is now below levels not seen since 1941.[6] This dismal record portrays[7] the stunning decline of America as a manufacturing superpower. And while a rise in productivity[8] has helped America maintain a prominent position in the world this has not resulted in manufacturing continuing to be an avenue for upward mobility for Americans.

So how do we re-industrialize America? How do we get back all the jobs that have been exported in the last 30 years? What will be the consequences of taking the bold steps necessary to make America once again the engine that drives the world's economy? What will be the result of failing to do so?

To set this discussion into its proper context first we must look at how America grew from a rustic agricultural nation on the edge of Western civilization into the greatest industrial superpower ever known.

In the interest of full disclosure I must confess that I am a life-long capitalist. I believe that capitalism is the only economic system ever devised by man that requires free choice as a necessary requirement. Every other system is either more or less a command economy. The defense and restoration of America's capitalist economy is today a hallmark of the conservative movement. Many people study the works of Milton Friedman[9] and Friedrich von Hayek.[10] Those of us who want to see economic opportunity unshackled espouse the principles of both the Chicago[11] and the Austrian Schools of Economics[12] as opposed to the theories of the Frankfurt School[13] which have moved America in the direction of a centrally planned economy.

Flying in the face of this conventional wisdom for the purposes of this discussion we must ask the question, was it capitalism that provided the environment which set America on the road to material riches and industrial power? Culture to humans is like water to a fish. It is everywhere. It provides the medium through which we move. However, since it is ever present it is not something we constantly notice or concentrate on. Most of those who read these words were raised in a time or by people who taught American History as a positive, ever-improving saga. We were taught that America never started a war and never lost one. We were taught that rugged individualism carved out an empire from a raw wilderness. We were taught that capitalism paved and paid the way.

At the hazard of being branded an apostate to conservatism I must continue to ask the question, was capitalism the catalyst for America's industrial power or do we labor under the after-glow of a time when American History was taught in such a way as to magnify present circumstances by projecting them into the past? Are we looking to a myth of free enterprise to recreate what it didn't create in the first place?

Was it capitalism that fostered the founding of the colonies which became the seedbed of the United States?

Mercantilism[14] was the economic system that proceeded capitalism in western civilization. This was a system of economic nationalism which sought to build a strong country by maintaining a favorable balance of trade and by being self-sufficient. This was one of the primary reasons why the sea-going European powers sought to establish colonies. They wanted to secure sources of raw materials for their developing industrial sectors and to control external markets allowing them to produce and sell products all within their domestic economy, keeping all the gold at home.

The term mercantilism was coined by Adam Smith[15] the philosophical father of capitalism, but it was not capitalism. Inherently Mercantilism necessitated a centrally planned and controlled economy. What benefitted the nation was permitted and encouraged. What didn't was prohibited and discouraged. It was under this system that the English colonies were founded. The first viable English colony in the New World, Virginia was founded by the Virginia Company[16] a joint stock company which was given a charter by James I. This charter, like subsequent charters given to the Massachusetts Bay Company[17] and proprietary charters given to individuals such as William Pennand the Lords Baltimore gave these companies and individuals monopolies within specific geographic areas. Government-imposed and enforced monopolies are a restraint of trade and by nature are incompatible with a free capitalist system.

The colonies founded upon this restraint of trade followed suit giving monopolies[18] to companies and individuals to do everything from making iron to importing. Government planning and control of the economy did not stop there. The colonial governments also granted subsidies, bounties, land grants, loans and money prizes to encourage the birth and prosperity of the industries and services desired. Through these actions the precursors of modern America were doing what is today reviled as inherently un-American, picking winners and losers.

If we fast forward to the founding of the United States do we find the unbridled free enterprise seen today to be the natural state of the Republic?

In 1791 Secretary of the Treasury Alexander Hamilton issued his third path-breaking report to Congress the Report on Manufactures.[19] Of all his reports this one is considered the most innovative. It provided a stark revelation of Hamilton's and his Federalist compatriots' vision for America and its economy. So did this report outline an economy based upon capitalism and free enterprise? No it did not. This report envisions[20] an America "independent of foreign nations for military and other essential supplies" this is the heart of a mercantilist program. Hamilton proposed subsidies to encourage industry. Some of the mercantilist policies advocated[21] by Hamilton encouraged the central government:

- To constitute a fund for paying the bounties.
- To constitute a fund for a board to promote arts, agriculture, manufactures, and commerce. Hamilton wanted the fund
  1. to defray the expenses of the emigration of artists, and manufacturers in particular branches of extraordinary.
  2. to induce the prosecution and introduction of useful discoveries, inventions, and improvements, by proportionate rewards.
  3. to encourage by premiums, both honorable and lucrative, the exertions of individuals and of classes.

The historical evidence of America's reliance upon protectionist and economic interventionist policies as tools in the building of our greatness can be found everywhere. The central government built, licensed, and encouraged roads[22] and canals[23] to foster interstate trade by providing monopolies, subsidies and grants. It fought wars to safeguard sea lanes[24] and to expand territory[25] and markets,[26] and it birthed,[27] regulated and controlled the financial industry from its very inception.

The incontrovertible evidence points to the fact that America was founded, launched, and nurtured as the successor to and the continuation of mercantilist not capitalist policies.

If these were the policies of economic nationalism which helped foster America's rise to industrial greatness wouldn't it seem appropriate for these policies to be the ones that would help it rise again? There is only one national figure who has consistently urged a return to economic nationalism, Patrick Buchanan.[28] He has pointed out for years that our rush to embrace the so-called free trade has put American workers at a decided disadvantage. The dissolution of tariff protection forced our workers to compete against people who will work for a small percentage of what Americans can afford to work for in societies with little or no regulation.

How do we get back all the jobs that have been exported in the last 30 years?

If we want to re-industrialize America we have to protect our markets and support our industry otherwise we will soon sink to a supplier of raw materials and a market to China and the other rapidly rising industrial powers of Asia.

What will be the consequences of taking the bold steps necessary to make America once again the engine that drives the world's economy?

Such a policy calculated to rebuild our industry and re-capture our domestic markets from China, Japan, and the four tigers of Asia[29] will carry as many risks as it does benefits. Just as any predator will react to resistance on the part of its prey so to if we enact tariffs on Chinese goods it may well ignite a trade war. Then again anything worth having is worth fighting for. If we want to once again rise to the top of the industrial world and once again have a favorable balance of trade we need to look at what is best for America not what is best for the U.N. or what is best for the globalization lobby.

What will be the result of failing to rebuild our industrial sector?

Some may deride this proposed return to mercantilist policies as isolationism. However, just as a nation without borders will soon cease to be a nation any nation that fails to protect and encourage its industry will find itself an agricultural and raw material colony in all but name for those nations which do.

★ DISPATCH TWENTY ★

How Long Did the Limits Last?

In 1798, a mere 10 years after the ratification of the Constitution war with France seemed imminent. In reaction to opposition regarding the policies of the government John Adams, hero of the Revolution, coauthor of the Declaration of Independence, one of the Framers of the Constitution, and the second President of the United States Congress passed the Alien and Sedition Acts.[1]

Congress eventually passed four of these laws in an effort to strengthen the Federal Government against internal dissent. The former supporters of the Constitution, now known as Federalists sponsored the legislation meant to silence political opposition which was coming mainly from the Democratic-Republicans and their leader Thomas Jefferson.

First Congress passed the Naturalization Act which required people to be residents of the United States for 14 years instead of 5 years before becoming eligible for American citizenship.

Then they passed the Alien Act which authorized the President to deport aliens who the government determined to be dangerous or a threat to the peace and/or safety of the United States. It must be remembered that while many believed America was under a threat of war this law was passed and enforced during peacetime.

Seeking to extend the power of the central government even further Congress next passed the Alien Enemies Act. This third act allowed the arrest, imprisonment, and deportation of aliens who were from an enemy country.

Finally Congress added the Sedition Act, aimed at any action deemed by the government to be treason. This included the publication of any material judged to be false, scandalous, or malicious. No matter what the Bill of Rights said the government declared these activities to be a severe misdemeanor that was punishable by both fine and imprisonment.

Under these bills 25 men, including numerous editors of newspapers, were arrested. In addition, their newspapers were shut down.

The net of suspicion was spread so far that it included Benjamin Franklin Bache, Benjamin Franklin's grandson who was the editor of a Philadelphia newspaper. He was charged with libeling President Adams. This arrest elicited a mounting public reaction against all four of the Alien and Sedition Acts.

Many Americans questioned the constitutionality of these laws. Indeed, public opposition to the Alien and Sedition Acts was so great that they were in part responsible for the election of Thomas Jefferson, a Republican, to the presidency in 1800. Once in office, Jefferson pardoned all those convicted under the Sedition Act, while Congress restored all fines paid with interest.

The unpopularity and questionable legality of these acts led to Adams being the first one-term president. And these actions by one of the foremost Framers and most vocal supporters during the ratification process used these oppressive laws to silence opposition. Here at the very beginning of the Constitutional Republic one of the architects of the document believed it gave him and Congress the power to silence the people when the people disagreed.

Jefferson and his Democratic-Republicans defeated Adams' bid for a second term by capitalizing on the public's disgust at what were perceived to be unconstitutional and repressive actions by the very people who wrote and led the fight for the adoption of the Constitution. Now those who portrayed themselves as the protectors of liberty would make sure that the limits placed upon the Federal Government were strictly observed.

In 1803, during their long wars with England and in need of financial relief France offered to sell Louisiana to the United States. This caused a novel situation and became the cause of a grave constitutional question and a major problem for President Thomas Jefferson and his ruling party. Seeing the opportunity to double the size of the United States, President Jefferson immediately wanted to purchase the territory.[2]

This was rather surprising in that Jefferson advocated a narrow or strict interpretation of the Constitution. And no matter how you read the document nowhere does it authorize the President or even the Congress to buy additional territory. Jefferson and his followers did not debate this point, they did not dispute this limitation but at the same time they felt the need to act quickly, and believed there was not time for the amendment process to legally change the Constitution.

This being the case, President Jefferson and his Democratic-Republicans merely passed legislation giving the President permission to sign a treaty obligating the United States to pay the money and to take possession of Louisiana. In addition, the Democratic-Republicans also appropriated the money to pay France for the territory. Where did Democratic-Republicans in Congress believe they acquired the authority to do this? They claimed to act under the provision of the Constitution (Article V, Section 3) which gave Congress the power to regulate the territories.

The third President and a compliant Congress interpreted the Constitution to do what they wanted to do even though it violated their own previously stated position.

As a third and final example of how soon the limited government promised by the Framers of the Constitution began to encroach upon the liberty it was meant to preserve let us look at the Monroe Doctrine.[3]

During the presidency of James Monroe's there occurred several revolutions against Spanish rule in South and Central America. The United States quickly recognized these newly established countries. Believing there was a strong possibility that European governments would intervene and try to reassert their control over the former colonies; President Monroe declared the doctrine in 1823. This doctrine declared that from that time forward America saw itself as the dominant power in the Western Hemisphere. It also warned that European interference in the Americas would not be allowed. The Doctrine consists of three principles:

1. The United States would remain neutral in European wars unless American interests were involved.

2. Both North and South America were no longer subject to colonization by European powers.

3. The United States would consider any and all attempt at European colonization in the New World as an "unfriendly act."

And although the United States did not have the military power to enforce these claims, the declaration had symbolic importance: announcing the United States' posture as the power to be reckoned with in the New World.

Monroe's Doctrine aggressively asserted the position of dominance claimed by the United States in the Americas, and it has been a cornerstone of American foreign policy ever since.

An interesting point that is little mentioned or considered is that this doctrine (and every doctrine proclaimed since) is not law but merely a declaration of a presidential policy. It is this fact that persuaded Monroe that as President he was authorized without any Constitutional authorization, to establish a foreign policy that commits the United States to military action without a declaration of war by Congress. Thus following in the footsteps of the second and the third our fifth president moved well beyond the limits the Constitution had imposed.

How long did the limits last? The Anti-Federalists were still active in politics as the warnings they gave were realized and the children of the Revolution took their first steps down the road to tyranny. These earliest assaults upon limits were followed by:

Jackson used the spoils system[4] to pack the federal bureaucracy with his supporters. Jackson advocated the removal of all Native Americans across the Mississippi in violation of numerous treaties passing the Indian Removal Act.[5] When the Supreme Court ruled that Georgia's expropriation and removal of the Cherokee was unconstitutional, referring to the Chief Justice Jackson said, "John Marshall has made his decision, now let him enforce it."[6] He then used the standing army the Anti-Federalists had warned against to complete the deportation acting as ruthlessly and as arrogantly as any Babylonian king. Lincoln decided that States which had voluntarily joined could not leave though this is stated nowhere in the Constitution.

Teddy Roosevelt ran roughshod over Latin America with his Big Stick diplomacy.[7] He provoked a revolution in Columbia, established Panama as a near colony, seized the Canal Zone, and in many ways used his big stick like a cudgel to establish and maintain an American Empire from Asia to the Dominican Republic in contravention to the advice of Washington and the words of the Constitution.

Wilson rounded up and interred Italians and Germans during WWI took over mines and factories, fixed prices, took over the transportation and communications networks, and strictly managed the production and distribution of food.[8]

FDR stretched the Constitution in so many ways it never snapped back. Since our first President for life established the bloated federal bureaucracy and its symbiotic military–industrial complex we have seen a succession of undeclared wars for peace, the welfare state, the Patriot Act, and preemptive war become emblems of a system that practice government of Washington, by Washington, and for Washington.[9]

Congress has declared war on only five occasions: the War of 1812; the Mexican War; the Spanish–American War, WWI, and WWII. However, this has not been the extent of our involvement in armed conflict. When American citizens have challenged the constitutionality of these wars without a declaration Federal Courts have ruled a declaration is not required.[10]

Ask yourself: How long did the limits last? Where did the limits go? How many limits are left? Which leads to the ultimate question: How can we get the limits back?

Keep the faith. Keep the peace. We shall overcome.

★ DISPATCH TWENTY-ONE ★

HUNKER IN THE BUNKER AND WAIT FOR THE RAIN

As those of you who follow these wandering pages know I have re-cently re-aligned my life to turn and face the strange changes that are overtaking Western Civilization with ever-increasing speed. Like ripples whose shape and size shifts but never leave the stream, change is the only constant in a society careening towards a cliff.

The descendants of those who built the empire no longer produce enough children to man the walls. The will to win and the desire to excel has been replaced by a complacency bred of bread, circuses, and entitle-ment checks distributed by a perpetually re-elected legislature designed to keep the marks from catching the con. A series of lack-luster presidents set the stage for collapse. One declares a new world order and then loses his bid for re-election to a saxophone playing party-boy. This surprise president sets the morality bar so low that his scurrilous actions and obvious lack of character corrupt the very fiber of our nation. The next two expand the government and spend us into oblivion.

Empires rise and empires fall. That is the way of the world and the lesson of History. From the fifteenth century through the twentieth century Western Civilization used a temporary advantage in technology to conquer the world. Where our military conquered we imposed our culture. Where we didn't gain political control the vision of our seemingly invulnerable strength and our unstoppable progress led local leaders to discard much of what was theirs to imitate what they coveted of ours.

For five centuries Western Civilization ruled supreme. It was our way or the highway so in our pride we decided ours was the High Way. Then in two spectacular bouts of societal suicide, WWI and WWII, we killed, maimed, and butchered ourselves. We wasted the accumulated riches of centuries and showed the millions of colonial subject people who were brought in to help kill whoever the enemy happened to be that Westerners weren't invulnerable, weren't unconquerable, and weren't even smart enough to avoid the slaughter or hide the evidence.

The destruction of the economies and populations of the various colonial powers inevitably led to the break-up of the empires and the rise of a bi-polar world that pitted a world-wide Communism that was inimical to everything Western Civilization stood for against a united West now led by the newest edition to their ranks: the United States.

We had allied ourselves with the Communists to defeat the Fascists. However the victory of 1945 vanished into 50 years of a Cold War that flashed hot enough times to kill many tens of thousands. This epic struggle brought the Communists to their knees and us to the edge of bankruptcy. As we defeated Communism its less threatening little brother Socialism crept in through the back door. We adopted the tenants of socialism: equality of outcome financed by expropriation of wealth and re-distribution to pacify our population through the long war. Today we are fast becoming all we have fought against for the last 60 years: a centrally-planned economy, a regimented society, and a totalitarian state.

This century-long series of debilitating wars sapped our will to reproduce just as technology gave us birth control and lax morals gave us abortion. This unholy trinity turned into a demographic time bomb that ensures the eventual submerging of the peoples of the West beneath waves of immigrants swarming in to take their place. The moral rot swilled out from Hollywood, and a reality show culture exemplified and condoned by the political elite inspires and reflects a hedonism that would have made Caligula blush. The entitlement mentality foisted and fostered by buy-a-vote-with-benefits governments has sapped people of the drive and desire to do anything more than sit on a couch and dream of their chance at the golden ring of 15 minutes of fame.

Sounds like a dismal picture doesn't it? The most depressing part of the whole thing is that it is true.

Empires rise and empires fall and it is our lot to live on the declining end of Western Civilization: the greatest empire of all time (so far).

No one ever gets to live in the world they were raised in. Time moves on and things change. However most generations don't watch the inversion of the world they grew up in. Today things which we thought were wrong are now right. Things that we thought were right are now wrong. What made you healthy yesterday kills you today. The wisdom of the ancients was once sought after in a world of constants today obsolesce often proceeds production in a microwave throw-away culture.

The world has been turned upside down.

Just as a British general marched out of Yorktown to surrender to a rag-tag bunch of summer soldiers, so we the children of those who stormed the beaches on D-Day to free Europe and end the darkness that was Nazism will wonder how were we defeated by those we had once so easily dominated?

The answer will be the same as it was for the British in the Revolution and for the Nazis in WWII: we defeated ourselves. Our overconfidence and our desire to have it all led us to forsake the values that brought about our success and the principles that made us who we were. While the Socialist Progressives march us off to the shabby future they have centrally-planned perhaps instead of the World Turned Upside Down we should sing a paraphrase of a line from the 1960s, "In tattered tuxedos they face the new heroes and crawl about in confusion. All the hands raised; they stand there amazed at the shattering of their own illusions."[1]

We stand at the edge of the abyss. We do not know what will be only that it will not be what it has been. Do not despair. Do not lose hope. Have faith in Christ. Follow Him and He will guide you to a safe harbor amidst the storm. I have found my place. I am preparing every day for the coming crescendo. My best advice is find Christ, find your place, and hunker down.

Keep the faith. Keep the peace. We shall overcome.

★ DISPATCH TWENTY-TWO ★

IF I WANTED TO MAKE AMERICA PROSPEROUS AGAIN

First, I would ask myself how did our ancestors build America from an agricultural colony on the edge of civilization into the number one manufacturing and commercial nation the world had ever known.

Why reinvent the wheel if round ones still roll?

The early American colonies of the British were founded based upon the economic ideas of Mercantilism.[1] Governmental regulation of industries, trade, and commerce characterized Mercantilism as every aspect of the economy was utilized for national policy. This was especially true with foreign trade, which was determined more by national aims rather than individual or local interests.

The definition of wealth began to change in the sixteenth century. During the Middle Ages, wealth was defined by the amount of productive land a nation possessed. As transportation, especially by sea, improved so did the ability to conduct foreign trade bringing with it an increase in the amount of (hard) cash (gold or silver) generated by that trade. The definition of wealth came to be the amount of gold a nation possessed. Therefore every nation sought to have a favorable balance of trade. They also sought to develop monopolistic type of environments wherein they provided their own raw materials thus avoiding imports which meant wealth flowing out and fostering the export of finished goods raising the level of wealth flowing in. Defining wealth as the accumulation of gold, the nations of Europe desired to conduct foreign trade on a larger scale, and they began looking for foreign sources of gold, silver, and raw materials.

This brings us to the British effort to develop North America as a source of wealth.

The Chesapeake colonies of Virginia and Maryland were the first successful British colonies in what was to become the United States of America. Though the initial colonists came looking for gold they soon learned that prosperity came not from a shovel but instead from a plow. It was tobacco that primed the pump and lifted the colonies from a burden to a benefit for the mother country. After years of mounting expenses for the British and years of starvation for the colonists the cultivation of tobacco brought prosperity. Virginia's production of tobacco grew from 200,000 pounds in 1624 to 3,000,000 pounds in 1638 overtaking the West Indies as the number one supplier of tobacco for all of Europe thus boosting Britain's balance of trade.

The cultivation of tobacco fostered a plantation system based upon indentured and slave labor. A gentrified class of great planters sought to replicate the social structure of Britain with a small number of very rich ruling a large number of small land holders who prospered to a certain extent but never enough to challenge the status quo. The wretched poor of Britain who had come to the Chesapeake colonies to find a better life did find more opportunity and the ability to advance from the landless poor to the ranks of yeoman farmer. However, there was little opportunity to enter the ranks for the gentry which became a type of American nobility.

New England, because of the soil, the climate, and the fact that there was no major cash crop that grew well in the area, did not lend itself to large plantations. Most farmers were operating at a subsistence level. If they did generate a surplus it was in crops that were not easily transported across the ocean, and these were also crops that could be grown in England and were not needed as imports.

This climatic and environmental adversity did not condemn New England to being a poor relation to the Chesapeake nobility. Instead the New English diversified, innovated, and used individual enterprise to not only match but to surpass Chesapeake and every other colony in the British Empire. Those who settled New England were Puritans who sought to purify the Anglican religion of ceremony and return it to what they saw as the simplicity of early Christianity.

They did not believe that good works brought salvation but they did believe that salvation brought good works. Therefore they sought to occupy their time with productive activity to glorify God through their labors. This was a manifestation of what the sociologist Max Weber later called, "The Protestant work ethic." Whatever you choose to call it, it was this drive to succeed no matter what the adversity that led the New English to look beyond the soil, beyond the climate and to the opportunity.

First they exploited the fisheries of the Northeast. In 1641 the New English caught 600,000 pounds of fish much of which was exported to Britain. By 1645 they were catching more than 6,000,000 pounds per year employing more than a thousand men on 440 ships. They came to dominate the fish trade shipping not only to Britain and its empire but also to Spain, Portugal, the Azores, Madeira, and the Canary Islands.

By the end of the 1600s the merchants of the New English coast began to circle the globe trading the fish, surplus crops, and lumber of their area to all parts of the British Empire. They became such shrewd traders that soon American ships were carrying trade from one colony to another even when the cargo didn't originate in New England. This secondary carrying trade generated a growing profit that in turn rebounded in a number of ways. The increased profits brought home financed increased industry and growth at home, and it also spawned a shipbuilding industry that exploited the vast resources of the northern forests.

Between 1674 and 1714 the New English built more than 1200 ships, totaling more than 75,000 tons. By 1700 there were 15 shipyards in Boston which produced more ships than all the rest of the British colonies combined. Only London had more shipyards. This was a significant engine of economic growth. To build one 150 ton merchant ship required as many as 200 workers, mostly skilled craftsmen. The shipyards also supported the growth of numerous enterprises to supply their needs such as saw mills, smithies, barrel makers, sail makers, iron foundries, and rope makers. In addition, the farmers of New England benefited by feeding the craftsmen, supplying the ships, and providing the timber.

By 1700 Boston was the third city of the Empire behind only London and Bristol and the New English shippers were earning freight charges for carrying produce and material that was neither produced, shipped to, or shipped from their home colony. The enrichment of the area spread prosperity far beyond the sphere of shippers, sailors, and their sundry suppliers. According to Boston's shipping register between 1697 and 1714 over 25% of the adult males in Boston owned shares in at least one ship.

All of these linkages produced an economy filled with diversification and development as opposed to the stratified monoculture of the Chesapeake colonies.

These trends continued as time went on leading to the industrial North eventually overwhelming the agricultural South. The expansion and growth of America was based upon a foundation of hard work and innovation born of adversity. Finding themselves in a hard place Americans found a way to prosper and grow like a young plant reaching for the Sun. Freed from the rigid restraints of the home country and then guaranteed freedom by the constitution and the limited government it provided America surged to the front ranks of nations.

Today, America labors under self-imposed adversity. We are in the grip of an oppressive Progressive Movement that after 100 years of incremental advance is poised to transform America[2] from what she has always been into what they want her to be. America has traditionally been a constitutionally limited Republic operating on democratic principles providing individual liberty and economic opportunity. The Progressives envision America as a centrally planned and highly regimented social democracy[3] where the wealth is spread around[4] from each according to their abilities to each according to their needs.

If I wanted to make America prosperous again I would take off the self-imposed shackles of a central government on steroids, stop imposing new regulations, and reduce taxes everywhere on everyone. Then I would stand back and watch our economy takes off like a rocket and we take our place beside our ancestors as free people with economic liberty and a will to succeed.

★ DISPATCH TWENTY-THREE ★

IF WE BLOW IT UP AGAIN IT WILL BLOW UP AGAIN

Back in 2007 when I was speaking of the crash to come I noted that we really didn't have to worry because our fearless and infallible leaders intuitively know the remedy. When the bubble bursts they will blow up another bubble.

The absolute triumph of Keynesian economics in America and the West has never been more on display than during our rocky journey through the Great Recession. An economic contraction which our leaders say is over and those of us who work and live in flyover country know is still grinding us down to the new normal. Troubled Asset Relief Program (TARP) was going to save the economy. It didn't. President Obama's porkulus stimulus was going to save the economy. It didn't. Quantitative Easing 1 (QE 1)and QE 2 were going to save the economy. They didn't.

Then along comes QE 3 with an open ended commitment to pump 85 billion per month into the economy, and presto-change-o alakazam and miraculously the stock market is breaking new highs and the real estate market is beginning to revive. Unemployment keeps inching down and even the Neocons over on Fox are telling us the cratered economy is showing signs of life. It turns out if you magically create trillions of dollars and drop them from helicopters across the country there seems to be more money blowing in the wind. As one very profitable prophet once said, "It doesn't take a weatherman to know which way the wind blows."

Hang on to your hats because a booming economy has to become part of the Obama legacy so that the transition to a centrally planned economy can ever be hailed as the prescription for success. Just as the booming economy of the 1990s is constantly brought up as "The prosperity we experienced during the Clinton years." If any politician ever attempts to restore economic freedom, or when there is another crash tries to blame on it too much regulation they will be demonized for a pathological fear of deficits, and seeking return to the old days of greed and avarice.

Those of us old enough to remember the Clinton years should know that it was the peace dividend and the Tech Boom Bubble which fueled the prosperity of the 1990s. We should also remember that it was a phony peace dividend since our military was engaged in interventions around the world during Clinton's depredations in the oval office. We should also remember that the Tech Boom flew through the air with billions in stock values for companies that made no profit and eventually delivered not prosperity but the crash of 2000.

Our Constitution was not written to be a living document that evolves over time. The words were never meant to take on new meanings with every passing generation. The accumulation of case law and judicial proclamations was not meant to supplant the written political contract that the Sovereign States individually decided to ratify. However, contrary to the oft stated desires of the Founders of our nation and the Framers of the Constitution the United States has evolved into a behemoth bureaucracy. In all bureaucracies instead of the best and the brightest rising to the top those who learn to pull the levers the best end up controlling the machine. Often the official leaders are merely telegenic front men for the powers behind the throne. The grifters who have gained power through elections filled with ineligible[1] voters,[2] outright frauds,[3] gerrymandering, and a two party system where-in Progressives control both parties use the living document ruse to turn the Constitution into a dead letter.

Crony capitalism has replaced free enterprise. Just watch the big gaming table at the New York Stock Exchange. Its volatile swings are dictated not by innovation, profits or production instead they are moved by real or projected government actions. Will the Fed keep creating money out of thin air? Will the EPA impose Cap-N-Trade? Will the imperial presidency use a foreign adventure to grasp more power? The banks act as willing accomplices of the Fed borrowing money at 0% interest and buying Treasuries at 3% helping to maintain the fiction that we aren't monetizing our debt and printing our way to prosperity.[4] The foreigners who used to crowd the treasury auctions know what is going on.[5] Today the biggest purchasers of American debt are American banks using the Fed's funny money.[6]

How many times must this Ponzi scheme economy show itself for what it is? How many times must this self-serving Progressive cabal be exposed for the hypocritical central-planning neo-fascists that they are? How many articles like this must be written before enough people wake up and do something? We glory in the American Revolution. It overthrew tyranny and established personal independence, individual freedom, and economic opportunity on a scale that had never been seen before in the world. This is something worth celebrating. However, the counter revolution has been in progress since Hamilton founded the first bank and John Adams threw his opponents in jail. The cost of freedom is eternal vigilance, and today's generation may be too busy watching the game to notice their country is being transformed into something they won't recognize by the time they get up for their seventh inning stretch.[7]

Any semblance of a freely functioning economy has vanished since Progressive leaders like FDR, LBJ, Nixon and Barrack H. Obama (BHO) birthed and nurtured government control and intervention as an 800 pound gorilla on steroids. The mirage of false prosperity is once again raising its crowned head out of the sea of financial calamity it created with the last bubble. A new bubble is forming and happy days will soon be here again with a chicken in every pot and a flat screen in every home. How many of our fellow citizens will be swept up in the coming Obama Boom? How many will be devastated when it all comes crashing down again?

The too-big-to-fail friends of the government will be made whole. The perpetually re-elected and their handlers will have their golden parachute pensions and plush jobs on K-Street[8] and at Fannie, Freddie[9] and crony filled board rooms across the country.[10] The only ones hurt will be those who do the real work, those who play by the rules. When the new bubble blows up the remedy is readymade: we'll just blow up another bubble. How could this ever go wrong?

★ DISPATCH TWENTY-FOUR ★

IF WE DON'T WIN WE LOSE

America's slide from the forefront of freedom to the swamp of collectivist social engineering didn't start with the current manager of our decline and his Cavalcade of Czars. It didn't start with President Obama's favorite foil and arch-nemesis the man the Corporations-Once-Known-as-the Mainstream-Media love to hate, George Bush, the Younger. It didn't start with the Bush–Clinton decade + 2 of continuous government growth, its thousand points of light or its Hillarycare.[1]

Even Ronaldus Magnus, the president Conservatives love and Progressives love to hate left Washington bigger than he found it.

Jimmy Carter not only walked[2] in the Inaugural Parade he walked us into the grip of a Department of Energy that works tirelessly to limit our energy production and a Department of Education that presides over the greatest decline in education in world History.[2] He chastised us in his malaise speech about our crisis of confidence never realizing it was our confidence in him not our country that was hobbling America. And what was his advice? Should we work harder, invent more, or launch out in bold new ways? No he suggested we wear sweaters and turn the heat down. Managing the decline has long been the theme song of those who see America's glory days in the rearview mirror instead of in the headlights as we travel towards the future.

What about Nixon? Forget about it! He gave us price controls,[3] OSHA, and the EPA. He took us off the gold standard,[4] proudly proclaimed "I am now a Keynesian,"[4] and left us at the mercy of the Federal Reserve, all this from the conservative wing of the Dualocracy which is the bi-polar Party of Power.

Lyndon Johnson and his Great Society, Medicare, Medicaid, and Food Stamp revolution created the entitlement monsters which are poised to devour the budget.

Though he cut taxes[5] to spur the economy, Kennedy with his phony missile gap[6] and foreign policy blunders[7] did little besides set the stage for Johnson.

Though he was the last president to cut the size of government and who made the hard choices to restrain growth, Eisenhower spent 8 years guiding the construction of the Military Industrial Complex[8] he warned[9] us about as he left the stage.

The Fair Deal[10] was merely Truman's election-driven attempt to increase the size, scope, and power of FDR's New Deal[11] which was a massive and unprecedented intrusion of the central government into the economic and social life of America.

FDR was the twentieth century poster boy when it comes to stretching the size of government and putting the stamp of entitlement as the cause on liberty's death certificate.

Hoover, contrary to FDR's story line and the accepted version of America's History, responded to the stock market crash with a massive extension of government and its programs. The Great Engineer, as he was known before his name became a household word for failed presidency, was a champion of government intervention, and though today his devotion to the tenets of laissez-faire are blamed for the depression when it was instead his federal interference that provided a deep recession for FDR to turn into the Great Depression.[12]

Silent Cal Coolidge[13] was America's last limited President. He limited himself and stayed within the confines of the Constitution.

Harding tried but died.[14]

Wilson used the War[15] he bragged[16] of keeping us out of as the excuse to arrest and detain citizens, seize control of the economy, foster segregation and racism, and generally slap the cuffs of a greatly expanded central government on America's wrists.

Taft was Teddy Roosevelt's handpicked successor. And although he continued the Progressive agenda of attacking business and expanding government he didn't do enough.[17] So Roosevelt broke with him and his presidency running against him splitting the Republican vote and opening the door for the Progressive Democrat Wilson.

Teddy was the grandfather of them all. His trust busting interventionism was Progressivism personified.[18]

Though this may be the genealogy of the current gang of statists who are poised to smother freedom, the struggle to keep constitutionally limited government, personal liberty, and economic freedom alive has been one long series of attack defenses declines and rebirths.

The second President, John Adams, was a man who helped write the Declaration of Independence and the Constitution. He was a man who worked tirelessly for the ratification of the Constitution. He also championed and signed the Alien and Sedition Acts[19] under which he arrested people who criticized him, his administration or his policies. From there it goes on and on.

Jefferson compromised his beliefs[20] about the limited power of the central government and purchased Louisiana without Constitutional authority, a good deal but a bad precedent. Monroe committed America to defending the entire Western Hemisphere. Polk sent American troops into territory internationally recognized as part of Mexico and then asked for a declaration of war when Mexican troops fired on those troops.[21] Lincoln suspended the right of habeas corpus whenever he needed to in order to maintain the Union though the Constitution does not grant that power to the Federal Government.[22] The 10th Amendment[23] strictly prohibits[24] the

Federal Government from having any powers not expressly delegated to it, and at least one state, Virginia, in their ratification convention expressly considered the Union voluntary and reserved the right to secede.[25]

From one battle to another America's freedom fighters have stood before the Leviathan of Central Government and clung relentlessly to the promises first set forth in the founding document of the United States of America, "We hold these truths to be self-evident, that all men are created equal, that they are endowed by their Creator with certain inalienable rights, that among these are life, liberty and the pursuit of happiness."[26] Considering that these uplifting and timeless words of human liberty were penned by a slaveholder and that it took four score and nine years for this stain to be removed from our nation we can see that our road away from serfdom has always been one of fits and starts.

Today we face the next great challenge. Progressivism, America's current variation on the age-old theme of government knows best is poised to break the bounds of limited government, regiment the people, and smother the economy. After more than 100 years of incremental growth in just over 4 years the promises of hope and change have broken the bank and mortgaged the future. One more term of this profligate spending and oppressive regulations and they will kill the golden goose.

The forces of freedom cannot afford to lose another election to the purveyors of class warfare and division. If we do this great experiment in limited government, personal freedom and economic liberty will have progressed from a new country on the margins of civilization to the greatest power the world has ever known, to just another socially engineered centrally planned economically shackled democracy voting itself benefits it can't afford.

Our adversaries believe they have stacked the deck by taking control of both major political parties which operate as two wings on the same bird of prey. They hope by nominating a Progressive in both parties there will be no way for the forces of freedom to prevail.

Our ranks are filled with those who have been in the trenches for a lifetime and are weary of the fight. They have been joined by the recently awakened who know little of the history and less of the tactics. Our opposition is comprised of the slickest, best funded, and most corrupt professional politicians, labor barons, and crony capitalists the world has ever seen with thousands of Occupy storm troopers thrown in for good measure. The odds are against us. The smart money is betting on the victory of the all-powerful government, lining up to get their deals and haul away the loot.

The odds have always been against us. We fought the greatest empire in the world to gain our freedom. We have persevered and prevailed against plot after plot to extinguish the light of liberty and in this battle too we must remember that the one we should never be forgotten told us long ago, "If my people, who are called by my name, will humble themselves and pray and seek my face and turn from their wicked ways, then I will hear from heaven, and I will forgive their sin and will heal their land."[27]

Yes, the blood of more than 54,000,000 innocent lives[28] cry out for justice, yes we as a people have legalized what should be unlawful and condoned what should be condemned. Yes, we have fallen from the high road and are weakened by an entitlement mentality and an addiction to entertainment. But we are the American people. We are, "We the People" and if we will but turn and acknowledge the one who has given us everything we have a chance.

The time is now. The place is here. We are the people we have been waiting for. We must rise to the occasion. We must win this battle because if we don't win we lose.

Keep the faith. Keep the peace. We shall overcome.

★ DISPATCH TWENTY-FIVE ★

IMMOVABLE OBJECT MEET THE IRRESISTIBLE FORCE

Many times in our history we've been confronted with what seemed like impossible odds.

In 1776 13 sparsely populated colonies clinging for life to the Atlantic seaboard surrounded by a forest that ran unbroken to the Mississippi dared to stand up to our imperial masters and say, "We hold these truths to be self-evident, that all men are created equal, that they are endowed by their Creator with certain unalienable rights, that among these are life, liberty and the pursuit of happiness."

No foreign king, no Prime Minister and no Parliament had the right to dictate to our ancestors what taxes to pay or how much they should be. Even though England at the time was the dominant superpower, the undersupplied and overmatched Americans refused to admit defeat. We lost New York. We lost battle after battle retreating more than we advanced, yet the prize of freedom overcame the penalty of failure, and against all odds victory was won.

When the pirates of Tripoli sought to extort tribute from us as they did from every other nation that passed through their waters our people rose up with a cry of, "Millions for defense but not a cent for tribute!" Gathering our miniscule navy and our brave marines the United States fought our way into the port of the pirates while a land force fought its way through the desert eventually claiming what the great powers of the day did not: the right to pass unmolested and the right to trade in freedom.

A generation later in our second war with England, the War of 1812,[1] we once again went toe-to-toe with the third largest army in the world and the largest navy the world had ever seen. The British defeated our attempt to invade Canada as they invaded our territory almost at will. Their armed forces ranged up and down our coast. They chased President Madison out of Washington and burned the White House. The only major battle we won was fought after the peace treaty was signed, yet we emerged bloody but vindicated. We had challenged the greatest empire in the world. We held our own winning new respect around the world.

Next, when the nations of Central and South America found the courage to rise up against their own colonial masters declaring their freedom with the hope of establishing free and independent republics modeled after the United States, President Monroe threw down the gauntlet to the rest of the world when he boldly presented his Doctrine.[2] Though our navy was miniscule and our army was almost nonexistent he relied upon the inherent strength of our people when he proclaimed the western hemisphere off limits to any power seeking to establish or re-establish colonies. We did not have the authority, we did not have the power, but we had the courage to say leave freedom alone so that our neighbors could develop their own lands for themselves.

In the Civil War America tore itself apart. For 4 long years the war raged killing more Americans than all our other wars put together. The powers of Europe believed the experiment in freedom was proving itself to be a failure. France moved to establish a sphere of influence in Mexico as the other great powers waited expectantly to pick up the pieces. As the war picked up momentum the emerging industrial might and burgeoning manpower of the new nation was pressed into service until by 1864 the Union Army was the largest and best equipped on earth and the Confederate Army was the second. Setting a pattern for all future wars the newest technology and the latest inventions such as railroads, iron-clad steam powered ships, telegraphs, repeating rifles, and machine guns first made their appearance in the American military. Against all odds we re-united our nation, sent France packing, and reaffirmed the Monroe Doctrine.

In WWI the two contending sides in Europe had bled each other dry on the fields of Flanders and fought to a stalemate. Then America sent our troops over there and didn't bring them back until it was over, over there. In WWII fascist dictators thought the Western democracies were decadent and ready to collapse with a good kick. And their plan seemed to be working until one of them made the mistake of kicking on our door, and we rose up like a giant from slumber and led the way in bringing their roofs down upon their heads.

As the Communist Colossus rose from the ashes of WWII to include Eastern Europe, and China America built NATO, held them at bay in Europe, and then stood almost alone to battle them as they tried to expand in Korea, Asia, and Central America. American blood and treasure was expended in torrents for five decades until the Soviet Union collapsed as a Christmas present to the world in 1991.[3] Against the uncounted hordes of the East and the fellow travelers in our midst we persevered and gained the victory.

Time and again when the odds were against us we, the American people have risen to the challenge. Whenever we have confronted a problem we have found some way to succeed. When President Kennedy challenged us to go to the Moon we did. When President Ragan challenged us to believe in ourselves again after the shame of Watergate, the forfeiture of our victory in Vietnam, and the Iran Hostage crisis we did.[4]

Today we face financial collapse and overwhelming debt. Today our adversaries aren't foreign dictators but our own elected officials who want to continue spending no matter what the voters say. Today the challenge is a system that doesn't work, a Congress that is bought and paid for, and a Progressive Movement that has managed to organize itself into power at every level in every branch and in both major parties.

No matter what the problems are, we're the American people. We're exceptional, and we can do it! It's time for every good citizen to come to the aid of our nation. We must stand for the solution or we'll fall before the problem. As a President who knew the way to grow an economy was to cut taxes once said, "We shall pay any price, bear any burden, meet any hardship, support any friend, oppose any foe, to assure the survival and success of liberty."[5] We've got to pick up the burden before Atlas shrugs. If we'll admit we have a problem we will find a solution. After all, we're the American people. Immovable Object Meet the Irresistible Force.

★ DISPATCH TWENTY-SIX ★

IMPERIAL REPUBLICS FALL

Historians spend their life looking backwards. Futurists spend their life looking forward. My goal has been to blend the two disciplines into one seamless endeavor.

When I was studying to become a Historian I came to a point where I had to declare a field of special study. This is where my obsession with current events intersected with my love for History. This is when I realized that current events are the forever unfolding always receding conveyor belt of reality. This is when I first verbalized the perception that as the future slides into the present and the present slides into the past our lives are the history of the future. Therefore in my writings I seek to frame the flow of today with the knowledge of yesterday to create a window into tomorrow.

History tells us that Imperial Republics fall. We have the examples of Athens1 and all the other grasping Greek republics that followed her. We have Rome[2] the example always deferred to of a republic that allowed empire to stifle freedom. The list however does not end there, we can look at Venice and the various republics of Renaissance Italy and of course the First Republic of France which was birthed in blood and died with a whimper as Napoleon grasped the Imperial crown. The siren song of empire has seduced republics down through history to trade in their freedom for power which eventually cost them both their freedom and the power.

Is it time to re-think America's international military commitments? Though settled by European kingdoms seeking empires the United States wasn't founded to become an empire. Individuals fought against the empire building tyrants until their determination and resolve won independence against all odds. Then, although the world was filled with despotic kings, our Framers gave us a Republic. However, it is worth remembering the exchange that took place between Ben Franklin, the elder statesman of the Constitutional Convention and an unknown woman. As he left Independence Hall he was asked, "Well Doctor what we have got a republic or a monarchy?" Appealing to his legendary wit Franklin replied, "A republic, if you can keep it."[3] We and our ancestors have been blessed by the Republic for hundreds of years. We've benefited from the liberty to live our lives and pursue our happiness. Now we've arrived at the "if you can keep it" phase of our journey.

At the cost of hundreds of billions and thousands of lives we doubled-down in Afghanistan. At the cost of over a trillion and thousands of lives we conquered Iraq and deposed Saddam to establish an ally for Iran. We spearheaded the bombing campaign in Libya and deposed Gaddafi so that Islamo-terrorists could attack our embassy and kill our diplomats. Our drones strike suspected enemies far and near. Troops have been dispatched to central Africa. And the perennial war drums still beat at the very mention of Iran.

We have sent our fellow citizens to fight long hard slogs in countries whose names are the very synonym for Quagmire. As our economy was being outsourced, our debt monetized, and our infrastructure crumbled we meekly followed our leaders deeper into thankless nation-building campaigns in nation after nation including one that's resisted and foiled every empire from Alexander to Moscow.

Instead of using our cruise missiles and stealth capabilities we fell into the trap announced and laid by Bin Laden. Whose strategy was as Lawrence Wright told us in his seminal book *Looming Towers* to, "lure America into the same trap the Soviets had fallen into: Afghanistan."[4] How did he plan to do it? "To continually attack until the U.S. forces invaded; then the mujahedeen would swarm upon them and bleed them until the entire American empire fell from its wounds. It had happened to Great Britain and to the Soviet Union. He was certain it would happen to America."

There were twists and turns on our journey from republic to empire.

George Washington[5] warned us to avoid foreign entanglements. Thomas Jefferson outlined the essential principles of our government which included this advice concerning foreign affairs, "peace, commerce, and honest friendship with all nations entangling alliances with none."[6]

For more than 100 years we concentrated on using our liberty to build a mighty nation. Then the temptation of empire captured the American imagination in the 1890s, a time when Europe was rushing to gobble up the last places open for colonization or carving up those areas unsuited for colonies into spheres of influence. Under President McKinley[7] the United States entered the scramble for colonies in the Spanish-American War winning Puerto Pico and the Philippines.[8]

Teddy Roosevelt[9] followed McKinley walking softly while carrying a big stick in the form of the Great White Fleet[10] and multiple intrusions into the sovereignty of Latin-American countries. After being re-elected on the promise to keep America neutral President Wilson[11] proclaimed America must fight WWI to "Make the World Safe for Democracy"[12] an adventure which cost over 300,000 casualties and which actually expanded the empires of England, France, and Japan. After the war, the Congress of the United States re-asserted control by rejecting the international entanglements of the League of Nations Treaty[13] returning to the traditional American foreign policy of freedom of trade and freedom of action.

Under FDR America fought an undeclared naval war[14] against Germany in 1940 and 1941 and imposed draconian embargoes against Japan[15] prior to Pearl Harbor. Once we were attacked we had to defend ourselves.

However, when WWII ended not with the defeat of totalitarianism but instead with the expansion of it in Eastern Europe the guiding light of American foreign policy seems to have been permanently extinguished. As the British Empire sailed into the sunset we filled the void taking up the role of leader of the West in the Cold War. For 46 years we faced the Soviets until they collapsed. Then instead of coming home we spread our wings even further embracing Eastern Europe promising to send young Americans to fight for Estonia and Slovakia among others, and so the sun never set upon the American Empire.

Not only is it against the founding principles of America to establish and maintain an empire of far-flung outposts, we cannot afford to be the Policeman of the world. We cannot afford to build nations for people who don't want them. How did a peaceful nation of free citizens become the advocate of pre-emptive attack and endless occupation? How much blood and treasure will we invest in Iraq, and what will be the result? A Shi'a[16] ally for Iran.[17] The war in Afghanistan was obviously defensive and retaliatory in nature given the Taliban's support for Al Qaeda. But 10 years later what's it all about? Are we really dedicated to building a modern nation for tribal people who have no sense of nationhood? Or have we walked into the same trap that brought the Soviets to their knees?

Currently the United States has armed forces in over 130 countries.[18] We're committed to defend most of these countries against aggression. Where were all these allies on 9/11? Where are they in Afghanistan? Why do we have treaties binding us to go to war to defend those who refuse to support us when we're attacked? If these policies are counter-productive are there any alternatives?

Close the foreign bases and bring our troops home. Station them on the borders to protect us from the on-going invasion of illegal immigrants who're overloading our systems. We have sealed and secured the mountainous border between the Koreas and we can secure our own borders if we have the wisdom and the will. If we need to project American power use the carrier battle-groups designed for that purpose. Protect America and rebuild our infrastructure instead of everyone else's. When asked what to do with the American Military after WWI Will Rogers said, "Get 'em all home, add to their number, add to their training, then just sit tight with a great feeling of security and just read about foreign wars. That's the best thing in the world to do with them."[19]

If we want to save the Republic we need to lose the empire or we can cling to the empire and lose both.

★ DISPATCH TWENTY-SEVEN ★

IS AMERICA A REPUBLIC OR AN EMPIRE?

I have written about the American Empire. I have advocated jettisoning the Empire to save the Republic. This topic has sparked debate and controversy even among the most dedicated readers. Usually the argument runs like this, "America is not an Empire, never has been and never will be," or "America's far-flung military deployments are not the garrisoning of an empire it is instead a forward defense of the homeland."

In a recent article along these lines, aptly entitled, "Republic or Empire?" in several publications there was spirited debate about whether or not America could be called an empire. Some people seemed to take offense at the very idea. Others who usually agree with my political stands find this and my other foreign policy positions such as bringing our troops home, concentrating on defending America, and equitable trade with all unacceptable. I present and promote these foreign policy positions as requirements for restoring limited government. It is my belief that as long as we are involved in endless war there is no real possibility to re-gain control of our government, our budget, or our future.

What I propose to do here is examine the hallmarks of empire and ask my readers to honestly ask themselves, "Is America a republic or an empire?"

First, it makes no difference whether it is the President, the Paramount Chief, an Augustus, the First Citizen, the Dear Leader, the Great Helmsman or der Fuehrer. It doesn't matter if it is an executive branch, a Politburo, a Central Committee, the Cabinet, or the collective leadership. Whatever form it takes, an empire is always dominated by a highly centralized executive power.

America was designed not to be an empire but instead to be a federal republic made up of a central government and state governments which were the precursors and creators of the central government. This central government founded upon and constrained by a written constitution originally presented the world with something new, a national government made up of divided co-equal powers. The Congress to make the laws, the executive to enforce the laws, and the judicial to judge if the laws conformed to the Constitution: the guiding light and touch-stone of American limited government. This worked well to establish and maintain a republic but it would not foster nor perpetuate an empire.

Thus the Constitution established the framework of what became known as the system of checks and balances. Only Congress could make laws, but the President could veto them. Congress could over-ride a president's veto, but the Supreme Court could declare laws unconstitutional making them null and void. The President is in charge of foreign policy and is the Commander-in-Chief of the armed forces, but the Congress controlled the purse and could cut off funding. Upon petition the Supreme Court could declare the actions of the President unconstitutional yet the president could appoint justices to the Supreme Court.

Did this work perfect? No, there were always swings one way or another. There have been powerful Supreme Courts such as under Chief Justices Marshall or Warren that changed the complexion of the country. There have been powerful Congresses such as the one from 1865 to the mid-1870s that virtually ignored presidents and set policy. There were powerful presidents such as Jackson or Lincoln. However the pendulum always swung back and forth. If you examined all three institutions there was one thing missing. Where was the sovereignty? Who was the nation?

In the highly centralized state, which is an empire whether personal or national, the leader or leadership operates according to the sentiments of the Sun King, Louis XIV of France who said, "I am the State."[1] During the birth of the American system, our Founders had spent more time debating this than any other aspect of the government, who would be the sovereign power. They had just fought and defeated one tyrant and they did not want to exchange one for another. They didn't trust the sovereignty of the nation in the hands of an executive because of the long and bloody history of Europeans with absolutism and divine right. They didn't trust an assembly after their recent history with the tyranny of the British Parliament and their Stamp Act,[2] Quartering Act[3] and other attempts to bring the colonies to their knees. They couldn't place it in the hands of the Supreme Court for that body would be merely judicial.

Instead they came up with a new idea in the world. They placed the sovereignty of the nation in the hands of *We the People.*

The Constitution is designed to empower the people not the government. Though today it is stretched and interpreted to give the government the power to do whatever it wants whenever it wants originally it was constructed to limit government.

We the People could vote the Congress in or out, we could choose our own president, and if the Supreme Court said something was unconstitutional that we wanted we could change the Constitution using a mechanism embedded within the document itself. For the first time no leader or oligarchy owned the state, instead the state belonged to the citizens.

What do we see in America today? We have a president who says, "We can't wait for an increasingly dysfunctional Congress to do its job. Where they won't act, I will."[4] When Congress after deliberation decides not to pass the Dream Act[5] giving amnesty to millions, the President uses an executive order to make it law by decree. When the Congress refuses to pass a Cap-and-Trade law[6] that many believe will hamstring our industry and hobble us in the race with other nations, the President orders his EPA department to enforce it anyway. Without consulting Congress the President takes us to war against Libya and deposes a government.[7]

These are the actions of an executive out of control.[8] Under the original American system if anyone would have asked, "Who speaks for the people?" the answer would have been the House of Representatives because they were elected every two years and were thus closest to the people. It wouldn't have been the Congress as a whole because under the original system the Senate was chosen by the various State legislatures and was designed to represent the States. It was the House which spoke for the people. Today it is the President who uses the bully pulpit magnified by a subservient press and a thousand government media pressure points and outlets saying in effect, I have a mandate from the people. I am the embodiment of their will. I am the state.

The next hallmark of an empire we will look at is that domestic policy becomes subordinate to foreign policy. The American President is constitutionally in charge of foreign policy so there is no better place for the holder of that office to act without any restraint. Treaties must be ratified, so our presidents began in the 1940s to forge personal agreements with the leaders of other countries that had all the force of treaties with none of the messy Senate confirmation required. Using their power as Commander-in-Chief of the armed forces modern presidents have also used their authority to start wars as in Kosovo and Libya, to sign cease fires as in Korea, and to commit America to the support of dictators and tyrants through deployments and equipment transfers, all without any Congressional oversight.

If we ask ourselves, has domestic policy really become subordinate to foreign policy think about whose infrastructure are we being taxed to rebuild? In Afghanistan and Iraq our money and our companies are building new schools while ours fall apart, we are building new roads in Afghanistan while we watch our own bridges crumbling. We give billions to countries and governments that despise us. We borrow money to give it away and then sometimes borrow it back[9] all in a bizarre[10] dance[11] balancing foreign interests at the expense of We the People.

Another hallmark of an empire is that the military mindset becomes ascendant to the point that civilians are intimidated. Think about the Defense budget. In 2012 it was over 600 billion dollars.[12] Does anyone believe Congress or anyone else really knows where all that money is going? The size,[13] scope[14] and unbelievable waste[15] in the defense budget stagger the imagination. However, to even question the defense budget will immediately get someone labeled as an isolationist who wants to gut our defense and surrender to the enemy.

Many people will argue that we are in a war and that during war of course the defense budget will be bloated. Can you remember any time since 1942 that we haven't been in a war? Yes, there were the brief days of the "Peace Dividend" under Clinton after the Soviet Union dissolved. And during those brief days of peace back in the 1990s we fought a war and enforced a decade long no-fly zone in Iraq, attacked Serbia, sent troops, planes or other assets to Zaire, Sierra Leone, Bosnia (numerous times), Herzegovina, Somalia, Macedonia, Haiti, Liberia, Central African Republic, Albania, Congo and Gabon, Cambodia, Guinea-Bissau, Kenya, Tanzania, Sudan, Afghanistan, and East Timor. And this was our only decade of peace since the 1940s, and to question any of this is considered tantamount to treason. We must ask ourselves, "Has the military mindset become ascendant to the point that civilians are intimidated?"

Perpetual war for peace has led the peaceful American people to be ensnared in the clutches of the military–industrial complex as President Eisenhower warned it would in 1961.[16]

All empires develop and maintain a system of satellite nations. When we hear of this we immediately think of the old USSR and their slave states in Eastern Europe. Advance the idea that America has satellite nations and people become irate. "How could you say such a thing about America?" Look at our so-called allies. Do they fit the description as satellite nations? A satellite nation is one that the empire deems is necessary for its own defense. It is also one that feels it cannot stand alone and wants the empire's protection.

That is the deal. The empire commits to protect the satellite and the satellite agrees to stand with its back against the empire facing a common foe. Added to that is the fact that we supply money and material to build the national defenses of our satellites/allies as well as economic aid and a preferential trade system. Think about these ideas and decide for yourself whether or not America has satellite nations ringing the heartland of the empire.

Another hallmark of empire is that a psychology or psychosis of pride, presumption, and arrogance overtakes the national consciousness. We are all familiar with the twenty-first century incantation of "Too big to fail." That was applied by our bailout happy leaders to their pet banks and companies during the opening days of the Great Recession. It is also an apt description for the way in which most Americans view our position as the most powerful nation on earth or as the silver-tongued talking heads like to say, the world's sole superpower. Since the end of WWI the United States has been the unchallenged mega power among the western block of nations. Since the dissolution of the Soviet Union we have towered like a colossus over the rest of the world. In the memory of most people now alive it has always been this way.

To most people the way it has been is the way it shall be. We speak of embracing change and of realizing that change is the only constant but few can really think that way. The familiar seduces us into thinking that the momentary circumstances of today are the unshakable foundations of tomorrow. To the children and grandchildren of the greatest generation the world will always gaze in awe at the great American eagle soaring above the world. Our navy rules the waves, our masses of fighters, bombers, and drones can reach out and touch any corner of the globe, our troops are the best trained, best equipped, and best led armies the world has ever seen, so such a mega power could never fall.

So it seemed to the inhabitants of Rome the eternal empire. So it seemed to the British when the Sun never set upon the union jack. And so it seems to us even though a rag-tag group like Al Qaeda defies our attempts to destroy them and continues to grow and multiply around the world. Even though the Taliban not only have withstood more than a decade of war they stand poised to reclaim their country as soon as we leave. Even though our deficit spending[17] and the national debt[18] it creates is leading us to a financial collapse that our own military leaders have identified as the greatest threat to our security[19] and our leader's only answer is more spending. This pride, presumption, and arrogance blind us to the enduring truth of what comes before a fall.

Finally an empire is the prisoner of history. A republic is not required to act upon the world stage. It can pick and choose its own way seeking its own destiny as a commonwealth of citizens. An empire must project its power for fear that if it doesn't another leviathan will arise to take its place. A free republic that has maintained its independence is able to decide where and when it will become involved. An empire is always the leader of a center of a heavy coalition comprising the imperial core and the associated or satellite nations. As such it is the collective security against the barbarian, the other that drives the actions of the empire.

In the parlance of our day it is our turn. It is our turn to be the policeman of the world, our turn to keep the peace, to guard civilization from the unwashed hordes who seek to turn back the clock and bring darkness into the world. We are a vanguard of stability in a world beset by chaos, and so were the British and the Romans before them.

Other writers may say something has been left off these hallmarks while others may say some of these don't apply. To all I would recommend a study of former empires to see if they agree these properties are found in all of them. Then ask ourselves, "Are these properties present in America today?" Once we have completed this process we will be able to answer the question for ourselves, "Is America an Empire?" If we decide, yes it is, we have to realize that there is a trajectory all empires follow: they rise and they fall.

We might decide that, we as the first empire that is not set-up to plunder wealth but instead to distribute wealth, are different, and therefore we will break the mold. We will stand while others have fallen. One look at our debt should persuade anyone that what we have built is as unsustainable as the British, the Roman, or any other empire we wish to use as a standard.

Do you say, "We can't be an empire because our president is elected." So were the emperors of the Holy Roman Empire, so were the kings of Poland. It is the empire that empowers our executive. Do you say, "We can't be an empire because we have a Congress." So did Athens, Rome, and Britain. Do you say, "We can't be an empire because we have freedom of speech, freedom of assembly, why we even have the freedom to own weapons." So did Athens, so did Rome, and so did Britain.

While we are yet on the glory side of the fall let us abandon the empire to save our republic. Let us resign from the great game of thrones, rebuild America, secure our own borders instead of those of Korea, or Afghanistan, and reaffirm our dedication to be the last best hope of mankind: a federal republic operating on democratic principles, securing our God-given liberties, providing personal freedom, individual liberty, and economic opportunity to all its citizens.

★ DISPATCH TWENTY-EIGHT ★

Is America Under Judgment?

All that follows I will preface with, "I believe." I am not attempting to establish theology for anyone or to declare that anyone who does not agree with me is a heretic. I am merely sharing my beliefs, grounded on study and prayer, since my opinion has been solicited on this topic more than once.

Many Christians today bring every conversation back to, "Do you think these are the last days?"

This may be based on a personal reading of the Book of Revelation in the Bible. It could be based on the broadcast sermons and teachings of any number of professional End Times preachers who have built careers on pointing to an apocalypse around the corner.

The signs of the times are always easy to read they just aren't so easy to interpret. Nero was the Antichrist as was Diocletian, King James II, Napoleon, Hitler, Stalin, and Mao. False Prophets have equally abounded from the Pope to Martin Luther, from Henry VIII to Rasputin to Jim Jones.

Is the End coming? Most certainly. Can we know when it is coming? Most certainly not. Since it is impossible to know when the end is coming I cannot believe that God would want us wasting any of the precious time He gives us speculating as to when it will arrive instead of being His witnesses to the world.

Since it is anti-biblical to believe we can know the date of the End,[1] it is obviously not a Godly use of our time to try and figure it out anyway. What can we know? Just as we can look at the clouds and know when a storm is coming or smell the wind and know when a rain is on the way, so to we can look at the present state of our nation and know the time of the season. If we use the analogy of a year's cycle it is obviously fall headed for the winter. It has been fall headed for the winter since the crucifixion of Christ: the fulcrum of History.

Some may ask, "Why has fall lasted so long?" The problem is we really don't know how long the previous winter and spring were. The belief that the Bible tells us that there were approximately X number of thousand years before Christ and there will be X number of years after Christ equaling 7,000 years as a week in God's time as taught by some popular TV preachers is based on the a tissue of strung-together scriptures and cherry-picked verses. Equally, the belief that the time from Adam and Christ is discernible from the Biblical text is based on the erroneous belief that the Bible is presented as a linear historical document.

While I believe that the Bible contains real History and that it is literally true I do not believe that it presents a year for year time-line type of presentation. The Old Testament is above all a spiritual History of how God chose one people and eventually one person to bring forth the Chosen One: Jesus Christ, the Messiah of the Jews and the Savior of man. I do not believe that by counting up the lives of everyone mentioned in Old Testament genealogies it is possible to know how many years elapsed between "Let there be light" and the birth, death, or resurrection of Christ.

Most of the names mentioned in the many Old Testament genealogies have no age associated with them so the would-be Biblical timeliner has to make a guess. Also when you compare the genealogies there are obvious overlaps, repetitions, and omissions. Compare the New Testament genealogies of Christ found in Luke and in Matthew and you will see the problem with genealogies as linear History.[2] Now multiply that by all the genealogies in the Old Testament and you will begin to see the problem with this method of calculating time.

The people who tell us that the Old Testament gives us an accurate count of the years between the beginning and the beginning of the end are the same ones who tell us that they can figure out from the book of Revelation when the end of time will come. They do this in spite of the fact that Christ Himself tells us in Matthew, "But about that day or hour no one knows, not even the angels in heaven, nor the Son, but only the Father."[3] Then to make the point again it was one of the last things He told us before ascending to Heaven in Acts, "It is not for you to know times or seasons which the Father has put in His own authority."[4]

Since we cannot know the day or the hour, the times or the seasons how godly can it be to spend so much time trying to figure it out? So much for trying to figure out when THE end is since it can't be done. However, I felt I had to deal with that before I moved on to the real subject of this dispatch: whether or not America is under judgment.

I believe that is a topic that can be discerned by anyone with eyes to see and ears to hear. I am not talking about the end of the United States. It is and will be called by the same name, waving the same flag. I will let you judge if it is the same country we grew up in.

Looking at the spiritual History of the Old Testament as a guide we see that Judah the southern kingdom of the Jews, the believing remnant that carried on the covenant after the apostatized Kingdom of Israel had been carried off into exile was finally delivered into the hands of its enemies because they had sacrificed their children to pagan gods and walked in the ways of the world.[5] Since 1972 when a case based upon a lie[6] was used by an activist Supreme Court to invent a constitutional right to abort babies over 54 million Americans have been deprived of the most fundamental right of all: Life.[7]

God does not condemn societies because of the sin within them because the same sins are in all peoples at all times. Rather God condemns societies for the sins they condone. Sodom, Gomorrah, and the cities of the plains were not destroyed because they were filled with more evil than the Canaanites that God eventually sent the Israelites to destroy. No, these cities were consumed by fire and brimstone because they gloried in what others did in shame.

Stroll down the streets of San Francisco. Flip the dial from the Modern Family to Two and a Half Men from The Jersey Shore to Glee and it seems Jerry Springer has defined the new America. On cable and satellite hard core porn fills the overnight hours while state after state legalizes pot on their way to legalizing everything. The government has taken over the numbers racket, calling it a lottery as they plunder the poorest amongst us by selling them false hope where winning is as likely as being struck with lightening.

What is the judgment of God on nations that have moved out from under His blessing by rejecting His guidance? He casts them down from the heights their former obedience had achieved. In the near future we may become the tail instead of the head as our leaders continue to wag the dog.

Alexis de Tocqueville one of the most astute observers of America said in the early 1800s "America is great because she is good, and if America ever ceases to be good, America will cease to be great." Now survey the current state of America for yourself. Don't accept the opinion of someone else, but make up your own mind. Is America good? The answer to that will provide the answer to the question posed in the title of this dispatch "Is America under Judgment?" For if we are not good what are we? And what is the result of that? Then remember God has told those who follow Him, "A thousand may fall at your side, and ten thousand at your right hand; but it shall not come near you."[8]

Keep the faith. Keep the peace. We shall overcome.

★ DISPATCH TWENTY-NINE ★

Is the Inertia Greater Than the Momentum?

The causes of our problems are not hard to see. Americans aren't obese because evil restaurateurs are forcing them to eat fried butter on a stick. We are bulging at the seams because we eat too much and exercise too little. Americans aren't trapped in upside down mortgages because evil bankers waylaid us and forced us to sign up for a house that was too big and cost too much. We're living in homes we can't afford because we wanted them and thought we deserved them even though we didn't have an income that could support them. Americans aren't buried in personal debt because credit card companies mailed us credit cards. We carry an average of $14,517 household debt[1] because we wanted what we wanted when we wanted it and couldn't wait until we could pay for it. And America isn't drowning in national debt[2] because we did anything more difficult to understand than electing people who bought our votes with entitlements we didn't need and couldn't afford.

The problem isn't that we don't know the answers. Instead it's that we don't want to face up to the fact that the free ride has to stop if we're going to get off before we land in the ash heap of History. America's economy is beginning to resemble one of those increasingly ridiculous action movies where the hero gets blown up, shot, stabbed, and hit with a brick only to jump up ready to roll. Every time a bubble bursts instead of allowing the economy to bottom out and correct itself the Government spends as it borrows[3] from foreign countries[4] and the Fed creates money[5] out of thin air to pay for it. It's time our leaders learn we have learned that blowing up a bubble to take the place of the last burst bubble is not building an economy.

127

As boom and bust turned into boom to boom to boom we have inevitably made our way to KABOOM!!!

The coming crash in this double-dip dilemma is going to be a double whammy. We are currently blowing up a new financial bubble providing Fed funds at near 0%[6] that the banks then loan out at 3–4% to the Fed by buying government bonds pumping more and more money into the system. And in a reprise of the 2000 dot.com crash[7] the social media bubble[8] is once again giving us billion dollar companies that aren't making any money for anyone except the gamblers in the stock market casino.

The Federal Government keeps inflating bubbles to avoid the real crash so that they can continue to buy votes with entitlements and pay for them with funny money. This postpones paying the piper, but it increases the bill when it finally comes.

Today the government Leviathan is devouring America's income.[9] In 2012 it's estimated that the central government will consume 24% of GDP kicking back 4% to the States and localities, the States will swallow 10% of GDP, and the local entities will inhale 11%. Subtracting the 4% Federal to State shell game the governance of America is today costing us 40% of America's production. On top of that the regulatory burden[10] grows heavier every day until everyone everywhere is in violation of something. And we wonder why industry isn't expanding? When you eat your seed corn and make impossible to follow guidelines for planting you can't expect a bumper crop.

With money pouring out of a 5» hose how can anyone take the politicians promises to cut the deficit and reduce the debt seriously? The most draconian plans suggested so far, such as Representative Ryan's doesn't balance until 2040[11] and that is only if future politicians decide to play nice and not buy votes with free goodies which is about as likely as a dog with fleas not scratching.

That's the problem: a dysfunctional government made up of klepto-maniacs writing phony checks on the future and a population addicted to easy money and unfunded entitlements.

What's the solution? We as a people must kick the entitlement habit. Like any addiction our national addiction to freebees has debilitated us. It has made us dependent on the outside stimulus. Where once families and churches took care of the needy we have been taught for generations that Uncle Sugar will do it, so we have let Uncle Sugar do it. How has that worked out? Ever since the government bureaucrats have stepped between the givers and the receivers welfare hasn't been well and it isn't fair. Many of us know people who need help who are denied and people who should be helping themselves who are riding in their Cadillacs to spend their food stamps.

After more than 15 trillion dollars and four decades of a war on poverty the percentage of Americans below the poverty line is higher than it was when we started.[12] There are more people on food stamps, more on disability and more that have just dropped out of the work force than ever before, and the only answer Washington seems to have is we haven't spent enough yet. That's like telling the heroin addict who almost died last night of an overdose that the problem was he didn't shoot up enough junk.

How do we stop spending? How do we balance the budget? This is like the question the backslider always asks, "How do I get back to God?" The answer to the backslider is, "You get back to God." The answer for the nation is, "we stop spending more than we bring in." The politicians have a way to make that solution work: raise taxes until income matches outgo. This brings up another problem: we can't eat the goose that lays the golden egg and expect to collect more eggs tomorrow. In any country that robs Peter to pay Paul eventually everyone changes their name to Paul. Case in point, we now have more people qualifying for disability each month than people finding jobs.[13]

Yes, this is a call for austerity. Yes, this will cause major dislocations. Yes, when drug addicts quit taking the poison their bodies have come to crave they get sick. In time drug addicts recover and once again become normal people able to stand on their own without the chemical prop of a debilitating drug. In time if we as a nation will kick the habit of cheap money and government handouts we will once again learn to stand on our own two feet, hold our head up high, and proudly say, "This is America the land of the free and the home of the brave."

If we will do this the last half of the twentieth century will be but a prelude to the American century. If we don't, the Sun will set on the American dream as we devour ourselves in an orgy of hedonism and self-gratification.

At the next election survey your choices and find people who have the courage to lead us in a return to fiscal responsibility before we face the coming collapse of the world we have known. For if we cast our bread upon the water it will return to us after many days, but if we sow the wind we will reap the whirlwind.

★ DISPATCH THIRTY ★

IS THE NECESSARY AND PROPER CLAUSE
EITHER NECESSARY OR PROPER?

I want to begin by saying that I believe the Preamble to the Declaration of Independence[1] and the Constitution,[2] with the Bill of Rights[3] included, comprise the most enlightened, ennobling, and beneficial documents ever penned by the hand of man. I also believe that the Constitution afforded the United States the greatest level of freedom and opportunity ever experienced by humanity. This freedom and opportunity in turn released the talents and abilities of the American people to build the greatest nation ever to exist, rising from 13 states exhausted and impoverished from years of war into a prosperous and powerful nation which by the end of the twentieth century stood upon the world stage as the uncontested sole superpower.

Simplicity is the essence of genius while over-simplification is the essence of fraud. In a picture perfect example of the truism "The victors write history" what we have been taught concerning the writing and ratification of the Constitution is actually a politically slanted version of the truth. This highly patrician account is also an example of over-simplification.

We are taught that the Articles of Confederation[4] were an abject failure because they were too weak. Shay's Rebellion scared the venerable leaders who had led and won the Revolution. George Washington and Co. came back from retirement to once again save the nation writing an "almost" divinely inspired document. There was only token dissent to the immediate acceptance of this tablet from the mount by some shadowy unknown people collectively called the "Anti-Federalists." However after some well-written articles by future leaders called the Federalists, We the People overwhelmingly voted for ratification and the Constitution immediately ushered in the blessings of liberty and opportunity for all rescuing the United States from anarchy and stagnation. Amen.

This is a thumb-nail sketch of what our thumb-nail sketch type history education once delivered as gospel in American public schools. Today, those lucky enough to live in a school district that still includes American History are instead treated to the progressive's litany of American crimes and debauchery. However, as our constitutionally limited government exceeds all previous limits, is either of these offerings good enough? Americans from all walks of life watch in stunned disbelief as the Federal Government on steroids swallows the economy, healthcare, the financial system, major manufacturing, the insurance industry, and anything else that doesn't move fast enough to get out of the way. Can the States themselves be far behind?

How did this come about? How did a government born in the shackles provided by a written constitution designed to limit its power swell into the all-powerful OZ?

Quite simply it was through the deception of the Progressives evolving our Constitution from a rock-solid framework limited to what it actually said into a living document that is constantly being re-interpreted. Thus without amendment, without debate, without a vote our leaders have nudged us from the land of liberty to the centrally-planned surveillance state which today sends the IRS after their enemies, leaves our borders open, our opportunities closed, and our sons and daughters manning hundreds of garrisons around the world.

One of the key tools in this century-long quest to transform America has been the use of the so-called elastic clauses in the Constitution. One major clause used to accomplish this is found in Article I, Section 8, Clause 18 which states, "The Congress shall have Power To ...make all Laws which shall be necessary and proper for carrying into Execution the foregoing Powers, and all other Powers vested by this Constitution in the Government of the United States, or in any Department or Officer thereof."[5]

There are several ways to look at this clause and its meaning. First we need to look at what is called "Original Intent," or what those who wrote the clause meant. Then we will look at what those who ratified the Constitution thought it meant. Finally we will look at how the Progressives interpret and re-interpret their favorite clause.

The necessary and proper clause was added to the Constitution by the Committee of Detail with no debate. Nor was it the subject of any debate during the remainder of the Convention. The reason why this clause was neither attacked nor defended during the Convention becomes clear from the statements of the Framers during the ratification process. James Wilson, one of the most eloquent defenders of the Constitution, a signer of the Constitution, and one of the first justices of the Supreme Court, said that this clause gave the Federal Government no more or other powers than those already enumerated in Section 8 of Article I and that "It is saying no more than that the powers we have already particularly given, shall be effectually carried into execution."[6] The Framers felt as if the clause was merely saying that which had been delegated could be used.

During the ratification debates this clause was a hot topic. Brutus proclaimed that through the Necessary and Proper Clause "This government is to possess absolute and uncontrollable power, legislative and judicial, with respect to every object to which it extends..."[7] the debate raged back and forth between the Federalists and the Anti-Federalists in newspapers, pamphlets, and on the floor of the ratification conventions.

Eventually the Federalists won the day and the Constitution was ratified. The result? The interpretation of this clause that was generally accepted by the ratification conventions was that it added no new or expandable powers to the federal government.

Since the New Deal era, Progressives have argued that the Necessary and Proper Clause expands the powers of the Federal Government to any extent it deems necessary and proper. In other words the federal government has all the power necessary to do whatever they want about anything they want. The executive department has been using this clause to grab power since Hamilton used it to found the First Bank of the United States in 1791. The Supreme Court has been stretching this clause since they ruled in Marbury v. Madison, 5 U.S. 137 (1803),[8] giving themselves the power of judicial review. This expansionist interpretation has been upheld by the Supreme Court on numerous occasions and is today the accepted opinion amongst the political-media-corporate establishment.

It is my belief that if we have a better understanding of where we came from and how we got here then we would have a better understanding of where we are. If we understand where we are perhaps we will see the way to get back to where we wanted to go when we started: back to a limited government of the people, by the people and for the people.

Knowing how a simple clause meant to say that what had been delegated could be used has evolved into near totalitarian power shows us that just as the present use of the Necessary and Proper Clause is neither necessary nor proper. And thus a government of the people, for the people and by the people has been hijacked and become something else.

No matter what we have been taught and no matter even what the reality was the reality is that the Constitution replaced the Articles of Confederation as the supreme law of the land. The announced purpose of the

Constitution's writing and adoption was to provide a limited government which respected both the rights of the States and the people. Since this was the stated and accepted purpose of the Constitution after two centuries and several decades how can *We the People* deny any longer that it has failed?

Failing and failure are two different things. Everyone who has ever succeeded has failed. It is falling forward from that failure which ultimately brings success. If the Constitution has failed what do we do now? Where's the reset button.

★ DISPATCH THIRTY-ONE ★

IT CAN'T HAPPEN HERE

Revolutions happened in other countries. The USSR, their satellite countries in Eastern Europe and Asia, African countries, and of course those banana republics somewhere down south, but one thing is for sure, it can't happen here. Following in the footsteps of giants who have used these prophetic words of Sinclair Lewis I want to examine how it did happen here.

In the America of George Washington, Thomas Jefferson, and James Madison, in the America we inherited from our forefathers we knew that there could never be a revolution. We had the Constitution with its checks and balances, its separation of powers, and its Bill of Rights. These were rock solid, carved in stone, and strong enough to preserve the Republic and safeguard the freedom of its people.

Besides the American people would not stand for some wannabe dictator and his brown, black or whatever color shirt followers marching through the streets and into the White House. The sons of the Pioneers wouldn't sit still for any attempt to curtail limited government, personal freedom, or economic opportunity. No way! No how! Others might accept censorship, surveillance, and rigged elections, but not us, not Americans. We had fought wars to defend our independence, wars to defeat totalitarianism; we had even fought wars to spread freedom. No, we wouldn't quietly allow homegrown tyrants grasp the levers of power.

I sounds so comforting, "It can't happen here." If you take a beginning Political Science class in either High School or College you will learn how the government works. How bills become laws, how the legislature is made up of the freely elected representatives of the people, how the President runs the executive branch and the Supreme Court sits atop the judicial branch. You will learn about the Declaration of Independence and how the Constitution was written to replace the Articles of Confederation which were too weak to work. Yes, you will learn all about how it's supposed to work.

In most schools you will also learn that the Constitution is a "living Document" that can be re-interpreted to fit every generation and every age. The results of 100 years of re-interpretation have led us to the brink of ruin and me to recommend that the study of the Constitution be moved from Political Science to History, since what rules us today is legal precedent and bureaucratic regulation. The courts use foreign laws and traditions to interpret our laws and traditions. The legislature passes laws they don't read filled with thousands of pages of vague platitudes and goals that the bureaucrats fill in with no oversight and the force of law. And the President does whatever he wants and no one says a thing.

So how did America fall for the oldest con in the world: "Give me your freedom and I'll give you security?"

Those who wished to gain power had no ideology or theology which inspired them. They only sought power for power's sake. They espoused whatever populist themes gave them the broadest support. To bring as many interest groups as possible into their coalition they embraced an "I'm okay you're okay" relativity that rejected absolutes and extoled the fringe as the mainstream.

And all the while the decedents of the blacksmiths and farmers who once congregated on corners to discuss the latest political pamphlet or to debate the merits of economic policy snoozed on the couch waking up long enough to go to work or watch the game.

The Revolutionaries of the New America first took root in the faculty lounges of academia providing the intellectual and cultural cover for an American movement that promoted the opposite of everything America stood for. From the classrooms of our colleges, came the next generations of teachers, journalists, lawyers, artists, and politicians. Soon it was common knowledge that our once rock-solid Constitution was a Living Document to be twisted and changed whenever those in power found the need.

From here it was just a matter of time until a revolution was accomplished through evolutionary change. Once the centers of power were secure in Washington, Hollywood, and in the media the trickle of change became a torrent and the torrent became a tsunami. Two wings on the same bird of prey, perpetually re-elected representatives from the twin headed party of power pander to the lowest common denominators, buying votes, using taxes to punish enemies, and tax money to reward friends.

Our tyrants-in-training have captured the government and the economy, created a dependent class of motor-voters, convinced people that a continually growing debt is sustainable, and turned the government into the one who picks winners and losers instead of a free economy. The slow slide down a slippery slope has accelerated into a precipitous procession over a predictable precipice. To those who have seen this coming it is like watching a slow motion train wreck. The coming destruction is not mitigated in the least by the decades or warning.

Our prideful boast of it can't happen here has become a heart wrenching analysis of how it did happen here. How did the Progressives capture our land and subvert our Republic? They did it gradually inch-by-inch, step-by-step. When they lost a round they held their gains and as soon as possible recovered their long march toward a totally transformed nation.

How they changed it brings us to the question, "How do we change it back?"

Violent revolt is both repugnant and obviously suicidal to people who understand that once that genie is out of the bottle there is no way to know which way it will go, except that the odds are heavily against it ever landing back in a stable land of limited government and personal freedom. The power of the state is overwhelming. Millions of shot guns, pistols, and even those terrible assault rifles we are constantly being lectured about would make no headway against Abrams tanks and F-18s.

There are only two ways to have a successful peaceful revolution. One: the vast majority of the people must go on strike and refuse to operate as a society until the changes have been made. Or two: it must happen gradually line upon line verse upon verse always keeping the goal in sight and moving forward at every opportunity. In other words we must do to the new establishment what they did to the old: not overthrow it, supplant it, and replace it in the hearts and minds of the people.

We can rest assured that all people at all times eventually yearn for freedom thus the stage is set by the very nature of man that God imprinted on us in His creation. Free choice is the natural state of man and in the end we will return to it. This pall of totalitarianism which is falling like a shadow across the land will one day awake to find the light of liberty that cannot be quenched forever.

What should we do? Education is the key. If you are not a teacher become one. Learn to show yourself approved. Teach anyone who will listen of freedom, of the true History of the American experiment. Become involved in any way you can to retake control of our education system so that we can train the coming generations to love freedom, truth, justice, and the American way.

And don't lose hope. God created us to be free, and though tyrants always seek to ensnare people in their self-serving systems we will one day be free again. Draw near to God and He will draw near to you. Remember that what we thought couldn't happen here has and what we think can't happen to us will. Freedom will rise from the ashes and one day the light of liberty will once again burn brightly in America the beautiful.

★ DISPATCH THIRTY-TWO ★

It's Not Over Till It's Over

The Civil War didn't end at the First Battle of Bull Run or at the Second for that matter. WWI didn't end at the First Battle of the Marne or at the Second. WWII didn't end at Midway.

After what we now knowingly call Gulf War I we celebrated with ticker-tape parades and fireworks as if we had defeated Hitler, Tojo, and Stalin all wrapped up in one. Yet a little more than 10 years later we had to go back into Iraq to finish the job, and we're still trying to finish it today. What should have been an incursion into Afghanistan has lingered on for more than a decade. The sad result of our nation-building in Iraq and Afghanistan will end with Iraq as Iran's most powerful ally and the Taliban back in power in Kabul.

One persistent question after politically directed wars is, "How do you win every battle and lose a war?" After sending the brave into Harm's Way the generalissimos of the home front drag the fighting out by hamstringing the warriors than when war is no longer a vote getter they throw the victory away through peace-at-any-price diplomacy.

I deeply appreciate the heroic scarifies of our troops, and I'm thankful they've provided a life of peace and safety for myself and my family. I celebrate the victories just as I mourn the losses in this long war. The death of an enemy leader can have momentous impact upon a war. The death of Attila ended his empire; the death of Hitler would have ended WWII earlier and did end it when it came. But the death of FDR did not end the war or change the strategy, and the death of Osama Bin Laden will not bring the end to this undeclared war.

The history of irregular warfare didn't begin with Al-Qaeda. It didn't begin with the Viet Cong. Irregular warfare has existed as long as there has been ill-equipped resistance to far-flung empires. The United States has battled irregular forces at home and in the far corners of the world since the Indian Wars. We fought irregular forces the first time we faced Islamic terrorists on the shores of Tripoli. After we conquered the Philippines from Spain we fought irregulars for years finally winning a war the Spanish never could. We've faced irregular forces in Lebanon, Somalia, Bosnia, Kosovo, Iraq, and Afghanistan. In some places we've prevailed in others we've withdrawn. At times we've even used irregular tactics ourselves such as the 3000 volunteers of Merrill's Marauders who fought behind Japanese lines in Burma during WWII.

A traditional military organization fighting irregular forces is more like trying to herd snakes than nail Jell-O to the wall, it may be hard but it isn't impossible. However, the initiative is on the side of the irregulars because they can strike here, there, and everywhere while the regular forces must protect important components of the infrastructure. Revolutionaries and other disaffected groups using irregular tactics have instinctively followed the advice of Mao Zedong who distilled the wisdom of Sun Tzu,[1] "The enemy advances, we retreat; the enemy camps, we harass; the enemy tires, we attack; the enemy retreats, we pursue."[2] As the regular forces move into an area the irregulars melt into the population. The disruptions in the lives of civilians create recruits for the irregulars. This is the force multiplier of the irregulars. Every action at suppression brings fresh resources to circumvent future actions.

This will be the inevitable result of the death of Osama Bin Laden. The immediate aftermath was wild jubilation on the part of a segment of our population, electioneering on the part of the administration, and a gross overestimation of the military significance. One man does not make a movement and one leader does not encompass the enemy in an irregular war.

This is especially true in the case of Bin Laden and his brain child Al-Qaeda. This organization is post-modern or perhaps pre-modern in style. It doesn't have a pyramid-shaped flowchart. It doesn't have a top-down command structure. In many ways it's more like a pyramid scheme where every franchise spins off new franchises and they spread out subdividing like amoebas into multiple places and shapes. These autonomous groups and rogue individuals are tied together by beliefs and ideology, united by tactics and strategy but each independent, separated and anonymous. No leader knows all the followers and few followers are connected directly to any leader. These international conspirators are not united by personal contacts or unified by strategic planning; instead they're forged into an inter-active whole by solidarity of purpose and continuity of world-view. In such a structure the death of any one person no matter how highly placed or inspirational will not have more than a marginal impact.

As omnipresent and as faceless as the Internet and as private and personal as family relations the tenuous filaments of the interlocking terror networks will prove more resilient than expected and more tenuous than imagined. One man's life can make a difference in the world, but one man's death rarely does. Grave yards are filled with indispensable people.

★ DISPATCH THIRTY-THREE ★

LEMMINGS AND THE CLIFF

We all think we are invincible. We all think we will have another day. Then one day there isn't another day and our day is done. Empires rise and empires fall and everyone always thinks, "We'll make it through this. We always have" then one time you don't. No one gets to live in the world they grew up in, because the only thing that never changes is that everything changes.

Though we won the race to the Moon, pioneered and financed the International Space Station we have witnessed the end of America's manned space program,[1] but not because of some grand explosion or tragedy. Past administrations faced these and soldiered on to boldly go where no man has gone before. It was not because of a lack of vision; our planners wanted to send Americans to Mars and beyond. It wasn't because of a lack of talent, or technical know-how. No the end of America's manned space program has arrived because America is in the grip of an administration focused on managing the decline of America even if they have to make the decline happen themselves.

Look at the economy. Though Nixon famously quipped, "I am now a Keynesian in economics."[2] Milton Friedman and the neo-classical economics of the Chicago School proved we can't spend our way to prosperity. We can't borrow our way to solvency, yet this administration has racked up the largest debt of any administration in History. Their first 800 billion dollar stimulus was such a failure even Mr. Obama can't keep a straight face when talking about the supposed shovel ready jobs. And what is this administration's answer to the continuation of the Great Recession? The President wants more spending and more debt, a policy which ensures the continued degradation of America's economic position in the world. From the undisputed leader of the world this administration is fundamentally transforming America into an economic dependency on China.[3]

Ever since the early 1980s and the Laffer Curve[4] provided the facts to prove what many economists had long known: within certain perimeters reducing taxes generates more revenue than raising them. Economists generally agree that raising taxes slows growth and reduces revenue especially during a recession. Yet in the current debt ceiling emergency what does the Obama Administration propose? They want to raise taxes. And how do they seek to achieve this masterstroke? By the most blatant application of class warfare rhetoric since Lenin climbed on a barricade in 1917.

If the President is to be believed, it is the tax credits given to the purchasers and operators of private jets that are one of the three causes of our current economic anemia. Conveniently it is forgotten by the President and by the Corporations Once Known as the Mainstream Media, who parrot his every word, that it was his own stimulus bill which created these tax credits to begin with. The second cause according to the President's teleprompter is tax breaks given to millionaires and billionaires. By millionaires and billionaires he means everyone earning more than the level needed to qualify for food stamps and Medicaid. And last but not the least are the billions of dollars in subsidies given to Oil Companies. Of course these aren't really subsidies they are tax credits[5] extended to domestic companies for the exploration and development of new oil resources. Never mentioned is the Democrats' pet corporation such as GE, which pays no federal taxes at all.

That's the economic plan: attack the private jet industry, tax the rich (anyone not on welfare), and penalize anyone attempting to actually solve America's dependence on countries that hate us for our energy. That won't lead us on the road back to prosperity or maybe that isn't the destination our leaders have chosen. Remember don't discount ulterior motives when the mistakes are so great stupidity seems like the only other answer.

Geo-politically, the endless wars for peace grind on even though everyone knows that since we left Iraq they have allied themselves with Iran and the moment we leave Afghanistan the Taliban will march into Kabul as Karsai, his crew, and our billions will take off for Geneva. Just as the President's best seller, *The Dreams of My Father* resembles the nightmares of others his Arab Spring looks more like the prelude to a twenty-first century Kristallnacht or the Middle East version of the March on Rome. Anyone except the willfully blind can see that the overthrown pro-Western dictators are being replaced by pro Al-Qaeda Muslim Brotherhood clones or a new round of military dictators. And after several years of the Obama drama America now leads from behind and cannot muster the wherewithal to defeat a tin pot dictator hated by his own people with a rag-tag army of mercenaries and children or to protect our own diplomats.

With a dismal record of retrenchment and failure such as this how did President Obama possibly win re-election?

However, we can't ignore the Lemming Effect. The political lemmings are those Americans who proudly ignore politics and economics, who get there news from John Stewart, Jay Leno or the major networks, this who vote for the same party their parents did just because that is what they do, in other words, Democrats. They will vote for the President even if they can't stand anything he's done and disagree with everything he says. After all he has a "D" after his name. Or as Lenin said, "The capitalists will sell us the rope we use to hang them."[6] With these millions of lemmings heading for the cliff Mr. Obama had a solid third of the electorate.

Luckily for the President and the Progressives the Republican leadership in Congress was dedicated to compromise when they should have stood their ground and they are experts at snatching defeat from the jaws of victory. They voted to raise the debt ceiling and alienated the majority of the Tea Party who could have been the salvation of the Party of Reagan.

Then the Republicans nominated the author of the model of Obamacare and took that off the table. And to cap it off Mr. Romney spent his most important debate experiences agreeing with everything the President said. And then with Mr. Christi's embrace of Obama after Hurricane Sandy the election was more a gift than a contest.

The Space Race is over, we won, but now we have capitulated. The Cold War is over, we won, but we squandered the opportunity to create a world of freedom to pursue wars without end. The greatest creditor in the world is now the greatest debtor. The greatest manufacturer is now the greatest importer of manufactured goods. Twenty-three years of Progressive presidents combined with a big-government, big-spending Congress has led us to the brink of the abyss. Our current debt levels are unsustainable and unless we act quickly the momentum of decline may become irreversible and irresistible.

However, we are the American people, we can stop this. We can throw the rascals out, reverse course and rebuild the land of the free and the home of the brave. We can do it. We must do it. Or, it won't get done.

How do we do it?

We can't let divisions divide us anymore. We must unite behind the strongest conservative and work together or we will all watch our beloved country swirl down the drain of History separately. Just as the Democrats and Independents took control of the Republican primaries in 2008 to nominate the Progressive McCain the conservative majority must take control in the future to ensure that a viable conservative is nominated. Otherwise the leaders of the Republican re-election machine will nominate an Obama-lite and the lights may go out on the greatest experiment in freedom ever devised as Hilary and Bill return to the White House.

Keep the faith. Keep the peace. We shall overcome.

★ DISPATCH THIRTY-FOUR ★

Liberty Makes Ignorance Necessary

If we knew everything in the past and the future there would be little need for freedom. If we could accurately know all that preceded our fleeting moment upon life's stage, if we could know all the consequences of our present desires, and if we could know what we would desire in the future we could then chart a course to perfection without any detours and so freedom of action would be unnecessary and central planning would make sense.

Freedom would not only be unnecessary but would also be very inconvenient. One free agent on this express to perfection would be the fly in the ointment and the monkey wrench in the gears. That one free person would rage against the machines, and would inevitably make an unforeseen choice and all the perfection would silently slip away.

In order to have the freedom to succeed there must also be freedom to fail. We all need the freedom to act upon circumstances that we don't fully understand to attain goals whose consequences we can't fully appreciate. Without this there is no freedom. We can pretend as the progressive advocates of central planning do that we can accurately predict the consequence of every action; however this is in Contrast to our real-world experience.

The reason failure is so prevalent is due to the fact that every individual is operating with imperfect knowledge of what is best or of what will eventually yield the best outcome that we must allow people the freedom to act upon their ignorance. In this way the independent and competitive choices of many individuals will eventually lead through trial-and-error to the development of the best. Since so many times the best emerges through accidental or unforeseen results of actions taken without complete knowledge of what the outcome would be we must leave room for accidents often guided by ignorance so that knowledge can grow.

It is an incontrovertible fact that as the fund of human knowledge grows the percentage that any one person can effectively know becomes smaller. In other words, as general knowledge increases individual ignorance also increases. Added to this is the constantly increasing complexity of our civilization and it becomes obvious that people must be allowed to act upon the knowledge they possess without regard to the vast amount of knowledge they do not possess. Otherwise no advancement would be possible, and we would live in a static society doomed to eventual demise.

It is this freedom to act in ignorance of all the consequences of their actions that allows the space for individual innovation. The greater the freedom of individuals to interpret the world according to their imperfect knowledge and to organize their efforts based upon their understanding of the world as they see it the greater the opportunity for the accidents which make up the majority of progress. If we take away the freedom to act upon our imperfect knowledge, or if we take away the freedom to fail we will also take away the engine of progress and condemn ourselves to a stagnant world of limited possibilities.

As one person tries something another may build upon their result whether it succeeds or fails. The ability to learn from and build upon the experience of others is the seedbed of innovation and the font of discovery. It is our ignorance of all but a small fragment of reality that causes probability and chance to play such a large portion in our activities. It is within this realm of probability and chance that the future grows.

This applies to social as well as technical fields. The favorable accidents which become the building blocks of a vibrant, successful society do not just happen. They are the result of someone taking a risk by doing something that hasn't been tried before without the complete knowledge of what the result will be. They include the chance of failure as well as success and often the success achieved is not the desired end result of the action when it was initiated. Freedom increases the opportunity for risk and opens the door to possibility.

When we look at the vast amount of knowledge that makes up the common store of information in the modern age and then look at the miniscule percentage that any one person could possibly gain, retain and understand we see that the difference between what the wisest knows and what the least wise knows is comparatively insignificant. Everyone is operating based upon imperfect knowledge and the acceptance of grand assumptions.

To tell you the truth I am not really sure how electricity works. Yet most of my life and lifestyle is predicated on the availability and use of electricity. Most people have no idea how the economy works yet we all base our lives upon the fact that it does. If we refused to act in areas where we had less than perfect knowledge we would do nothing. One of the big differences between an advocate of liberty and an advocate of central planning is that those who see liberty as man's natural state understand that no one person or group is wise enough to make all the decisions for everyone. Central planners by definition believe they are wise enough to do so.

The case for liberty made by such Enlightenment thinkers as John Milton and John Locke provided the philosophical foundation for the Framers as they wrote our Constitution. They based their arguments for liberty on the realization that human ignorance and our need to act in the face of ignorance is a basic component of reality.

Every application of the tenets of Liberty reflect our need to give these actions based upon ignorance the widest possible scope to interface with chance and probability of uncertainty. Certainty is unattainable in this life outside of a cultural straightjacket that restricts choice and eliminates the freedom to fail. Such a society will be stagnant, stunted and doomed. Without the freedom to fail on an individual basis and then fall forward from that failure a society has short-circuited the conveyor belt of individual success and charted the course to eventual systemic failure. The former USSR was a textbook example of this scenario.

If we wish to avoid the trash heap of History we must be wise enough to learn that though acting upon ignorance may increase the odds of failure if we try to eliminate failure so that everyone gets a trophy and everyone succeeds we have consigned ourselves to the dead end that always awaits anyone or any society that believes perfection is attainable on this earth.

For it isn't failing that marks a failure it is the refusal to rise from failure and move on to success. We learn by failing. We achieve by using our freedom to fail as a launching pad for success. We fail because of our ignorance. We succeed because of our failures.

★ DISPATCH THIRTY-FIVE ★

LIBERTY TYRANNY AND THE RULE OF LAW

A foundational difference between a country that enjoys the benefits of limited government, individual liberty, personal freedom and economic opportunity, and one that suffers under the yoke of tyranny is that the former observes the rule of law and the latter witnesses the rule of whim.

John Locke the intellectual font from which our founders drank long and deep said, "The end of law is not to abolish or restrain, but to preserve and enlarge freedom. For in all the states of created beings capable of law, where there is no law, there is no freedom."[1]

Many people who see themselves as defenders of the common man give their support to people and programs that restrict liberty and relegate most citizens to the role of pawns in the puzzle factory of central planning. These low-information voters and starry-eyed fellow-travelers either wake up for elections voting for the party their parents did or they believe the demagogues who sell them some version of Utopia. The former are just taking a commercial break between reality shows while the latter honestly believe that one more program will actually usher in heaven on earth and there will be a computer on every desk, a cell phone in very hand and all will be right with the world, Kum ba yah, my lord, Kum ba yah.

The problem with the low-information voters is that they really don't care enough to find out what is happening and they believe whatever the Corporations Once Known as the Mainstream Media tell them. You can't do much in the face of militant apathy. The inertia outweighs the momentum. All we can do is wait for reality to shout loud enough to wake them up.

The starry-eyed fellow-travelers however might be reachable with a reasonable discussion. They are after all seeking after a better world. However, they have swallowed everything the progressive educational system has been swilling out for the last few generations. Less is more: man-made global warming, it takes a village; America is to blame for the troubles of the world, capitalism, bad socialism, good, etc.

In this essay I wish to address these fellow citizens and hope to convince them that when they sign on to the various progressive plans for central planning whether it is for healthcare or of the whole economy it inevitably leads to violations of the rule of law, a breakdown of the social contract and the loss of liberty.

When attempting to plan an entire economy or even of a large part, as the 1/6 that represents healthcare, it is impossible for any piece of legislation to specify every detail for every circumstance. Therefore the laws when passed though they may be thousands of pages long will be large guidelines empowering agencies and bureaucrats to write the specifics with the force of law. Thus the representatives of the people actually delegate their power to unelected individuals who can make law with the wave of a pen. The form of a representative government operating according to democratic principles is maintained while in reality we have rule by decree and an autocratic regime.

James Madison, the Father of the Constitution and our fourth president told us, "It will be of little avail to the people that the laws are made by men of their own choice if the laws be so voluminous that they cannot be read, or so incoherent that they cannot be understood."[2]

In these attempts to control and plan entire economies or of large segments of economies those who direct those economies must choose between outcomes. One outcome advances the plan and one does not.

Obviously since the plan is the plan so whatever obstructs its accomplishment is less desirable than what moves it towards its goal. Therefore the planners must encourage one thing and discourage another. This all comes down to limiting choices and picking winners and losers.

Coal is bad because it slows the progress towards a zero carbon footprint and according to the pet pseudo-science of the day contributes to the global warming that in reality is cyclical and ended more than a decade ago. Therefore coal production and use must be discouraged.

Solar power is good because it is renewable and once you are past the production of the solar panels it causes no pollution. Therefore solar panel production must be encouraged even when it is an inefficient power source. Even after billions of dollars have been poured into boondoggles which profited no one except campaign contributors and other progressive stake-holders good money must follow bad for the plan must go on.

This choosing of winners and losers according to a predetermined plan by unelected members of the nomenclature restricts the liberty of people to work and prosper as they will while rewarding others who make poor investments and some who even go bankrupt leaving the tax payers to clean up the mess.[3]

This is the opposite of the rule of law. Laws to be fair have to apply to everyone. When a nation lives under the rule of law the government does not deny individuals of opportunities or rights. Whenever a government launches out on the road to Utopia it is necessary that it micromanage the economy making specific decisions relating to the actual needs of people with regard to the plan. They must slow some down and speed some up if they want everyone to arrive at the desired location at the desired time.

When law ceases to be generally applied and instead arbitrarily chooses between what one can do and what another may not do, and these choices are different, then the law is no longer creating a level playing field it is building a maze.

Aristotle taught us that, "The only stable state is the one in which all men are equal before the law."[4] That great Roman Cicero said, "We are in bondage to the law so that we might be free."[5]

★ DISPATCH THIRTY-SIX ★

No Joke

Fido, Casper the Friendly Ghost and Juan Valdez walk into a polling place. No this isn't the beginning of a joke it was a key part of the Chicago Plan to re-elect the worst President in American History.

The Voter Participation Center (VPC),[1] a left wing organization whose work to register Democrat voters exemplifies the process used for generations in Chicago to ensure the Outfit/Machine[2] maintains control of the government, the power, and the swag. The VPC is mass mailing pre-printed voter registration forms to selected voter blocks known to be part of the Democrat coalition, African-Americans, Latinos, young adults, and single women. In their effort to extend the Chicago system to the rest of the country VPC mailed nearly 200,000 third-party voter registration forms to Virginia residents in June. This has resulted in more than 15,000 new voters being registered.

However, there are a few problems with this exercise in Chicago-style democracy. They are violating rules set forth in the state code and the Virginia Constitution requiring that voters fill out their own form. The State Board of Elections, which the group says pre-approved their forms and their methods, has asked the group to stop filling in the forms prior to sending them to the people,[3] and pointing to the errant forms they have also raised questions concerning how the group obtained lists of registered voters. In addition,[4] according to Justin Riemer, the Virginia State Board of Elections' deputy secretary, forms have been sent by the group to "deceased infants, out-of-state family members, and non-U.S. citizens, among others."[5]

Given the fact that these forms can be mailed in and that the Federal Government will sue any State that has the chutzpah to require a photo ID to vote don't be surprised when in this, the most crucial election of our lives Fido, Casper, or Juan are allowed to cast their vote to continue the occupation of Washington by the Progressive Statists and their totalitarian plans.

The list of problems with Democrat voting procedures that have ensured their iron-fisted rule in the tottering hulks of our once great cities is as long as it is disturbing. There are the great Democrat machines that have used every form of voter fraud and intimidation to dominate the urban political scene in America for generations in places such as Philadelphia,[6] the Military,[7] and of course the Mecca of corruption President Obama's adopted hometown and political base, Chicago.[8] In East St. Louis[9] and Indianapolis[10] there are actually more registered voters than eligible citizens.

The Obama Justice Department circled the country like a bird of prey waiting to pounce on any jurisdiction that attempts to purge the dead, the illegal immigrants, or felons from the voting lists, it is apparent that voter fraud has been elevated from a crime to a national policy.[12] Attorney General Holder sued Florida,[12] Georgia,[13] and Texas[14] while investigating Pennsylvania.[15] Yet there is no time or resources spent on investigating 16 counties in Texas with more voters on the rolls than in the census or 16 jurisdictions in Illinois that also have more registered than eligible.

In the 2008 election there was no interest in prosecuting the clear case[16] of voter intimidation by the New Black Panther Party who patrolled voting locations armed with clubs while making racist statements to voters.[17] While the professional civil rights activists screamed about voter suppression because of requirements to show a photo ID to vote the most reprehensible case of voter suppression of all is the campaign waged to limit the vote of our active duty military.[18] By the way Mexico and South Africa among many others require a photo ID to vote.

Any attempt to slow the growth of phantom voters is met vigorously by the Federal Government with strident accusations of racism saying that anyone who requires a photo ID to vote might as well burn a cross on the White House lawn. This is patently absurd. It takes a photo ID to do many things people do every day. You need a photo ID to:

- Get a Driver's license
- Buy alcohol
- Buy cigarettes
- Apply for welfare
- Apply for food stamps
- Cash a check
- Purchase a firearm
- Make any large credit card purchase
- Open a bank account
- Rent an apartment
- Be admitted to a hospital
- Get a marriage license

And yet according to Attorney General Holder any jurisdiction that requires a photo ID to vote is placing an undue burden on minorities akin to a poll tax collected by a man in a white hood. But for security purposes you needed a photo ID to get into the NAACP meeting to hear Mr. Holder speak in a state he sued over their requirement of a photo ID to vote.[19] In addition Mexico[20] requires a photo ID to vote as does South Africa.[21] Though I doubt if either of these countries will be accused of suppressing the vote by doing so by any of our Civil Rights Professionals. The irony never ends in a world that is fast becoming the theater of the absurd.

Add into the mix that most states offer free IDs and provisional ballots that are counted once ID is verified to anyone who shows up without an ID, and it's easy to see the righteous battle against voter ID is really a reprehensible defense of voter fraud.

Passing over the debates of who is Barack Obama, where did he come from, and what motivates him we must deal now with the Fete Accompli. He has been legally sworn in and has run the country into the ground for almost four years with another four to go. We cannot afford four more years of the Progressive's spend us into oblivion with the Cloward–Piven Strategy[22] as national policy. We face another four years of international support[23] for the Muslim Brotherhood's march to power in Middle East and serial apology tours.[24] We cannot afford another four years of trillion dollar yearly deficits. We have got to support politicians who will stand in the breach and work to stop or at least slow this express to oblivion.

If we don't end this soon the Progressives will end it later.

If we don't reassert our devotion to constitutionally limited government, personal liberty, and economic freedom we will sink into a quagmire of endless entitlements for the idlers paid for by plundering the productive. The opponents of liberty are lined up to steal elections, but we can overwhelm them if we will all show up and vote. Make sure every Patriot is registered, and do anything and everything you can to make sure everyone you know votes, because you can bet Fido, Casper the Friendly Ghost and Juan Valdez will. And that's no joke.

Keep the faith. Keep the peace. We shall overcome.

★ DISPATCH THIRTY-SEVEN ★

NOT WORTH A CONTINENTAL

The Federal Reserve System (the Fed) was established in 1913 as one of the cornerstones of the Progressive agenda.[1] It was established and advertised as a way to stop the boom and bust cycle which has always been a fixture of capitalist economies. Historically, the Fed is America's third Central Bank. The First and Second Banks of the United States were born out of Alexander Hamilton's ideas as expressed in his famous Second Report on Public Credit in 1790.[2] The first bank was allowed to expire and the last was ultimately killed by Andrew Jackson in 1833.[3] Jackson believed the Bank had too great an influence politically and economically.

The United States grew to become the greatest industrial power on earth in the next 80 years without a central bank.

Established in 1913, the Federal Reserve is America's central bank. It is semi-independent/semi-public depending on which role is needed to justify its actions.[4] It is run by a board of seven Governors. These Governors are nominated by the President and confirmed by the Senate. Led by a Chairman who is also appointed by the President and confirmed by the Senate these eight people control a system of 12 Regional Federal Reserve Banks which have numerous branches throughout the United States.

The Fed can expand or contract the money supply in many ways. They print money both physically and digitally, they set interest rates, they can loosen or tighten the regulations for lending, and they can purchase debt from the Treasury. Most of these measures are neither understood nor noticed by the general public. This helps build and maintain the impression of a mysterious institution behind a curtain-pulling levers and pressing buttons secretly controlling the economy. In many ways this impression is correct.

Ben Bernanke is the current Chairman of the Federal Reserve. Some believe that this is the most important post in the United States because the Federal Reserve controls our economy through its control of the money supply. Mr. Bernanke acquired the nickname Helicopter Ben from a speech he delivered in 2002 entitled, "Deflation: Making Sure 'It' Doesn't Happen Here."[5]

In this famous speech he said, "The sources of deflation are not a mystery. Deflation is in almost all cases a side effect of a collapse of aggregate demand—a drop in spending so severe that producers must cut prices on an ongoing basis in order to find buyers. Likewise, the economic effects of a deflationary episode, for the most part, are similar to those of any other sharp decline in aggregate spending—namely, recession, rising unemployment, and financial stress."[6] This is a well-stated summation of the problem of deflation.

As a defense against the ravages of deflation the Chairman of the Federal Reserve never actually said he would drop money from a helicopter. What he said was, "The U.S. government has a technology, called a printing press (or today, its electronic equivalent), that allows it to produce as many U.S. dollars as it wishes at no cost."[7] Which was coupled by later analysts and pundits with the statement, "A money-financed tax cut is essentially equivalent to Milton Friedman's famous 'helicopter drop' of money."[8]

In the popular imagination this has been shortened into the oft misquoted belief that he said he would get in a helicopter and drop bales of money to combat deflation.

The collapse of the Housing Bubble in 2008 brought the American economy to a standstill and threatened to escalate into a systemic collapse of major banks and other financial institutions. To stop the wheels from coming off the commercial cart the politicians reacted with unusual speed and vigor. George Bush famously said, "I've abandoned free market principles to save the free market system"[9] when he advocated and passed the Troubled Asset Relief Program (TARP) which was designed to buy mortgage-backed securities in an effort to inject money into the American banking system and thus restart the economy. This 700 billion dollar fund (later resized to 475 billion) was eventually used instead to bailout major banks, AIG, and buy GM and Chrysler with only 22 billion ever going to buy toxic assets.[10]

This was followed by President Obama's stimulus bill which cost another 800 billion and was supposedly designed to kick start the economy by providing jobs. The Congressional Budget Office eventually evaluated that each of these shovel-ready jobs cost 4.1 million.[11] Then again as our President later joked, "Shovel-ready was not as shovel-ready as we expected."[12]

Spending government money to prime the economic pump cannot work. The government doesn't produce anything. It must either take the money out of the economy through taxation taking from the productive for the benefit of the unproductive or print the money thus causing inflation. The government does not create wealth. All it can do is redistribute it. When the government is in the business of picking winners and losers we all lose freedom, liberty, and opportunity.

Inflation is a rise in the general level of prices related to an increase in the volume of money and the resulting loss of value of currency. The Progressives didn't invent inflation. The Obama Administration isn't the first to resort to inflation to keep the ball rolling without the pain of tax increases. America was born in inflation. During the Revolution one of the greatest problems was how to finance the war. America was effectively blockaded by the massive British fleet and unable to trade with the rest of the world. So the government printed the money they needed, and printed and printed and printed until the money was effectively worthless coining instead of wealth the shameful saying, "Not worth a Continental."[13] These early ancestors to our dollar were eventually redeemed at 100 to 1.

Helicopter Ben has already overseen two rounds of monetary inflation referred to by the mysterious name of Quantitative Easing (QE)[14] which is a fancy way of saying the Fed floods the banks with money. The staggering size of these have only now begun to come to light showing that since the 2008 collapse the Fed has flushed more than 16 trillion dollars[15] out of the pockets of taxpayers and into the hands of banks and corporations both foreign and domestic designated by the Federal Government as too big to fail. That is more money in four years than the entire national debt[16] which has taken 236 years to accumulate and QE 3 is an open-ended commitment to keep printing at the rate of over 80 billion per month as long as necessary.

While running for office and telegraphing his distributive goals Mr. Obama said we need to spread the wealth around.[17] Chairman Bernanke has said the government can produce as many U.S. dollars as it wishes at no cost.[18] However, no matter what these two wannabe puppet masters may believe there is no free lunch. In their insolated ivory-tower gated-community world they may never have to pay the tab for their misguided attempts to create wealth with the wave of their hand. Those of us who work for a living and live in the world of family budgets will. The money we earn will be worth less and less and less until it is worthless. The money we have saved will lose value day-by-day. Someday people may not say, "It's not worth a Continental." They may instead say, "It's not worth a dollar."

The problem with getting older is you can remember when what we now pay at the pump was a car payment, and what we now pay for groceries was a house payment. The central-planners behind the curtain in OZ may tell us there is no inflation, but our eyes and our wallets tell us something else: the truth.[19]

★ DISPATCH THIRTY-EIGHT ★

ORGANIZED ANARCHY LEADS TO ONE LAST QUESTION

In the topsy-turvy world of twenty-first century America those who live by the kindness of strangers wish to dictate how much kindness they deserve changing the strangers from benefactors to victims. We have reached a point where our national motto should be "Stand and Deliver" as a runaway government devours everything in sight in an effort to satisfy the growing demands of their pre-programmed supporters.

America has taken such a bizarre turn that oxymorons are the only things that make sense any more. Organized anarchy has exploited militant apathy to create regulated liberty so that producers must provide for slackers and the informed must follow the dictates of the willfully ignorant. You can't fix stupid but there is a cure for ignorance. If we could just get these products of public education and sports hypnosis to take off the blinders long enough to understand the meaning behind the matrix perhaps we could garner one more electoral victory to stop us before we step off the cliff. Except of course the Corporations Once Known as the Mainstream Media are working as hard as they can to make sure our choice always comes down to Tweedle De and Tweedle Dum.

Our Progressive era seeks to change the old adage, "Those who refuse to learn from History are doomed to repeat it" to "Those who refuse to learn from History doom the rest of us to repeat it." The patients have seized control of the asylum. The land of the free and the home of the brave is transforming into the land of the free lunch and the home of the knaves. Symbiosis is the living together in more or less intimate association or close union of two dissimilar organisms as in parasitism. What we are witnessing today is symbiosis on steroids wherein the parasite isn't merely along for the ride but instead demands the driver's seat.

Looking at the almost bewildering explosion of reality we call today our minds behold the organized anarchy of the Occupy Everywhere Movement that is spreading around the world. We are now witnessing a government supported revolution akin to Mao's Cultural Revolution. This isn't a revolt of the 99% seeking to devour the 1% it is the 46%[1] that pay no federal taxes seeking to increase the production from their 54% milk cows. To call forcing one segment of the population to work to support another segment of the population paying your fair share makes theft a contribution and bondage a responsibility.

The people involved express a variety of causes. They want a bailout for home owners who are upside down or in foreclosure. At the same time they want those who accepted the bailout on Wall Street prosecuted. They want[2] student loans forgiven, wars stopped, big corporations downsized, and an end to capitalism. Many politicians and their major media publicity machine have embraced the movement labeling it the Progressive version[3] of the Tea Party. This is a window on the future. Showing the silent majority what is to come: a shabby world where the Lilliputians have not only bound Gulliver they have harnessed him to the cart and forced him to be their beast of burden.

By seeking the destruction of capitalism instead of seeking to break the umbilical cord between the crony capitalists and their bought and paid for politicians what they really seek is to force us to worship the myth of free enterprise as we sacrifice the energy and inventiveness of the productive on the altar of the indolent.

It is time to lay our cards on the table. It is time to call a spade a spade. Capitalism is an economic system characterized by private or corporate ownership of capital goods, by investments that are determined by private decisions, prices, and production. The distributions of goods in a capitalistic system are determined by competition in a free market. Socialism is an economic system characterized by collective or governmental ownership and administration of the means of production and distribution of goods. Fascism is an economic system that exalts the nation above the individual and that stands for a centralized autocratic government with severe economic regimentation. Essentially fascism is socialism pretending to be capitalism since private ownership exists in a government straightjacket.

Which of these systems do we have? Which of these systems is staring us in the face every day?

I challenge anyone and everyone to take this test. Watch the stock market for one month. Watch its ups and downs. What you will see is that the market does not move because of innovation or production, instead it moves in response to government actions, statements, and policies. While we still have private ownership the government is increasingly regulating and controlling the economy. Take the test. Review the definitions above and you decide. Which of these systems do we have? Or does it have us?[4]

America has never experienced a truly capitalistic system. We were born under mercantilism. We grew to power under Henry Clay's American System of nationalistic paternalism.[5] We have flirted with socialism in a mixed system since FDR reshuffled the deck and institutionalized the New Deal. And now we struggle to maintain some visage of freedom at the edge of a crony capitalism whose Progressive public–private security blanket has become the pillow that smothers all incentive. We have morphed from a representative republic operating on democratic principles into a state wholly owned by a good old boy coalition composed of the perpetually re-elected, the unions, and the crony capitalists: the Outfit.[6,7]

The over educated under informed[8] lemmings that call themselves the 99% are being duped by the Outfit.[9] They are a collective battering ram assailing the last remnants of American individualism.[10] They are using the threat[11] of social[12] unrest to demand the final triumph of "I want what I want" over "I get what I earn."

What's the cure for the Great Recession? Is it more government spending and more government control as the Outfit and their 99% fellow-travelers tell us? Is it "Drill baby drill" and a return to a golden-age of pure capitalism that never really existed?

First we must understand our situation. What is the cause of the chronic state of our anemic recovery? Is it as our president tells us and the world: Americans are soft[13] arrogant[14] and lazy?[15] Or have we finally reached the tipping point? Have we finally reached the point where all the Peters being robbed to pay for Paul's vacation have decided to change their name to Paul? Is this a recession or is it a strike? The central planners look at the wreckage of a once great economy that their programs have gutted and say, "You can't make an omelet without breaking some eggs." They should be asking "How many omelets can they make if the goose doesn't lay any more golden eggs?"

Which leads to one last question: "Who is John Galt?"

★ DISPATCH THIRTY-NINE ★

OWENS' LAW OF OSCILLATING PYRAMIDS
Which explains:
The Cyclical Rise and Fall of Bureaucracy
While at the same time answering the age-old question:
"What happened to the Maya?"
OR
I'M NOT GIVING YOU ANYMORE CORN TO BUILD PYRAMIDS

INTRODUCTION

"The Mayas were intelligent; they had a highly developed culture. They left behind not only a fabulous calendar but also incredible calculations. They knew the Venusian year of 584 days¼" (p.55)

Von Daniken, Erich. Chariots of the Gods? Bantam Books: New York.

For years people wondered where did these peaceful geniuses go. Did the mother ship come down and carry them back to Jupiter or wherever peaceful geniuses come from? Did they evolve into a higher state of being?

All this wondering provided the gist for popular speculation and pseudoscientific pontification for many years or at least until Yuri Valentinovich Knorosov and other linguists translated the Mayan language. Then it was learned that they might not have been so peaceful after all, and as a matter of fact they may have been one of the most warlike of all peoples. And low and behold archeological data began to supply the required evidence and the problem was solved: the Mayan had destroyed themselves in an orgy of fire and arrows. It all seemed so neat, scientific, and profitable.

Then some smart aleck historian, who also happened to be an organizational leadership researcher, made the mistake of interviewing some of the Native Americans who today make-up a sizable portion of the population of Guatemala and Mexico who happen to look surprisingly like the people depicted in the Mayan bas-reliefs. And inconvenient as it may seem once all this speculation, pontification, and general wondering had made several careers and helped some otherwise starving publishers buy much needed yachts and mansions this eager young researcher emerged from the wilds of Northern Arizona and declared, "The Maya had NOT disappeared after all."

"What!" Cried the popular speculators.

"Away with him!" Yelled the enraged pseudoscientific pontificators.

"Quick, have him write a book about it!" Yelled the copious publishers from their thousand foot yachts docked outside their hundred room mansions.

Since it is impossible to categorically answer the question, "What?" and since no one really ever feels like following the Red Queen's advice and conveniently being, "Away withed." I figured I might as well at least write an article and do my little part to help keep poor, disadvantaged publishers supplied with at least enough caviar, truffles and European blended coffees to avert any relief from the high cholesterol and gout which serve as their red badge of courage.

So where did the Maya go? To quote one of my sources, "We got tired of giving those guys all our corn to build pyramids so we moved to the next valley and kept our corn for ourselves or something like that."

This somehow brings me to the breakthrough Organizational Leadership concepts that should make my career as a leadership expert and hopefully get me an invitation to sip European coffee and eat truffles on one of those yachts.

Are you ready?

Here they come:

1. Bureaucracy is a good thing.
2. History supports the theory that bureaucracy is fundamental to the human condition.
3. Bureaucracies all start out as pyramids with a large base, a small peak, and a proportional center, which adequately supports the top and adequately covers the base.
4. Bureaucratic pyramids all eventually become diamonds as they bloat in the middle.
5. All organizational diamonds eventually collapse due to the bloated weight of the expanded center.
6. The top is always lost in the crash.
7. A majority of the center plunges back to the base.
8. The natural leveling process of change never leaves a level playing field.
9. A new peak immediately appears because there is always a point that rises above the field.
10. The remaining middle coalesces to support the new peak in order to accentuate and solidify its difference from the base.
11. Another pyramid establishes itself on the ruins of the preceding one.

I call this **Owens' Law of the Oscillating Pyramid**. I propose that this Law explains the cyclical rise and fall of bureaucracy. This Law is based upon observation and research and also upon the fact that eventually the costs outweigh the benefits and someday, somewhere someone is going to yell, "I'm not giving you anymore of my corn to build pyramids!"

The collapse of the Soviet Union provided a perfect example of this phenomenon. For decades, this highly bureaucratic "Evil Empire" had enforced its rule by giving benefits to one group (the communists) to brutalize and dominate other groups (everyone else). As the model predicted the Soviet system admitted more and more people into the middle of the pyramid thus bloating the mid-level brutalizers and increasing the number of people who supposedly had a stake in the system. But unfortunately for the Evil Empire the inefficiencies of the system didn't allow the pyramid to provide the material advantages needed to continue the inflation nor to even sustain the growing weight of the middle level. Therefore, with no incentive to continue supporting the regime the pyramid collapsed.

Bureaucracy = hierarchical structure, division of labor, written rules, and records.

This has been evident since the beginning of time.

Examples:

- Revolution every generation
- Revolutionary youth becoming Reactionary adults
- Luther from 99 theses to peasant revolt
- British bureaucracy "the ministry" goes on though ministers may come and go.

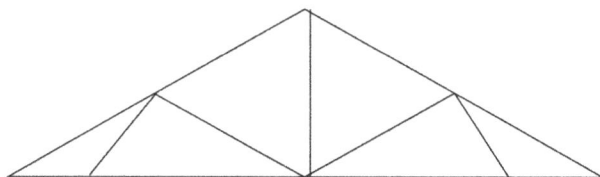

Pyramids are made of pyramids, each department or group has a head, and each head is supported by layers.

When a pyramid falls these component pyramids tend to seek independence (Chinese mandarins—Roman Empire) and then they begin to coalesce into succeeding pyramids, such as exemplified by the successive Egyptian and Chinese dynasties or the Frankish Empire of Charlemagne.

Signs that the end of a pyramids cycle is approaching:

- "I was just following orders," or "That's the way we've always done it," as an excuse for doing things that common sense tells us are foolish.
- Malicious obedience. When a subordinate follows the non-sensical orders of superiors in the hopes that doing so will bring about change.
- Geritocracy. Look at Congress. Almost automatic re-election ensures a constantly aging pool of leaders with a vested interest in maintaining the status quo.

In modern American society we have moved from Truman's "The buck stops here," to Clinton's "It depends on what the meaning of the word 'is' is."[2] From Bill Gates leading an industry to change the world to octegenarian politicians whose secretaries have to turn on their computers deciding what shape that industry should take.

At the time of the American Revolution there was no direct taxation instead there were taxes on various transactions which in total added up to a miniscule percentage of their income. Today, for many it is now over 50%. How much corn are we willing to give to those we don't trust to do things we don't want? How long can this continue? We are spending the money of the unborn to pay for the repose of the unproductive. This is the ultimate expression of taxation without representation.

The Oscillating Pyramid Cycle:

Formless base—pinnacle dominated true pyramid—bloated middle diamond shaped twin pyramid—out of balance wobble (component pyramids strive for increasing individual autonomy)—collapse

The Historical Opportunity to Break this Cycle:

The Israelites at Mt. Sinai instead of accepting God's offer to reinstate a personal relationship they reject this and demanded that Moses build them a social pyramid instead.

Proposed Exception to the Rule:

Steady-state primitive (Neolithic, pre-agriculture) societies both ancient and modern have been advanced as being different than the cultures of the present and therefore by implication exempt from this theory of bureaucratic/organizational structure. There is not enough social or organizational data to make informed statements about unknown cultures. Everyone that has been extensively studied and reported on exhibited the pyramidal, hierarchical social structure and rule-based operation even if a lack of writing precluded the development of true bureaucracy.

Long-running societies (China, India, and Rome) exhibit this oscillating character within the ebb and flow of civil war and dynastic change.

In modern democracies, elections are designed to provide stability through a peaceful, periodic change in the pinnacle thereby allowing the base to exert influence and buy into the existence of the pyramid through nationalism. Economic self-interest has also become a major factor in modern democracies. Periodic major changes, Andrew Jackson, FDR, etc. change the tenor but not the shape as the middle continues to bloat. Modern democracies are still too new of a phenomenon to contend that they will break the pattern and at the moment they appear to be textbook cases of its operation.

Change of Focus for Modern Consideration:

Bureaucracy is a GOOD thing. The oscillating nature of its natural lifecycle should be understood, recognized, appreciated, and factored into current calculations for what it is, the natural course of human organization. Change is a constant component of life.

So the next time you're standing in line to renew whatever permit happens to need renewing at the time tell yourself that, "Bureaucracy is a GOOD thing." Tell yourself that about a thousand times as you wait for the clerk who has been standing at the window for ten minutes waiting to open the window at exactly 9 AM and not one second sooner. And as your mind numbs through this exercise you can comfort yourself with the thought, "Eventually all pyramids fall," as you fight to keep yourself from standing on a chair and yelling,

"I'M NOT GIVING YOU ANYMORE CORN TO BUILD PYRAMIDS!"

Then again as every pyramid falls another takes its place. That is Owens' Law of Oscillating Pyramids.

DISPATCH FORTY ★

★

Positively Negative

The Corporations Once Known as the Mainstream Media constantly trumpets the claim that President Obama was a Professor of Constitutional Law. And when he was campaigning he charged that President Bush was not respecting the Constitution when he fired eight prosecutors saying, "I was a constitutional law professor, which means unlike the current president I actually respect the Constitution."[1]

In this long over-looked quote from a radio interview a Pre-President Obama laments the negative liberties he sees as a flaw in the Constitution and waxes eloquent in defense of the redistribution of wealth and the positive power of an intrusive welfare state.[2]

"If you look at the victories and failures of the civil rights movement and its litigation strategy in the court I think where it succeeded was to invest formal rights in previously dispossessed people, so that now I would have the right to vote. I would now be able to sit at the lunch counter and order as long as I could pay for it I'd be o.k. But, the Supreme Court never ventured into the issues of redistribution of wealth, and of more basic issues such as political and economic justice in society. To that extent, as radical as I think people try to characterize the Warren Court, it wasn't that radical. It didn't break free from the essential constraints that were placed by the founding fathers in the Constitution, at least as its been interpreted and Warren Court interpreted in the same way, that generally the Constitution is a charter of negative liberties. Says what the states can't do to you. Says what the Federal Government can't do to you, but doesn't say what the Federal Government or State government must do on your behalf, and that hasn't shifted and one of the, I think, tragedies of the civil rights movement was, um, because the civil rights movement became so court focused I think there was a tendency to lose track of the political and community organizing and activities on the ground that are able to put together the actual coalition of powers through which you bring about redistributive change. In some ways we still suffer from that."[3]

Unfortunately for this radical interpretation, liberty is a negative. Personal liberty is always and only possible when and where external control stops. We have the liberty to think as we wish because no one can control or even know our true inner thoughts. We do not have the liberty to steal; society has placed limits on that action which are enforced by external control. The Framers of our Constitution knew this which explains why our foundational document includes restrictions on the power of government not restrictions on individuals. Unless governmental control over the individual was limited there would be no liberty.

This has been common knowledge in our Republic since John Hancock signed his John Hancock and we declared to the world that the United States of America was going to be something different. We were determined to break free of the entangling state control stifling the monarchies of Europe. We would be a new type of nation where individual liberty, opportunity, and free enterprise would unleash the pent-up creativity and ingenuity would make real the genius of a free people. However, over the years many have fallen asleep, lulled into a trance by the prosperity and security this freedom from state control has fostered.

Slowly the knowledge of what gave vent to this prosperity and security has been lost and generations of Americans have been taught by state schools that free enterprise is evil and state paternalism is good. Generations have been bred to see governmental support, direction, and control as necessary and proper. They have ingested the poison of dependence metastasizing the debilitating life on the dole to the point where they see their continued receipt of stolen goods as an entitlement. So many have fallen for the licentious materialistic hedonism masquerading as life in a post-modern America that when asked, "What is the American Dream?" many will reply "To own your own home." A response and a belief which made the congressionally mandated Fannie/Freddie induced housing bubble possible if not inevitable.[4]

This shows the negative results of the positive reinforcement of materialism over intellectualism. The correct response to the question, "What is the American Dream?" is Individual liberty and opportunity. Once this was common knowledge among an engaged American public who realized that no one fought and died to own a home, people owned homes in America before the revolution. It was freedom that was the object of the Revolution and it is the individual liberty and opportunity that freedom enables that is the American Dream. And today in America this individual liberty and opportunity has now become the object of ridicule in schools pushing a green agenda and a socialist future. The demand for a return to individual liberty and opportunity has become the disparaged slogan on signs at Tea Parties.

Our leaders have embraced instead the idea of "Positive Liberty" which is an oxymoron. By this they mean that the state should actively intervene in the lives of people to provide them with all that is necessary for lives lived as the leaders think they should be. What they are really New Speaking of is Socialism disguised as democracy. However, the increase of governmental power over people does not equate to liberty it equates to serfdom and only the Progressive New Speak of a post-modern America could call this decrease of freedom an increase of liberty or democracy.

Alexis de Tocqueville said, "Democracy extends the sphere of in-dividual freedom socialism restricts it. Democracy attaches all possible value to each man; socialism makes each man a mere agent a mere number. Democracy and socialism have nothing in common but one word: equality. But notice the difference: while democracy seeks equality in liberty, socialism seeks equality in restraint and servitude."[5]

This positive liberty is the handmaiden of the other new positive that our progressive leaders wish to foist upon us: positive equality. The real equality, the one our ancestors fought and died for is equality of opportunity which is a negative, forcing the government stays out of the way and the people go as far as their investment of time, talent and treasure can take them.

In our new progressive world the government is supposed to act to create an equality of outcome so that all are equal all the time. This type of collective equality is to be advanced and protected by the all-powerful state pushing down some, lifting others until all are equal at all times. This equality of outcome becomes an unlimited reality that is conceived of as the goal of society. Unfettered democracy defined as the participation of all in the political process either as rulers, dispensers or consumers becomes not only the goal but the means and the end in and of itself.

Thus our Constitutional Scholar-in-Chief is leading us step-by-step away from the individual liberty and opportunity that are the guardians of the American Dream and into a negative representation of our positive values. With another four years this administration will succeed in fundamentally transforming America.[6]

One last quote from Alexis de Tocqueville "The American Republic will endure, until politicians realize they can bribe the people with their own money."[8]

PS: Don't take the bribe.

★ DISPATCH FORTY-ONE ★

Putting the Paste Back in the Tube

We all know that trying the same thing over and over expecting different results is a popular definition of insanity. And we also know that putting the paste back in the tube is a popular illustration of an impossible task.

I tested the first truism mentioned above as a young man whose motto should have been, "I'll never do that again—I just did it again." For some reason just as not going to school didn't lead to improved job prospects and attempting to spend every day at a party didn't lead to happiness. Over and over I valiantly kept trying to rock-n-roll all night and party every day. I applied my patented hangover cure. Stay drunk. I figured it wasn't the drinking that caused the hangover it was the getting sober, and I tried my best to avoid hangovers from the time I was 15 until I was 30. Then at 30 I had my Come-to-Jesus moment, meaning I literally came to Jesus. With His guidance I found another path which included school and working which yielded a different result including a soul mate for a wife, a son to be proud of, and a wonderful life.

Turning to the second truism mentioned above, as a person who actually tried putting toothpaste back in the tube I can attest that it deserves its symbolism as impossible. At best you can manage to get a little back in the tube. But the process is messy, frustrating and in the end so fruitless that it's laughable. All of which brings me to my question for this dispatch. Can those of us who believe in limited government, personal liberty, and economic freedom walk America back from the cliff to which the embrace of Progressive leadership and its collectivist mindset, one hundred years of reinforcement by indoctrination, and an addiction to entitlements have led us?

How best to describe the problem we face? Often a good example will expose a basic problem better than any technical explanation. Look at the debate[1] we had about the payroll tax extension. Both wings of the Party of Power continued the baseline inspired fiction that you have to pay for tax cuts when all they ever do is allow those who earn money to keep it. The Democratic wing, always seeking to divide America into interest groups, contended the only way to pay for tax cuts on one segment of the population is to tax someone else. Therefore they proposed to pay for the extension by taxing millionaires and billionaires.[2] The Republican Progressives proposed cutting federal salaries to pay for it[3] an approach which sounds as if it should appeal to those seeking to re-limit the central government.

Looking at the first solution, taxing the rich to give to the un-rich is merely more of the same spreading-the-wealth-around income distribution socialism which is the hallmark of the Democratic wing of the Party of Power.

Turning to the second solution it sounds good while in reality it is more baseline thinking where cutting a proposed increase is a cut even though the budget still increases.[3] Instead of cutting proposed increases in salaries why not cut some of the tens of thousands of new bureaucrats which have been added in just the last two years?[4] Merely cutting the proposed increases in salaries of the hordes of federal drones is like re-arranging the deck chairs on the Titanic. It may look better but ultimately it really won't help keep the ship of state afloat. This is typical of the governance proposed by the big government Republican wing of the Party of Power. It may look good, it may even sound good, but when you peel back the onion the deficits continue and the debt goes up.

Peering through the fog generated by the media amplified rhetoric the entire debate is bogus because the original payroll tax cut was a trap to begin with. It put money in the pocket of every person who receives a pay check by letting each of us keep a little more of the money we earned. But the payroll tax is what supports the current recipients of Social Security.[5] There is no Trust Fund. That is a fiction, since the money goes directly to the general funds to be replaced by IOUs that aren't worth the paper they would be printed on if they weren't electronic. If this money is taken away Social Security loses even the illusion of a pay-as-you-go system and is starkly revealed for what it is: welfare for seniors, a Ponzi scheme that makes Bernie Madoff look like a piker.[6]

It is time for my generation to admit we have been ripped off for every cent ever extorted from us for Social Security, and the only way we can receive benefits is to have the government extort it from our children and give it to us. By decreasing the plunder taken from the kids and instead taking it from the perennial enemies of the Democratic Progressives, the most productive, Social Security is revealed for what it is: just another welfare entitlement. And merely lowering the salary of a bloated bureaucracy perpetuates the growth and legitimizes the recent exponential expansion of a centrally-planned government that has run amuck. It also makes social security visible as the Ponzi scheme it has always been.

Europe is exploding because the bill is coming due for countries that have played this social welfare shell game for generations. Austerity is the word that is igniting riots and strikes from Athens to London. Faced with the possibility that they won't be able to retire at 50 with full pensions, generous benefits, and guaranteed vacations people are throwing fire bombs and toppling governments.

Western Civilization was born in the Mid-East, was launched as a world embracing power from Europe, and culminated in the great experiment of America. Today Western Civilization teeters on the edge of destruction. Our Federal Reserve is pumping out funny money faster than anyone can count trying to prop up the European launching pad as we abandon our occupation of the Middle Eastern cradle and fear for the continued vitality of its American summit. Western Civilization burns while our Party of Power plays the fiat financial fiddle. Will we continue the shadow dance pretending we have a limited government or will we muster up the courage to tell our media enhance perpetually re-elected puppet masters that he who pays the piper calls the tune?

★ DISPATCH FORTY-TWO ★

REAL HOPE FOR A CHANGE

Hope and change were the magic words that swept a relatively unknown, inexperienced Barack Obama into the Oval Office. He campaigned as the one able to fix the Bush economy. Once in office he has protested that he didn't know how bad the economy was even though that was what he had run his campaign on. He has spent the majority of his first term and successfully campaigned for his second blaming everyone else for everything.

His signature accomplishments, the stimulus, Obamacare and the Dodd-Frank financial reform have done more to harm than help. Serial vacations and weekly golf outings aside, President Obama has worked hard and has so far managed to turn a recession into the Great Recession. Now he has won re-election with the message, "More of the same" with no solution in sight.

The solution to our current malaise is not more of the same. It isn't spreading the wealth around in a step-by-step slide into socialism. The solution isn't even a return to the status quo as it stood before the current administration began its war on American exceptionalism. We cannot return to a system that alternates between Republican and Democratic Progressives. We must make a break with the post-Reagan past. We must return to the fundamentals that made America the greatest nation the world has ever known: individual liberty and free enterprise safe guarded by a written constitution, and a federal representative republic operating on democratic principles

The solution is simple. How we get there is the subject of this article and hopefully a sign pointing in the direction of change.

First we have to unleash the primary engine of our greatness, our people.

Currently a tax system that no one, not even the people who write it, can understand depresses creativity and entrepreneurship by penalizing anyone who excels with the aptly named progressive tax. Income tax had been declared unconstitutional by the Supreme Court in 1894.[1] So Congress led the way in proposing and passing the 16th Amendment which allowed for not only an income tax but a graduated income tax.[2] The first income tax law provided for a graduated tax with a top rate of 7%. And when it was stated during the debate that someday the rate might reach an unbelievable 50% the speaker was laughed to scorn. Yet, by 1961 the top rate had climbed to 91% with the 50% rate beginning at the $16,000 level.[3] These rates were cut dramatically under Ronald Reagan and a wave of growth was ignited that blazed for decades.[4]

However they have been creeping back up ever since. But it isn't the rates whatever they are that we should stand against. It is instead the idea behind them. If we want a level playing field and if we want everyone to pay their fair share what we need is a flat tax. Everyone, whether they make $1,000, $10,000 or $10,000,000 pays the same percentage with no deductions and no tax credits. Everyone pays. Everyone contributes. If you earn money you join with all other earners to support the nation. Trying to tax our way out of debt elicits a paraphrase of Parkinson's Law, "Expenditures always rise to meet income."

Next we have to unleash our corporations.

Today America has the highest corporate tax rate in the world. This makes us uncompetitive and unattractive to foreign capital.[5] First of all tax on corporate profits is a double tax because corporations are owned by stock holders. When the profits are distributed to the owners of the stock they are responsible for this as income. Therefore the corporate tax is a double tax which is obviously unfair and an inhibition to growth and productivity. I do not propose to lower the corporate tax rate. I propose we eliminate it entirely. This would strike a blow for true equality, freedom, and fairness. It would also take a giant step in the direction of making America once again the most attractive place in the world for those who want the freedom to excel.

I would couple this with an immediate moratorium on federal regulations and a roll back on those which have shackled our economy since the beginning of the progressive era. Take the oil industry for example. If we would cut the ideologically driven threads which bind this giant we could unleash the power of our vast reserves, free ourselves from dependence on our enemies and create millions of jobs.[6] "Drill Baby Drill" could become the slogan for a general renewal of American-free enterprise. We need to cut the red tape that strangles us and let freedom ring.

What about foreign Affairs?

Internationally we need to return to the policies which guided us from being a raw undeveloped nation on the edge of civilization to the pinnacle of world power. This foreign policy is superbly summed up by one of the most under-rated presidents in American History, John Quincy Adams in his statement, "America goes not abroad, in search of monsters to destroy. She is the well-wisher to the freedom and independence of all. She is the champion and vindicator only of her own."[7] To return to America's traditional foreign policy we need to end the undeclared wars. Stop maintaining garrisons in more than 100 nations around the world, bring our troops home, and guard our own borders.[8] We need to quit trying to build nations for people who don't even like us, so come home and rebuild our own infrastructure which was once the envy of the world is now a crumbling reminder of what we could once accomplish.

We also need to return the control of America's money to Congress where it belongs according to the Constitution.[9] The perpetually re-elected have abdicated their responsibility to create money to the Federal Reserve. Originally instituted to abolish the business cycle and manage the economy this central bank has presided over the devaluation of American currency and the inflation of one bubble after another which has led to one crash after another.[10]

It is instructive to remember, that Marx in his Manifesto of the Communist Party called for, "Centralization of credit in the hands of the state, by means of a national bank with State capital and an exclusive monopoly." And that Thomas Jefferson said, "The central bank is an institution of the most deadly hostility existing against the Principles and form of our Constitution. I am an Enemy to all banks discounting bills or notes for anything but Coin. If the American People allow private banks to control the issuance of their currency, first by inflation and then by deflation, the banks and corporations that will grow up around them will deprive the People of all their Property until their Children will wake up homeless on the continent their Fathers conquered." We must free ourselves from this privately and secretly owned corporation that controls our monetary system and our economy.[11]

Lenin once said, "The surest way to destroy a nation is to debauch its currency."[12] The Federal Reserve Bank has inflated our currency almost beyond recognition and to re-establish our nation as the greatest experiment in human freedom that it was meant be we must reverse this trend. To do this we must stop the deficit spending which drives our debt and creates the need for politicians to inflate our currency to hide their mismanagement. We need to cut current deficit spending, cap future spending, and begin to pay down the debt. Only by actually becoming responsible once again will we create the certainty of value that sound money portrays. Inflation is a dishonest tax upon all we earn and the silent thief of all we save.

Our current leaders work to manage the decline of America.[13] However, those of us who refuse to accept the inevitability of this decline can turn it around. We can stand in the gap and bring forth the re-birth of America. So, if we have the will and the courage we can have some real hope for a change.

★ DISPATCH FORTY-THREE ★

REAL REBELS AND THE COUNTER REVOLUTION

Think of America's Founders. These were real rebels.

Sam Adams agitated against the imposition of taxes. He penned the petitions which brought forth the rallying cry "No taxation without representation!" While avoiding violence he led the effort to organize resistance to tyranny. He founded the Committee of Correspondence in Massachusetts and inspired its spread to the other colonies. He organized boycotts of British goods and the public trial of the British soldiers involved in the Boston Massacre.

In a world of divine right kings where the common man was a pawn to be exploited and demeaned James Madison made these revolutionary statements, "The powers delegated by the proposed Constitution to the federal government are few and defined. Those which are to remain in the State governments are numerous and indefinite."[1] And, "An ELECTIVE DESPOTISM was not the government we fought for; but one which should not only be founded on free principles, but in which the powers of government should be so divided and balanced among several bodies of magistracy, as that no one could transcend their legal limits, without being effectually checked and restrained by the others."[2]

Patrick Henry did more than say, "Give me liberty or give me death."[3] Before the Revolution, as a member of the Assembly in Virginia he led in the formation of a resistance movement against the tyranny of the British crown. During the Revolution he served in the Continental Congress that passed the Deceleration of Independence. After the Revolution he was not afraid to stand up against the desire of many to impose a

Constitution without a Bill of Rights leading in the fight to maintain the greatest amount of individual liberty and the strongest limits to the central authority possible under the new Federal Government. As if he could see the convolutions which currently threaten to swallow the Republic Mr. Henry reminded us at the beginning of our national experiment in limited government, "When the American spirit was in its youth, the language of America was different: Liberty, sir, was the primary object."[4]

Today the world is turned upside down. The so-called radical rebels of the 1960s now own or control most things including the government. The anti-establishment has become the establishment and the silent majority is being told to remain silent while this progressive minority transforms our nation into what their collectivist programmers have taught them it should be. And yet they still see themselves as the rebels fighting a faceless bureaucracy for freedom never realizing they have met the enemy, and they are them.

All of this made me think about my old friend the professional revolutionary and something hit me. He has always considered himself a rebel. And considering he has made a living out of being a spokesman for the movements dedicated to destroying the America we have always known that kind of made sense at one time.

But in reality he is now and has consistently in the past loyally spouted the logical progression of the anti-American, anti-capitalist garbage that many of the teachers at our good old public High School tried to shove into our young skulls full of mush. He also sounds exactly like all of our contemporaries who have spent a lifetime drinking at the well of the Corporations Once Called the Mainstream Media. Though they see themselves as deep thinkers it has always been obvious they receive their programming, their news and views from the major networks, and the transcripts in the print media. They spout the same anti-traditional values pro-socialism talking points time after time.

Their representatives have spent decades chipping away at the America we love in the movies, on television, and in songs. They have gained control of one component of society at a time: education, the media, the board room, the Congress, and finally the White House. Through patience and planning they have gained control of the entire federal government and the elites of most areas of society. Therefore I cannot see why we should continue referring to them as rebels merely because they see themselves that way.

When you listen to their current spokesmen such as the Daily Show, Bill Maher, or any of the MSNBC line up they come off as so hip and so cutting edge when in fact they agree 100% with the current administration and its collectivist anti-life New Age agenda. What's rebellious about that? That's like saying Pravda was a radical spokesman for change when they parroted whatever the leaders of the former USSR had to say.

Today my friend the professional rebel is actively helping recruit and train the brown shirt Occupy troops? They may rail against Wall Street but that same Wall Street promotes and funds the very people these protesters vote for. Someone is being used for something, but they never seem to wake up to ask, "Why should we pay no attention to the man behind the curtain?"

I can no longer consider myself a conservative. What is there left to conserve? I am a radical and a rebel, because I advocate for limited government, personal liberty, and economic freedom. These 1960s retreads who continue to advocate for the progressive collectivists who have won their revolution and now occupy the seats of power are faux rebels: organizational apparatchiks spouting the party line.

Look at how revolutionary some of our real rebels still sound today:

Sam Adams said, "The Constitution shall never be construed... to prevent the people of the United States who are peaceable citizens from keeping their own arms."[5] And "The liberties of our country, the freedom of our civil constitution, are worth defending against all hazards: And it is our duty to defend them against all attacks."[6] He also said, "Our contest is not only whether we ourselves shall be free, but whether there shall be left to mankind an asylum on earth for civil and religious liberty."[7]

Patrick Henry said, "Guard with jealous attention the public liberty. Suspect everyone who approaches that jewel. Unfortunately, nothing will preserve it but downright force. Whenever you give up that force, you are inevitably ruined."[8] And, "We are not weak if we make a proper use of those means which the God of Nature has placed in our power... the battle, sir, is not to the strong alone it is to the vigilant, the active, the brave."[9] When thinking of his most famous statement we should keep it in context and recall the whole quote, "Is life so dear or peace so sweet as to be purchased at the price of chains and slavery? Forbid it, Almighty God! I know not what course others may take, but as for me, give me liberty, or give me death!"[10]

So the next time the nightly faux news shows are filled the antics of the faux rebels demonstrating for more government power, or the next time one of your relatives or old friends wants to fill your ear with their oft repeated mantras for the collectivist establishment tell yourself, "This is the time for real rebels and the counter revolution."

And if pointing out the transparent hypocrisy of the faux rebels of today should ever be considered too rebellious for the faint of heart let me share one more quote from Patrick Henry, "If this be treason, make the most of it!"[11]

★ DISPATCH FORTY-FOUR ★

RIDE TO THE SOUND OF THE GUNS

He graduated with the highest number of demerits and at the bottom of his class. He was the poster child for graduating by the skin of your teeth. Yet he also became the youngest Major General in American History and the man General Sheridan believed did more than any other to win the Civil War. He was a fighting commander whose standing order in combat was, "Ride to the sound of the guns!" Perhaps it flowed from the fact that while at West Point George Armstrong Custer didn't study very much, that he had only one strategy, and only one tactic. The strategy was victory, and the tactic was charge.[1]

Although our current crop of military leaders are made up of politicians who have learned how to pull the levers and work the system in a way they resemble the always ready for action Custer. They appear to be a one trick pony. Unfortunately that trick is kowtowing to the political leadership telling them exactly what they want to hear when what they need to hear might be the exact opposite.

For a decade between 1979 and 1989 the United States military and Intelligence establishments were intimately involved in supporting the Mujahedeen insurgents of Afghanistan battle against the invading Soviets.[2] We supplied weapons, training, Intel, and logistical support. We had many field operatives, soldiers, and analysts who were deeply conversant with all the nuances of the military and political realities in Afghanistan.

Yet when our leaders decided to invade the country to flush out Al Qaeda[3] and punish the Taliban[4] for sheltering them, military leaders who should have known better presented and approved plans that even a layman could see would lead to a new insurgency against America as the next invaders. These leaders bowed to the dictates of modern America post-Vietnam strategy delivering a campaign with minimum casualties and victory in name not in fact. Instead of using the expert professional American forces needed to produce a real victory they relied on mercenary indigenous warriors who with the help of our firepower pushed the Taliban to the wall and then let them walk out the back door.

What is the result? Ten years later we are still fighting and taking casualties in a war scheduled to end like a bad movie in 2014 or...? Having never sealed the border between Afghanistan and Pakistan we are fighting an enemy that can not only melt into the civilian population it can rest and regroup in safe havens attacking our isolated and exposed garrisons almost at will.

Even at this point, after President Obama's surge, an army of less than 200,000 trying to pacify a nation the size of Texas with the most forbidding terrain on the planet isn't going to work. After the investment of half a trillion dollars and more lives, limbs, and blood this mission teeters on the brink of failure. Our only allies in the country are hopelessly compromised and corrupt characters who have little relevance outside their palaces and little interest beyond funneling our money out of the country for their post-war retirement.

Where are the military leaders with the courage of Custer? Where are the ones who will hazard their career to speak truth to power? If an untutored armchair general with no more information than is commercially available can see that if we don't seal the border and provide enough troops to hold the territory we capture we will never win why can't military experts? Where are the generals who demand what they really need to win and ready to resign if they don't get it? If General Petraeus[5] had done this (and if he hadn't been compromised by scandal) he would have had a lock on the Republican nomination and the White House in 2012.

What about our fearless media? Where are the nightly counts of the fallen that graced the network newscast when Bush the Younger was in office? Where are the anti-war demonstrators who stood guard outside his Texas ranch and dogged his speeches? Where are the American people? Why is no one asking how can it take more than a decade to train an Afghan army to protect their own country from their own people? In WWII we trained and deployed more than 10 million soldiers, sailors and marines. We equipped armies, air forces, and navies and defeated all comers in less than 4 years. Now we cannot secure one country in more than a dozen years?

I am not saying that after the sneak attack of 9/11 we shouldn't have responded. We should have immediately devastated our enemies and their allies telling the Taliban if it happened again it would happen again. Al Qaeda had been attacking us for a decade, and we knew exactly where they were. With B-2s and cruise missiles we had the capability to decapitate them without the necessity of boots on the ground. We needed to strike hard and fast. We should have had the political and military leadership to take them out within 24 hours. Instead we dithered around until Al Qaeda and their Taliban hosts were dispersed and disappeared. We didn't do what we should have done and instead did do what we shouldn't have done producing a decade long occupation in a land that has defeated or outlasted every invader.

How should we have dealt with the on-going threat of Al Qaeda: a non-state enemy? Instead of fighting undeclared wars we should have followed the Constitution and granted Letters of Marque and Reprisal[6] which would have granted compensation and legal authority to private firms or individuals to exact retribution upon the perpetrators of the attack. Such action is not only authorized by the Constitution but it is also recognized by International Law. Send in the military equivalent of

Dog the Bounty Hunter. Let Blackwater[7] do the job, and see what free enterprise can accomplish.

What we need are military officers with the bravado of Custer. We need military leaders willing to hazard all, even their careers and officers who are willing to walk into the Oval Office and say we're fighting the wrong war, the wrong way, in the wrong place, and at the wrong time. We need officers who remember that they have sworn in to uphold the Constitution of the United States not an administration, not a career, and not a pension.

What we need is another Custer. Without one what we may get is another Little Bighorn.

★ DISPATCH FORTY-FIVE ★

SMOKE AND MIRRORS

Like a sleight-of-hand-artist on a busy street with a briefcase that turns into a table, three walnuts shells and a pea the perpetually re-elected and their town criers in the Corporations Once Known as the Mainstream Media appear to be perennially able to fool the perpetually distracted by pulling a metaphorical quarter out of their ear.

I know a professional revolutionary. We grew up together. He has correctly diagnosed America's disease as a corporate cult[1] in a symbiotic relationship with a corrupt government. He deftly outlines the general theory, although not the specifics of how crony capitalists and political hacks have crafted a system wherein money laundering has become national policy. The political hacks fleece the sheeple through taxes and inflation. They give the money to their accomplices in the flimflam corporations who funnel huge chunks of cash back to the hacks for re-election. Every few years the sheeple rouse themselves out of their media-induced coma long enough to be herded to the polls to vote for more of the same.

Yes, the professional revolutionaries and their government-educated followers have correctly diagnosed the disease. However, they have prescribed poison instead of medicine. Their answer to the curse of Corporatism's[2] National Socialism[3] is less nationalism and more socialism. Since corporatism has built a coffin our body politic cannot seem to claw its way out of, the professional revolutionaries prescribe cutting out the crony capitalists and giving the whole operation to the political hacks. In other words if the black shirts[4] have ruined the country let's try the reds.

That would be as transparent as fighting the most horrendous war in human history because Hitler attempted to pull Poland into his freedom smothering embrace and then giving Poland to Stalin.[5]

Headlines and talking heads scream for days, "The Super Committee cannot fail or the sky will fall!" Endless hours in the 24-hour news cycle are devoted to debating, "Will the Super Committee succeed or will they fail?" Meanwhile most of the sheeple are consumed with concern about the NBA strike, a celebrity drowning 30 years ago, or was Kim's wedding a set-up all along. Then we're told the Super Committee failed accompanied by endless squabbling about who caused the failure.

It is all nothing but Kabuki, a form of Japanese drama based on popular legends and characterized by elaborate costumes, stylized acting.

Remember how the Super Committee became so super? It didn't come from another planet with a red sun and lower gravity. It was instead the Frankenstein created as the cover for another rise in the debt ceiling. The Tea Party had just made a Herculean effort in the 2010 elections and achieved an historical sweep of the House of Representatives. Over 60 newly minted congressmen owed their seat at the table of plenty to the greatest grassroots movement America has seen in generations. They had campaigned on changing the culture of corruption in Washington, stopping the deficit spending, severing the cord to the crony capitalists, and paying down the national debt.

Before they could even arrive the Republican leadership colluded with a recently humiliated inexperienced president and a recently repudiated Democratic leadership to extend the Bush tax cuts in exchange for more spending in the lamest of all lame duck sessions. Then as soon as the fresh troops arrive they raise their hands in salute to the same old Republican leadership, renew the patriot Act, pass a series of continuing resolutions allowing the drunken sailors to continue spending, and then vote to raise the debt ceiling by another few trillions. Oh but they fought! They wrangled and they refused to give the Spender in Chief more trillions of our great grandchildren's money unless he agreed to a Super Committee backed up by automatic cuts and automatic tax increases in future deficits totaling trillions of dollars in cuts. This was a drama worthy of as Washington turns. If it was a joke it wouldn't be funny.

To begin with the Super Committee wasn't filled with deficit hawks and balanced budget advocates. It was instead filled with the most partisan members from both wings of the Party of Power guaranteeing there would be no settlement. Obviously the plan all along was for the automatic cuts and taxes to come into play, over the next 10 years. In other words the spendaholics of this Congress are going to place limits on the credit card of following Congresses who have the ability to vote away the limits any time they want to. How could that ever fail?

The smoke and mirrors of political theater is meant to hide the fact that all they're arguing over is to reduce the yearly deficits way off there in the future somewhere. All they ever discussed was slowing[6] the rate of increase. Even if the most draconian plan so far introduced by the young firebrand Representative Ryan had been adopted the budget still went up every year, and the national debt still grew every year. And though there would have been more and more spending with no end to the red ink in sight Ryan was portrayed as pushing Grandma off the cliff and a large percentage of the population believes it. This is baseline budgeting wherein the proposed budget becomes the base for what is cut. In other words our leaders can cut all day and the spending still goes up.[7]

It is time to tell our hypnotized fellow citizens to take the blinders off. Wake up! The house is on fire and the firemen are pouring gasoline on the flames.

The system is broke and it is becoming very clear that all the king's horses and all the king's men can't put this thing together again. The spending[8] goes on every second of every minute of every hour of every day. The tax code that ostensibly is designed to pay for it all is in reality a bewildering maze meant to trap those unsophisticated enough not to hire an army of tax lawyers and accountants while legally recognized persons such as GE file 57,000 page tax returns on 14 billion in profits and pays no tax at all.

While the hemorrhaging[9] of our descendant's wealth goes on night and day we are being set up for the next battle to raise the debt ceiling, the balanced budget amendment. Even if this long threatened turkey could finally make it to the block what good is a balanced budget amendment? The spendthrifts we call a government can still spend all they want as long as they raise enough money to pretend to cover at least the on budget[10] portion of the swag. And where do you think they will raise the money? They will either raise taxes or print money. Either way we pay so they can play. What we need is a spending amendment that limits spending to a prescribed percentage of the GDP.

At one time the best tongue-in-cheek advice for coping with the policies of the convention of confidence men masquerading as the American government was get a government job and study Spanish. Now the situation has descended even beyond the black humor of that cynical joke. Today the best advice may be to hunker in the bunker, store food, and learn enough History so that you can tell those who come after what America used to be.

In 2010 I thought it was time to take the gloves off and tell America the emperor has no clothes. To do so this advocate of the Constitution and limited government wrote *The Constitution Failed*.[11] A book which places current events in a constitutional and historical context proving that while our nation was founded upon a document meant to limit government we now stand face-to-face with an unlimited government. I believed it was time to sound the alarm. I thought people were ready to admit the terrible truth; our government does little more than tip its hat to the Constitution while doing whatever it wants. The first step in solving any problem is admitting you have a problem. The second is recognizing what that problem is. My hope was that *The Constitution Failed* would help people recognize and identify the problem so that we the people can reach a solution.

When it was first published and I was doing book signing tours people would come up and yell in my face, "How dare you say the Constitution has failed." Today in the same situation people come up and say, "I know that's right." Yet, nothing has changed and we are still on a rollercoaster ride over the edge.

As one who has been pounding this drum and singing this song for fifty years all I can do is wonder, will the drowning Lady Liberty finally see the life preserver as she goes down for the last time? Will she finally grasp the Constitution as the only thing that has ever guaranteed limited government, personal freedom and economic opportunity in America? Will she remember her past and save her future or will she sink beneath the waves of government regulation and drown in the red tape of an all-powerful central government?

I wrote *The Constitution Failed* to make a difference. I wrote it because I see my beloved country walking off a cliff into the abyss of socialism and I am compelled to throw out the life line.

I am writing this present book in the hopes that perhaps it will do some good. I want to see the re-birth of limited government. I want to see personal liberty and economic freedom continue to exist in this: the last best hope of mankind. And I'm ready to put my life, my fortune and my sacred honor on the line for limited government, personal liberty and economic freedom.

★ DISPATCH FORTY-SIX ★

Step-by-step Inch-by-inch

How do you fundamentally transform a nation from what it has been to what a clique of ideologues wants it to be? The easiest way is to convince the general population that what the would-be masters want is what the people want. Those seeking to subvert a culture must take a long view. They must realize that this will be a multistage project that will take generations to achieve.

As an example that will strike home and ring true to every engaged American let's look at how the Progressives have incrementally moved us from the best educated, most politically engaged population in History to a flock of militantly apathetic fans. Couch potatoes waiting for the next game or reality show unaware how our government operates and impatient with anyone who tries to explain it to them. How were we nudged[1] from the most self-reliant people in the world to a line of people waiting hat in hand for the next transfer payment?

The first goal was the educational system.[2] Capture that and it was possible to raise up generations who either thought as they did or who didn't think at all. Dumb it down, exchange confused thinking for critical thinking and soon the people who once asked hard questions will swallow easy answers. The best place to start is at the colleges and universities. If you can convince a generation of teachers that the snake-oil you're selling will cure everything you will soon have them indoctrinating[3] generations that the sickness is really the cure.

A target of particular interest was journalism schools. Once these schools become factories churning out carbon copies it isn't necessary to have an official propaganda ministry. The journalists themselves will self-censor anything that doesn't fit the reality they imbibed along with the Kool-aide. Once the editorial boards and the human resource departments are filled with clones none but clones need apply. Today the portals of American media are filled with people who don't even know someone who is pro-life. They don't know anyone who sympathizes with the Tea Party. So those on the other side are always the other. There is no understanding or compassion for thoughts and ideas they find foreign and alien even though they represent the thinking of the majority of Americans. So as we cling to our Bibles and our guns the megaphones of the public discourse represent mainstream America as a fringe while holding up a cross section of the Jerry Springer Show or the Gong Show as the new normal.

The next target in America's transition from a society built upon individualism, self-reliance and innovation into a centrally-planned experiment in utopian collectivism might have been the hardest or it might have been the easiest: capitalism itself.

As layer after layer of regulations entangled the economy there came a tipping point. This was reached when government interference in the economy became the dominant feature. Then business decisions were no longer made because they were right but instead because of how they intersected with government policy. Look at the stock market today. It no longer moves due to innovation or even speculation it instead moves like a marionette to the strings pulled by the Federal Reserve. It reacts to real, perceived or imagined government actions.

No longer do we have Henry Fords or J. D. Rockefellers moving and shaking the economy to build industries. Now we have crony capitalists who use their connections to get sweetheart deals, tax subsidies and bailouts. Too Big to Fail has replaced Laissez-faire and it is no longer what you know but who you know that brings success in America.

The most insidious aspect of this incremental transformation of America is what it has done to truth. Once thought to be an objective reality, in a centralized utopia truth must become whatever endorses and supports the efforts to reach the designated goals. If necessary, good becomes bad, up becomes down and dark becomes light if that is what is required to make the assumptions and conclusions of the planners plausible.

War becomes peace. Inequality becomes equality. Pork becomes stimulus. Stonewalling and taking the fifth becomes the most transparent administration in history and the destruction of the greatest health system ever known becomes affordable care.

As the meanings of words change it becomes increasingly hard to hold an intelligent conversation, because no one is sure what anyone else means. This cannot be viewed as the natural evolution of language. This is a direct by-product of the effort to centrally-plan a society. Since all efforts must be bent to the centrally directed goals all thoughts must be shaped to conform to the politically correct thoughts of the leaders. All other thoughts become suspect and are held up to ridicule.

The prevailing mood of cynicism and the general intellectual climate that this produces brings about the loss of even the meaning of truth. Truth becomes relative. It is wholly dependent upon political consid-erations as the spirit of independent inquiry itself disappears. Under the constant barrage of the all-embracing central government and their willing allies in the media the belief in the power of rational conviction fades from view and only the official line seems to make sense to those who through either apathy or complacency swallow the party line and march in lock-step from freedom to serfdom.[4]

The desire to force people to accept a creed and to salute the flag is nothing new. What is new is the justification for doing so that lies at the basis of our current round of communal thought control. It is believed by some that there is no real freedom of thought in any society at all. The thoughts of the masses have always been and will always be shaped by what we now call propaganda or governmental advertising by the laws and regulations of the leaders and the example of the upper classes. Those who wish to regiment thought and control opinion act as if since this is so it is incumbent upon them to direct the thoughts of the masses into a desirable direction. Or in other words a direction that supports the movement towards the goals and objectives previously chosen by the central planners.

Incrementally, step-by-step, inch-by-inch[5] the highly individualistic descendants of the pioneers have become a mob clamoring for bread and circuses. Dependent upon government for their very livelihood a large portion, perhaps a majority of the electorate, eagerly embrace the thinking needed to justify robbing their fellow citizens through transfer payments to subsidize their lifestyle. Society becomes rigid and any deviance from the proscribed way of thinking is ostracized. Any attempt to break free of the stranglehold of political correctness on the thoughts and opinions of a once free people must be punished. The best that we can hope is that since we have gone step-by-step and inch-by-inch eventually, slowly we will turn.

In George Orwell's classic 1984 it was the thought police that monitored and directed the thoughts of an entire nation. On a smaller scale the sadistic captain of the chain-gang in Cool Hand Luke phrased it this way when re-ferring to people who tried to break out of the system, "You run one time, you got yourself a set of chains. You run twice you got yourself two sets. You ain't gonna need no third set, 'cause you gonna get your mind right."

★ DISPATCH FORTY-SEVEN ★

SUPREME CONTEMPT

Recently President Obama made this remarkable statement, "Ultimately, I'm confident that the Supreme Court will not take what would be an unprecedented, extraordinary step of overturning a law that was passed by a strong majority of a democratically elected Congress."[1] For someone reputed to be a former professor of Constitutional Law at the University of Chicago this statement is hard to explain. Any high school student in a sophomore American History class knows there are many precedents for the Supreme Court making laws passed by Congress null and void. As a matter of fact, in the system of government tradition has delivered to us overturning laws as unconstitutional has been an important power of the Supreme Court for more than 200 years.

And if the primary content of the President's statement isn't strange enough the supporting information is wrong. Obamacare wasn't passed by a strong majority in Congress. In reality the final vote in the House vote was 220 to 215.[1] Every Republican and 34 Democrats voted against the law.[2] In the Senate the vote was 60 Democrats and Independents voting for and 39 Republicans voting against.[3] The Democrats, even though they controlled both houses of Congress knew they would lose enough of their own members that it was going to be a close vote so they moved the bill outside the regular order of business and used a legislative maneuver known as reconciliation to avoid giving the Republicans the opportunity to filibuster the law.[4]

What is the context of these current pressure tactics being used by the executive branch on the judicial branch?

Soon after taking office in 1829, President Andrew Jackson a long time Indian fighter spearheaded one of his signature pieces of legislation through Congress: the Indian Removal Act.[5] This act gave the president the power to negotiate treaties with the various tribes which still existed in America East of the Mississippi. These treaties, often accepted either under duress or under questionable circumstances seized the lands of the tribes and forced them to move West to the Indian Territory in what is today Oklahoma. The time for fighting had passed and most of the tribes quietly left their ancestral lands.

One tribe decided to try another route. The Cherokee Nation had adopted the ways of the Europeans. They devised their own written language and wrote their own Constitution. They had their own plantations, printing presses, and businesses. They also had their own lawyers and instead of going on the warpath as their ancestors had done they went to court to fight the orders from the State of Georgia which dispossessed them of their land.

In two cases; Cherokee Nation v. Georgia (1831) [6] and Worcester v. Georgia (1832),[7] the United States Supreme Court considered whether or not it had the power to enforce the rights of Native American nations in disputes between them and the States. In Cherokee Nation v. Georgia, the Court ruled that it lacked jurisdiction to review the claims of any Indian nation within the United States. In Worcester v. Georgia, the Court ruled that only the Federal Government not the States had the power to regulate the Indian nations.

What the ruling in Worcester v. Georgia meant was that Georgia could not legally seize the Cherokee lands. It was at this junction when referring to the majority opinion written by Chief Justice John Marshall that President Andrew Jackson made one his most famous statements, "Mr. Marshall has made his decision. Now let him enforce it!"[8] Instead of enforcing the ruling the Federal Government joined with Georgia in expelling the Native Americans and the result was the Trail of Tears as the Cherokee lost their lands and moved west.[9]

Franklin D. Roosevelt legislating Keynesian economic philosophy in the New Deal sought to end the Depression through government spending and central control. With massive majorities in both houses of Congress the President's agenda was enacted as quickly as possible. Then less than three years after the New Deal began to transform America the Supreme Court began overturning some of the central portions of Roosevelt's program.

In response to this resistance to his vision FDR decided to pack the court with Justices who would support his laws.[10] What he proposed was that for any justice over the age of 70 who refused to retire, the President could appoint a new Justice to sit beside the current Justice and do his work. If his plan had been adopted and none of the then current Justices retired he would have been able to appoint six new Justices. Since he couldn't force the conservative Justices to retire he sought in this way to outnumber them and thus change the ideological complexion of the court. As the President moved ahead in his attempt to pack the court the Supremes started ruling in his favor which eventually stopped the need for his effort to influence the court through overwhelming appointments. Then time and attrition did what he had tried to do with legislation. By 1941, four Justices had retired and two had died consequently by the end of his presidency seven of the nine Justices were Roosevelt appointees.[11]

Now we come full circle to President Obama and his obvious attempt to belittle and intimidate the court. Should anyone be surprised? This is nothing more than standard operating procedure for a Chicago politician. It is also a normal technique for a community organizer who has been trained in the tactics of Saul Alinsky.[12] No, we shouldn't be surprised but we could have expected more of anyone who has been entrusted with the highest office in the land. It is just such crude strong-arm tactics such as this which open Mr. Obama up to charges of being a typical South Chicago thug. If he wishes to avoid such charges he needs to avoid such actions.

The above brief review clearly shows that this was not the first attempt of a president to influence the court. However coming from one who is constantly extolled as a constitutional scholar it is certainly disquieting. As a constitutional scholar the President would obviously know when he took the opportunity during his 2010 State of the Union Speech to bash[13] the Supreme Court over their ruling in was improper form and poor etiquette leaving no other interpretation to his words than a conscious effort to alter the traditional system of checks and balances and the power relationship between the separate branches of the federal government.

★ DISPATCH FORTY-EIGHT ★

THE COMING CONTRACTION

The party's over and it's time to pay the bill. Our government has been on a spending binge for as long as I can remember. With Clinton and Newt's slight-of-hand accounting back in the late 1990s notwithstanding, which wouldn't withstand the level of scrutiny we give a tab at our local burger joint, there have been yearly deficits every year since I was born back in the 1940s. The debt[1] piled up to a record amount under Bush the Younger, and under Obama it has sky rocketed to the point where people have actually begun to notice that the emperor has no clothes.

It isn't that our nation is broke since our assets still outweigh our debt, but who wants to sell Yellowstone to satisfy the Chinese? It isn't just our government who has buried us buying $640 toilet seats, $436 hammers, or a $797,400 outhouse. All of us have had an apple out of that sack. We have pushed our personal credit to the max, our plastic to the limit, and our "Gotta have it now" culture to the breaking point. It isn't just the 51% who pay no federal taxes[2] but seem to have an insatiable appetite for federal services that are to blame. Those of us who make enough to merit a tax target on our backs have also drunk deep from the government trough. Social Security, Medicare, disaster relief, and student loans have added billions if not trillions to the national debt transferring money to the middle class.

All of us have contributed to this problem.[3] If not by accepting the money or services ourselves than by voting for people who've made careers doling out the plunder, robbing Peter to pay Paul, buying votes, and corrupting the system. The entire edifice of Western Civilization teeters on the brink of financial collapse due to the last three generations squandering the as yet unearned income of the next three. We invested the great grand kid's future in Ponzi schemes so that we could play today and they could pay tomorrow. This is the national version of "I will gladly pay you Tuesday for a hamburger today."

Our lack of interest allowed politicians to run amuck. Our personal greed and lack of restraint have all of us living in houses made of plastic cards. We look at Greece and ask for whom the bell tolls ignoring the answer that it tolls for thee.

The enemies of capitalism learned the wisdom of Alinsky that "Change comes from power and power comes from organization."[4] They followed gurus such as Richard Andrew Cloward[5] and Francis Fox Piven[6] the two Columbia professors who advocated overwhelming the government bureaucracy with entitlement demands.[7] They followed leaders such as Barney Frank and Christopher Dodd who have pushed legislation that created the bubbles and then strangled the recovery. Now these well-organized and well-financed Progressives have come to the end game. In the great tradition of all socialist power grabs now that the crisis they created has arrived they have taken to the streets.

The Corporations Once Known as the Mainstream Media are fell all over themselves trying[8] to equate[9] the Occupy Everywhere Movement with the Tea Party.[10] I've known the Tea Party. The Tea Party is a friend of mine, and this is no Tea Party. I have attended many Tea Party events and they were all peaceful. They all respected the police and stayed within the limits of lawful protest. When the events were over they left the areas cleaner than when they arrived. The only people arrested at Tea Party events have been Progressive street thugs who have attempted to disrupt a peaceful protest. The liberal version is trashing every place they lay their head and threatening violence.[11] In all the Tea Party events over the last few years not one persona has been arrested. In the Occupy Movement in just a few weeks hundreds had to be hauled away.[12] There were multiple thefts and even rapes reported at Occupy events.[13]

I personally know a professional agitator who glories in the title of the Rude Guy. He has made a lifestyle out of pushing for the socialist agenda he imbibed as a youth in public school. He has spent decades moving from protest to protest advocating an end to capitalism while supporting himself through the sale of his books and paintings. This Rude Guy has moved from the implosion of Europe to what some enemies of our nation are calling the American Spring[14] seeking free room and board in New York to continue his work. Given the fact that Van Jones has spent years, George Soros has spent millions through his front groups, and that professional organizers are flocking in from around the world it is hard to buy the Corporate Media line that this Occupy Everywhere Movement is spontaneous.

However, there are the Howard Beale types who want to scream "I'm mad as hell and I'm not going to take it anymore!" And there are also the young party people who are looking for an opportunity to have an experience, to recreate the golden years of the 1960s when they fantasize the Summer of Love produced something of value besides a generational overdose and a rise in Socially Transmitted Diseases. These naive sheep will be driven before the organizers into the police truncheons. It is these unengaged warm bodies being interviewed nightly. These are the ones who come across as unfocused, confused, and almost comical. They do not represent the well-oiled machinery behind the curtain.

The list of millionaire entertainers who stop by to step out of their air-conditioned limousine to shout, "Power to the people" as they shake their bejeweled fists grows every day. The union bosses express solidarity and send in their shock troops.[15] Leading Democrats praise the movement.[16] The Chairman of the Democratic National Committee, Debbie

Wasserman Schultz, has said the Occupy Everywhere Movement is more in the mainstream than the current crop of Republican candidates for president. This movement is not spontaneous, and it is not going to end well. In some places the leaders of this leaderless movement are calling for violence and socialism.[17] In other places they are leaving the public square to march on private residences to intimidate and threaten.[18] Is this organized anarchism or militant apathy?

Some of the issues their signs rail against: bank bailouts, corporate welfare, and other aspects of crony capitalism are issues they do share with the Tea Party. However, the Tea Party Movement has directed their anger at government which is the culprit as far as wasting our national treasure to support their donors. The Occupy Movement is focused on attacking the donors who have received the payouts. The people who invested with Bernie Madoff thought they had found the goose that laid golden eggs, and yes they did receive unrealistic and what are now called unearned payouts, but at the end of the day it wasn't the investors who were arrested it was Madoff. The Tea Party offers concrete proposals: end the over spending, cut taxes and regulations, and free the economy to free the people. The Occupy Movement offers no solution besides more of the same government intervention that caused the problems to begin with.

As stated at the beginning, we have all had a hand in leading our great nation to the edge of the abyss. And it seems as if our inability to agree upon who the culprits are or what the answers are may push us over the edge. A great contraction in our economy and in our life styles is coming. We must choose. Are we willing to make the changes that will right the ship of state and begin to bail out the rushing tide of debt that threatens to capsize us? Or, will we continue to argue ourselves into paralysis until our creditors demand the austerity we dread?

The one thing worse than being poor is being poor again. Most of us individually and all of us as a nation have been living far beyond our means charging extravagance to a credit card that has reached its limit. We can either send back the steak and have a hamburger on our own now or eventually sit powerless as our card is cut up by the foreign maître d'. We can either change our menu from caviar to corn flakes now or end up eating rubber biscuits as we wash dishes in the back room.

One thing is for sure the contraction is coming; it is how we want to deal with it that is the question.

★ DISPATCH FORTY-NINE ★

The Constitution Failed

People often ask me, "How could you write a book entitled *The Constitution Failed?*" If the Constitution was written to ensure a limited government and if today we have an unlimited central government my question is, "How can anyone contend that the Constitution hasn't failed?"

We know that for the last 100 years the Progressives have sought progress by changing the Constitution, which was written to establish unbreakable boundaries for government, without recourse to the amendment process. The Framers knew that without these boundaries government would grow into a millstone around the neck of the American people. Instead of a document establishing solid limits the Progressives say it is a living document that can be re-interpreted with each passing year evolving into whatever the current leaders may desire.

Our twin-headed Progressive party of power expands and twists the General Welfare, the Commerce, and the Supremacy clauses to sanction any executive, legislative, judicial, or regulatory action they wish to impose whether it's a welfare state, energy policies, or the mandatory purchase of insurance. However, nothing is more symbolic of the current irrelevance of the Constitution to our leaders than the utter contempt they hold for the 9th and 10th Amendments.

Back during the original debate to ratify the Constitution these two sentinels of limited government were forced upon the proponents of a strong central government by those much maligned patriots the Anti-Federalists. The Constitution never would have been ratified without an assurance that the first order of business for the new government would be the ratification of the Bill of Rights. The capstone of these sacred rights is the 9th and the 10th Amendments which state:

The 9th Amendment, "The enumeration in the Constitution, of certain rights, shall not be construed to deny or disparage others retained by the people."

The 10th Amendment, "The powers not delegated to the United States by the Constitution, nor prohibited by it to the States, are reserved to the States respectively, or to the people."

I present the following examples of how our Progressive central government infringes upon the rights of the States and the people:

Term limits:

While in almost every instance that voters have had an opportunity to voice their opinion they have overwhelmingly approved term limits, and the courts have just as consistently overturned the will of the people. Through ballot initiatives and Constitutional amendments to State Constitutions the people have spoken, but instead of the voice of the people[1] we hear the commands of the elites.

The Supreme Court in a classic five-to-four decision in U.S. Term Limits v. Thornton (1995) said the states don't have the authority to limit the terms of their own congressional delegations. They further ruled that unless the Constitution is amended neither the states nor Congress has the power to limit the number of terms members of Congress can serve. Dissenting Justice Clarence Thomas pointed out that the majority ignored the clear meaning of the Tenth Amendment. Since there is no explicit denial of the power to limit terms to the States in the Constitution the 10th Amendment clearly states this power is reserved to the States.

Immigration:

When the Governor and legislators of Arizona attempted to address the hundreds of thousands of illegal immigrants who are pouring over their borders with Mexico each year they first had to admit that the Federal Government was not enforcing their own laws. After the central government ignored their petitions and pleas for help for years the government of Arizona acted to protect their citizens passing a law which merely stated that the State would enforce the current immigration laws.

Immediately, the Justice Department sued to block the law, contending that it violates the U.S. Constitution. The Arizona law was subsequently struck down by the Federal Courts using the Supremacy Clause for their justification. Judge Richard Paez, said, "By imposing mandatory obligations on state and local officers, Arizona interferes with the federal government's authority to implement its priorities and strategies in law enforcement, turning Arizona officers into state-directed [Homeland Security] agents."[2] When it reached the 9th U.S. Circuit Court of Appeals a three-judge panel said, "Congress has given the federal government sole authority to enforce immigration laws, and that Arizona's law violates the Supremacy Clause of the Constitution."[3] The Federal Government has abdicated its responsibility to protect Arizona from invasion and in their opinion a law that requires law enforcement officials to enforce the law goes too far.

The intrusive actions of the Transportation Security Administration (TSA):

Legislators in Texas decided to take action to protect their citizens from what many considered to be overly aggressive pat-downs. The reaction of the TSA to Texas attempting to protect their citizens from the molestation the Federal l Agency calls a pat-down is indicative of the attitude our central government has towards any infringement of their absolute power. On their website *The TSA Blog* the gatekeepers of the air said, "What's our take on the Texas House of Representatives voting to ban the current TSA pat-down? Well, the Supremacy Clause of the U.S. Constitution (Article VI, Clause 2) prevents states from regulating the federal government." This says it all. As far as our Federal masters are concerned there is no limit to their power.[4]

Obamacare: Mandating action and penalizing inaction:

The Federal Government is attempting to enforce the mandatory purchase provisions of Obamacare alternately as authorized by the Commerce Clause and as a tax, depending on which argument they think a judge will uphold.[5] This massive invasion of personal liberty is currently being challenged by 28 States as being beyond the bounds of the Constitution.[6] Currently two judges have ruled it unconstitutional and three have ruled it constitutional. If this is provision wherein not taking an action is considered either engaging in commerce and thereby subject to regulation or if a non-action is taxable what is left of our precious freedom? What other non-actions will now be under the power of the government. If a government can control our non-actions what does that say about their power over our actions?

What happened? The Supreme Court led by the "Conservative" Chief Justice Roberts ruled the Obamacare mandate is constitutional because it is a tax.[7] When the administration orchestrated its passage they specifically said it was not a tax. If it is a tax it is inherently unconstitutional since all tax laws must originate in the House[8] and Obamacare originated in the Senate.[9] The statists will contort themselves into any shape they need to advance their agenda.

By ignoring the unambiguous meaning of the 9th and 10th Amendments and by stretching and twisting the meanings of a few vague clauses the Progressive leaders of our Federal Government have interpreted our

Constitution to mean anything needed to do anything desired. Once the words lose their meanings, once the sentences can mean anything the Progressives want, what power does the Constitution have to limit government?

Ultimately this is a message of hope because I trust in the ability of the American people to solve any problem they confront. However, we have to admit there is a problem before we can solve it, and if we refuse to admit there is a problem we have no chance of solving it. The problem is our limited government has become unlimited and does whatever it wants. How can I say, "The Constitution Failed"?[10] What I am saying is our system is broken, it is no longer functioning as designed, and we need a re-set button.

★ DISPATCH FIFTY ★

The Corrupt Bargain

In American History slogans, catch phrases, and grand titles have often come to serve as signposts marking out eras and pointing the way to popular notions of what passes for an understanding of the national mood or circumstance in a particular period of time. Examples include: "Millions for defense but not one cent for tribute!"[1] A slogan which spurred us on to our first undeclared war against the Barbary Pirates. "Remember the Maine!"[2] a slogan used by the newspapers at the end of the nineteenth century to gin up support for a war against Spain, and a war which launched the United States as a colonial power. "The Square Deal," the "New Deal" the "Fair Deal," and the "Great Society" all designate government programs aimed at the redistribution of wealth, and of course "Camelot" immediately brings forth visions of the youthful, inspiring, inept, and immoral Kennedy years.

In an effort to advance the cause of verbal economy by recycling a catch phrase from the past, I propose that we label House Speaker John Boehner's proposed plan for raising the debt limit as "The Corrupt Bargain."

Looking back the original Corrupt Bargain[3] refers to the compromise which defeated a hero, elected a president, and ultimately led to that president's defeat.

In 1824, as today, America's political system was under unbearable stress. There were two major political parties; the Federalists[4] who were the political descendants of Hamilton and the centralized government party and the Democratic-Republicans[5] who were the political heirs of Jefferson and the Anti-Federalists.

During the election of 1824 the Federalists collapsed as a party while there were five major candidates and scores of minor ones running as Democratic-Republicans. The candidate officially backed by the Democratic-Republican Party was William H. Crawford, the Secretary of the Treasury under President Monroe. He had been chosen by the Democratic-Republican Caucus in Congress and had little popular support.

The confusing outcome of this election showed the growing power of an electorate fast outgrowing the original restrictive voting practices of the Federalist era and beginning to display the impact of mass appeal campaigning. Andrew Jackson, the hero of the battle of New Orleans came out on top with 99 electoral votes and 43% of the popular vote. John Quincy Adams, the son of the second president and Monroe' secretary of state, won 84 electoral votes and 30% of the popular vote. Crawford won 41 electoral votes. Henry Clay, the Speaker of the House came in fourth with 37 electoral votes. Since no one had enough electoral votes to win, the election was thrown into the House of Representatives. They had to choose between the top three candidates, which immediately disqualified Clay, and since Crawford had very little popular support it was immediately seen as a contest between Jackson and Adams.

In this situation Clay, as Speaker of the House, held the commanding position. He held similar views in most areas to Adams and had actually split that wing of the party siphoning off enough votes to deny Adams a win. However, Clay was an outspoken opponent of Jackson, and after more than a month of bargaining he threw his support behind Adams securing his election as the sixth president. Adams then appointed Clay as his Secretary of State a post that had been the stepping-stone to office for the four previous presidents.

While this politically expedient arrangement worked well for the election it did not work out so well for the administration or for the future of either Adams or Clay. The supporters of Jackson branded it as the "Corrupt Bargain" and used it to immediately launch the bitter 1828 presidential campaign. The Jackson Democrats pointed to the Adams–Clay bargain as the symbol of a corrupt system wherein Washington elites disregarded the will and interests of the people to pursue their own ends.

All of which brings us to Speaker Boehner and his various plans,[6] trial balloons, and phone interviews he is presenting to the nation as a means of raising the debt limit over and over and over. And make no mistake about it that is his goal. He is a career politician and a quintessential Washington insider. He and the other leaders of the Republican Congressional Caucus are as attuned to the voice of their constituents as the Democratic-Republican Caucus was in 1824. The grassroots Tea Party which swept the 2010 elections and which made him Speaker clearly want an end to yearly deficits and to an ever-increasing debt. Yet every plan the perpetually-re-elected Republicans present including Paul Ryan's, merely cuts the present deficit and slows the growth of the debt, but they do not end the deficit spending or reduce the debt. In other words they propose to drive us to the poorhouse a little slower than their Democrat opponents.

These same neo-conservative progressives caved during the lame duck session after the paradigm shifting election of 2010 breathing life into the freshly hobbled Obama Administration by agreeing to a stealth stimulus in return for an extension of all the Bush tax cuts. They caved during the series of continuing resolution battles allowing more spending in exchange for cuts in discontinued programs and layoffs of non-existent federal workers. They have either colluded or have been out-maneuvered by an administration determined to fundamentally transform America.

Now they stand with the strongest card conservatives have held since the Clinton impeachment debacle. A card dealt by the hard work and strategies of the Tea Party. This card is the ability of the House to just say no to any more deficit spending. By refusing to pass a bill to raise the debt limit the House can stop our slide into the financial abyss. When a shopaholic has maxed out all their credit cards and reached the limit of their available lines of credit the answer is not to give them a higher limit or new cards.

Yes, the alternative will be tough but we have spent our way into this corner and we have to work and save our way out. Since neither party seems willing to drain the swamp it is time to flood the swamp with calls, letters, and visits. Demand that our representatives represent us and not themselves or their fellow insiders. Stop the deficits! Pay down the debt! And don't make a Corrupt Bargain that will lead us and our posterity further down the road to serfdom. Don't sacrifice the future for the ex- pediency of the present. Don't mortgage the innocent lives of the unborn for the fleeting luxury of a self-indulgent present or we will all endure a shabby future in a second-rate Chinese financial dependency that was once the land of the free and the home of the brave.

★ DISPATCH FIFTY-ONE ★

THE FORBIDDEN WORD IMPEACH

What does History tell us about the impeachment of an American President? It has only happened twice.

Today Lincoln is an icon. His Roman style temple and oversized statue dominate one end of the National Mall. But in 1864 he was an embattled president caught in a war he couldn't win and running against George B. McClellan, a popular general who said he could end it. Even History was against Lincoln. No president had won a second term in over 30 years. Mr. Lincoln needed all the allies he could muster to win. So the first Republicans led by the President tried to split the opposition. They changed the party name to the National Union Party and chose a Southern Democrat as a running mate. In a surprise to everyone including Lincoln, he won re-election positioning Johnson one heartbeat away from the Oval Office.

After the worst mistake by a Southern sympathizer since the attack on Fort Sumter, the assassination of Lincoln, Andrew Johnson[1] assumed the presidency and almost immediately ran afoul of the Radical Republicans who had a three to one majority in Congress and who wanted to punish the South. Johnson was the only Southern Senator to remain loyal to the Union. He served as the Union imposed military governor of Tennessee until chosen to run for Vice President. A mere 41 days into Lincoln's second term Johnson was sworn in. When he sought to allow the South a path back into the Union that re-imposed limitations upon the freed slaves and ensured the rise of ex-Confederates to power, he was impeached for breaking a law concerning the firing of appointees. After a contentious trial one vote stood between him and conviction and he was acquitted.[2]

Johnson and his presidency survived, barely. He was afterwards relegated to irrelevancy and served as a mere caretaker until General Grant came along to become the face of Reconstruction. In this first impeachment battle the President was acquitted, but Congress won.

If you ask the average person who lived through the national ordeal why was President Clinton impeached they will inevitably say it was because of his scandalous tryst with a young intern in the Oval Office. Though this was a shameful betrayal of trust, it was not the reason he was impeached. He wasimpeached[3] for perjury and obstruction of justice in a legal matter that had nothing at all to do with Monica Lewinsky. And even though Clinton was later found in contempt[4] by a federal judge for lying under oath and was later disbarred for ethical violations it was the leadership of the House that impeached him that paid the political price. The Senate which on a strict party line vote (all the Progressives voted to acquit), came out relatively unscathed. Today we are constantly told by the Progressive Press Mr. Clinton is a beloved elder statesman.[5]

Etched upon the memory of the Republican wing of the party of power is the knowledge that unless there is a Senate willing to convict there is no glory in being a House ready to indict.

Republics rise and republics fall. They rise due to the explosion of creativity and production which always accompanies freedom, and they fall when demagogues convince a majority that they deserve a free ride at the expense of a minority. The good thing about History is that if we are wise enough we can learn from other people's mistakes. If we aren't going to allow History to instruct us we should at least be wise enough to allow it to warn us.

Our History teaches us that the impeachment process is possible to initiate but difficult to consummate. So what are we to do if History warns us that what we are witnessing is the fall of our republic? Have we learned enough from History to navigate our way through to a safe harbor, or are we helpless in the face of a hurricane of transformation?[6]

Due to the information developed by the American intelligence community and the bravery of Navy Seal Team Six we learned that the leader of Al Qaeda, the fraternity of terrorists America finds itself endlessly destroying, was not hiding in a cave. He was instead living in a compound barely 1,000 yards from the military academy of our principle ally in our decade long undeclared war. Today's Hitler is dead, yet the war goes on as if nothing has happened. We have victory after victory with no conclusion and no peace in sight.

Looking at our current economic and social situation America appears more like an occupied nation than the victor of the Cold War and the sole remaining Super Power on Earth. Perhaps it is time to conceptualize the idea that our existential enemy is not a rag-tag group of malcontents dedicated to turning back the clock by six centuries. The enemy that poses a mortal threat to our way of life is instead the home-grown Progressive Movement that has labored for more than a century to subvert our education, corrupt our politics, and evolve their way from constitutionally limited government to central planning and total control.

The visible head of the Progressive Movement today is President Barack Obama. As portrayed by the Corporations Once Known as the Mainstream Media he is not just an Alinsky[7] style community organizer, he is a constitutional scholar. We are told endlessly that he was a Professor of Constitutional Law at the University of Chicago. Leaving the reality of these claims aside it is sufficient to say that this constitutional scholar professes to believe that the Constitution is a flawed document because it does not provide for positive rights[9] such as guarantees of housing, jobs, etc. The kind of rights that the constitutions of the Soviet Union did and of Red China does provide its slaves, I mean citizens. Not to worry our constitutional scholar-in-chief also believes that our Constitution, written to set strict limits on the federal government is a living document[10] that each generation is free to interpret: that is, change at will.

President Obama has presided over the most calamitous decline in American prestige and influence since his fellow Progressive Jimmy Carter disgraced the office. Mr. Obama's apology tours, his over-the-top spending which are nothing less than cross-generational theft are eclipsed by his blatant assaults upon the very core of his responsibility: the integrity of the Constitution.

The President of the United States is sworn[11] to preserve, protect, and defend the Constitution, but instead Mr. Obama has trampled upon the letter as well as the spirit of this document meant to define the perimeters of federal power.

These unconfirmed Czars[12] rule like potentates over shadow departments dispensing huge budgets in effect creating a parallel government outside of citizen scrutiny or control.[13] Appointees at the National Labor Relations Board work at subordinating the nation to organized labor. A rogue justice department provides guns to Mexican cartels,[14] refuses to prosecute obvious instances of voter intimidation, gives a pass to Islamist groups,[15] and stonewalls Congress,[16] while aggressively going after peaceful pro-life demonstrators[17] and America's Sheriff Joe Arpaio.[18] They suestates[19] that try to enforce immigration laws they ignore and seek to try the perpetrators of 9/11 in a New York trial that would parade itself through our national consciousness like a Broadway production of Khalid Sheikh Mohammed Superstar.[20]

Beyond these abuses of power there are two glaring examples of the type of blatant transgressions of clear constitutional limits which, if not addressed set a precedent that may stand in the future as signs of the times that were missed at the time. If not addressed, they will point accusing fingers at a generation asleep at the switch when the bounds of limited government were finally breached.

Ruling by decree from Chicago-on-the-Potomac our Leader has taken us to war without even consulting Congress[21] and made recess appointments while Congress was in session.[22]

Mr. Obama has said he can rule[23] without Congress because he can't wait.[24] He traveled the country at tax payer expense campaigning for four more years to seal the deal, inflaming class warfare, and dispensing government giveaways to buy votes. These two egregious affronts to the Constitution lie at the feet of the Washington Monument passed over by the media and explained away by the government's propaganda arm. And what does the loyal opposition do? They huff and they puff but actually they do nothing.

Only two Congressmen,[25] had the integrity to point out that presidents are not allowed to take us to war by whim. And only one[26] had the courage to point out that making high-level appointments without Senate confirmation while the Senate is in session is more than bad form: it is unconstitutional and more compatible with a dictatorship than a republic.

We stand before the yawning maw of collectivism presided over by a self-proclaimed transformational president[27] seeking to change us from what we have been to what he thinks we should be. Mr. Obama is supported by what amounts to a personality cult in the media and a legion of fellow citizens addicted to either distributing or receiving the dole. The Republican candidates are standing in a circular firing squad working hard at allowing the Progressive Media make them look like the bar scene from Star Wars. At the same time the media gives the President a pass for everything from gas prices to artificially deflated unemployment figures. If America as we have known her is to survive, we must elect a Congress with enough courage and enough votes to do what must be done. The

Congress we have now is passive in the face of serial provocations and outright illegality. They will not call Mr. Obama to account on anything so he feels free to do everything.

He has won again so we all lose unless when we get another chance we replace those who merely go along to get along with those who are willing to speak the forbidden word…Impeach!

★ DISPATCH FIFTY-TWO ★

THE MAN WHO WOULD BE KING

In 114 BC, Rome was a democratic republic. Representatives elected by popular vote served as the Consuls to rule as executives, the Consuls appointed the members of the Senate and the Senate by controlling the purse ran Rome. The Empire was conquered in the name of the Senate and the People of Rome, symbolized by the ever present SPQR seen on every Roman standard in every gladiator movie you have ever watched.

At the beginning of the first century BC sovereignty in Rome resided in the People, which may have inspired the most famous attribution of sovereignty in American History, "We the People" as the proclaimed authors of the Constitution. The power in republican Rome resided in the people. In a revolution that was by then legendary, they had banished their kings and established themselves as a free republic where the people assembled together to elect the Consuls, the magistrates, and made all major decisions such as whether or not to go to war. And far beyond mere words much of what was early Rome was the target the Founding Fathers shot at when they established our later day republic.

And yet, by 14 AD, when Augustus died, popular elections were but a memory. Power was no longer located in the people, or in their assemblies, or their appointed representatives in the Senate, instead power was concentrated in an Imperial Palace which was guarded, unapproachable, and foreboding.

How did this revolution occur? What led the freedom loving Romans to lay down their liberty and put on the yoke of oppression? Later Romans who longed for the freedom their ancestors had discarded pointed to 133 BC when a rich young man named Tiberius Gracchus[1] bought his way into the office of Tribune, an executive position one step below magistrate that was meant to protect the interests of the poor. Gracchus used his office to curry personal power by giving bread and circuses to the people paid for by the public treasury. Eventually he hit on a very popular plan. He proposed to seize the lands of the rich and give them to the poor and he imposed this under his own authority, an authority he lacked under the Roman constitution. Later when he put himself forward for a second term in opposition to custom and law he was assassinated by a group of Senators.

Several generations of corrupt politicians using the same formula sought to buy personal power and popular adoration by looting the public treasury to give the people ever-increasing benefits. Finally another rich young ruler arose by the name of Julius Caesar. He rose through various public offices eventually gaining the office of Proconsul or Governor of Gaul (France). He knew that to be a true Roman hero and paramount leader he needed to be a successful conqueror, so that is what he spent the next nine years doing. He conquered not only all of Gaul but much of central Europe even leading the first Roman expedition to Britain. While he accomplished this he sent back well-written dispatches to Rome which were published and widely distributed recounting his bravery and skill as a general.

All of this was too much for his political rivals in Rome. They gained enough votes to have him branded a traitor which meant little in Gaul where he had absolute power thanks to his well-trained and veteran army. His rivals promised his arrest and conviction if and when he returned to the capitol. However Caesar was not to be denied so he compounded the accusations of his treason with a treasonable act leading his army across the Rubicon River to Rome.

With his troops behind him Caesar secured all power and after many adventures to suppress the forces loyal to the old order he had a compliant Senate elect him dictator for life. As his grasp of power solidified it became clear his rule would be the end of the republic. Breaking completely with tradition he began to wear purple, the color of royalty in public. Finally when his chief Lieutenant, Anthony, publicly offered him a crown it was too much and just as with Gracchus 100 years before, Caesar was assassinated by a group of senators.

Caesar was followed by Augustus, the first Emperor of Rome who was never called Emperor. He was instead known by the republican sounding title of princeps, or first citizen. Kings were hated in Rome. The traditions of the Republic ran deep. Both Gracchus and Caesar had been killed because people thought they would make themselves king. The genius of Caesar's nephew and successor was that Augustus made himself king in all but name while keeping the outward forms of the Republic.[2] The elections were rigged, the Senate only did what they were told, and the people were kept happy by giveaways from the public treasury and kept in line by a smothering blanket of laws and regulations.

Fast forward to the 20th century and two other would be kings include Mussolini[3] who decreed that calendars in Italy should begin again with October 29, 1922 the date he assumed power as the first day of year one. He proclaimed the Fascist Era was the dawn of a new age.[4] And Hitler[5] who said his National Socialist Nazis would reign for a thousand years.[6]

In America today we have a leader who campaigned on a platform of cutting taxes and regulations. A man who when the economy melted down said if he didn't solve the problem in three years he wasn't worthy of a second term.[7] In a classic example of bait and switch he walked over his promises[8] to restore American greatness and suddenly announced five days before the election that he would instead transform America.[9]

Presidents are elected to preserve, protect and defend the constitution. Nowhere in the job description does it mention anything about transforming America. He was elected to do one job and decided instead to do another. TARP[10] was passed to clear the toxic assets out of the banks and restart the system but instead was used[11] to seize controlling interests in AIG, GM and Chrysler and in general assert government ownership over a significant portion of the American economy. The stimulus[12] was passed to re-energize the economy but instead it became a gift bag for the President's supporters and a slush fund for his re-election.[13]

Mr. Obama, with the Corporations Once Known as the Mainstream Media clearing his way and covering his tracks, compares himself to Lincoln, Teddy Roosevelt, FDR, and Reagan. He ridicules those who cling[14] to the old ways, and decrees that he can rule without Congress[15] because he can't wait.[16] His spending[17] has impoverished future generations and will eventually sink the ship of state. His foreign policy ignores our allies and empowers our enemies. Instead of uniting our country to get out of the hole dug by generations of failed Progressive boondoggles and giveaways he incites class warfare while the welfare rolls expand daily.

Whether we are dealing with one man devoted to personal aggrandizement or merely a teleprompter reading front man for a well-oiled CABAL we are face to face with someone who has been positioned by the generosity of American voters to do irreparable damage to our nation. We had one last chance to save the republic as we have known it. The Republicans who operate as the other half of the party of power nominated another big government operator who promises little more than driving us to the poor house a little slower with new wars along the way.

What we need is a man who will work as president to re-impose the limits of the constitution. We need a man who will educate Americans as to what a constitutional government is and what it should do and not do. We need a leader who will reverse course and take us back to the days of individual liberty, personal freedom, and economic liberty. We need a leader who isn't afraid to jettison the empire to save the republic. Now is the time for such a leader. If only enough Americans recognize the signs of the times and rally round the flag. If the Progressives win they will still call it America but it won't be the America we remember.

Just as the Rome of Caligula and Nero still called itself a republic so too in the coming era of Progressive centralization and control will our beloved country still be America. The Constitution will remain on display in Washington. However, in the world turned upside down liberty will be circumscribed by political correctness and freedom will be defined by government regulations. Our schools and media will assure us that we are the most free and prosperous nation on earth while other countries that have gained their freedom pass us by. History as it is taught in America today tries to tell us that socialism works.[18] It doesn't. It leads to a stunted, shabby future where everyone sinks to the level of the lowest common denominator. What we need is a rebirth of republicanism with a small "r" and a big dream.

Keep the faith. Keep the peace. We shall overcome.

★ DISPATCH FIFTY-THREE ★

THE NATURE OF THINGS

When my grandmother was born a horse was the normal means of transport. When my granddaughter was born the International Space Striation was the brightest light in the night's sky. In other words, things change. When I sat on the couch and watched the first man walk on the moon with my grandmother she didn't believe it was real. When I tell my low-information neighbors that the International Space Striation is the brightest light in the night's sky they don't believe it is true. In other words, human nature doesn't change.

To allow our leaders, our fellow citizens, our own kith and kin the charitable label of misguided dreamers is the closest I can come to innocently explaining their roles as either accomplices or instigators of our national decline. I try to tell myself they are as Lenin and Stalin are reputed to have called them, "Useful Idiots:"[1] well-meaning people who genuinely believe central planning will help the needy. I try not to let myself think the Progressives and their supporters are actually extremely corrupt and evil people who are actively attempting to transform our beloved experiment in freedom into another forced labor camp striving to achieve Utopia.[2]

The problem with utopian dreams is that they always end in dystopian realities. Lenin's dream of a worker's paradise transformed itself into Stalin's nightmare of the gulags, starvation, and the eventual destruction of their nation. Mussolini's dream of a return to the glories of Rome led directly to the loss of the empire they had and the destruction of their nation. Hitler's dream of a Thousand Year Reich led directly to the Gestapo, the Holocaust, the worst war in History, and the destruction of their nation.

How can we believe we can follow a dream of utopia to any other end than the one everyone else has arrived at: the dust bin of History?

Some may say, "But we are Americans, and we have always done the things others could not do." You will find no more ardent believer in American Exceptionalism than I. I truly believe, not that diversity is our strength but instead that the blending of all into a uniquely American hybrid has created the most talented, most dynamic, and most successful nation the world has ever known. It is not the will or the talents of our homegrown American collectivists that I question; it is the very nature of collectivism that I maintain makes the accomplishment of their utopian dream impossible.

People can have the best of intentions; however, if they believe they can take from Peter to pay Paul without making Peter resent the fact that he has less than he had before don't know Peter very well. And if they think they can set Paul up as a perpetual recipient of the swag taken from Peter without creating a pool of Paul's who constantly want more and who resent those who do the distributing they have never worked in a soup kitchen, a food bank, or a giveaway store for more than a day.

The vast majority of people are not by nature altruistic milk cows, and they resent it when that is how they are viewed by the nameless faceless bureaucracy necessary to make the machinery of utopia crank out the shabby imitation of perfection they deliver. Conversely the vast majority of people are not by nature perpetual mooches content to stand with their hands out waiting for the nameless faceless bureaucracy to deliver the bare minimum needed to survive which is always the bounty that actually drops from the utopian extruder.

I contend that a collectivist redistribution Utopia whether it is called Progressive, Socialist, Communist, Fascist, or merely the right thing to do is contrary to the nature of humanity.

People by nature want to be self-reliant. They want to make things better for themselves and their children. People want to strive for something noble, and they want to feel as if their lives matter. Yet in an industrial world divided into haves and have nots it is easy to understand how the frustration of being a have not can convince someone that there needs to be a more equitable division of the material goods which modern civilization abundantly provides.

Having come from a blue collar family and having spent the majority of my life as a self-employed boom or bust house painter I can well relate to not having health insurance because you can't afford it, I couldn't. I can relate to having mornings where you don't know what you will feed your family that night because I have had those days. I know what it is like to be a high school dropout who can't get anything except a menial low paying job, because I have been that person. Yes, I can relate to the situations which might make a person believe we need to spread the wealth around.

I also know what it feels like to have to get food stamps and other things from public and private assistance just to make it through the day because I have done so. I know how the welfare people make you feel, the way they treat you as if you are trying to take their personal money or the dispense their confiscated wealth with the pious condescension of pity.

What I can't relate to is either thinking it is a good thing to consign our fellow citizens to such a life or to being satisfied with such a life.

Not only do welfare states corrupt both the dispensers and the recipients it also carries the seeds of its own destruction. Eventually the recipients will want more than the dispensers are willing to give, and revolution or collapse will be the end result.

In addition, since redistribution as a state policy always means stealing from Peter to pay Paul, ultimately the thief will need a gun.

Though Peter may be a nice person and at first say, "Sure I can contribute something to help poor old Paul," if poor old Paul never gets back on his feet sooner or later Peter will wonder why Paul doesn't start providing for himself. At that point the contributions are no longer voluntary and they must be taken one way or another. There is also the question of how many Pauls can Peter carry without either shrugging like Atlas or becoming a Paul himself in self-defense. As Margret Thatcher taught us, "The problem with socialism is that you eventually run out of other people's money."[3]

Plunder empires always collapse. Utopias always end up eating the goose that laid the golden egg. Central planning and collectivism: the Progressive dream for a Great Society has never, can never, and will never succeed. It just isn't natural.

★ DISPATCH FIFTY-FOUR ★

The Question is, "What's the Answer?"

In politics and economics as in everything in life there always seems to be more questions than answers.

Some answers previously shared:

Politically speaking, I have said before in these columns that I no longer consider myself to be a conservative because there is nothing left to conserve. Instead I consider myself a Liberal in the classical sense: in the tradition of Jefferson and Paine a believer in human liberty. The once proud name of Liberal has been coopted and fundamentally transformed by the Socialists who have followed the advice of one of their early leaders, Norman Thomas, "The American people will never knowingly adopt Socialism. But under the name of 'liberalism' they will adopt every fragment of the Socialist program, until one day America will be a Socialist nation, without knowing how it happened."[1]

I say it is time to reclaim the name.

In the economic realm, I am unabashedly a believer in capitalism. The reason for this is that it is the only system ever devised by man that requires freedom as a foundation for it to exist. Every other economic system ever tried is a centrally-planned command system. The king, the dictator, or the politburo decides how many widgets the country needs and that is how many widgets the country gets and everyone works at the widget factory.

As a child of the Cold War who had Marx shoved down his throat by Socialist teachers from grade school through college, I rebelled when one of my History professors told me that economics was the lynchpin of History. It wasn't until after the fall of the Evil Empire that I was able to appreciate this truth. It is interesting to note that before we adopted the German style of College education in the 1890s Economics, History and Political Science were all one discipline. How can we understand any one of them without the others? One legged stools do not stand very well. Information in a vacuum is still a vacuum.

So what is the question?

How can America continue to exist politically as a Republic with a constitutionally limited government dedicated to personal liberty, economic freedom and individual opportunity if our central government destroys competition?

The support of competition does not make someone an anarchist as Senate Majority Leader Harry Reid accuses.[2]

The use of competition as an organizing mechanism in society precludes the use of certain types of coercive regulations. However, it does not preclude the use regulations or guidelines. There are important reasons why the negative aspects of this statement have been stressed by the advocates of competition while the positive have been neglected by its opponents.

It is necessary that all parties in the market place must be free to buy and sell at any price which they can agree on. It is also necessary that everyone should be free to produce, sell and buy anything that can be produced or sold. It is also necessary that everyone has equal and free access into the trades.

Any attempt to control or regulate prices or quantities of commodities deprives competition of its ability to bring about the effective coordination of individual efforts because price changes then are no longer able to correctly act as a reliable guide for an individual's actions.

This is not an iron-clad rule. As long as any restrictions placed on all potential producers affect all producers the same and are not used as an indirect method for controlling prices and quantities. All such restrictions impose extra costs however if they are imposed evenly competition can survive if not thrive. For example, it is generally agreed that regulations to control the use of poisonous substances, to limit working hours, or to require sanitary conditions are both desirable and necessary.

The only question here is: are the social advantages gained by these regulations greater than the economic costs they impose. Neither is the existence of social services incompatible with freedom as long as their organization and operation is not designed to restrict competition.

Thus it is shown that the advocates of competition and economic freedom are not anarchists demanding a Laissez-faire anything goes free-for-all. They admit the need for safety and agree that as long as things are equal things are fair.

The fairness of competition is shown in one of its primary foundational principles: that the owner of private property benefits from all the useful services rendered and is liable for all the damages caused to others by its use. When it becomes impossible to make the enjoyment of certain services dependent on payment or if the damages from its use are deflected then competition is ineffective as a social organizer because the price system has been disrupted.

Thus both restrictions on the use of property and bailouts which transfer the cost of failure from those who made the bad decisions to the taxpayers cause the market to become unhinged from reality and the creature of government direction. We see licenses, permits, and other regulations control who can engage in what economic activity. Look at the stock market. Does it rise or fall because of innovation? Do the efforts of people to create and market new products lead the DOW to new heights? No. The market rises and falls on whether or not the Fed is going to continue pumping fiat money into the system.

The rules of the game have been so distorted by the government that honest and open competition is almost impossible. This is why the underground economy flourishes, because it the only place where free competition still exists. And people will always yearn to be free. No matter how governments try to chain their citizens down with webs of regulations and nets of laws Gulliver will always struggle and strain against the ties that bind until he breaks free.

It is obvious to all that President Obama has succeeded in his goal of fundamentally transforming America.[3] For example, his massive stimulus4 that paid off5 campaign debts to unions and donors and his mountains of new regulations6 on everything from banking to coal to student loans. There is the never-ending FED pump7 which just keeps pouring more money into an already bloated bubble in an effort to make a socialized crippled economy at least look like it works. And of course there is Obamacare which effectively socializes one-sixth of the entire economy.8 The combination of these policies breaks the back of competition and sound the death knell of the great experiment in freedom begun in 1776. Drip by drip, inch-by-inch we have been moved closer to the goal. Now it is the Health Care take-over and the flood of fiat currency that leads the way to a terminal case of bankruptcy, a systems collapse, and as our Progressive leaders hope the dawn of a new day.

When the invisible hand[9] has been tied and competition weighted in favor of government chosen winners and losers, when the electoral game has been stacked in favor of a two headed Progressive Republicrat party of unlimited power, pride and ambition, when equal justice under the law applies only to citizens and not to officials, the Question is, "What's the Answer."

That answer might be, "How long?"

How long before we the American people demand that our nation founded in revolution against tyranny reject the empire and restore the Republic? We can all see that the emperor has no clothes. We all know the deck has been stacked, the game rigged, and the winners chosen. How long before we demand that we are allowed to live in a nation where we will be judged by the content of our character and not by our membership in a protected or favored group, our political contributions or whether or not we have saluted the party line?

As we watch our beloved nation transformed it might be well to remember what our second President John Adams once said, "a Constitution of Government once changed from Freedom, can never be restored. Liberty, once lost, is lost forever."[10] Then again he also said, "Remember democracy never lasts long. It soon wastes, exhausts, and murders itself. There never was a democracy yet that did not commit suicide."[11]

★ DISPATCH FIFTY-FIVE ★

THE RATIFICATION DEBATE PART ONE

While it is not my usual routine to write articles in a series, in honor of our nation's 235th birthday I want to take some time to examine in depth the process that led to the ratification of the Constitution.

Context:

To understand the debate over the ratification of the Constitution it is necessary to first establish the context, for the study of a text without a context is a pretext.

Was the Constitution the first document produced to form the United States of America? Does it mark the beginning of our nation and its government?

No, before there was a Constitution there was a United States of America. This nation was not formed under the auspices of the Constitution the Constitution was formed under the auspices of the United States.

Years before there was a Constitution there were the Articles of Confederation and it was at the final ratification of this document that the United States of America officially was born. Prior to this the United States had declared their independence however it was with the ratification of the Articles that an actual nation was birthed by the federation of the several States. The Articles of Confederation are often over-looked and much maligned. They were drafted in 1777 by the same Continental Congress that passed and proclaimed the Declaration of Independence. The Articles acknowledged the inherent sovereignty of the constituent States while at the same time establishing a league of friendship and perpetual union.

The Articles of Confederation:

The Articles of Confederation were written, debated and ratified during the Revolutionary War when the States were fighting for their lives against the overbearing Imperial government intent upon reducing all of them to mere appendages of the London based bureaucracy. In consequence, they reflect the lack of confidence felt in any highly centralized state power. The States were jealous of their ability to control their internal affairs. These privileges had been won in various ways in the different States but in each of them they had gained the authority of custom and tradition. And in every State they were held dear and looked upon as necessary for a free and prosperous nation. Therefore the Articles while creating a central government that could address such issues as war and peace most of the actual power was reserved to the individual States.

The maintenance of the sovereignty, freedom and independence of the individual States was facilitated by the fact that under the Articles there was no Executive or Judicial branches in the central government only a legislature that consisted of only one house. This one house Congress was composed of committees of delegates appointed by the States. Congress was charged with the responsibility to prosecute the Revolution, declare war, maintain the Army and Navy, establish relations with other government, send and receive ambassadors and other functions such as establish policies for any territories acquired that were not under State control.

In the depths of war the Articles of Confederation were adopted by the Second Continental Congress on November 15, 1777. The Articles actually became the official and original organic document establishing the government of the United States of America on March 1, 1781 when Maryland, the last of the 13 States ratified the document.

Today we reap the fruits of the reality that winners write history. For 200 plus years we have all been taught that the Articles of Confederation were an abject failure. We are lectured on the fact that they did not have the power to create or sustain a viable nation. It is common knowledge that if they would have continued in force there would have been wars between the states and a dysfunctional economy.

Yes, this is what we are taught. This is what every school child for 10 generations has learned as the bedrock of civics and the study of American politics and History. However, does the accepted History fit the facts?

What were some of the accomplishments of the Articles of Confederation?

- The government of the United States was established under the Articles not the Constitution.
- The government as established under the Articles successfully fought and won the Revolutionary War
- The government as established under the Articles concluded the peace which gained not only the independence of the 13 original colonies but all the land east of the Mississippi River and south of Canada.
- The government as established under the Articles established diplomatic relations with the rest of the world and worked successfully to get the new United States of America recognized as an independent nation.
- The government as established under the Articles negotiated our first treaty with a foreign power (France).
- The government as established under the Articles led all the States to renounce their claims to the western lands.
- The government as established under the Articles passed the Land Ordinance of 1785 which provided for the survey and sale of the western lands surrendered by the original 13 States. These sales provided income for the new nation without taxation
- The government as established under the Articles through the set aside of land established federal support for a public education system.
- The government as established under the Articles passed the North-west Ordinance of 1787 which provided the process through which

every subsequent State after the original 13 became States, with full equality with the original States.

- The government as established under the Articles outlawed slavery in the Northwest Territory.
- The government as established under the Articles passed a Bill of Rights that protected the settlers of territories from abuses of power.

This is a very long list of positive accomplishments for a government that is portrayed as an abject failure. This brings us to the question, "What was the problem?" a question I will address in the next dispatch.

★ DISPATCH FIFTY-SIX ★

THE RATIFICATION DEBATE PART TWO

Picking up where I left off in my review of the ratification debate I want to address the question I raised at the end of the last Dispatch, "What was the problem?"

If the government as established under the Articles had so many successes how did it end up being replaced by the government as established under the Constitution?

There were some perceived and actual weaknesses of the government as established under the Articles of Confederation:

- The national government was too weak as compared to the State governments.
- There was only a unicameral legislature that represented the States and nothing to directly represent the people.
- There was not a separate executive department to carry out and enforce the acts of Congress.
- There was no national court system to interpret the meaning of the laws passed by Congress leaving them open to differing interpretations in the separate States.
- Congress didn't have the power to levy taxes. It was instead dependent on State donations, which were levied on the basis of the value of land within the various states.
- Congress did not have the exclusive right to coin money. Each state retained the right to coin money. Without a uniform monetary system the coins of one state might not be accepted in another, hampering commerce.
- There was no mechanism to adjudicate disputes between the states.
- The individual States were not precluded from having their own foreign policies including the right to make treaties.
- Each State had one vote in Congress with no respect to size or population.

- It required 9 out of the 13 states to approve the passage of major laws, approve treaties, or declare war.
- The amendment process was cumbersome requiring a unanimous vote.

Some of these weaknesses caused actual problems during the Articles short tenure, and some were merely perceived as possible sources of problems in the future.

So how did we get from the Articles of Confederation to the Constitution?

It was commerce that proved to be the catalyst for the transition between the Articles and the Constitution.

Disputes concerning navigation on the Potomac River between Maryland and Virginia led the calling of a conference between five states at Annapolis, Maryland, in 1786. Alexander Hamilton was one of the delegates. He successfully convinced the delegates that these issues of commerce were too intertwined with primarily economic and political concerns to be properly addressed by representatives of only five states. Instead he proposed that all of the states send representatives to a Federal Convention the following year in Philadelphia. At first Congress was opposed to this plan. However, when they learned that Virginia would send George Washington they approved of the meeting. Elections of delegates were subsequently held in all of the States except Rhode Island which ignored the summons.

The Convention had been authorized by Congress merely to draft proposals for amendments to the Articles of Confederation. However, as soon as it convened they decided on their own to throw the Articles aside and instead create a completely new form of government.

Was the writing of the Constitution legal? Who gave the Federal Convention authority to discard the Articles of Confederation which had been duly ratified by all 13 States? Was this a counter-revolution?

The answers to these questions have been debated by historians and constitutional scholars for hundreds of years, but in reality the answers are moot. Whether the Federal Convention had any legal sanction to do what they did doesn't matter. The action was eventually accepted by the Congress, the ratification conventions were held in the various States, and eventually it was ratified becoming the supreme law of the land.

Now we are ready to look at the Great Debate between the Federalists and the Anti-Federalists.

First, what about the terms, "Federalist" and "Anti-Federalist" how appropriate were they during the debate?

New Speak is nothing novel in politics, and the concept of words having power to shape reality was not invented by George Orwell. Look at the original debate of the ratification of the Constitution, and as a consequence how we have studied, learned, and even shaped the debate in this lecture concerning the ratification of the Constitution.

Think about the central term itself. Federalism refers to decentralized government. Those who supported the Constitution, who advocated that it replace the Articles of Confederation, which if nothing else established a decentralized system of government, called themselves "Federalists," even though they wanted a more centralized government. This left the supporters of the Articles, who wanted a decentralized government, to be known then and forever as the "Anti-Federalists," when in fact they were the true Federalists.

So much for the straightforward clarity of Historical fact, everything must be examined and everything interpreted.

In the study of the debate for the ratification of the Constitution a common mistake made is the shallowness of the study. In a good school the average student will be exposed to perhaps two of the Federalist Letters and none of the Anti-Federalist Letters, which is like trying to understand an answer without knowing the question. In this abbreviated look at the subject we will look at both sides in general instead of seeking an overview of the topic leaving the specifics to a personal study, which will without a doubt enrich the understanding of any who find the motivation for such an endeavor.

The Federalist and Anti-Federalist papers were actually published as newspaper articles for the general public. This in itself tells us much about the comparative state of public education and awareness between the American general public in the late Eighteenth century and the early Twenty-first century. When we examine the two sets of papers and dwell upon the vocabulary and the breadth and depth of the philosophical, political, and economic ideas expressed we are immediately struck by the fact that the average person in America today would not be able to understand the sophisticated and specialized vocabulary let alone grasp the ideas. And yet these were not published in journals for the educated elite. These were published in general circulation newspapers and were actually debated and referenced across the dinner tables and around the workshops of America.

In the next Dispatch we will look deeper into these two sets of documents that have had such a profound effect upon America and find out exactly who the Federalists and the Anti-Federalists were and why does it matter to us today?

★ DISPATCH FIFTY-SEVEN ★

The Ratification Debate Part Three

Concluding my three part series in celebration of our nation's 235th Birthday, we will look at arguments advanced by both sides. In the last Dispatch we ended with the question, who were the Federalists and the Anti-Federalists and why does it matter to us today? In this Dispatch we will learn the answers to the questions. Who was debating? What did they have to say? Who won? And, why does it matter to us today?

The Federalist Papers

The Federalist Papers are a collection of 85 essays published in New York newspapers. They outline how the government, as proposed in the Constitution, would operate and why this highly centralized type of government was the best for the United States of America. All of the essays were signed by "PUBLIUS." To this day there is some dispute as to who authored some of the articles. However, after much study the consensus is generally believed that Alexander Hamilton wrote 52, James Madison wrote 28, and John Jay wrote 5.

Just as in every state, the debate over the ratification of the Constitution was intensely followed by the public in New York. Immediately after the conclusion of the Convention, the Constitution came under intense criticism in many New York newspapers. Echoing the sentiments of several of the prominent men who had been delegates to the Convention some contributors to the newspapers said the Constitution diluted the rights Americans had fought for and won in the recent Revolutionary War.

As one of the leading designers and loudest proponents of the Constitution Alexander Hamilton worried that the document might fail to be ratified in his home state of New York. Therefore, Hamilton, a well-trained and well-spoken lawyer, decided to write a series of essays refuting the critics and pointing out how the new Constitution would in fact benefit Americans. In the Convention Hamilton had been the only New York delegate to sign the Constitution after the other New Yorkers walked out of the Convention, because they felt the document being crafted was injurious to the rights of the people.

Hamilton was in favor of a strong central government having proposed to the Convention a president elected for life that had the power to appoint state governors. Although these autocratic ideas were thankfully left out of the finished document Hamilton knew that the Constitution, as written, was much closer to the kind of government he wanted than the one which then existed under the Articles of Confederation.

Hamilton's first essay was published October 27, 1787 in the New York Independent Journal signed by "Publius." At that time the use of pen names was a common practice. Hamilton then recruited James Madison and John Jay to contribute essays that also used the pen name "Publius."

James Madison, as a delegate from Virginia, took an active role participating as one of the main actors in the debates during the Convention. In addition he also kept the most detailed set of notes and personally drafted much of the Constitution.

John Jay of New York had not attended the Convention. He was a well-known judge and diplomat. He was in fact a member of the government under the Articles currently serving as the Secretary of Foreign Affairs.

The tripartite "Publius" wrote al 85 essays that were written and published between October 1787 and August 1788; all were published in newspapers of the State of New York. But their popularity, readership, and impact were not limited to New York. They were in such great demand that they were soon published in a two volume set.

The Federalist essays, also known as the Federalist Papers, have served two distinct purposes in American history. Primarily the essays helped persuade the delegates to the New York and other State Ratification Conventions to vote for the Constitution. In later years, The Federalist Papers have helped scholars and other interested people understand what the writers and original supporters of the Constitution sought to establish when they initially drafted and campaigned for ratification.

Knowing that the Federalist Papers were written by such luminaries as Hamilton, the first Secretary of the Treasury; James Madison, the fourth President of the United States; and John Jay, the first Chief Justice of the Supreme Court, the question asked is, who were these Anti-Federalists who dared speak against the founding of the greatest nation that has ever existed: Some fringe people who didn't want the blessing of truth, justice, and the American way?!

The Anti-Federalist Papers

The list of Anti-Federalist leaders included George Mason, Edmund Randolph, Elbridge Gerry, Samuel Adams, Patrick Henry, Richard Henry Lee, and even though he was not in the country at the time, Thomas Jefferson.

There is one major difference between the Federalist Papers and the Anti-Federalist Papers: the former are compact and relatively unified the latter are not really a single series of articles written by a united group with a single purpose as the Federalist Papers were. Instead there were many different authors and they were published all over the country in pamphlets and flyers as well as in newspapers. Among the many the most important are: John DeWitt—Essays I–III, The Federal Farmer—Letters I and II, Brutus Essays I-XVI, Cato, Letters V and VII.

The first of the Anti-Federalist essays was published on October 5, 1787 in the Philadelphia Independent Gazetteer. This was followed by many more published throughout the country which charged that any new government formed under the auspices of the Constitution would:

- be injurious to the people because it lacked a Bill of Rights;
- discriminate against the South with regard to navigation legislation;
- give the central government the power to levy direct taxation.;
- lead to the loss of state sovereignty;
- represent aristocratic politicians bent on promoting the interests of their own class.

The Federalists had the momentum from the beginning. They were wise enough to appropriate the name Federalist, since federalism was a popular and well-understood concept among the general public even though their position was the opposite of what the name implied. They also had the support of most of the major newspapers and a majority of the leading men of wealth if not of all the original revolutionary patriots. They also used a tactic of trying to rush the process as much as possible calling for conventions and votes with all dispatch. And in the end these tactics combined with the great persuasion of the Federalist Papers and the prestige of General Washington carried the day. The Constitution was ratified on June 21, 1788.

Although the Anti-Federalists lost their struggle against the ratification of the Constitution their spirited defense of individual rights, personal liberty, and their deep-rooted suspicion of a central governmental power became and remain at the core American political values. Their insistence upon the absolute necessity of the promise of enumerated rights as a prerequisite for ratification established the Bill of Rights as the lasting memorial to their work.

★ DISPATCH FIFTY-EIGHT ★

THE REVOLUTION PASSED IN THE NIGHT

Many things are holding the headlines hostage, the terrorist attacks, the crippling effects of Obamacare, the prospect of expanding war in Syria, and as always Iran.

There is one over-riding constant that defines as it divides the present era: the fact that America has a President who advances values and policies diametrically opposed to the traditional beliefs of a vast number of Americans. From bowing to foreign leaders to not knowing how many states there are, from vowing to fundamentally transform America to actually doing it, President Obama is to many the Manchurian Candidate.

Elected the first time on a vague promise of hope and change he has been re-elected on a blatant promise to re-distribute the wealth and complete the transformation of America into a centrally-planned welfare state. His bureaucratically imposed policies such as Cap-n-Trade and the Dream Act are blatant end runs around the authority of a Congress that overwhelmingly rejected both. The alarming reality we all must face is that for the first time in American history we may actually have a president who rejects America's traditional belief in personal freedom, individual liberty and economic opportunity.

Barack Obama is blatant in his collectivist and redistributionist rhetoric. Such as:

> "In America, we have this strong bias toward individual action. You know, we idolize the John Wayne hero who comes in to correct things with both guns blazing. But individual actions, individual dreams, are not sufficient.

We must unite in collective action, build collective institutions and organizations."[1] Emphasis added.

"And what would help minority workers are the same things that would help white workers: the opportunity to earn a living wage, the education and training that lead to such jobs, labor laws and tax laws that *restore some balance to the distribution of the nation's wealth* ..." Emphasis added.

"But the Supreme Court never ventured into the issues of redistribution of wealth, and more basic issues such as political and economic justice in society. And to that extent, as radical as I think people try to characterize the Warren Court, it wasn't that radical. It didn't break free from the essential constraints that were placed by the founding fathers in the Constitution, at least as it's been interpreted. And the Warren Court interpreted in the same way, that generally the Constitution is a charter of negative liberties—says what the states can't do to you—says what the Federal Government can't do to you—but it doesn't say what the Federal Government or State government must do on your behalf.

And that hasn't shifted and one of the, I think, the tragedies of the civil rights movement was because the civil rights movement became so court-focused I think there was a tendency to lose track of the political and community organizing and activities on the ground that are able to put together the actual coalitions of powers through which you *bring about redistributive change.* In some ways we still suffer from that ..."[2] Emphasis added.

These positive rights are what Progressives have been trying to establish since FDR floated his idea of a second Bill of Rights which included

- The right to a useful and remunerative job in the industries or shops or farms or mines of the nation.
- The right to earn enough to provide adequate food and clothing and recreation.
- The right of every farmer to raise and sell his products at a return which will give him and his family a decent living.

- The right of every businessman, large and small, to trade in an atmosphere of freedom from unfair competition and domination by monopolies at home or abroad.
- The right of every family to a decent home.
- The right to adequate medical care and the opportunity to achieve and enjoy good health.
- The right to adequate protection from the economic fears of old age, sickness, accident, and unemployment.
- The right to a good education.

Now all of these sound great and in a perfect world might make up a laundry list of prizes falling out of the cornucopia of utopia. In a real world they would mandate a government large enough to provide everything and powerful enough to take everything away.

The whole idea of having a constitution is to limit the government which is in essence a charter of negative liberties.

President Obama goes on to state,

> Now, just as there was in Teddy Roosevelt's time, there is a certain crowd in Washington who, for the last few decades, have said, let's respond to this economic challenge with the same old tune. 'The market will take care of everything,' they tell us. If we just cut more regulations and cut more taxes—especially for the wealthy—our economy will grow stronger. Sure, they say, there will be winners and losers. But if the winners do really well, then jobs and prosperity will eventually trickle down to everybody else. And, they argue, even if prosperity doesn't trickle down, well, that's the price of liberty.
>
> Now, it's a simple theory. And we have to admit, it's one that speaks to our rugged individualism and our healthy skepticism of too much government. That's in America's DNA. And that theory fits well on a bumper sticker. But here's the problem: It doesn't work. It has never worked.[3]

And of course there is his infamous "You didn't build that"[4] statement which exposes his complete misunderstanding of what it takes to start and grow a business.

With a leader such as this whose basic understanding of America is at such odds with those who once constituted the majority of the citizens and the continuity of our History is it any wonder that so many feel as if they are living in a conquered nation?

Conquered by who? As Pogo once told us, "We have met the enemy and he is us."[5]

Or as Garet Garrett, quipped as he chronicled the fall of the Republic and the rise of the American Bureaucratic Empire said, "There are those who still think they are holding the pass against a revolution that may be coming up the road. But they are gazing in the wrong direction. The revolution is behind them. It went by in the Night of Depression, singing songs to freedom."[6]

★ DISPATCH FIFTY-NINE ★

THE SUN IS SETTING TELL EVERYONE YOU KNOW

If we say nothing while watching someone walk off a cliff and plunge to their death we would be criminally negligent. If we ride past a home in the early morning and see smoke rising from the roof and don't call 911 we would be criminally negligent. Today, as we watch our nation walk off a cliff, as we watch the smoke rise from the home of the brave and the land of the free, if we do not do all we can to raise the awareness of our fellow Americans we are criminally negligent.

Those who are awake to the coming end of limited government have watched this slow motion train wreck for our entire lives. We have watched as inch-by-inch the Federal Government has lured our fellow citizens into one entitlement trap after another. We have wondered when they will wake up and pay attention.

Election after election we have marveled at the shallowness of the debate. One side says, "If you elect them they will gut the safety net and throw Grandma off the cliff!" And after every election no matter who wins the safety net becomes more of a hammock. The other side says, "If you elect them they will gut the defenses and whoever the currently fashionable model of a barbarian horde happens to be will soon stifle freedom, walk upon Old Glory and turn us all into slaves." And after every election the defense budget grows and the policeman of the world continues to walk the beat.

Blind justice may be good but a blind electorate is falling for these two straw man arguments electing demagogues whose motto might as well be, "You know I'm lying but you like what I say." The social safety net will not be eliminated by any of these empty suits. It will instead become the sack the cats are sewn in before the crazy guy throws it in the river. The defense budget will not be gutted. It won't even be reduced. Baseline budgeting and secret off budget black ops funding will make sure our 900 base 130 country overseas empire continues to make sure the sun never sets on the stars and stripes.

As each constitutional guarantee falls by the wayside we wonder when enough people will turn off the game, forget about the vampires, the hoarders, and the dysfunctional non-reality reality stars and realize our nation and our children's heritage is being transformed into what our ancestors fought a revolution to be rid of?

Most of us, even the comatose can recite, "We hold these truths to be self-evident, that all men are created equal, that they are endowed by their Creator with certain unalienable Rights, that among these are Life, Liberty, and the pursuit of Happiness."[1] Our assembly line public education has drilled the words if not the meaning into our heads.

What our one more brick in the wall system hopes we don't recall is the next line, "That to secure these rights, Governments are instituted among Men, deriving their just powers from the consent of the governed,"[2] And they pray that we don't shout the next line, "That whenever any Form of Government becomes destructive of these ends, it is the Right of the People to alter or to abolish it, and to institute new Government, laying its foundation on such principles and organizing its powers in such form, as to them shall seem most likely to affect their Safety and Happiness."[3]

When a government uses the excuse of security to assert the right to collect[4] our phone records monitor electronic communications,[5] and generally read our e-mail without a warrant,[6] to arrest and detain American citizens on American soil without a warrant,[7] and hold them indefinitely without trial, to wage war without declaration or even congressional approval what we have here is more than a failure to communicate. What we have is a central government establishing a tyranny in the name of providing security.

Ben Franklin told us, "Those who desire to give up freedom in order to gain security will not have, nor do they deserve, either one."[8]

Think of the 2012 presidential race, what did we get?

Looking for substance we tuned into the ad nauseam insipid debates organized and orchestrated by a partisan press merely trying to make the Republicans look like the bar scene from Star Wars. What did we hear? In the primaries with lone exception of Ron Paul we heard one after another big government professional calling for less spending, less regulations and more war. Out of that list all we had a chance to get was more war. And the lone exception is continuously relegated to the status of an also ran by every news organization including the supposedly conservative one.

On the other side we were offered four more years of this: four more years of total transformation until we wake up one day in the Progressive version of Heaven: a cradle-to-grave nanny state fighting endless wars for peace. Regimented, controlled, secure and listening as the same comatose voters who brought us to this place repeat the pabulum that jumps off the teleprompters into the mouths of the info-announcers as if these were their own opinions.

And what did we get, the travesty of the comedic Obamacare roll-out and the resurgence of Al-Qaeda around the world. Together these twin catastrophes expose the utter falsehood of the president's twin campaign slogans; "Bin Laden is dead and GM is alive"[9] and "If you like your plan you can keep your plan Period"[10]

We cannot and we must not allow this to happen without at the very least exerting every effort to wake up anyone within the sound of our voice. To do this we of course must be awake and aware ourselves.

If we do not know where we came from how can we know where we are? If we don't know where we are, how can we know where we are going?

We must study to show ourselves approved. If we lose the foundation how will the structure stand? We must know and understand the constitutional and historical underpinnings of this noble experiment in human freedom if we are to preserve it. We must know and understand the flow of current events if we wish to shape the future.

Study, learn, share, and look for the lights in the tower. One if by land and two if by sea, we must recognize the signs of the times and try to wake up as many people as we can. The time is late, the hour is dark, but the right shall prevail.

Forty-seven years ago a young pre-rap poet songwriter tried to wake people up to the intrusion of government and the need to recognize it when he said, "Maggie comes fleet foot face full of black soot talkin' that the heat put plants in the bed but the phone's tapped anyway Maggie says that many say they must bust in early May orders from the D.A. Look out kid Don't matter what you did. Walk on your tiptoes don't try 'No-Doz' better stay away from those that carry around a fire hose keep a clean nose watch the plain clothes you don't need a weatherman to know which way the wind blows."[11]

Knowing which way the wind blows should tell us that we must do our duty to save our country or it will be lost. I don't know about you but in the future when my grandchildren ask, "What did you do to hold back the night?" I want to be able to say more than, "I didn't notice the darkness."

Keep the faith. Keep the peace. We shall overcome.

DISPATCH SIXTY

The Uncivil War

In American schools the Civil War is a one trick pony. It was all about slavery and that is all it was about.

There can be no doubt that slavery is a blight upon the History of the United States. It was incompatible with the inspiring words of our Declaration of Independence, "We hold these truths to be self-evident, that all men are created equal, that they are endowed by their Creator with certain unalienable Rights, that among these are Life, Liberty and the pursuit of Happiness."[1]

The very idea of chattel slavery wherein one person can own another and their children, and their children's children unto the furthest generation is an abomination. The South saw this as their peculiar institution,[2] and they had built an entire culture upon slavery as an economic necessity. For a variety of reasons even the Southern Churches supported and attempted to justify the practice.[3] However, all of this being said slavery was not the only issue at stake in the Civil War.

There was one other that took center stage in the minds of many: State's Rights.

In the decades that had passed since the ratification of the Constitution slavery had been steadily abolished in the Northern states while remaining prevalent in the South. This inexorably led to the issue of slavery becoming intertwined in the issues of States Rights,[4] Federalism[5] and the growing power of the Federal Government.

The proponents of States rights appealed to the 10th Amendment which states, "The powers not delegated to the United States by the

Constitution, nor prohibited by it to the States, are reserved to the States respectively, or to the people."[6] This had been added to the original Constitution due to the intellectual and political pressure from the Anti-Federalists. This Amendment was meant to reassure people of the limited nature of the Federal Government and that with the few exception specifically delegated to the Federal Government by the States the States and the people were free to continue exercising their sovereign powers.

President Lincoln did not see the Civil War as a war to end slavery until that became necessary to stop European powers from recognizing the South.[7]

Lincoln said in his 1st Inaugural Address, "I have no purpose, directly or indirectly, to interfere with the institution of slavery in the States where it exists. I believe I have no lawful right to do so, and I have no inclination to do so."[8]

Lincoln was on record as saying, "My paramount object in this struggle is to save the Union, and is not either to save or to destroy slavery. If I could save the Union without freeing any slave I would do it, and if I could save it by freeing all the slaves I would do it; and if I could save it by freeing some and leaving others alone I would also do that. What I do about slavery, and the colored race, I do because I believe it helps to save the Union; and what I forbear, I forbear because I do not believe it would help to save the Union. I shall do less whenever I shall believe what I am doing hurts the cause, and I shall do more whenever I shall believe doing more will help the cause."[9]

Lincoln also said, "Do the people of the South really entertain fears that a Republican administration would, directly, or indirectly, interfere with their slaves, or with them, about their slaves? If they do, I wish to assure you, as once a friend, and still, I hope, not an enemy, that there is no cause for such fears."[10] Obviously his object was to maintain the Union at all costs and ending slavery (or not) was to him merely a means to that end.

That Lincoln himself was on record as believing that the invasion of the States was unlawful is shown by another quote from his 1st Inaugural Address, "That the maintenance inviolate of the rights of the States, and especially the right of each State to order and control its own domestic institutions according to its own judgment exclusively, is essential to that balance of power on which the perfection and endurance of our political fabric depend; and we denounce the lawless invasion by armed force of the soil of any State or Territory, no matter what pretext, as among the gravest of crimes."[11] Yet in this same address he proclaims his belief that the Union is perpetual and the he has sworn an oath to preserve it.

However there were very basic and foundational problems with the entire effort to preserve the Union. For one thing it was known by all that it was a voluntary union entered into by sovereign States. It was also known that the Federal Government only has those powers which are expressly delegated. Nowhere in the document does it say the Federal Government has the power to force States to remain in the Union.

In addition, three states—New York, Rhode Island, and Virginia included "resumption clauses," which would allow the states to leave the union to "resume" their status as independent states.

New York declared, "That the Powers of Government may be reassumed by the People, whensoever [sic] it shall become necessary to their Happiness."[12]

Rhode Island said, "That the powers of government may be reassumed by the people whensoever [sic] it shall become necessary to their happiness."[13]

Virginia stated, "Do in the name and in behalf of the People of Virginia declare and make known that the powers granted under the Constitution being derived from the People of the United States may be resumed by them whensoever [sic] the same shall be perverted to their injury or oppression."[14]

Everyone loves to quote Lord Acton when he says things like, "Power tends to corrupt and absolute power corrupts absolutely."[15] Or, "Liberty is not a means to a higher political end. It is itself the highest political end."[16]

Most are not aware of the correspondence that took place between Lord Acton and Robert E. Lee after the Civil War. In that correspondence Lord Acton said,

> "I saw in State Rights the only availing check upon the absolutism of the sovereign will, and secession filled me with hope, not as the destruction but as the redemption of Democracy. The institutions of your Republic have not exercised on the old world the salutary and liberating influence which ought to have belonged to them, by reason of those defects and abuses of principle which the Confederate Constitution was expressly and wisely calculated to remedy. I believed that the example of that great Reform would have blessed all the races of mankind by establishing true freedom purged of the native dangers and disorders of Republics. Therefore I deemed that you were fighting the battles of our liberty, our progress, and our civilization; and I mourn for the stake which was lost at Richmond more deeply than I rejoice over that which was saved at Waterloo."[17]

To which Lee answered,

> "I yet believe that the maintenance of the rights and authority reserved to the states and to the people, not only essential to the adjustment and balance of the general system, but the safeguard to the continuance of a free government. I consider it as the chief source of stability to our political system, whereas the consolidation of the states into one vast republic, sure to be aggressive abroad and despotic at home, will be the certain precursor of that ruin which has overwhelmed all those that have preceded it."[18]

I know that States Rights has been tarred with the broad brush of racism; however, I reject that attempt to restrict the speech of a free people along with all of the strangulating impediments of political correctness.

America was designed to be a federal republic which operates on democratic principles. The continuing attempts to curtail the freedom of actions of the States and to transform the United States into a centrally-planned democracy run counter to our founding documents, our History, and, our nature.

Here's another Lord Acton quote people seem to overlook, "Socialism means slavery."[20]

★ DISPATCH SIXTY-ONE ★

THOSE WHO READ THE PAST WRITE THE FUTURE

Unfortunately most of what we are taught in History survey classes in American schools consists of simplistic formulas. Formulas designed to persuade those forced to attend the government controlled education mills that they should ride the same ideological hobby horses as whoever currently has the power to select textbooks and prescribe curricula. Whether it was the rabidly pro-American imperial History of yesteryear that pushed lines such as, "We never started a war and never lost one," and "We turned a raw wilderness into a civilized nation." Or, if it is the rabidly anti-American propaganda of today spouting lines such as, "America was founded by deists who used serial genocide and economic fascism to steal a nation, pollute the earth, and poison the sea"? Neither of these highly subjective views are correct. Both versions are merely two sides of an extremely myopic view which does not seek to discover nor promote the truth but instead seek to mold the next generation into what they think will be foot soldiers in their own crusade.

History, if it has any value at all is that it fulfills two goals. First, the study of History should provide context. A text without a context is a pretext and we must have context so we can understand how we as a people became who we are, how the world became what it is, and where it might go next. Secondly, the study of History should help us learn from and hopefully avoid the mistakes made by those who have gone before so we can leave a better world to those who come after. However, as stated above, these are rarely the goals of History education. The reason why is summed up in a joke only Historians seem to get.

Objectivity

Most people in the world believe objectivity exists. They act as if the stories presented in survey of history classes are "the facts ma'am and nothing but the facts." I was once part of this blissful herd. I was a self-taught Historian before I took the plunge and studied to become a card carrying member of the profession. I was captured by the allure of History when I was nine years old. Nothing in the world made any sense. What I was taught and saw at home conflicted 180 degrees from what I was taught at church. What I was taught at church conflicted 180 degrees from what I was taught at school. What I saw on the streets appeared real because it seemed to be the way the world actually worked, but it was out of synch with my home my church and my school. Not knowing myself well enough to know that I am a person who operates best when things make sense and the world appears orderly I was confused and uncomfortable living in a world so out of joint.

Consequently when I learned in the third grade that there were histories of the world available I latched onto them like a drowning man latches onto a life preserver. I began reading History books every day. They became my raft in a swirling sea of confusion creating an orderly world of sequential reality that I used to build my bridge to the first positive value of History, gaining a coherent understanding of how we as a people became who we are, how the world became what it is, and where it might go next. However, I was a rebellious child, a child who never moved to the second value of History. I never learned to profit from the mistakes of those who went before. Following those in my family who went before I walked out of traditional education at age 16 figuring I knew enough to make my way in the world. Twenty plus years of manual labor later I thought it might be a good idea to finish my education.

When I finished my Bachelor degree in History I realized that a Bachelor degree in History is good for two things, it can help you become the manager of the electronics department at Wal-Mart and it opens the door for a Master Degree in History. Since I was determined to become a History professor, I chose the latter. On my first day of graduate school this budding self-taught Historian had to grit my teeth as a professor told our class, "There are no facts, and History is only what Historians say it is."

Of course I had to run up after class to argue, "How can you say there are no facts? Look at the Vietnam War. We know it happened. We know when it started and when it ended. Those are facts and we can know them!" After listening calmly to my impassioned tirade the professor quietly said, "Maybe there's another side to that story."

This rude awakening sent me on a journey of discovery: searching for the other side of the story. Along the way I contributed my first chapter in a History book. My research helped me realize there is more than one side to every story. There are often conflicting facts, overlapping time-lines, and always another way to look at everything. The truth of this is displayed in an endless series of quotes. Napoleon once said, "History is a set of lies agreed upon."[1] Voltaire said, "History is a pack of lies we play on the dead."[2] Ambrose Bierce said, "God alone knows the future, but only an historian can alter the past."[3] And one of my favorite philosophers, Anonymous sagely added, "The certainty of history seems to be in direct inverse ratio to what we know about it."[4]

What is the purpose of this self-revealing stroll down memory lane? It isn't for the purpose of either self-actualization or confession. Both of those goals were achieved long ago. It is instead my attempt to lead you my loyal reader (for those will be the only ones left after such a lesson in historiography) to the second value of the study of History. I am encouraged by the multitudes of people who are today engrossed in this study. So many of the recently awakened yearn to know the History of America, they long to know how our Constitution was written by whom and why.

I am here to remind everyone we need to look at all sides, consider every angle, and remember everyone has a point of view, even Historians, and objectivity is in reality subjectivity in a grey flannel suit.

Remember that second value of History? It should help us learn from and hopefully avoid the mistakes made by those who have gone before so we can leave a better world to those who come after. If we merely exchange the unabashedly anti-American lenses of the present for the unquestioning pro-American lenses of the past we will be blind to what we really need to see.

The complexity of reality defies the easy interpretations of partisan politics. Has America always been right? No, the jingoistic refrain of "My country right or wrong" will lead those who blindly salute it into supporting what is wrong as easily as what is right. Has America always been wrong? No, the view currently used to indoctrinate the youth in our public schools which sees America as an imperialistic power that used genocide, racism, and naked aggression to build a hegemonic empire forget all the good America has accomplished. This view presents an America bent on maintaining the privileges of the rich over the rights of the poor and leads those who imbibe its venom into ignoring that America was founded as the world's greatest experiment in personal liberty and economic freedom.

Both views are too simplistic for people who want to break free of the matrix and see the world for what it truly is: a struggle between those who wish to control mankind for their own benefits and those who wish to see man set free so he can become all that he may be.

This is a call for those who have taken the bread and circus blinders off their eyes not to replace them with another set. Today we don't have to rely on what we have been taught. We can use the Internet as a portal into every perspective imaginable, histories beyond counting, and all the great works of mankind. Read broadly, study extensively and think for yourself. Don't exchange the purveyors of self-serving pap on the left for the purveyors of self-serving pap on the right. Open both ears, hear both sides, use the mind God gave you, and find the center path.

America has done some things wrong. America has done some things right. When it all is brought to the scales, when enough is seen to grasp the big picture, it is the non-objective view of this Historian that America has provided more freedom for more people than any other country that has ever existed. It is also my opinion that powers of anti-freedom have sought to regain control since the Revolution, and if those who have been too busy working and raising families don't spend enough time to learn what History teaches we will soon earn the reward for the failure to hold on to the past. We will lose the future.

DISPATCH SIXTY-TWO ★

Tomorrow Begins Today

Today America's leaders, ignoring the example of Dr. Kissinger, have abandoned realpolitik.[1] Otto von Bismarck; the Iron Chancellor who united Germany coined the term. In its original German it means "the politics of reality." According to the tenets of realpolitik, foreign policy has only one purpose: the security of the state. Instead our leaders have subverted it to crusading for the touchy feely advancement of causes and ideologies.

The visit of Hu Jintao,[2] the President of Communist China, in 2011 revealed the fruits[3] of this strategy. Prior to his arrival he demeaned the status of our currency and announced that he would not compromise over trade deals radically skewed in China's favor. And why should he? He, along with the rest of the world, have taken their measure of our current leadership and they know even if they don't receive the infamous bow they will receive the deference reserved for everyone except our traditional allies.

Our trade policies[4] force us to open our markets while those of our trading partners are blocked by fees and regulations. Our foreign policy is littered with wars we aren't allowed to win and we won't stop fighting. Our once dominate high technology has been given away or stolen. Our once predominate industrial base has been shipped overseas. And our once prevailing credit surplus has been changed into the biggest debt in History. This is the record of the last 20 years, and a record that reminds me of an old song, "Once I built a railroad, I made it run, made it race against time. Once I built a railroad; now it's done. Brother, can you spare a dime?"

Ronald Reagan emerged through the ridicule and derision of the establishment to take realpolitik to its logical conclusion: engineering the destruction of the Evil Empire and the absolute ascendancy of the United States. Since he left the scene our Presidents have led a steady advance to the rear. The North American Free Trade Act (NAFTA) opened the flood gates as so-called free trade that gutted our industrial base. Social engineering and the colossal spending it requires have bankrupted us.

Are we to be the generation that drops the ball? Each generation of Americans has bequeathed to their posterity a land stronger than they received. We were handed the unquestioned leadership of the world and after less than two decades we have frittered it away. If we are to reverse the slide we must make the decision that from this day forward we will chart a new course. From this day forward we will face reality and do the hard things necessary to reclaim our greatness and preserve the heritage of America for our children.

What are the solutions to the seemingly unsolvable problems we face? They aren't hard; mostly they're just common sense. Our government and We the People must stop over spending and live within your means. Lower or repeal all taxes. Cut the regulations on everything. Abandon so-called free trade[5] and seek equitable trade. End the wars. Quit being the policeman of the world. Bring our troops home. Seal the borders. Admit that Social Security has been a Ponzi scheme since day one. Realize that all the money we've paid into it over the years has been flushed down a rat hole. It isn't there.

Now figure out a fix with that in mind. Drill baby drill and approve a few permits to build some new refineries while you're at it. And if we must buy oil quit buying it from people who hate us in areas where they don't want us. Instead buy our oil from Mexico. This would pump money into our neighbor's economy instead of Al Qaeda's and perhaps our neighbor's citizens might want to stay in their own country. Quit apologizing for our past and put America first.

If we're to have a tomorrow we must make today count. We must live each day as a day worth living for each day lived is one less we have to live, and there are only so many days. Today is the day to make tomorrow happen.

★ DISPATCH SIXTY-THREE ★

Truth Justice and the American Way

Who in their wildest dreams ever thought we would see a headline that says, "China Urges U.S. to Protect Creditors by Raising Debt?"[1] For those of us who grew up in an America that was the undisputed leader of the free world locked in the Herculean task of containing the godless hordes of the Communist East, an America that was the largest manufacturer, largest creditor, and the economic engine that drove the world's economy until recently it was unimaginable. We watched as America fought wars around the edges of the creeping red menace. We worked to elect the leaders and pay the taxes that built a 600 ship navy, the best equipped armies in history, and the Space Based Initiative all of which eventually convinced even the Soviets that their centrally-planned monstrosity couldn't compete as it collapsed of its own weight.

Yes, except for the pages of MAD magazine, Cracked, or Rolling Stone until recently such a headline would have been unimaginable. Today, after 23 years of Progressive leadership it has become the truth. Communist China is warning us to make provisions to pay our creditors in the face of a declining credit rating and an ever-growing debt. Have they ever heard of the GM bond holders?

If you've ever been to a Tea Party rally or if you grew up in America before it became politically incorrect to love our country you will remember these words, "I pledge allegiance to the Flag of the United States of America and to the Republic for which it stands, one nation, indivisible, with liberty and justice for all." This is our hallowed Pledge of Allegiance.

It ends by announcing to the world our dedication to Justice.

In a world still run by kings, empires, and tyrannical despots as America rose to become a capitalist colossus of opportunity, we proclaimed that instead of the whims of the privileged riding roughshod over the rights of man we as a nation believed in an objective justice that wasn't swayed by birth or purchased by fraud. For more than 200 years this honorable standard was our goal. It wasn't always perfectly applied, and it was sometimes cruelly circumvented by prejudice and avarice, but at least it was our goal. The statue of Lady Justice wears a blindfold so that she is not influenced by what can be seen and she holds the scales which weigh the truth.

Martin Luther King called us to be more than we had been and all that we can be when he said, our children "will not be judged by the color of their skin but by the content of their character."[2] That this call was not for something new but instead a fulfillment of our original design is shown in Dr. King's plea that America, "live out the true meaning of its creed: 'We hold these truths to be self-evident: that all men are created equal.'" This was ever the goal: blind justice. This was ever the light which shone from the beacon in the hand of Lady Liberty: freedom to rise above our birth, liberty to rise to the level of our efforts, and justice for all.

Today the Progressives have shackled us to a creed of political correctness[3] which for the first time in our history makes Americans fearful of the penalties for what they say, write, and think. The Progressive ideology of from each according to their abilities to each according to their need, their dedication to the end of American Exceptionalism through globalization, and their worship of the myth of man-made global warming has created a toxic atmosphere where justice has no blindfold and her scales are tipped by the corruption of political power, crony capitalism, and interest groups on steroids.

In the face of these assaults on who we are and what we can do the American people refuse to give up! In the face of the best government money can buy taxing us to penury and spending us to poverty the American people continue to produce, to work, and to hope. In a world where our Progressive leaders have raised stealing from Peter to pay Paul into a national policy the American people have refused to go quietly into that dark night. On the day taxes were due thousands upon thousands of dedicated Americans gathered in city parks, town squares, and fields to proclaim America is still the home of the brave and the land of the free.

This is the American way. We have faced adversity many times. We have stood up to be counted when kings and emperors sought to squash the freedom of man under the weight of their divine right pride. We have shouldered the burden when dictators sought to clamp their totalitarian yoke upon the neck of the world and we will stand before these self-inflated ideologues who seek to smother freedom under a centrally-planned economy and a regimented society. Other countries have shown that when you rob Peter to pay Paul eventually Peter changes his name to Paul and that in the face of a stacked deck they will pretend to work as the government pretends to pay. In America today millions are rising up and saying we will not have a nation drowning in debt and limited in power! We will not leave a broken dream to our children! We will work tirelessly to preserve truth, justice and the American way.

Keep the faith. Keep the peace. We shall overcome.

★ DISPATCH SIXTY-FOUR ★

Tyranny is as Tyranny Does

During a recent 4th of July celebration of America's independence, Hillsdale College, a bastion of constitutional education and a powerhouse in the promotion of liberty, announced a "Read the Declaration" campaign. This campaign encouraged people who were gathered to celebrate the victory of freedom over tyranny to read the Declaration of Independence in its entirety.

Many of our fellow citizens have never read this foundational document. Many may have stopped after famous second sentence of the preamble, "We hold these truths to be self-evident, that all men are created equal, that they are endowed by their Creator with certain inalienable rights that among these are life, liberty and the pursuit of happiness."[1] In the Dream Time before political correctness, no child left behind, and the dumbing down of America most of us memorized that sentence in grade school and never forgot it.

Sadly many of those same people never read or remembered anything in the document after that sentence. The rest of the Declaration is a litany of the reasons why our ancestors felt that they needed "to dissolve the political bands which have connected them with another, and to assume among the powers of the earth, the separate and equal station to which the Laws of Nature and of Nature's God entitle them."[2] Or as they expressed it, "a decent respect to the opinions of mankind requires that they should declare the causes which impel them to the separation."[3]

The litany that sought to enlighten the opinions of mankind was a long list of the grievances they had with the King of Great Britain: George III.

I believe it would be a good exercise to see how many items on this list would make sense today if we substituted "The Federal Government" or "The President" for the "He." Give it a try and see what you think. See what conclusions you draw from the exercise.

America was born out of the desire for people to be free from what they perceived to be tyranny.

At this stage in America's History we seem to have come full circle. That which we rejected at our birth we find encumbering us once again. Through our own indifference we have forged our own chains and allowed the low-information voters to become the majority of those whose votes are counted. Those who should represent the true majority have been sidelined and cast aside almost as subjects in an occupied state.

However people are willing to bear with injustice long and to suffer the insufferable in silence. As our ancestors framed it, "Prudence, indeed, will dictate that governments long established should not be changed for light and transient causes; and accordingly all experience hath shown, that mankind are more disposed to suffer, while evils are sufferable, than to right themselves by abolishing the forms to which they are accustomed."[4]

Our ancestors finally reached the end of their rope when they stated, "But when a long train of abuses and usurpations, pursuing invariably the same object evinces a design to reduce them under absolute despotism, it is their right, it is their duty, to throw off such government, and to provide new guards for their future security."[5] Obviously we have not reached this state. The tyranny which we face holds the seats of power. It calls itself by the old names and all the old forms are still in place. Just as there was still a Senate in Rome even after Octavian became Augustus.[6]

Looking at our present day litany:

- The President refuses to enforce laws duly passed by the legislature and signed by the executive.[7]

- The Justice department incites racial division and covertly interferes in the judicial process.[8]

- The administration spies on its citizens[9] and mandates that its employees spy[10] on each other with legal penalties for those who fail to report.

- The Federal Reserve creates money without any oversight and irreparably damaging the earnings[11] and savings[12] of the American people.

- The Federal Government which is charged with protecting every state from invasion[13] has refused to secure[14] our borders and allowed tens of millions of people to enter and stay illegally adversely impacting every aspect of American life.

- The IRS has targeted[15] groups and individuals that hold opinions opposing the Obama administration.

- The President has made recess appointments[16] when Congress was in session; he has waged war[17] without Congressional approval or notification, he took an apology tour[18] around the world, he casts our allies aside,[19] and he promotes our enemies.[20]

Look at this long train of abuses and the subjugation of our God-given rights to a capricious and overbearing perpetually re-elected government dominated by two parties that are merely two heads on the same bird of prey. At such a time as this it is good to recall "That to secure these rights, governments are instituted among men, deriving their just powers from the consent of the governed. That whenever any form of government becomes destructive of these ends, it is the right of the people to alter or abolish it, and to institute new government, laying its foundation on such principles and organizing its powers in such form, as to them shall seem most likely to affect their safety and happiness."[21]

A word to the wise they say is sufficient. After 50 years of ringing the bell of liberty I am beginning to wonder.

It is to the preservation of limited government, personal liberty and economic opportunity that we the descendants of the founders and the children of the Framers should "with a firm reliance on the protection of divine Providence" and "for the support of this Declaration ... mutually pledge to each other our Lives, our Fortunes and our Sacred Honor."[22]

Be vigilant in the protection of freedom.

Keep the faith. Keep the peace. We shall overcome.

★ DISPATCH SIXTY-FIVE ★

UNCLE SAM PLAYS YOU PAY

America is careening towards a financial Armageddon. The President proposed a budget for 2012 that projected a deficit of 1.6 trillion dollars. That is trillion with a "T." Gone are the innocent days when one of the perpetually re-elected could quip, "A billion here and a billion there and soon we're talking about real money."[1] Now billions disappear into the federal sinkhole at the rate of 4.08 billion per day.[2] What does a trillion look like?[3] If you went into business the day Jesus was born, and you lost a million dollars a day, 365 days a year, it would take you until October 2737 to lose a trillion dollars.

According to the Congressional Budget Office (CBO) the budget deficit just for February 2011 hit $223 billion, which means more debt was added in just that one month than was added in all of 2007.[4] The personal share of the federal debt borne by every tax-paying citizen is now increasing at the rate of $50 per day seven days a week, 364 days a year. That is an increase of $1,500 per month and $18,250 per year per tax payer.[5]

That sounds serious. However, it doesn't appear as if our elected officials take it seriously at all. The Republicans propelled into the majority by the grass-roots activism, high energy and victories of the Tea Party Movement promised to cut 100 billion from the 2011 budget. President Obama submitted that budget which spends 3.7 trillion with a deficit of 1.6 trillion dollars in 2010. It was never passed even though the Democrats controlled both houses of Congress and the White House. This left the door open for the Republicans to use the continuing resolutions necessary to keep the government operating as vehicles to wring spending cuts from the Democrats. After theatrical bi-weekly dramas these cuts were in the range of 10 to 12 billion dollars.

Then finally, with the Democrats imposing an artificial deadline for the passage of a budget that was almost half expended and which they had failed to pass when they had undisputed control, the two parties of power struck what they hailed as a "Historic" compromise. They first told us they slashed 38 billion from the budget. The actual number, according to the Congressional Budget Office has since dwindled down and down until today it is estimated to be less than a billion.[6] The Federal Government will still increase the national debt by more than a trillion dollars per year and our leaders expect us to celebrate their conversion to fiscal sanity. Isn't the definition of insanity to continue doing the same thing and expect different results? Just because they're crazy doesn't mean we have to cheerfully put on an economic straightjacket and walk voluntarily into a padded cell at the poor house.

Representative Paul Ryan (R. WI) introduced a budget[7] which he says takes on the sacred cows and gores the sacred bulls by cutting six trillion from the projected budgets of the next 10 years. The Democrats immediately assaulted this plan as cruel, heartless, and inadequate.[8] The President announces his latest plan which he assures us he meant to introduce all along once someone else had opened the debate. In his plan Mr. Obama plans to cut the projected deficit by stopping waste and abuse in government programs and by taxing the rich.

There are two problems with this approach: if we had all the money politicians have promised to save by stopping waste and abuse we would have a surplus, and the rich don't have enough money. It has been estimated that if you confiscated every dime every person who makes over one million dollars per year makes it would only generate enough money to run our debt-addicted government for less than one year. What would we do for the next year? And the fact of the matter is that the tax increases that the President wants are not confined to the rich. They would target everyone with a combined gross income above 250,000.[9] That group includes most small business people. This approach will take money out of the pockets of the greatest creators of jobs: small business people. And it still won't generate enough money to stop the red ink.

The battle looms over and over to raise the debt limit.[10] This is an inside-the-belt-way shell game wherein the parties of power each beat their chests and growl at each other about who is the most responsible before they both vote to increase the limit on their collective credit card. Wouldn't it be great if we could all just raise the limit on our credit cards indefinitely? And now with the Federal Reserve buying our own debt to finance the repayment maybe we could increase the limits on all our cards so that we can pay our Visa with our MasterCard and our MasterCard with our Discover and our Discover with our Visa. How could that ever go wrong?

The storyline we are supposed to believe now is that in exchange for raising the debt limit there must be meaningful movement towards a balanced budget amendment.[11] That sounds so encouraging. If we just had a balanced budget amendment the problem will be solved. As always there are several spare balanced budget amendments lying around in Congress waiting for enough votes or at least an opportunity to get to the floor for a debate before they are stuffed back in a committee until the next time the shopaholics on the Potomac need to convince the great unwashed in fly-over country that this time they are serious about curbing their over-spending.

But even if they were passed what good would they do? The President and the Democrats have already shown that they think the way to solve the deficit problem is to raise taxes. The Republicans have a plan that appears very dramatic but at the end of a decade still would not end the deficit spending, which means the debt is still growing.[12]

The International Monetary Fund has looked at these plans and says it appears America is not serious about dealing with its addiction to debt. If we don't do something soon our creditors are going to stage an intervention, and they will dictate how we must restructure our lives and our nation if we want any more credit. And we are addicted to credit.

A balanced budget amendment merely requires a balanced budget, and budgets can be balanced by increasing taxes instead of decreasing spending. What we need instead is a spending amendment which would limit federal expenditures to a reasonable percentage of the nation's income.[13] The amendment should also include a designated manner in calculating the nation's income so that it can't be changed in creative ways to raise the spending limit with smoke and mirrors. If we can't stop the spending we will eventually destroy our credit, collapse our economy, and curtail our liberty. In other words, no matter what we the people want Uncle Sam will continue to spend, spend, spend as long as we pay, pay, pay.

DISPATCH SIXTY-SIX

We Can Trust Us

L istening to the lies of the politicians as presented by the prattle of the biased it is easy to lose hope in a secular sense. My hope in an eternal sense is founded on the rock of an unshakable faith in Jesus and so it cannot be shaken. However, in the secular, resting as it must upon the shifting sands of man in America today, hope as a measured commodity is all too often hopeless. Seeking for hope in current events, a diamond among the discards and a point of light in a sea of darkness, is seeking something positive among the gathering gloom of an empire in eclipse.

I don't know about you but I cannot focus on the negative trends of our current situation for long without at least contemplating depression and I don't mean the economic kind. I am thankful I have a peace that passes all understanding and a hope that cannot be taken away, and I am also glad that I have a sense of History which gives me a context to frame the "now." For if all we have is "now" it can always be changed with the next headline, the next news bulletin or the next press release. Having a historical context brings things into focus fitting the events of today into flow of time from yesterday to tomorrow.

Truth often becomes the victim of expediency. For what seems true at the moment may end up as the lie of the hour. Politicians bend truth like gravity bends light: the heavier the perceived need the greater the unperceived distortion. Lies can become so widely believed that truth is swallowed in truism. Lies become the accepted wisdom of professional pundits chattering endlessly supporting that which ultimately must fall for those who seek to surf a tsunami into a safe harbor. The news is filled with half-truths and as my second favorite philosopher, Anonymous once said, "Beware of half-truths, you may have gotten the wrong half."

We live in a twilight time. Twilight by definition is a time when two sources of light pierce the gloom, that quivering moment when both the Sun and the Moon hold back the darkness. The darkness of confusion is dispelled by the brightness of truth but it is disputed by refracted light of opinion masquerading as truth.

Casting about for something solid in the midst of the swirling fog of conflicting facts, shifting observations, and contradictory visions in the secular sense I must focus on one thing: the people. I trust the American people. I trust them to make the right choice when presented with unvarnished reality. I trust them to do what must be done to preserve the bequest of our forefathers for the inheritance of our posterity.

The Declaration of Independence[1] was written to proclaim the righteousness of the actions of "One people" with the courage to declare to a world sold into bondage that our liberty was founded upon truth. "We hold these truths to be self-evident, that all men are created equal, that they are endowed by their Creator with certain unalienable Rights that among these are Life, Liberty and the pursuit of Happiness."

We the People wrote the Constitution in order to perfect that which had been founded upon the truth.[2] "We the People of the United States, in Order to form a more perfect Union, establish Justice, insure domestic Tranquility, provide for the common defense, promote the general Welfare, and secure the Blessings of Liberty to ourselves and our Posterity, do ordain and establish this Constitution for the United States of America."

It is to this one people, this "We the people" that I look for secular hope, political peace, and the eventual solution to our current cultural conundrum. The popular definition of a conundrum is a problem without a solution. However it also has another meaning, a riddle whose answer is or involves a pun. Since I am referring to the second meaning I will present the riddle, "How is liberalism the solution to the problem of liberalism?"

In our through-the-looking-glass world politicians use the actual truth to obscure the obvious truth. Congressman Joe Early (D-Mass) at a press conference to answer questions about the House Bank scandal said, "They gave me a book of checks. They didn't ask for any deposits."[3] While I'm sure it is true he was given a book of checks, obviously one needs to make deposits if one is to honestly write checks. In the same manner the leaders of our free country promote socialism as the solution to the problems socialism has caused knowing that you cannot honestly write checks if you don't make deposits. Capitalism makes the deposits and socialism wants to write the checks. As Churchill said "Socialism is a philosophy of failure, the creed of ignorance, and the gospel of envy, its inherent virtue is the equal sharing of misery."[4]

We are awash in polls. Every campaign and every major news source constantly trumpet polls many of which contradict each other. No matter what the polls say I believe that the American people still believe in freedom. I believe that they still believe in the equality of opportunity and the opportunity of equality. We all aren't the same. Each of us is born with a particular set of talents and each of us uses those talents in a certain way. It is my belief, that given the level playing field of individual liberty and economic freedom, the vast majority of Americans will work hard to earn what they deserve. This is my secular hope. Heaven on earth is not possible but given individual liberty and economic freedom inherently promised in the perfect union We the People sought to create we can at least avoid remaining in the hell of socialism the Progressives are currently foisting upon us, and as Churchill also said "If you're going through hell, keep going."[5]

Oh, by the way, the answer to the riddle, "How is liberalism the solution to the problem of liberalism?" is that Classical Liberalism promotes the general welfare by promoting the limitation of government and the liberty of the individual in order to better serve the whole. Welfare Liberalism erodes the general welfare by expanding the government at the expense of the individual in order to better serve the individual. Thus Classical Liberalism is the solution to the problems caused by Welfare Liberalism. And that's the truth which brings me to one last Churchill quote for the day, "The truth is incontrovertible. Malice may attack it. Ignorance may deride it. But in the end, there it is."[6]

Don't be discouraged by the blather of the pontificating politicians or confused by the conflicting ruminations of the professional talkers. When all is said and done we can trust us. We the people will eventually come down on the side of truth, justice, and the American way.

★ DISPATCH SIXTY-SEVEN ★

We Know the Problem … What's the Answer?

These weekly Dispatches, which I am privileged to submit for your consideration, elicit many comments and questions. The most common of which can be summed up as, "I agree with your analysis, appreciate the Historical context, but how about some practical suggestions."

If you are one of the many who have sent me those emails, posted those replies, made those phone calls, or asked me in person this Dispatch is for you.

To fully address these questions we have to look at two levels: the macro and the micro. We need practical suggestions for the very large and the very small. We need practical suggestions for the societal and cultural level and the personal level.

First of all we need some historical context for our current situation. In some ways we are unique, we are America after all. And in some ways what is happening to us has happened many times before. As I have often said in these Dispatches if History doesn't actually repeat itself it does rhyme.

The French Revolution occurred between 1787 and 1799.[1] It was the first to try to attempt to replicate the phenomenon of the American Revolution which overthrew the age-old tyranny of divine right kings and landed aristocracy replacing it with a federal republic operating on democratic principles based upon limited government, personal liberty, and economic freedom.

The American Revolution inspired the French to believe they too could break free of the chains and breathe the fresh air of freedom. However, it lost something in the translation. Perhaps because the French didn't have the long tradition of limited self-government and human rights which had grown up in England since the Magna Carta had been forced on a reluctant

King John in 1215. Perhaps it was because the French had endured centuries of the cruelest servitude under the most absolute of absolute monarchs.

Whatever the reason once the French broke free of the cultural, societal, and personal restraint of the Old Regime which had persecuted and exploited them for so long the French people sought to exact revenge. They sought to cut the former ruling class out of society and while they were at it establish a completely new regime in its place. The French, always famous for philosophers, had produced one who had a tremendous influence on the thinking of the Founders of our country and the Framers of the Constitution: Jean-Jacques Rousseau.[2]

However, Rousseau had two sides. On one side he eloquently expressed the idea that government was established upon a social contract between the rulers and the ruled and that to have any legitimacy government must base itself upon the consent of the governed. Thus empowering the governed to decide when that contract has been violated and giving them a philosophical basis for change. Our forefathers based their work upon this side.

On the other side, Rousseau argued against private property. And that it is the role of the state to impose freedom, equality, and justice for all within the state regardless of the view of the majority. Thus empowering a minority to decide what constitutes freedom, equality, justice, and justifying the use of state power to mold society to fit the vision of the few. On this side Rousseau is considered the father of modern socialism and communism. This is the side that the leaders of the French Revolution chose to follow.

Another difference is that by 1787 France had been a highly centralized nation for centuries. The local governments served at the pleasure of the central authority and they could be established or overthrown upon the whim of the ruler. In America we had the experience of 13 separate colonies each with their own particular history and each with their own particular traditions. In America this led to the establishment of a Federal Republic with sovereignty resting in the people and the States and only delegated by them to the central government.

These differences led to the corruption of the French Revolution into The Terror[3] a period between 1793 and 1794 when France was surrounded by enemies and pressed on every side. The Leaders of the Revolution felt as if there were agents and sympathizers of their enemies everywhere and they proceeded to execute thousands of their own people in order to secure freedom. The Terror eventually led to a military dictatorship which evolved into an Empire with a monarch at least as absolute as the one they had overthrown in 1787.

Unfortunately for humanity suffering under the yoke of absolute rulers and their crony elites, subsequent revolutions have tended to follow the French model instead of the America. The Mexican Revolution (1810–1821)[4] was part of a wide ranging revolt against the once great Spanish Empire (1808–1826).[5] From the Rio Grande to Tierra del Fuego revolutions cast aside the foreign rule of Spain and established home-grown republics. All of these republics modeled their initial declarations of independence on America's but the successor regimes all came to model some variation of the French. The people rose up in righteous indignation against an oppressive system and in the end found themselves under one military dictator after another. They fought to gain their liberty and merely traded one elite for another as the iron heel of tyranny maintained its stand on the throat of liberty.

Other revolutions, the Russian (1917) and the Cuban (1952–1959) are further examples of the trend. What begins as an attempt to bring the blessing of limited government, personal liberty, and economic freedom to people ends up bringing instead a tyranny usually more cruel than the one against which the people originally rebelled.

As can be seen by this litany of subverted revolutions it is usually violence that brings the fall of the former tyranny and facilitates the rise of the latter. One example of a revolution that came about through an election would be the Nazi revolution in 1932. Another would be the current regime of Hugo Chavez in Venezuela. A revolution by way of the ballot box, but a revolution nonetheless.

Today America is in the midst of a revolution. America has elected a President who has vowed to fundamentally transform America.[6] He promised this to his adoring supporters before his election, and he has worked tirelessly to bring it about. He is an Alinsky style community organizer who is working to organize[7] our community by occupying[8] the center of power and the streets at the same time. He follows the Cloward/Piven Strategy[9] spending us into oblivion in the name of saving the economy. He has seized major portions of the economy[10] and shoved national health insurance, a financial sector take-over, and undeclared war down the throats of a passive American public. Polls show that vast majorities do not want what he is selling but he is closing the deal anyway.[11]

Mr. Obama campaigned day and night for another term, and a term that will be without restraint for a President who has already said he can rule without Congress.[12] He will most likely appoint at least one more Supreme Court Justice and solidify America's passage from a Federal Republic to a European style social democracy.

That is the context, so what should patriotic Americans do now? As I said at the beginning to fully address these questions we have to look at two levels: the macro and the micro. We need practical suggestions for the very large and the very small. We need practical suggestions for the societal and cultural level and the personal level.

On the macro level we need to do everything in our power to make sure Barack Obama does not gain a compliant Congress controlled by Harry Reid and Nancy Pelosi. We need to contribute our time, our talent, and our treasure to making sure his accomplices are defeated and defeated decisively in November 2014. Whom should we support? My advice is study the opposition candidates, and support the one who stands for limited government, personal liberty, and economic freedom. Choose the ones that most credibly support a return to constitutional government.

I realize that the Republicans are for the most part merely Progressives who call themselves conservatives to win elections and then spend their time making deals to further the Progressive agenda. It often comes down to the point of choosing the lesser of two evils. The problem with choosing the lesser of two evils is that you are still choosing evil. However in this instance with code blue on one side and a slow fall off a high cliff on the other we may want to choose the one who will drive us to the poor house a little slower. At least that way we will have more time to prepare and perhaps another opportunity to make the logical choice and vote for a return to constitutional government.

On the micro level I am reminded of many people I have met over the years who have escaped from any one of the hell-holes socialist revolutions have produced in the last 100 years. Whether it is Poland, or Russia, or Cuba they have told me over and over that they see the same things happening here that once swallowed their homelands. They have told me how they cry at night as they see central planning and social engineering consuming America. They have tearfully asked me, "Where can we go now? We escaped tyranny looking for freedom and now we see the same thing coming here?"

In answer to their questions I have asked one of my own, "How can we survive the coming darkness?" One by one they have all given me the same advice, "Get out of the cities, get yourself some land where you can grow your own food, and do all you can to protect your family and preserve the traditions of liberty."

In other words, head for the hills and hunker down. Personally my wife and I have made this choice. We have decided to sacrifice whatever portions of our modern life styles and lucrative careers must be jettisoned to maintain what is truly important: our family, our lives, and our liberty. We saw this coming and made a five-year plan which is now coming to fruition. Myself and many others have been sounding the alarm from the watchtowers for years.

Now is the time for all good citizens to come to the aid of our nation. We must stand up for our heritage. We must do battle in the marketplace of ideas, and we must engage in the struggle at the ballot box, but we must also prepare to save some seed corn in case the winter does descend. We must preserve what we can so we can begin again. So "that this nation, under God, shall have a new birth of freedom—and that government of the people, by the people, for the people, shall not perish from the earth."[13]

Keep the faith. Keep the peace. We shall overcome.

★ DISPATCH SIXTY-EIGHT ★

We Must Know Who We Are to Decide What We Will Be

Forget about the debate the government parties and the geriatric media want us to have, "Are you a Republican or a Democrat?" The debate we need to have concerns what we were meant to be, not who they tell us we should be. Instead we should discuss issues of substance such as, "Are we a Republic or a Democracy?" for this will lead us to the truth. In today's polarized political atmosphere Conservatives shout "Republic!" while Progressives scream, "Democracy!" In truth, neither term fully describes the boldest experiment to provide individual freedom and release human potential in the history of mankind. There is a third term needed if we are to grasp the qualities which makes us who we are.

The United States was birthed in the fire of revolution against the denial of personal freedom and the expropriation of resources by an authoritarian government. The first attempt to balance the rights of the people, the prerogatives of their local states and the need for a centralized structure to face other nations on the world stage, the Articles of Confederation[1] proved inadequate. Then the Framers crafted a constitution establishing a federal republic designed to operate on democratic principles.

All three terms democratic,[2] federal,[3] and republic[4] are needed to express the unique nature of the American Experiment. Not one of them conveys the strength of the three and therefore cannot stand alone. Together they outline the form of government and the manner in which it shall be chosen, yet even these loaded terms leave unstated the inner essence of the last best hope of humanity. For it is the separation of powers,[5] private property rights,[6] and the checks and balances[7] built into the system that has safe guarded liberty and unleashed the potential of the American people.

The fact that instead of a reasoned debate about who we are, where we came from, and how we got here we stand on opposite sides of barricades shouting slogans at each other highlights the need for all of us to educate ourselves in the history of the principles and values upon which our country was founded. The current public educational process is a government-mandated system that forces teaching to a test that's forgotten as soon as it's passed.

The teaching of American History has been presented as a boring jumble of names and dates for a few semesters in 12 years since before any of us were born. It's time for anyone who wants to understand what's going on in our rapidly evolving political landscape to dig in and educate ourselves. We cannot allow those who want to subvert the home of the brave and the land of the free either to the right or to the left in order to sway us with slogans and catch phrases. We have to know enough to know when we're being conned by ideologues with a hidden agenda.

Ideologues reduce all things to the dimensions of their own thoughts. They oversimplify and overload words with meaning effectively blocking the channels of communication. They turn complex political, social and economic principles into cat-calls, catch-phrases and campaign slogans designed to move masses to emotional responses not individuals to reasoned reactions. It was the ideologue Karl Marx who reduced history to a conflict between capital and labor, charged all problems to the inequalities of capitalism, projected a continually deteriorating situation and then pointed to communism as the only answer.

We must resist the temptation to reduce our American experiment to an ideology. We cannot allow this bait-and-switch tactic to lead us to the mirage of a collectivist utopia. We need to understand this would deny and distort the constitutionally limited government we inherited. Ideologies start with a conception of mankind as made-up of interchangeable parts projects universally comprehensive answers and ends with enforced uniformity in society. In contrast America has facilitated diversity, individualism and a variety of life paths.

So, "Are we a Republic or a Democracy?" First of all, we need to understand these are not equivalent or interchangeable terms. Today both republic and democracy have become loaded with ideological baggage as in the Democratic Peoples Republic, or Social Democracy.[8]

To be specific: republic describes a form of government wherein representatives stand in place of others to deliberate, decide and lead. Democracy means from the people. But there is the third term that must be reckoned with if we're to understand America: federal. Federal means a form of government in which a union of States recognizes a central authority while retaining certain residual powers of government. Putting this all together, the United States of America was designed to be a federation of States with a republican form of government chosen through a democratic process.

Those who declare we're a democracy want majority rule while striving to build a majority of people dependent on the government following the dictum of tax, tax, tax, spend, spend, spend, elect, elect, elect. Those who say we're a republic have problems with the direction taken by the representatives whose very existence proclaims this to be a republic. This is where the third word fully impacts the other two. The federal nature of the American experiment declares to all that this is an elected representative government of limited power and separated authority. We are not a centrally-planned unitary government based on mob-rule. If we will learn who we are perhaps then we will see clearly who we will be.

★ DISPATCH SIXTY-NINE ★

WHAT'S THE REASON?

Just as the pursuit of perfection can often end in the sacrifice of what is good so too the worship of reason often results in the exaltation of mediocrity and the circumscription of reasonable thought and action.

Daily the Progressives aggressively push forward against positions which have long been the traditional battle lines of the conservative movement. The front lines in the culture war move ever closer to the transformed America they envision.[1] First prayer was expelled from School. Then the sexual revolution wave peaked with the nullification of state abortion laws by the Supreme Court and then crashed into the main-stream with condoms and birth-control distributed to school children. Divorce became common-place, and out-of-wedlock births account for the majority in several demographics.[2] Pornography is a constitutional right and as close as a mouse click away in most homes.

Those who want to hold on to the America we were raised in are ridiculed in the press, movies, and by our elected officials as a wild-eyed fringe of traditionalist America-firsters clinging to our guns and Bibles.[3] This is why it is important to examine the place of reason as opposed to tradition in the operation of society.

To paraphrase the infamous phrase of George Bush the Younger, "I have sacrificed free market principles to save the free market system,"[4] I would say, "At times we must suspend the rule of reason for reason to flourish." Or follow in the footsteps of David Hume who was said to have turned against the Enlightenment its own weapons to whittle down the claims of reason by the use of rational analysis.[5]

It is the ability to think in symbols and imagine abstract things that sets man apart from the rest of the animal kingdom. Therefore at the outset let me say this is not an appeal for irrationality or any type of transcendental mysticism. It is instead meant to be a rational examination of the anti-rationalistic position which is necessary for the preservation of individual freedom, personal liberty, and economic opportunity, and the only conditions under which reason can flourish and evolve. For the attempt to apply reason and reason alone to the organization of society's intricately woven interface of conventions stifles creativity, leaves no place for innovation, and is ultimately unreasonable.

When we attempt to apply the laws of science or the mechanical practices of engineering to human activity we run the risk of building a maze so perfect the mouse can never find the cheese. Or in other words we can seek to make our processes so ideal that there is no room for free thinking, free action, or for the splashes of genius that are the real catalysts of societal evolution.

Those who stand by the idea that reason and reason alone should shape the future must of necessity seek to abandon tradition; for traditions are not built upon reason. They are built upon trial and error. That which doesn't work is discarded, and that which works becomes accepted through use and time. However it is impossible to completely disregard tradition. Every day each of us moves through life acting upon hundreds of unconscious rules and procedures that we don't think about because they were bred into us by those who raised us. It is the consensus of a common culture and heritage which makes a people one, E Pluribus Unum.

Those who worship reason believe that they can design a perfect society, a Utopia, and that all of their dreams of perfection will stand the light of day. History proves over and over that those who seek to guide the evolution of man through the evolution of society do not create the heaven on earth they advertise.

Look to the French Revolution which cast down Christ and enshrined Reason as their God.[6] It didn't produce the liberty, equality, and fraternity it promised; instead it brought forth the Terror, dictatorship, war and ruin.[7] The Russian Revolution overthrew the absolute monarchy of the Romanovs and installed an even more absolute dictatorship that promised a worker's paradise and delivered the gulags, starvation, and collapse.[8]

When those who think they are wise enough to make everyone's decisions about everything try to manufacture a society that looks like their computer models they must use coercion to force those who do not accept their vision to act as if they did. Rules, regulations and red tape bind the human spirit and prevent the growth of the un-designed, the unforeseen, and smother the spark of genius. As counter-intuitive as it may sound a free society will always be in large measure a tradition bound society. For traditions, though they may seem to be unbreakable at times, are always evolving while rules are cast in concrete.

Patrick Henry told us, "Virtue, morality, and religion. This is the armor, my friend, and this alone that renders us invincible. These are the tactics we should study. If we lose these, we are conquered, fallen indeed . . . so long as our manners and principles remain sound, there is no danger."[9]

John Adams said, "Our Constitution was made only for a moral and religious people. It is wholly inadequate to the government of any other."[10]

Our virtue is embodied and defended in our traditions. Once these walls have fallen how can our virtue stand unprotected assailed on all sides in what is becoming an alien culture?

The ethics of virtue tells us "Virtue is determined by the right reason. Virtue requires the right desire and the right reason. To act from the wrong reason is to act viciously. On the other hand, the agent can try to act from the right reason, but fail because he or she has the wrong desire. The virtuous agent acts effortlessly, perceives the right reason, has the harmonious right desire, and has an inner state of virtue that flows smoothly into action. The virtuous agent can act as an exemplar of virtue to others."[11]

The virtuous person acts in the way they do because it is their nature. They have imbibed the virtue of their society and they act naturally as an embodiment of the good. They have absorbed the traditions and they act as they do without thought, without regard or reliance on reason. They do not question what is right or wrong. They know what is right or wrong and act accordingly. They follow tradition.

The worshipers of reason reject the traditions that have grown up organically in society and design their own. They reject the good and seek the perfect. The problem is that perfection is impossible in this life. Perfection does not belong to the realm of man. The air castles and utopias of the rationalistic social engineers may look good on paper; however they never materialize into anywhere we can live.

Why is it hell the Progressives will deliver instead of the heaven they promise? This is what has traditionally happened and that's the reason.

★ DISPATCH SEVENTY ★

When the Have Nots Become the Haves

Saul Alinsky the political thinker who seems to have had more impact on President Obama than any other was very clear in his most important book about what his motives were and what he was aiming at,

> "What follows is for those who want to change the world from what it is to what they believe it should be. 'The Prince' was written by Machiavelli for the Haves on how to hold power. 'Rules for Radicals' is written for the Have-Nots on how to take it away."

With the November Revolution of 2008 which gave us one party rule for two years the Progressive Democrat party saw their chance and they took it. Within the two years it took for the people to realize they needed some balance the Progressives passed Obamacare which effectively gives government control one sixth of the economy.[1] They passed Dodd-Frank which gives them extensive control over the financial sector.[2] When they couldn't push Cap-N-Trade even through a rubber-stamp Congress the President imposed it by executive order.[3] When they likewise failed to muster enough of their own hacks to pass the Dream Act once again it was imposed by fiat.[4]

The anti-capitalist programs of the Progressive Bush Administration's final days were continued and amplified by the Obama Administration[5] TARP was followed by the Stimulus. The takeover of AIG and the auto industry was followed by force feeding money into the economy for years of quantitative easing as the casino we call the stock market soars.

The unemployment numbers reported by the government have become totally unhinged from reality as the real rate stays at levels which would easily shine the light of truth on the fiction of a recovery.[6]

According to the government's own Bureau of Labor Statistics the real unemployment rate (U-6) has been continuously above 13% for the last year.[7] This information is readily available (one click of the mouse) and yet the media (including Fox) have told us day-by-day that it is falling and is now down to 7.2. This typifies the manufactured reality the Federal Government and the Corporations Once Known as the Mainstream Media shovel into the public trough. If the plagiarized opinions I hear my fellow citizens share everyday are any indication the average person accepts the fiction as reality.

New research from the Republicans on the Senate Budget Committee shows that over the last five years, the U.S. has spent about $3.7 trillion on welfare.[8]

> "We have just concluded the 5th fiscal year since President Obama took office. During those five years, the Federal Government has spent a total $3.7 trillion on approximately 80 different means-tested poverty and welfare programs. The common feature of means-tested assistance programs is that they are graduated based on a person's income and, in contrast to programs like Social Security or Medicare, they are a free benefit and not paid into by the recipient, "

says the minority side of the Senate Budget Committee.[9]

The minority side also states that, "The enormous sum spent on means-tested assistance is nearly five times greater than the combined amount spent on NASA, education, and all federal transportation projects over that time."[10] And the staggering sum of $3.7 trillion is not even the entire amount spent on federal poverty support, as states contribute more than $200 billion each year primarily in the form of free low-income healthcare.

The goal has always been to get enough people receiving benefits to out-vote the ones paying for the benefits. In the fourth quarter of 2011, (the last full year for which statistics are available) 49.2% of Americans received benefits from one or more government programs.[11]

In total, the Census Bureau estimated, 151,014,000 Americans out of a population then estimated to be 306,804,000 received benefits from one or more government programs during the last three months of 2011. Those 151,014,000 beneficiaries equaled 49.2% of the population.

This included 82,457,000 people—or 26.9% of the population—who lived in households in which one or more people received Medicaid benefits.

At the same time a large number of Americans no longer pay any federal taxes. Even the Progressive Huffington Post states, "Some 76 million tax filers, or 46.4% of the total, will be exempt from federal income tax in 2011." Using the same year as a way of fair comparison.[12]

Just imagine an undisciplined out-of-control shopaholic whose credit limit has just been extended. Now they can continue overspending without any accountability. That shopaholic is the U.S. government.[13]

In the week since Congress reached a temporary deal to suspend the U.S. government's debt ceiling the Treasury department has added another $375 billion in new debt.[14]

The suspension of a cap on U.S. debt, which was previously fixed at $16.69 trillion, means the Treasury department can spend whatever amount of money it wants.[15]

How much money will the U.S. government put on our grandchildren's credit card by the next debt ceiling deadline? At the current rate of deficit spending which is $375 billion per week, U.S. public debt will reach $22.70 trillion by February 7, 2014.

All these transfer payments impoverish the working middle class who pay the biggest share of their income in taxes and empower those who receive the benefits, often being the same ones who pay no taxes. Thus the have-nots become the haves fulfilling the goal of the Alinsky inspired community organizing program which has become Americas' master plan.

As the have-nots rise to become the haves and the haves descend to become the have-nots the cycle repeats itself in an endless spiral of social warfare and the only ones who really benefit are those whose goal is power irrespective of who has what.

This is why the President and his advisors seem so oblivious to the turmoil[16] and destruction[17] the implementation of their plans causes. The goal of the President[18] and of the other Progressive leaders has always been universal single payer insurance no matter what they had to say to sell it.[19] Obamacare was always seen as a half-step in the direction of total government control.[20] So what do a few speed bumps along the way matter when the goal is to totally transform America?[21]

Our current administration seems to have no respect for the law.

The Affordable Care Act (Obamacare) forbids the Federal Government from enforcing the law in any state that opted out of setting up its own healthcare exchange.[22] This may change once the Supreme Court rubberstamps the power-grab.

The Obama administration has ignored that part in the law, enforcing all of its provisions even in states where the federal government is operating the insurance marketplaces on the error-plagued Healthcare.gov website.

Thirty-six states chose not to set up their exchanges, a move that effectively froze Washington, D.C. out of the authority to pay subsidies and other pot-sweeteners to convince citizens in those states to buy medical insurance. However, the IRS overstepped its authority promising to pay subsidies in those states anyway.

The imperious leaders of the have-nots now have the government, and tradition, laws, and history all take a back seat to the alliance of Progressives who want to have it all.

★ DISPATCH SEVENTY-ONE ★

WHEN WILL ENOUGH BE ENOUGH

When taxes become destructive they've surpassed the consent of the governed bending to the will of tyranny. When regulations strangle competition instead of securing it from evil combinations they've become counterproductive and defeat the very purpose for which they were proposed. When foreign entanglements bleed the nation but do not secure the peace or defeat the enemy they've become interventionist vehicles for vested interests. When spending becomes a hemorrhaging of assists leading to national bankruptcy those who continue to pile debt upon debt seek not the good of the nation but instead its destruction. When leaders selected to unite instead do all they can to divide they no longer advance the interest of the whole and are instead partisan leaders in a factional fight.

A social contract is one made between a people and their government. It is an agreement whereby the people surrender certain aspects of their independence for the guarantee of corporate security and the enjoyment of a general welfare. In the case of most countries this is an unwritten and unconscious arrangement built upon tradition and precedent as in the case of England. However in the United States we have an actual contract, the Constitution. This was ratified by the original states and the subsequent states were formed under it and admitted as full partners to it.

All contracts may be legitimately changed over time as long as there are mechanisms either within the document or established by the document to do so. Within our Constitution there is an amendment process and it has been amended 27 times so far. Whether we agree with those amendments or not they have been legally ratified and accepted thus becoming part of the document. However, over the years our government structure has been changed and our manner of life transformed more by the informal changes than by the formal. Nowhere in the Constitution is the central government given the power to wage unending undeclared war. Nowhere is the central government given the right to ignore the requirement to protect the states from invasion. Nowhere is there found any basis for executive orders, signing statements or bureaucratic regulations to have the force of law without legislative action by Congress.

Well-connected rabble rousers now say equality will not be achieved until everything is equal in everybody's house. Leveling the playing field has finally thrown off its cloak of deceit and exposed itself as, "From each according to their ability to each according to their need." The professional civil rights entrepreneurs who've extorted vast amounts of personal wealth with threats of boycotts and demonstrations have been unmasked as the true purveyors of prejudice seeking to keep race and gender differences alive for their own benefit. Union bosses build political empires using the legally forced dues of members with more money spent on political activity than on member service. The union bosses ride in limousine comfort from board meetings to political rallies while their members lose jobs. The pensions of the bosses are golden parachutes while the pensions of the members are underfunded.

The Land of the Free is held captive, locked in a two party system where both parties are merely two heads on the same bird of prey. Both parties are dedicated to more spending and bigger government. Both parties exploit gerrymandering of districts and overwhelming corporate donations to ensure a hierarchy of the perpetually re-elected using a system of seniority to enhance their power. Legal barriers exist at every turn to stop any new parties from gaining the access that might deflect the central government from its ever-increasing growth toward totalitarianism.

When will enough be enough? When will citizens rise in their righteous anger and demand not a New Deal, not a Great Society, a New Frontier or a Fundamentally Transformed America but instead their original deal. The one we wrested from the hands of the tyrant King George. The one we've fought to establish and defend from Yorktown to Kandahar and the right of a people to be free to live as they desire, to work for their own benefit and choose their own destiny. Free from the smothering governmental control which has been the lot of most people in most places since the beginning of time. When will the yoke of tyranny become too heavy to be borne? What will be the spark that lights the torches and brings the incensed villagers to the gate of the castle demanding, "Bring the monster out!" so that a stake can be driven through the heart of tyranny and freedom can return to the land?

When that day comes what will we the people do? Will we try to resurrect the government of old that ultimately brought us full circle or will we be bold enough to forge a new the social contract and design better ways to ensure that the beast of tyranny doesn't once again break the chains of restraint.

★ DISPATCH SEVENTY-TWO ★

WHERE DID THIS DEBT COME FROM ANYHOW?

Have you ever wondered where the National Debt came from? Do you wonder who started it? Do you ask yourself is the National Debt constitutional? I believe that a lack of Historical knowledge and context is a major contributing factor in our current state of political deterioration. Unless we know where we came from we cannot truly appreciate where we are and we have no point of reference to guide us to where we want to go.

The National Debt didn't start under Barak Obama or George Bush. It didn't start under FDR or Wilson or Lincoln. So where did it come from and when did it start?

The National Debt and the economic outlook inherent in its creation have not only been with us since the beginning it was one of the most powerful arguments for the ratification of the Constitution. I may have just lost many of the recently awakened. I most assuredly lost those who worship the Constitution as American Scripture and the Framers as demigods who brought the tablets down from on high.

Don't misunderstand the intent of the following article. It is not to malign the Constitution. I believe it is the greatest political document to come from the hand of man. I have spent a life time testifying to its importance and working to educate people as to its continued relevance. However I also believe we need to know the History of its development, ratification and the continuing saga of its effectiveness. If we don't learn from History we will be forced to learn from our own mistakes. It's always less painful to learn from the mistakes of others.

At the turn of the twentieth century Historian Charles Beard published *An Economic Interpretation of the Constitution of the United States* and set off a debate that still rages around the idea that the Constitution was a product of a conflict between competing economic interests. The argument goes like this: the Founders, who supported a strong, centralized government and favored the Constitution during its drafting and ratification, were men whose primary economic interests were marked by extensive personal property. They consisted primarily of people involved in commerce such as merchants, shippers, bankers, speculators, private and public securities holders, southern planters and all they could influence. Those who opposed the ratification of the Constitution were supporters of a decentralized government that already existed under the Articles of Confederation. These were people whose economic interests were connected to real estate. They consisted primarily of isolated, subsistence non-commercial farmers and laborers, people who were often also debtors, and the people they could influence although their leaders such as Jefferson were also men of wealth. This article fits into that debate.

Building within the above outlined framework, although James Madison is generally called the Father of the Constitution when it comes to economic concerns I believe the title should belong to Alexander Hamilton.

When the Annapolis Convention[1] which was called in September, 1786 to deal with economic concerns failed to attract enough state delegations for a quorum Hamilton requested permission[2] from the Congress of the Confederation to call another convention[3] in Philadelphia for the purpose[4] of proposing amendments to the Articles of Confederation.[5] Once they closed the doors though they had no authority,[6] the delegates from the 12 states attending wrote a new constitution. Then ignoring the provision of the Articles which required unanimous consent to alter the nature of the American government the Framers sent the Constitution out to be ratified by special ratification conventions by-passing the State legislatures.

Alexander Hamilton[7] was born in the West Indies. By the time he was 15 his father was bankrupt. At 16, he moved to New York and went to work in an accountant's office. He was a self-made man who put himself through Columbia University and personally raised artillery regiments for the Revolution. He spent most of the war as Washington's top aide. Hamilton had a desire to create a central government both politically and financially strong.

Once the Constitution was ratified and Washington elected as the first president he chose Hamilton as his Secretary of the Treasury. Hamilton hit the ground running. He soon submitted three ground-breaking reports[8] to Congress, one of which impacts the present discussion.

His Report on Public Credit[9] caused controversy because of its social and financial implications. During the Revolution the Confederation and the individual States had run up large debts to both foreign and domestic individuals. Hamilton proposed that the Federal Government assume all the war debt of the States which helped the measure gain approval in Congress. These debts had devalued in worth due to the inflation. As the debts lost their value they were bought up by speculators at a fraction of their face value. Hamilton proposed to redeem them at their original value giving tremendous profits to the speculators, many of whom were prominent in Congress and State governments. The new national government was short on cash, so Hamilton proposed to pay the war debt by issuing interest-bearing bonds, and thus the national debt was born at the dawn of the Republic. It has existed ever since. It has never been paid down to zero and it never will be.

Is the national debt constitutional? Yes, in two ways. Article VI among other things states, "All Debts contracted and Engagements entered into, before the Adoption of this Constitution, shall be as valid against the United States under this Constitution, as under the Confederation."[10] And because the 14th Amendment states, "The validity of the public debt of the United States, authorized by law, including debts incurred for payment of pensions and bounties for services in suppressing insurrection or rebellion, shall not be questioned."[11] So the Constitution both in its original form and as amended both validates the debt and takes the question of its legality off the table.

Over the hundreds of years since its inception our nation has continuously had a National Debt. Every President has faced it when they took office and every President has left it for their successor. Some have reduced it, most have increased it. At times it has contributed to our strength and stability. At first by helping to establish the credit of the United States and then by proving the trustworthiness of our government, no one ever doubted redemption. Today the National Debt[12] soars beyond the perceived ability to redeem. It races ahead at an average rate of $3.93 billion per day which is $163,750,000 dollars per hour, $2,729,166.66 per minute and, $45,486 per second.[13] We all know from our personal finances debt in and of itself isn't a bad thing. We also know unsustainable debt is. No one can afford to spend more than they make forever. Of course they have their own printing press then they can do it until no one accepts the paper anymore. Then they will do something else.

Stand by for something else.

★ DISPATCH SEVENTY-THREE ★

WHERE'S THE OUTRAGE?

I n the best line of a lackluster campaign Bob Dole challenged the voters who were swallowing the liberal line of the Corporations Once Known as the Mainstream Media "Where's the outrage?"[1] At the time they were carrying water for Bill Clinton in the 1996 election. By that time Mr. Clinton's Bimbo Eruptions[2] and complete lack of ethics had become common knowledge but the unengaged in fly-over country were lapping up the Clinton mantra "Character Doesn't Matter" and preparing to not vote in droves.[3]

Today we face a crisis that is more pertinent to the beating heart of American liberty than whether or not the President is or is not a morally challenged serial abuser of women or what "is" means.[4] Today we again face a challenge that was also presented to us by Mr. Clinton 12 years ago when he waged in an unconstitutional wag-the-dog air war against Yugoslavia that even some of his supporters speculated was more about diverting attention from his Oval Office escapades than anything else.[5]

This re-run of Clinton's war by decree prompts this writer to ask: Who has the right to commit America to war? Who has the right to send our soldiers into harm's way? Does America go to war by the act of Congress or by the whim of the Executive?

In this matter, which strikes at the heart of the American Experiment no one in Congress, except Ron Paul and Dennis Kucinich, two polar opposites from the right and the left, had the integrity to ask these questions. The media totally abdicated its watchdog role. This is a matter that should be at the forefront of the consciousness of the American people. We should have risen up and demanded an explanation. But instead, since our Congressional leaders ignored it and the media treated the only two elected officials who did speak out as if they wore aluminum hats, our fellow citizens hit the mental snooze button, and rolled over to watch a reality show so that they could ignore reality.

On March 19, 2011 President Obama's administration declared war on Libya by launching 112 Tomahawk missiles at targets within the country.[6] I say the administration declared war because the United States Congress was not consulted. Congressional leaders weren't even advised of these acts of war until 90 minutes before the bombs started falling.[7] And this was not really consultation. Rep. Mike Rogers (R-MI), the chairman of the House Permanent Select Committee on Intelligence, said "I wouldn't call it consultation as much as laying it out."[8] President Obama had spent time consulting with the U.N.[9] and the Arab League[10] but he couldn't be bothered with consulting the United States Congress? All of which brings me back to the quote from Bob Dole, "Where's the outrage?"

The Constitution in Article I, Section 8[11] ever wary of giving the executive too much power gave Congress the exclusive power to declare war. Ever since Harry Truman decided for domestic political reasons[12] to call a war in Korea that cost 54,229[13] American lives a Police Action our Presidents have followed the guns and butter policies of peace at home and war abroad. However Johnson,[14] Bush I,[15] and Bush II 16 sought and received Congressional approval before committing America to war in all but name. Before Obama only "Where is the Outrage" Clinton presumed to have the power to wage war by Executive Order.[17]

Today we are again faced with an out-of-control administration that believes it can involve America in a war on the whim of the executive instead of the act of Congress. They pointed toward the War Powers Act as a fig leaf to cover their actions. This administration is headed by a lawyer and filled with lawyers, and yet they presumably did not know that the War Powers Act specifically says, "The constitutional powers of the President as Commander-in-Chief to introduce United States Armed Forces into hostilities, or into situations where imminent involvement in hostilities is clearly indicated by the circumstances, are exercised only pursuant to (1) a declaration of war, (2) specific statutory authorization, or (3) a national emergency created by attack upon the United States, its territories or possessions, or its armed forces."[18] And it is clear that not even one of the three circumstances explicitly named by the Act applied to the situation of our attack upon Libya.

The President has said he doesn't need Congressional Approval,[19] the Corporations Once Known as the Mainstream Media repeats[20] that the President has the authority, and the Justice Department says the President has all the authority he needs for the war in Libya.[21]

However, due to President Obama's clear circumvention of Congressional approval and his egregious and erroneous appeal to the War Powers Act, I am stating categorically that his attack upon Libya is an abuse of executive power and an unconstitutional action. This is not my opinion alone. Many Americans from constitutional law experts to his own Progressive Democrats are beginning to say the same thing,[22] which brings me back to the quote from Bob Dole, "Where's the outrage?"

If this is a blatant abuse of power and an unconstitutional act leading to war I also say this rises to the level of an impeachable offense. In this I find myself standing for the first time with the most liberal Democrats.[23] And in another departure from tradition I am also in agreement with Vice President Joe Biden when he once said, "Launching an attack without congressional approval is an impeachable offense."[24] No matter what the administration says, no matter what the media says, we the people need to hold those who would violate the constitutional limitations of our government to account or they will continue to transgress the limits and do whatever they want.

In another quote that seems as relevant today as it was 15 years ago Senator Dole asked, "When do the American people rise up and say, 'Forget the media in America! We're going to make up our minds! You're not going to make up our minds!' This is about saving our country!"[25]

★ DISPATCH SEVENTY-FOUR ★

Which Words Work

What words mean is important. The ability to speak, to transfer complex and symbolic knowledge from one person to another is one of the hallmarks of humanity. When words lose their meaning communication loses its ability to transmit thoughts. Obviously words can change their meanings over time. One example is the word prevent. This word now means to stop something from happening. Hundreds of years ago it meant for one thing to happen before another: pre-event.

This is natural and is the organic outgrowth of how people speak. All languages change over time. What isn't natural is when, for ideological reasons, groups work to change the meanings of words to either confuse the discussion or to attract support from people who normally would not lend them their support.

Leaving aside the natural organic change of meanings and looking instead at the contrived control of meaning for political purposes we recognize the need to establish precise meanings to convey precise thoughts.

A perfect example is how the words liberty and democracy have become intertwined and confounded. Knowing that equality before the law is a necessary bridge on the road to liberty advocates of liberty rightfully believe that all citizens should have a share in making the law. This is where the advocates of liberty and the proponents of the democracy movement share a preference for a means while they do not necessarily share a preference for the ends.

The advocates of liberty standing on the foundation of the enlightenment thinking of the 18th century and the classical liberal traditions of the 19th see democracy as a means for limiting the coercive power of government no matter what form that government may take. Conversely to the dogmatic democrat the only legitimate limit on government power is the current majority opinion.

The difference between these two positions is starkly revealed if we understand what each side sees as the opposite of their idea. To the dogmatic democrat it is authoritarianism and to the classical liberal it is totalitarianism. Neither of these two opposites excludes the other. It is possible for a democracy to use totalitarian methods, and an authoritarian government might implement the principles of liberty.

Both of these terms democracy and liberty are used in vague and wide references by those who seek to lead our people. Their precise meanings have been blurred by this usage to the point where many people confound them and believe if they can vote they have liberty. However if we can return the meaning to these words we will find that it is possible to separate the two and find clarity.

The doctrine of liberty deals with what laws ought to be. The doctrine of democracy deals with the manner of determining what will be the law.

The advocates of liberty agree that it is best if only what the majority accepts should be law however they do not agree that all majority-driven law is always good law. They seek to persuade the majority that the principles of liberty should be the hallmark of all laws. They accept that majority rule is the fairest method of deciding what the laws are. They do not agree that this gives the majority the unlimited authority to decide what the laws ought to be.

The doctrinaire democrat holds that majority opinion not only decides what the law should be and that this majority opinion is also the measure of what is good law.

Therefore when we confound the concept of liberty with the use of democratic action it is natural to accept that everything democratically decided upon is an advance for liberty. One has only to look at the fact that the German people voted to give Hitler dictatorial powers to see that this is an illusion.

For while the principles of liberty are one of the paths which may be chosen through democratic action the use of democratic action does not preclude other choices and it says nothing about what is the proper role of government. While the spread of democracy, especially the idea of one-man-one-vote, has advanced the cause of liberty in many nations there is nothing that demands it do so. In America today many popular policies are advanced on the merit that they are the democratic desire of a majority. This does not necessarily mean that they will advance the cause of liberty. To require a citizen to purchase certain products such as healthcare and to use the coercive power of the state to enforce it may have passed as part of a democratic procedure; however, this does not advance the cause of liberty.

Giving someone the power to vote does not magically give them the knowledge or the information as to how to vote. When the franchise is extended to more and more low-information voters this may advance the cause of democracy; however, it does not advance the cause of liberty. Low-information voters are easily manipulated by demagogues who exploit the desires of the day to build their own kingdoms and enhance their own power without regard to our constitutional limits.

We have a growing mass of low-information voters, a progressive government who makes it their business to shape the majority opinion, and a media that is dedicated to the government party. This is the prescription for a totalitarian democracy. The constraining hand of the constitution and tradition has fallen away and the manipulated voice of the majority calls for more entitlements, more regulation, more government to solve the problems caused by entitlements, regulations and government.

We have come full circle. In our revolution the advocates of liberty rose up against an autocrat to demand freedom. They then used that freedom to craft a government limited in power so that people could live their lives and build their fortunes without oppression. Today we have elected leaders who have progressed past these limits. Leaders who seek to control every aspect of life. We may have reached the dreams of the democratic fathers however these dreams are turning into the nightmares of our Founders: advocates of liberty one and all.

★ DISPATCH SEVENTY-FIVE ★

WHO NEEDS ROBIN HOOD?

"It's time to level the playing field."[1] "The rich need to pay their fair share."[2] "We have to end tax breaks for millionaires and billionaires."[3] These are some of the stock phrases used by President Obama and his administration to fire up their troops to picket private homes, gin up mobs to protest success and to channel America towards the future they envision. Like a one trick pony or an extremely inept coach the Progressives' playbook has only one option. It's a Hail Mary pass they run over and over: class warfare. From Marx to Chavez the collectivists have always played the same card from each according to the ability to each according to their need.[4]

Over a century of propaganda and indoctrination has conditioned most Americans to accept one of the most insidious aspects of class warfare as a natural and respectable feature of our government: progressive taxation. At its core progressive taxation is the quintessential action of the Trojan horse the Progressives have constructed to transform America from a representative republic with a capitalist economy into a centrally planned socialist democratic republic.[5]

The shock troops for this movement which has captured the leadership of both major parties is made up of the Corporations Once Known as the Mainstream Media, unions, crony capitalists, and a conglomeration of front groups and organizations, many of which receive[6] vast[7] amounts of government money. These interest groups constantly agitate for Progressive policies and carry the water for Progressive politicians. They also contribute time, money and resources for the election campaigns of the very Progressive politicians who vote to give them government grants in a circular money laundering scheme which if not illegal is certainly immoral.

Who are these Progressives in America today? They're the most vocal proponents of the manmade global warming hoax. They serve as willing acolytes for their Nobel Prize winning high priest. After failing to pass their much desired Cap-N-Trade they are regulating it into existence through the Environmental Protection Agency.[8]

They are also the same ones who after leading the charge against integration, standing in the school house door and attacking peaceful demonstrators with everything from fire hoses to clubs they support every media starved Civil Rights professional who will rant and rave on cue to keep America's deepest wound festering.

They use Political Correctness to monitor and manage the discussion. Political Correctness is the Progressives' version of New Speak and the coin of their realm. Many of these verbal add-ons are merely variations and expressions on the over-riding theme of take from the evil rich to help the deserving poor, with a good dose of "We've got to do it for the children" thrown in for good measure. Political Correctness is strangling free speech and pushing many into a cone of silence wherein they no longer have the liberty to express their opinions without retaliation on the job or in school.

People who wish to take from the rich and give to the poor never create wealth themselves. They always want to take from one and give to another so they can drain off a living in between exulting in the power to decide who deserves the blessings of their charity. And they always seem to get more than anyone else.

The massive frauds and waste of the Federal Government shows where this is headed. As they swallow more of the economy their ineptitude seems to grow in direct proportion to the size of the swag. Take for instance the stimulus slush-fund of 2009. Billed as a way to create jobs this bill spent $278,000 for every job created.[9] In terms of the national debt President Obama is spreading the wealth[10] around at an astounding rate of 3.94 billion dollars per day in deficit spending alone.[11] He has gone beyond taxing the rich and is now taxing the unborn.

Looking back at the battle cry of "Tax the rich" that symbolizes the inequity it is the Progressive tax system which some often confuse this with the story of Robin Hood. They say he stole from the rich to give to the poor. They point to Robin and say that is all they want to do, take some of the excess wealth held by the rich and distribute it to the unfortunate.

Unfortunately for them such a translation of the Robin Hood myth turns the story on its head. After returning from a war of choice initiated by an absentee king in the Middle-East Robin learned that his estate had been taxed away. Finding this level of abuse intolerable he became an outlaw stealing the ill-gotten loot government agents were extorting from the people in the form of taxes and then returned the money to those who had actually earned it.

Wait a minute maybe we do need Robin Hood today!

★ DISPATCH SEVENTY-SIX ★

WHO VOTES FOR DEMOCRACY?

D emocracy! Democracy! Democracy! This is the mantra that we hear from Tahrir Square[1] to Yemen[2] from Belarus[3] to Wall Street[4] protestors who are on the march around the world demanding Democracy!

Democracy has long been the cover for all manner of despotic totalitarian regimes creating hellholes for their own people and nightmares for the rest of us. One needs only to recall that even though the popular myth of Hitler being elected is demonstrably false, he lost[5] the only election he ever ran in which he ever ran. Though unelected he was however appointed Chancellor in 1933 after his Nazi Party became the largest single party through democratic elections.[6] His ghoulish regime achieved total power when 90% of the German people voted[7] to make Hitler the Führer or undisputed dictator of their nation. And who can forget the many Democratic People's Republics that have graced the world with their despotic presence, East Germany, Cuba, Laos, Vietnam and North Korea. The cover of democracy and the votes of the people have been used to legitimize the most insidious forms of human depravity.

It is popular among conservatives to decry the nation-wide and world-wide demand for democracy as if it were something new under the Sun. It is also popular to point out that the United States of America was founded as a representative Republic not as a Democracy. The representative nature of the Republic was enshrined in both the Articles of Confederation and the Constitution. The difference is proudly pointed out that we are a representative republic which operates on democratic principles NOT a democracy.

It is not quite as popular to point out that though our representative Republic has always operated on democratic principles in the beginning that democracy did not spread out very far. The franchise was restricted only to males of the Caucasian persuasion who owned a certain amount of property. The dirty little secret teachers of American History survey classes fought for years to keep from their impressionable students was that even though Wilson led America into fighting WWI to make the world safe for democracy[8] and FDR led us into WWII as the Arsenal of Democracy[9] the Founders of our country went to great lengths to protect our Republic from the perils of democracy.

Examples of the Founders distaste for democracy are easy to find:

James Madison said, "Democracies have ever been spectacles of turbulence and contention; have ever been found incompatible with personal security, or the rights of property; and have, in general, been as short in their lives as they have been violent in their deaths."[10]

John Adams said, "Remember, democracy never lasts long. It soon wastes, exhausts, and murders itself. There never was a democracy yet that did not commit suicide"[11] and, "The experience of all former ages had shown that of all human governments, democracy was the most unstable, fluctuating and short-lived."[12]

Alexander Hamilton said, "It has been observed that a pure democracy if it were practicable would be the most perfect government. Experience has proved that no position is more false than this. The ancient democracies in which the people themselves deliberated never possessed one good feature of government. Their very character was tyranny; their figure deformity."[13]

The circle of American democracy was at first drawn closely around the ruling circle of intellectuals, lawyers and men of property because they feared the tyranny of those unable or unwilling to learn the rudiments of

History, Economics or Governance. However, as time passed spurred on by a combination of their desire to participate and the cajoling of those who wanted to rule them people began to agitate for an extension of the franchise and for one reason or another the circle began to expand until by the 1830s throughout the United States most Caucasian males could vote. By comparison in Britain at the same time less than 10% could vote.

The watchword in America became democracy, not in the speeches of the first Progressives in the 1890s but in the voices of their great grandfathers in the second generation after our Revolution. Within a generation leadership passed from Washington, Jefferson, Madison and other statesmen with grand visions of liberty and freedom to partisan leaders of political factions. The stirring and deeply reflective tone of the Federalist and Anti-Federalist Papers was replaced by clever slogans designed to move the masses and win votes.

Alexis de Tocqueville is often quoted to show the high state of American involvement and participation in the democratic process. He is less often quoted in his assessment of that process, "The most able men in the United States are very rarely place at the head of affairs."[14] He pointed to the character of a democracy where people ignored important issues, disdained intellectuals who were informed of these issues and instead were moved by "the clamor of a mountebank [a demagogue] who knows the secret of stimulating their tastes."[15]

In the recent past President Bush in 2005 during his second inaugural speech declared the doctrine that bears his name by saying, "It is the policy of the United States to seek and support the growth of democratic movements and institutions in every nation and culture, with the ultimate goal of ending tyranny in our world."[16] Since that time democratic elections have brought us Hamas as the elected representatives of the Palestinian People,[17] Islamists have won[18] the first post-Arab Spring election in Tunisia and who can forget that Hugo Chavez has won multiple elections in Venezuela. There is also our new partner in our latest military adventure Yoweri Museveni Uganda's President-for-Life who was democratically elected[19] as was his more famous predecessor Idi Amin Dada.[20]

The democratic revolution which began in America a generation after the establishment of our representative Republic has grown through the roughshod years of Jackson, the tax, tax, tax, spend, spend, spend, elect, elect, elect days of FDR and has morphed into the Occupy Everywhere Movement that polluted our cities and clamored for the predictable goal of pure democracy, "From each according to their ability to each according to their need."[21]

We are witnessing the tyranny not of the majority but instead of the majority of voters coming to fruition. In America in a typical election only 50% or less of eligible voters bothers to cast their ballot.[22] Many congressional districts are gerrymandered into personal possessions, local counties, cities and states belong to good-old-boy networks and the Senate is the province of millionaire media stars. The uninformed elect the unqualified to give them what is unearned.

Or as Alexander Fraser Tyler said, "A democracy cannot exist as a permanent form of government. It can only exist until the voters discover that they can vote themselves largesse from the public treasury. From that moment on, the majority always votes for the candidates promising the most benefits from the public treasury with the result that a democracy always collapses over loose fiscal policy, always followed by a dictatorship. The average age of the world's greatest civilizations has been 200 years."[23]

Mr. Tyler also sagely added, "These nations have progressed in this sequence: From bondage to spiritual faith; from faith to great courage;

from courage to liberty; from liberty to abundance; from abundance to selfishness; from selfishness to complacency; from complacency to apathy; from apathy to dependency; from dependency back again to bondage."[24]

The democratic revolution begun in America 200 years ago has circled the globe. The leaders of the Egyptian revolutionaries have come to New York to join the protesters at Zuccotti Park to chant, the mantra, "Democracy Now!" Looking at the paradise on earth replicated from New York to Oakland in these demonstrations supported by the unions,[25] Democrats[26] and the President[27] I only have one question, "Who will vote for that?"

★ DISPATCH SEVENTY-SEVEN ★

WHO WILL WIN THE WAR AGAINST INCOME INEQUALITY?

From each according to their ability to each according to their need was the hollow promise of the Soviet Union. It was long known to be merely the cover for a ruthless Communist Party that pretended to build a worker's paradise while in fact enslaving a nation for its own gain.

Today this infamous lie has been resurrected in America as the war against income inequality.

The war on poverty has failed. After decades of propaganda, trillions of dollars, and tens of thousands of regulations there is no less poverty in America than when LBJ sounded the charge of the contrite brigade. Of course it was a shell game all along. The idea that you could take money out of one pocket and put it in another while dropping some along the way aptly describes the effort to tax the rich to alleviate poverty. If all the money that has been expropriated to end poverty had been given directly to the poor we would have ended poverty.

However this isn't what happened. It was never what was intended to happen. It will never happen because instead of a direct wealth transfer the loot is filtered through politicians, programs and bureaucrats who all siphon off enough to make sure the pennies that eventually dribble out of the welfare pipeline have little resemblance to the dollars that went in. They certainly don't want to actually eliminate the poor since their campaign slogans and their jobs would evaporate with them.

Anyone who has ever stood hat-in-hand at a welfare office knows the scorn dished out with the meager fare always makes the meal a little less satisfying than imagined. Jesus told us that "The poor will always be with you."[1] Yet somehow the political savants who hold sway are always able to convince the low-information voters that they will end poverty, or as we call it today, income inequality.

The only equality that is compatible with freedom is equality before the law. By this I mean that whenever society, as expressed through government, makes rules they should apply to everyone the same. In other words, if a millionaire commits murder and a homeless person commits murder they should both stand before the same tribunal charged with the same crime. Or if a tax is passed everyone should pay the same percentage. We know that in the first case the difference between a dream team of lawyers and a public defender may mitigate the equality just as in the second case a progressive tax system will distort it. However, this goal of equality before the law is the only one where actual equality is what is required to make it work.

All other types of equality, of income or opportunity or outcome require inequality. If this sounds like circular thinking don't be surprised; it is.

Since people are obviously not equal in talents, abilities, resources, or nature the only way to make everyone start in the same place and end up in the same place is to treat them differently. Some must be slowed down and some must be artificially pushed forward. Some must get less than they earn so that some can get more. This is the dirty little secret hidden behind the campaign slogan to end income inequality. In reality it is just another way to describe income redistribution or as our president calls it, "Spread the wealth around."[2]

Those who make their living selling these illusions are supported by those who make their livings distributing the loot and by all those who think they will get something for nothing. Unfortunately after generations of Progressive education, incremental socialism, and the sloth that is the bread by the bread and circus culture of the couch potato this may now be a majority of the votes counted.

Having sunk beneath the contempt of the Russian people and drown in the red capitalism of the Chinese, it seems as if the infection of class envy co-joined to state power has emerged from the faculty lounge and fastened its death grip on America. In the 2012 election the campaign slogan, "GM is alive and Bin Laden is dead"[3] trumped a devastated economy to re-elect the inspiration of the IRS and the excuser of Benghazi. If the war against income inequality proves the media-enhanced key to return Nancy Pelosi to the Speakership and retain Harry Reid as the agenda setting leader of the Senate, the Progressives will know they have two years to seal the deal.

We will still call it the United States of America. We will still tell ourselves we are free, prosperous, and powerful; however, we may all be whistling in the wind. Our politicians may win their war to end income inequality as they seek an American version of a worker's paradise. The comatose voters may even notice that things aren't quite like they used to be, but then half-time will be over and that will be that.

Look at the results of the 2012 election. GM is moving overseas after ripping off the American tax payers. Al-Qaeda is marching to victory. Think about the pledge that gained passage for Obamacare, "If you like your plan you can keep your plan. Period." Reflect on this swindle and ask yourself how equal will anything be if we swallow the next big lie: ending income inequality. Ask yourself who will win the war against income inequality. The answer is those who distribute the loot will keep the lion's share.

As an added bonus this war against income inequality as a campaign tool to fool the masses is leading us further into the unconstitutional waters our president has sailed for so long.[4] Brazenly saying, "We're not just going to be waiting for legislation in order to make sure that we're providing Americans the kind of help they need. I've got a pen and I've got a phone."[5]

The question here is, "Will anyone in the House have the courage to do something about it?"

★ DISPATCH SEVENTY-EIGHT ★

WHOSE RESPONSIBILITY IS IT?

God makes all of us to be round pegs in round holes. In a free society if we end up a round peg in a square hole…that's on us.

There is no feeling worse than believing we have squandered our talents, wasted our life, and made no difference in our short time upon the world stage. If we live in a society that chooses what, where, and how we do things it is easy to feel as if the opportunity to become who we were created to be was stolen. However, in a free society where we can choose for ourselves the responsibility for those choices as well as the freedom belongs to us.

Freedom does not merely mean that each individual bears the responsibility and the burden of choosing their path. In a free society it also means that each individual will also receive either the praise or the blame that results from those choices. Freedom and responsibility cannot be separated if either is to have a realistic bearing upon the individual. If you cannot choose you are not responsible. If you can you are. A society cannot call itself free unless individuals ultimately occupy the positions and bear the consequences resulting from their own actions. For that society to remain stable the individuals need to recognize that their positions and the concurrent consequences are the result of their own choices and actions.

A free society can only offer the opportunity to choose, and in a society of free agents this can only provide the chance for success. The outcome always depends on the accidental interactions between circumstances and others. Someone who has taken their destiny into their own hands while cognoscente of what they cannot control will concentrate their attention on what they can as if these are the only aspects of the endeavor which matter. Circumstances and chance will either be advantageous or limiting. Only the individual will know whether they have made the most advantageous use of either their talents or their circumstances; therefore, the responsibility for their actions resides with them.

In America today the knowledge of and the belief in this link between freedom and responsibility has become as rare as the honest man Diogenes spent a life time looking for. Today victimhood has been raised to an art form. It is inspired and rewarded by a complex system of laws and social conventions that offers praise for the helpless pawn and reviles the individual who succeeds. Driven by the apathy and antagonism it elicits from those who accept the arguments that "You can't fight city hall" and "It wasn't my fault" even the word responsibility disappears from the vocabulary of motivation from the pulpit to the hustings.

The I'm OK you're OK culture that accepts infanticide, suicide, and much else of what was once known as vice as not only morally acceptable but as civil rights flees from moralizing. This throw-away culture elects people of the lowest morals and of the most glaring narcissism: media rock stars who rule instead of lead and who trample upon the freedoms our forefathers fought and died for. This is not only accepted it is voted for since if our leaders are morally bankrupt it is all right for us to do whatever feels good. If our leaders are attempting to weld the shackles of a totalitarian gulag in every sphere of life, we truly are deprived of choice and are mere victims.

If you attempt to tell people that they are responsible for their choices and their conditions, it will often provoke outright hostility. These people have been taught that society has made them what they are. It has determined their position in life and it is nothing but external circumstances that decide whether they succeed or fail. They have rejected all responsibility because they fear it and in consequence they have rejected freedom.

In a large part this is a development that is not purely either religious or political in nature. The rise of science and of the attempt to apply it to our understanding of humanity leads to several conclusions which are incompatible with freedom.

The first of these misapplied axioms is that everything is governed by iron-clad laws. While this may apply to thermodynamics, it does not relate in the same fashion to free agents in a free society. Thoughts are infinite and new thoughts can always inspire new choices. The second axiom erroneously used to understand human action is the idea of universal determinism. The idea that all things are the inevitable consequence of prior action directed by inherently immutable outside forces precludes spontaneity and freedom of choice. In such a system human will becomes an illusion and reality a maze with always only one way out.

Of course based on reality as experienced by everyone it has to be admitted that except on rare occasions the outcomes of human action could not be predicted and the results of particular circumstances interacting with particular individuals could not be foreseen. However, from genetics to economics from sociology to politics the belief that everything is determined by laws eliminates the space for a belief in freedom of the will and the responsibility which its operation engenders.

Those who accept the determinist position assert that it is genetics shaped by education tempered by society that constructs and controls all of us. We are all the product of both nature and nurture and we exist within a grid designed, created, and controlled by society. Whatever we are and whatever we become it isn't our fault and it isn't our choice or our effort. This position was summed up brilliantly in the statement, "You didn't build that." If you accomplished something you didn't do it on your own just as if you fail it isn't because of you, you're merely a victim and as such society owes you support.

Divorced from morality and excluded from personal experience by education and an ever more regimented society, responsibility has become a legal concept. There are intricate webs of laws used to determine liability in the case of negatives while the "You didn't build that" mentality erodes the concept of responsibility for success. Once the link between choice and responsibility has been severed one of the major motivators for excellence has been silenced. For the greatest significance of this fundamental concept is that a feeling of responsibility for one's own choices is its role in guiding the decisions and actions for free people.

If nothing is ever your fault, if nothing is ever your achievement what does it matter what you choose or what you do? If we are to be free we must bear the responsibility of that freedom or else we will search our whole life to learn whose responsibility is it.

★ DISPATCH SEVENTY-NINE ★

WHY CAN'T WE CHANGE?

Paths with no obstacles usually lead nowhere. Among those who hallow the Constitution you will find no more loyal devotee to this document that helped continue the limited government established under the Article of Confederation. There is no one who believes more passionately than the author of this article that the Constitution provided the space for the individual freedom, personal liberty, and economic opportunity needed to foster the growth of the greatest nation this world has ever seen

However, it is only necessary to read *The Gilded Age* by Mark Twain to see how corruption and greed, crony capitalism, and lobbyists have been building their own kingdoms since before any of us were born. And just as it doesn't take a weather man to know which way the wind blows it doesn't take a constitutional scholar to know at this time and in this place the Constitution has failed.[1]

Look at the path America is on. Do you think our current leaders or our current policies will lead to a renewing of America or to its slide into the second tier of nations? Think about the directions laid out for us.

We are told by the Progressives who lead us that perpetual continuation of unemployment payments for the long-term unemployed is good for the economy and good for jobs.

If unemployment creates jobs and is good for the economy why don't we just give it to everyone who doesn't have a job in perpetuity, and make it a thousand dollars a week for good measure?

Increase the minimum wage to $10.10. This will create jobs and help the economy. Our leaders say there are just too many people laboring for the current starvation wage of $7.25.[2] While according to CNN Money, "An estimated 3.6 million people were paid hourly rates at or below the federal minimum in 2012, down from 3.8 million a year earlier. Just under 60% of all U.S. workers are paid hourly, according to the U.S. Bureau of Labor Statistics. An estimated 4.7% of those hourly workers make minimum wage or less, down from 5.2%, a year earlier. That share is the lowest since 2008."[3] That's quite a few people: 3.6 million, and obviously worthy of notice.

However, when 16 million people[4] had their healthcare plans cancelled due to Obamacare we were told this was an insignificant number.[5] As with everything connected to Obamacare, the numbers of those who have lost insurance coverage as a result are sketchy. Some sources say more than 4.2 million Americans have now seen their health insurance policies canceled due to the new regulations.[6] The President's spokesman said that 14 million losing their healthcare is just a "small sliver" of the population.[7]

We must increase food stamps. This is the only humane thing to do since so many go to sleep hungry at night, and besides it will create jobs and it's good for the economy.

If food stamps spur economic growth why not just give them to everyone and on a handy plastic card that works at marijuana stores and casinos.

We must have comprehensive immigration reform, the code words for amnesty because it will create jobs and it's good for the economy, besides the illegals have earned the right to be citizens.[8] This comes not from some general in La Raza it comes from our own Secretary of Homeland Security. If illegal immigrants have earned the right to be citizens why don't we just dispense with borders and give citizenship to every undocumented democrat who can walk across the line.

Look at these continuing soap operas we find as our national policy. These are transparent wealth transfers, give aways, and oxymoronic programs building bridges to nowhere. All passed by the gerrymandered representatives of K Street that make up the perpetually re-elected representatives of our nation and lame excuses for leadership proposed by empty suits who have occupied the White House since Reagan went home to California.

What's a patriot to do? There is a remedy in the Constitution for the failure of the Constitution. It is found in Article V which describes the amendment process[9] which provides two ways to amend the Constitution: either Congress initiates an amendment or the States can call for a Constitutional Convention to consider amendments. The first method has resulted in 27 amendments[10] the second method has never been used.

Many people fear a Constitutional Convention. Many believe that it would open a can of worms and lead to the destruction of our limited government. Our limited government has already been co-opted by the Progressives and turned into a Leviathan which is quickly devouring every limit and every freedom in its path.

What we have is not working, and it hasn't worked for quite some time. I believe that Article V at least provides a method to attempt to return to limited government peacefully. Let's give peace a chance. I believe that the principles of liberty can win in the marketplace of ideas. Let us engage in a debate to save our present and the future of our children. To continue the way we are going leads to a democratic totalitarianism of the majority.

If we could find the faith and the courage to call a Constitutional Convention for what should we advocate?

I propose we do as our ancestors, the Framers of our Constitution, did when they were called upon to propose amendments to the Articles of Confederation. I propose we write a completely new document. Where do I get the chutzpa, the hubris to call for such an outcome?

By remembering why governments exist at all, "That to secure these rights, governments are instituted among men, deriving their just powers from the consent of the governed."[11] And never forgetting "That whenever any form of government becomes destructive of these ends, it is the right of the people to alter or abolish it, and to institute new government, laying its foundation on such principles and organizing its powers in such form, as to them shall seem most likely to effect (sic) their safety and happiness."[12]

Our system is broken and all the king's horses and all the king's men can't put it back together again. If we stay within the bounds of what has been done in the past what are we to do? Propose a Balanced Budget Amendment or a Spending Restriction Amendment? Or perhaps an amendment that says, "The Constitution means what it says not what judges interpret it to say" and then stand back while the Supreme Court interprets that.

If we continue to play the same game by the same rules, we will lose the same hand because the deck is stacked. This is when we need to remember: paths with no obstacles usually lead nowhere.

Let us be as bold and brave as our forefathers. Let us propose fundamental change and roll the dice. If you don't swing the bat then you don't have a chance to hit the ball. If we continue on the road we are traveling the only thing left to say is an attempt to explain how and why we let freedom slip from our grasp.

I believe that no one is as smart as everyone, so the ideas I am proposing I do not see as the beginning and end of debate. I see them instead as a starting point. Let's join together, demand a hearing, and move forward in an attempt to reinstate limited government and preserve this last best hope of mankind.

First of all I stand for retaining the amendments with the exception of the 16th and 17th and enshrining them within the original document.

I propose eliminating the office of President and changing to a parliamentary style government that is based upon the majority in the House electing a Prime Minister who is head of government and head of State. Elections for the House should continue on a two-year basis.

I propose that we keep the Senate but that it reverts to its original intent as the representatives of the States and those Senators are once again elected by the legislatures of the States and serve at their pleasure.

I propose stronger guarantees for the States in a renewed Federalism: a true confederation similar to that of Switzerland.

I propose that since the scope of Federal jurisdiction will be severely restricted, the Federal Court System along with its power of judicial review be abolished. The State court systems are well able to handle the civil and criminal cases brought within their boundaries.

I propose that the Supreme Court be abolished and replaced by a Constitutional Court similar to Germany's. This court would be physically removed from the capital, and it shall have no jurisdiction beyond Judicial Review having the power to declare laws and actions of the Federal Government unconstitutional. The Congress shall have the power to override these rulings by a three-quarter majority in both houses. Judges shall serve four-year terms with only two terms allowed.

I know that these proposals will make some people very upset. I know these proposals will make some quit reading this History of the Future. I also know that if we do not do something to break the log jam the river will not flow free.

Yes, there are what seem to be insurmountable obstacles to change. I know these obstacles are daunting, and they will not be overcome by the timid. However, paths with no obstacles usually lead nowhere, and if what we have is no longer working, why can't we change.

Keep the Faith. Keep the peace. We shall overcome.

DISPATCH EIGHTY ★

★

WHY CENTRAL PLANNING WON'T WORK

Failure to plan is planning to fail. This truism has been a guiding light in my life and in the lives of countless others. Without planning we would never accomplish much in life. The haphazard serendipity of chance rarely adds up to a consistently positive result. We all know people who seem like they can fall into a sewer and come up smelling like roses. Most of us come up smelling like something quite different if we take the same fall.

On an individual basis planning is absolutely critical. For society some things also need planning such as coining money, defending the nation, and delivering the mail. All of these require planning and for all of these things it is possible to plan realistically and effectively.

There is no argument between the citizen supporters of constitutionally limited government and our perpetually re-elected Progressive collectivists and the fellow-travelers who support them about this. Some planning is both necessary and good. However, this is where we part company. Those who believe in a constitutionally limited government do not believe that it is possible or advisable to try to run an economy and a society through central planning.

The very attempt to use central planning short circuits the myriad of personal decisions which make up the routine functions of a free economy and that is the bedrock of a free society. Every group that advocates central planning, no matter what they call themselves are Utopians who believe that they can do a better job making decisions for everyone than everyone can make for themselves. That is the essence of the nanny-state: government knows better and must protect us from our own bad choices.

There is one common feature that is clearly a part of all the various collectivist systems no matter what they call themselves. They all call for the deliberate organization of society to accomplish identifiable social goals. That a free society lacks this focus and its activities are guided by the personal whims and feelings of individuals all seeking their own good is always the complaint of the Utopians.

This brings the basic difference between the collectivists and the advocates of personal liberty into stark relief. The different types of collectivists: Socialists, Communists, Fascists, and Progressives may differ as to the specific societal goals towards which they want to drive their populations, and they may differ in their methods depending upon the amount of control they exert over the choices of others. However, much they differ from each other; they all uniformly differ from the advocates of individual freedom in that they wish to regiment all of society and all its resources to achieve whichever set of goals their particular brand of collectivism sees as the pathway to Nirvana.

Whatever the social goal is whether it's called the great leap forward, a worker's paradise, a classless society, the common good, the general welfare, or the Great Society it doesn't take much reflection to see that these terms are so vague it's impossible to determine their exact meaning so that any specific course of action could be decided upon. It's like a war on terror, or drugs, or obesity how are you supposed to know when the goal has been reached or victory achieved?

The welfare and happiness of people cannot be measured on a scale of more or less. There are too many variables. There are too many possible combinations of circumstances that can become either negatives or positives depending upon another set of widely diverse situations. The "good" of any society cannot be expressed as simply or succinctly as the collectivists pretend. It is just too complex.

To direct all of society's energy and resource by one plan assumes that every need and desire is given a rank in order of importance and a place in order of time. It also assumes that an absolute lineal order of occurrences must proceed from every action. If this happens that will automatically occur. Besides asserting through action that it is possible to order all things as one desires it also inherently expresses the idea that there is one universal set of ethics by which good and bad are obviously seen by the planners. All of these assumptions, assertions, and expressions are not only false they are obviously false. No one is as smart as everyone.

The very idea of having a universally accepted and complete code of ethics is beyond the scope of human experience. People are constantly choosing between different values as they go through their daily life. What is best today in this situation may not be best tomorrow in that situation. However, when all of society and all of its resources are to be harnessed and driven in one direction toward a preselected set of goals such a universal and complete set of ethics are not only a necessity they are a prerequisite for success. Since this is unattainable success is also unattainable. If this sounds harsh please view the tattered hulks and broken lives which litter the history of all Utopian collectivist societies.

Only God can plan the end from the beginning. Only God has an ultimate and a true ethical code that is universally applicable to all people in all situations. Only God has a right to order events to suit Hi purposes. He created all things, and all things exist because He holds them up. All things are His, and He has the ability and the right to do with them as he pleases.

The problem we face is that collectivism puts the state in the place of God. Collectivists believe that government, through its bureaucracy, can make decisions and take action that could only work if designed and carried out with the aid of omniscience and omnipotence neither of which qualities have ever or will ever belong to government.

A scientist once said to God, "You're not so much. We have learned how to make life in our laboratories."

God answered, "Is that so."

The scientist proudly said, "Yes it is and I am willing to have a contest with you right now to see who can make life faster and better."

"All right," God said, "let's go." With that God stooped down and picked up some dirt and started molding it into a man as the scientist grabbed his test tubes and started pouring liquids from one to another.

Just as God was about to blow the breath of life into His creation, he looked at the scientist and said, "Hey! Get your own dirt."

There is one thing I have learned in this life: God is God and I am not and neither is anyone or anything else. Sounds like a pretty basic lesson; however, it took me about half of my life to learn. If we could only get those entrusted with our government to learn the same thing, maybe we would stop our slow slide into that long dark night.

★ DISPATCH EIGHTY-ONE ★

Why Did We Write It in the First Place?

Besides regulating the division of authority, constitutions written to limit government must contain substantive rules. They need to establish general principles which will govern the specific acts of the legislature. Therefore, the essence of a constitution involves not only a hierarchy of power and authority but it also establishes a hierarchy of laws. The founding principles built into the structure of the document itself are of a general nature. They proceed from a higher authority designed to control the content of the later specific laws which are enacted by the representative and delegated legislature elected subsequent to the establishment of the constitutionally limited government.

The idea of a higher law which governs legislation is an old one. In the 1700s, at the time of the writing of our Constitution, it was known as the Law of Nature, the Law of God, or the Law of Reason. It was the idea of enshrining this higher law into a written constitution which would be the foundation for a real world government that was the genius of the Framers.

The difference between the Constitution and any subsequent law enacted by the government it founded is like the difference between laws in general and their specific application by the courts in a particular case. Just as a judicial ruling is considered sound, only if it is based upon the law and not on the mere opinion of the jurist, so too laws themselves are considered legitimate only if they conform to the higher law. In the same way that we want to prevent a judge from breaking from the law for some consideration of a specific person or idea, so too we do not want the legislature to break the general rules to fulfill any immediate or temporary goals.

In the personal lives we all lead we know that often we are tempted to sacrifice long-standing principles for immediate gain. This is a human trait that all share and only the highly disciplined avoid. So too legislatures, made up of fallible men, are therefore in desperate need of unbreakable higher laws that will constrain them from doing collectively what we all do individually.

Just as an individual will hesitate or at least contemplate the implications of violating a long-held principle for an immediate gain, so too a legitimate and responsible legislature will be reluctant to break established general laws for new specific aims. To violate a particular principle at a particular time for a specific purpose is different than saying that principle is null and void.

Passing laws that either benefit or penalize specific people or making legislation retroactive is different than saying that to do so is correct. If a legislature passes laws that infringe upon the personal liberty or the property rights of individuals during a war or to achieve some monumental national goal is far different than stating that such rights can be infringed with impunity. It is to mark these differences that every piece of legislation is supposed to have a clause that identifies where the authority for it is found in the Constitution.

It is also for this purpose that general principles should not be promulgated by the legislature but instead by another body. It is appropriate that this other body should have a suitable time to deliberate so that any establishment or change in the general principles can be fully debated, considered, and amended if necessary.

It is not that a Constitution provides an absolute limit on the will of the people. Looking to our Constitution, which is the model for all such documents which are truly meant to limit the power of government, there is the amendment process which has been used 27 times to change the higher laws of our general principles. Constitutions are meant to act as a check on the ability of a temporary majority from imposing its will in any manner it chooses. In other words, the social contract agreed to by the people who allow the governance of temporary and shifting majorities in particular situations is based upon the belief that every majority implicitly agrees to abide by the general principles which embody the higher law.

Consequently, no one and no group has complete freedom to impose upon the rest of society any laws or any regulations that it wants. The very essence of constitutionalism rests upon the foundational belief that all power and authority will be exercised within the framework of the general principles and higher law that the constitution creates. People are chosen to assume power to legislate, govern, or adjudicate because it is believed they will do what is right. Not because it is believed that whatever they do is right. Legitimate authority in a constitutional system rests on the belief that power is not a physical fact but a decision on the part of the people to willingly obey.

Looking at the current situation in America today we have a President who in a 2001 interview expressed his innermost thoughts about the Constitution. He stated:

> "If you look at the victories and failures of the civil rights movement and its litigation strategy in the court I think where it succeeded was to invest formal rights in previously dispossessed people, so that now I would have the right to vote. I would now be able to sit at the lunch counter and order as long as I could pay for it I'd be o.k. But, the Supreme Court never ventured into the issues of redistribution of wealth, and of more basic issues such as political and economic justice in society. To that extent, as radical as I think people try to characterize the Warren Court, it wasn't that radical. It didn't break free from the essential constraints that were placed by the founding fathers in the Constitution, at least as it's been interpreted and Warren Court

interpreted in the same way, that generally the Constitution is a charter of negative liberties. Says what the states can't do to you. Says what the Federal government can't do to you, but doesn't say what the Federal government or State government must do on your behalf, and that hasn't shifted and one of the, I think, tragedies of the civil rights movement was, um, because the civil rights movement became so court focused I think there was a tendency to lose track of the political and community organizing and activities on the ground that are able to put together the actual coalition of powers through which you bring about redistributive change. In some ways we still suffer from that." [1]

That is as clear a statement of the way our Progressive leaders view America's founding document, a charter of negative liberties.

As F. A Hayek told us in *The Constitution of Liberty*, "Only a demagogue can represent as 'antidemocratic' the limitations which long-term decisions and the general principles held by the people impose upon the power of temporary majorities."

Think of what we had. Look at what we've got. Imagine where we're going.

Keep the faith. Keep the peace. We shall overcome.

★ DISPATCH EIGHTY-TWO ★

WHY DO WE OBEY?

How can a law be illegitimate? Isn't this an oxymoronic question? It is a question that brings us to the concept that there can be a difference between what is legal and what is right. This is the debate between those who believe in Legal Positivism and those who believe in Natural Rights.

Legal positivists "believe that the only legitimate sources of law are those written rules, regulations, and principles that have been expressly enacted, adopted, or recognized by a governmental entity or political institution, including administrative, executive, legislative, and judicial bodies."[1] In other words, whatever the government says is legal is right.

While those who believe in Natural Law believe "all written laws must be informed by, or made to comport with, universal principles of morality, religion, and justice, such that a law that is not fair and just may not rightly be called law."[2] Any law which is contrary to Natural Law is not a legitimate law. For example, a law that says it is legal to murder others would be seen by all to be illegitimate in a moral sense even though it would be technically legal.

That this is the concept under which the United States was first formulated is self-evident when we read that incomparable document which was issued by the Continental Congress as a justification for its war and its purpose: the Declaration of Independence. In its opening paragraph, the preamble which all school children once memorized, this document explains itself thusly: "When in the Course of human events, it becomes necessary for one people to dissolve the political bands which have connected them with another, and to assume among the powers of the earth, the separate and equal station to which the Laws of Nature and of Nature's

God entitle them, a decent respect to the opinions of mankind requires that they should declare the causes which impel them to the separation."[3]

This brings us to the first debate of this essay. Is God supreme and consequently His laws binding upon all people and all nations? Or is man supreme and all nations amendable to his will and purpose and all his laws supreme until they are changed?

When they decided to adopt the phrase "Laws of Nature and of Nature's God" the 56 signers of the Declaration based the foundation of our country on a legal standard of freedom. They sought to impress this mold into all the various forms of government to follow. This legal standard of freedom they adopted was that God's law was supreme and that this law inherently gives man freedom. The phrase "Laws of Nature and of Nature's God" referred to the laws that God as the Creator of the universe established for the governance of people, nations, and nature. Throughout History these laws have been described as the laws of Creation, God's Creation laws, or as the Founders of our nation chose to call them, the Laws of Nature and of Nature's God. These laws, whatever they are called, are ascertained through an examination of God's creation, the text of the Bible, and instinct or reason.

The decision of the Founders to expressly rely upon God's law was not a casual one. The debate concerning the basis of law had raged on both sides of the Atlantic for many years before and after the Declaration was drafted. After years of reflection on the Declaration of Independence, its principle author, Thomas Jefferson, stated in 1825 that its central point was "not to find out new principles, or new arguments, never before thought of, not merely to say things which had never been said before; but to place before mankind the common sense of the subject."[4]

That this is a generally accepted theory has been affirmed by the world in the universal acceptance of the correctness of the Nuremburg Trials after WWII.[5] The Nazis who were on trial universally sought to defend themselves on the grounds that everything they did was legal and that they were just following the orders of the legally constituted government. This defense was universally rejected. The world came together and said in effect there is a higher law.

Today, in America it is the accepted practice that our federal legislature enacts laws which direct the apparatus of government as to how it should operate. It is also accepted practice that the same body enacts laws which establish rules for how ordinary individuals should live their lives. This duality obscures the truth that though it is necessary and proper for the government to administer the labor of those who have been hired to carry out its will this does not translate into an objective right to administer the individual efforts of its citizens.

The distinguishing characteristic between a free society and a command society is that in a free society there is a recognized sphere of personal action which stands apart from the public sphere. In a free society it is recognized that within the private sphere an individual cannot be ordered about at the whim of government bureaucrats. It is also recognized that in the public sphere individuals should only be required to obey laws which are generally applicable to all. It used to be the proud declaration of free people that as long as they kept within the bounds of known law they didn't need to ask by your leave of anyone, they were sovereign of their own life.

This, however, was a declaration grounded on the belief that laws should be of a general nature; they should be clearly stated and knowable.

Today our Progressive leaders pass laws composed of thousands of pages written in the clear and precise language of government new Speak insurance papers by saying, "We have to pass it to know what's in it."[6] We also have the spectacle of the man who was in charge of writing the tax code for decades when he is caught cheating[7] on his taxes saying, "I personally feel that I have done nothing morally wrong."[8] While Mr. Rangle was never indicted for tax evasion since he is above the laws he passes, he was found guilty of violating the rules of the House for the same charges.[9]

There is little that is more important to a free society than laws being clear and certain. If people do not know what the law is, there will be paralysis. In totalitarian societies people never know when they might be accused of breaking a law or rule that they may not even be aware of. In authoritarian and totalitarian societies the apparatus of government is not used merely to operate the necessary functions of civil administration rather it is used to coerce citizens to obey.

Article II, Section 1 of the Articles of Impeachment filed against President Nixon was about the abuse of power. It stated, "He has, acting personally and through his subordinated and agents, endeavored to obtain from the Internal Revenue Service, in violation of the constitutional rights of citizens, confidential information contained in income tax returns for purposes not authorized by law, and to cause, in violation of the constitutional rights of citizens, income tax audits or other income tax investigation to be initiated or conducted in a discriminatory manner."[10]

Nixon "endeavored to obtain from the Internal Revenue Service, in violation of the constitutional rights of citizens, confidential information." He "endeavored to obtain," but he never did obtain this information. The IRS turned him down and turned him in. Today, the Obama regime after years of hiding documents and sending their operatives to Congress to either misleading, lying, or pleading the fifth has finally been exposed by documents obtained through a Freedom of Information request that was enforced by a judge.11 It has definitively been learned that the IRS persecution of conservative groups was not the work of a few rogue agents in a district office. The targeting of the Tea Party groups was directed by the IRS Headquarters in Washington.[12]

We have come full circle. From a nation founded upon the Laws of Nature and of Nature's God, we have allowed the Progressives and their Living Document to lead us to a land governed by the laws of man. The children of the Founders and the descendants of the Framers now cower before an all-powerful corporate state that passes laws no one reads, regulates everything, and employs armies of bureaucrats to harass us into obedience and conformity.

Looking at the contradiction between what we were created to be and what we have become, the question why do we obey comes to mind. Is it that we are too timid to follow in the footsteps of Washington, Jefferson, and Henry? Is it that we have developed a habit of following the directions of our leaders? Or is it that we have a respect for the rule of law?

In the face of continued abuse the timid grow bold, old habits are broken, and when respect is lost it is not easily regained.

One day there will be one abuse too many. And in that day the people of America will recall that the same people who based our society on the Laws of Nature and of Nature's God also said, "We hold these truths to be self-evident, that all men are created equal, that they are endowed by their Creator with certain unalienable Rights, that among these are Life, Liberty and the pursuit of Happiness, "That to secure these rights, Governments are instituted among Men, deriving their just powers from the consent of the governed, That whenever any Form of Government becomes destructive of these ends, it is the Right of the People to alter or to abolish it, and to institute new Government, laying its foundation on such principles and organizing its powers in such form, as to them shall seem most likely to affect their Safety and Happiness. Prudence, indeed, will dictate that Governments long established should not be changed for light and transient causes; and accordingly all experience hath shown, that mankind are more disposed to suffer, while evils are sufferable, than to right themselves by abolishing the forms to which they are accustomed. But when a long train of abuses and usurpations, pursuing invariably the same Object evinces a design to reduce them under absolute Despotism, it is their right, it is their duty, to throw off such Government, and to provide new Guards for their future security."[13]

Why do we obey? Ask yourself, why do I obey, and you will have the answer, because We the People is merely you and I waiting to recall who we are, how we got here, and what we are supposed to be.

★ DISPATCH EIGHTY-THREE ★

WHY DOES AFFIRMATIVE ACTION END AT THE GRIDIRON?

Have you ever pondered the fact that everyone being endowed with equal rights by our creator works out so naturally while the equality of outcome that our Progressive would-be-masters seek to impose is impossible to achieve without treating people differently? Have you ever noticed that whenever the government wishes to give anyone anything they have to first take it from someone else?

Since everyone obviously has different skills, talents, and ambitions people inevitably perform and produce at different levels. Therefore, to make everyone end up in the same place, it is necessary to hold some back and artificially advance others.

For example, if we wanted to treat everyone equally with regard to taxes, we would have a flat tax with no deductions as in everyone pays 10%. If you make one million dollars or one thousand dollars, you pay 10%. That would be equal treatment before the law and in my opinion that would be fair. However, in the Progressives version of a fair tax system designed to promote equality, people who earn different amounts are taxed at different rates. If you earn more you pay more. That may sound good to some, but how is it fair?

In education if equality was really the desired result, then everyone would be judged by the same standards for admission regardless of race, creed, color, or any other mitigating factor. Everyone would take the same tests and everyone would be graded exactly the same with admission based upon the score. In the world of American Academia as administrated by the Progressives categories of people are judged by different standards and they call this fairness.

Look at the bewildering array of social programs that have been implemented to ensure equality and fairness in the Progressive Utopia. From food stamps and free cell phones to state subsidized education in criminal justice for convicted felons, these ill-conceived and often abused programs turn the safety net into a hammock that beg the question Ayn Rand was known to ask, "At whose expense?"[1] If someone gets free food, free education; free anything the question we should ask is, at whose expense? The next question should be, do those who are paying the freight for this pleasure cruise do so voluntarily or are they being coerced? If they are being coerced into paying for someone else's benefits, what makes this any different than theft?

It's as if the Progressives have tried to change our original national motto from "E Pluribus Unum" to "Stand and Deliver" or have they changed our present national motto "In God We Trust" to "You Can't Fight City Hall." Or as if the new national anthem should be, "Happy Days Are Here Again—Unless You Work For a Living."

One of the most often quoted and misquoted statements concerning History tells us, is that those who do not learn from History are doomed to repeat it and today we are seeing the fruits of this truism. The two great revolutions of the eighteenth century, the American and the French, were mirror images of each other in several important ways. The American Revolution made a declaration[2] to the entire world that the rights they sought were endowed upon all men by their creator. The French in the Declaration of the Rights of Man[3] placed government as the source of these rights. The American Revolution sought to rid themselves of an all-powerful government with a limited government so that individuals could be free to prosper on their own. The French sought to replace an all-powerful government based upon birth with an all-powerful government based on merit believing that where the former one wanted to maintain the status quo with elites on top while the latter one would promote equality with elites on top.

The American experiment created the freest, richest, most powerful country in the History of the world. In France after the Terror,[4] after the Triumvirate,[5] and after the Empire[6] the people saw that they had merely replaced one elite group with another. Then the Kings came back.[7]

In America today our federally controlled education has led to generations of people who have never learned History or Civics. Now the progressive Pied Pipers are leading the uninformed to exchange the equality of opportunity our Founders established for the equality of outcome Europe has chased after since the French Revolution. With a public not knowing enough to know the difference these bait and switch tactics seem to be working, and after 100 years of a living document the Constitution is nearly dead.[8]

We have one more election to stem the tide as we look for a chance to reverse the flow and return America to limited government, individual freedom, and economic opportunity. Above all we must avoid one party rule in Washington. If we miss this opportunity we may soon experience the equality of mediocrity as we descend into the collectivist pit of self-immolation. This pit is typified by big government programs meant to redress some perceived inequality. Redressing inequality sounds good. The problem lies in the fact that to do so you need a big enough government to enforce the desired result, and governments are made up of fallible people who all have their own prejudices and desires.

James Madison, in Federalist 51 reflected that, "If men were angels, no government would be necessary. If angels were to govern men, neither external nor internal controls on government would be necessary."[8] Men aren't angels. Which is why he continued, "In framing a government which is to be administered by men over men, the great difficulty lies in this: you must first enable the government to control the governed; and in the next place oblige it to control itself."[9]

One program which serves as a fitting example of the impossibility of living a consistent life when trained, framed and constrained by the attempts to impose an artificial man-made, government enforced equality is Affirmative Action.[10]

Why Does Affirmative Action End at the Gridiron?

Even the Colleges that are the most rapid in their interpretation and enforcement of Affirmative Action seem to forget these artificial standards when it comes to their sports teams. Have you ever wondered why that is so? Because they want the best players on the field no matter what the ratios of black, white, yellow, red, straight, gay or other.

Don't fall for the siren song of something for nothing, for affirmative this, and equality that. Don't let the perpetually re-elected hucksters fool you with their promise of a fair shot, a square deal, or of making someone else pay their fair share. When everything is put in one pot and it is supposed to be divided equally it always seems that those who do the dividing get the fairest share of all.

★ DISPATCH EIGHTY-FOUR ★

WHY GRIDLOCK IS A GOOD THING

Gridlock is one of the greatest blessings bestowed upon us by the Framers. It is a natural result of the checks and balances built into the system to stop any temporary majority from fundamentally changing the country. If it wasn't for the checks and balances, FDR would have completely socialized the country back in the 1930s. If it wasn't for them now BHO would simply impose his agenda on us. Wait a minute I think he is.

Living as the occupants of an occupied nation those of us who believe limited government, personal freedom, and economic liberty are good things have to face up to the fact that a cadre of political savants who advocate for the collectivization of the American experiment have maneuvered their way into the halls of power. They have captured the media, the unions, Hollywood, and a large segment of education. The elections have been gerrymandered into a parody of democracy. Political Correctness dries up free speech and Affirmative Action uses racial quotas and discrimination while saying they are doing it to increase integration.

It takes a conspiracy theory wrapped in a spiral of silence to pretend the foregoing isn't true. Every day the regime is bent on fundamentally changing this country from a representative republic founded upon respect for the laws of nature and of nature's God into a centrally-planned social safety net. Our education system spends more money per capita than any other, and instead of academic superstars we produce illiterate whiners with high self-esteem.

The borders are open to a mass migration from the third world. Free trade has gutted our industrial base. Our foreign policy is in tatters as the conquerors of the republic allow our ambassadors to be murdered, our citizens to be unfairly imprisoned, and our national interests to be sacrificed for hidden goals and secret agendas.

America the beautiful where have you gone? From sea to shining sea your people watch as the alabaster cities rot into bankrupt hulks where socialism has failed. At the same time, those who exemplify and lead the destruction of the once proud land of the free and home of the brave point to the very instrument which provided the opportunity for humanity to excel in the bright sunshine of freedom.

Seeing gridlock not as a brake upon the ambitions of temporary ruling factions to establish themselves as permanent oligarchies, President Obama attacks the structure of government as created by the Framers of the Constitution.[1]

One of the greatest mistakes ever foisted upon this country by the Progressives was the passing of the 17th Amendment[2] to the Constitution. This change to the Constitution was pushed through in the early days of the 20th century, finally becoming law in 1913. This amendment took the election of U.S. Senators away from the state legislatures and made them part of the march toward democracy that has always been a hallmark of the progressive movement.

Before the 17th Amendment the Senators had acted as the representatives of the States preserving the federal nature of our government. Since its passage the various states must hire lobbyists to represent them in Washington as if they were just another interest group. This has given us the best government money can buy and left the States at the mercy of a central bureaucracy on steroids.

Now President Obama, as the leader and spokesman of our Progressive masters is railing against the fact that every state has two senators. In his political cradle the paragon of party politics, Chicago Mr. Obama described to a small group of wealthy supporters several hurdles to keeping Democrats in control of the Senate and possibly re-capturing the House. One of those hurdles, according to the President, is that each state regardless of its population has two Senate seats. Or as Mr. Obama said, "Obviously, the nature of the Senate means that California has the same number of Senate seats as Wyoming. That puts us at a disadvantage."[3]

The President noted that the congregation of Democrat voters in big cities gives Republicans an advantage in rural states affecting both the elections for the House and the Senate. Of course, it is those very concentrations and the massive political machines' support that allow the democrat Party to control so many States and their electoral votes. In essence what Mr. Obama is complaining about is that while Democrat control of big city machines has perhaps locked up the electoral keys to the White House, they are not able to translate that into a lock on the legislative side for a true one-party state.

If you will remember the last time they were able to pull off this hat trick (2008–2010) they shoved Obamacare and the Dodd-Frank Wall Street Reform and Consumer Protection Act, or as it is also known as, the Federal Reserve Empowerment Law down our throats.[4] This has so-cialized one sixth of our economy, has entrenched crony capitalism, and enshrined too-big-to-fail.[5]

The Progressives from the Ivory Tower to the White House have worked tirelessly for over 100 years to change the iron-clad guarantees of the Constitution into a Living Document which is as firm as Jell-O and as clear as mud. They want a one-party state and a unified central-ized government to efficiently complete their transformation.[6] It is in the interests of all lovers of liberty to vote for divided government so that we can bask in the light of gridlock. For when the lawyers in Washington and the bureaucratic minions aren't able to do anything, maybe we will have a chance to do something.

The biggest hurdle we have in maintaining the safety of gridlock is that the Progressives have captured the leadership of both major parties. They have also rigged elections in such a way as to almost eliminate the possibility for a minor party to win. Using our ballots strategically we must find ways to keep the Progressives from gaining one more shot at one-party rule. We must maintain some breathing room so that freedom doesn't suffocate.

Why is gridlock a good thing? It might be our last chance to get something done.

★ DISPATCH EIGHTY-FIVE ★

WHY HAVE A BILL OF RIGHTS?

In any free society that area of life which is left to the sole discretion of the individual includes all actions that are not specifically forbidden by a general law.

In our nation when it came time for the ratification of the Constitution, it would have been impossible to gain the votes needed if the backers of a centralized national government had not promised that the first thing they did was pass a Bill of Rights.[1] It had been asserted by the proponents of liberty that to enumerate such a list would eventually become a statement that only those rights enumerated were protected. However, it was generally believed certain rights were so important and so open to suppression that fundamental guarantees were needed. In consequence, the Constitution was lengthened to include the first 10 amendments as the opening business of Congress.

Over time the argument that these enumerated rights would come to be seen as the only ones protected has certainly come to pass, which is another of the assertions of the Anti-Federalists that have stood the test of time. However, it has also been shown that without these constitutional protections these enumerated rights would have long ago been relegated to the ash heap of History.

Even with the protection of the Bill of Rights there has been a steady chipping away at the rights our forefathers thought were so important. A Supreme Court that has abrogated onto itself the power to nullify the will of the people as expressed in legislation and to invent rights that are nowhere enumerated debates whether or not "shall not be infringed" really means it is legal to restrict.

In our age of seemingly endless technological change we must admit that any enumerated list of rights cannot be complete. What about surveillance? Does our right to privacy which has been asserted to allow tens of millions of abortions extend to our growing Orwellian Omni-present surveillance state? Does the state have a right to follow us with drones? To take our lives without due process? To collect our emails, our phone calls or keep a ledger of where we go? Under President Bush people demonstrated because his administration wanted to see the records of library withdrawals. Under President Obama the populace is silent about the most egregious violations of our rights.

What about the rights of the States? Do they have the right to be protected from invasion? Do they have the right to pass and enforce laws that call for local agencies to enforce the federal laws that the central government refuses to enforce? Ever since the 17th Amendment[2] stripped the States of their representation in Congress, our federal system has been debilitated to the point of paralysis. Today, the central government runs roughshod over the States demanding that they stand by helplessly as their citizens are harassed and their sovereignty is evaporated.

If the Bill of Rights is to remain as any type of bulwark against tyranny, it must be accepted that they contain a general assumption that government is restrained from infringing upon the traditional rights that we have enjoyed. If we stand ideally by while our rights are redefined to irrelevance, we will one day wake up to find ourselves in a prison camp we once called the United States of America.

We have experienced over the course of the last 200 years that the Constitution could be no more than a somewhat porous protection from the assumption of total power by a centralized government. Today we endure levels of control and taxation that make the causes of our own Revolution pale in comparison. It is hard not to believe that if Washington, Henry, and that generation were with us today they wouldn't be issuing declarations and raising the alarm, "The totalitarians are coming! The totalitarians are coming!!"

The only protection of this creeping corruption of our constitutionally limited government is an informed public. If the people sleep the tyrants dream. They dream of ordering society to match whichever version of a Utopian pyramid scheme they adopt to fool the people. It matters little whether they call it communism, fascism, or progressivism, a re-education camp is a prison by another name. It matters little whether we call it censorship or political correctness. It matters little whether we call it taxes or penalties. It matters little whether we call it coercion or regulation.

What does matter is whether we are truly free or free only in name. Can we do what we want or can we merely do what is allowed?

Outside the bounds of the constitutionally established amendment process, the Progressives have used the fiction of a Living Document to make the Constitution a dead letter. Executive orders, signing statements, court decisions, and the bewildering framework of regulation stretch the power of government while restricting the freedom of the people.

Empires rise and empires fall. Some fall due to invasion and some due to suicide. The European Empires committed suicide in two fratricidal World Wars that destroyed their cities and left their people shell-shocked and unwilling to bear the burden of power.

Today we watch while our great republic jettisons the world girdling empire it inherited from the exhausted Europeans. We stand mute as our leaders abandon the leadership not only of the free world but of the world itself. Not for the noble cause of reasserting freedom at home but instead because we have spent ourselves into bankruptcy with bread and circuses to amuse the masses while a clique of elites concentrates power. We have empty suits leading representatives who have gerry-mandered their way to perpetual election presiding over an unelected bureaucracy that rules by decree.

Does liberty still ring or has the bell finally cracked beyond repair? Why do we have a Bill of Rights? So we can remember who we once were.

★ DISPATCH EIGHTY-SIX ★

WHY I AM NO LONGER A CONSERVATIVE REPUBLICAN

Maybe it's just me but I'm tired of the same old same old in our politics. The big-box monopoly parties have morphed into two sides of the same coin, two heads on the same bird of prey. Today our choice boils down to the Conservative Republican tax and spend, infringe personal liberty, and outsource or sovereignty policies or the Liberal Democrat tax and spend, infringe personal liberty, and outsource or sovereignty policies. But of course, since we don't want to throw away our vote we must vote for one of the big boys. Conservative? Liberal? Tweedle Dee Or Tweedle Dum?

As a voter I've had my Damascus Road experience, the scales have fallen from my eyes. They may brand it as throwing away my vote, however, I have reached the point where I would rather make my vote count by voting for someone who might actually try to find a different way to operate our government besides taxing like the Sun King and spending like a drunken sailor.

And what might this difference that I am voting for be? How about this for radical: let's return to constitutional government? WOW! What a concept.

How did we arrive at the current situation? James Madison in his speech to the Virginia Ratifying Convention, June 16, 1788 said, "There are more instances of the abridgement of the freedom of the people by the gradual and silent encroachment of those in power, than by violent and sudden usurpation." We didn't get here all in one jump. First the camel said, "Can I just stick my nose in your tent to stay warm?" and finally the generous man found himself out in the cold as the camel settled down for a nice warm nap, one inch at a time.

The compassion of our people built a safety net for those who needed help, and the greed of the lazy have turned it into a hammock. America, the Land of the Free has turned into America, from each according to their abilities to each according to their need. The willingness to share our heritage has led America to welcome more immigrants each year than the rest of the world combined, and the abuse of our generosity has turned into a migration invasion that threatens to overwhelm us and destroy the future of our children. Taxes imposed to meet the ever-swelling demands of government have turned into a blatant wealth re-distribution program that makes most pyramid schemes look fair. Sometimes I think our government looks at a productive citizen as merely a source of residual income. Or as the ads promise, our leaders lay on the beach of self-importance and our checks just keep pouring in. We are no longer respected as Citizens. Instead, we are coveted as consumers, or human capital.

Albert Einstein said, "Insanity: doing the same thing over and over again and expecting different results."[1]

If we want a different world we have to start at the only place we have the absolute sovereign ability to make a change, that is, we must start with ourselves.

I quit the Republican Party once it was obvious that the Republican majority in Congress I had spent my entire adult life working for was just a change in leadership and not a change in direction. I quit calling myself a conservative after the second Bush debacle made it obvious that the conservative movement had been hijacked by the neocons and I realized that you can't defend a captured position. You can't conserve what has already been lost. I realized that we as a people, we as a federation of States, need to find a different way.

One thing I know, no one person can do this alone. No one group can do it. To make any headway in the face of the electoral monopoly held by the party of power, the many third party groups are going to have to coalesce into an effective opposition. We can't let divisions divide us any more, egos will have to be suppressed, and we will have to bond together with everyone dedicated to limited government, personal liberty, and economic freedom.

None of us can roll this big rock up this steep hill by ourselves. However, together we can.

Winston Churchill said, "If you will not fight for the right when you can easily win without bloodshed, if you will not fight when your victory will be sure and not so costly, you may come to the moment when you will have to fight with all the odds against you and only a precarious chance for survival. There may be a worse case. You may have to fight when there is no hope of victory, because it is better to perish than to live as slaves."[2]

Looking at the increasing speed with which the Progressive regime is building its command and control structure, the future is invading the present at an ever accelerating pace. Their living document has made the Constitution a dead letter. Their mixed economy has as many people on the dole as on the job. The Fed's printing press is burying us, our children, and their grandchildren taking out a mortgage on lives that haven't been lived and spending money from taxes on work that hasn't been done.

We must unite if these United States are to once again become the land of the free and the home of the brave instead of the land of the free lunch and the home of the knave.

Quoting Ben Franklin, "We must hang together, gentlemen...else, we shall most assuredly hang separately."[3]

★ DISPATCH EIGHTY-SEVEN ★

WHY LAW VS ANTI-LAW IN AMERICA

America was founded upon the principles of Natural Law. The Progressives led us into the realms of Legal Positivism. The vast government apparatus they have constructed has progressed into a dystopian fantasy land beyond law where faceless bureaucrats in an alphabet soup of departments create regulations with the force of law from thin air. Such is the journey from tyranny to tyranny for 10 generations. Such is the journey from law to anti-law.

We built this Republic on the foundation of Natural Law.

The opening sentence of the Declaration of Independence is unarguably the most famous.[1] Countless American students have memorized it, regurgitated it for exams, and many can still recite it many years later.

"When in the Course of human events, it becomes necessary for one people to dissolve the political bands which have connected them with another, and to assume among the powers of the earth, the separate and equal station to which the Laws of Nature and of Nature's God entitle them, a decent respect to the opinions of mankind requires that they should declare the causes which impel them to the separation."

While many will point to this preamble as a statement of why the Declaration was made few in our present generation can define what Thomas Jefferson was referring to, which was a common term and a common understanding at the time of its composition, "the Laws of Nature and of Nature's God."

In his book, *The Five Thousand Year Leap*, by Dr. W. Cleon Skousen, he points out that "...the debates in the Constitutional Convention and the writings of the Founders reflect a far broader knowledge of religious, political, historical, economic, and philosophical studies."[2] He also states, "The thinking of Polybius, Cicero, Thomas Hooker, Coke, Montesquieu, Blackstone, John Locke, and Adam Smith salt-and-peppered their writings and their conversations. They were also careful students of the Bible, especially the Old Testament, and even though some did not belong to any Christian denomination, the teachings of Jesus were held in universal, respect and admiration."[3]

The ancient Roman Cicero was a victim of turbulent power politics and eventually killed for writing against the dictatorship of Caesar, but in his writings *On the Republic* and *On the Laws* he spoke about Natural Law. He spoke of it as True Law or Right Law. "True law is right reason in agreement with nature; it is of universal application, unchanging and everlasting;…It is a sin to try to alter this law, nor is it allowable to repeal any part of it, and it is impossible to abolish it entirely. We cannot be freed from its obligations by senate or people…one eternal and unchangeable law will be valid for all nations and all times, and there will be one master and ruler, that is God, over us all, for he is the author of this law,…."[4]

Introduced in 1766, Blackstone's became the law book of the Founding Fathers. In fact political scientists have shown that Blackstone was one of two most frequently invoked political authorities of the Founders. Like Cicero more than a thousand years before Blackstone recognized Natural Law as the sure foundation of human society when he stated, "Upon these two foundations, the law of nature and the law of revelation (the law of nature's God), depend all the human laws; that is to say, *no* human laws should be suffered to contradict these."[5]

In essence what all this means is that there are laws greater than any laws man can make; therefore, there are areas which are beyond legislation. In America we attempted to safeguard those areas such as individual liberty, personal freedom, and economic opportunity with a constitution.

This Constitution was written to limit the power of government to those powers and only those powers which had been specifically delegated to it.

The final amendment in the Bill of Rights reads, "The powers not delegated to the United States by the Constitution, nor prohibited by it to the states, are reserved to the states respectively, or to the people." It would be hard to be any more direct. However, this amendment has been interpreted into irrelevancy as the Progressives made their long march to power.

The Progressives nudged us into Legal Positivism:

Throughout the last 25 years if we spoke of "the laws of nature" many Americans would think we are speaking of doing whatever comes naturally as typified in the saying, "If it feels good do it." Most seem not to consider the relevance or even the existence of absolute truth or God's Law.

To the leaders of today and the compliant populace they and their government-controlled schools have indoctrinated man's law as supreme. The epitome of this is extolled in the belief in a "Living Constitution." One in which everything is constantly evolving, and where people, legislatures, and courts do not seem to be concerned with a constitution meant to limit the power of government. Instead, they say relevance and necessity drives them to interpret a constitution which empowers government to do anything it decides is necessary.

This brings us to the legal philosophy which undergirds this assault upon traditional American law: Legal Positivism.

This legal philosophy posits that law consists exclusively of that which is created and directed by the human will. In other words, with the limiting guide of Natural Law removed the appropriateness of government action becomes a question of mere legality. Anything which has become law is acceptable. The Final Solution of the Third Reich was legal. The purges of Stalin were legal.

As one German professor intellectually paving the way for the Nazi dictatorship stated in his analysis of the death of limited government after WWI, "fundamentally irretrievable liberty of the individual … gradually recedes into the background and the liberty of the social collective occupies the front of the stage."[6] He further notes that this change in the emphasis of freedom from the individual to the collective signaled the "emancipation od democratism from liberalism." Remember that in this context Liberalism had its original meaning, which is advocating liberty, and not its corrupted American meaning, advocating for exactly what the good professor was describing.

This newly liberated democracy equates the state with the legal code. Whatever the majority decides is legal is right. This leads inevitably to the position that there are no limits to the power of the legislator. There are no natural rights and no fundamental and inviolable liberties.

Turning traditional reasoning on its head, the proponents of Legal Positivism advanced the position that when a state is bound by law it is an unfree prisoner of the law. They reasoned that in order for a state to act with true justice it must be free of the law. Since personal freedom and the rule of law are inseparable as Legal Positivism overtakes a state, personal freedom becomes progressively more proscribed until the individual is enmeshed in a bewildering web of laws.

By the end of the twentieth century, America was tangled in law after law. The Federal laws alone fill more volumes than anyone could carry: libraries full of laws written by lawyers often weighing out the gnat while swallowing the camel. There were laws about this and laws about that, until finally there were laws about everything. Until even those we have elected to protect and defend the Constitution believe, as one Congressman said, "The Federal Government can do most anything in this country."[8]

Today we are entering the rule of Anti-Law.

With the prevalence of omnibus bills numbering thousands of pages written to read like telephone books with addendums and commentaries in insurance speak, the legislature has abdicated its power to bureaucrats who fill in the blanks.

The situation is typified by statements by some of the leaders of the post-constitutional Obama Congress. From the former Speaker of the House Nancy Pelosi's famous, "We've got to pass the bill to find out what's in the bill,"[7] to perpetual incumbent Congressman Conyers outburst, "I love these members, they get up and say, 'Read the bill.' What good is reading the bill if it's a thousand pages and you don't have two days and two lawyers to find out what it means after you read the bill?"[9]

The philosophical position of the rule of bureaucracy has been best stated by Soviet political theorists attempting to explain and justify that great prison of nations: the USSR. One put it this way, "Since it is impossible to distinguish between laws and administrative regulations, this contrast is a mere fiction of bourgeois theory and practice."[10] Perhaps the best description of the Soviet position is from another Russian, "What distinguishes the Soviet system from all other despotic governments is that ... it represents an attempt to found the state on principles which are the opposite of those of the rule of law ... and it has evolved a theory which exempts the rulers from every obligation or limitation."[11]

Or as a Communist Theorist summed it up, "The fundamental principle of our legislation and our private laws, which the bourgeois theorist will never recognize is: everything is prohibited which is not specifically permitted."[13]

Here we are in a land strangled by regulation. Our elected officials pass laws they don't read about things they don't understand and unelected bureaucrats fill in the gaps. As can be seen in the IRS scandal, they see themselves as above the law and there seems to be no way to make them accountable. Like a runaway train involved in a slow motion wreck, the citizens stand helplessly as our nation implodes. We can vote for one of the parties of power; however, they are merely two heads on the same bird of prey. No matter which one is in power the government grows and grows.

How do we end this death spiral? How did Washington, Jefferson, and Adams do it? We started with the Declaration of Independence so we might as well end there.

"We hold these truths to be self-evident, that all men are created equal, that they are endowed by their Creator with certain unalienable Rights, that among these are Life, Liberty and the pursuit of Happiness. That to secure these rights, Governments are instituted among Men, deriving their just powers from the consent of the governed. That whenever any Form of Government becomes destructive of these ends, it is the Right of the People to alter or to abolish it, and to institute new Government, laying its foundation on such principles and organizing its powers in such form, as to them shall seem most likely to affect their Safety and Happiness."

These were dangerous words then, and they are dangerous words now. Let each citizen swear to do and be whatever is necessary to preserve, protect, and defend the Constitution. God bless America.

Keep the faith. Keep the peace. We shall overcome.

★ DISPATCH EIGHTY-EIGHT ★

WHY LIBERTY DIES

To understand why liberty is imperiled in our country today we must first state clearly and unequivocally what is liberty. Then and only then can we understand what is necessary for its preservation as well as see what is undermining it today. Liberty is the absence of coercion and the freedom to act upon your own will within the perimeters of not infringing the freedom of action of others. The only way that has been found among the societies of man to ensure, promote, and protect liberty is through the rule of law.

The rule of law means that government is not allowed to coerce an individual except through the enforcement of a previously known and explicitly stated principle of limited government. This principle places a limit upon the power of government to legislate by calling into question what sorts of laws are legitimate and which is not. This looks beyond individual statutes to the very nature of legislation itself. This differs markedly with the modern notion of the rule of law that holds as long as all the actions of a government comply with the law it is meeting the standard. It is well to remember that under this definition both the Nazis and the Soviets operated under the rule of law.

This modern definition is actually an oxymoron. If a government passes a law which says that it can do whatever it wants than everything it does is legal. Hitler passed the Enabling Act and accomplished this in one fell swoop.[1]

Because the rule of law is an absolute limitation on all legislation it cannot be a law of the same order as that passed by a legislature. No Legislator can effectively limit himself through legislation since he can

578e3

tankl

always amend that legislation at a later date. Constitutions can make the infringement of pre-decided basic principles more difficult; however, as we have seen in our own Progressive land of the Living Document limitations can be re-defined away through courts and tradition.

The rule of law can only prevail where its basic principles are an organic part of the culture of the people. They must be part of the commonly held beliefs and standards of a majority of the people or they will be jettisoned as soon as they restrain that majority from following the path of least resistance and living as they believe they should. For if the rule of law is the common belief it will be followed closely and guarded jealously. If it is seen as impractical or as an impediment to life as the majority wish to live it, it will be soon rejected and replaced. Such a society will gladly embrace tyranny and arbitrary rule as long as they are convinced that they can now live as they want to live.

In our nation we have built a rather impressive framework to restrain the government: our Constitution. Though it has been interpreted into meaninglessness in many ways, it is still given lip service and is still the penultimate law of the land. However, there is one glaring hole that is currently being exploited to make an end-run around its remaining provisions: the rise of the Federal Bureaucracy.

We have gone to great lengths to limit what powers the elected officials of our government possess and left open the door for appointed officials to run roughshod over our lives. The legislature passes vague thousand-page laws and then the bureaucrats interpret them any way they desire with little or no oversight. Elected officials, even the perpetually re-elected gerrymandered creatures of today come and go. The bureaucracy lives forever. When the elected officials cannot find the power to impose the Progressive agenda they do it through the bureaucrats they have appointed.

When they couldn't pass Cap-N-Trade, they imposed it through the EPA.[2] When they can't pass gun restrictions they have their bureaucrats buy up all the ammunition and make it almost impossible for the people to obtain any.[3] When they can't pass amnesty they impose it through regulations[4] and edicts.[5] The control of private land is taken through wet lands regulations.[6] Between the out-of-control legislators-for-life and their appointed regulators we are told to do everything from what kind of light bulbs[7] to buy to how many gallons we can use to flush a toilet.[8]

Liberty is being eaten away inch-by-inch and day-by-day, legislated, and regulated into oblivion. When our government can't pass laws or impose regulations they will utilize the IRS,[9] the NSA,[10] or anyone of a hundred of their alphabet agencies to spy on us or intimidate us into silence. Common Core[11] is coming for the kids. Amnesty is coming for the jobs.[12] Political Correctness is coming for free speech.[13]

Unless patriots stand-up the country will fall. It will still be called the United States of America. People will still say the pledge of Allegiance. They will still sing the national anthem and salute the flag but will it be the same country that our forefathers fought and died for? Will it still be the land of the free and the home of the brave? Or will it be something else: a place where the rule of law once protected its citizens from the rule of men until the laws of men overwhelmed the laws of nature and of nature's God?[14]

Jean-Jacques Rousseau one of those who inspired the Framers of the Constitution reminded us, "Free people, remember this maxim: we may acquire liberty, but it is never recovered if it is once lost."[15]

Barry Goldwater said, "Equality, rightly understood as our founding fathers understood it, leads to liberty and to the emancipation of creative differences; wrongly understood, as it has been so tragically in our time, it leads first to conformity and then to despotism."[16]

The enemies of freedom also speak of liberty. Vladimir Lenin said, "It is true that liberty is precious; so precious that it must be carefully rationed."[17]

Benito Mussolini said, "The truth is that men are tired of liberty."[18]

The controllers of men may try to use the language of liberty to subvert liberty; however, the God given spirit of man shall always strive to become what God meant for us to be, free people in a free world."

Norman Vincent Peale said, "Once we roared like lions for liberty; now we bleat like sheep for security! The solution for America's problem is not in terms of big government, but it is in big men over whom nobody stands in control but God."[19]

Winston Churchill told us, "If you will not fight for right when you can easily win without bloodshed; if you will not fight when your victory is sure and not too costly; you may come to the moment when you will have to fight with all the odds against you and only a precarious chance of survival. There may even be a worse case. You may have to fight when there is no hope of victory, because it is better to perish than to live as slaves."[20]

And every school child should know that Patrick Henry famously said, "Is life so dear or peace so sweet as to be purchased at the price of chains and slavery? Forbid it, Almighty God! I know not what course others may take, but as for me, give me liberty, or give me death!"[21]

Why does liberty die? Because people allow it.

DISPATCH EIGHTY-NINE

WHY SOCIAL SECURITY HURTS SOCIETY AND ISN'T SECURE

The concept of a social safety net is well accepted throughout the Western World. The idea that some provision should be made for those who through no fault of their own are unable to provide for themselves first appeared as a state policy in Germany in the nineteenth century as the Iron Chancellor, Bismarck, sought to co-opt the popular appeal of socialism and strengthen the newly founded German Imperial state. The idea struck a chord in the hearts of most people in Europe and in the hearts of its descendants around the world.

In days gone by the family, the parish church and the local community had filled this need. However, with the growth of cities and the near total separation of these urban populations from the land, it became necessary for the wider community to accept this responsibility.

It was inevitable that since some sort of agency or bureau was needed to supervise the distribution of such aid, this public apparatus would follow the trajectory of all bureaucracy: growth. Mission creep would inevitably set in as the bureaucrats would seek to build their kingdom. Services would increase so that the servicers would increase and one layer would insulate another. From providing the bare necessities to those who through no fault of their own could not do so, we have reached a stage where the modern ideal of fairness intersects and we have the self-selected indigent demanding a living wage for doing nothing.

This amounts to those who make provision for themselves being forced to make provision for those who don't. This must necessarily be so because the only way such a system to exist for any length of time is for it to become compulsory upon all to contribute for the benefit of some. This then brings into play the economic truth that whatever you subsidize you get more of and viola the welfare rolls keep growing as the benefits keep increasing.

One of the tricks used to sell this scam to an unwitting nation was the use of the word insurance. Everyone was familiar with the concept of insurance: pay a premium and expect coverage if the event insured against occurs. The government called it Social Security Insurance and it seemed so reasonable. The problem is the money has always gone directly into the general fund. Therefore, it was spent today with no provision for tomorrow. Combine that with yearly deficit spending and the inevitable growth of the national debt and the money coming in has no relationship to the money going out.

It is a Ponzi scheme pure and simple and it always has been. FDR and his Brain Trust social engineers knew that from the start. The problem with a Ponzi scheme is that eventually the music stops and there are never enough chairs. The most successful Ponzi scheme we know of was with Bernie Madof. It eventually came crashing down, and it was a pittance compared to the tenuous superstructure we have built up with Social Security.

In 2013, Social Security ran a $71 billion deficit.[1] This means there have been four years of consecutive cash-flow deficits, which means that the inflow is less than the outflow. According to the 2014 annual report from the programs' trustees, the combined 75-year unfunded obligation of the Social Security and Disability Insurance Trust Funds (referred to collectively as the OASDI Trust Fund) is $13.4 trillion.[2] That is a $1.1 trillion increase from last year's unfunded obligation of $12.3 trillion, and this is without calculating the tens of millions more who will enter the System under President Obama's amnesty decree.[3]

Does anyone really believe we are ever going to make that whole? Are we ever going to take enough out of other portions of our budget to fund these obligations? If we don't eventually someone will have to pay the piper. If it isn't us it will be our children or their children on and on until it crashes against the reality that the cupboard is bare.

This so-called insurance meant from the beginning not merely compulsory insurance it also meant compulsory membership in a unitary system controlled and enforced by the state. The main reason such a centralized system is widely accepted as necessary was the administration convenience and the economy of scale that alone could make provision for everyone at once. This is nothing except a government monopoly. Not a closed monopoly where no one can compete against the 800 pound gorilla, but an open monopoly where everyone is forced to participate even if they make provisions for themselves and never take recourse to the guaranteed payout.

Even though competition is possible the accepted principle that all sheltered monopolies become inefficient over time applies here. Just because the pyramid hasn't collapsed yet does not mean that Social security earns the praise it garners as a successful program. As the saying which typifies government inefficiency goes, it still equates to having the DMV run your retirement plan.

How has a system that was sold to the American public as a means to relieve the abject poverty of a few morphed into a tool for wealth distribution? How has the once vigilant American public been convinced in not only the efficiency but the necessity of a program which is little more than a new way of packaging the discarded aims of Socialism? It was done incrementally.

It reminds me of the story about the two pastors who meant at a conference. Pastor A was approached by Pastor B who had once been the pastor at A's current church, but he had been thrown out because he tried to move the piano from the right side of the platform to the left.

Pastor B: Hi, I heard you have moved the piano from the right side of the platform to the left side and that the people love you there. When I tried it they threw me out faster than the Holy Spirit can say Jesus. How did you do it?

Pastor A: One inch every six months.

What won't be accepted today will be accepted ten years from now if we move there slowly. This is classic Alinsky, and is straight out of his Rules for Radicals.

Whereas the people of the West fought for 50 years to resist the smothering embrace of Communism, we have allowed ourselves to accept it by degrees under other names until what we have is in many ways indistinguishable from what they tried to make us accept. The practice of the welfare state's attempt to bring about a just distribution for everyone who has reached a certain age by distributing incomes in such proportions and amounts as it sees fit is merely another method under a new name of achieving Marx's long promised goal, "From each according to his ability to each according to their need."

It is of paramount importance that we understand the difference in a situation where a society decides to prevent the utter destitution of a few and a situation in which the state assumes the right to determine the just portion everyone must pay and the just portion everyone receives with state sponsored coercion to back it all up. Individual freedom, personal liberty, and economic opportunity are profoundly threatened when the state is given the exclusive power to provide certain services.

This system was designed in the 1930s. It has been tweaked and massaged several times since then; however, it is in essence a 1930s construct. Whenever someone suggests finding a new way to provide for any or all of the needs now associated with the Social Security System we are greeted with visions of heartless robber barons throwing grandma off a cliff. However, it is eminently reasonable that when the best available solution based on the best available knowledge is frozen in place it becomes the most efficient way to prevent any new knowledge ever being applied to the problem.

When our desire to provide out of the public treasury for those in need is combined with a system for compelling everyone to make provision against being in need we have in effect created a third system. This is a system under which people in certain circumstances such as old age or disability are provided for without consideration of whether or not they are able to take care of themselves or not. Under this system everyone is provided with the standard of which the government has deiced they should have. With no means testing we have the specter of people who make $100,000 per year receiving pensions forcefully taken from contributions from people who make $15,000 per year.

With the current average life span and the caps on the amount of income eligible for taxation almost everyone who lives long enough collects more than they ever pay in. How is that supposed to work?

Since most people want to earn what they receive and do not want a hand-out, the reality of the SS Ponzi scheme has been wrapped in enough insurance type language to fill a phone book. This has become an effort through concealment to persuade the public to accept what is in reality an income redistribution plan. This was instituted and has evolved from an acceptable half-measure designed to induce hard-working people to accept what they haven't earned and yet think it is fair, because they have paid in. No matter that they routinely receive far more than they ever pay in.

One last aspect of this corrupt bargain that transfers the wealth from future generations to the present is that the SS administration uses some of the funds gained through compulsory deductions to employ publicity agencies to convince the majority of payees that the system needs to constantly expand. Some of the money is also spent to lobby Congress for this constant expansion. This amounts to nothing less than a group of self-interested executives allowed public funds to agitate for a larger organization to administer which means even bigger budgets for publicity and lobbying. It is a self-perpetuating pyramid scheme that uses the money of the victims to gain authority over ever larger portions of the victim's income and lives.

All this superstructure has been built over generations by the elected representatives of the people and the bureaucrats they employ. However, I believe it is doubtful if Americans would have turned their backs on the work ethic which made us great and embraced spreading the wealth around as a tool for social engineering. If they had fully known where they were headed and what the end result would be: a centrally planned collectivist entitlement machine hurtling towards a fiscal cliff, they would have rebelled.

When we add this all up we find that the scales are now weighted against individual liberty, personal freedom, and economic opportunity. In the end after every deduction and every benefit, Social Security hurts society and it isn't secure.

DISPATCH NINETY

WHY THE CONGRESS MUST REIGN IN THE SUPREME COURT

"We hold these truths to be self-evident, that all men are created equal, that they are endowed by their Creator with certain unalienable Rights that among these are Life, Liberty and the pursuit of Happiness." Please notice that this, the foundational sentence of the American way of life does not say "endowed by the Supreme Court."[1]

Ever since the Supreme Court took unto itself the power to void laws passed by the representatives of the people in Marbury V. Madison[2] the black-robed Justices have acted and Americans have accepted them as if they are the source and the summit of what is and what isn't allowed in America. In most cases since the middle of the twentieth century, the high court has sided with whatever the central government wanted to do in the way of extending its power and curtailing rights which any person who can read plainly sees protected in the document they are sworn to defend.

However, in Article III of the Constitution, the one that outlines the judicial branch, after specifically enumerating which types of cases the Supreme Court shall try it says , "In all the other Cases before mentioned, the Supreme Court shall have appellate Jurisdiction, both as to Law and Fact, with such Exceptions, and under such Regulations as the Congress shall make."[3]

We often hear of obscure clauses of the Constitution which have been stretched and strained to sweep more power and authority into the never satisfied maw of the Federal Leviathan such as:

The "Necessary and Proper Clause" which is found in Article I, Section 8, Clause 18 states, "To make all Laws which shall be necessary and proper for carrying into Execution the [enumerated] Powers, and all other Powers vested by this Constitution in the Government of the United States, or in any Department or Officer thereof."[4] This is also known as the "Elastic Clause" because Congress and Presidents have stretched it to give them powers the Founders never would have dreamed possible outside a tyranny.

The "Commerce Clause" found in Article I, Section 8, Clause 3 states, "to regulate Commerce with foreign Nations, and among several States, and with the Indian Tribes."[5] This is the go-to clause for the Progressive's conquest of America. This is the clause that was used in the 1930s by FDR to implement most of the New Deal. It was used by LBJ in the 1960s to impose the Great Society. And it is being used by BHO in the 21st century to shackle us with the social democracy brand of socialism which has devastated Europe and which has been repudiated by our former adversaries in the Cold War.

In the Supreme Court decision Wickard v. Filburn in 1942[6] it was handed down from on high that wheat farmer growing wheat on his own property for his own use can be legally regulated under the commerce clause because not selling your wheat and using it yourself is actually competing with wheat that is sold and is therefore commerce. This is the same clause the Obama Administration originally used as a defense to say they can fine people for not buying insurance arguing that not buying insurance is commerce.

Yes, these two clauses have been stretched and interpreted beyond any semblance of rationality to restrict and restrain Americans in the enjoyment of the freedom and liberty which should be our birthright, yet the clause which clearly states that Congress has the power to reign in the Court has been ignored.

Forget all the posturing about abortion by all the so-called conservatives in Congress. Has there ever been a concerted, protracted, or sustained effort to remove abortion from the jurisdiction of the Supreme Court? No there hasn't. And yet tomorrow, or even today Congress could pass a law stating that abortion is an exception to the court's jurisdiction and with the signing of this law by the president Roe V. Wade would be null and void, and all state laws affecting abortion would once again be in effect. And this same procedure could be used for the representatives of the people to take back control of the law and the country from the Court.

The Congress is elected. The Supreme Court is appointed. Congress can be replaced. The Justices of the Supreme Court serve for life. They could be impeached and removed; however, none have ever been removed and the likelihood of that happening is remote. There are checks and balances in the process of passing laws. The Senate is a check on the House and the House on the Senate. The President is a check on Congress and Congress is a check on the President. There is a check designed to restrain the Supreme Court from becoming a black-robed committee of kings: Article III, Section 2, Clause 2 giving Congress the power to create exceptions to the Court's jurisdiction. However, tradition and the desire of professional politicians to demagogue about issues instead of solving them keeps the perpetually re-elected from reigning in these want-a-be demigods.

Thursday June 28, 2012 will live in the memory of all patriotic Americans as a day of infamy along with Pearl Harbor, and 9/11. This is the day the Supreme Court ruled that if the Central government can't force American citizens to do what they want them to do one way they can do it another.

When the Obama Administration and their co-conspirators, the Progressive Democratic Party in Congress, rammed Obamacare through Congress they argued that the fines imposed under the individual mandate upon anyone who didn't purchase health insurance wasn't a tax,[7] but that it was a penalty allowable under the Commerce Clause. According to the Constitution all tax bills must begin in the House.[8] Obamacare began in the Senate;[9] however, that was all right since the fines weren't taxes they were penalties.

When the issue got to court and it became clear there wasn't a majority ready to declare not buying insurance was commerce the Obama Administration argued there was no standing to litigate the individual mandate and the fine it imposed because it is a tax. Through the looking glass inside the beltway and behind the curtain, it's a penalty[10] when that argument works and it's a tax when that argument works.[11]

Sophistry is defined as "Reasoning that appears sound but is misleading or fallacious. In Metaphysics, Aristotle defines sophistry as 'wisdom in appearance only.'"[12] When we look at that definition from now on it will be hard not to see the face of Chief Justice Roberts who today showed his true colors as the midwife of totalitarianism. While declaring unconstitutional the very arguments used to pass the law the majority declared the law constitutional based upon the very arguments its opponents used to try and defeat the bill. Up is down, right is wrong, and the government can do whatever it wants.

When addressing the Supreme Court it has been said, "There is no power above them to control any of their decisions. There is no authority that can remove them, and they cannot be controlled by the laws of the legislature. In short, they are independent of the people, of the legislature, and of every power under heaven. Men placed in this situation will generally soon feel independent of heaven itself."[13]

The balance between the central government and the once free citizens it is attempting to turn into dumbed down helpless dependents has been significantly changed. As predicted by the Anti-Federalists, the courts have been used over and over to expand the power of the central government to the detriment of the States and the citizens. With this decision we crossed a threshold; we passed a tipping point and are no longer at the edge of the abyss. We are careening down the cliff into the fearful embrace of totalitarianism. An over-the-top Supreme Court has given the green light to an out-of-control Progressive Administration, and as of today there are no checks and there is no balance.[14]

Those of us who love liberty and are dedicated to limited government must contact our representatives and demand that the Supreme Court be brought under control. Something must be done to preserve liberty or the United States we have loved will become the one we have dreaded. An all-powerful central government will continue to grow and bend all things to its will. We must return to the literal definition of constitutional government or this living document will be the death of freedom and the graveyard of liberty.

Keep the faith. Keep the peace. We shall overcome.

★ DISPATCH NINETY-ONE ★

Why the Welfare State Isn't Well and It Isn't Fair

Throughout most of the 19th and 20th centuries Socialism had a fairly precise definition, a somewhat clear program, and a generally agreed upon goal. The definition of Socialism was some variant of Karl Marx's well-known statement, "From each according to the ability to each according to their need."[1] Socialism's program was the nationalization of all means of production, exchange, and distribution. Socialism's goal was the use of all three in a comprehensive plan to bring about some chimera of social justice.

There were two general schools or roads socialists followed to utopia, Marxism[2] and Fabianism.[3] Both were variants of Socialism. They differed mainly in their stated ultimate ideal of a Socialist State and how to get there.

The Marxists said they believed that in a fully Socialist State the State itself would wither away, and all that would be left was a classless society basking in the sunshine of social justice for all. The method advocated by the Communists to achieve this social nirvana was revolutionary change leading to a dictatorship of the working class (proletariat) which ruthlessly exterminated the old society and built the new.

The Fabians saw their road to social justice leading through a highly centralized government built up gradually by democratic means slowly gaining control of the levers of power and gradually implementing its program of bureaucratic control until complete social justice was achieved.

In Europe these schools of thought were explicit and open forming political parties and vying for power either through the ballot or from the barrel of a gun. In America the engrained belief in personal liberty, individual freedom, and economic opportunity were too strong to allow the open development of any party that openly claimed Socialism as their philosophy. Therefore, the gradualist approach of the Fabians became the incremental approach of the Progressives.

Starting with Teddy Roosevelt and Woodrow Wilson, massively redirecting society under FDR, and moving ever forward under every president, except Ronald Reagan, the Progressives have slowly built the web upon which America now is bound.

With the fall of the Soviet Union and of its satellite empire, communism finally lost its great patron. It had long since lost its allure in the reality of a brutal dictatorship that ground its people into the dirt in the race to social justice. So in the West Socialism has gone underground in the Green Movement, the vast network of community organizing groups, and in the Democrat Party. Many of the leaders of the Party now openly call themselves Progressives. All of them champion the idea of a Living Constitution that is evolving from the old American ideal of individualism toward a new collectivist ideal of social justice.

As long as the ideas and goals of Socialism were just that: ideas and goals, it all sounded good and many intellectuals as well as many members of the general public bought into the lofty sounding fairness of social justice. However, once the Socialists gained actual power in the USSR and later in its satellite empire the crushing reality of its brutish methods and the soul killing dullness of its execution dimmed the glow. It changed its image from a rising sun of opportunity into the glare of an interrogation lamp.

This is where the insidious and dangerous character of the new underground Socialists in the plethora of underground manifestations reveals itself. Today we don't have a socialist state in America; instead we have a welfare state. Unlike Socialism the welfare State has no precise definition. The attempt to understand all its implications is like trying to take a picture of fog: it obscures the picture, however, it cannot be seen as anything solid. The leaders of this homegrown style of Socialism: Progressivism, have learned that by incrementally increasing the level of governmental control over private industry and individuals they can still achieve the Socialist goal of income redistribution without the stigma of advocating an admittedly authoritarian dictatorship.

All they have to do is speak in vague terms of the general good and spreading the wealth around and the low-information citizens nurtured in state schools will stand in line to proudly vote for hope and change. Never realizing that the prosperity Paul thinks he is voting out of Peter's pocket will not reach him as it is syphoned off to feed an ever-growing bureaucracy needed to transfer the wealth.

As long as the danger to liberty came from self-declared Socialists who were openly pursuing collectivist goals and as long as there was the glaring disconnect of a brutal dictatorship saying it was oppressing its own people in the quest for social justice, it was easy to argue that the tenets of Socialism were false. There were examples to show that it would not achieve its goals, that its execution was brutish, and that it would inevitably produce results which most Socialists themselves would find abhorrent.

The situation is different when we face the Welfare State. It has no definite form and is instead a conglomeration of diverse and sometimes even contradictory elements. Some of these elements may seem to make a free society more attractive such as something for everyone while others such as the means to take from one to give to another are incompatible with freedom.

I am not in any way advocating for no government. I am advocating for limited government. There are many things which most will agree are beneficial to society and which are legitimate concerns for government such as defense, the mail system, taxes appropriate to a limited role, and the judiciary. Most people today would also agree that some form of a safety net is possible in a free society to protect against risks common to all.

However, here it is important to differentiate between two views of this type of protection. There is limited protection which can be achieved for all and absolute security which can never be achieved.

The first of these types of protection is against severe poverty: the assurance of a minimum level of support for everyone. The second is the guarantee of a certain standard of life which is determined by comparing the standard enjoyed by one group against that enjoyed by another. In other words, the difference is between the protection of an equal minimum income for all and the protection of a particular income for particular groups. This is the goal of the Welfare State that brings us back to "From each according to their ability to each according to their need" or as our current Progressive President puts it, "Spreading the Wealth Around."[4]

To accomplish this, the coercive power of the State is used to ensure that particular people get particular things which in turn require discrimination between people and unequal treatment. Some are forced to give while others receive. This is incompatible with a free society. Thus the welfare State which aims at social justice inevitably leads back to Socialism with its coercive power and arbitrary methods. In addition though some of the aims of the Welfare State such as income equality can only be achieved through the use of methods which are incompatible with freedom all of the aims may be pursued in that fashion.

The primary danger is that once the aims of the Welfare State have been accepted as legitimate it is then tacitly assumed that the use of means which are contrary to freedom are acceptable. The ends justify the means and the rule of law is sacrificed in the name of social justice.

Ultimately we arrive at a place where the criticism of the generally accepted goals of the Welfare State leads automatically to negative labels. If you point out that Obamacare is socialized medicine you are throwing grandma over the cliff. If you point out that common core is indoctrination you are against education. If you point out that progressive taxation is inherently discriminatory and unfair you are the friend of millionaires and billionaires and the enemy of the poor. If you point out that government regulations are strangling business you are against clean air and consumer safety.

Our Progressive leaders always point to the shining city on a hill where everyone has everything. Our low-information fellow citizens never seem to realize that a government which ceases to administer limited resources put under its control for a specific purpose will instead use its coercive power to ensure that people are given what some bureaucrat decides they need. They never connect the dots. They do not understand that when larger and larger segments of the population come to depend on the government for everything, eventually it will be the decision of those in authority what anyone receives. This isn't freedom. This isn't what America was or what it is supposed to be. And this is why the Welfare State isn't well and it isn't fair.

★ DISPATCH NINETY-TWO ★

Why We Need a Third Party

It has happened just as foretold. The Progressive Republicans joined with their Democrat fellow-travelers and once again sold our inheritance for a bowl of promises. In 2010 we voted for an end to the out-of-control spending and what did we get? Three and a half trillion steps closer to the abyss.[1]

Fast forward to 2014 and we did it again. We sent Washington a loud wake-up call that out here in fly-over country we are tired of this slow motion slide into collectivism. And what is the first thing our shiny new majorities do? Re-elect the same tired old progressive leadership that has compromised its way from debt to debt and legislation to regulation. Does anyone think for a moment this crowd of Democrat lite that call themselves Republicans are going to do anything to stop the emperor who has no clothes?

Does anyone think they will use their power of the purse to reign in President Obama from doing things that he himself said he couldn't do because he wasn't an emperor?[2] Does anyone think they will do anything to bring out the truth about the IRS or Benghazi? They may play politics with investigations and hearings but at the end of the day the administration will not be called to account for turning the light out on America's time in the sun.

It's time to admit that when you fall off a cliff it doesn't matter much if you were pushed or if you walked. The fall might not be so bad but that sudden stop at the end isn't so good.

Maybe it's just me but I'm tired of the same old same old in our politics. The big-box monopoly parties have morphed into two sides of the same coin. Today we choose between the Conservative Progressives' policies of tax and spend, infringe personal liberty, and outsource our sovereignty or the Liberal Progressives' policies of tax and spend, infringe personal liberty, and outsource our sovereignty. We've been caught on the horns of a dilemma trying to choose between Tweedledee and Tweedledum, and since we don't want to throw our vote away we must vote for one of the big boys after which the campaign promises dissolve and we're hung out to dry.

As a voter I've had my Damascus Road Experience. The scales have fallen from my eyes. I've reached the point where I would rather vote for someone who might actually try finding another way to operate our government besides taxing like the Sun King and spending like a drunken sailor whose credit card limit is constantly raised and who can print his own money.

It's time to stop talking. It's time to take action. The Founders of our nation dedicated their lives, their fortunes, and their sacred honor to birth our state and this noble experiment. It's time for us to do the same. This nation was conceived as a representative republic designed to operate on democratic principles. For over 100 years the Progressives have worked to transform the land of the free and the home of the brave into a People's Democratic Republic. What's the difference? The difference between a Democracy and a People's Democracy is "the difference between a jacket and a straight-jacket."[3]

How did we arrive at the current situation?

James Madison our fourth president and the chief architect of the U.S. Constitution said, "There are more instances of the abridgement of the freedom of the people by the gradual and silent encroachment of those in power, than by violent and sudden usurpation."[4] We didn't get here all in one jump. First the camel said, "Can I just stick my nose in your tent to stay warm?" and finally the generous man found himself out in the cold as the camel settled down for a nice warm nap, one inch at a time.

The compassion of our people built a safety net for those who needed help and the greed of the lazy turned it into a hammock. America, the

Land of the Free is being transformed[5] into an America that is dedicated to the unsustainable achievement of, from each according to their abilities to each according to their need.[6] When you rob Peter to pay Paul, eventually Peter changes his name to Paul and the house of cards tumbles down.[7]

The willingness to share our heritage led America to welcome more immigrants each year than the rest of the world combined,[8] and the abuse of our generosity turned into a migration invasion that threatens to overwhelm us and destroy the future of our children. Taxes imposed to meet the ever-swelling demands of government have turned into a blatant, wealth re-distribution program[9] that makes most pyramid schemes look fair. It's as if our predatory government looks at a productive citizen as merely a source of residual income. Or as the ads promise, our Progressive leaders lay on the beach of self-importance and our checks just keep pouring in. We're no longer respected as Citizens. Instead, we're coveted as consumers or human capital.

It's time for action.

We as citizens who love our country must break the logjam caused by an imperial presidency, an abdicating legislature, an activist court, a suffocating bureaucracy, and the strangulation of regulation. The constant growth of government destroys freedom for "as government expands liberty contracts."[10]

It's time to actively work for America's acceptance of a different way.

And what might this different way be?

Something radical, something that almost strains the bounds of the imagination, something that would immediately unleash the bent-up energy of a free people: a return to constitutionally limited government!

But how do we get there from here? We need to build a new party to win the reins of government from the two-headed bird of prey which has assumed perpetual power through perpetual re-election. What we need now are citizens willing to sacrifice their repose and enter the arena. We need non-professionals to clean up the mess and right the ship of state.

What we don't need is one more election where the Conservative Progressives replace the Liberal Conservatives because as Albert Einstein said, "Insanity is doing the same thing over and over again and expecting different results."[11]

We need a new party. We must work to unite the Tea Party Movement with the many splinter parties which hold the same basic values. We must reclaim our liberty from the professional politicians and professional radicals who have manipulated the system to achieve unlimited power which they use to spend us into insolvency, tax us into poverty, and regulate us into serfdom.

This new party must siphon off all the conservatives who are members of the twin party out of habit or family tradition. This new party must rise fast and work hard. It must capture the center and the right declaring boldly that it will defend what America stands for but not necessarily all that stands for America. The time has come to fight for the right before we are swallowed by the wrong.

Winston Churchill said, "If you will not fight for the right when you can easily win without bloodshed, if you will not fight when your victory will be sure and not so costly, you may come to the moment when you will have to fight with all the odds against you and only a precarious chance for survival. There may be a worse case. You may have to fight when there is no hope of victory, because it is better to perish than to live as slaves."[12]

We can't let divisions divide us or they will bury us. United we stand, divided we fall. None of us can do this alone but together we can.

Keep the faith. Keep the peace. We shall overcome.

★ DISPATCH NINETY-THREE ★

WHY WE NEED CAPITALISTS

At one time in America most people were financially independent. I don't mean by this that most people were wealthy. What I mean is that they worked for themselves as opposed to working for someone else as a hired laborer. People were farmers, or craftsmen, trappers, or frontiersmen. Thomas Jefferson pictured America as a republic based upon the yeoman farmer.

That day has passed. Today most people who work are employed by someone and draw a wage. As a matter of fact, in America today it is not overstating the matter to say that of those who earn their own living the vast majority are exclusively wage earners.

Combine this with the reality of our modern infatuation with democracy and it is no wonder that the majority of voters continue to elect people who are pro-worker and anti-free enterprise. This is aptly reflected in our labor laws and the radicalized National Labor Relations Board. It is also reflected in the progressive income tax, the fact that corporate income is taxed twice, once as income to the corporation and secondly as income when the same money is distributed to shareholders. It is further manifested in the bewildering array of regulations that spews forth from Washington strangling business in red tape.

The masses of wage earners have fallen prey to the siren songs of demagogues. These pied pipers point to the visible difference between the rewards earned by those who risk their capital and their personal efforts to start and build an enterprise and those who earn wages to work for those enterprises. These differences in reward are labeled as unfair. It is either intimated or stated directly that those who start enterprises and build their bigger reward have done so by taking from those who earn a smaller reward by working for the enterprises they build.

We hear endlessly about a fair deal, a level playing field, and building ladders to the middle class. Government control is offered as a gateway to utopia where those who earn too much give to those who earn too little; from each according to their ability to each according to their need. The Svengalis of redistribution seek to mesmerize people removed from anything except doing a proscribed task for an agreed upon amount, and that free enterprise is the cause of the unfairness they portray as America's legacy. Combine those who succumb to this delusion among the wage earners to those who are living off the dole and we have a solid majority dedicated to restricting freedom to gain security. A bargain our Founders warned us leads to having neither.

This is where we stand today. The entrepreneur is looked down upon as a parasite on the economic life of the wage earners. They are portrayed in movies, on TV, and by our leaders as grasping schemers who care nothing for the environment or their fellow man, and the only reason they aren't throwing grandma off the cliff is because someone is watching. Try to remember the last time Outside of an Ayn Rand novel or movie that you saw capitalists portrayed as anything positive in America.

This is a trap; a trap that swallowed Russia and held it captive for generations, and a trap that impoverished Eastern Europe and turned China into one big internment camp. Those who spent most of the 20th century sitting in the dirt eating leaves as a result of their campaign against free enterprise have broken their chains and are today the Tigers of East Asia and the power houses made of BRIC.

Entrepreneurs are necessary. They are the engine which makes the wheels of innovation turn. They are the ones willing to take a risk. They will turn away from the guaranteed wage and the benefits all our parents taught us were necessary for a good life. They are the ones willing to take the chance and hazard their all for something others can't see. They are the ones who build the organizations for others to work within. Without them economies stagnate, suffocate, and die.

If the government were to take over every business in America and ensure that every wage earner could continue to earn their daily bread does anyone think this would be the America that we have known? Does anyone believe it would be the America that grew from 13 impoverished war weary states on the edge of civilization into the greatest power the world has ever known? This has been tried before and everywhere it has ever been tried it has failed. Don't believe the political savants who tell us this time it will work. The ones who's every words say they will do it differently and whose every program proves they are doing it the same.

In Russia the government actually took ownership of everything, and then ran it all into the ground. In Italy and Germany they tried it another way. They allowed for private ownership but with strict government control. Here in our American version we are following the Italian and German path with crony capitalism building fortunes on political access. Our stock market does not move in response to innovation and enterprise, rather it moves in tandem with government policies. Too-Big-to-Fail makes the cronies at the top wealthy as they plunder the assets, buy back the stock, and enrich their friends with options making sizable campaign donations along the way to those who make it all legal. Then when the bubbles burst they get bailed out and the tax payers foot the bill.

If we are to survive let alone thrive we have got to open the way for the innovator. We have got to once again encourage the risk taker, quit punishing success, and stop subsidizing failure.

To give a good day's work for a day's wage is an honorable thing. To be a faithful and responsible employee is something we can teach our children. However, without the new energy and markets created by innovative entrepreneurs the system will eventually stop growing. When the pie stops growing everyone ends up fighting over the size of their piece. When the pie stops growing and the population keeps growing everyone's piece must get smaller, except of course for those who do the dividing.

Why do we need capitalists? So that everyone else can have a job.

★ DISPATCH NINETY-FOUR ★

WHY WORRY WHEN YOU CAN PRAY

I am often asked, "How can you stay focused so intently upon the situations and circumstances surrounding America's current condition of managed decline without succumbing to the mind-chilling depression it warrants?"

How can I watch with the contextual awareness of an Historian the seemingly unstoppable advance of the progressives in their quest to rebuild America in their own image without falling victim to the lure of apathy and the thrill of the games?

What is it that allows me to gaze daily at the man-caused disasters which befall us as we morph from our nation to the Obamanation without embracing the nihilism so common to the citizens of falling empires?

There is one common solution to these apparent paradoxes. There is one answer to these discomforting questions. Because there is one name that stands above all nations, all circumstances, and all names and that name is Jesus.

If it wasn't for my rock solid faith in Jesus I would despair. If it wasn't for my faith in Jesus I would turn away from the shame of our surrender, the enormity of our decline, and the potential of our looming defeat. As a believer in limited government, personal liberty, and economic freedom without Jesus I would give-up. I would look at the reality of our situation and admit the subjugation of my nation to this band of looting Utopians who have gathered the reins of power and are leading us like sheep to the slaughter into a dystopian future of unlimited government, personal servitude, and a centrally-planned economy.

However, I do have Jesus as my personal Savior. I confess Him as my Lord and Savior. I believe that God has raised Him from the dead, and that he will come again.

Yes, I follow current events, the History of the Future,[1] like a housewife follows her people on any other soap opera. I tune in every day to see what new perils Lady Liberty faces, and what dastardly deeds Simon Lagree Obama will perpetrate upon the chained and restrained citizens who watch helplessly as their nation floats on an ice flow of freedom constantly melting beneath them. Yet just like those readers of Uncle Tom's cabin so long ago I have my Tom. I have my joy and the lifter of my head. I have Jesus. So I know that no matter what happens here and no matter what may happen to me or mine, He will be my reward.

The followers of some other religion who say they are a religion of peace may have declared war upon us. They have adopted a policy of convert or die. However, I know that Jesus has already won the war. I know that He has already died for me and though this body may perish He has already done all the dying I will ever have to do.

It was not always this way. Yes, I have always been obsessed with current events. Yes, I have always studied History, economics, and political science. Yes, I have always been aware of the context and the goal of the Progressive horde. However, there was a time when I didn't have this hope that lives inside of me. There was a time when the thought of being a pawn in a rigged game, being the citizen of an occupied nation sold by low-information voters to one demagogue after another, intent upon the subversion of the Constitution, drove me to despair. Watching the incremental surrender caused me to embrace a philosophy of militant apathy. I didn't care and I couldn't stand anyone who did.

This led to a hollowness that made any success or pleasure I experienced seem futile and merely a diversion. I was an atheist. I didn't believe in God. I didn't believe in spirits. All I believed in was what I could see, and all I could see was the decay of something once promising: the selling of the land of the free and the home of the brave for a bowl of pottage called entitlement. At the age of 30, I had reached my limit. I was convinced nothing meant anything. I was sure that my nation on its way to freedom had turned around and looked longingly at the chains of tyranny they had broken and was turning before my eyes into a pillar of salt. It seemed no one could read the handwriting on the wall, and I was playing the fiddle while Rome burned.

There came a time when I was saying to myself over and over, "I've got to try something, I've got to try something." I was a drug addict, an alcoholic, and I thought if I could just find a better high or a smoother whiskey all my anxieties would disappear. No matter what I tried it didn't work. The rotting stench of decay still filled my mind. I couldn't take my eyes off the slow motion train wreck that has been America's path. I was thinking the unthinkable and wondering if there was any reason to go on? I didn't believe in an afterlife. I believed that here was all there was. So I thought if I wasn't here the sorrow would stop. Yet something within me still clutched at straws and kept saying, "I've got to try something, I've got to try something."

Then one day as I went about my work saying this to myself over and over, I heard someone say, "Why don't you try Jesus." As a devout believer in Militant Apathy and a devout non-believer in everything else, I turned to follow my regular pattern of smashing in the face of anyone foolish enough to mention Jesus to me, and no one was there. I was in a church for a secular reason at the time and there was no one else in the entire building. I know because I looked. I had distinctly heard an answer to my perennial question, "Why don't you try Jesus" yet I knew no one else was there.

As an atheist who didn't believe in anything except the visible, that was, to say the least, disconcerting. I started attending that church the next week. It was Christian church. I knew from my youth the Christianity, which I had rejected in that same youth, was built upon the Bible so I started reading.

I read Mathew, Mark, Luke, and John. By the time I finished John I knew I had to make a decision. All of this was either true or it was false. If it was false it was just another lie in a world filled with lies. But if it was true it was the most important truth in the world. I knew from my study of History that many of the early followers of Jesus including Matthew, Mark, Luke, and John were killed because of their faith. I also knew that each of them had been given the opportunity to reject Jesus, admit what they had written and what they preached was lies and live, or they could affirm the truth of what they said and die. I knew they had all chosen death rather than say it was a lie.

Then I reasoned, if this story, this good news about a God who became flesh, paid the price of all sin by dying a sinless death upon a cross, and who purchased our everlasting life by defeating death rising from the grave was a lie they would have known it since they wrote it. They would have known there was no Savior, no salvation, and that their death would have been final. They would have known all this, and they would have chosen life over death. They didn't. They chose death in this life, because they believed in a life after this life: the life their writing told us about.

At that moment I asked Jesus to be my Savior. Suddenly a light burst forth in my being that has never gone out. A joy replaced the sadness. Hope replaced depression as I chose life over death, and I have spent every day since then trying to live for Him because He chose to live for me. Since that day it has never been about who I am but about what He' done, and not about what I've done but about who He is.[2]

Jesus Christ my Lord and Savior.

If you are overwhelmed by the calamity which is looming in our future, by the soul crushing sadness of living as citizens of a city on the hill that is committing suicide before our eyes.

Turn your eyes upon Jesus,

Look full in His wonderful face,

And the things of earth will grow strangely dim,

In the light of His glory and grace.

So why worry when you can pray….;--)

★ DISPATCH NINETY-FIVE ★

WOULD WE THE PEOPLE RATIFY THE CONSTITUTION TODAY?

We the People are the opening words of the preamble to the Constitution. Many patriots glory in that name, "*We the People.*"[1] They hold it aloft as a banner against the encroachment of an ever-expanding central government. In the minds of many it is connected somehow to Lincoln's famous description of America's government, "Of the People, by the people and for the people."[2]

Both of these were revolutionary terms when first spoken.

The people of the founding generation did not think of themselves as "Americans," instead they saw themselves as citizens of their respective States. The 13 colonies, with the singular exception of North and South Carolina, were each founded as separate entities. Each had its own history and relationship with the crown. They banded together for the Revolution during which they established the Continental Congress under the Articles of Confederation. This established a Confederation composed of 13 independent States.

When the secretly drafted Constitution was finally revealed to the public many of the leading lights of the Revolution were enraged by what they saw as a counter-revolution seeking to supplant the legally constituted Confederation of States in favor of a consolidated central government. Some of them say that the truth was revealed in the first three words, "We the People" instead of "We the States of America."

Every school child can recite the most famous words of Patrick Henry, "Give me liberty or give me death." You probably said those words in your head before you read them once you saw his name. He is synonymous with America's defiance to tyranny. While these famous words ring in the heads of all, few know his opinion on the Constitution.

At the Virginia Ratification Convention in 1788, Patrick Henry said,

> And here I would make this inquiry of those worthy characters who composed a part of the late federal Convention. I am sure they were fully impressed with the necessity of forming a great consolidated government, instead of a confederation. That this is a consolidated government is demonstrably clear; and the danger of such a government is, to my mind, very striking. I have the highest veneration for those gentlemen; but, sir, give me leave to demand, What right had they to say, We, the people? My political curiosity, exclusive of my anxious solicitude for the public welfare, leads me to ask, Who authorized them to speak the language of, We, the people, instead of, We, the states? States are the characteristics and the soul of a confederation. If the states be not the agents of this compact, it must be one great, consolidated, national government, of the people of all the states.[3]

Ever since the Civil War fatally warped the original federal structure and we the People became a reality, the central government of the United States has assumed more and more power until today totalitarianism appears to be within its grasp. I am not referring to the crude overt totalitarianism of a Nazi Germany or a Soviet Russia; instead I am referring to a soft totalitarianism, a kind of nanny-state smothering of individual freedom, personal liberty, and economic opportunity. After the complete subjugation of the States to the central government by the Lincoln administration combined with the increased mobility of the modern era, we the people actually became the way most people think of themselves.

In America, today we have a president, who in a 2001 interview expressed his innermost thoughts about the Constitution,

> If you look at the victories and failures of the civil rights movement and its litigation strategy in the court, I think where it succeeded was to invest formal rights in previously

dispossessed people, so that now I would have the right to vote. I would now be able to sit at the lunch counter and order as long as I could pay for it I'd be o.k. But, the Supreme Court never ventured into the issues of redistribution of wealth, and of more basic issues such as political and economic justice in society. To that extent, as radical as I think people try to characterize the Warren Court, it wasn't that radical. It didn't break free from the essential constraints that were placed by the founding fathers in the Constitution, at least as it's been interpreted and Warren Court interpreted in the same way, that generally the Constitution is a charter of negative liberties. Says what the states can't do to you. Says what the Federal Government can't do to you, but doesn't say what the Federal Government or State government must do on your behalf, and that hasn't shifted and one of the, I think, tragedies of the civil rights movement was, um, because the civil rights movement became so court focused I think there was a tendency to lose track of the political and community organizing and activities on the ground that are able to put together the actual coalition of powers through which you bring about redistributive change. In some ways we still suffer from that.[4]

That is a clear statement of the way our Progressive leaders view America's founding document, a charter of negative liberties. A charter that they believe needs to be expanded with a Second Bill of Rights first proposed by FDR in his 1944 State of the Union Address,

1. A realistic tax law—which will tax all unreasonable profits, both individual and corporate, and reduce the ultimate cost of the war to our sons and daughters. The tax bill now under consideration by the Congress does not begin to meet this test.

2. A continuation of the law for the renegotiation of war contracts—which will prevent exorbitant profits and assure fair prices to the Government. For two long years I have pleaded with the Congress to take undue profits out of war.

3. A cost of food law—which will enable the Government (a) to place a reasonable floor under the prices the farmer may expect for his

production; and (b) to place a ceiling on the prices a consumer will have to pay for the food he buys. This should apply to necessities only; and will require public funds to carry out. It will cost in appropriations about 1% of the present annual cost of the war.

4. Early re-enactment of the stabilization statute of October, 1942. This expires on June 30, 1944, and if it is not extended well in advance, the country might just as well expect price chaos by summer. We cannot have stabilization by wishful thinking. We must take positive action to maintain the integrity of the American dollar.

5. A national service law—which, for the duration of the war, will prevent strikes, and, with certain appropriate exceptions, will make available for war production or for any other essential services every able-bodied adult in this Nation.[4]

According to Cass R. Sunstein, the former administrator of the White House Office of Information and Regulatory Affairs, President Obama not only believes in FDR's Second Bill of Rights he seeks to implement them,

> As the actions of his first term made clear, and as his second inaugural address declared, President Barack Obama is committed to a distinctive vision of American government. It emphasizes the importance of free enterprise, and firmly rejects "equality of result," but it is simultaneously committed to ensuring both fair opportunity and decent security for all.

In these respects, Obama is updating FDR's Second Bill of Rights.5

We are in the grip of the Federalists on steroids bent on redistributing their way to total power. The question before us today is, "Would we the people ratify the Constitution today?"

Even Conservatives believe in a safety net. Everyone contributes to and hopes to receive from Social Security. No one wants people dying in the streets because they can't get medical care, so Medicaid is available to the uninsured. Of course Medicare is considered a right for anyone over 65. Unemployment is an accepted part of the safety net as are food stamps. If you add up what is already accepted and expected then throw Obamacare into the mix and you see we have become a society addicted to entitlements all of which would fail the test of a strict interpretation of the Constitution.

The 10th Amendment says, "The powers not delegated to the United States by the Constitution, nor prohibited by it to the States, are reserved to the States respectively, or to the people."7 The power to do any of these entitlements is not delegated anywhere in the document as it is written, only as it is interpreted.

So would we the people ratify the Constitution as it is written today? I think not. A living document has turned the Constitution into a dead letter and the entitlements we have all accepted have turned the descendants of the Founders, Framers, and Pioneers into supplicants standing before the federal throne waiting for a check.

Only a re-birth of self-reliance, a renaissance of historical perspective, and renewed political activity have a chance to bring about a rebirth of liberty in the land of the free and the home of the brave.

Keep the faith. Keep the peace. We shall overcome.

★ DISPATCH NINETY-SIX ★

Yes America Did Build That

I have often been tempted to believe that the greatest contribution of the British people to the world has been the limited liability corporation. It was the development of this concept that created the environment for the invisible hand of capitalism to create the dynamic free economy. And it was that free economy not conquest or empire that lifted the masses of Western Civilization out of abject poverty.

Economically that concept maybe the greatest contribution of the British to the world, however, when viewed as a whole the greatest contribution of the British people is the reality of a limited government. It is limited government which has allowed the freedom and independence necessary for humanity to do what humanity was created to do: exercise its individual free choice.

The people of Great Britain, the political forefathers of American liberty, fought for centuries to establish individual freedom. Beginning as abject servants of an absolute king they struggled to carve out a space for the recognition of personal independence. Through battles and death, fire and sword, through revolution and repression the people of Britain won inch-by-inch a space for humanity to breathe free.

Most of us have heard of the Charter of Liberties in 1100 which declared that the King was subject to the law. The Magna Carta of 1215 asserts the writ of habeas corpus, trial by one's peers, representation of nobility for taxation, and a ban on retroactive punishment. The Petition of Right of 1628 asserts the specific rights and liberties of England that the King is prohibited from infringing. The Habeas Corpus Act of 1679 is a procedural device to force the courts to examine the lawfulness of a prisoner's detention. And finally, there was the Bill of Rights of 1689, the result of the Glorious Revolution, securing Parliamentary Sovereignty over the King and Courts.

All of these were fought for and won for all British citizens back when the United States were 13 separate colonies proud to be part of the British Empire. Americans saw themselves as British. They believed that they had the same rights as any other British citizen and that they were not second-class citizens. It was their stand upon these rights which became the seedbed of the American Revolution.

When Americans claimed that they were British citizens with all the rights and privileges this entailed, they pointed to the charters given to the first settlers. The First Virginia Charter, signed by King James in 1606, stated clearly:

> wee doe, for us, our heires and successors, declare by theise presentes that all and everie the parsons being our subjects which shall dwell and inhabit within everie or anie of the saideseverall Colonies and plantacions and everie of theire children which shall happen to be borne within the limitts and precincts of the said severall Colonies and plantacions shall have and enjoy all liberties, franchises and immunites within anie of our other dominions to all intents and purposes as if they had been abiding and borne within this our realme of Englande or anie other of our saide dominions.[1]

And, the "Charter of Massachusetts Bay" which was issued in 1629 that proclaimed:

> Wee doe hereby for Us, our Heires and Successors, ordeyne and declare, and graunte to the saide Governor and Company and their Successors, That all and every the Subjects of Us, our Heires or Successors, which shall goe to and inhabite within the saide Landes and Premisses hereby mentioned to be graunted, and every of their Children which shall happen to be borne there, or on the Seas in goeing thither, or retorning from thence,shall have and enjoy all liberties and

> Immunities of free and naturall Subjects within any of the
> Domynions of Us, our Heires or Successors, to all Intents,
> Constructions, and Purposes whatsoever, as if they and ev-
> erie of them were borne within the Realme of England.[2]

Then after popular uprisings and resistance compelled the British Parliament to repeal the Stamp Act they passed the Declaratory Act (1766), which said that the British Parliament's taxing authority, was the same in America as in Great Britain. Americans believed that they could only be taxed with the approval of their local assemblies. In this law the parliament also declared its complete authority to make binding laws on the American colonies "in all cases whatsoever."[3]

Patriots such as James Otis and Sam Adams in Massachusetts and Patrick Henry in Virginia called it treason. They insisted that this action destroyed all that their British ancestors had fought for. If you make a careful examination of the arguments of the Founders before the Declaration of Independence or if you look at the arguments set forth in that hallowed document, you will see that all of the arguments were based upon the ancient rights which had been won by the British people. It was not until they realized that the solid foundation which they believed stood beneath their freedom was in reality a sand bar in the river of politics did they declare their independence and fight to win it.

Once they had won the long hard fight and proudly stood as 13 independent nations on the edge of what was becoming a trans-Atlantic civilization did they see that if they were to preserve the freedom they had won they needed something more than a tradition and stronger than a promise. This is when America made its first great contribution to the world: the concept of a written constitution. Yes America you did build that.

From their British roots and from the writings of the Enlightenment giants such as John Locke's *Two Treatises on Government* (1689 and 1690), Baron de Montesquieu in *The Spirit of the Laws* (1748), Jean-Jacques Rousseau's *The Social Contract* (1762), Immanuel Kant's *What is Enlightenment?* and his *Groundwork of the Metaphysics of Morals* and Adam Smith's *Wealth of Nations*, the Framers wrote a constitution to limit government. For they realized without the binding chains of limitation any government will inevitably accumulate such power that it will eventually trample upon the rights of its citizens. Sadly we have learned that even with a written constitution the same thing will eventually occur.

Our forefathers understood that any document which establishes a government and delineates which powers belong to it, and which expressly states, "The powers not delegated to the United States by the Constitution, nor prohibited by it to the states, are reserved to the states respectively, or to the people"[4] is purposefully limiting the power of the central government. In addition, this document is extremely clear in dividing the powers of government into separate parts as described by Montesquieu in *The Spirit of the Laws*. In this work Montesquieu proposed separating the power of government among a legislature, an executive, and a judiciary. This approach presented a government which did not centralize all its powers in an executive. There should be no imperial presidency.

It was the genius of the Framers to construct a constitution which they believed was strong enough to stand the test of time and the lust for power among those chosen to represent the people. They believed as Madison said, "The powers delegated by the proposed Constitution to the federal government are few and defined."[5] This is America's great contribution to civilization: a government in chains so that the people could be free for when a government is free, the people are in chains.

Then along came the Progressive Movement, Teddy Roosevelt, Woodrow Wilson, FDR, LBJ, and now BHO. They have used the fiction of a Living Document to turn the Constitution into a dead letter. They have progressed past the limitations on the government not by following the amendment process but instead by ignoring and interpreting then calling precedent tradition. Inch-by-inch, step-by-step slowly they turned the greatest experiment in human freedom ever devised into another welfare state kleptocracy promising a worker's paradise for those who don't work by plundering those who do.

The blush is off the rose. The scam is plain to see. The emperor has no clothes, "If you like the plan you have, you can keep it. If you like the doctor you have, you can keep your doctor, too."[7] You can't spend more than you make forever.[8] Eventually the note comes due.

The political actions of our Framers followed the lead of philosophers so too the Progressives have followed their own philosophical leaders.

Marx taught them "From each according to his ability to each according to his need."[9] He also taught that capitalism will wither away and then a dictatorship of the proletariat will build a worker's paradise.[10] His disciples attempted to put this into practice in that great prison-house of nations: the USSR.

Lenin taught them, "The way to crush the bourgeoisie is to grind them between the millstones of taxation and inflation"[11] and "The best way to destroy the capitalist system is to debauch the currency"[12] and of course "The goal of socialism is communism."[13]

Stalin elaborated on this further, "Education is a weapon whose effects depend on who holds it in his hands and at whom it is aimed"[14] and "Print is the sharpest and the strongest weapon of our party"[15] and also "Ideas are more powerful than guns. We would not let our enemies have guns, why should we let them have ideas."[16]

Following these precepts the enemies of freedom have captured the education system and systematically worked to dumb down our people.

They have captured the major media and turned it from a watchdog to a lap dog swilling out propaganda to a populace entranced by bread and circuses.

It is our duty to keep the light of freedom alive, to teach our true History, and to instill in our children and in the minds of any who will listen, limited government is essential for freedom. Let us work to restore the limits so our children may be free.

Keep the faith. Keep the peace. We shall overcome.

★ DISPATCH NINETY-SEVEN ★

YESTERDAY'S TOMORROW IS TODAY

S cience fiction has predicted many of today's realities from cell phones to tablets. Many things that are today part of History like walking on the moon, organ transplants, and space stations were once flights of fancy.

Futurists build current events on a foundation of History to provide a launching pad for visions of what is to come. One of the most widely recognized Futurists is Alvin Toffler whose seminal works include Future Shock and The Third Wave.[1] He is also the one who told us, "Change is not merely necessary to life - it is life."[2]

Here is my question for today "Is Ray Kurzweil a Futurist?"

The Wall Street Journal has described Kurzweil as "the restless genius." Forbes calls him "the ultimate thinking machine." He has been ranked by Inc. Magazine as #8 among entrepreneurs in the United States, He has also been called "the rightful heir to Thomas Edison," while according to PBS he is one of 16 "revolutionaries who made America."

His inventions are breathtaking and they impact our lives on a daily basis. These inventions include the first CCD flat-bed scanner, the first omni-font optical character recognition, the first print-to-speech reading machine for the blind, the first text-to-speech synthesizer, the first music synthesizer capable of recreating the grand piano and other orchestral instruments, and the first commercially marketed large-vocabulary speech recognition.[3]

Today, many websites attribute Mr. Kurzweil with accurate predictions about where the world will be tomorrow. In his latest book, *The Singularity is Near*[4] he describes the singularity as a reference to the theoretical limitlessness of exponential expansion that will see the merging of our biology with the staggering achievements of "GNR" (genetics, nanotechnology, and robotics) to create a species of unrecognizably high intelligence, durability, comprehension, memory, and so on. This is a bold prediction; however, bold predictions do not a Futurist make.

There is a fundamental difference between someone who is a professional writer and observer of humanity such as Toffler and someone who is a technological genius with almost unlimited resources who is actively working to make his predictions reality. Toffler reads studies and interviews on his way to predictions of where society and technologies will go next. Kurzweil traded in his massive private business built upon his inventions to become Google's Director of Engineering whose sole job is to make the company's computers smarter than humans.[5] He is working every day to improve artificial intelligence and then wed that to cutting edge robotics and human interface to produce the very singularity he is predicting.[6]

Reaching back to the science fiction genre which I referenced earlier we are looking at the rise of the machines, the coming of the cylons, skynet, and the matrix. These of course are all fiction; however, the reality we face brings this question to my mind, "Once we design and build machines that are smarter than we are and they design and build machines that are smarter than they are what do they need us for?"

Artificial Intelligence (AI) foresees a time when machines not only rival but surpass human capabilities. Once this happens will we know when these super intelligent machines cross the threshold from hyper abilities to self-awareness? These scenarios are troubling, even terrifying yet most people would dismiss them as the science fiction they mirror. There is another aspect of this technological revolution that is not quite as far-fetched and not quite as unbelievable: automation.

We have lived with automation all of our lives. People have been displaced by innovation since the Sumerian water wheel took the place of people with buckets bringing water from rivers into their fields. I can remember people telling me in the 1970s, "I'm a keypunch operator, I'll always have a job." Today machinists, tool and dye makers, auto workers, and many people have been replaced by machines. Tomorrow white collar workers will face the same fate as so many of their blue collar brethren.[7] Why do we need accountants when machines can fill in the same programs they use today to figure taxes and current accounts? Who needs teachers when lectures can be delivered by speech technology, questions answered by Watson type question answers, and tests grade themselves?

Look to Futurists like Toffler who are predicting where we are headed and look to inventors like Kurzweil who are telegraphing where they are headed and a collage of futures points to the tomorrow today will become.

It is my contention that we as a people, as a society, and as a civilization need to address this soon approaching brave new world. When I speak to people about these coming changes the almost universal reaction is, "Not in my lifetime." I believe this is a combination of wishful thinking, hiding our heads in the sand, and having no idea what is going on around us.

This is a social dislocation approaching at speeds unforeseen. I don't believe these changes are decades away. I believe within a decade they will be upon us. Large percentages of blue and white collar workers will be displaced. Machines will take the place of humans in many areas and humans will not be able to compete with them. If we allow this to come upon us with no preparation, we will be swamped by the rising tide of change and drowned in the tsunami of innovation.

Change is accelerating as the interconnectedness of communication accelerates the cross-polarization of ideas. After tens of thousands of years the use of the wheel had not spread all the way around the world. Today something is invented in America this morning, improved in India this afternoon, and spawning new ideas tomorrow in China. We cannot contain the explosion of technology because someone somewhere will always seek to move beyond the known to the unknown. No matter what glories we have beheld yesterday tomorrow is coming whether today is ready or not.

Long ago Toffler told us, "Future shock is the shattering stress and disorientation that we induce in individuals by subjecting them to too much change in too short a time."[8] He also predicted and predated Kurzweil's Singularity when he said, "The next major explosion is going to be when genetics and computers come together. I'm talking about an organic computer—about biological substances that can function like a semiconductor."[9]

How long will it before our cars drive themselves, 3-D printers create human organs, and the government has the ability to monitor everyone at once? How long will it be before you cannot tell the difference between speaking to a computer on the phone and speaking to a human?

Failure to plan is planning to fail. If we as a society do not stop living in yesterday and face up to the challenges of today we will sacrifice our future.

★ DISPATCH NINETY-EIGHT ★

You Didn't Build That

We can't know what we don't know; however, we can know that we don't know or as Socrates taught us the recognition of our ignorance is the beginning of wisdom.

The society and civilization in which any human lives and operates is like water to a fish. Something they move around in, something they need to survive, it is also something they don't even notice. If we wish to understand the world in which we live we need to realize that the civilization which serves as our support and framework is based upon vast amounts of knowledge those who fill its ranks give no thought to whatsoever.

It is also necessary to understand that civilization isn't something consciously created by man. Civilizations build up over time by humans interacting with and attempting to modify their surroundings. As such our civilizations are more accretions than structures.

What our civilization is today is no more the conscious product of some master plan than the course of a river. Life flows into the channels of least resistance and is moved by forces that act upon it. We can no more predict what our civilization will look like in a few generations than one of our 17th century ancestors could have described the lives we live today.

What will be invented tomorrow that will change the future in ways we could never imagine? More than thirty years ago in 1983 who would have thought we would all walk around with minicomputers we call cell phones? Or that there would be hundreds of television stations? Or a worldwide Internet that can cross-pollenate thought at the speed of light? What may be around the next corner is anyone's guess. One thing is for sure, 30 years from now we will live in ways we never imagined today.

This is the foundational problem that undergirds and eliminates the possibility of success from any of the Utopian central-planning schemes that litter History and of the ones we are trying today. The planners cannot take the place of masses of people living, innovating, and creating. No one person or group can substitute their decisions for the independent decisions of everyone else without short circuiting the system and causing civilization to stall out. No one is as smart as everyone.

If two minds are better than one how much better are 100,000 or 1 million or billions? Over and over those who think they and they alone are intelligent, far seeing or inspired enough to shape the future have grabbed the reins of power and tried to impose their vision on the world around them. Sooner or later reality comes along and teaches them that it just won't work. We have people trying to guide trillion dollar economies who know nothing of economics, and people trying to guide History who know nothing of History. We are surrounded by political savants who know how to get elected and not much else. Some even have the hubris to list running a campaign as a life skill that qualifies them to run the lives of everyone around them.[1]

What is even more bizarre than this is that people believe them and vote them into office based on such sketchy experience and vague promises as hope and change. Then when the Rube Goldberg[2] plans they devise fall apart and everyone is worse off than before the savants say, "You just didn't give us enough power to accomplish the task. What we need now is more of the same." Time after time civilizations have fallen for this siren song of perfection. And time after time civilizations have fallen because they did.

Why does this destructive desire to trade freedom for the promise of utopia always fail? Because it's based on the erroneous idea that humanity created civilization and therefore it is possible to alter its institutions, operations, and mechanisms whenever and however we please.

This assertion would be valid only if we had created civilization deliberately with full knowledge of what we were doing while we were doing it. In a way it is true that humanity has made its civilization in that it was not brought here by some aliens who placed us in it like animals in the artificial habitat of a zoo. Civilization is the product of the combined actions of hundreds of generations living their lives, making choices, succeeding and failing, rising and falling. This, however, does not mean civilization is the conscious product of human design or that any one individual or group can completely comprehend all of its functions or what is required for its continued existence.

The very idea that humanity sprang from the earth with a mind able to conceive civilization and then proceeded to systematically create it does not fit the anthropological or historical record. Our minds themselves are the product of the constant adjustments we make as we attempt to adapt to our surroundings.

Is it nature or nurture is an age-old debate.

The reality is that it is both. Our minds are what they are, unbelievably intricate bio-computers able to think in symbolic terms and extrapolate beyond what is known to what is imagined. They are the wonder upon which civilization is built; however, they did not design and then initiate civilization. If they were, all we would have to do to reach a higher plane of civilization is imagine it and then make it happen. The fact that civilization has advanced by fits and starts shows that some things work and some things don't. It is the constant adjustment that moves us forward.

Believing the lie that man is the measure of all things is the trap the Utopians fall into: that man in and of himself has the capacity to control History. It seems so enticing and yet it never works because that isn't how civilizations grow. They grow by the friction between our present conditions and our dreams. They grow by the incessant revision of what is into what we want it to be. Our current experience shapes our course deviations in so many ways that cannot be foretold leading in a zigzag fashion from the present to the future.

The weathermen who have a hard time accurately predicting what the weather will be like five days from now seem ever ready to tell us what it will be like 500 years from now. The economic forecasters who are surprised every month by what the economy did last month have no problem making absolute statements about how actions today will guide our multifaceted economy for years in the future.

Man knows not his time and we cannot know the future. In other words, we can't know what we don't know. About the best we can do is know that we don't know.

★ DISPATCH NINETY-NINE ★

You Say You Want a Revolution

Our revolution changed the world. Our Declaration of Independence proclaims self-evident truths.[1] "That all men are created equal, they're endowed by their Creator with unalienable rights, among these are life, liberty and the pursuit of happiness. These words shook a world held in the vise-grip of hereditary privilege inspiring people around the globe. Our Constitution established a representative republic with a limited government of the people, by the people, and for the people."[2]

We've watched as our constitutionally limited government grew until today, it's a leviathan running amok like Godzilla in Tokyo smashing things and scaring boy scouts. Today, the Federal Government is the largest employer in America, states are the largest employers in the states, and counties are among the largest employers in the counties get the picture? Government is on a rampage and unless Mothra is going to fly in to save the day we'll have to deal with Frankenstein-on-the-Potomac ourselves.

Such brazen power-plays as the Executive branch issuing the Legislature an ultimatum,[3] either pass Cap-N-Trade[4] or we'll impose it administratively through command-and-control[5] make the dramatic changes in our political culture shockingly apparent.[6] Has our balance of powers melted away under the glare of executive orders, signing statements and now ultimatums?[9] Some people say this is evolution. To others it's devolution. Our hard-won and dearly-paid-for Republic is devolving into a command-and-control all-encompassing central-state.

With political dynasties bequeathing congressional seats like hereditary fiefdoms, it's becoming hard to explain why we left the British Empire.

Today we not only have taxation without representation[8] as congressional party-line voters ignore their constituents, we also have representation without taxation[9] as the perpetually re-elected Lords and Ladies represent the illegal immigrants and the professional welfare hammock-riders.

These big government social planners may believe they've achieved their community organizing goals fulfilling Historian Will Durant paraphrase of Lincoln's famous quote, "It may be true that you can't fool all the people all the time, but you can fool enough of them to rule a large country."[10] They may believe their revolutionary administration will fundamentally change America,[11] however, if they'd step 20 miles outside the Beltway obviously there's a counter-revolution brewing.[12] The Tea Party is overtaking the Republican Party in popularity. It has already supplanted them at the grassroots of the conservative movement. By 2010 an avalanche of voters thronged the polling places demanding their country back.

Following the tactics of Saul Alinsky brought the Obama-Acorn-SEIU coalition control of the Democratic Party and the country but following the Cloward-Piven Strategy[13] for overwhelming the system to impose an alternative system is going to lead to a complete repudiation of this radical departure from traditional American politics and economics. We aren't Venezuela. Even after decades of legislative efforts to progressively create a permanent underclass of government dependents who'll follow the leader to the next looting of productive members of society, the majority in this country still want freedom and opportunity not cradle-to-grave mediocrity.

We can and should stage a counter-revolution against this growing tyranny. A peaceful, lawful revolution at the ballot box and if you're talking about destruction, you can count me out. The last thing we need in this crowded theater full of combustible emotions is either a match or someone shouting fire. Any incident right now would trigger a massive response. Just as the executive is using the EPA to impose the onerous restrictions of a Cap-N-Trade style economy stunting strangulation of regulations he's also using ICE to change the enforcement of immigration policy and cook the books without any messy debate.

Ruling by decree, "I have a pen and I have a phone,"[14] are hardly compatible with constitutionally-limited government. We're told the administration has solutions. They sold us a solution to heal the greatest healthcare system in the world "If you like your plan you can keep your plan. Period"[15] like a pig-in-a-poke. They claim to have a solution to save or create jobs while we lose jobs every month, a draconian solution for the man-made global warming hoax, a solution for endless wars for elusive peace. You say you have a solution. We'd all love to see the plan.

They say they want a contribution. Back in the good old change we could believe in days the dialogue of class warfare[16] repeated that no one making under 250,000, or was it 150,000, or was it …anyway only the evil rich would have to pay a dime of new taxes. Watch out! You might find out you're rich come next April 15th.

Everyone has known since at least that tax-cutting wild man JFK that cutting taxes increases revenue to the government and raising them lowers revenue. Since the government knows raising taxes lowers revenue and since they're raising taxes to increase revenue what are they trying to do? Complicated tax codes are used as a way to incentivize and de-incentivize behavior.

If you want more widgets give tax breaks for buying widgets. If you want less widgets tax widgets. Using that for a guide notice what's being pushed and what's being pulled? Taxes on producers and tax breaks for non-producers imagine tax cuts for people who don't pay taxes and tax increases for those who do. Taking the money of producers to bailout the greedy, reward the cronies and support the lazy. It's time to tell the statists at the ballot box if they want money for things we hate they're going to have to wait.

Executive orders and signing statements have been used in Republican and Democrat administrations for years to change the constitution without changing the Constitution. Now sweeping new powers by regulators threatens to make Congress irrelevant as an all-powerful executive branch grows like a malignant tumor. Don't lose heart, don't despair, don't you know it's going to be all right?

Keep the faith, keep the peace, organize and
win the day. We shall overcome.

★ DISPATCH ONE HUNDRED ★

You Should Ask Whose Property Is It

Even for someone who learned at their grandmother's knee that what's mine is mine and what's yours is negotiable the knowledge that some things are mine and some things aren't came early. The whole idea of freedom rests upon the idea that within the wider world there is society which is a smaller circle that outlines what is personal and what is communal. Even in monasteries where monks have taken vows of poverty they refer to my cell, my candle, and my prayers.

Private property is an essential ingredient of a free society.

Two of the greatest rewards derived from the study of History are the ability to build upon the achievements of others and the opportunity to learn from the mistakes of others. One of the greatest calamities caused by the failure to study History is a lack of context.

Most people live their lives as if History began the day they were born and they forever live in a constantly flowing and ever changing now. George Orwell said in his epic dystopian novel 1984 that, "He who controls the past controls the future. He who controls the present controls the past."

The Progressives captured the majority of American education long ago and have taught generations of Americans that capitalism is bad and socialism is good. They have also taught children since at least the 1950s that America has been a grasping imperialistic power that has prospered by taking from others. We are seeing the fruits of this propaganda today.

Instead of memorizing the Declaration of Independence, our children have memorized the outlandish theories of Al Gore. Instead of learning the truth they have been indoctrinated with an inconvenient truth that is inconvenient because it isn't true. They have been taught from History books that have more about Nelson Mandela than they do about George Washington. And this is not a new thing. I am in my 60s and I was thrown out of public schools for standing up for capitalism by people who were pushing socialism.

If we want to recapture the future we have to recapture the present, so that we can recapture the past. Today, those of us who believe in limited government, individual freedom, and economic opportunity live as subjects in a land dominated and occupied by people who act as if America should pay a penalty or do penance for being the greatest country to have ever existed. We must regain and preserve our heritage of knowledge by regaining knowledge of our History or it will be erased from the consciousness of our children and replaced with the inconvenient lies of a shabby Progressive future. A future where the Sun is setting for the West rising in the East, and a paternal government seeks to take the place of god.

If we want to save America, we must begin at the beginning. Most people think the Constitution is the beginning. Even though our Progressive masters seek to re-interpret it to bring about our end, it wasn't our beginning. Before the Constitution came The Declaration of Independence.[1] This is the seminal document proclaiming to the world a new nation not ruled by kings had appeared upon the stage. This Declaration did not spring freshly from the imagination of Thomas Jefferson. It was not born in a vacuum. Jefferson was a student of Philosophy and History.

When Jefferson wrote the Declaration of Independence he built many of the ideas on the works of John Locke one of the greatest influences on the Framers. Locke had written in The Second Treatise of Civil Government, "The state of nature has a law of nature to govern it, which obliges every one: and reason, which is that law, teaches all mankind, who will but consult it, that being all equal and independent, no one ought to harm another in his life, health, liberty, or possessions..."[2]

This in turn inspired George Mason to write in The Virginia Declaration of Rights[3] which was published just before the Declaration of Independence in 1776, "That all men are by nature equally free and independent, and have certain inherent rights, of which, when they enter into a state of society, they cannot, by any compact, deprive or divest their posterity; namely, the enjoyment of life and liberty, with the means of acquiring and possessing property, and pursuing and obtaining happiness and safety."

Today the concept of private property is out of fashion as our collectivist rulers try to build a classless society on such misunderstood and elastic phrases as the Pursuit of Happiness[4] and the Necessary and Proper Clause.[5]

Looking at the works and words of our founders and of those who framed the Constitution, it is plain to see that the phrase Pursuit of Happiness was everywhere used as meaning the right to own, control, and use private property which brings us to economics.

In a capitalistic system people own, control, and use their own private property for their own devices. The opposite of that is Communism which advocates the state ownership of all property. Portraying itself as half way in between is Socialism which seeks to extract a portion of the rewards of private property for the benefit of those who do not own it. A malignant form of socialism with a capitalist veneer, Fascism advocates private ownership and total state control of its use.

Looking at capitalism we see the miracle that was the United States. In just a little over 150 years we rose from being 13 impoverished, war ravaged states loosely bound together into a colossus that strode upon the world stage saving freedom first from fascism and then from communism.

One of the founders of the Soviet nightmare Leon Trotsky said of the communistic system he helped create, "In a country where the sole employer is the state. Opposition means death by slow starvation. The old principle, he who does not work shall not eat, has been replaced by a new one: who does not obey shall not eat."[6]

And although Socialists try to play the part of sentimental reformers who are only out to help the children their ultimate agenda shows that they are in reality merely a stalking horse for their communist big brother. One socialist site puts it this way, "In Socialism, the laborer is the direct manager of their means of production, and receives the whole of their production. In Capitalism, the laborer is dominated by a Capitalist, who directs production and sets wages."[7]

As for the Fascists their program may sound familiar,

> "We ask that government undertake the obligation above all of providing citizens with adequate opportunity for employment and earning a living. The activities of the individual must not be allowed to clash with the interests of the community, but must take place within the confines and be for the good of all. Therefore, we demand: ... an end to the power of financial interest. We demand profit sharing in big business. We demand a broad extension of care for the aged. We demand ... the greatest possible consideration of small business in the purchases of the national, state, and municipal governments. In order to make possible to every capable and industrious [citizen] the attainment of higher education and thus the achievement of a post of leadership, the government must provide an all-around enlargement of our system of public education.... We demand the education at government expense of gifted children of poor parent. The government must undertake the improvement of public health—by protecting mother and child, by prohibiting child labor—by the greatest possible support for all groups concerned with the physical education of youth. [W]e combat the ... materialistic spirit within and without us, and are convinced that a permanent recovery of our people can only

proceed from within on the foundation of The Common Good Before the Individual Good."[8]

Ask yourself where are we today? The government issues regulations at the mind numbing rate of 68 per day[9] According to a study by the American Action Forum, regulations that went into effect in 2013 cost Americans $112 billion—or $447 million for each of the 251 days the federal government was open.[10] This study also predicts that the regulatory burden will increase to $143 billion in 2014.[11] Who controls the property you own? Who reaps the benefit of your labor? Tax Freedom Day the day after which you have worked enough to pay your taxes and can now start working for yourself gets later each year. In 2013, it was April 18th, five days later than it was in 2012.

F. A. Hayek tells us in The Constitution of Liberty, "True coercion occurs when armed bands of conquerors make the subject people toil for them, when organized gangsters extort a levy for 'protection,' when the knower of an evil secret blackmails his victim, and, of course, when the state threatens to inflict punishment and to employ physical force to make us obey its commands."[12]

John Locke told us, "Every man has a property in his own person. This nobody has a right to, but himself."[13] He also said, "All wealth is the product of labor,"[14] and "Government has no other end, but the preservation of property."[15] These are the bedrocks upon which our system was originally built. The next time you receive your pay look at the deductions. Ask yourself for whose benefit do you toil? Then look around you and think of the taxes you pay, the regulations you must follow, and the rules you must obey; then ask yourself, whose property is it?

CONCLUSION

THE GREAT CIVIL DEBATE

There have been calls for a return to civility in our speech. I heartily second that motion, believing as I do that civility should always be the hallmark of discussion among ladies and gentleman. However, that has not been the topic of this book.

I seek to call my fellow Americans not to a more civil debate but to The Great Civil Debate. This is the debate we need if we are to move beyond the gridlock of right versus left, the vitriol of Democrat versus Republican, and the hysteria of a coming conservative authoritarianism or a looming socialist one. The debate I'm calling for is not an innovation in American History. Instead it's a re-play of a previous event and the sequel to our preliminary event: the debate over the ratification of the Constitution. What we need now is a debate over the relevance of the Constitution with regard to the actions of the Federal Government.

From the day the Constitution was signed, September 17, 1787 to the day it was ratified June 21, 1788, this country rang with the impassioned speeches and stirring essays of both the opponents and the proponents of this our founding document. Today is the day and now is the time for the debate to once again stir the hearts of the nation, will we have a limited government, personal liberty, and free enterprise or are we going to have something else? There's no greater admirer of the United States Constitution then the author of this book. None can be found who gives more veneration to the Framers or who pays more attention to its words.

However, after 226 years there's no one more convinced that we've reached an historical impasse. The Constitution is still in force. It has been amended 27 times, but it has not been supplanted. Yet, it's all but ignored by the Federal Government. Our continually expanding federal bureaucracy tips its hat to the commerce clause or uses the elastic necessary and proper clause as a political fig leaf to do whatever they want. This being the current situation this book is in fact an intervention. It's well known that until a problem is recognized there's no hope for a solution. Therefore, since every other commentator I'm aware of dances around the 800 pound gorilla in the middle of the room, I'll acknowledge the obvious and take the afore-mentioned primate as my dancing partner and say what must be said: the Constitution has failed.

This is not to say that it is a flawed document, a vehicle for ulterior motives, or that it has always been a failure. This is not to say that I'm offering or advocating for a replacement. As I mentioned earlier, there is no greater admirer of the United States Constitution than the author of this book. What I do mean to say is that this great document which birthed and sustained a limited government for more than 200 years has now become effectively irrelevant.

The proof for this sad statement can be seen in the unguarded rhetoric of the movers and shakers of our now unlimited government. When asked where in the Constitution a warrant for mandated healthcare could be found one Congressman answered, "I don't worry about the Constitution."[1] Another Congressman said, "There's nothing in the Constitution that says that the federal government has anything to do with most of the stuff we do. It means what we say it means."[2] When asked a question about the constitutionality of healthcare legislation former Speaker of the House Nancy Pelosi's response was, "Are you serious?"[3]

And we have a President who writes that the Constitution is not "… static but rather a living document, and must be read in the context of an ever-changing world."[4] No wonder a liberal pundit finds it odd that a candidate for Congress would promise to consider the constitutionality of legislation saying, "That certainly isn't the job of Congress. They should just pass whatever they want and let the courts worry about it later."[5] These examples are joined by volumes of others, which show that not only is the Constitution irrelevant to these leaders it has become so accepted as irrelevant that they no longer even have to pay lip service to the integrity of the document they've sworn to uphold and defend.[6]

We need a reset button. We need to return to limited government. But how do we get there from here? The Tenth Amendment which says, "The powers not delegated to the United States by the Constitution, nor prohibited by it to the States, are reserved to the States respectively, or to the people"[7] has been emasculated through court rulings.[8] The legal system has moved from original intent to precedent. From what the words mean to what can we say the words mean. This tsunami of change is led by the Progressives who believe that we need to evolve past the ideas and procedures devised and set down by the Framers and create a New America. A transformed America[9] founded not on the equality of opportunity[10] but on the equality of outcome[11] these big government leaders in both parties seek not mere equal justice for all but social justice, not free enterprise but central planning.[12]

The great debate of our founding has broken down and become the great shouting match of an elephant trumpeting as a jackass brays. We have become a dysfunctional political circus masquerading as a functional democracy. We get to vote. However, all we get to do is choose which party drives us over the cliff. We never get to choose another direction.

We know that the Progressives who smoothly appropriated the name of Liberals are dedicated to collectivism, centralization, and regimentation so we can see they will not provide us with a new direction.

Since America was founded as a representative republic based upon limited government and dedicated to individual liberty, personal freedom, and economic opportunity predicated on man's natural rights whether they were called Anti-federalists, Whigs, or Republicans being a conservative initially meant standing up for this as the status quo. However, it has become obvious the conservative movement had been hijacked by semi-reformed Progressives known as Neocons reaching across the aisle compromising freedom for power. We can see that these fellow-travelers won't provide us with a new direction.

You can't conserve what has already been lost. We as a people, we as a federation of States need to find a different way, a new direction.

One thing I know, no one person can do this alone. No one group can do it. To make any headway in the face of the electoral monopoly held by the party of power, the many third party groups are going to have to coalesce into an effective opposition, the country party. We can't let divisions divide us any more, egos will have to be suppressed, and we will have to bond together with everyone dedicated to limited government, personal liberty, and economic freedom. If we want the land of the free we must be brave.

None of us can roll this big rock up this steep hill by ourselves. However, together we the people can if we will. Ben Franklin told us, "We must hang together, gentlemen...else, we shall most assuredly hang separately."[13]

It may take generations in the dark before we once again value the light enough to risk the sacrifice of safety to gain freedom. Therefore, it is well to remember that Franklin also said, "They that can give up essential liberty to obtain a little temporary safety deserve neither liberty nor safety."[14]

People are talking past each other. We see a great convergence where the people of the extreme right and the people of the extreme left find themselves agreeing on the brutishness of the government. From both directions the deteriorating situation of our freedom is apparent. Both sides see the problem it is only the answer that eludes us and the habit of reflexively arguing that keeps us from uniting for the cause of freedom without which neither side will long endure.

Two monologues in the same room builds cacophony not compromise, confusion not consensus. We must first begin a dialogue if we are ever to have a conversation. As a society we must be united or we will be divided and divided societies always fall. One can impose the peace of a graveyard one cannot impose peace in a society that is at war with itself. If we stand on opposite sides of barricades shouting slogans at each other civility has been lost in partisanship and community has collapsed into civil discord.

This book which is meant as a philosophical intervention sadly begins with the assessment based upon the current reality that the Constitution has failed. However, it ends on a note of hope. We are the descendants of the Pioneers, the offspring of the Framers, and we can do this. We can find a way within the legal framework of the Constitution itself to press that reset button. We can solve this problem, because we're Americans and we are a can-do, get-it-done people.

However, if we refuse to admit there's a problem we will be doomed to suffer silently in the shadows as our beloved city on the hill becomes a lost dream in the twilight of freedom. Instead, let us start The Great Civil Debate. How can we restore limited government, ensure liberty, and revitalize free enterprise? How can we get there from here?

Let action follow philosophy as the future slides into the present, the present slides into the past, and our lives are the history of the future.

Keep the faith. Keep the peace. We shall overcome.

Dr. Robert R. Owens

NOTES

Introduction

1. Orwell, George, Animal Farm, Sparks Notes, http://www.sparknotes. com/lit/animalfarm/section10.rhtml (accessed December 10, 2014).

Dispatch One

1. Washington Times 8-4-11 http://communities.washingtontimes.com/ neighborhood/stimulus/2011/aug/4/debt-ceiling-agreement-fiscal-band-aid-mortal-woun/ (accessed December 18, 2013).

2. The Quotation Collect, Ronald Wilson Reagan http://www.quotationcollection. com/author/Ronald-Wilson-Reagan/quotes (accessed December18, 2013).

3. Revolutionary War and Beyond, James Madison Quotes, http://www. revolutionary-war-and-beyond.com/james-madison-quotes-5.html (accessed December 18, 2013).

4. You Tube, http://www.youtube.com/watch?v=_cqN4NIEtOY (accessed December 18, 2013).

5. The Quotation Page, http://www.quotationspage.com/quote/36121.html (accessed December 18-, 2013).

6. The Cold war Museum, The Fall of the Soviet Union, http://www.coldwar. org/articles/90s/fall_of_the_soviet_union.asp (accessed December 18, 2013).

7. Snopes, http://www.snopes.com/politics/soapbox/borderpatrol.asp (accessed December 18, 2013).

8. You Tube, http://www.youtube.com/watch?v=RZcEHLr4gBg (accessed December 18, 2013).

9. Quotation Collection, Ronald Wilson Reagan http://www.quotationcollection. com/author/Ronald-Wilson-Reagan/quotes (accessed December 18, 2013).

10. Brainy Quote, http://www.brainyquote.com/quotes/quotes/a/alber-teins133991.html (accessed December 18, 2013).

11. Political Punch, http://abcnews.go.com/blogs/politics/2009/02/obamas-budget-a/ (accessed December 18, 2013).

12. Bedard, Paul, U.S. News and World Report, August 3, 2011, http://www.usnews. com/news/washington-whispers/articles/2011/08/03/report-obama-adminis-tration-added-95-billion-in-red-tape-in-july (accessed December 18, 2013).

13. John Petrie's Collection of Winston Churchill Quotes, http://jpetrie.myweb. uga.edu/bulldog.html (accessed December 18, 2013).

Dispatch Two

1. Yogi Berra Quotes, http://www.mindspring.com/~hsstern/maewest/y_berra. htm (accessed December 18, 2013).

2. U.S. Department of Defense, http://www.defense.gov/news/newsarticle. aspx?id=65432 (accessed December 18, 2013).

3. Franc, Michael, The heritage Foundation, "Beyond The $800 Hammer," http://www.heritage.org/research/commentary/2001/06/beyond-the-800-hammer (accessed December 18, 2013).

4. Abate, Tome, SFGATE, "Military waste under fire / $1 trillion missing -- Bush plan targets Pentagon accounting" May 18, 2003, http://www.sfgate. com/news/article/Military-waste-under-fire-1-trillion-missing-2616120. php (accessed December 18, 2013)

5. Stephey, M. J., Time Magazine, "The Bretton Woods System," October 21, 2008, http://content.time.com/time/business/article/0,8599,1852254,00. html (accessed December 18, 2013).

6. Reynolds, Alan, Townhall.com, "What 'Guns and Butter' Means," December 18, 2003, http://townhall.com/columnists/alanreyn-olds/2003/12/18/what_guns_and_butter_means/page/full (accessed December 18, 2013).

7. Investopedia, http://www.investopedia.com/terms/s/smithsonian-agree-ment.asp (accessed December 18, 2013).

8. Investopdedia, http://www.investopedia.com/terms/d/dirtyfloat.asp (accessed December 18, 2013).

9. Yogi Berra Quotes, http://www.mindspring.com/~hsstern/maewest/y_berra. htm (accessed December 18, 2013).

10. Ibid.

11. Ibid.

12. Ibid.

13. Ibid.

Dispatch Three

1. Douthat, Ross, New York Times, "Going for Bolingbroke," July 27, 2013, http://www.nytimes.com/2013/07/28/opinion/sunday/douthat-going-for-bolingbroke.html?_r=2& (accessed December 18, 2013)

2. Brainy Quote, http://www.brainyquote.com/quotes/authors/k/karl_marx. html (accessed December 18, 2013).

3. Luhby, Tami, CNN Money, "Government Assistance Expands," February 7, 2012, http://money.cnn.com/2012/02/07/news/economy/government_assistance/index.htm (accessed December 18, 2013).

4. Roife, Rebecca, The Washington Post, "American on Food Stamps," July 11, 2013, http://www.washingtonpost.com/wp-srv/special/politics/food-stamps/ (accessed December 18, 2013).

5. Melchior, Jullian Kay, National Review Online, "Me and My Obamaphone," August 1, 2013, http://www.nationalreview.com/article/354867/me-and-my-obamaphones-jillian-kay-melchior (accessed December 18, 2013).

6. Investopedia, http://www.investopedia.com/terms/m/mixed-economic-system.asp (accessed December 18, 2-13).

7. You Tube, http://www.youtube.com/watch?v=KrefKCaV8m4 (accessed December 18, 2013).

8. Davenport, David, Forbes, "President Obama's Executive Power End Run Around The Constitution," January 16, 2013, http://www.forbes.com/sites/daviddavenport/2013/01/16/president-obamas-executive-power-end-run-around-the-constitution/ (accessed December 18, 2013).

9. Trottman, Melanie, Jess Bravin and Michael R. Crittenden, The Wall Street journal, "Court Throws Out Recess Picks," January 25, 2013, http://online.wsj.com/news/articles/SB10001424127887324039504578263772492524536 (accessed December 18, 2013).

10. The Economist, "America's border troubles, north and south," January 25, 2005, http://www.economist.com/node/4318265 (accessed December 18, 2013).

11. Famous Quotes, http://www.larrywillis.com/quotes.html (accessed December 18, 2013).

12. Ibid.

13. Ibid.

14. Ibid.

15. Ibid.

16. Ibid.

17. Ibid.

18. Ibid.

Dispatch Four

1. The Constitution, http://constitutionus.com/ (accessed December 18, 2013).

2. Web Guide, Primary Documents in American History, The Articles of Confederation, http://www.loc.gov/rr/program/bib/ourdocs/articles.html (accessed December 18, 2013).

3. Internet Encyclopedia of Philosophy, Social Contract theory, http://www. iep.utm.edu/soc-cont/ (accessed December 18, 2013).

4. Drexel University, Constitution of the United States, Preamble to the Bill of Rights, http://www.drexel.edu/usconstitution/billOfRights/preamble/ (accessed December 18, 2013).

5. Drexel University, Constitution of the United States, Amendment X, http://www.drexel.edu/usconstitution/billOfRights/amendment10/ (accessed December 18, 2013).

6. U.S. Constitution Online, Constitutional Amendments, The Amendment process, http://www.usconstitution.net/constam.html#process (accessed December 18, 2013).

7. You Tube, http://www.youtube.com/watch?v=KrefKCaV8m4 (accessed December 18, 2013).

Dispatch Five

1. Internet Encyclopedia of Philosophy, Social Contract theory, http://www. iep.utm.edu/soc-cont/ (accessed December 18, 2013).

2. U.S. Constitution Online, Constitutional Amendments, The Amendment process, http://www.usconstitution.net/constam.html#process (accessed December 18, 2013).

3. Joe Clarke.net, Al Sharpton, May 15, 2012, http://www.joeclarke.net/2010/05/ al-sharpton-demands-that-everything.html (accessed December 18, 2013).

4. Brainy Quote, http://www.brainyquote.com/quotes/quotes/k/karl-marx136396.html (accessed December 18, 2013).

5. Pleuger, Gilbert , New Perspective Vol 9, No 1, "Totalitarianism," http:// www.history-ontheweb.co.uk/concepts/totalitarianism.htm (accessed December 18, 2013).

6. Amazon.com, "New Deal or Raw Deal," http://www.amazon.com/New-Deal-Raw-Economic-Damaged/dp/1416592229 (accessed December 18, 2013).

7. U.S. History, "Lyndon Johnson's Great Society," http://www.ushistory.org/ us/56e.asp (accessed December 18, 2013).

8. Kennedy and the New frontier, http://countrystudies.us/united-states/history-120.htm (accessed December 18, 2013).

9. You Tube, http://www.youtube.com/watch?v=KrefKCaV8m4 (accessed December 18, 2013).

Dispatch Six

1. Dunn, J.R., American Thinker, "Liberalism and Mass Shootings,: November 9, 2013, http://www.americanthinker.com/2013/09/liberalism_and_mass_shootings.html (accessed December 18, 2013).

2. Brainy Quote, http://www.brainyquote.com/quotes/keywords/crisis.html (accessed December 18, 2013).

3. Find Law, second Amendment, http://constitution.findlaw.com/amendment2/amendment.html (accessed December 18, 2013).

Dispatch Seven

1. Amazon.com, "The Constitution Failed," http://www.amazon.com/Constitution-Failed-PH-D-Robert-Owens/dp/1609579615/ref=sr_1_1?ie=UTF8&qid=1372328556&sr=8-1&keywords=the+constitution+failed+owens (accessed December 18, 2013).

2. U.S. Constitution Online, The Tenth Amendment, http://www.usconstitution.net/xconst_Am10.html Accessed 12-18-13 (accessed December 18, 2013).

3. You Tube, http://www.youtube.com/watch?v=KrefKCaV8m4 (accessed December 18, 2013).

Dispatch Eight

1. Christianity Today Library, "Why did Columbus Sail?," July 1, 1992, http://www.ctlibrary.com/ch/1992/issue35/3509.html (accessed December 18, 2013).

2. Excerpts from Christopher Columbus' Log, 1492 A.D., http://www.franciscan-archive.org/columbus/opera/excerpts.html (accessed December 18, 2013).

3. Pluralism, http://www.udel.edu/htr/American/Texts/pluralism.html (accessed December 18, 2013).

4. You Tube, Apology Tours, http://www.youtube.com/watch?v=DAXA0WVwxiE (accessed December 18, 2013).

5. You Tube, Not a Christian country, http://www.youtube.com/watch?v=tmC3IevZiik (accessed December 18, 2013).

6. Gallup, Americans believe in God, http://www.gallup.com/poll/147887/americans-continue-believe-god.aspx (accessed December18, 2013).

7. Pew Research, Religion & Public Life Project, Religious Landscape Survey, http://religions.pewforum.org/reports (accessed December 18, 2013).

8. Gary North's Specific Answers, The Bible mandates free market capitalism. It is anti-socialist, http://www.garynorth.com/public/department57.cfm (accessed December 18, 2013).

9. Brainy Quote, Churchill, http://www.brainyquote.com/quotes/quotes/w/winstonchu164131.html (accessed December 18, 2013).

10. LyricsFreak, http://www.lyricsfreak.com/p/paul+simon/sounds+of+silence_20559740.html (accessed December 18, 2013).

11. PopMarket, http://www.azlyrics.com/lyrics/bobdylan/gottaservesomebody.html (accessed December 18, 2013).

12. Bible Gateway, Joshua 24:15, http://www.biblegateway.com/passage/?search=Joshua%2024:15&version=NKJV (accessed December 18, 2013).

Dispatch Nine

1. Declaration of Independence, http://www.ushistory.org/declaration/document/ (accessed 12-18-13).

2. You Tube, Fundamentally Transform America http://www.youtube.com/watch?v=_cqN4NIEtOY (accessed December 18, 2013).

3. U.S. History, Truman Defeats Dewey, http://www.u-s-history.com/pages/h898.html Accessed 12-18-13 (accessed December 18, 2013).

4. Time Magazine, Clinton V. Congress: The Race is set, http://content.time.com/time/magazine/article/0,9171,983003,00.html (accessed December 18, 2013).

5. Dallas News, "Obama's road trip to Texas: make Ted Cruz-Republicans the face of Washington opposition," http://trailblazersblog.dallasnews.com/2013/05/obamas-road-trip-to-texas-make-ted-cruz-republicans-the-face-of-washington-opposition.html/ (accessed December 18, 2013).

6. Bible gateway, 2 Chronicles 7:13-15, http://www.biblegateway.com/passage/?search=2%20Chronicles+7:13-15&version=NKJV (accessed December 18, 2013).

7. Declaration of Independence, http://www.ushistory.org/declaration/document/ (accessed December 18, 2013).

8. InfoPlease, "John F. Kennedy's Inaugural Address," http://www.infoplease.com/ipa/A0878607.html (accessed December 18, 2013).

Dispatch Ten

1. Declaration of Independence, http://www.ushistory.org/declaration/document/ (accessed December 18, 2013).

2. Your Dictionary, "Equality Before the Law," http://www.yourdictionary.com/equality-before-the-law#law (accessed December 18, 2013).

3. Stanford Encyclopedia of Philosophy, Equality of Opportunity, http://plato.stanford.edu/entries/equal-opportunity/ (accessed December18, 2013).

4. The Founder's Constitution, "Article 1, Section 9, Clause 8," http://press-pubs. uchicago.edu/founders/tocs/a1_9_8.html (accessed December 18, 2013).

5. Bill of Attainder, http://www.techlawjournal.com/glossary/legal/attainder. htm (accessed December18, 2013).

6. The Founder's Constitution, "Article 1, Section 9, Clause 8," http://press-pubs. uchicago.edu/founders/tocs/a1_9_8.html (accessed December 18, 2013).

7. Charters of Freedom, The Bill of Rights, http://www.archives.gov/exhibits/ charters/bill_of_rights_transcript.html (accessed December 18, 2013).

8. The Literature Network, http://www.online-literature.com/orwell/ani-malfarm/10/ (accessed December 18, 2013).

9. Equality of Opportunity and Equality of Outcome, http://www.ourcivilisa-tion.com/cooray/btof/chap20.htm (accessed December 18, 2013).

Dispatch Eleven

1. MSNBC, "Obama says stimulus spending must pick up," http://www. nbcnews.com/id/31508658/ns/business-stocks_and_economy/ (accessed December 20, 2013).

2. KRUGMAN, PAUL, New York Times, "Green Shoots and Glimmers," April 16, 2009, http://www.nytimes.com/2009/04/17/opinion/17krugman. html?_r=1& (accessed December 20, 2013).

3. Reuters, "Obama: U.S. in worst crisis since Depression," October 7, 2008, http://www.reuters.com/article/2008/10/08/usa-politics-debate-economy-idUSN0749084220081008 (accessed December 20, 2013).

4. Zibel, Eve, Fox News, "Biden: 'We Misread How Bad the Economy Was,'" July 5, 2009, http://www.foxnews.com/politics/2009/07/05/biden-misread-bad-economy/ (accessed December 20, 2013).

5. QB, "It's the economy stupid," http://quotationsbook.com/ quote/5097/#sthash.m1vGWCde.dpbs (accessed December 20, 2013).

6. Reich, Robert, The American Prospect, "It's the Economy, Stupid -- But Not Just the Current Slowdown," December 5, 2007, http://prospect.org/article/its-economy-stupid-not-just-current-slowdown (accessed December 20, 2013).

Dispatch Twelve

1. You Tube, Michael Savage Explains the Mental Disorder of Liberalism, http:// www.youtube.com/watch?v=AEwVcsHnf3o (accessed December 20, 2013).

2. PsyBlog, Propaganda Techniques in Michael Moore's Fahrenheit 9/11, http://www.spring.org.uk/2007/11/9-propaganda-techniques-in-michael. php (accessed December 20, 2013).

3. HelpMe.com, "Upton Sinclair's The Jungle as Socialist Propaganda," http://www.123helpme.com/view.asp?id=16385 (accessed December 20, 1203).

4. You Tube, Fundamentally Transform America, http://www.youtube.com/watch?v=KrefKCaV8m4 (accessed December 18, 2013).

5. Lamb, Henry, WND, "Defining 'social democracy,'" http://www.wnd.com/2002/03/13255/ (accessed December 20, 2013).

6. Modern History Project, "On July 19, 1962, Khrushchev said: "The United States will eventually fly the Communist red flag" http://modernhistoryproject.org/mhp?Article=FinalWarning&C=7.8 (accessed December 20, 2013).

7. I Go Pogo, "I have met the enemy and he is us," http://www.igopogo.com/we_have_met.htm (accessed December 20, 2013).

Dispatch Thirteen

1. Kenny, Thomas, About.com, "What is the Fiscal Cliff?," http://bonds.about.com/od/Issues-in-the-News/a/What-Is-The-Fiscal-Cliff.htm (accessed December 20, 2013).

2. TAU, BYRON, Politico, "Intelligence community: U.S. out as sole superpower by 2030," December 12, 2012, http://www.politico.com/politico44/2012/12/intelligence-community-us-out-as-sole-superpower-by-151519.html (accessed December 20, 2013).

3. Sahadi, Jeanne, CNN Money, "Why the U.S. can't inflate its way out of debt," March 23, 2010, http://money.cnn.com/2010/03/10/news/economy/inflation_debt/index.htm (accessed December 20, 2013).

4. JFK Experience, "Favorite JFK Quotes," http://www.jfkexperience.com/jfk-resources/favorite-jfk-quotes/ (accessed December 20, 2013).

5. Durden, Tyler, End of America, "Thought Experiment: Why Obama Wants The Fiscal Cliff," December 12, 2012, http://www.zerohedge.com/news/2012-12-05/guest-post-thought-experiment-why-obama-wants-fiscal-cliff (accessed December 30, 2013).

6. You Tube, Fundamentally Transform America http://www.youtube.com/watch?v=_cqN4NIEtOY (accessed December 18, 2013).

7. EconBrowser, "Return to the gold standard," September 1, 2012, http://www.econbrowser.com/archives/2012/09/return_to_the_g.html (accessed December 20, 2013).

8. Fox News.com, "Social Security Plan Cutoff to Be 55," http://www.foxnews.com/story/2005/02/02/social-security-plan-cutoff-to-be-55/ (accessed December 20, 2013).

Dispatch Fourteen

1. Joyce, Helen, Plus Magazine, "Adam Smith and the invisible hand," http://plus.maths.org/content/adam-smith-and-invisible-hand (accessed December 21, 2013).

2. Brainy Quote, Friedrich August von Hayek Quotes, http://www.brainyquote.com/quotes/authors/f/friedrich_august_von_haye_2.html (accessed December 21, 2013).

3. SubtleTea.com, "The Wit and Wisdom of Thomas Paine," http://www.subtletea.com/thomaspainequotes.htm (accessed December 21, 2013).

4. American Christian Heritage, "Where is the king of America," http://acheritagegroup.org/blog/?p=69 (accessed December 21, 2013).

5. The Founder's Constitution, "Constitutional Government," http://press-pubs.uchicago.edu/founders/documents/v1ch17s9.html (accessed December 21, 2013).

6. U.S. Government: The Balance of Power, http://library.thinkquest.org/J0110221/USGovernment.html (accessed December 21, 2013).

7. Kelly, Martin, About.com, "Lincoln Suspended the Writ of Habeas Corpus," http://americanhistory.about.com/b/2010/10/23/lincoln-suspended-the-writ-of-habeas-corpus.htm (accessed December 21, 2013).

8. Kline, Malcolm A., Accuracy in Media, "Progressive Segregation," http://www.aim.org/briefing/progressive-segregation/ (accessed December 21, 2013).

9. This Nation.com, "What is an Executive Order," http://thisnation.com/question/040.html (accessed December 21, 2013).

10. GGA Quotes, "Constitution," http://giga-usa.com/quotes/topics/constitution_t001.htm (accessed December 21, 2013).

Dispatch Fifteen

1. U.S. Government Spending, http://www.usgovernmentspending.com/debt_deficit_history (accessed December 21, 2013).

2. Hamilton, Alexander, second Report to Congress, http://american_almanac.tripod.com/hambank.htm (accessed December 21, 2013).

3. Legal Theory Lexicon, "Strict Construction and Judicial Activism," http://lsolum.typepad.com/legal_theory_lexicon/2004/05/legal_theory_le_3.html (accessed 12-21-13).

4. USLegal: Definitions, "Enumerated Power Law & Legal Definition," http://definitions.uslegal.com/e/enumerated-power/ (accessed December 21, 2013).

5. _____, "Implied Power Law & Legal Definition," http://definitions.uslegal.com/i/implied-power/ (accessed December 21, 2013).

6. Hamilton, Alexander, "ARGUMENTS FOR THE CREATION OF A NATIONAL BANK," http://american_almanac.tripod.com/forbank.htm (accessed December 21, 2013).

7. Trumbore, Brian, Buy And Hold, "William Duer and the Crash of 1792," http://www.buyandhold.com/bh/en/education/history/2000/8699.html (accessed December 21, 2013).

8. Ibid.

9. U.S. History, "Second Bank of the United States," http://www.u-s-history.com/pages/h256.html (accessed December 21, 2013).

10. FederalReserveEducation.org, "The History of the Federal Reserve," http://www.federalreserveeducation.org/about-the-fed/history/ (accessed December 21, 2013).

11. Global Research, "Who Owns the Federal Reserve?," http://www.globalresearch.ca/who-owns-the-federal-reserve/10489 (accessed December 21, 2013).

12. Investopedia, "Business Cycle," http://www.investopedia.com/terms/b/businesscycle.asp#axzz1ZLhdVkIq (accessed December 21, 2013).

13. The U.S. Constitution, "The First Bank of the United States," http://www.nps.gov/history/history/online_books/butowsky2/constitution5.htm (accessed December 21, 2013).

14. U.S. Constitution Online, The Tenth Amendment, http://www.usconstitution.net/xconst_Am10.html (accessed December 18, 2013).

15. Brainy Quote, Yogi Berra, http://www.brainyquote.com/quotes/quotes/y/yogiberra141506.html (accessed December 21, 2013).

Dispatch Sixteen

1. You Tube, Fundamentally Transform America http://www.youtube.com/watch?v=_cqN4NIEtOY (accessed December 18, 2013).

2. The Washington Post, "McDonald's may get its way with health-care law," http://voices.washingtonpost.com/blogpost/2010/10/mcdonalds_may_get_its_way_with.html (accessed December 21, 2013).

3. Cover, Matt, CNS News.com, "30 Percent of Employers to Drop Health Coverage Because of Obamacare," June 7, 2011, http://www.cnsnews.com/news/article/30-percent-employers-drop-health-coverage-because-obamacare (accessed December 21, 2013).

4. Cline, Andrew, The American Spectator, "No, You Can't Keep Your Current Health Coverage," September 30, 2012, http://spectator.org/articles/38846/no-you-cant-keep-your-current-health-coverage (accessed December 21, 2013).

5. Ellerson, Lindsey, ABC News.com, "President Obama Continues Questionable "You Can Keep Your Health Care" Promise," July 16, 2010, http://abcnews.go.com/blogs/politics/2009/07/president-obama-continues-questionable-you-can-keep-your-health-care-promise/ (accessed December 21, 2013).

6. NBC Politics, "Obama health care promise named 'Lie of the Year,'" http://nbcpolitics.nbcnews.com/_news/2013/12/12/21880402-obama-health-care-promise-named-lie-of-the-year (accessed December 21, 2013).

7. Investor's Insights.com, "Government Takeover Revisted," http://www.investorsinsight.com/blogs/forecasts_trends/archive/2010/07/27/financial-reform-or-government-takeover-revisited.aspx (accessed December 22, 2013).

Dispatch Seventeen

1. BARBOZA, DAVID, Economix, "China Poised to Lead World in Patent Filings," October 6, 2010, http://economix.blogs.nytimes.com/2010/10/06/china-poised-to-lead-world-in-patent-filings/?_r=1 (accessed December 22, 2013).

2. DirectorBlue, Hotair, "DemCare: a tidal wave of regulations, taxes, fees, bureaucracies, waiting lines, bankruptcies and seniors denied medical care are on the way," March 28, 2010, http://hotair.com/greenroom/archives/2010/03/28/demcare-a-tidal-wave-of-regulations-taxes-fees-beauracracies-waiting-lines-bankruptcies-and-seniors-denied-medical-care-are-on-the-way/ (accessed December 22, 2013).

3. Miller, Emily, Human Events, "Senate Dems' New Proposal To Weaken Filibuster," January 2, 2011, http://www.humanevents.com/2011/01/03/senate-dems-new-proposal-to-weaken-filibuster/ (accessed December 22, 2013).

4. "The Road to Serfdom," http://www.amazon.com/s/ref=nb_sb_noss?url=search-alias%3Daps&field-keywords=the+road+to+serfdom&x=0&y=0 (accessed December 22, 2013).

5. Morley, Robert, The Trumpet.com, "The Death of American Manufacturing," February 2006, http://www.thetrumpet.com/article/2061.904.80.0/economy/the-death-of-american-manufacturing (accessed December 22, 2013).

6. Elfenbein, Eddy, Crossing Wall Street, "24 Scary Facts About the U.S. Economy," October 13, 2010, http://www.crossingwallstreet.com/archives/2010/10/24-scary-facts-about-the-u-s-economy.html (accessed December 22, 2013).

7. McCormack, Richard, The American Prospect, "The Plight of American Manufacturing," December 21, 2009, http://prospect.org/article/plight-american-manufacturing (accessed December 22, 2013).

8. Grove, Andy, Bloomberg Business Week Magazine, "How America can Create Jobs," July 1, 2010, http://www.businessweek.com/magazine/content/10_28/b4186048358596.htm (accessed December 22, 2013).

9. McCormack, Richard, The American Prospect, "The Plight of American Manufacturing," December 21, 2009, http://prospect.org/article/plight-american-manufacturing (accessed December 22, 2013).

10. Drucker, Peter F., The Atlantic Online, "Really Reinventing Government," February 1995, http://www.theatlantic.com/past/politics/polibig/reallyre.htm (accessed December 22, 2013).

Dispatch Eighteen

1. Said What?, Churchill Quote, "Those that fail to learn from history, are doomed to repeat it," http://www.saidwhat.co.uk/quotes/political/winston_churchill/those_that_fail_to_learn_from_2804 (accessed December 22, 2013).

2. Quote DB, Mark Twain Quote, "History doesn't repeat itself, but it does rhyme," http://www.quotedb.com/quotes/3038 (accessed December 22, 2013).

3. PBS, American Experience. "Durant's Big Scam," http://www.pbs.org/wgbh/americanexperience/features/general-article/tcrr-scam/ (accessed December 22, 2013).

Dispatch Nineteen

1. CBO, Economic and Budget Issue Brief, "What Accounts for the Decline in Manufacturing Employment?," February 18, 2004, http://www.cbo.gov/sites/default/files/cbofiles/ftpdocs/50xx/doc5078/02-18-manufacturingem-ployment.pdf (accessed December 22, 2013).

2. Perry, Mark J., A E Ideas, "Manufacturing's Death Greatly Exaggerated," December, 23, 2009, http://www.aei-ideas.org/2009/12/manufacturings-death-greatly-exaggerated/ (accessed December 22, 2013).

3. Ibid.

4. Ibid.

5. Ibid.

6. Ibid.

7. All Employees Manufacturing, http://research.stlouisfed.org/fred2/data/MANEMP.txt (accessed December 22, 2013).

8. Perry, Mark J., A E Ideas, "Manufacturing's Death Greatly Exaggerated," December, 23, 2009, http://www.aei-ideas.org/2009/12/manufacturings-death-greatly-exaggerated/ (accessed December 22, 2013).

9. Library of Economic Liberty, The Concise Encyclopedia of Economic, "Milton Friedman," http://www.econlib.org/library/Enc/bios/Friedman.html (accessed December 22, 2013).

10. Klein, Peter G., Ludwig von Misses Institute, "Biography of F. A. Hyek 1899-1992," http://mises.org/page/1454/Biography-of-F-A-Hayek-18991992 (accessed December 22, 2013).

11. Business Dictionary, "Chicago School of Economics," http://www.businessdictionary.com/definition/Chicago-school-of-economics.html (accessed December 22, 2013).

12. Boettke, Peter J., Library of Economic Liberty, Concise Encyclopedia of Economics, "The Austrian School of Economics," http://www.econlib.org/library/Enc/AustrianSchoolofEconomics.html (accessed December 22, 2013).

13. The Frankfurt School, http://www.marxists.org/subject/frankfurt-school/ (accessed December 22, 2013).

14. LaHaye, Laura, Library of Economic Liberty, The Concise Encyclopedia of Economics, "Mercantilism," http://www.econlib.org/library/Enc/Mercantilism.html (accessed December 22, 2013).

15. Library of Economic Liberty, The Concise Encyclopedia of Economics, "Adam Smith," http://www.econlib.org/library/Enc/bios/Smith.html (accessed December 22, 2013).

16. National Park Service, Historic Jamestowne, "The Virginia Company of London," http://www.nps.gov/jame/historyculture/the-virginia-company-of-london.htm (accessed December 22, 2013).

17. U.S History, "Second Bank of the United States," http://www.u-s-history.com/pages/h256.html (accessed December 21, 2013).

18. Fedrico, P. J., Heinonline, "Colonial Monopolies and Patents," http://heinonline.org/HOL/LandingPage?collection=journals&handle=hein.journals/jpatos11&div=76&id=&page (accessed December 22, 2013).

19. The Founder's Constitution, Republican Government, "Hamilton's Report on Manufactures," http://press-pubs.uchicago.edu/founders/documents/v1ch4s31.html (accessed December 22, 2013).

20. Ibid.

21. Ibid.

22. Crumrin, Timothy, Conner Prairie, "Road Through the Wilderness: The Making of the National Road," http://www.connerprairie.org/Learn-And-Do/Indiana-History/America-1800-1860/The-National-Road.aspx (accessed December 22, 2013).

23. McNamara, Robert, About.com, 19th Century History, "Albert Gallatin's Report on Roads, Canals, Harbors, and Rivers," http://history1800s.about.com/od/canals/a/gallatinreport.htm (accessed December 22, 2013).

24. Williams, Nathan, History News Network, "How Did the United States Defeat the Barbary Pirates?," http://hnn.us/article/287 (accessed December 22, 2013).

25. U.S. Mexican War, http://www.pbs.org/kera/usmexicanwar/war/ (accessed December 22, 2013).

26. U.S History, "Spanish-American War," http://www.u-s-history.com/pages/h3617.html (accessed December 22, 2013).

27. USHistory.org, "The First bank of the United States," http://www.ushistory.org/tour/first-bank.htm (accessed December 22, 2013).

28. Patrick J. Buchanan Official Website, http://buchanan.org/blog/ (accessed December 22, 2013).

29. Rosenberg, Matt, About.com, "Pacific Rim and Economic Tigers," http://geography.about.com/od/urbaneconomicgeography/a/econtigers.htm (accessed 12-22-13).

Dispatch Twenty

1. How Stuff Works, "Alien and Sedition Act," http://history.howstuffworks.com/revolutionary-war/alien-and-sedition-act.htm (accessed December 22, 2013).

2. Kelly, Martin, About.com "Jefferson and the Louisiana Purchase," http://americanhistory.about.com/od/thomasjefferson/a/tj_lapurchase.htm (accessed December 22, 2013).

3. All American Patriots, "1823: Monroe Doctrine," http://www.allamerican-patriots.com/american_historical_documents_1823_monroe_doctrine (accessed December 22, 2013).

4. U.S. History, "Spoils System," http://www.u-s-history.com/pages/h326.html (accessed December 22, 2013).

5. History Net.com, "Indian Removal Act," http://www.historynet.com/indian-removal-act (accessed December 22, 2013).

6. History Central.com, "Indian Removal Act," http://www.historycentral.com/Indians/RemovalAct.html (accessed December 22, 2013).

7. Campaign for Liberty, "Teddy Roosevelt and His Big Stick," http://www.campaignforliberty.org/members-posts/teddy-roosevelt-and-his-big-stick/ (accessed December 22, 2013).

8. Encyclopedia of the New American Nation, "Judiciary Power and Practice - War and the courts," http://www.americanforeignrelations.com/E-N/Judiciary-Power-and-Practice-War-and-the-courts.html (accessed December 22, 2013).

9. Ibid.

10. Ibid.

Dispatch Twenty-one

1. Cowboy Lyrics.com, "Phil Ochs: Ringing of Revolution," http://www. cowboylyrics.com/lyrics/ochs-phil/ringing-of-revolution-11450.html#. T89_a8X-5p8 (accessed December 22, 2013).

Dispatch Twenty-two

1. LaHaye, Laura, Library of Economic Liberty, The Concise Encyclopedia of Economics, "Mercantilism," http://www.econlib.org/library/Enc/Mercantilism.html (accessed December 22, 2013).

2. Fundamentally Transform America http://www.youtube.com/watch?v=_cqN4NIEtOY (accessed December 18, 2013).

3. The Free Dictionary, "Social Democracy," http://www.thefreedictionary. com/social+democracy (accessed December 22, 2013).

4. Spread the Wealth Around, http://www.youtube.com/watch?v=RZcEHLr4gBg (accessed December 18, 2013).

Dispatch Twenty-three

1. Daudani, Ray, NBC 12, "10,000 dead found on Virginia voter rolls," August 14, 2012, http://www.nbc12.com/story/19237542/10000-dead-found-on-virginias-voter-rolls (accessed December 22, 2013).

2. Schmidt, Marcus, Times Dispatch, "Thousands of Virginia Voters on the Rolls in Other States," http://www.timesdispatch.com/news/state-regional/government-politics/thousands-of-va-voters-on-the-rolls-in-other-states/article_3ce0c700-9ac9-53c1-8bfa-54619d917feb.html (accessed December 22, 2013).

3. Barack Obama Voter Fraud 2012, November 8, 2012, http://obamavoter-fraud.blogspot.com/ (accessed December 22, 2013).

4. Graham, Peter, PBS News Hour, "Are Banks Borrowing from the Fed at Low Interest and Making Money Buying U.S. Treasuries?," http://www.pbs.org/newshour/business-desk/2010/05/are-banks-borrowing-from-the-f.html (accessed December 22, 2013).

5. CBS Money Watch, "Foreigners Reduce Stakes in U.S. Treasury," February 16, 2010, http://www.cbsnews.com/news/foreigners-reduce-stakes-in-us-treasury/ (accessed December 22, 2013).

6. Jutia Group, "Banks Biggest Buyers of U.S. Treasury Securities: Bank of America (NYSE: BAC), JPMorgan Chase (NYSE: JPM), Citigroup (NYSE: C), Wells Fargo (NYSE: WFC)," November 3, 2009, http://jutiagroup.com/20091103-banks-biggest-buyers-of-u-s-treasury-securities-bank-of-america-nyse-bac-jpmorgan-chase-nyse-jpm-citigroup-nyse-c-wells-fargo-nyse-wfc/ (accessed December 22, 2013).

7. Fundamentally Transform America http://www.youtube.com/watch?v=_cqN4NIEtOY (accessed December 18, 2013).

8. Birnbaum, Jeffrey H., Washington Post: Politics, "Hill a Steppingstone to K Street for Some," July 27, 2005, http://www.washingtonpost.com/wp-dyn/content/article/2005/07/26/AR2005072601562.html (accessed December 22, 2013).

9. Overby, Peter, NPR, "How Fannie, Freddie Became Kings Of The Hill," July 15, 2008, http://www.npr.org/templates/story/story.php?storyId=92540620 (accessed December 22, 2013).

10. McIntyre, Douglas A. and Brian Zajac, NBC News: Business, "Retirement plan: The corporate boards that love ex-politicians," July 13, 2012, http://www.nbcnews.com/business/retirement-plan-corporate-boards-love-ex-politicians-826388 (accessed December 22, 2013).

Dispatch Twenty-four

1. Noyes, Rich, News Busters, "Today's Push for ObamaCare Matches Media Spin for HillaryCare in 1990s," September 9, 2009, http://newsbusters.org/blogs/rich-noyes/2009/09/09/todays-push-obamacare-matches-media-spin-hillarycare-1990s (accessed December 22, 2013).

2. Peterson, Paul E., The Hoover Institute, "The Decline and Fall of American Education," January 30, 2003, http://www.hoover.org/publications/hoover-digest/article/6325 (accessed December 22, 2013).

3. The Econ Review, "President Nixon Imposes Wage and Price Controls," http://www.econreview.com/events/wageprice1971b.htm (accessed December 22, 2013).

4. On the Issues, "Richard Nixon on the Budget and the Economy," http://www.ontheissues.org/celeb/Richard_Nixon_Budget_+_Economy.htm (accessed December 22, 2013).

5. You Tube, Income Tax Cut, JFK Hopes To Spur Economy 1962/8/13, http://www.youtube.com/watch?v=aEdXrfIMdiU (accessed December 22, 2013).

6. Reeves, Richard, Washington Post, "Missile Gaps and Other Broken Promises," February 10, 2009, http://100days.blogs.nytimes.com/2009/02/10/missile-gaps-and-other-broken-promises/?_r=0 (accessed December 22, 2013).

7. Craughwell, Thomas J. with M. William Phelps, History News Network, "Failures of the Presidents: JFK's Bay of Pigs Disaster," http://hnn.us/article/55759 (accessed December 22, 2013).

8. Military Industrial Complex, http://www.militaryindustrialcomplex.com/what-is-the-military-industrial-complex.asp (accessed December 22, 2013).

9. Eisenhower, Dwight, "Military-Industrial Complex Speech, Dwight D. Eisenhower, 1961," http://www.h-net.org/~hst306/documents/indust.html (accessed December 22, 2013).

10. History Channel, This Day in History, "Truman delivers his Fair Deal speech," http://www.history.com/this-day-in-history/truman-delivers-his-fair-deal-speech (accessed December 22, 2013).

11. U.S. History, The New Deal, http://www.u-s-history.com/pages/h1851.html (accessed December 22, 2013).

12. Rothbard, Murray N.. Lew Rockwell.com, "Herbert Hoover's Depression," http://archive.lewrockwell.com/rothbard/rothbard184.html (accessed December 22, 2013).

13. History Channel, Calvin Coolidge, http://www.history.com/topics/calvin-coolidge (accessed December 22, 2013).

14. White House, Warren Harding, http://www.whitehouse.gov/about/presidents/warrenharding (accessed December 22, 2013).

15. Higgs, Robert, The Independent Institute, "How War Amplified Federal Power in the Twentieth Century," July 1, 1999, http://www.independent.org/publications/article.asp?id=113 (accessed December 22, 2013).

16. Presidential Campaign Slogans, Wilson, http://www.presidentsusa.net/1916slogan.html (accessed December 22, 2013).

17. Examiner.com, "The Taft-Roosevelt Rift: Taft the Trust Buster," December 15, 2010, http://www.examiner.com/article/the-taft-roosevelt-rift-taft-the-trust-buster (accessed December 22, 2013).

18. U.S. History, The Trust Buster, http://www.ushistory.org/us/43b.asp (accessed December 22, 2013).

19. U.S. History, "Alien and Sedition Act," http://www.ushistory.org/us/19e.asp (accessed December 22, 2013).

20. Kelly, Martin, About.com "Jefferson and the Louisiana Purchase," http://americanhistory.about.com/od/thomasjefferson/a/tj_lapurchase.htm (accessed December 22, 2013).

21. U.S. Mexican War, http://www.pbs.org/kera/usmexicanwar/war/ (accessed December 22, 2013).

22. Longley, Robert, About.com, "Lincoln Issues Proclamation Suspending Habeas Corpus Rights," http://usgovinfo.about.com/od/historicdocuments/a/lincolnhabeas.htm (accessed December 22, 2013).

23. U.S. Constitution Online, The Tenth Amendment, http://www.usconstitution.net/xconst_Am10.html (accessed December 18, 2013).

24. Tenth Amendment Center, "About the Tenth Amendment," http://tenthamendmentcenter.com/about/about-the-tenth-amendment/ (accessed December 22, 2013).

25. Imbriale, Kenneth S., "A Brief Examination of the Legality of Secession in the United States," http://www.historyvortex.org/LegalitySecession.html (accessed December 22, 2013).

26. Declaration of Independence, http://www.ushistory.org/declaration/document/ (accessed December 18, 2013).

27. Biblegateway, 2 Chronicles 7:13-15, http://www.biblegateway.com/passage/?search=2%20Chronicles+7:13-15&version=NKJV (accessed December 18, 2013).

28. Ertelt, Steven, LifeNews.com, "54,559,615 Abortions Since Roe vs. Wade Decision in 1973," January 23, 2012, http://www.lifenews.com/2012/01/23/54559615-abortions-since-roe-vs-wade-decision-in-1973/ (accessed December 22, 2013).

Dispatch Twenty-five

1. The War of 1812, http://www.gatewayno.com/history/war1812.html (accessed December 22, 2013).

2. Encyclopedia Britannica, "The Monroe Doctrine," http://www.britannica.com/EBchecked/topic/390243/Monroe-Doctrine (accessed December 22, 2013).

3. Collapse of the Soviet Union, http://sfr-21.org/collapse.html (accessed December 22, 2013).

4. Amazon.com, "America Won the Vietnam War," http://www.amazon.com/America-Won-Vietnam-Robert-Owens/dp/1594672954/ref=sr_1_1?ie=UTF8&qid=1387757469&sr=8-1&keywords=america+won+the+vietnam+war+owens (accessed December 22, 2013).

5. Brainy Quote, Kennedy, http://www.brainyquote.com/quotes/quotes/j/johnfkenn114918.html (accessed December 22, 2013).

Dispatch Twenty-six

1. Rise and Fall of Athenian Greatness, http://www.augie.edu/dept/history/athe.htm (accessed December 24, 2013).

2. Gill, N. S., About.com, "End of the Roman Republic," http://ancienthistory.about.com/od/romerepublic/p/endRepublic.htm (accessed December 23, 2013).

3. Benjamin Franklin Quotes, http://quotes.liberty-tree.ca/quotes_by/benjamin+franklin (accessed December 23, 2013).

4. Kakutani, Michiko, New York Time: Books, "The Evolution of Al Qaeda and the Intertwining Paths Leading to 9/11," http://www.nytimes.com/2006/08/01/books/01kaku.html?pagewanted=all&_r=0&gwh=BF4D89E00EE004B8C7C7E58E5A38F7AA&gwt=pay (accessed December 23, 2013).

5. Yale Law School: The Avalon Project, "Washington's farewell Address 1796," http://avalon.law.yale.edu/18th_century/washing.asp (accessed December 23, 2013).

6. Vance, Laurence M., Lew Rockwell.com, "Jeffersonian principles," http://archive.lewrockwell.com/vance/vance17.html (accessed December 23, 2013).

7. Knowledgerush, "William McKinley," http://www.knowledgerush.com/kr/encyclopedia/William_McKinley/ (accessed December 23, 2013).

8. U.S. History, "Spanish-American War," http://www.u-s-history.com/pages/h3617.html (accessed December 22, 2013).

9. The White House, "Theodore Roosevelt," http://www.whitehouse.gov/about/presidents/theodoreroosevelt (accessed December 23, 2013).

10. Naval History and Heritage, "The Great White Fleet," http://www.history.navy.mil/faqs/faq42-1.htm (accessed December 23, 2013).

11. The White House, "Woodrow Wilson," http://www.whitehouse.gov/about/presidents/woodrowwilson/ (accessed December 23, 2013).

12. History Matters, "Making the World "Safe for Democracy": Woodrow Wilson Asks for War," http://historymatters.gmu.edu/d/4943/ (accessed December 23, 2013).

13. PBS: Woodrow Wilson, "League of Nations," http://www.pbs.org/wgbh/amex/wilson/portrait/wp_league.html (accessed December 23, 2013).

14. O'Connor, Jerome, Real Clear History, "FDR's Undeclared Atlantic War," http://www.realclearhistory.com/2012/09/04/fdr039s_undeclared_atlantic_war_3306.html (accessed December 23, 2013).

15. Buchanan, Patrick J., "Why Di Japan Attack Us?," http://www.theamericancause.org/patwhydidjapan.htm (accessed December 23, 2013).

16. OWR, "General Essay on Shi'a Islam," http://www.philtar.ac.uk/encyclopedia/islam/shia/ (accessed December 23, 2013).

17. Central Intelligence Agency: World Fact Book, "Iran," https://www.cia.gov/library/publications/the-world-factbook/geos/ir.html (accessed December 23, 2013).

18. Global Security.org: Military, "Where are the Legions? [SPQR]Global Deployments of US Forces," http://www.globalsecurity.org/military/ops/global-deployments.htm (accessed December 23, 2013).

19. Quotation Collection, "Will Rogers," http://www.quotationcollection.com/quotation/23/quote (accessed December 23, 2013).

Dispatch Twenty-seven

1. HyperHistpory.com, "Louis XIV," http://www.hyperhistory.com/online_n2/people_n2/persons6_n2/louis.html (accessed December 23, 2013).

2. U.S. History, "The Stamp Act," http://www.ushistory.org/declaration/related/stampact.htm (accessed December 23, 2013).

3. _____, "The Quartering Act of 1765," http://www.ushistory.org/declaration/related/quartering.htm (accessed December 23, 2013).

4. The White House, "We can't wait," http://www.whitehouse.gov/economy/jobs/we-cant-wait (accessed December 23, 2013).

5. Martin, Adam, The Wire, "Obama's New Immigration Policy Looks a Lot Like the DREAM Act," June 15, 2012, http://www.thewire.com/politics/2012/06/obamas-new-immigration-policy-looks-lot-dream-act/53600/ (accessed December 23, 2013).

6. Picket, Kerry, The Washington Times, "EPA imposes Obama's cap and trade regs- energy prices 'skyrocket,'" August 20, 2011, http://www.washingtontimes.com/blog/watercooler/2011/aug/20/picket-obama-08-energy-prices-will-skyrocket-under/ (accessed December 23, 2013).

7. Paul, Rand, The Washington Times, "Obama's unconstitutional Libyan war," June 15, 2011, http://www.washingtontimes.com/news/2011/jun/15/obamas-unconstitutional-libyan-war/ (accessed December 23, 2013).

8. Kumar, Anita, McClatchy DC: Watching Washington and the World, "Obama turning to executive power to get what he wants," March 19, 2013, http://www.mcclatchydc.com/2013/03/19/186309/obama-turning-to-executive-power.html (accessed December 23, 2013).

9. MailOnline.com, "U.S. gives billions of dollars in foreign aid to world's richest countries - then asks to borrow it back," June 3, 2011, http://www.dailymail.co.uk/news/article-1393960/US-gives-billions-foreign-aid-worlds-richest-countries-asks-borrow-back.html (accessed December 23, 2013).

10. Angle, Jim, Fox News, "Senators Outraged U.S. Borrowing Big From China While Also Giving It Aid," October 24, 2011, http://www.foxnews.com/politics/2011/10/24/senators-outraged-us-borrowing-big-from-china-while-also-giving-it-aid/ (accessed December 23, 2013).

11. Fox News, "U.S. Offers Foreign Aid to Countries Holding Billions in Treasury Securities," June 3, 2011, http://www.foxnews.com/politics/2011/06/02/us-offers-foreign-aid-to-countries-holding-billions-in-treasury-securities/ (accessed December 23, 2013).

12. Reuters, "U.S. House approves $649 billion for defense in 2012," July 8, 2011, http://www.reuters.com/article/2011/07/08/usa-budget-defense-idUSN1E6670UA20110708 (accessed December 23, 2013).

13. Wheeler, Winslow, Breaking Defense, "The Military Imbalance: How The U.S. Outspends The World," March, 16, 2012, http://breakingdefense.com/2012/03/the-military-imbalance-how-the-u-s-outspends-the-world/ (accessed December 23, 2013).

14. Business Wire, "Defense Spending in North America - A look at the leading players, market size and forecasts to 2016," July 31, 2012, http://www.businesswire.com/news/home/20120731006013/en/Research-Markets-Defense-Spending-North-America--#.UrhT2bRzYqM (accessed December 23, 2013).

15. Thompson, Loren, Forbes, "How To Waste $100 Billion: Weapons That Didn't Work Out," December 19, 2011, http://www.forbes.com/sites/lorenthompson/2011/12/19/how-to-waste-100-billion-weapons-that-didnt-work-out/ (accessed December 23, 2013).

16. Eisenhower, Dwight, "Military-Industrial Complex Speech, Dwight D. Eisenhower, 1961," http://www.h-net.org/~hst306/documents/indust.html (accessed December 22, 2013).

17. Dave Manuel.com, "A History of Surpluses and Deficits in the United States," December 23, 2013, http://www.davemanuel.com/history-of-deficits-and-surpluses-in-the-united-states.php (accessed December 23, 2013).

18. U.S. Debt Clock.org, http://www.usdebtclock.org/ (accessed December 18, 2013).

19. Bamett, Laura, The Huffington Post: Politics, "Adm. Mike Mullen: 'National Debt Is Our Biggest Security Threat,'" May, 25, 2011, http://www.huffingtonpost.com/2010/06/24/adm-mike-mullen-national_n_624096.html (accessed December 23, 2013).

Dispatch Twenty-eight

1. Bible Gateway, Acts 1:7, http://www.biblegateway.com/passage/?search=acts%201:7&version=NKJV (accessed December 23, 2013).

2. Fairchild, Mary, About.com, "Compare Matthew's Genealogy to Luke's Genealogy of Jesus Christ," http://christianity.about.com/od/biblefactsandlists/a/jesusgenealogy.htm (accessed December 23, 2013).

3. Bible Hub, Matthew 24:36, http://biblehub.com/niv/matthew/24-36.htm (accessed December 23, 2013).

4. Bible Gateway, Acts 1:7, http://www.biblegateway.com/passage/?search=acts%201:7&version=NKJV (accessed December 23, 2013).

5. Bible Gateway, 2 Kings 21:5-13, http://www.biblegateway.com/passage/?search=2%20Kings%2021:5-13&version=NKJV (accessed December 23, 2013).

6. Folger, Janet, "24 Years of Abortion on Demand Based on Lies," http://www.pregnantpause.org/abort/lies.htm (accessed December 23, 2013).

7. Politifact, "Chris Smith says more than 54 million abortions have been performed since U.S. Supreme Court decided Roe v. Wade," http://www.politifact.com/new-jersey/statements/2012/mar/18/chris-smith/chris-smith-says-more-54-million-abortions-have-be/ (accessed December 23, 2013).

8. Bible Gateway, Psalm 91:7, http://www.biblegateway.com/passage/?search=Psalm%2091:7&version=NKJV (accessed December 23, 2013).

Dispatch Twenty-nine

1. Nerd Wallet Finance, "American Household Credit Card Debt Statistics: 2013," http://www.nerdwallet.com/blog/credit-card-data/average-credit-card-debt-household/ (accessed December 23, 2013).

2. U.S. Debt Clock.org, http://www.usdebtclock.org/ (accessed December 18, 2013).

3. National Priorities Project, "Borrowing and the National debt," http://nationalpriorities.org/budget-basics/federal-budget-101/borrowing-and-federal-debt/ (accessed December 23, 2013).

4. Tavakoli, Janet, Business Insider, "IMMINENT THREAT: Foreign Borrowings Will Lead To The Destruction Of The US Financial System," October 30, 2011, http://www.businessinsider.com/clear-and-present-danger-foreign-borrowing-poses-an-imminent-threat-to-the-us-dollar-and-us-financial-system-2011-10 (accessed December 23, 2013).

5. Paul, Ron, "The Fed and the Debt," http://archive.lewrockwell.com/paul/paul740.html (accessed December 23, 2013).

6. Deadline News.com, "Two More Years of 4% Interest Rates?" http://www.deadlinenews.com/2012/02/24/two-more-years-of-4-interest-rates/ (accessed December 23, 2013).

7. Beattie, Andrew, Investopdeia, "The Dotcom Crash," http://www.investopedia.com/features/crashes/crashes8.asp#axzz22PItNZAS (accessed December 23, 2013).

8. Farrell, Paul B., Market watch, "The Real Crash is dead ahead as 2008 is forgotten," http://www.marketwatch.com/story/the-real-crash-is-dead-ahead-as-2008-is-forgotten-2012-07-31 (accessed December 23, 2013).

9. U.S. Government Spending, http://www.usgovernmentspending.com/debt_deficit_history (accessed December 21, 2013).

10. Duncan, Kevin, The Daily Caller, "The Growing Regulatory State," http://dailycaller.com/2011/10/20/the-growing-regulatory-state/ (accessed December 23, 2013).

11. Klein, Ezra, The Washington Post, "For some conservatives, even Ryan does not go far enough," March 22, 2012, http://www.washingtonpost.com/blogs/wonkblog/post/wonkbook-for-some-conservatives-even-ryan-does-not-go-far-enough/2012/03/22/gIQAMIuSTS_blog.html (accessed December 23, 2013).

12. Beatty, W. A., American Thinker, "All the Dependency Pieces Are Falling into Place," July 30, 2012, http://www.americanthinker.com/2012/07/all_the_dependency_pieces_are_falling_into_place.html (accessed December 23, 2013).

13. T. B. Rickert's Call, "More Americans joining disability than finding jobs," July 18, 2012, http://tbrickert.wordpress.com/2012/07/18/more-americans-joining-disability-than-finding-jobs/ (accessed December 23, 2013).

Dispatch Thirty

1. Declaration of Independence, http://www.ushistory.org/declaration/document/ (accessed December 18, 2013).

2. U.S. Constitution Online, Constitutional Amendments, The Amendment process, http://www.usconstitution.net/constam.html#process (accessed December 18, 2013).

3. Charters of Freedom, The Bill of Rights, http://www.archives.gov/exhibits/charters/bill_of_rights_transcript.html (accessed December 18, 2013).

4. Library of Congress, The Articles of Confederation, http://www.loc.gov/rr/program/bib/ourdocs/articles.html (accessed December 23, 2013).

5. The United States Constitution, http://constitutionus.com/ (accessed December 23, 2013).

6. The Founder's Constitution, "Article 1, Section 8, Clause 18," The Necessary and Proper Clause, http://press-pubs.uchicago.edu/founders/print_documents/a1_8_18s5.html (accessed December 23, 2013).

7. Excerpt from Essay No. 1 by Brutus, "FEDERALIST POWER WILL ULTIMATELY SUBVERT STATE AUTHORITY" http://www.ucs.louisiana.edu/~ras2777/conlaw/antfed17.html (accessed December 23, 2013).

8. Our Documents, "Marbury v. Madison," http://www.ourdocuments.gov/doc.php?flash=true&doc=19 (accessed December 23, 2013).

Dispatch Thirty-two

1. About Sun Tzu, http://www.thetao.info/artofwar.thetao.info/china/suntzu.htm (accessed December 23, 2013).

2. QB, "The enemy advances, we retreat; the enemy camps, we harass; the enemy tires, we attack; the enemy retreats, we pursue," http://quotationsbook.com/quote/44984/#sthash.xmCTFsaK.dpbs (accessed December 23, 2013).

Dispatch Thirty-three

1. Mail Online, "The shuttle as you've never seen it before: Space Station astronauts capture Atlantis re-entering the atmosphere from above ...hours before it is wheeled into hangar for the last time," http://www.dailymail.co.uk/sciencetech/article-2017122/Space-Shuttle-Atlantis-makes-historic-final-landing-Nasas-30-yr-programme-ends.html (accessed December 23, 2013).

2. Club Troppo, "Did Nixon really say "we are all Keynesians now"?," http://clubtroppo.com.au/2009/02/15/pedantic-fact-checking-did-nixon-really-say-we-are-keynesians-now/ (accessed December 23, 2013).

3. Your Tube, Fundamentally Transform America, http://www.youtube.com/watch?v=KrefKCaV8m4 (accessed December 18, 2013).

4. Laffer, Arthur, The Heritage Foundation, "The Laffer Curve: Past, Present, and Future," June 1, 2004, http://www.heritage.org/research/reports/2004/06/the-laffer-curve-past-present-and-future (accessed December 23, 2013).

5. Leach, Andrew, Alberta Oil, "The fine line between a subsidy and a tax credit," June 1, 2011, http://www.albertaoilmagazine.com/2011/07/insights-do-targeted-tax-incentives-work/ (accessed December 23, 2013).

6. Get a Quote a Day, Lenin Quotes, "The Capitalists will sell us the rope with which we will hang them," http://quotes.liberty-tree.ca/quotes_by/vladimir+ilyich+lenin (accessed December 23, 2013).

Dispatch Thirty-five

1. Brainy Quote, John Locke, http://www.brainyquote.com/quotes/quotes/j/johnlocke401229.html (accessed December 23, 2013).

2. Federalist No. 62, James Madison, http://www.constitution.org/fed/federa62.htm (accessed December 23, 2013).

3. CARROLL, CONN, The Washington Examiner, "Obama donor gained nearly $1 billion in tax credits in Solyndra bankruptcy," September 19, 2013, http://washingtonexaminer.com/day-4-obama-donor-gained-nearly-1-billion-in-tax-credits-in-solyndra-bankruptcy/article/2536031 (accessed December 23, 2013).

4. Do One Thing: Quotes for a Better World," Rule of Law Quotes: Aristotle, "The only stable state is the one in which all men are equal before the law," http://www.doonething.org/quotes/law-quotes.htm (accessed December 23, 2013).

5. Search Quotes, Tullius Cicero quotes, "We are in bondage to the law so that we might be free," http://www.searchquotes.com/quotation/We_are_in_bondage_to_the_law_so_that_we_might_be_free/32084/ (accessed December 23, 2013).

Dispatch Thirty-six

1. Hester, Wesley P., Times Dispatch, "Romney camp asks Va. to probe voter forms," July 25, 2012, http://www.timesdispatch.com/news/update-romney-camp-asks-va-to-probe-voter-forms/article_46e1b142-4c67-569a-b9c6-4ff2edca7d27.html (accessed December 24, 2013).

2. Chicago's Outfit and the Machine, http://www.gangresearch.net/Chicago-Gangs/outfit/index.html (accessed December 24, 2013).

3. Hester, Wesley P., Times Dispatch, "Romney camp asks Va. to probe voter forms," July 25, 2012, http://www.timesdispatch.com/news/update-romney-camp-asks-va-to-probe-voter-forms/article_46e1b142-4c67-569a-b9c6-4ff2edca7d27.html (accessed December 24, 2013).

4. Ibid.

5. Ibid.

6. Farmelant, Scott, Philadelphia City Paper, "Dead Men Can Vote," http://archives.citypaper.net/articles/101295/article009.shtml (accessed December 24, 2013).

7. Atlas Shrugs, "Massive Voter Fraude: Military Vote Suppressed," http://atlasshrugs2000.typepad.com/atlas_shrugs/2012/11/more-voter-fraud-military-absentee-ballots-not-counted.html (accessed December 24, 2013).

8. Live Leak, "More Democratic Voter Fraud Found in Chicago IL," http://www.liveleak.com/view?i=331_1288233022 (accessed December 24, 2013).

9. Huston, Warner Todd, Publius Forum, "East St. Louis: More Voters Registered Than Citizens That Live There," March 28, 2011, http://www.chicagonow.com/publius-forum/2011/04/east-st-louis-more-voters-registered-than-citizens-that-live-there/ (accessed December 24, 2013).

10. Huston, Warner Todd, News Busters, "Indiana: More Registered to Vote Than Eligible, Media Misses Story," http://newsbusters.org/blogs/warner-todd-huston/2008/10/09/indiana-more-registered-vote-eligible-media-misses-story (accessed December 24, 2013).

11. Investors.com, "Justice Department Encourages Voter Fraud The Chicago Way," http://news.investors.com/ibd-editorials/060112-613434-justice-department-promotes-voter-fraud-in-florida.htm?p=full (accessed December 24, 2013

12. Fox News, "Justice Department sues Florida over effort to purge voter rolls of non-citizens," http://www.foxnews.com/politics/2012/06/12/justice-department-sues-florida-over-purging-voter-rolls-as-expected/ (accessed December 24, 2013).

13. Atlanta Business Chronicle, "Justice Department sues Georgia over voting," http://www.bizjournals.com/atlanta/news/2012/06/27/justice-department-sues-georgia-over.html (accessed December 24, 2013).

14. Jackson, Henry C., Washington Times, "Texas, Justice Department square off over voter ID law," http://www.washingtontimes.com/news/2012/jul/9/texas-justice-square-off-over-voter-id-law/ (accessed December 24, 2013).

15. International Business Times, "Justice Dept. Tells Pa. Its Voter ID Law Is Under Investigation," July 23-2012, http://www.ibtimes.com/justice-dept-tells-pa-its-voter-id-law-under-investigation-730237 (accessed December 24, 2013).

16. Spakovsky, Hans von, The Heritage Network, "The New Black Panther Party Evidence on Voter Intimidation," July 21, 2010, http://blog.heritage.org/2010/07/21/the-new-black-panther-party-evidence-on-voter-intimidation/ (accessed December 24, 2013).

17. You Tube, "Security" patrols stationed at polling places in Philly, http://www.youtube.com/watch?v=neGbKHyGuHU (accessed December 24, 2013).

18. Hedgecock, Roger, U-T San Diego, "Suppressing the Military Vote," July 24, 2012, http://www.utsandiego.com/news/2012/jul/24/suppressing-the-military-vote/ (accessed December 24, 2013).

19. Pavlich, Katie, Townhall.com, "NAACP Requires Photo I.D. to See Holder Speak in State Being Sued Over Voter ID," July 3, 2012, http://townhall.com/tipsheet/katiepavlich/2012/07/10/naacp_requires_photo_id_to_see_holder_speak (accessed December 24, 2013).

20. Agren, David, USA Today, "Mexico's national voter IDs part of culture," January 25, 2012, http://usatoday30.usatoday.com/news/world/story/2012-01-22/mexico-national-voter-ID-cards/52779410/1 (accessed December 24, 2013).

21. Pollak, Joel B., Breitbart, "Sorry, Jesse Jackson: South Africa Has Photo ID Voting," December 6, 2013, http://www.breitbart.com/Big-Government/2013/12/06/Sorry-Jesse-Jackson-South-Africa-Has-Photo-ID-Voting (accessed December 24, 2013).

22. The Obama File, "Cloward-Piven Strategy," http://www.theobamafile.com/_opinion/Cloward-Piven.html (accessed December 24, 2013).

23. Belman, Ted, American Thinker, "Why is Obama in bed with the Muslim Brotherhood?," February 26, 2012, http://www.americanthinker.com/2012/02/why_is_obama_in_bed_with_the_muslim_brotherhood.html (accessed December 24, 2013).

24. You Tube, Apology Tours, http://www.youtube.com/watch?v=DAXA0WVwxiE (accessed December 18, 2013).

Dispatch Thirty-seven

1. Rothbard, Murray N., Ludwig von Mises Institute, "Origins of the Federal Reserve," November 13, 2009, http://mises.org/daily/3823 (accessed December 24, 2013).

2. U.S. History, "Report on Public Credit," http://www.u-s-history.com/pages/h441.html (accessed December 24, 2013).

3. History.com: This Day in History, "Andrew Jackson shuts down Second Bank of the U.S.," http://www.history.com/this-day-in-history/andrew-jackson-shuts-down-second-bank-of-the-us (accessed December 24, 2013).

4. Lapidos, Juliet, Explainer, "Is the Fed Private or Public?," http://www.slate.com/articles/news_and_politics/explainer/2008/09/is_the_fed_private_or_public.html (accessed December 24, 2013).

5. The Federal Reserve Board, Remarks by Governor Ben S. Bernanke, "Deflation: Making Sure 'It' Doesn't Happen Here," November 21, 2002, http://www.federalreserve.gov/BOARDDOCS/SPEECHES/2002/20021121/default.htm (accessed December 24, 2013).

6. Ibid.

7. Quora, Bernanke Quotes, "The U.S. government has a technology, called a printing press," http://www.quora.com/What-are-some-iconic-Ben-Bernanke-quotes (accessed December 24, 2013).

8. Ibid.

9. Live Leak, "Bush: 'I've Abandoned Free Market Principles To Save The Free Market System,'" http://www.liveleak.com/view?i=4a2_1229470578 (accessed December 24, 2013).

10. Bloomberg Business Week Magazine, "Where Di the TARP Money Go?," http://www.businessweek.com/magazine/content/10_41/b4198029792387.htm (accessed December 24, 2013).

11. Hoft, Jim, Gateway Pundit, "CBO Finds Obama Stimulus May Have Cost As Much as $4.1 Million Per Job," June 5, 2012, http://www.thegatewaypundit.com/2012/06/cbo-finds-obama-stimulus-may-have-cost-as-much-as-4-1-million-per-job/ (accessed December 24, 2013).

12. Fox Nation, "Obama Jokes at Jobs Council: 'Shovel-Ready Was Not as Shovel-Ready as We Expected,'" http://nation.foxnews.com/president-obama/2011/06/13/obama-jokes-jobs-council-shovel-ready-was-not-shovel-ready-we-expected (accessed December 24, 2013).

13. History Wired, "Not worth a Continental," http://historywired.si.edu/object.cfm?ID=437 (accessed December 24, 2013).

14. Investopdedia, "Quantitative Easing," http://www.investopedia.com/terms/q/quantitative-easing.asp#axzz1xlltQbSk (accessed December 24, 2013).

15. Greenstein, Tracey, Forbes, "The Fed's $16 Trillion Bailouts Under-Reported," September 20, 2011, http://www.forbes.com/sites/traceygreenstein/2011/09/20/the-feds-16-trillion-bailouts-under-reported/ (accessed December 24, 2013).

16. U.S. Debt Clock.org, http://www.usdebtclock.org/ (accessed December 18, 2013).

17. You Tube, Spread the Wealth Around, http://www.youtube.com/watch?v=RZcEHLr4gBg (accessed December 18, 2013).

18. Quora, Bernanke Quotes, "The U.S. government has a technology, called a printing press," http://www.quora.com/What-are-some-iconic-Ben-Bernanke-quotes (accessed December 24, 2013).

19. Macke, Jeff, Breakout, "Bernanke: There Is No Inflation (and If There Were, We Could Stop It)," April 5, 2011, http://finance.yahoo.com/blogs/breakout/bernanke-no-inflation-were-could-stop-20110405-093226-104.html (accessed December 24, 2013).

Dispatch Thirty-eight

1. Eichier, Alexander, Huffington Post, "46 Percent of Americans Exempt From Federal Income Tax in 2011," June 28, 2011http://www.huffington-post.com/2011/06/28/46-percent-of-americans-e_n_886293.html (accessed December 26, 2013).

2. Schoen, Douglas, U.S. news, "Occupy'-ers Seek Dissolution of Democracy, End of Capitalism," October 19, 2011, http://www.usnews.com/debate-club/is-occupy-wall-street-the-next-tea-party-movement/occopy-ers-seek-dissolution-of-democracy-end-of-capitalism-occupy-ers-seek-dissolution-of-democracy (accessed December 26, 2013).

3. Ibid.

4. Cunningham, Paige Winfield, The Washington Times, "Paul: Obama health care more fascism than socialism," http://www.washingtontimes.com/blog/inside-politics/2011/nov/16/paul-obama-health-care-more-fascism-socialism/ (accessed December 26, 2013).

5. McNamara, Robert, About.com: 19th Century History, "American System (Economic Ideas Advanced by Henry Clay)," http://history1800s.about.com/od/1800sglossary/g/americansysdef.htm (accessed December 26, 2013).

6. Chicago's Outfit and the Machine, http://www.gangresearch.net/Chicago-Gangs/outfit/index.html (accessed December 24, 2013).

7. NewsAlert, "The Political Corruption Behind Barack Obama and Chicago," January, 6, 2008, http://nalert.blogspot.com/2008/01/political-corruption-behind-barack_06.html (accessed December 26, 2013).

8. The Guardian, "Wall Street protesters: over-educated, under-employed and angry," http://www.theguardian.com/world/2011/sep/19/wall-street-protesters-angry (accessed December 26, 2013).

9. Guido, Jessica, NBC 5 Chicago, "Controversial Professor Bill Ayers Speaks With Occupy Chicago Protesters," November 17, 2011, http://www.nbcchi-cago.com/news/local/Controversial-Professor-Bill-Ayers-Speaks-With-Oc-cupy-Chicago-Protestors--134045388.html?dr (accessed December 26, 2013).

10. Schoen, Douglas, U.S. news, "Occupy'-ers Seek Dissolution of Democracy, End of Capitalism," October 19, 2011, http://www.usnews.com/debate-club/is-occupy-wall-street-the-next-tea-party-movement/occopy-ers-seek-dissolution-of-democracy-end-of-capitalism-occupy-ers-seek-dissolution-of-democracy (accessed December 26, 2013).

11. Rappleye, Hannah, New York Post, "OWS protesters cause mayhem across the city, 275 arrested," November 17, 2011, http://nypost.com/2011/11/17/ows-protesters-cause-mayhem-across-the-city-275-arrested/ (accessed December 26, 2013).

12. Smith, Emily, CBS 2 New York, "OWS Protesters Chant 'Follow Those Kids!' As Small Children Try To Go To School On Wall Street: Tiny Tots, Some As Young As 4, Overwhelmed By Hostility, Crush Of Humanity," November 17, 2011, http://newyork.cbslocal.com/2011/11/17/ows-protesters-chant-follow-those-kids-as-small-children-try-to-go-to-school-on-wall-street/ (accessed December 26, 2013).

13. Goldberg, Jonah, National Review Online, "Wait, Is Malaise French for "Soft"?," September, 29, 2011, http://www.nationalreview.com/corner/278769/wait-malaise-french-soft-jonah-goldberg (accessed December 26, 2013).

14. You Tube, America's Shame: Obama Calls U.S. "Arrogant" & "Dismissive" in Speech in France, http://www.youtube.com/watch?v=OLZer0P9l1M Accessed December 26, 2013).

15. MRCTV, "Obama Says Americans "Lazy," http://www.mrctv.org/videos/obama-says-americans-lazy (accessed December 26, 2013).

Dispatch Forty

1. Gensert, William L., American Thinker, "The Transformational Tyrant," January 17, 2012, http://www.americanthinker.com/2012/01/the_transformational_tyrant.html (accessed December 26, 2013).

2. MR. Conservative "Obama Rants That The Constitution Is A 'Charter of Negative Liberties,'" http://www.mrconservative.com/2013/06/18984-obama-rants-that-the-constitution-is-a-charter-of-negative-liberties/ (accessed December 26, 2013).

3. You Tube, Obama: Constitution Flawed - Missing Redistribution of Wealth, http://www.youtube.com/watch?v=sMJS4CP3OC0 (accessed December 26, 2013).

4. Wallison, Peter J. & Edward J. Pinto, Forbes, "A Government-Mandated Housing Bubble," February 16. 2009, http://www.forbes.com/2009/02/13/housing-bubble-subprime-opinions-contributors_0216_peter_wallison_edward_pinto.html (accessed December 26, 2013).

5. Good Reads, "Alexis de Tocqueville quotes," http://www.goodreads.com/author/quotes/465.Alexis_de_Tocqueville (accessed December 26, 2013).

6. You Tube, Fundamentally Transform America

7. Good Reads, "Alexis de Tocqueville quotes," http://www.goodreads.com/author/quotes/465.Alexis_de_Tocqueville (accessed December 26, 2013).

Dispatch Forty-one

1. Helderman, Rosalind S., The Washington Post, "Democratic, Republican payroll tax cut extension plans both blocked by Senate," December 8, 2011, http://www.washingtonpost.com/blogs/2chambers/post/democratic-republican-payroll-tax-cut-extension-plans-both-blocked-by-senate/2011/12/08/gIQAmRzvfO_blog.html (accessed December 26, 2013).

2. Ledderman, Josh, The Hill, "Schumer: Democrats will pay for payroll tax-cut with millionaire's tax," November 27, 2011, http://thehill.com/video/senate/195527-schumer-democrats-will-pay-for-payroll-tax-cut-extension-with-millionaires-tax (accessed December 26, 2013).

3. Limbaugh, Rush, Liberty New Online, "BASELINE BUDGETING MAKES REAL FEDERAL BUDGET CUTS IMPOSSIBLE," August 2, 2011, http://www.libertynewsonline.com/article_301_30876.php (accessed December 26, 2013).

4. CARROLL, CONN, The Heritage Network, "Federal Workforce Continues to Grow Under Obama Budget," February 22, 2011, http://blog.heritage.org/2011/02/22/federal-workforce-continues-to-grow-under-obama-budget/ (accessed December 26, 2013).

5. Faier, Brian, Bloomberg Business Weekly, "Obama Payroll Tax Cuts Seen Undermining Social Security," December 9, 2011, http://www.businessweek.com/news/2011-12-09/obama-payroll-tax-cuts-seen-undermining-social-security.html (accessed December 26, 2013).

6. Samuelson, Robert J., Newsweek, "Social Security Is Middle-Class Welfare," March 6, 2011, http://www.newsweek.com/social-security-middle-class-welfare-66119 (accessed December 26, 2013).

Dispatch Forty-two

1. Political Vel Craft, "Personal Income Tax Violates U.S. Supreme Court Ruling ~ Privately Owned Federal Reserve Violates U.S. Constitution & President Kennedy's Executive Orders," http://politicalvelcraft.org/2011/09/08/u-s-supreme-court-struck-down-personal-income-tax-president-kennedy-struck-down-federal-reserve-both-not-enforced/ (accessed December 26, 2013).

2. Terrell, Ellen, Library of Congress: Business Reference services, "History of the US Income Tax," February 2004, http://www.loc.gov/rr/business/hottopic/irs_history.html (accessed December 26, 2013).

3. Chamberlain, John, The Freeman, "The Progressive Income tax," April 1, 1981, http://www.fee.org/the_freeman/detail/the-progressive-income-tax#axzz2oawA5yDo (accessed December 26, 2013).

4. The Ronald Reagan Presidential Foundation and Library, "The Second American Revolution: Reaganomics," https://www.reaganfoundation.org/economic-policy.aspx (accessed December 26, 2013).

5. Politifact, "Pat Toomey says U.S. has highest corporate tax rates in the world," http://www.politifact.com/truth-o-meter/statements/2011/jan/03/pat-toomey/pat-toomey-says-us-has-highest-corporate-tax-rates/ (accessed December 26, 2013).

6. Kudlow, Larry, Real Clear Markets, "Unleash the Great American Energy Industry," march 31, 2011, http://www.realclearmarkets.com/articles/2011/03/31/unleash_the_great_american_energy_industry_98939.html Accessed 12-26-13 (accessed December 26, 2013).

7. _____, John Quincy Adams, http://www.quotationspage.com/quote/32145.html (accessed December 26, 2013).

8. Politifact, "The U.S. military "'s in 130 countries. We have 900 bases around the world,'" http://www.politifact.com/truth-o-meter/statements/2011/sep/14/ron-paul/ron-paul-says-us-has-military-personnel-130-nation/ (accessed December 26, 2013).

9. U.S. Constitution Online, Article 1 Section 8, http://www.usconstitution.net/xconst_A1Sec8.html Accessed 12-26-13 (accessed December 26, 2013).

10. Investopedia, The Federal Reserve: Introduction, February 25, 2009, http://www.investopedia.com/university/thefed/#axzz1XM8i0e4c (accessed December 26, 2013).

11. Porter, George, The U. S. Federal Reserve System, http://www.converge.org.nz/pirm/fr_paul.htm (accessed December 26, 2013).

12. Get a Quote a Day, Lenin Quotes, "The Capitalists will sell us the rope with which we will hang them," http://quotes.liberty-tree.ca/quotes_by/vladimir+ilyich+lenin (accessed December 23, 2013).

13. Faith and Freedom Network and Foundation, "President Obama Is 'Managing The Decline Of America,'" February 22, 2010, http://blog.faithandfreedom.us/2010/02/president-obama-is-managing-decline-of.html#.UryuV7RzYqM (accessed December 26, 2013).

Dispatch Forty-three

1. Revolutionary War and Beyond, James Madison Quotes, http://www.revolutionary-war-and-beyond.com/james-madison-quotes-5.html (accessed December 18, 2013).

2. Ibid.

3. Related Information: Patrick Henry, http://www.ushistory.org/declaration/related/henry.htm (accessed December 27, 2013).

4. Brainy Quotes, Patrick Henry, http://www.brainyquote.com/quotes/authors/p/patrick_henry.html (accessed December 27, 2013).

5. _____, Samuel Adams, http://www.brainyquote.com/quotes/authors/s/samuel_adams.html?gclid=CNq_nZOz164CFUPc4AodsitAdg (accessed December 27, 2013).

6. Ibid.

7. Ibid.

8. _____, Patrick Henry, http://www.brainyquote.com/quotes/authors/p/patrick_henry.html (accessed December 27, 2013).

9. Ibid.

10. Ibid.

11. Ibid.

Dispatch Forty-four

1. The Free Dictionary, George Armstrong Custer, http://encyclopedia2.thefreedictionary.com/Custer%2c+George+Armstrong (accessed December 27, 2013).

2. Zallman, Amy, About.com, "War in Afghanistan -- the History behind the U.S. War in Afghanistan," http://terrorism.about.com/od/warinafghanistan/ss/AfghanistanWar_3.htm (accessed December 27, 2013).

3. Wander, Andrew, The Guardian/The Observer, "A history of terror: Al-Qaeda 1988-2008," July 12, 2008, http://www.theguardian.com/world/2008/jul/13/history.alqaida (accessed December 27, 2013).

4. History of the Taliban, http://www-pub.naz.edu/~aamghar6/History%20of%20the%20Taliban.htm (accessed December 27, 2013).

5. Reuters, "General Petraeus hangs up uniform, warns on budget," http://www.reuters.com/article/2011/08/31/us-usa-petraeus-idUSTRE77U5HU20110831 (accessed December 27, 2013).

6. U.S. Constitution Online, Article 1 Section 8, http://www.usconstitution.net/xconst_A1Sec8.html (accessed December 26, 2013).

7. The New York Times, "Articles about Blackwater Worldwide," http://topics.nytimes.com/top/news/business/companies/blackwater_usa/index.html (accessed December 27, 2013).

Dispatch Forty-five

1. Amazon.com, "The Corporate Cult," http://www.amazon.com/Corporate-Cult-More-What-Women/dp/1589390423/ref=sr_1_2?ie=UTF8&qid=132 2141274&sr=8-2 (accessed December 27, 2013).

2. Mills, David G., Information Clearing House, "It's the Corporate State, Stupid," http://www.informationclearinghouse.info/article7260.htm (accessed December 27, 2013).

3. Gordon, David, Ludwig von Mises Institute, "Nazi Economic Policy," January 2, 2009, http://mises.org/daily/3274 (accessed December 27, 2013)

4. Spartacus Educational, "The Black Shirts," http://www.spartacus.schoolnet.co.uk/SPblack.htm (accessed December 27, 2013).

5. _____, "Yalta Conference," http://www.spartacus.schoolnet.co.uk/2WWyalta.htm (accessed December 27, 2013).

6. Hays, Don, The Hill, "THERE ARE NO CUTS! – The fallacy of baseline budgeting," http://thehill.com/blogs/congress-blog/economy-a-budget/195099-there-are-no-cuts-the-fallacy-of-baseline-budgeting (accessed December 27, 2013).

7. Ferrara, Peter, Forbes, "A Budget Cutting Deal That Boosts Federal Spending," August 4, 2011, http://www.forbes.com/sites/peterferrara/2011/08/04/a-budget-cutting-deal-that-boosts-federal-spending/ (accessed December 27, 2013).

8. U.S. Debt Clock.org, http://www.usdebtclock.org/ (accessed December 18, 2013).

9. Ibid.

10. Tax Policy Center, "Taxes and the Budget: What does it mean for a government program to be 'off-budget'?," http://www.taxpolicycenter.org/briefing-book/background/taxes-budget/off-budget.cfm (accessed December 27, 2013).

11. Amazon.com, "The Constitution Failed," http://www.amazon.com/Constitution-Failed-PH-D-Robert-Owens/dp/1609579615/ref=sr_1_1?ie=UTF8&qid=1372328556&sr=8-1&keywords=the+constitution+failed+owens (accessed December 18, 2013).

Dispatch Forty-six

1. The Blaze, "Cass Sunstein's New Presidential Appointment Is Almost Hard to Believe…Especially Considering a Paper He Once Wrote," August 26, 2013, http://www.theblaze.com/stories/2013/08/26/cass-sunsteins-new-presidential-appointment-is-almost-hard-to-believe-especially-considering-a-paper-he-once-wrote/ (accessed December 27, 2013).

2. DeMar, Gary, The Political Outcast, "How Liberals Captured the Nation through 'Free' Education," http://politicaloutcast.com/2012/12/how-liberals-captured-the-nation-through-free-education/ (accessed December 27, 2013).

3. Norris, Chuck, Republic-Main Street, "Public Education: Progressive In-doctrination Camps," March 8, 2011, https://republicmainstreet.wordpress.com/2011/03/08/chuck-norris-public-education-progressive-indoctrination-camps/ (accessed December 27, 2013).

4. Amazon.com, "The Road to Serfdom," http://www.amazon.com/s/ref=nb_sb_noss?url=search-alias%3Daps&field-keywords=the+road+to+serfdom&x=0&y=0 (accessed December 22, 2013).

5. Day, Rebecca, "'SLOWLY I TURNED': A PIECE OF AMERICA'S POP CULTURE," http://www.niagarafallsreporter.com/slowly.html (accessed December 27, 2013).

Dispatch Forty-seven

1. Final Vote Results for Roll Call 887, November, 7, 2009, http://clerk.house.gov/evs/2009/roll887.xml (accessed December 27, 2013).

2. The Washington Post, "House Democrats pass historical health-care legislation," http://www.washingtonpost.com/wp-srv/special/politics/votes/house/finalhealthcare/ (accessed December 27, 2013).

3. United States Senate, "H.R. 3590 (Patient Protection and Affordable Care Act)," http://www.senate.gov/legislative/LIS/roll_call_lists/roll_call_vote_cfm.cfm?congress=111&session=1&vote=00396 (accessed December 27, 2013).

4. Darling, Brian, Human Events, "Your Guide to Budget Reconciliation and Obamacare," september 22, 2009, http://www.humanevents.com/2009/09/22/your-guide-to-budget-reconciliation-and-obamacare/ (accessed December 27, 2013).

5. PBS: Judgment Day, "Indian Removal," http://www.pbs.org/wgbh/aia/part4/4p2959.html (accessed December 27, 2013).

6. Cornell University Law School: Legal Information Institute, "THE CHEROKEE NATION v. THE STATE OF GEORGIA," http://www.law.cornell.edu/supremecourt/text/30/1 (accessed December 27, 2013).

7. PBS: New Perspectives on the West, "Worcester v. Georgia," http://www.pbs.org/weta/thewest/resources/archives/two/worcestr.htm (accessed December 27, 2013).

8. Two Documents on Indian Removal (1830s), http://www.pinzler.com/ushistory/indremsupp.html (accessed December 27, 2013).

9. U.S. History, "The Trail of Tears — The Indian Removals," http://www.ushistory.org/us/24f.asp (accessed December 27, 2013).

10. PBS: American Experience, "Presidential Politics," http://www.pbs.org/wgbh/americanexperience/features/general-article/fdr-presidential/ (accessed December 27, 2013).

11. Ibid.

12. Fund, John, Real Clear Politics, "Obama's Affinity for Saul Alinsky." March 29, 2012, http://www.realclearpolitics.com/2012/03/29/obama039s_affinity_for_saul_alinsky_276330.html (accessed December 27, 2013).

13. Moran, Terry, ABC News, "State of the Union: The Slam, the Scowl and the Separation of Powers," January 28, 2010, http://abcnews.go.com/Politics/State_of_the_Union/state-of-the-union-president-obama-justice-alito-political-theater/story?id=9688639 (accessed December 27, 2013).

Dispatch Forty-eight

1. U.S. Debt Clock.org, http://www.usdebtclock.org/ (accessed December 18, 2013).

2. Politifact, "John Cornyn says 51 percent of American households pay no income tax," http://www.politifact.com/truth-o-meter/statements/2011/jul/08/john-cornyn/john-cornyn-says-51-percent-american-households-pa/ (accessed December 27, 2013).

3. FactCheck.org, "Who Caused the Economic Crisis?," http://www.factcheck.org/2008/10/who-caused-the-economic-crisis/ (accessed December 27, 2013).

4. Discover the Networks.org, "Saul Alinsky," http://www.discoverthenetworks.org/individualProfile.asp?indid=2314 (accessed December 27, 2013).

5. NASW Foundation, "Richard A. Cloward (1926 - 2005)," http://www.naswfoundation.org/pioneers/c/cloward.htm (accessed December 27, 2013).

6. Five Colleges Archives& Manuscript Collections, "Frances Fox Piven," http://asteria.fivecolleges.edu/findaids/sophiasmith/mnsss52_bioghist.html (accessed December 27, 2013).

7. Coppock, Nancy, American Thinker, "The Cloward/Piven Strategy of Economic Recovery," February 7, 2009, http://www.americanthinker.com/2009/02/the_clowardpiven_strategy_of_e.html (accessed December 27, 2013).

8. CNN, "How Occupy Wall Street compares to the tea party," October, 13, 2011, http://news.blogs.cnn.com/2011/10/13/how-occupy-wall-street-compares-to-the-tea-party/ (accessed December 27, 2013).

9. Rainey, James, Los Angeles Times, "On the Media: Tea party, Occupy Wall Street share a moment," October 12, 2011, http://articles.latimes.com/2011/oct/12/entertainment/la-et-onthemedia-20111012 (accessed December 27, 2013).

10. Boyle, Catherine, CNBC, "Occupy Wall Street 'Bookend to Tea Party': Jon Corzine," http://www.cnbc.com/id/44855426 (accessed December 27, 2013).

11. PJ Media, "Occupy L.A. Speaker: Violence will be Necessary to Achieve Our Goals," October 11, 2011, http://pjmedia.com/tatler/2011/10/11/occupy-l-a-speaker-violence-will-be-necessary-to-achieve-our-goals/ (accessed December 27, 2013).

12. News Talk WCHB, "700 Arrested In Brooklyn Bridge "Occupy Wall St." Protest," October 3, 2011, http://wchbnewsdetroit.com/2347942/700-arrested-in-brookyln-bridge-occupy-wall-st-protest/ (accessed December 27, 2013).

13. Occupy Protests Plagued by Reports of Sex Attacks, Violent Crime," November 9, 2011, http://www.foxnews.com/us/2011/11/09/rash-sex-attacks-and-violent-crime-breaks-out-at-occupy-protests/ (accessed December 27, 2013).

14. Huffington Post, "Masoud Jazayeri, Iran General, Calls Wall Street Protest American Spring," http://www.huffingtonpost.com/2011/10/09/masoud-jazayeri-wall-street_n_1002598.html (accessed December 27, 2013).

15. Hall, Mike, AFL-CIO, "Union Movement Opens 'Arms and Hearts' to Occupy Wall Street Activists," October 9, 2011, http://www.aflcio.org/Blog/Corporate-Greed/Union-Movement-Opens-Arms-and-Hearts-to-Occupy-Wall-Street-Activists (accessed December 27, 2013)

16. Klein, Rick, ABC News, "Democrats Seek to Own 'Occupy Wall Street' Movement," October 10, 2011, http://abcnews.go.com/Politics/democrats-seek-occupy-wall-street-movement/story?id=14701337 (accessed December 27, 2013).

17. Portnoy, Howard, Hotair, "Occupy L.A.: We will need violence (and socialism!) to attain our goals," October 12, 2011, http://hotair.com/greenroom/archives/2011/10/12/occupy-l-a-we-will-need-violence-and-socialism-to-attain-our-goals/ (accessed December 27, 2013).

18. Riley, Charles, CNN Money, "Occupy Wall Street... mansions," October 12, 2011, http://money.cnn.com/2011/10/10/news/economy/occupy_wall_street_protest/index.htm (accessed December 27, 2013).

Dispatch Forty-nine

1. Patrick J. Buchanan Official Web Site, "Let the People Rule," http://buchanan.org/blog/let-the-people-rule-169 (accessed December 27, 2013).

2. De Vogue, Ariane, ABC News, "Arizona Immigration Law: Enforcement Blocked by Circuit Court," April 11, 2011, http://abcnews.go.com/Politics/arizona-immigration-law-enforcement-blocked-circuit-court/story?id=13350124 (accessed December 27, 2013).

3. NBC News, "Court Rules Against Arizona Immigration Law," http://www.nbcnews.com/id/42537304/ns/politics-more_politics/t/court-rules-against-arizona-immigration-law/#.Ur2yubRzYqM (accessed December 27, 2013).

4. The TSA Blog, "Texas House of Representatives Seeking to Ban Current TSA Pat-Down," http://blog.tsa.gov/2011/05/texas-house-of-representatives-seeking.html (accessed December 27, 2013).

5. Levy, Robert A., Cato Institute, "The Taxing Power of Obamacare," April 20, 2010, http://www.cato.org/publications/commentary/taxing-power-obamacare (accessed December 27, 2013).

6. Somin, Ilya, The Volokh Conspiracy, "Number of States Challenging the Constitutionality of Obamacare Rises to 28," January 19, 2011, http://www.volokh.com/2011/01/19/number-of-states-challenging-the-constitutionality-of-obamacare-rises-to-28/ (accessed December 27, 2013).

7. Republic Magazine, "John Roberts, Constitutional Traitor: Chief Justice Approves Obamacare Tax Mandate," June 28, 2012, http://www.republicmagazine.com/news/john-roberts-constitutional-traitor-chief-justice-approves-obamacare-tax-mandate.html (accessed December 27, 2013).

8. Heritage Guide to the Constitution, "Origination Clause," http://www.heritage.org/constitution/#!/articles/1/essays/30/origination-clause (accessed December 27, 2013).

9. McCarthy, Andrew C. National Review Online, "Obamacare's Unconstitutional Origins," October 5, 2013, http://www.nationalreview.com/article/360460/obamacares-unconstitutional-origins-andrew-c-mccarthy (accessed December 27, 2013).

10. Amazon.com, "The Constitution Failed," http://www.amazon.com/Constitution-Failed-PH-D-Robert-Owens/dp/1609579615/ref=sr_1_1?ie=UTF8&qid=1372328556&sr=8-1&keywords=the+constitution+failed+owens (accessed December 18, 2013).

Dispatch Fifty

1. Pirates in America: Tripolitan War, http://nefertiti67.tripod.com/pirates/id1.html (accessed December 28, 2013).

2. U.S. History, "Remember the Maine!" http://www.ushistory.org/us/44c.asp (accessed December 28, 2013).

3. Robert McNamara, About.com, "The Election of 1824 Was Decided in the House of Representatives: The Controversial Election was Denounced as 'The Corrupt Bargain,'" http://history1800s.about.com/od/leaders/a/electionof1824.htm (accessed December 28, 2013).

4. U.S. History, "Federalist Party," http://www.u-s-history.com/pages/h445.html (accessed December 28, 2013).

5. Encyclopedia Britannica, "Democratic-Republican Party," http://www.britannica.com/EBchecked/topic/498833/Democratic-Republican-Party (accessed December 28, 2013).

6. Stanley, Paul, The Christian Post, "John Boehner Tries to Rally Support for Debt Plan," July 27, 2011, http://www.christianpost.com/news/boehners-plan-had-soft-support-with-gop-prospects-improving-quickly-52932/ (accessed December 28, 2013).

Dispatch Fifty-one

1. The White House, "Andrew Johnson," http://www.whitehouse.gov/about/presidents/andrewjohnson (accessed December 29, 2013).

2. The History Place: Impeachment Proceedings, "Andrew Johnson," http://www.historyplace.com/unitedstates/impeachments/johnson.htm (accessed December 29, 2013).

3. _____, "Bill Clinton," http://www.historyplace.com/unitedstates/impeachments/clinton.htm (accessed December 29, 2013).

4. Conservapedia, "Bill Clinton" http://conservapedia.com/Bill_Clinton (accessed December 29, 2013).

5. Daily Kos, "Bill Clinton: Elder Statesman to the World," http://www.dailykos.com/story/2009/09/24/785901/-Bill-Clinton-Elder-Statesman-to-the-World# (accessed December 29, 2013).

6. You Tube, Fundamentally Transform America http://www.youtube.com/watch?v=_cqN4NIEtOY (accessed December 18, 2013).

7. Geraghty, Jim, National Review Online, "The Alinsky Administration," May 14, 2009, http://www.nationalreview.com/articles/227500/alinsky-administration/jim-geraghty (accessed December 29, 2013).

8. Patton, David A.. Newsmax, "Obama: Constitution is 'Deeply Flawed,'" http://www.newsmax.com/InsideCover/obama-constitution/2008/10/27/id/326165 (accessed December 29, 2013).

9. Kuligowski, Monte, American Thinker, "A Clear Danger: Obama, a 'Living Constitution,' and 'Positive Rights,'" http://www.americanthinker.com/2010/10/a_clear_danger_obama_a_living.html (accessed December 29, 2013).

10. Sweetness and Light, "Obama: Constitution is Living Document," http://sweetness-light.com/archive/obama-constitution-is-living-document#.UsA6UrRzYqM (accessed December 29, 2013).

11. SunServer.com, "Presidential Oath of Office," http://www.sonserver.com/america/oath01.htm (accessed December 29, 2013).

12. Glenn Beck, "List of Obama's Czars," Augist 21, 2009, http://www.glennbeck.com/content/articles/article/198/29391/ (accessed December 29, 2013).

13. McAuliff, Michael, Huffington Post, "Obama Tells Congress He's Keeping His

Czars," April 15, 2011, http://www.huffingtonpost.com/2011/04/15/obama-czars-signing-statement_n_849963.html (accessed December 29, 2013).

14. Antle, James, Real Clear Politics, "Fast & Furious Scandal Festers," February 19, 2012, http://www.realclearpolitics.com/2012/02/19/fast_amp_furious_scandal_festers_273734.html (accessed December 29, 2013).

15. McCarthy, Andrew C., National Review Online, "Obama Gives Islamists a Walk," April 20, 2011, http://www.nationalreview.com/articles/265206/obama-gives-islamists-walk-andrew-c-mccarthy (accessed December 29, 2013).

16. Liberty News, "Justice Department 'Stonewalling' Congressional Investigators?," February 2, 2012, http://www.libertynews.com/2012/02/justice-department-stonewalling-congressional-investigators/ (accessed December 29, 2013).

17. Ertelt, Steven, LifeNews.com, "Obama Administration Accused of Targeting Peaceful Pro-life Advocate," May, 17, 2011, http://www.lifenews.com/2011/05/17/obama-admin-accused-of-targeting-peaceful-pro-life-advocate/ (accessed December 29, 2013).

18. Investors.com, "Arpaio Unjustly in Justice Department Crosshairs," December 16, 2011, http://news.investors.com/ibd-editorials/121611-595048-arpaio-arizona-immigration-border-sb1070-panthers-.htm (accessed December 29, 2013).

19. Human Events, "Obama Sues Arizona, Gives Sanctuary to Law Breakers," July 26, 2010, http://www.humanevents.com/2010/07/26/obama-sues-arizona-gives-sanctuary-to-lawbreakers/ (accessed December 29, 2013).

20. Jackson, David, The Oval, "Obama Still Thinks 9/11 Suspects Should be Tried in New York," April 17, 2011, http://content.usatoday.com/communities/theoval/post/2011/04/obama-still-thinks-911-suspects-should-be-tried-in-federal-court/1#.UsBCjLRzYqM (accessed December 29, 2013).

21. Ackerman, Bruce, FP, "Obama's Unconstitutional War," March 31, 2011, http://www.foreignpolicy.com/articles/2011/03/24/obama_s_unconstitutional_war#sthash.wzGMirLw.geoiZAaJ.dpbs (accessed December 29, 2013).

22. Kerpen, Phil, the daily Caller, "Obama's illegal NLRB appointments are even more outrageous than his appointment of Cordray," January 6, 2012, http://dailycaller.com/2012/01/06/obama-illegal-nlrb-appointments-even-more-outrageous-than-cordray-appointment/ (accessed December 29, 2013).

23. Brownfield, Mike, Heritage Foundation, "Constitution, Anyone? Obama Promises to Rule... Without Congress," December 14, 2011, http://blog.heritage.org/2011/12/14/constitution-anyone-obama-promises-to-rule-without-congress/ (accessed December 29, 2013).

24. The White House, "We can't wait," http://www.whitehouse.gov/economy/jobs/we-cant-wait (accessed December 23, 2013).

25. You Tube, "Ron Paul, Dennis Kucinich on "Freedom Watch" talk Obama's Illegal, Unconstitutional Attack on Libya," http://www.youtube.com/watch?v=Se_YPdp5T1Q (accessed December 29, 2013).

26. Watson, Paul Joseph, Infowars.com, "Ron Paul Likens Obama to "Dictator" Over 'Recess Appointments,'" January 6, 2012, http://www.infowars.com/ron-paul-likens-obama-to-dictator-over-recess-appointments/ (accessed December 29, 2013).

27. Raasch, Chuck, USA Today, "Obama aspires to a transformational presidency," April 16, 2009, http://usatoday30.usatoday.com/news/opinion/columnist/raasch/2009-04-16-raasch-column-04162009_N.htm (accessed December 29, 2013).

Dispatch Fifty-two

1. Quotes of the Founding Fathers: The Importance of a Moral Society: http://www.free2pray.info/5founderquotes.html (accessed December 31, 2013).

2. Quotes on Liberty and Virtue, http://www.liberty1.org/virtue.htm (accessed December 31, 2013).

3. You Tube, Obama's Millionaires and Billionaires, http://www.youtube.com/watch?v=Koi_5o9mTsU (accessed December 31, 2013).

4. Noah Webster Quotes, http://www.seekfind.net/NoahWebster.html (accessed December 31, 2013).

5. Quotes on Liberty and Virtue, Samuel Adams, http://www.liberty1.org/virtue.htm (accessed December 31, 2013).

6. _____, Thomas Jefferson, http://www.liberty1.org/virtue.htm (accessed December 31, 2013).

7. _____, Samuel Adams, http://www.liberty1.org/virtue.htm (accessed December 31, 2013).

8. _____, Douglas McArthur, http://www.liberty1.org/virtue.htm (accessed December 31, 2013).

9. Bible Gateway, Proverbs 14:34, http://www.biblegateway.com/passage/?search=Proverbs+14%3A34&version=NKJV (accessed December 31, 2013).

Dispatch Fifty-two

1. Tiberius Gracchus, http://www.roman-empire.net/republic/tib-gracchus.html (accessed December 31, 2013).

2. From the Roman Republic to the Roman Empire, http://www.international-relations.com/History/RepublictoEmpire.htm (accessed December 31, 2013).

3. Spartacus Educational: Benito Mussolini, http://www.spartacus.schoolnet. co.uk/2WWmussolini.htm (accessed December 31, 2013).

4. Britt, Lawrence, Rense.com, "Fourteen Defining Characteristics of Fascism," http://www.rense.com/general37/char.htm (accessed December 31, 2013).

5. Spartacus Educational: Adolf Hitler, http://www.spartacus.schoolnet.co.uk/ GERhitler.htm (accessed December 31, 2013).

6. _____, Nazi Party, http://www.spartacus.schoolnet.co.uk/ GERnazi.htm (accessed December 31,1203).

7. Glenn Beck, "Obama says if it's not fixed in 3 years I'm done," http:// www.glennbeck.com/2012/02/02/flashback-obama-says-if-its-not-fixed-in-3-years-im-done/ (accessed December 31, 2013).

8. Fox News.com, "A Brief Look at Candidate Obama's 2008 Campaign Promises," http://www.foxnews.com/politics/2011/04/05/brief-look-at-candidate-obama-2008-campaign-promises/ (accessed December 31, 2013).

9. You Tube, Fundamentally Transform America http://www.youtube.com/ watch?v=_cqN4NIEtOY (accessed December 18, 2013).

10. Investopedia, "Troubled Asset Relief Program – TARP," http:// www.investopedia.com/terms/t/troubled-asset-relief-program-tarp. asp#axzz1mYhRb3H0 (accessed December 31, 2013).

11. CNN Money, "bailout tracker," http://money.cnn.com/news/storysupplement/economy/bailouttracker/ (accessed December 31, 2013).

12. _____, "What's in Obama's stimulus plan," http://money.cnn. com/2011/09/08/news/economy/obama_stimulus_plan/index.htm (accessed December 31, 2013).

13. Hawkins, Awr, Brietbart, "Stimulus Money: A Slush Fund for Unions and Democrats," http://www.breitbart.com/Big-Government/2012/05/04/ stimulus-money-a-slush-fund-for-unions-and-democrats (accessed December 31, 2013).

14. Christianity Today, "Obama: 'They cling to guns or religion,'" April 13, 2008, http://www.christianitytoday.com/gleanings/2008/april/obama-they-cling-to-guns-or-religion.html (accessed December 31, 2013).

15. Brownfield, Mike, Heritage Foundation, "Constitution, Anyone? Obama Promises to Rule... Without Congress," December 14, 2011, http://blog. heritage.org/2011/12/14/constitution-anyone-obama-promises-to-rule-without-congress/ (accessed December 29, 2013).

16. Simendinger, Alexis, Real Clear Politics, "Obama's "We Can't Wait" Juggling Act," January 20, 2012, http://www.realclearpolitics.com/articles/2012/01/20/obamas_we_cant_wait_juggling_act.html (accessed December 31, 2013).

17. Jeffrey, Terence P., CNS News.com, "Obama Has Now Increased Debt More than All Presidents from George Washington Through George H.W. Bush Combined," October 5, 2011, http://cnsnews.com/news/article/obama-has-now-increased-debt-more-all-presidents-george-washington-through-george-hw (accessed December 31, 2013),

18. Everyone around the World says; Socialism WORKS!", http://www.pa-oracle.com/SocialismWORKS!/index.php?sw=Fascist%20Italy (accessed December 31, 2013).

Dispatch Fifty-three

1. Pollard, Jerry, Defeat Communism, "Useful Idiots," May 26, 2013, http://defeatcommunism.com/profiles/blogs/5467818:BlogPost:61704 (accessed January 2, 2014).

2. You Tube, Fundamentally Transform America http://www.youtube.com/watch?v=_cqN4NIEtOY (accessed December 18, 2013).

3. Good Reads, "Margaret Thatcher Quotes," http://www.goodreads.com/author/quotes/198468.Margaret_Thatcher (accessed January 2, 2014).

Dispatch Fifty-four

1. Norman Thomas Quotes, http://quotes.liberty-tree.ca/quote_blog/Norman.Thomas.Quote.FFB1 (accessed January 2, 2014).

2. Tea Party.org, "Harry Reid calls Tea Party 'Fanatics,' 'Anarchists,'" September 23, 2013, http://www.teaparty.org/harry-reid-calls-tea-party-fanatics-anarchists-28626/ (accessed January 2, 2014).

3. You Tube, Fundamentally Transform America http://www.youtube.com/watch?v=_cqN4NIEtOY (accessed December 18, 2013).

4. Investors.com, "Wasted Stimulus," August 16, 2011, http://news.investors.com/ibd-editorials/081611-581654-wasted-stimulus.htm (accessed January 2, 2014).

5. The Center for Public Integrity, "Obama rewards big bundlers with jobs, commissions, stimulus money, government contracts, and more," June 15, 2011, http://www.publicintegrity.org/2011/06/15/4880/obama-rewards-big-bundlers-jobs-commissions-stimulus-money-government-contracts-and (accessed January 2, 2014).

6. The Weekly Standard, "Obama's Regulatory Rampage," January 28, 2013, http://www.weeklystandard.com/articles/obama-s-regulatory-rampage_696381.html (accessed January 2, 2014).

7. GOP.gov, "The Federal Reserve Pumps More Money," http://www.gop.gov/policy-news/12/09/13/the-federal-reserve-pumps-more (accessed January 2, 2014).

8. Breitbart, "Obamacare's Cost Of Control," http://www.breitbart.com/ Big-Government/2013/07/28/Obamacare-s-Cost-Of-Control (accessed January 2, 2014).

9. Investopedia, "Definition of 'Invisible Hand,'" http://www.investopedia.com/ terms/i/invisiblehand.asp (accessed January 2, 2014).

10. The Quotation Page, John Adams, "But a Constitution of Government once changed from Freedom, can never be restored. Liberty, once lost, is lost forever," http://www.quotationspage.com/quote/34444.html (accessed January 2, 2014)

11. Brainy Quotes, John Adams, "Remember, democracy never lasts long. It soon wastes, exhausts, and murders itself," http://www.brainyquote.com/ quotes/quotes/j/johnadams124799.html (accessed January 2, 2014).

Dispatch Fifty-eight

1. Thinking Catholic Strategic Center, Obama Quote, "In America, we have this strong bias toward individual action," http://www.thinking-catholic-strategic-center.com/anti-american-quotes.html (accessed January 2, 2014).

2. _____, Obama Quote, "But the Supreme Court never ventured into the issues of redistribution of wealth, and more basic issues such as political and economic justice in society," http:// www.thinking-catholic-strategic-center.com/anti-american-quotes.html (accessed January 2, 2014).

3. Atlas Shrugs, "Obama's Anti-Capitalism Speech in Kansas," December 6, 2011, http://atlasshrugs2000.typepad.com/atlas_shrugs/2011/12/obamas-anti-capitalism-speech-in-texas-kansas.html (accessed January 2, 2014).

4. You Tube, Obama: If You've Got A Business, You Didn't Build That, http:// www.youtube.com/watch?v=YKjPI6no5ng (accessed January 2, 2014).

5. I Go Pogo, "I have met the enemy and he is us," http://www.igopogo.com/ we_have_met.htm (accessed December 20, 2013).

6. Garrett, Garet, Ludwig von Misis Institute, "The Revolution Was," January 26, 2008, http://mises.org/daily/2726 (accessed January 2, 2014).

Dispatch Fifty-nine

1. Declaration of Independence, http://www.ushistory.org/declaration/document/ (accessed December 18, 2013).

2. Ibid.

3. Ibid.

4. Sledge, Matt, The Huffington Post, "NSA Phone Records Collection Can't Be Challenged By The Callers, Government Argues," October 2, 2013, http://www.huffingtonpost.com/2013/10/02/nsa-phone-records-collection_n_4032985.html (accessed January 2, 2014).

5. Abdo, Alex, ACLU, "The Most Important Surveillance Order We Know Almost Nothing About," December 30, 2013, https://www.aclu.org/blog/tag/government-surveillance (accessed January 2, 2014).

6. Rosenzweig, Paul, The Heritage Foundation, "Is the Government Reading Your E-Mail?," March 21, 2013, http://blog.heritage.org/2013/03/21/is-the-government-reading-your-e-mail/ (accessed January 2, 2014).

7. Wolverton, Joe, New American, "Obama Signs 2013 NDAA: May Still Arrest, Detain Citizens Without Charge," January 5, 2014). http://www.thenewamerican.com/usnews/constitution/item/14120-obama-signs-2013-ndaa-may-still-arrest-detain-citizens-without-charge (accessed January 2, 2014).

8. Think Exist.com, Benjamin Franklin Quotes, "Those who desire to give up freedom in order to gain security will not have, nor do they deserve, either one," http://thinkexist.com/quotation/those_who_desire_to_give_up_freedom_in_order_to/12888.html (accessed January 2, 2014).

9. Jackson, David, The Oval, "Biden: Bin Laden is dead, General Motors is alive," April 26, 2012, http://content.usatoday.com/communities/theoval/post/2012/04/biden-bin-laden-dead-gm-is-alive/1#.UsWrr7RzYqN (accessed January 2, 2014).

10. Holan, Angie Drobnic, Politifact, "Lie of the Year: 'If you like your health care plan, you can keep it,'" December 12, 2013, http://www.politifact.com/truth-o-meter/article/2013/dec/12/lie-year-if-you-like-your-health-care-plan-keep-it/ (accessed January 2, 2014).

11. BobDylan.com, "Subterranean Homesick Blues," http://www.bobdylan.com/us/songs/subterranean-homesick-blues (accessed January 2, 2014).

Dispatch Sixty

1. Declaration of Independence, http://www.ushistory.org/declaration/document/ (accessed December 18, 2013).

2. U.S. History, "The Peculiar Institution," http://www.ushistory.org/us/27.asp (accessed January 2, 2014).

3. Matthews, Terry, "The Convenient Sin," http://www.liberalslikechrist.org/about/slavery&southernchurches.html (accessed January 2-=, 2014).

4. The Free Dictionary, "State's Rights," http://legal-dictionary.thefreedictionary.com/States%27+Rights (accessed January 2, 2014)

5. PBS: Constitution USA with Peter Sagal, "Federalism," http://www.pbs.org/tpt/constitution-usa-peter-sagal/federalism/#.UsXhOrRzYqM (accessed January 2, 2014).

6. Tenth Amendment Center, "About the Tenth Amendment," http://tenthamendment-center.com/about/about-the-tenth-amendment/ (accessed December 22, 2013).

7. Civil War Trust, "10 Facts about the Emancipation Proclamation," http://www.civilwar.org/education/history/emancipation-150/10-facts.html (accessed January 2, 2014).

8. Bartleby.com, "Abraham Lincoln: First Inaugural Address," http://www.bartleby.com/124/pres31.html (accessed January 2, 2014).

9. New York Times, "A LETTER FROM PRESIDENT LINCOLN.; Reply to Horace Greeley. Slavery and the Union The Restoration of the Union the Paramount Object," August 24, 1862, http://www.nytimes.com/1862/08/24/news/letter-president-lincoln-reply-horace-greeley-slavery-union-restoration-union.html Accessed January 2, 2014).

10. Abraham Lincoln Research Site, "ABRAHAM LINCOLN QUOTES ABOUT SLAVERY (Including Sources)," http://rogerjnorton.com/Lincoln95.html (accessed January 2, 2014).

11. Bartleby.com, "Abraham Lincoln: First Inaugural Address," http://www.bartleby.com/124/pres31.html (accessed January 2, 2014).

12. Yale Law School: The Avalon Project, "Ratification of the Constitution by the State of New York; July 26, 1788," http://avalon.law.yale.edu/18th_century/ratny.asp (accessed January 2, 2014).

13. U.S. Constitution Online, "Rhode Island's Ratification," http://uscon-stitution.net/rat_ri.html (accessed January 2, 2014).

14. Yale Law School: The Avalon Project, "Ratification of the Constitution by the State of Virginia; June 26, 1788," http://avalon.law.yale.edu/18th_century/ratva.asp (accessed January 2, 2014).

15. Brainy Quotes, Lord Acton, http://www.brainyquote.com/quotes/authors/l/lord_acton.html (accessed January 2. 3014).

16. Ibid.

17. Free Republic, "THE LORD ACTON - GENERAL LEE CORRESPONDENCE," http://www.freerepublic.com/focus/news/828843/posts (accessed January 2, 2014).

18. Ibid.

19. Brainy Quotes, Lord Acton, http://www.brainyquote.com/quotes/authors/l/lord_acton.html (accessed January 2, 2014).

Dispatch Sixty-one

1. Brainy Quote, Napoleon, http://www.brainyquote.com/quotes/quotes/n/napoleonbo161968.html (accessed January 6, 2014).

2. The Quotation Page, Voltaire, http://www.quotationspage.com/quotes/Voltaire (accessed January 6, 2014).

3. History News Network: Quotes about History, http://hnn.us/article/1328 (accessed January 6, 2014).

4. Ibid.

Dispatch Sixty-two

1. U.S. History, "Henry Kissinger," http://www.u-s-history.com/pages/h1966.html (accessed January 9, 2014).

2. Jakarta Globe, "Hu Jintao's Visit Ends Any Dreams of the US and China Sharing the World Stage," January 25, 2011, http://www.thejakartaglobe.com/archive/hu-jintaos-visit-ends-any-dreams-of-the-us-and-china-sharing-the-world-stage/418948/ (accessed January 9, 2014).

3. Watson, Paul Joseph, Infowars.com, "10 Ways In Which China Humiliates The United States," http://www.prisonplanet.com/10-ways-in-which-china-humiliates-the-united-states.html (accessed January 9, 2014).

4. Masch, Vladimir A., Bloomberg Business Week, "U.S. Trade Policy Needs Revamping," http://www.businessweek.com/debateroom/archives/2007/02/us_trade_policy_needs_revamping.html (accessed January 9, 2014).

5. Scott, Robert E., Economic Policy Institute, "The high price of 'free' trade," http://www.epi.org/publication/briefingpapers_bp147/ (accessed January 9, 2014).

Dispatch Sixty-three

1. Wassener, Bettina and Matthew Saltmarsh, New York Times, "China Urges U.S. to Protect Creditors by Raising Debt," July 14, 2011, http://www.nytimes.com/2011/07/15/business/global/china-urges-us-to-take-responsible-action-on-debt.html?_r=0 (accessed January 9, 2014).

2. U.S. Constitution Online, "The I Have a Dream Speech," http://www.usconstitution.net/dream.html (accessed January 9, 2014).

3. Lind, Bill, Accuracy in Academia, "The Origins of Political Correctness," http://www.academia.org/the-origins-of-political-correctness/ (accessed January 9, 2014).

Dispatch Sixty-four

1. Declaration of Independence, http://www.ushistory.org/declaration/document/ (accessed December 18, 2013).

2. Ibid.

3. Ibid.

4. Ibid

5. Ibid.

6. Gill, N. S., About.com, "Octavianus Becomes the First Roman Emperor Augustus Caesar," http://ancienthistory.about.com/od/augustusbio/a/aa092397Augustu.htm (accessed January 11, 2014).

7. Boyle, Matthew, Breitbart, "Obama Admin Can Pick Which Laws to Enforce," April 24, 2013, http://www.breitbart.com/Big-Government/2013/04/24/Big-Sis-declares-Obama-has-power-to-pick-which-laws-to-enforce-as-immigration-bill-would-grant-admin-more-authority (accessed January 11, 2014).

8. Howley, Patrick, The daily caller, "Justice Department facilitated anti-Zimmerman protests," July 10, 2013, http://dailycaller.com/2013/07/10/doj-provided-security-for-anti-zimmerman-protests/ (accessed January 11, 2014).

9. Huffington Post, "NSA Admits Listening To U.S. Phone Calls Without Warrants," June 15, 2013, http://www.huffingtonpost.com/2013/06/15/nsa-phone-calls-warrants_n_3448075.html (accessed January 11, 2014).

10. Landay, Jonathan S. and Marisa Taylor, McClatchy DC, 'Obama's plan to predict future leakers unproven, unlikely to work," July 9, 2013, http://www.mcclatchydc.com/2013/07/09/196211/linchpin-for-obamas-plan-to-predict.html#.Ud3pIW0UoXU (accessed January 11, 2014).

11. International Business Times, "Fistful of Dollars: How the Federal Reserve destroyed America," May 1, 2011, http://www.ibtimes.com/fistful-dollars-how-federal-reserve-destroyed-america-211927 (accessed January 11, 2014).

12. Gilani, Shah, Money Morning, "Federal Reserve Has Destroyed the Meaning of Saving," December, 15, 2012, http://moneymorning.com/2012/12/15/the-federal-reserves-magic-act-is-destroying-america/ (accessed January11, 2014).

13. Heritage Guide to the Constitution, "Guarantee Clause," http://www.heritage.org/constitution/#!/articles/4/essays/128/guarantee-clause (accessed January 11, 2014).

14. Gibson, Dave, Examiner.com, "Obama refuses to secure border, sues states for trying to protect themselves," August 4, 2011, http://www.examiner.com/article/obama-refuses-to-secure-border-sues-states-for-trying-to-protect-themselves (accessed January 11, 2014).

15. Breitbart, "IRS Scandal," http://www.breitbart.com/Topics/B610D48D3EE0D-AFBF4FECE5BEA5F7D43/IRS-Scandal (accessed January 11, 2014).

16. Liptak, Adam, The New York Times, "Justices to Hear Case on Obama's Recess Appointments," June 24, 2013, http://www.nytimes.com/2013/06/25/us/justices-agree-to-hear-case-on-presidents-recess-appointments.html?_r=2& (accessed January 11, 2014).

17. Ackerman, Bruce, FP, "Obama's Unconstitutional War," March 31, 2011, http://www.foreignpolicy.com/articles/2011/03/24/obama_s_unconstitutional_war#sthash.wzGMirLw.geoiZAaJ.dpbs (accessed December 29, 2013).

18. The Blaze, "Words Matter 2012 Presents: Clips From Obama's 'Apology Tour,'" October 23, 2012, http://www.theblaze.com/stories/2012/10/23/words-matter-2012-presents-clips-from-obamas-apology-tour/ (accessed January 11, 2014).

19. Sowell, Thomas, Redding.com, "Obama casts U.S. allies aside," http://www.redding.com/news/2011/feb/09/thomas-sowell-obama-casts-us-allies-aside/?print=1 (accessed January 11, 2014).

20. Rubin, Barry, PJ Media, "It's Official: Obama Administration Promotes Islamist Regimes; Insists They are Moderate," November 8, 2011, http://pjmedia.com/barryrubin/2011/11/08/it%E2%80%99s-official-obama-administration-promotes-islamist-regimes-insists-they-are-moderate/ (accessed January 11, 2014).

21. Declaration of Independence, http://www.ushistory.org/declaration/document/ (accessed December 18, 2013).

Dispatch Sixty-five

1. Brainy Quote, Everett Dirksen, "A billion here, a billion there" http://www.brainyquote.com/quotes/authors/e/everett_dirksen.html (accessed January 15, 2014).

2. U.S. Debt Clock.org, http://www.usdebtclock.org/ (accessed December 18, 2013).

3. Dawson, Lindsey, Grown Ups.com, "What is a Trillion Anyway," http://www.grownups.co.nz/read/lifestyle/entertainment/lindsey-dawson-trillion (accessed January 15, 2014).

4. The Washington Times, "Obama spending hits new records," March 8, 2011, http://www.washingtontimes.com/news/2011/mar/8/obama-spending-hits-new-records/ (accessed January 15, 2014).

5. Ibid.

6. Fenhoz, Tim, National Journal, "CBO Says Budget Deal Will Cut Spending by Only $352 Million This Year," April 13, 2011, http://www.nationaljournal.com/budget/cbo-says-budget-deal-will-cut-spending-by-only-352-million-this-year-20110413 (accessed January 15, 2014).

7. Fraser, Alison Acosta, The Foundry, "Chairman Ryan's Budget Resolution Changes America's Course," April 5, 2011, http://blog.heritage.org/2011/04/05/morning-bell-chairman-ryans-budget-resolution-changes-americas-course/ (accessed January 15, 2014).

8. Rutten, Tim, Los Angeles Times, "Paul Ryan's budget blueprint would push the aged into poverty," April 9, 2011, http://articles.latimes.com/2011/apr/09/opinion/la-oe-rutten-ryan-budget-20110409 (accessed January 15, 2014).

9. Beach, William W., Rea S. Hederman, Jr., John L. Ligon, Guinevere Nell and Karen Campbell, Ph.D. The Heritage Foundation, "Obama Tax Hikes: The Economic and Fiscal Effects," September 20, 2010, http://www.heritage.org/research/reports/2010/09/obama-tax-hikes-the-economic-and-fiscal-effects (accessed January 15, 2014).

10. Sahadi, Jeanne, CNN Money, "Debt ceiling FAQs: What you need to know," May, 18, 2011, http://money.cnn.com/2011/01/03/news/economy/debt_ceiling_faqs/index.htm (accessed January 15, 2014).

11. Spellerberg, Shirley, Real Clear Conservatives, "IS A BALANCED BUDGET AMENDMENT A DANGEROUS GIMMICK?," March 3, 2011, http://realclearconservatives.com/2011/03/30/is-a-balanced-budget-amendment-a-dangerous-gimmick/ (accessed January 14, 2015).

12. U.S. Debt Clock.org, http://www.usdebtclock.org/ (accessed December 18, 2013).

13. Darling, Brian, Human Events, "The Balanced Budget Debate Begins," March 2, 2011, http://blog.heritage.org/2011/03/02/the-balanced-budget-debate-begins/ (accessed January 15, 2014).

Dispatch Sixty-six

1. Declaration of Independence, http://www.ushistory.org/declaration/document/ (accessed December 18, 2013).

2. The Constitution, http://constitutionus.com/ (accessed December 18, 2013).

3. Funny Quotes from Famous People, http://cmgm.stanford.edu/~lkozar/Famous_Quotes.html (accessed January 15, 2014).

4. Brainy Quote, Churchill, http://www.brainyquote.com/quotes/quotes/w/winstonchu164131.html (accessed December 18, 2013).

5. Ibid.

6. Ibid.

Dispatch Sixty-seven

1. Fordham University, "French Revolution," http://www.fordham.edu/halsall/mod/modsbook13.asp (accessed January 15, 2014).

2. Lucidcafe': Library, "Jean-Jacques Rousseau." http://www.lucidcafe.com/library/96jun/rousseau.html (accessed January 15, 2014).

3. Wilde, Robert, About.com "The Terror," http://europeanhistory.about.com/od/thefrenchrevolution/a/hfr7.htm (accessed January 7, 2014).

4. Minster, Christopher, About.com, "The Mexican Revolution," http://latina-mericanhistory.about.com/od/thehistoryofmexico/a/mexicanrevo.htm (accessed January 15, 2014).

5. Encyclopedia Britannica, "The Wars of Independence," http://www.britannica.com/EBchecked/topic/331694/history-of-Latin-America/60878/The-wars-of-independence-1808-26 (accessed January 15, 2014).

6. You Tube, Fundamentally Transform America http://www.youtube.com/watch?v=_cqN4NIEtOY (accessed December 18, 2013).

7. Hillyer, Quinn, The American Spectator, "Alinsky to Obama to Occupiers," October 21, 2011, http://spectator.org/articles/36719/alinsky-obama-occupiers (accessed January 15, 2014).

8. You Tube, "Obama Supports Occupy Wall Street," http://www.youtube.com/watch?v=aH99q2CRNZg (accessed January 15, 2014).

9. Coppock, Nancy, American Thinker, "The Cloward/Piven Strategy of Economic Recovery," February 7, 2009, http://www.americanthinker.com/2009/02/the_clowardpiven_strategy_of_e.html (accessed December 27, 2013).

10. LeVine, Steve and Theo Francis, Bloomberg Business Week, "Now, Obama 'Owns' General Motors," April 1, 2009, http://www.businessweek.com/bwdaily/dnflash/content/apr2009/db2009041_951044.htm (accessed January 15, 2014).

11. Conservapedia, "Barack Hussein Obama's unlawful acts," http://www.conservapedia.com/Barack_Hussein_Obama%27s_unlawful_acts (accessed January 15, 2014).

12. Brownfield, Mike, Heritage Foundation, "Constitution, Anyone? Obama Promises to Rule... Without Congress," December 14, 2011, http://blog.heritage.org/2011/12/14/constitution-anyone-obama-promises-to-rule-without-congress/ (accessed December 29, 2013).

13. Abraham Lincoln Online, "The Gettysburg Address," http://www.abrahamlincolnonline.org/lincoln/speeches/gettysburg.htm (accessed January 15, 2014).

Dispatch Sixty-eight

1. U. S. Constitution Online, Articles of Confederation, http://www.usconstitution.net/consttop_arti.html (accessed January 28, 2014).

2. Lewis, Laura dawn, Government Structures 101, http://www.couplescompany.com/features/politics/structure1.htm (accessed January 29, 2014).

3. The Free Dictionary, "Federalism," http://www.thefreedictionary.com/federal (accessed December 29, 2014).

4. Your Dictionary, "Republic," http://www.yourdictionary.com/republic (accessed January 29, 2014).

5. Kelly, Martin, About.com, "Separation of Powers," http://americanhistory.about.com/od/usconstitution/g/sep_of_powers.htm (accessed January 29. 2014).

6. Alchian, Armen A., Library of Economics, "Property Rights," http://www.econlib.org/library/Enc/PropertyRights.html (accessed January 29, 2014).

7. U. S. Constitution Online, "Checks and Balances," http://www.usconstitution.net/consttop_cnb.html (accessed January 29, 2014)

8. Encyclopedia Britannica, "Democratic-Republican Party," http://www.britannica.com/EBchecked/topic/498833/Democratic-Republican-Party (accessed December 28, 2013).

Dispatch Sixty-nine

1. Fundamentally Transform America http://www.youtube.com/watch?v=_cqN4NIEtOY (accessed December 18, 2013).

2. You Tube, Jayson, Sharon, USA Today, "More Kids Born out of Wedlock," http://usatoday30.usatoday.com/NEWS/usaedition/2012-04-12-Cohabiting---with-kids---_ST_U.htm (accessed February 4, 2014).

3. Obama small town guns and religion comments, http://www.youtube.com/watch?v=DTxXUufI3jA (accessed January 7, 2014).

4. You Tube, Bush: "I've abandoned free market principles to save the free market system," http://www.youtube.com/watch?v=Tmi8cJG0BJo (accessed January 6, 2014).

5. Tame, Chris R., "THE REVOLUTION OF REASON: PETER GAY, THE ENLIGHTENMENT, AND THE AMBIGUITIES OF CLASSICAL LIBERALISM," http://mises.org/journals/jls/1_3/1_3_7.pdf (accessed February 4, 2014).

6. Conservapedia, "Cult of Reason," http://www.conservapedia.com/Cult_of_Reason (accessed January 7, 2014).

7. Wilde, Robert, About.com "The Terror," http://europeanhistory.about.com/od/thefrenchrevolution/a/hfr7.htm (accessed January 7, 2014).

8. Collapse of the Soviet Union, http://sfr-21.org/collapse.html (accessed December 22, 2013).

9. Quotes on Liberty and Virtue, Patrick Henry, http://www.liberty1.org/virtue. htm (accessed February 4, 2014).

10. _____, John Adams, http://www.liberty1.org/virtue. htm (accessed February 4, 2014).

11. Internet Encyclopedia of Philosophy, "Virtue Ethics," http://www.iep.utm. edu/virtue/ (accessed February 4, 2014).

Dispatch Seventy

1. Leonhardt, David, New York Times, "Challenge to Health Bill: Selling Reform," July 21, 2009, http://www.nytimes.com/2009/07/22/business/ economy/22leonhardt.html?_r=1& (accessed February 4, 2014).

2. Morrissey, Ed, Hot Air, "Dodd-Frank costs US financial sector 24 million man-hours per year for compliance," April 17, 2012, http://hotair.com/ archives/2012/04/17/dodd-frank-costs-us-financial-sector-24-million-man-hours-per-year-for-compliance/ (accessed February 4, 2014).

3. Picket, Kerry, The Washington Times, "EPA imposes Obama's cap and trade regs- energy prices 'skyrocket,'" August 20, 2011, http://www.washington-times.com/blog/watercooler/2011/aug/20/picket-obama-08-energy-prices-will-skyrocket-under/ (accessed December 23, 2013).

4. Koffler, Keith, The Whitehouse Dossier, "Obama Imposes Partial Dream Act by Fiat," June 15, 2012, http://www.whitehousedossier.com/2012/06/15/ obama-imposes-dream-act-fiat/ (accessed February 4, 2014).

5. CARROLL, CONN, The Heritage Network, "Bush's Betrayal of Free-Market Principles Now Complete," December 30, 2008, http://blog.heritage. org/2008/12/30/bushs-betrayal-of-free-market-principles-now-complete/ (accessed February 4, 2014).

6. Diamond, Dan, Forbes, "Why The 'Real' Unemployment Rate Is Higher Than You Think," July 5, 2013, http://www.forbes.com/sites/dandia-mond/2013/07/05/why-the-real-unemployment-rate-is-higher-than-you-think/ (accessed February 4, 2014).

7. Bureau of Labor Statistics, "Alternative measures of labor underutilization," http://www.bls.gov/news.release/empsit.t15.htm (accessed February 4, 2014).

8. Halper, Daniel, The Weekly Standard, "U.S. Spent $3.7 Trillion on Welfare Over Last 5 Years," October 23, 2013, http://www.weeklystandard.com/ blogs/report-us-spent-37-trillion-welfare-over-last-5-years_764582.html (accessed December 4, 2014).

9. Ibid.

10. Ibid.

11. Jeffrey, Terence P., CNS News.com, "49% of Americans Get Gov't Benefits; 82M in Households on Medicaid," October 23, 2013, http://cnsnews.com/news/article/terence-p-jeffrey/census-49-americans-get-gov-t-benefits-82m-households-medicaid (accessed February 4, 2014).

12. Eichier, Alexander, Huffington Post, "46 Percent of Americans Exempt From Federal Income Tax in 2011," June 28, 2011, http://www.huffingtonpost.com/2011/06/28/46-percent-of-americans-e_n_886293.html (accessed December 26, 2013).

13. Delegge, Ron, EFF Guide, "Will U.S. Public Debt Reach $22 Trillion by Feb. 2014?," October 23, 2013, http://archive.etfguide.com/commentary/1138/Will-U.S.-Public-Debt-Reach-$22-Trillion-by-Feb.-2014/ (accessed February , 2014).

14. Hook, Janet and Kristina Peterson, The wall Street journal, "Congress Passes Debt, Budget Deal," October 18, 2013, http://online.wsj.com/news/articles/SB10001424052702303680404579139212598765046 (accessed February 4, 2014).

15. Ibid.

16. McCormack, John, The Weekly Standard, "Millions of Americans Are Losing Their Health Plans Because of Obamacare," October 23, 2013, http://www.weeklystandard.com/blogs/millions-americans-are-losing-their-health-plans-because-obamacare_764602.html (accessed February 4, 2014).

17. McLaughlin, Seth, The Washington Times, "Obamacare's troubles a sign of things to come," October 23, 2013, http://www.washingtontimes.com/blog/inside-politics/2013/oct/23/gop-rep-obamacares-troubles-sign-things-come/ (accessed February 4, 2014).

18. You Tube, "Obama on single payer health insurance," http://www.youtube.com/watch?v=fpAyan1fXCE (accessed February 4, 2014).

19. Roy, Avik, Forbes, "Sen. Harry Reid: Obamacare 'Absolutely' A Step Toward A Single-Payer System," August 10, 2013, http://www.forbes.com/sites/theapothecary/2013/08/10/sen-harry-reid-obamacare-absolutely-a-step-toward-a-single-payer-system/ (accessed February 4, 2014).

20. Ibid.

21. You Tube, "Fundamentally Transform America," http://www.youtube.com/watch?v=KrefKCaV8m4 (accessed December 18, 2013).

22. Martosko, David, Mail Online, "Federal judge suddenly green-lights lawsuit that could stop Obamacare in its tracks," October 22, 2013, http://www.dailymail.co.uk/news/article-2471978/Bombshell-Federal-judge-suddenly-green-lights-lawsuit-stop-Obamacare-tracks.html (accessed February 4, 2014).

Dispatch Seventy-two

1. Encyclopedia Britannica, "Annapolis Convention," http://www.britannica.com/EBchecked/topic/26190/Annapolis-Convention (accessed February 5, 2014).

2. Constitution Facts.com: About the Founding Fathers, Alexander Hamilton, http://www.constitutionfacts.com/us-founding-fathers/about-the-founding-fathers/ (accessed February 5, 2014).

3. U. S. History, "The Constitutional Convention," http://www.u-s-history.com/pages/h368.html (accessed February 5, 2014).

4. This Nation.com, "The Constitutional Convention," http://thisnation.com/textbook/constitution-convention.html (accessed February 5, 2014).

5. U. S. Constitution Online, "Articles of Confederation," http://www.usconstitution.net/consttop_arti.html (accessed January 28, 2014).

6. Constitution Facts.com: About the Founding Fathers, http://www.constitutionfacts.com/us-founding-fathers/about-the-founding-fathers/ (accessed February 5, 2014).

7. U.S. History, "Alexander Hamilton," http://www.u-s-history.com/pages/h367.html (accessed February 5, 2014).

8. The Library of Congress, "Alexander Hamilton: A Resource Guide," http://www.loc.gov/rr/program/bib/hamilton/memory.html (accessed February 5, 2014).

9. The Founder's Constitution, Article 1, Section 8, Clause 2, "Alexander Hamilton: Report on Public Credit," http://press-pubs.uchicago.edu/founders/documents/a1_8_2s5.html (accessed February 5, 2014).

10. U. S. Constitution Online, "Debts, Supremacy Oaths," http://www.usconstitution.net/xconst_A6.html (accessed February 5, 2014).

11. U.S. Constitution Online, "Amendment 14," http://www.usconstitution.net/xconst_Am14.html (accessed February 5, 2014).

12. U.S. Debt Clock.org, http://www.usdebtclock.org/ (accessed December 18, 2013).

13. Ibid.

Dispatch Seventy-three

1. Seelye, Katherine D., New York Times, "DOLE IS IMPLORING VOTERS TO 'RISE UP' AGAINST THE PRESS," October 26, 1996, http://www.nytimes.com/1996/10/26/us/dole-is-imploring-voters-to-rise-up-against-the-press.html (accessed February 12, 2014).

2. Bradly, Tahman, ABC News, "Friends Feared New Clinton Bimbo Eruptions," June 1, 2008, http://abcnews.go.com/blogs/politics/2008/06/article-friends/ (accessed February 12, 2014).

3. Humorous Quotes, Bill Clinton, "Character doesn't matter," http://gopcapitalist.tripod.com/stupidquotes.html#character (accessed February 12, 2014).

4. Chatterbox, "Bill Clinton and the Meaning of 'Is,'" http://www.slate.com/articles/news_and_politics/chatterbox/1998/09/bill_clinton_and_the_meaning_of_is.html (accessed February 12, 2014).

5. FrontLine, http://www.pbs.org/wgbh/pages/frontline/shows/kosovo/etc/press.html (accessed February 14, 2014).

6. Knickerbocker, Brad, The Christian Science Monitor, "US leads 'Odyssey Dawn' initial attack on Libya," http://www.csmonitor.com/USA/Military/2011/0319/US-leads-Odyssey-Dawn-initial-attack-on-Libya (accessed February 14, 2014).

7. Letter From the Capitol, "Libya: Will Sarko Save the Day?" March 24, 2011 http://www.letterfromthecapitol.com/letterfromthecapitol/2011/03/libyan-update.html (accessed February14, 2014).

8. Galloway, Lana, "Obama's Libya Briefing to Congress: 'Involvement to Be a Matter of Days, Not Weeks,'" http://www.obamashitlist.com/2011/03/19/obama%E2%80%99s-libya-briefing-to-congress-%E2%80%9Cinvolvement-to-be-a-matter-of-days-not-weeks%E2%80%9D/ (accessed February 14, 2014).

9. Wilson, Scott, with Colum Lynch and Karen DeYoung, The Washington Post, "Obama administration seeks more U.N. authority to intervene in Libya," http://www.washingtonpost.com/politics/as-gaddafi-gains-wests-window-closes/2011/03/16/ABlGYNh_story.html (accessed February 14, 2014).

10. Freeman, Colin, Nick Meo in Benghazi and Patrick Hennessy, The Telegraph, "Libya: Arab League calls for United Nations no-fly zone," http://www.telegraph.co.uk/news/worldnews/africaandindianocean/libya/8378392/Libya-Arab-League-calls-for-United-Nations-no-fly-zone.html (accessed February 14, 2014).

11. U.S. Constitution Online, "Article 1 Section 8," http://www.usconstitution.net/xconst_A1Sec8.html (accessed December 26, 2013).

12. Shmoop, "The Korean War," http://www.shmoop.com/korean-war/politics.html (accessed February 14, 2014).

13. Korean War Casualty Statistics, http://www.zzwave.com/cmfweb/history/krwarcost.html (accessed February 14, 2014).

14. Yale Law School: The Avalon Project, "The Tonkin Gulf Incident," http://avalon.law.yale.edu/20th_century/tonkin-g.asp Accessed February 14, 2014).

15. Infoplease, "The Persian Gulf War. http://www.infoplease.com/ipa/A0001293.html (accessed February 14, 2014).

16. The Center for Media and Democracy, "Congressional Action on the Iraq War," http://www.sourcewatch.org/index.php?title=Congressional_actions_on_the_Iraq_War (accessed February 14, 2014).

17. Hahn, Michael, Lexis Nexis, "The Conflict in Kosovo: A Constitutional War?" https://litigation-essentials.lexisnexis.com/webcd/app?action=DocumentDisplay&crawlid=1&doctype=cite&docid=89+Geo.+L.J.+2351&srctype=smi&srcid=3B15&key=05e43c2b719ed5f4902c926ae18bd620 (accessed February 14, 2014).

18. Yale Law School: The Avalon Project, "War Powers Resolution," http://avalon.law.yale.edu/20th_century/warpower.asp (accessed February 14, 2014).

19. Dayen, David, FDL, "Obama Asserts Authority for Libya Mission Without Congressional Action," http://news.firedoglake.com/2011/03/21/obama-asserts-authority-for-libya-mission-without-congressional-action/ (accessed February 14, 2014).

20. Shear, Michael D., The Caucus, "Obama Defends 'Limited' Role in Libya," http://thecaucus.blogs.nytimes.com/2011/03/28/obama-defends-limited-role-in-libya/?_php=true&_type=blogs&_php=true&_type=blogs&_r=1 (accessed February 14, 2014).

21. Savage, Charlie, The caucus, "Justice Memo Upholds Libya Strikes," http://thecaucus.blogs.nytimes.com/2011/04/07/justice-memo-upholds-libya-strikes/ (accessed February 14, 2014).

22. Morrissey, Ed, Free Republic, "Democrats catching impeachment fever? Obama's actions in Libya Unconstitutional," March 20, 2011, http://www.freerepublic.com/focus/f-news/2691955/posts (accessed February 14, 2014).

23. Meyers, Jim and Dan Weil, Newsmax, "Dems Rip Obama on Libya, Bring Up 'Impeachable Offense'!," March 22, 2011, http://www.newsmax.com/Headline/obama-kucinich-randpaul-libya/2011/03/22/id/390339 (accessed February 14, 2014).

24. Fox Nation, "Biden Flashback: Launching an Attack Without Congressional Approval Is an Impeachable Offense," http://nation.foxnews.com/libya/2011/03/23/biden-flashback-launching-attack-without-congressional-approval-impeachable-offense (accessed February 14, 2014).

25. Seelye, Katherine D., New York Times, "DOLE IS IMPLORING VOTERS TO 'RISE UP' AGAINST THE PRESS," October 26, 1996, http://www.nytimes.com/1996/10/26/us/dole-is-imploring-voters-to-rise-up-against-the-press.html (accessed February 12, 2014).

Dispatch Seventy-five

1. New York Post, "OBAMA TASK FORCE TO 'LEVEL PLAYING FIELD,'" January 30, 2009, http://nypost.com/2009/01/30/obama-task-force-to-level-playing-field/ (accessed February 18, 2014).

2. The Oval, "Obama: Rich should pay 'fair share' of debt reduction," July 25, 2011, http://content.usatoday.com/communities/theoval/post/2011/07/obama-opposes-short-term-debt-deal-from-boehner/1#.UwPh0IVfTKk (accessed February 18, 2014).

3. Gandel, Joe, The Moderate Voice, "Obama Weekly Video Address: Tax Breaks for Millionaires and Billionaires Must Be On the Table in Debt Ceiling Talks," July 2, 2011, http://themoderatevoice.com/115208/obama-weekly-video-address-tax-breaks-for-millionaires-and-billionaires-must-be-on-the-table-in-debt-ceiling-talks/ (accessed February 18, 2014).

4. The Quotation Page, Karl Marx http://www.quotationspage.com/quote/36121.html (accessed December 18, 2013).

5. You Tube, "Fundamentally Transform America" http://www.youtube.com/watch?v=_cqN4NIEtOY (accessed December 18, 2013).

6. Horowitz, Carl, National Legal and Policy Center, "HUD Still Funds ACORN Affiliate Despite Ban" July 19, 2011, http://nlpc.org/stories/2011/07/19/hud-still-funds-acorn-housing-affiliate-despite-ban (accessed February 18, 2014).

7. Ertelt, Steven, LifeNews.com, "Planned Parenthood Gets $363M in Tax Money, Abortions Rise," December 16, 2010, http://www.lifenews.com/2010/12/16/planned-parenthood-gets-363m-in-tax-money-abortions-rise/ (accessed February 18, 2014).

8. Picket, Kerry, The Washington Times, "EPA imposes Obama's cap and trade regs- energy prices 'skyrocket,'" August 20, 2011, http://www.washington-times.com/blog/watercooler/2011/aug/20/picket-obama-08-energy-prices-will-skyrocket-under/ (accessed December 23, 2013).

9. America's Watchtower, "The stimulus spent $278,000 for every job saved or created," July 5, 2011, http://americaswatchtower.com/2011/07/05/the-stimulus-spent-278000-for-every-job-saved-or-created/ (accessed February 18, 2014).

10. You Tube, "Spread the Wealth Around," http://www.youtube.com/watch?v=RZcEHLr4gBg (accessed December 18, 2013).

11. U.S. Debt Clock.org, http://www.usdebtclock.org/ (accessed December 18, 2013).

Dispatch Seventy-six

1. Making Cities Livable, "Tahrir Square and the birth of Democracy?" http://www.livablecities.org/articles/tahrir-square-and-birth-democracy (accessed July 27, 2014).

2. Anti-War.com, "180,000 Attend Yemen Pro-Democracy Protests," http://news.antiwar.com/2011/02/25/180000-attend-yemen-pro-democracy-protests/ (accessed July 27, 2014).

3. DW, "Hoping for Ukrainian protest success in Belarus," http://www.dw.de/hoping-for-ukrainian-protest-success-in-belarus/a-17434895 (accessed July 27, 2014).

4. Daily Tracker, "Occupy Wall Street Shows People Want Democracy, Not Corporatocracy," http://finance.yahoo.com/blogs/daily-ticker/occupy-wall-street-shows-people-want-democracy-not-152011256.html (accessed July 27, 2014).

5. Adolf Hitler's Rise to Power, http://www2.dsu.nodak.edu/users/dmeier/Holocaust/hitler.html (accessed July 27, 2014).

6. A Teacher's Guide to the Holocaust, "The Rise of the Nazi Party," http://fcit.usf.edu/holocaust/timeline/nazirise.htm (accessed July 27, 2014).

7. The History Place, "The Triumph of Hitler," http://www.historyplace.com/worldwar2/triumph/tr-fuehrer.htm (accessed July 27, 2014).

8. History Matters, "Making the World "Safe for Democracy": Woodrow Wilson Asks for War," http://historymatters.gmu.edu/d/4943/ (accessed December 23, 2013).

9. American Rhetoric, "The Great Arsenal of Democracy," http://historymatters.gmu.edu/d/4943/ (accessed July 27, 2014).

10. Democracy Reform, "Did America's Founders want Democracy?" http://democracyreform.blogspot.com/2006/11/did-americas-founders-want-democracy.html (accessed July 27, 2014).

11. Ibid.

12. Ibid.

13. The Quotation Page, Alexander Hamilton, http://www.quotationspage.com/quote/27458.html (accessed July 27, 2014).

14. Democracy In America Alexis de Tocqueville 1831, "Chapter XIII: Government Of The Democracy In America – Part I," http://www.marxists.org/reference/archive/de-tocqueville/democracy-america/ch13.htm (accessed July 27, 2014).

15. Ibid.

16. NPR, "President Bush's Second Inaugural Address," http://www.npr.org/templates/story/story.php?storyId=4460172 (Accessed July 27, 2014).

17. Rosenberg, M. J., The American Conservative, "Who Elected Hamas," http://www.theamericanconservative.com/articles/who-elected-hamas/(accessed July 27, 2014).

18. ABC News, "Protests break out as Islamists win Tunisian election," http://www.abc.net.au/news/2011-10-28/tunisian-islamists-win-election/3605366 (accessed July 27, 2016).

19. The Guardian, "It means Yoweri Museveni wants to be Uganda's president for life," http://www.theguardian.com/world/2011/feb/16/uganda-election-yoweri-museveni-kizza-besigye (accessed July 27, 2014).

20. Boddy-Evans, Alistair, About.com African history, "Idi Amin Dadda," http://africanhistory.about.com/od/biography/a/bio_amin.htm (accessed July 27, 2014).

21. The Quotation Page, Karl Marx http://www.quotationspage.com/quote/36121.html (accessed December 18, 2013).

22. History Learning Place, "Voting Patterns in America," http://www.historylearningsite.co.uk/voting_patterns_in_america.htm (accessed July 27, 2014).

23. Famous Quotes, Alexander Fraser Tyler, http://www.famousquotessite.com/famous-quotes-6934-alexander-fraser-tyler-cycle-of-democracy-1770.html Accessed July 27, 2014).

24. Ibid.

25. Brady, Jeff, NPR, "Unions Assume A Support Role For Occupy Movement," October 29, 2011, http://www.npr.org/2011/10/29/141794777/unions-assume-a-support-role-for-occupy-movement (accessed July 27, 2014).

26. Klein, Rick, ABC News, "Democrats Seek to Own 'Occupy Wall Street' Movement," October 10, 2011, http://abcnews.go.com/Politics/democrats-seek-occupy-wall-street-movement/story?id=14701337 (accessed December 27, 2013).

27. Boyer, Dave, The Washington Times, "Obama: MLK would have backed 'Occupy' protests," October 16, 2011, http://www.washingtontimes.com/news/2011/oct/16/obama-king-would-have-backed-occupy-wall-street/ (accessed July 27, 2014).

Dispatch Seventy-Seven

1. Bible Gateway, Matthew 26:11, https://www.biblegateway.com/passage/?search=Mt++26:11 (accessed July 30, 2014).

2. You Tube, "Spread the Wealth Around," http://www.youtube.com/watch?v=RZcEHLr4gBg (accessed December 18, 2013).

3. Google, GM is alive and Bin Laden is Dead, https://www.google.com/search?q=GM+is+alive+and+Bin+Laden+is+dead&client=firefox-a&hs=zaX&rls=org.mozilla:en-US:official&tbm=isch&tbo=u&source=univ&sa=X&ei=CRXYUonHI4-osASVi4G4BQ&ved=0CDUQsAQ&biw=1787&bih=813&dpr=0.9 (accessed July 30, 2014).

4. Yahoo News, Obama to Dems: I'll act with or without Congress, http://news.yahoo.com/obama-dems-39-ll-act-without-congress-004736977--politics.html (accessed July 30, 2014).

5. CBS News, "Obama On Executive Actions: 'I've Got A Pen And I've Got A Phone,'" http://washington.cbslocal.com/2014/01/14/obama-on-executive-actions-ive-got-a-pen-and-ive-got-a-phone/ (accessed July 30, 2014).

Dispatch Seventy-nine

1. Amazon.com, "The Constitution Failed," http://www.amazon.com/Constitution-Failed-PH-D-Robert-Owens/dp/1609579615/ref=sr_1_1?ie=UTF8&qid=1372328556&sr=8-1&keywords=the+constitution+failed+owens (accessed December 18, 2013).

2. Lowery, Annie, The New York Times, "Raising Minimum Wage Would Ease Income Gap but Carries Political Risks," February 13, 13, http://www.nytimes.com/2013/02/13/us/politics/obama-pushes-for-increase-in-federal-minimum-wage.html?pagewanted=all&_r=2& (accessed July 30, 2914).

3. CNN Money, "Minimum wage jobs on the decline," http://money.cnn.com/2013/02/27/news/economy/minimum-wage/ (accessed July 30, 2014).

4. McCormack, John, The Weekly Standard, "Millions of Americans Are Losing Their Health Plans Because of Obamacare," October 23, 2013, http://www.weeklystandard.com/blogs/millions-americans-are-losing-their-health-plans-because-obamacare_764602.html (accessed February 4, 2014).

5. Red Flag, "Carney Dismisses 14 Million Losing Their Health Insurance Because of Obamacare As A "Small Sliver" of The Population…," http://www.redflagnews.com/headlines/carney-dismisses-14-million-losing-their-health-insurance-because-of-obamacare-as-a-small-sliver-of-the-population (accessed July 30, 2014).

6. Fox News.com, "New Numbers: 4.2M Americans Dropped From Health Plans," http://foxnewsinsider.com/2013/11/07/how-many-americans-have-lost-their-health-insurance-under-obamacare (accessed July 30, 2014).

7. Red Flag, "Carney Dismisses 14 Million Losing Their Health Insurance Because of Obamacare As A "Small Sliver" of The Population…," http://www.redflagnews.com/headlines/carney-dismisses-14-million-losing-their-health-insurance-because-of-obamacare-as-a-small-sliver-of-the-population (accessed July 30, 2014).

8. Finger, Richard, Forbes, "Homeland Security Secretary: 11 Million llegals Have "Earned The Right To Be Citizens". Oh Really?," http://www.forbes.com/sites/richardfinger/2014/01/28/3302/ (accessed July 30, 2014).

9. National Register, "The Constitutional Amendment Process," http://www.archives.gov/federal-register/constitution/ (accessed July 30, 2014).

10. Quizlet, Constitutional Amendments 1-27, http://quizlet.com/5149242/constitutional-amendments-1-27-flash-cards/ (accessed July 30, 2014).

11. Declaration of Independence, http://www.ushistory.org/declaration/document/ (accessed December 18, 2013).

12. Ibid.

Dispatch Eighty-one

1. You Tube, "2001 Obama WBEZ Interview," https://www.youtube.com/watch?v=OkpdNtTgQNM (accessed July 30, 2014).

Dispatch Eighty-two

1. The Free Dictionary, "Legal Positivism," http://legal-dictionary.thefreedictionary.com/Legal+Positivism (accessed July 30, 2014).

2. Ibid.

3. Declaration of Independence, http://www.ushistory.org/declaration/document/ (accessed December 18, 2013).

4. American History, "Letters of Thomas Jefferson," http://www.let.rug.nl/usa/presidents/thomas-jefferson/letters-of-thomas-jefferson/jefl282.php (accessed July 30, 2014).

5. History.com, "The Nuremberg Trials," http://www.history.com/topics/world-war-ii/nuremberg-trials (accessed July 30, 2014).

6. You Tube, "Spread the Wealth Around," http://www.youtube.com/watch?v=RZcEHLr4gBg (accessed December 18, 2013).

7. Vincent, Isabel, New York Post, "The case against Charlie Rangle," http://nypost.com/2009/10/04/the-case-against-charlie-rangel/ (accessed July 30, 2014).

8. Wright, C. Edmund, American Thinker, "Why Geithner and Rangel Matter," January 16, 2009, http://www.americanthinker.com/2009/01/why_geithner_and_rangel_matter.html (accessed July 30, 2014).

9. Newman, Andy, The New York Times, "Rangel's Ethics Violations," November `16, 2010, http://cityroom.blogs.nytimes.com/2010/11/16/rangel-found-to-have-violated-multiple-ethics-rules/?_php=true&_type=blogs&_r=0 (accessed July 30, 2014).

10. Watergate.info, "Articles of Impeachment," http://watergate.info/impeachment/articles-of-impeachment (accessed July 30, 2014).

11. Factcheck.org, "IRS Officials Misled Congress, Public," May 21, 2013, http://www.factcheck.org/2013/05/irs-officials-misled-congress-public/ (accessed July 30, 2014).

12. Judicial Watch, "New Documents Show IRS HQ Control of Tea Party Targeting" May 14, 2014, http://www.judicialwatch.org/press-room/press-releases/judicial-watch-new-documents-show-irs-hq-control-tea-party-targeting/ (accessed July 30, 2014).

13. Declaration of Independence, http://www.ushistory.org/declaration/document/ (accessed December 18, 2013).

Dispatch Eighty-three

1. Good Reads, https://www.goodreads.com/author/quotes/432.Ayn_Rand Accessed 11-24-14 (accessed July 30, 2014).

2. Declaration of Independence, http://www.ushistory.org/declaration/document/ (accessed December 18, 2013).

3. Yale Law School: The Avalon Project, Declaration of the Rights of Man – 1789, http://avalon.law.yale.edu/18th_century/rightsof.asp (accessed November 24, 2014).

4. About Education, "The Terror 1793 – 94," http://europeanhistory.about.com/od/thefrenchrevolution/a/hfr7.htm (accessed November 24, 2014).

5. Wilde, Robert, About.com, "French Revolution 101," http://europeanhistory.about.com/od/thefrenchrevolution/p/ovfrenchrev.htm (accessed November 24, 2014).

6. Ibid.

7. Wells, H. G., A Short History of the World, Bartleby.com, "The French Revolution and the Restoration of Monarchy in France," http://www.bartleby.com/86/55.html (accessed November 24, 2014).

8. Constitution Society, "The Federalist #51," http://www.constitution.org/fed/federa51.htm (accessed November 24, 2014).

9. Ibid.

10. Snyder, Neil, The American Thinker, "Enough with Affirmative Action Presidents," October 10, 2012, http://www.americanthinker.com/articles/2012/10/enough_with_affirmative_action_presidents.html (accessed November 24, 2014).

Dispatch Eighty-four

1. Boyer, Dave, The Washington Times, "Obama blames Founding Fathers' 'structural' design of Congress for gridlock," May 23, 2014, http://www.washingtontimes.com/news/2014/may/23/obama-blames-structural-design-congress-gridlock/ (accessed November 24, 2014).

2. Our Documents, 17th Amendment, http://www.ourdocuments.gov/doc.php?flash=true&doc=58 (accessed November 24, 2014).

3. Boyer, Dave, The Washington Times, "Obama blames Founding Fathers' 'structural' design of Congress for gridlock," May 23, 2014, http://www.washingtontimes.com/news/2014/may/23/obama-blames-structural-design-congress-gridlock/ (accessed November 24, 2014).

4. Borowski, Julie, Freedom Works, "Repeal it: Dodd-Frank Entrenches Crony Capitalism," August 2, 2011, http://www.freedomworks.org/content/repeal-it-dodd-frank-entrenches-crony-capitalism (accessed December 2, 2014).

5. Ghei, Nita, The Washington Times, "The crony-capitalist triumph," July 20, 2011, http://www.washingtontimes.com/news/2011/jul/20/the-crony-capitalist-triumph/ (accessed December 2, 2014).

6. You Tube, "Fundamentally Transform America" http://www.youtube.com/watch?v=_cqN4NIEtOY (accessed December 18, 2013)

Dispatch Eighty-five

1. Bill of Rights, http://www.constitution.org/billofr_.htm (accessed December 2, 2014).

2. Our Documents, 17th Amendment, http://www.ourdocuments.gov/doc.php?flash=true&doc=58 (accessed December 2, 2014).

Dispatch Eighty-six

1. Think Exist.com, Albert Einstein Quotes, http://thinkexist.com/quotation/insanity-doing_the_same_thing_over_and_over_again/15511.html (accessed December 2, 2014).

2. Quote DB, Winston Churchill, ""If you will not fight for the right when you can easily win without bloodshed ... ," http://www.quotedb.com/quotes/2531 (accessed December 2, 2014).

3. Quote World, Benjamin Franklin, "We must hang together, gentlemen... else, we shall most assuredly hang separately." http://www.quoteworld.org/quotes/4954 (accessed December 2, 2014).

Dispatch Eighty-seven

1. Declaration of Independence, http://www.ushistory.org/declaration/document/ (accessed December 18, 2013).

2. Alder, Carolyn, In Search of the American Constitutional Paradigm, "God's Law the Foundation of Free Government," http://www.freedomformula.us/articles/gods-law-the-foundation-of-free-government/ (accessed December 2, 2014).

3. Ibid.

4. Ibid.

5. Ibid.

6. Baume, Sandrine, E-International Relations, "Hans Kelsen and the Case for Democracy," May 8, 2013, http://www.e-ir.info/2013/05/08/hans-kelsen-and-the-case-for-democracy/ (accessed December 2, 2014).

7. Bowling, Marqurite, The daily Signal, "We have to pass the bill so you can find out what is in it," March 10, 2010, http://dailysignal.com/2010/03/10/video-of-the-week-we-have-to-pass-the-bill-so-you-can-find-out-what-is-in-it/ (accessed December 2, 2014).

8. "PETE STARK: - The Federal Government can do most anything in this country," https://www.youtube.com/watch?v=W1-eBz8hyoE (accessed December 2, 2014).

9. Blumenthal, Paul, The Sunlight Foundation, "Rep. Conyers: Don't Read the Bill," July 27, 2009, http://sunlightfoundation.com/blog/2009/07/27/rep-conyers-dont-read-the-bill/ (accessed December 2, 2014).

10. Stuchka, Peter, Distinguish between law and administrative regulation, http://books.google.com/books?id=ENQjPm-S7UEC&pg=PA351&lpg=PA 351&dq=peter+stuchka+distinguish+between+law+and+administrative+re gulation&source=bl&ots=lGrbneJgfT&sig=jIy-7RXIDdvWmg2LX7cWJpPb Es&hl=en&sa=X&ei=XfQzVLaECoakyATU5IKgCg&ved=0CCMQ6AEwA A#v=onepage&q=peter%20stuchka%20distinguish%20between%20law%20 and%20administrative%20regulation&f=false (accessed December 2, 2014).

11. Hyak, F. A., "What distinguishes the Soviet system from all other despotic governments" http://books.google.com/books?id=ENQjPm-S7UEC&pg= PA351&lpg=PA351&dq=hyak+What+distinguishes+the+Soviet+system+f rom+all+other+despotic+governments&source=bl&ots=lGrbneJkdO&sig =Cb9sT56UrYk6IA13Y8UgCBI8LrA&hl=en&sa=X&ei=1PUzVNnKE4P6 yATu9ILQCA&ved=0CCAQ6AEwAA#v=onepage&q=hyak%20What%20 distinguishes%20the%20Soviet%20system%20from%20all%20other%20 despotic%20governments&f=false (accessed 1December 2, 2014).

12. Ibid.

Dispatch Eighty-eight

1. History Place.com, World War Two In Europe, "Hitler's Enabling Act," http://www.historyplace.com/worldwar2/timeline/enabling.htm (accessed December 2, 2014).

2. Picket, Kerry, The Washington Times, "EPA imposes Obama's cap and trade regs- energy prices 'skyrocket,'" August 20, 2011, http://www.washington-times.com/blog/watercooler/2011/aug/20/picket-obama-08-energy-prices-will-skyrocket-under/ (accessed December 23, 2013).

3. Minter, Frank, Forbes, "Is The Obama Administration The Cause Of Gun Ammunition Shortages?," http://www.forbes.com/sites/frank-miniter/2013/10/20/is-the-obama-administration-the-cause-of-gun-am-munition-shortages/ (accessed December 2, 2014).

4. National Report, "Obama Issues Executive Order Granting Amnesty to Illegals who Enroll in Obamacare," http://nationalreport.net/obama-issues-executive-order-granting-amnesty-illegals-enroll-obamacare/ (accessed December 2, 2014).

5. Judicial watch, "Uncovers Documents from DHS Detailing Obama Plan to Impose DREAM Act by Suspending Illegal Alien Deportations," http://www.judicialwatch.org/press-room/press-releases/jw-uncovers-documents-dhs-detailing-obama-plan-impose-dream-act-suspending-illegal-ali/ (accessed December 2, 2014).

6. Right Edition, "Got a wet yard? EPA will take control," October 23, 2013 http://rightedition.com/2013/10/23/got-wet-yard-epa-will-take-control/ (accessed December 2, 2014).

7. NBC News, "Hey! Who turned out the lights? Incandescent bulb ban just one of new year's new laws" December 30, 2013 http://usnews.nbcnews.com/_news/2013/12/30/22114574-hey-who-turned-out-the-lights-incandescent-bulb-ban-just-one-of-new-years-new-laws?lite (accessed December 2, 2014).

8. Deziel, Chris, SF Gate, "The Federal Regulations on Toilet Gallons," http://homeguides.sfgate.com/federal-regulations-toilet-gallons-88640.html (accessed December 2, 2014).

9. Real Clear Politics, "History of IRS Abuse," May 15, 2013, http://www.realclearpolitics.com/lists/irs-scandal/ (accessed December 2, 2014).

10. Electronic frontier Foundation, "Timeline of NSA Domestic Spying," https://www.eff.org/nsa-spying/timeline (accessed December 2, 2014).

11. Gabbay, Tiffany, The Blaze, "Indoctrination and Data Mining in Common Core: Here's Why America's Schools May Be in More Trouble Than You Think," http://www.theblaze.com/stories/2013/03/27/indoctrination-and-data-mining-in-common-core-heres-why-americas-schools-may-be-in-more-trouble-than-you-think/ (accessed December 2, 2014).

12. Vadum, Matthew, Frontpage Mag, "Amnesty and Attack on American Workers," http://www.frontpagemag.com/2013/matthew-vadum/amnesty-and-the-attack-on-american-workers/ (accessed December 2, 2014).

13. Snyder, Michael, Info Wars, "19 Shocking Examples Of How Political Correctness Is Destroying America," http://www.infowars.com/19-shocking-examples-of-how-political-correctness-is-destroying-america/ (accessed December 2, 2014)

14. Declaration of Independence, http://www.ushistory.org/declaration/document/ (accessed December 18, 2013).

15. Brainy Quotes, Jean-Jacques Rousseau, "Free people, remember this maxim: we may acquire liberty, but it is never recovered if it is once lost," http://www.brainyquote.com/quotes/authors/j/jeanjacques_rousseau.html (accessed December 2, 2014).

16. _____, Liberty Quotes, http://www.brainyquote.com/quotes/keywords/liberty_2.html (accessed December 2, 2014).

17. _____, Vladimir Lenin, http://www.brainyquote.com/quotes/authors/v/vladimir_lenin.html (accessed December 2, 2014).

18. _____, Liberty Quotes, http://www.brainyquote.com/quotes/keywords/liberty_2.html (accessed December 2, 2014).

19. Proverbia, Liberty, Norman Vincent Peal, http://en.proverbia.net/citastema.asp?tematica=704 (accessed December 2, 2014).

20. Hawkins, John, Town Hall.com, "The 40 Greatest Quotes From Winston Churchill," http://townhall.com/columnists/johnhawkins/2013/01/19/the-40-greatest-quotes-from-winston-churchill-n1492794/page/full (accessed December 2, 2014).

21. Brainy Quotes, Liberty Quotes, http://www.brainyquote.com/quotes/keywords/liberty_2.html (accessed December 2, 2014).

Dispatch Eighty-nine

1. Greszler, Rachel and Romina Boccia, The Heritage Foundation, "Social Security Trustees Report: Unfunded Liability Increased $1.1 Trillion and Projected Insolvency in 2033," August 4, 2014, http://www.heritage.org/research/reports/2014/08/social-security-trustees-report-unfunded-liability-increased-11-trillion-and-projected-insolvency-in-2033 (accessed December 3, 2014).

2. Ibid.

3. Hughes, Brian, Washington Examiner, "Fight brewing over Social Security benefits for illegal immigrants," November 29, 2014, http://www.washingtonexaminer.com/fight-brewing-over-social-security-and-medicare-for-illegal-immigrants/article/2556750 (accessed December 3, 2014).

Dispatch Ninety

1. Declaration of Independence, http://www.ushistory.org/declaration/document/ (accessed December 18, 2013).

2. Kelly, Martin, About.com, "Marbury v. Madison," http://americanhistory.about.com/od/judicialbranch/p/marbury.htm (accessed December 4, 2014).

3. Cornell University Law School: Legal Information Institute, Article III, U.S. Constitution http://www.law.cornell.edu/constitution/articleiii (accessed December 4, 2014).

4. U.S. Constitution Online, "Article 1 Section 8," http://www.usconstitution.net/xconst_A1Sec8.html (accessed December 26, 2013).

5. Ibid.

6. Lawnix, Wickard v. Filbum, http://www.lawnix.com/cases/wickard-filburn.html (accessed December 4, 2014).

7. Klingebiel, Jacqueline, ABC News, "Obama: Mandate is Not a Tax," September 2, 2009, http://abcnews.go.com/blogs/politics/2009/09/obama-mandate-is-not-a-tax/ (accessed December 4, 2014).

8. U.S. Constitution Online, "Article 1 Section 7," http://www.usconstitution.net/xconst_A1Sec7.html (accessed December 4, 2014).

9. Capitol Hill on NBC News, "Health Care: A timeline of the overhaul bill's passage," http://www.nbcnews.com/id/35986022/ns/politics-capitol_hill/t/health-care-timeline-overhaul-bills-passage/#.VIBokckZGpB (accessed December 4, 2014).

10. Slack, Kevin, The New Your Times, "Arguing That Health Mandate Is Not a Tax, Except When It Is," March 26, 2012, http://www.nytimes.com/2012/03/27/health/policy/arguing-that-health-mandate-is-not-a-tax-except-when-it-is.html?_r=1& (accessed December 4, 2014).

11. Ibid.

12. Nordquist, Richard, About Education, "Sophistry," http://grammar.about.com/od/rs/g/Sophistry.htm (accessed December 4, 2014).

13. Odom, Thomas H., Federal Constitutional Law: Introduction to Interpretive Methods ..., Volume 1 / Google Books, http://books.google.com/books?id=9PbXK83ru00C&pg=PT75&lpg=PT75&dq=There+is+no+power+above+them+to+control+any+of+their+decisions&source=bl&ots=hNx_LHsnFG&sig=haX8zMXm0RGeqge52D71saFRx1w&hl=en&sa=X&ei=rW2AVLz8CteBygTus4GwBg&ved=0CCAQ6AEwAA#v=onepage&q=There%20is%20no%20power%20above%20them%20to%20control%20any%20of%20their%20decisions&f=false (accessed December 4, 2014).

14. Constitution Society, "To the Citizens of the State of New-York," October 18, 1787, http://www.constitution.org/afp/brutus01.htm (accessed December 4, 2014).

Dispatch Ninety-one

1. Brainy Quotes, Karl Marx Quotes, http://www.brainyquote.com/quotes/authors/k/karl_marx.html (accessed December 18, 2013).

2. Business Dictionary.com, "Marxism," http://www.businessdictionary.com/definition/Marxism.html (accessed December 9, 2014).

3. Info Please.com, "Fabian Society," http://www.infoplease.com/encyclopedia/history/fabian-society.html (accessed December 9, 2014).

4. You Tube, "Obama Spreading the wealth around," https://www.youtube.com/watch?v=OoqI5PSRcXM (accessed December 9, 2014).

Dispatch Ninety-two

1. Picht, Jim, The Washington Times, "The debt ceiling agreement: a fiscal band-aid on mortal wounds," http://communities.washingtontimes.com/neighborhood/stimulus/2011/aug/4/debt-ceiling-agreement-fiscal-band-aid-mortal-woun/ (accessed December 9, 2014).

2. Kessler, Glenn, The Washington Post, "Obama's royal flip-flop on using executive action on illegal immigration," http://www.washingtonpost.com/blogs/fact-checker/wp/2014/11/18/obamas-flip-flop-on-using-executive-action-on-illegal-immigration/ (accessed December 8, 2014).

3. Quotation Collection, "Ronald Reagan," http://www.quotationcollection.com/author/Ronald-Wilson-Reagan/quotes (accessed December 9, 2014).

4. Revolutionary War and Beyond, James Madison Quotes, http://www.revolutionary-war-and-beyond.com/james-madison-quotes-5.htm (accessed December 9, 2014).

5. You Tube, "Fundamentally Transform America," http://www.youtube.com/watch?v=KrefKCaV8m4 (accessed December 18, 2013).

6. The Quotation Page, Karl Marx http://www.quotationspage.com/quote/36121.html (accessed December 18, 2013).

7. The Cold War Museum, The Fall of the Soviet Union, http://www.coldwar.org/articles/90s/fall_of_the_soviet_union.asp (accessed December 18, 2013).

8. Snopes. "Border Patrol" http://www.snopes.com/politics/soapbox/border-patrol.asp (accessed December 9, 2014).

9. You Tube, "Obama Spreading the wealth around," https://www.youtube.com/watch?v=OoqI5PSRcXM (accessed December 9, 2014).

10. Quotation Collection, "Ronald Reagan," http://www.quotationcollection.com/author/Ronald-Wilson-Reagan/quotes (accessed December 9, 2014).

11. Brainy Quote, Albert Einstein, http://www.brainyquote.com/quotes/quotes/a/alberteins133991.html (accessed December 9, 2014).

12. Good Reads, "Winston Churchill Quotes," http://www.goodreads.com/quotes/106588-if-you-will-not-fight-for-right-when-you-can (accessed December 9. 2014).

Dispatch Ninety-four

1. Owens, Robert R. The Constitution Failed, http://www.amazon.com/Constitution-Failed-PH-D-Robert-Owens/dp/1609579615/ref=sr_1_1?ie=UTF8&qid=1350471788&sr=8-1&keywords=the+constitution+failed+owens (accessed November 24, 2014).

2. Casting Crowns, Lyrics, "Who am I," http://www.azlyrics.com/lyrics/castingcrowns/whoami.html (accessed December 9, 2014).

Dispatch Ninety-five

1. The Constitution, http://constitutionus.com/ (accessed December 18, 2013).

2. Abraham Lincoln Online, "The Gettysburg Address," http://www.abrahamlincolnonline.org/lincoln/speeches/gettysburg.htm (accessed January 15, 2014).

3. The Founder's Constitution, Patrick Henry, Virginia Ratifying Convention, http://press-pubs.uchicago.edu/founders/documents/preambles14.html (accessed December 9, 2014).

4. You Tube, "2001 Obama WBEZ Interview," https://www.youtube.com/watch?v=OkpdNtTgQNM (accessed July 30, 2014).

5. The Heritage Foundation, FDR's Second Bill of Rights, http://www.heritage.org/initiatives/first-principles/primary-sources/fdrs-second-bill-of-rights (accessed December 9, 2014).

6. Sunstein, Cass, Bloomberg View, "Obama, FDR and the Second Bill of Rights," http://www.bloombergview.com/articles/2013-01-28/obama-fdr-and-the-second-bill-of-rights (accessed December 9, 2014).

7. U.S. Constitution Online, Amendment 10, http://www.usconstitution.net/xconst_Am10.html (accessed December 9, 2014).

Dispatch Ninety-six

1. American History, "The First Virginia Charter 1606," http://www.let.rug.nl/usa/documents/1600-1650/the-first-virginia-charter-1606.php (accessed December 9, 2014).

2. American History, "Charter Of Massachusetts Bay 1629," http://www.let.rug.nl/usa/documents/1600-1650/charter-of-massachusetts-bay-1629.php (accessed December 9, 2014).

3. The Declaratory Act, http://www.ushistory.org/declaration/related/declaratory.htm (accessed December 9, 2014).

4. U.S. Constitution Online, Amendment 10, http://www.usconstitution.net/xconst_Am10.html (accessed December 9, 2014).

5. Good Reads, "James Madison Quotes,' http://www.goodreads.com/quotes/23893-the-powers-delegated-by-the-proposed-constitution-to-the-federal (accessed December 9, 2014).

6. Tampa Bay Times, PoliticFact.com, "Obama: 'If you like your health care plan, you'll be able to keep your health care plan," http://www.politifact.com/obama-like-health-care-keep/ (accessed December 9, 2014).

7. U.S. Debt Clock.org, http://www.usdebtclock.org/ (accessed December 18, 2013).

8. Brainy Quotes, Karl Marx Quotes, http://www.brainyquote.com/quotes/authors/k/karl_marx.html (accessed December 18, 2013).

9. Marx and Lenin, http://www.chsbs.cmich.edu/fattah/courses/modern-thought/marx.htm (accessed December 9, 2014).

10. Brainy Quotes, Vladimir Lenin, http://www.brainyquote.com/quotes/authors/v/vladimir_lenin.html (accessed December 2, 2014).

11. Ibid.

12. Ibid.

13. _____, Joseph Stalin Quotes, http://www.brainyquote.com/quotes/authors/j/joseph_stalin.html (accessed December 9, 2014).

14. Ibid.

15. Ibid.

Dispatch Ninety-seven

1. Amazon.com, Alvin Toffler, http://www.amazon.com/Alvin-Toffler/e/B000AP5YBK/ref=sr_tc_2_0?qid=1394667707&sr=8-2-ent (accessed December 9, 2014).

2. Brainy Quotes, Alvin Toffler Quotes, http://www.brainyquote.com/quotes/authors/a/alvin_toffler.html (accessed December 9, 2014).

3. Kurzweil Technologies, "A Brief Career Summary of Ray Kurzweil," http://www.kurzweiltech.com/aboutray.html (accessed December 9, 2014).

4. Amazon.com, "The Singularity Is Near: When Humans Transcend Biology," http://www.amazon.com/The-Singularity-Is-Near-Transcend/dp/0143037889 (accessed December 9, 2014).

5. McGee, Matt, Search Engine land, "Ray Kurzweil's Job At Google: Beat IBM's Watson At Natural Language Search," http://searchengineland.com/ray-kurzweils-job-google-beat-ibms-watson-natural-language-search-185149 (accessed December 9, 2014).

6. Ibid.

7. Waters, Richard, The Big Read, "Technology: Rise of the replicants," http://www.ft.com/intl/cms/s/2/dc895d54-a2bf-11e3-9685-00144feab7de.html#axzz2vnXoaFPR (accessed December 9, 2014).

8. Brainy Quotes, Alvin Toffler Quotes, http://www.brainyquote.com/quotes/authors/a/alvin_toffler.html (accessed December 9, 2014).

9. Ibid.

Dispatch Ninety-eight

1. Hot Air, "Obama's answer on experience: But I'm such a great campaigner!," September 2, 2008, http://hotair.com/archives/2008/09/02/obamas-answer-on-experience-but-im-such-a-great-campaigner/ (accessed December 9, 2014).

2. Dictionary.com, "Rube Goldberg," http://dictionary.reference.com/browse/rube+goldberg (accessed December 9, 2014).

Dispatch Ninety-nine

1. Declaration of Independence, http://www.ushistory.org/declaration/document/ (accessed December 18, 2013).

2. Abraham Lincoln Online, "The Gettysburg Address," http://www.abrahamlincolnonline.org/lincoln/speeches/gettysburg.htm (accessed January 15, 2014).

3. Fox nes.com, " Administration Warns of 'Command-and-Control' Regulation Over Emissions," http://www.foxnews.com/politics/2009/12/09/administration-warns-command-control-regulation-emissions/ (accessed December 9, 2014).

4. Brandon, Doug, Cato Institute, "Cap 'n Trade: The Ultimate Pork-Fest," July 2, 2009, http://www.cato.org/blog/cap-n-trade-ultimate-pork-fest (accessed December 9, 2014).

5. Nimmo, Kurt, InfoWars.com, "EPA Threatens 'Command-and-Control' Economy to Push Climate Change Agenda," December 9, 2009, http://www.infowars.com/epa-threatens-command-and-control-economy-to-push-climate-change-agenda/ (accessed December 9, 2014).

6. Political Culture of the United States, http://academic.regis.edu/jriley/421elazar.htm (accessed December 9, 2014).

7. The Free Dictionary, "Separation of Powers," http://legal-dictionary.thefreedictionary.com/Balance+of+powers (accessed December 9, 2014).

8. United States History, "No Taxation Without Representation," http://www.u-s-history.com/pages/h640.html (accessed December 10, 2014).

9. Aronoff, Alan, America Thinker, "Representation Without taxation," http://www.americanthinker.com/articles/2009/04/representation_without_taxatio.html (accessed December 12, 2014).

10. Browse Quotes, Abraham Lincoln, "You may fool all the people some of the time; you can even fool some of the people all the time; but you can't fool all of the people all the time," http://quotationsbook.com/quote/45358/ (accessed December 10, 2014).

11. You Tube, "Fundamentally Transform America" http://www.youtube.com/watch?v=_cqN4NIEtOY (accessed December 18, 2013).

12. Thomas, Andrew, American Thinker, "Beware the Counterrevolution," August 16, 2009, http://www.americanthinker.com/articles/2009/08/beware_the_counterrevolution.html (accessed December 10, 2014).

13. Poe, Richard, DiscovertheNetworks.org, The Cloward-Piven Strategy," 2005, http://www.discoverthenetworks.org/Articles/theclowardpiven-strategypoe.html (accessed December 10, 2014).

14. Obama On Executive Actions: 'I've Got A Pen And I've Got A Phone'," January 14, 2014, http://washington.cbslocal.com/2014/01/14/obama-on-executive-actions-ive-got-a-pen-and-ive-got-a-phone/ (accessed December 10, 2014).

15. You Tube, "Obama if you like your plan you can keep your plan," https://www.youtube.com/watch?v=wfl55GgHr5E (accessed December 10, 2014).

16. Daily News, "Obama's search for an enemy: The President keep beating the class warfare drum," March 7, 2009, http://www.nydailynews.com/opinion/obama-search-enemy-president-beating-class-warfare-drum-article-1.368969 (accessed December 10, 2014).

Dispatch One Hundred

1. Declaration of Independence, http://www.ushistory.org/declaration/document/ (accessed December 18, 2013).

2. Locke, John, Constitution Society, "The Second Treatise of Civil Government," http://www.constitution.org/jl/2ndtreat.htm (accessed December 10, 2014).

3. The Virginia Declaration of Rights, Constitution Society, http://www.constitution.org/bcp/virg_dor.htm (accessed December 10, 2014).

4. Declaration of Independence, http://www.ushistory.org/declaration/document/ (accessed December 18, 2013).

5. The Free Dictionary, "Necessary and Proper Clause," http://legal-dictionary.thefreedictionary.com/Necessary+and+Proper+Clause (accessed December 10, 2014).

6. Good Reads, "Leon Trotsky Quotes," http://www.goodreads.com/quotes/319203-in-a-country-where-the-sole-employer-is-the-state (accessed December 10, 2014).

7. Property and Socialism, http://www.punkerslut.com/propertyessays.html (accessed December 10, 2014).

8. National Socialist Party of Germany (NAZI) Quotes, http://quotes.liberty-tree.ca/quotes_by/national+socialist+party+of+germany+%28nazi%29 (accessed December 10, 2014).

9. Starr, Penny, CNSNEWS.com, "6,125 Proposed Regulations and Notifications Posted in Last 90 Days--Average 68 per Day," November 9, 2012, http://cnsnews.com/news/article/6125-proposed-regulations-and-notifications-posted-last-90-days-average-68-day (accessed December 10, 2014).

10. Batkins, Sam, AAF, "A Regulatory Flurry: The Year in Regulation, 2013," http://americanactionforum.org/research/a-regulatory-flurry-the-year-in-regulation-2013 (accessed December 10, 2014).

11. Ibid.

12. Hayek, F. A., The Constitution of Liberty, "True Coercion," http://books.google.com/books?id=nh_ZYYZJj8C&pg=PA79 &lpg=PA79&dq=hayek+True+coercion+occurs+when+armed+ bands+of+conquerors&source=bl&ots=KmFVhd2bjk&sig=GI ZEZTjVF7D8SC8oToCWF08wN0I&hl=en&sa=X&ei=TCkPU-G6fl2QW434GoAQ&ved=0CC4Q6AEwAg#v=onepage&q=hayek%20 True%20coercion%20occurs%20when%20armed%20bands%20of%20 conquerors&f=false (accessed December 10, 2014).

13. Brainy Quote, John Locke, http://www.brainyquote.com/quotes/quotes/j/ johnlocke151490.html (accessed December 10, 2014).

14. Brainy Quote, John Locke, http://www.brainyquote.com/quotes/quotes/j/ johnlocke118856.html (accessed December 10, 2014

15. Brainy Quote, John Locke, http://www.brainyquote.com/quotes/quotes/j/ johnlocke383067.html (accessed December 10, 2014).

Conclusion

1. You Tube, "Congressman says 'I don't worry about the Constitution'," https:// www.youtube.com/watch?v=lgh-q4t0kzM (accessed December 10, 2014).

2. The Sovereign Investor Daily, "Have You Read the U.S. Constitution?," http://thesovereigninvestor.com/diversified-investments/have-you-read-the-u-s-constitution/ (accessed December 10, 2014).

3. Ibid.

4. Ibid.

5. Tanner, Michael, National Review Online, "Democrats: The Constitution is 'Weird'," http://www.nationalreview.com/articles/248102/democrats-constitution-weird-michael-tanner (accessed December 10, 2014).

6. Gill, Kathy, AboutNews.com, "Oaths of Office for federal Officials," http://uspolitics.about.com/od/usgovernment/a/oaths_of_office_4.htm (accessed December 11, 2014).

7. U.S. Constitution Online, Amendment 10, http://www.usconstitution. net/xconst_Am10.html (accessed December 9, 2014).

8. Tenth Amendment Center, "A Constitutional Coup d'etat," http://tenth-amendmentcenter.com/2009/08/31/rob-natelson-a-constitutional-coup-detat/ (accessed December 11, 2014).

9. Krauthammer, Charles, Real Clear Politics, "Obama's Plan to Transform America," December 12, 2008, http://www.realclearpolitics.com/articles/2008/12/obamas_plan_to_transform_ameri.html (accessed December 11, 2014).

10. Stanford Encyclopedia of Philosophy, Equality of Opportunity, http://plato.stanford.edu/entries/equal-opportunity/ (accessed December 18, 2013).

11. Economic expert.com, "Equality of Outcome," http://www.economicexpert.com/a/Equality:of:outcome.html (accessed December11, 2014).

12. Beck, Glenn, Fox news, "What is 'Social Justice?'", http://www.foxnews.com/story/2010/03/23/what-is-social-justice/(accessed December 11, 2014).

13. USHistory.org, Benjamin Franklin Quotes, http://www.ushistory.org/franklin/quotable/singlehtml.htm (accessed January 4, 2015).

14. Ibid.

BIBLIOGRAPHY

Abate, Tome, SFGATE, "Military waste under fire / $1 trillion missing -- Bush plan targets Pentagon accounting" May 18, 2003, http://www.sfgate.com/news/article/Military-waste-under-fire-1-trillion-missing-2616120.php (accessed December 18, 13).

ABC News, "Protests break out as Islamists win Tunisian election," http://www.abc.net.au/news/2011-10-28/tunisian-islamists-win-election/3605366 (accessed July 27, 2014)

Abdo, Alex, ACLU, "The Most Important Surveillance Order We Know Almost Nothing About," December 30, 2013, https://www.aclu.org/blog/tag/government-surveillance (accessed January 2, 2014).

About Education, "The Terror 1793 – 94," http://europeanhistory.about.com/od/thefrenchrevolution/a/hfr7.htm (accessed November 24, 2014).

About Sun Tzu, http://www.thetao.info/artofwar.thetao.info/china/suntzu.htm (accessed December 23, 2013).

Abraham Lincoln Online, "The Gettysburg Address," http://www.abrahamlincolnonline.org/lincoln/speeches/gettysburg.htm (accessed January 15, 2014).

Abraham Lincoln Research Site, "ABRAHAM LINCOLN QUOTES ABOUT SLAVERY (Including Sources)," http://rogerjnorton.com/Lincoln95.html (accessed January 2, 2014).

Ackerman, Bruce, FP, "Obama's Unconstitutional War," March 31, 2011, http://www.foreignpolicy.com/articles/2011/03/24/obama_s_unconstitutional_war#sthash.wzGMirLw.geoiZAaJ.dpbs (accessed December 29, 2013).

Adm. Mike Mullen: 'National Debt Is Our Biggest Security Threat'," May, 25, 2011, http://www.huffingtonpost.com/2010/06/24/adm-mike-mullen-national_n_624096.html (accessed December 23, 2013).

Adolf Hitler's Rise to Power, http://www2.dsu.nodak.edu/users/dmeier/Holocaust/hitler.html (accessed July 27, 2014).

Agren, David, USA Today, "Mexico's national voter IDs part of culture," January 25, 2012, http://usatoday30.usatoday.com/news/world/story/2012-01-22/mexico-national-voter-ID-cards/52779410/1 (accessed December 24, 2013).

Alchian, Armen A., Library of Economics, "Property Rights," http://www.econlib.org/library/Enc/PropertyRights.html (accessed January 29, 2014).

Alder, Carolyn, In Search of the American Constitutional Paradigm, "God's Law the Foundation of Free Government," http://www.freedomformula.us/articles/gods-law-the-foundation-of-free-government/ (accessed December 2, 2014).

All American Patriots, "1823: Monroe Doctrine," http://www.allamericanpatriots.com/american_historical_documents_1823_monroe_doctrine (accessed December 22, 2013)

All Employees Manufacturing, http://research.stlouisfed.org/fred2/data/MANEMP.txt (accessed December 22, 2013).

Amazon.com, Alvin Toffler, http://www.amazon.com/Alvin-Toffler/e/B000AP5YBK/ref=sr_tc_2_0?qid=1394667707&sr=8-2-ent (accessed December 9, 2014).

_____, "America Won the Vietnam War," http://www.amazon.com/America-Won-Vietnam-Robert-Owens/dp/1594672954/ref=sr_1_1?ie=UTF8&qid=1387757469&sr=8-1&keywords=america+won+the+vietnam+war+owens (accessed December 22, 2013).

_____,"New Deal or Raw Deal," http://www.amazon.com/New-Deal-Raw-Economic-Damaged/dp/1416592229 (accessed December 18, 2013).

_____, "The Constitution Failed," http://www.amazon.com/Constitution-Failed-PH-D-Robert-Owens/dp/1609579615/ref=sr_1_1?ie=UTF8&qid=1372328556&sr=8-1&keywords=the+constitution+failed+owens (accessed December 18, 2013).

_____, "The Corporate Cult," http://www.amazon.com/Corporate-Cult-More-What-Women/dp/1589390423/ref=sr_1_2?ie=UTF8&qid=1322141274&sr=8-2 (accessed December 27, 2013).

_____, "The Road to Serfdom," http://www.amazon.com/s/ref=nb_sb_noss?url=search-alias%3Daps&field-keywords=the+road+to+serfdom&x=0&y=0 (accessed December 22, 2013).

_____, "The Singularity Is Near: When Humans Transcend Biology," http://www.amazon.com/The-Singularity-Is-Near-Transcend/dp/0143037889 (accessed December 9, 2014)

American Christian Heritage, "Where is the king of America," http://acheritagegroup.org/blog/?p=69 (accessed December 21, 2013).

American History, "Charter Of Massachusetts Bay 1629," http://www.let.rug.nl/usa/documents/1600-1650/charter-of-massachusetts-bay-1629.php (accessed December 9, 2014).

_____, "Letters of Thomas Jefferson," http://www.let.rug.nl/usa/presidents/thomas-jefferson/letters-of-thomas-jefferson/jefl282.php (accessed July 30, 2014).

_____, "The First Virginia Charter 1606," http://www.let.rug.nl/usa/documents/1600-1650/the-first-virginia-charter-1606.php (accessed December 9, 2014).

American Rhetoric, "The Great Arsenal of Democracy," http://historymatters.gmu.edu/d/4943/ (accessed July 27, 2014).

America's Watchtower, "The stimulus spent $278,000 for every job saved or created," July 5, 2011, http://americaswatchtower.com/2011/07/05/the-stimulus-spent-278000-for-every-job-saved-or-created/ (accessed February 18, 2014).

Angle, Jim, Fox News, "Senators Outraged U.S. Borrowing Big From China While Also Giving It Aid," October 24, 2011, http://www.foxnews.com/politics/2011/10/24/senators-outraged-us-borrowing-big-from-china-while-also-giving-it-aid/ (accessed December 23, 2013).

Anti-War.com, "180,000 Attend Yemen Pro-Democracy Protests," http://news.antiwar.com/2011/02/25/180000-attend-yemen-pro-democracy-protests/ (accessed July 27, 2014).

Antle, James, Real Clear Politics, "Fast & Furious Scandal Festers," February 19, 2012, http://www.realclearpolitics.com/2012/02/19/fast_amp_furious_scandal_festers_273734.html (accessed December 29, 2013).

Aronoff, Alan, America Thinker, "Representation Without taxation," http://www.americanthinker.com/articles/2009/04/representation_without_taxatio.html (accessed December 24, 2014).

A Teacher's Guide to the Holocaust, "The Rise of the Nazi Party," http://fcit.usf.edu/holocaust/timeline/nazirise.htm (accessed July 27, 2014).

Atlanta Business Chronicle, "Justice Department sues Georgia over voting," http://www.bizjournals.com/atlanta/news/2012/06/27/justice-department-sues-georgia-over.html (accessed December 24, 2013).

Atlas Shrugs, "Massive Voter Fraude: Military Vote Suppressed," http://atlasshrugs2000.typepad.com/atlas_shrugs/2012/11/more-voter-fraud-military-absentee-ballots-not-counted.html (accessed December 24, 2013).

_____, "Obama's Anti-Capitalism Speech in Kansas," December 6, 2011, http://atlasshrugs2000.typepad.com/atlas_shrugs/2011/12/obamas-anti-capitalism-speech-in-texas-kansas.html (accessed January 2, 2014).

Barnett, Laura, The Huffington Post: Politics, "Adm. Mike Mullen: 'National Debt Is Our Biggest Security Threat'," May, 25, 2011, http://www.huffingtonpost.com/2010/06/24/adm-mike-mullen-national_n_624096.html (accessed December 23, 2013).

Barack Obama Voter Fraud 2012, November 8, 2012, http://obamavoterfraud.blogspot.com/ (accessed December 22, 2013).

BARBOZA, DAVID, Economix, "China Poised to Lead World in Patent Filings," October 6, 2010, http://economix.blogs.nytimes.com/2010/10/06/china-poised-to-lead-world-in-patent-filings/?_r=1 (accessed December 22, 2013).

Bartleby.com, "Abraham Lincoln: First Inaugural Address," http://www.bartleby.com/124/pres31.html (accessed January 2, 2014).

Batkins, Sam, AAF, "A Regulatory Flurry: The Year in Regulation, 2013," http://americanactionforum.org/research/a-regulatory-flurry-the-year-in-regulation-2013 (accessed December 10, 2014).

Baume, Sandrine, E-International Relations, "Hans Kelsen and the Case for Democracy," May 8, 2013, http://www.e-ir.info/2013/05/08/hans-kelsen-and-the-case-for-democracy/ (accessed December 2, 2014).

Beach, William W., Rea S. Hederman, Jr., John L. Ligon, Guinevere Nell and Karen Campbell, Ph.D. The Heritage Foundation, "Obama Tax Hikes: The Economic and Fiscal Effects," September 20, 2010, http://www.heritage.org/research/reports/2010/09/obama-tax-hikes-the-economic-and-fiscal-effects (accessed January 15, 2014).

Beattie, Andrew, Investopdeia, "The Dotcom Crash," http://www.investopedia.com/features/crashes/crashes8.asp#axzz22PItNZAS (accessed December 23, 2013).

Beatty, W. A., American Thinker, "All the Dependency Pieces Are Falling into Place," July 30, 2012, http://www.americanthinker.com/2012/07/all_the_dependency_pieces_are_falling_into_place.html (accessed December 23, 2013).

Beck, Glenn, Fox news, "What is 'Social Justice?'," http://www.foxnews.com/story/2010/03/23/what-is-social-justice/ (accessed December 11, 2014).

Bedard, Paul, U.S. News and World Report, August 3, 2011, http://www.usnews.com/news/washington-whispers/articles/2011/08/03/report-obama-administration-added-95-billion-in-red-tape-in-july (accessed December 18, 2013).

Belman, Ted, American Thinker, "Why is Obama in bed with the Muslim Brotherhood?," February 26, 2012, http://www.americanthinker.com/2012/02/why_is_obama_in_bed_with_the_muslim_brotherhood.html (accessed December 24, 2013).

Benjamin Franklin Quotes, http://quotes.liberty-tree.ca/quotes_by/benjamin+franklin (accessed December 23, 2013).

Benko, Ralph, Fox News, "Forty Years Ago Today Nixon Took Us Off the Gold Standard," August 15, 2011, http://www.foxnews.com/opinion/2011/08/15/forty-years-ago-today-nixon-took-us-off-gold-standard/ (accessed December 22, 2013).

Bible Gateway, Acts 1:7, http://www.biblegateway.com/passage/?search=acts%201:7&version=NKJV (accessed December 23, 2013).

_____, Joshua 24:15, http://www.biblegateway.com/passage/?search=Joshua%2024:15&version=NKJV (accessed December 18, 2013)

_____, Matthew 26:11, https://www.biblegateway.com/passage/?search=Mt++26:11 (accessed July 30, 2014).

_____, Proverbs 14:34, http://www.biblegateway.com/passage/?search=Proverbs+14%3A34&version=NKJV (accessed December 31, 2013).

_____, Psalm 91:7, http://www.biblegateway.com/passage/?search=Psalm%2091:7&version=NKJV (accessed December 23, 2013).

_____, 2 Chronicles 7:13-15, http://www.biblegateway.com/passage/?search=2%20Chronicles+7:13-15&version=NKJV (accessed December 18, 2013).

_____, 2 Kings 21:5-13, http://www.biblegateway.com/passage/?search=2%20Kings%2021:5-13&version=NKJV (accessed December 23, 2013).

Bible Hub, Matthew 24:36, http://biblehub.com/niv/matthew/24-36.htm (accessed December 23, 2013).

Bill of Attainder, http://www.techlawjournal.com/glossary/legal/attainder.htm (accessed December 18, 2013).

Birnbaum, Jeffrey H., Washington Post: Politics, "Hill a Steppingstone to K Street for Some," July 27, 2005, http://www.washingtonpost.com/wp-dyn/content/article/2005/07/26/AR2005072601562.html (accessed December 22, 2013).

Bloomberg Business Week Magazine, "Where Did the TARP Money Go?," http://www.businessweek.com/magazine/content/10_41/b4198029792387.htm (accessed December 24, 2013).

Blumenthal, Paul, The Sunlight Foundation, "Rep. Conyers: Don't Read the Bill," July 27, 2009, http://sunlightfoundation.com/blog/2009/07/27/rep-conyers-dont-read-the-bill/ (accessed December 2, 2014).

Boettke, Peter J., Library of Economic Liberty, Concise Encyclopedia of Economics, "The Austrian School of Economics," http://www.econlib.org/library/Enc/AustrianSchoolofEconomics.html (accessed December 22, 2013).

BobDylan.com, "Subterranean Homesick Blues," http://www.bobdylan.com/us/songs/subterranean-homesick-blues (accessed January 2, 2014).

Borowski, Julie, Freedom Works, "Repeal it: Dodd-Frank Entrenches Crony Capitalism," August 2, 2011, http://www.freedomworks.org/content/repeal-it-dodd-frank-entrenches-crony-capitalism (accessed December 2, 2014).

Bowling, Marqurite, The daily Signal, "We have to pass the bill so you can find out what is in it," March 10, 2010, http://dailysignal.com/2010/03/10/video-of-the-week-we-have-to-pass-the-bill-so-you-can-find-out-what-is-in-it/ (accessed December 2, 2014).

Boyer, Dave, The Washington Times, "Obama blames Founding Fathers' 'structural' design of Congress for gridlock," May 23, 2014, http://www.washingtontimes.com/news/2014/may/23/obama-blames-structural-design-congress-gridlock/ (accessed November 24, 2014).

_____, "Obama: MLK would have backed 'Occupy' protests," October 16, 2011, http://www.washingtontimes.com/news/2011/oct/16/obama-king-would-have-backed-occupy-wall-street/ (accessed July 27, 2014).

Boyle, Catherine, CNBC, "Occupy Wall Street 'Bookend to Tea Party': Jon Corzine," http://www.cnbc.com/id/44855426 (accessed December 27, 2013).

Boddy-Evans, Alistair, About.com African history, "Idi Amin Dadda," http://africanhistory.about.com/od/biography/a/bio_amin.htm (accessed July 27, 2014).

Boyle, Matthew, Breitbart, "Obama Admin Can Pick Which Laws to Enforce," April 24, 2013, http://www.breitbart.com/Big-Government/2013/04/24/Big-Sis-declares-Obama-has-power-to-pick-which-laws-to-enforce-as-immigration-bill-would-grant-admin-more-authority (accessed January 11, 2014).

Brady, Jeff, NPR, "Unions Assume A Support Role For Occupy Movement," October 29, 2011, http://www.npr.org/2011/10/29/141794777/unions-assume-a-support-role-for-occupy-movement (accessed July 27, 2014).

Bradly, Tahman, ABC News, "Friends Feared New Clinton Bimbo Eruptions," June 1, 2008, http://abcnews.go.com/blogs/politics/2008/06/article-friends/ (accessed February 12, 2014).

Brainy Quote, Albert Einstein, http://www.brainyquote.com/quotes/quotes/a/alberteins133991.html (accessed December 9, 2014).

_____, Alvin Toffler Quotes, http://www.brainyquote.com/quotes/authors/a/alvin_toffler.html (accessed December 9, 2014).

_____, Churchill, http://www.brainyquote.com/quotes/quotes/w/winstonchu164131.html (accessed December 18, 2013).

_____, Crisis Quotes, http://www.brainyquote.com/quotes/keywords/crisis.html (accessed December 18, 2013).

_____, Everett Dirksen, "A billion here, a billion there" http://www.brainyquote.com/quotes/authors/e/everett_dirksen.html (accessed January 15, 2014).

_____, Friedrich August von Hayek Quotes, http://www.brainyquote.com/quotes/authors/f/friedrich_august_von_haye_2.html (accessed December 21, 2013).

_____, Jean-Jacques Rousseau, "Free people, remember this maxim: we may acquire liberty, but it is never recovered if it is once lost," http://www.brainyquote.com/quotes/authors/j/jeanjacques_rousseau.html (accessed December 2, 2014).

_____, John Adams, "Remember, democracy never lasts long. It soon wastes, exhausts, and murders itself," http://www.brainyquote.com/quotes/quotes/j/johnadams124799.html (accessed January 2, 2014).

_____, John Locke, http://www.brainyquote.com/quotes/quotes/j/johnlocke401229.html (accessed December 2, 2013).

_____, John Locke, http://www.brainyquote.com/quotes/quotes/j/johnlocke151490.html (accessed December 10. 2014).

_____, John Locke, http://www.brainyquote.com/quotes/quotes/j/johnlocke118856.html (accessed December 10, 2014).

_____, John Locke, http://www.brainyquote.com/quotes/quotes/j/johnlocke383067.html (accessed December 10, 2014).

_____, Joseph Stalin Quotes, http://www.brainyquote.com/quotes/authors/j/joseph_stalin.html (accessed December 9, 2014).

_____, Karl Marx Quotes, http://www.brainyquote.com/quotes/authors/k/karl_marx.html (accessed December 18, 2013).

_____, Karl Marx, http://www.brainyquote.com/quotes/quotes/k/karlmarx136396.html (accessed December 18, 2013).

_____, Kennedy, http://www.brainyquote.com/quotes/quotes/j/johnfkenn114918.html (accessed December 22, 2013).

_____, Liberty Quotes, http://www.brainyquote.com/quotes/key-words/liberty_2.html (accessed December 2, 2014).

_____, Lord Acton, http://www.brainyquote.com/quotes/authors/l/lord_acton.html (accessed January 2, 2014).

_____, Napoleon, http://www.brainyquote.com/quotes/quotes/n/napoleonbo161968.html (accessed January 6, 2014).

_____, Patrick Henry, http://www.brainyquote.com/quotes/authors/p/patrick_henry.html (accessed December 27, 2013).

_____, Samuel Adams, http://www.brainyquote.com/quotes/authors/s/samuel_adams.html?gclid=CNq_nZOz164CFUPc4AodsitAdg (accessed December 27, 2013).

_____, Vladimir Lenin, http://www.brainyquote.com/quotes/authors/v/vladimir_lenin.html (accessed December 2, 2014).

_____, Yogi Berra, http://www.brainyquote.com/quotes/quotes/y/yogiberra141506.html (accessed December 21, 2013).

Brandon, Doug, Cato Institute, "Cap 'n Trade: The Ultimate Pork-Fest," July 2, 2009, http://www.cato.org/blog/cap-n-trade-ultimate-pork-fest (accessed December 9, 2014).

Breitbart, "Obamacare's Cost Of Control," http://www.breitbart.com/Big-Government/2013/07/28/Obamacare-s-Cost-Of-Control (accessed January 2, 2014).

_____, "IRS Scandal," http://www.breitbart.com/Topics/B610D48D3EE0D-AFBF4FECE5BEA5F7D43/IRS-Scandal (accessed January 11, 2014).

Britt, Lawrence, Rense.com, "Fourteen Defining Characteristics of Fascism," http://www.rense.com/general37/char.htm (accessed December 31, 2013).

Brownfield, Mike, Heritage Foundation, "Constitution, Anyone? Obama Promises to Rule... Without Congress," December 14, 2011, http://blog.heritage.org/2011/12/14/constitution-anyone-obama-promises-to-rule-without-congress/ (accessed December 29, 2013).

Browse Quotes, Abraham Lincoln, "You may fool all the people some of the time; you can even fool some of the people all the time; but you can't fool all of the people all the time," http://quotationsbook.com/quote/45358/ (accessed December 10, 2014).

Buchanan, Patrick J., "Why Di Japan Attack Us?," http://www.theamerican-cause.org/patwhydidjapan.htm (accessed December 23, 2013).

Bureau of Labor Statistics, "Alternative measures of labor underutilization," http://www.bls.gov/news.release/empsit.t15.htm (accessed February 4, 2014).

Business Dictionary.com, "Chicago School of Economics," http://www.businessdictionary.com/definition/Chicago-school-of-economics.html (accessed December 22, 2013).

_____, "Marxism," http://www.businessdictionary.com/definition/Marxism.html (accessed December 9, 2014).

Business Wire, "Defense Spending in North America - A look at the leading players, market size and forecasts to 2016," July 31, 2012, http://www.businesswire.com/news/home/20120731006013/en/Research-Markets-Defense-Spending-North-America--#.UrhT2bRzYqM (accessed December 23, 2013).

Campaign for Liberty, "Teddy Roosevelt and His Big Stick," http://www.campaignforliberty.org/members-posts/teddy-roosevelt-and-his-big-stick/ (accessed December 22, 2013).

Capitol Hill on NBC News, "Health Care: A timeline of the overhaul bill's passage," http://www.nbcnews.com/id/35986022/ns/politics-capitol_hill/t/health-care-timeline-overhaul-bills-passage/#.VIBokckZGpB (accessed December 4, 2014).

CARROLL, CONN, The Heritage Network, "Bush's Betrayal of Free-Market Principles Now Complete," December 30, 2008, http://blog.heritage.org/2008/12/30/bushs-betrayal-of-free-market-principles-now-complete/ (accessed February 4, 2014)

_____, "Federal Workforce Continues to Grow Under Obama Budget," February 22, 2011, http://blog.heritage.org/2011/02/22/federal-workforce-continues-to-grow-under-obama-budget/ (accessed December 26, 2013).

_____, The Washington Examiner, "Obama donor gained nearly $1 billion in tax credits in Solyndra bankruptcy," September 19, 2013, http://washingtonexaminer.com/day-4-obama-donor-gained-nearly-1-billion-in-tax-credits-in-solyndra-bankruptcy/article/2536031 (accessed December 23, 2013).

Casting Crowns, Lyrics, "Who am I," http://www.azlyrics.com/lyrics/castingcrowns/whoami.html (accessed December 9, 2014).

CBO, Economic and Budget Issue Brief, "What Accounts for the Decline in Manufacturing Employment?", February 18, 2004, http://www.cbo.gov/sites/default/files/cbofiles/ftpdocs/50xx/doc5078/02-18-manufacturingemployment.pdf (accessed December 22, 2013).

CBSDC, "Obama On Executive Actions: 'I've Got A Pen And I've Got A Phone'", January 14, 2014, http://washington.cbslocal.com/2014/01/14/obama-on-executive-actions-ive-got-a-pen-and-ive-got-a-phone/ (accessed December 10, 2014).

CBS Money Watch, "Foreigners Reduce Stakes in U.S. Treasury," February 16, 2010, http://www.cbsnews.com/news/foreigners-reduce-stakes-in-us-treasury/ (accessed December 22, 2013).

CBS News, "Obama On Executive Actions: 'I've Got A Pen And I've Got A Phone,'" http://washington.cbslocal.com/2014/01/14/obama-on-executive-actions-ive-got-a-pen-and-ive-got-a-phone/ (accessed July30, 2014).

Central Intelligence Agency: World Fact Book, "Iran," https://www.cia.gov/library/publications/the-world-factbook/geos/ir.html (accessed December 23, 2013).

Chamberlain, John, The Freeman, "The Progressive Income tax," April 1, 1981, http://www.fee.org/the_freeman/detail/the-progressive-income-tax#axzz2oawA5yDo (accessed December 26, 2013).

Charters of Freedom, The Bill of Rights, http://www.archives.gov/exhibits/charters/bill_of_rights_transcript.html (accessed December 18, 2013).

Chatterbox, "Bill Clinton and the Meaning of 'Is,'" http://www.slate.com/articles/news_and_politics/chatterbox/1998/09/bill_clinton_and_the_meaning_of_is.html (accessed February 12, 2014).

Occupy Protests Plagued by Reports of Sex Attacks, Violent Crime," November 9, 2011, http://www.foxnews.com/us/2011/11/09/rash-sex-attacks-and-violent-crime-breaks-out-at-occupy-protests/ (accessed December 27, 2013).

Chicago's Outfit and the Machine, http://www.gangresearch.net/Chicago-Gangs/outfit/index.html (accessed December 24, 2013).

Christianity Today, "Obama: 'They cling to guns or religion,'" April 13, 2008, http://www.christianitytoday.com/gleanings/2008/april/obama-they-cling-to-guns-or-religion.html (accessed December 31, 2013).

Christianity Today Library, "Why did Columbus Sail?," July 1, 1992, http://www.ctlibrary.com/ch/1992/issue35/3509.html (accessed December 18, 2013).

Civil War Trust, "10 Facts about the Emancipation Proclamation," http://www.civilwar.org/education/history/emancipation-150/10-facts.html (accessed January 2, 2014).

Cline, Andrew, The American Spectator, "No, You Can't Keep Your Current Health Coverage," September 30, 2012, http://spectator.org/articles/38846/no-you-cant-keep-your-current-health-coverage (accessed December 2, 2013).

Club Troppo, "Did Nixon really say "we are all Keynesians now"?," http:// clubtroppo.com.au/2009/02/15/pedantic-fact-checking-did-nixon-really- say-we-are-keynesians-now/ (accessed December 23, 2013).

Conservapedia, "Bill Clinton" http://conservapedia.com/Bill_Clinton (accessed December 29, 2013).

Constitution Facts.com: About the Founding Fathers, Alexander Hamilton, http://www.constitutionfacts.com/us-founding-fathers/about-the-found- ing-fathers/ (accessed February 5, 2014).

Constitution Society, "The Federalist #51," http://www.constitution.org/fed/ federa51.htm (accessed November 24, 2014).

CNN, "How Occupy Wall Street compares to the tea party," October, 13, 2011, http://news.blogs.cnn.com/2011/10/13/how-occupy-wall-street-compares- to-the-tea-party/ (accessed December 27, 2013).

CNN Money, "bailout tracker," http://money.cnn.com/news/storysupple- ment/economy/bailouttracker/ (accessed December 31, 2013).

_____, "Minimum wage jobs on the decline," http://money.cnn. com/2013/02/27/news/economy/minimum-wage/ (accessed July 30, 2014).

_____, "What's in Obama's stimulus plan," http://money.cnn. com/2011/09/08/news/economy/obama_stimulus_plan/index.htm (ac- cessed December 31, 2013).

Collapse of the Soviet Union, http://sfr-21.org/collapse.html (accessed December 22, 2013).

Coppock, Nancy, American Thinker, "The Cloward/Piven Strategy of Econom- ic Recovery," February 7, 2009, http://www.americanthinker.com/2009/02/ the_clowardpiven_strategy_of_e.html (accessed December 27, 2013).

Conservapedia, "Cult of Reason," http://www.conservapedia.com/Cult_of_ Reason (accessed January 7, 2014).

_____, "Barack Hussein Obama's unlawful acts," http://www.conservapedia. com/Barack_Hussein_Obama%27s_unlawful_acts (accessed January 15, 2014).

Cornell University Law School: Legal Information Institute, Article III, U.S. Constitution http://www.law.cornell.edu/constitution/articleiii (accessed December 4, 2014).

_____,"THE CHER- OKEE NATION v. THE STATE OF GEORGIA," http://www.law.cornell. edu/supremecourt/text/30/1 (accessed December 27, 2013).

Constitution Society, "To the Citizens of the State of New-York," October 18, 1787, http://www.constitution.org/afp/brutus01.htm (accessed December 4, 2014).

Cowboy Lyrics.com, "Phil Ochs: Ringing of Revolution," http://www.cowboy-lyrics.com/lyrics/ochs-phil/ringing-of-revolution-11450.html#.T89_a8X-5p8 (accessed December 22, 2013).

Cover, Matt, CNS News.com, "30 Percent of Employers to Drop Health Coverage Because of Obamacare," June 7, 2011, http://www.cnsnews.com/news/article/30-percent-employers-drop-health-coverage-because-obamacare (accessed December 21, 2013).

Craughwell, Thomas J. with M. William Phelps, History News Network, "Failures of the Presidents: JFK's Bay of Pigs Disaster," http://hnn.us/article/55759 (accessed December 22, 2013).

Crumrin, Timothy, Conner Prairie, "Road Through the Wilderness: The Making of the National Road," http://www.connerprairie.org/Learn-And-Do/Indiana-History/America-1800-1860/The-National-Road.aspx (accessed December 22, 2013).

Cunningham, Paige Winfield, The Washington Times, "Paul: Obama health care more fascism than socialism," http://www.washingtontimes.com/blog/inside-politics/2011/nov/16/paul-obama-health-care-more-fascism-socialism/ (accessed December 26, 2013).

Daily Kos, "Bill Clinton: Elder Statesman to the World," http://www.dailykos.com/story/2009/09/24/785901/-Bill-Clinton-Elder-Statesman-to-the-World# (accessed December 29, 2013).

Daily News, "Obama's search for an enemy: The President keep beating the class warfare drum," March 7, 2009, http://www.nydailynews.com/opinion/obama-search-enemy-president-beating-class-warfare-drum-article-1.368969 (accessed December 10, 2014).

Daily Tracker, "Occupy Wall Street Shows People Want Democracy, Not Corporatocracy," http://finance.yahoo.com/blogs/daily-ticker/occupy-wall-street-shows-people-want-democracy-not-152011256.html (accessed July 27, 2014).

Dallas News, "Obama's road trip to Texas: make Ted Cruz-Republicans the face of Washington opposition," http://trailblazersblog.dallasnews.com/2013/05/obamas-road-trip-to-texas-make-ted-cruz-republicans-the-face-of-washington-opposition.html/ (accessed December 18, 2013).

Darling, Brian, Human Events, "The Balanced Budget Debate Begins," March 2, 2011, http://blog.heritage.org/2011/03/02/the-balanced-budget-debate-begins/ (accessed January 15, 2014).

_____, Human Events, "Your Guide to Budget Reconciliation and Obamacare," September 22, 2009, http://www.humanevents.com/2009/09/22/your-guide-to-budget-reconciliation-and-obamacare/ (accessed December 27, 2013).

Daudani, Ray, NBC 12, "10,000 dead found on Virginia voter rolls," August 14, 2012, http://www.nbc12.com/story/19237542/10000-dead-found-on-virginias-voter-rolls (accessed December 22, 2013).

Dave Manuel.com, "A History of Surpluses and Deficits in the United States," December 23, 2013, http://www.davemanuel.com/history-of-deficits-and-surpluses-in-the-united-states.php (accessed December 23, 2013).

Davenport, David, Forbes, "President Obama's Executive Power End Run Around The Constitution," January 16, 2013, http://www.forbes.com/sites/daviddavenport/2013/01/16/president-obamas-executive-power-end-run-around-the-constitution/ (accessed December 18, 2013).

Dawson, Lindsey, Grown Ups.com, "What is a Trillion Anyway," http://www.grownups.co.nz/read/lifestyle/entertainment/lindsey-dawson-trillion (accessed January 15, 2014).

Day, Rebecca, "'SLOWLY I TURNED': A PIECE OF AMERICA'S POP CULTURE," http://www.niagarafallsreporter.com/slowly.html (accessed December 27, 2013).

Dayen, David, FDL, "Obama Asserts Authority for Libya Mission Without Congressional Action," http://news.firedoglake.com/2011/03/21/obama-asserts-authority-for-libya-mission-without-congressional-action/ (accessed February 14, 2014).

Deadline News.com, "Two More Years of 4% Interest Rates?" http://www.deadlinenews.com/2012/02/24/two-more-years-of-4-interest-rates/ (accessed December 23, 2013).

Declaration of Independence, http://www.ushistory.org/declaration/document/ (accessed December 18, 2013).

Delegge, Ron, EFF Guide, "Will U.S. Public Debt Reach $22 Trillion by Feb. 2014?," October 23, 2013, http://archive.etfguide.com/commentary/1138/Will-U.S.-Public-Debt-Reach-$22-Trillion-by-Feb.-2014/ (accessed February 4, 2014).

DeMar, Gary, The Political Outcast, "How Liberals Captured the Nation through 'Free' Education," http://politicaloutcast.com/2012/12/how-liberals-captured-the-nation-through-free-education/ (accessed December 27, 2013).

Democracy In America Alexis de Tocqueville 1831, "Chapter XIII: Government Of The Democracy In America – Part I," http://www.marxists.org/reference/archive/de-tocqueville/democracy-america/ch13.htm (accessed July 27, 2014)

Democracy Reform, "Did America's Founders want Democracy?" http://democracyreform.blogspot.com/2006/11/did-americas-founders-want-democracy.html (accessed December 24, 2014).

De Vogue, Ariane, ABC News, "Arizona Immigration Law: Enforcement Blocked by Circuit Court," April 11, 2011, http://abcnews.go.com/Politics/arizona-immigration-law-enforcement-blocked-circuit-court/story?id=13350124 (accessed December 27, 2013).

Deziel, Chris, SF Gate, "The Federal Regulations on Toilet Gallons," http://homeguides.sfgate.com/federal-regulations-toilet-gallons-88640.html (accessed December 2, 2014).

Diamond, Dan, Forbes, "Why The 'Real' Unemployment Rate Is Higher Than You Think," July 5, 2013, http://www.forbes.com/sites/dandiamond/2013/07/05/why-the-real-unemployment-rate-is-higher-than-you-think/ (accessed February 4, 2014).

Dictionary.com, "Rube Goldberg," http://dictionary.reference.com/browse/rube+goldberg (accessed December 9, 2014).

DirectorBlue, Hotair, "DemCare: a tidal wave of regulations, taxes, fees, bureaucracies, waiting lines, bankruptcies and seniors denied medical care are on the way," March 28, 2010, http://hotair.com/greenroom/archives/2010/03/28/demcare-a-tidal-wave-of-regulations-taxes-fees-beauracracies-waiting-lines-bankruptcies-and-seniors-denied-medical-care-are-on-the-way/ (accessed December 22, 2013).

Discover the Networks.org, "Saul Alinsky," http://www.discoverthenetworks.org/individualProfile.asp?indid=2314 (accessed December 27, 2013).

Do One Thing: Quotes for a Better World," Rule of Law Quotes: Aristotle, "The only stable state is the one in which all men are equal before the law," http://www.doonething.org/quotes/law-quotes.htm (accessed December 23, 2013).

Douthat, Ross, New York Times, "Going for Bolingbroke," July 27, 2013, http://www.nytimes.com/2013/07/28/opinion/sunday/douthat-going-for-bolingbroke.html?_r=2& (accessed December 18, 2013).

Drexel University, Constitution of the United States, Amendment X, http://www.drexel.edu/usconstitution/billOfRights/amendment10/ (accessed December 18, 2013).

_____, Constitution of the United States, Preamble to the Bill of Rights, http://www.drexel.edu/usconstitution/billOfRights/preamble/ (accessed December 18, 2013).

Drucker, Peter F., The Atlantic Online, "Really Reinventing Government," February 1995, http://www.theatlantic.com/past/politics/polibig/reallyre. htm (accessed December 22, 2013).

Duncan, Kevin, The Daily Caller, "The Growing Regulatory State," http://dailycaller.com/2011/10/20/the-growing-regulatory-state/ (accessed December 23, 2013).

Dunn, J.R., American Thinker, "Liberalism and Mass Shootings,: November 9, 2013, http://www.americanthinker.com/2013/09/liberalism_and_mass_shootings.html (accessed December 18, 2013).

Durden, Tyler, End of America, "Thought Experiment: Why Obama Wants The Fiscal Cliff," December 12, 2012, http://www.zerohedge.com/news/2012-12-05/guest-post-thought-experiment-why-obama-wants-fiscal-cliff (accessed December 30, 2013).

DW, "Hoping for Ukrainian protest success in Belarus," http://www.dw.de/hoping-for-ukrainian-protest-success-in-belarus/a-17434895 (accessed July 27, 2014).

EconBrowser, "Return to the gold standard," September 1, 2012, http://www.econbrowser.com/archives/2012/09/return_to_the_g. html (accessed December 20, 2013).

Economic expert.com, "Equality of Outcome," http://www.economicexpert. com/a/Equality:of:outcome.html (accessed December 11, 2014).

Eichier, Alexander, Huffington Post, "46 Percent of Americans Exempt From Federal Income Tax in 2011," June 28, 2011, http://www.huffingtonpost. com/2011/06/28/46-percent-of-americans-e_n_886293.html (accessed December 26, 2013).

Eisenhower, Dwight, "Military-Industrial Complex Speech, Dwight D. Eisenhower, 1961," http://www.h-net.org/~hst306/documents/indust.html (accessed December 22, 2013).

Eland, Ivan, The Cato Institute, "The U.S. Military: Overextended Overseas," July 24, 1998, http://www.cato.org/publications/commentary/us-military-overextended-overseas (accessed December 26, 2013).

Electronic frontier Foundation, "Timeline of NSA Domestic Spying," https://www.eff.org/nsa-spying/timeline (accessed December 2, 2014).

Elfenbein, Eddy, Crossing Wall Street, "24 Scary Facts About the U.S. Economy," October 13, 2010, http://www.crossingwallstreet.com/archives/2010/10/24-scary-facts-about-the-u-s-economy.html (accessed December 22, 2013).

Ellerson, Lindsey, ABC News.com, "President Obama Continues Questionable "You Can Keep Your Health Care" Promise," July 16, 2010, http://abcnews.go.com/blogs/politics/2009/07/president-obama-continues-questionable-you-can-keep-your-health-care-promise/ (accessed December 21, 2013).

Encyclopedia Britannica, "Annapolis Convention," http://www.britannica.com/EBchecked/topic/26190/Annapolis-Convention (accessed February 5, 2014).

_____, "Democratic-Republican Party," http://www.britannica.com/EBchecked/topic/498833/Democratic-Republican-Party (accessed December 28, 2013).

_____, "Social Democracy," http://www.britannica.com/EBchecked/topic/551073/social-democracy (accessed January 29, 2014).

_____, "The Monroe Doctrine," http://www.britannica.com/EBchecked/topic/390243/Monroe-Doctrine (accessed December 22, 2013).

_____, "The Wars of Independence," http://www.britannica.com/EBchecked/topic/331694/history-of-Latin-America/60878/The-wars-of-independence-1808-26 (accessed January 15, 2014).

Encyclopedia of the New American Nation, "Judiciary Power and Practice - War and the courts," http://www.americanforeignrelations.com/E-N/Judiciary-Power-and-Practice-War-and-the-courts.html (accessed December 22, 2013).

Englund, Eric, Lew Rockwell.com, "The Federal Reserve Has Destroyed the Meaning of Saving," September 7, 2001, http://www.lewrockwell.com/2001/09/eric-englund/the-fed-corrupts-everything/ (accessed January 11, 2014).

Equality of Opportunity and Equality of Outcome, http://www.ourcivilisation.com/cooray/btof/chap20.htm (accessed December 18, 2013).

Ertelt, Steven, LifeNews.com, "Planned Parenthood Gets $363M in Tax Money, Abortions Rise," December 16, 2010, http://www.lifenews.com/2010/12/16/planned-parenthood-gets-363m-in-tax-money-abortions-rise/ (accessed February 18, 2014).

_____, "54,559,615 Abortions Since Roe vs. Wade Decision in 1973," January 23, 2012, http://www.lifenews.com/2012/01/23/54559615-abortions-since-roe-vs-wade-decision-in-1973/ (accessed December 22, 2013).

_____, LifeNews.com, "Obama Administration Accused of Targeting Peaceful Pro-life Advocate," May, 17, 2011, http://www.lifenews.com/2011/05/17/obama-admin-accused-of-targeting-peaceful-pro-life-advocate/ (accessed December 29, 2013).

Everyone around the World says; Socialism WORKS!», http://www.paoracle.com/SocialismWORKS!/index.php?sw=Fascist%20Italy (accessed December 31, 2013).

Examiner.com, "The Taft-Roosevelt Rift: Taft the Trust Buster," December 15, 2010, http://www.examiner.com/article/the-taft-roosevelt-rift-taft-the-trust-buster (accessed December 22, 2013).

Excerpts from Christopher Columbus' Log, 1492 A.D., http://www.franciscan-archive.org/columbus/opera/excerpts.html (accessed December 18, 2013).

Excerpt from Essay No. 1 by Brutus, "FEDERALIST POWER WILL ULTI-MATELY SUBVERT STATE AUTHORITY" http://www.ucs.louisiana.edu/~ras2777/conlaw/antfed17.html (accessed December 23, 2013).

FactCheck.org, "Who Caused the Economic Crisis?," http://www.factcheck.org/2008/10/who-caused-the-economic-crisis/ (accessed December 27, 2013).

_____, "IRS Officials Misled Congress, Public," May 21, 2013, http://www.factcheck.org/2013/05/irs-officials-misled-congress-public/ (accessed July 30, 2014).

Faier, Brian, Bloomberg Business Weekly, "Obama Payroll Tax Cuts Seen Undermining Social Security," December 9, 2011, http://www.businessweek.com/news/2011-12-09/obama-payroll-tax-cuts-seen-undermining-social-security.html (accessed December 26, 2013).

Fairchild, Mary, About.com, "Compare Matthew's Genealogy to Luke's Genealogy of Jesus Christ," http://christianity.about.com/od/biblefactsandlists/a/jesusgenealogy.htm (accessed December 23, 2013).

Faith and Freedom Network and Foundation, "President Obama Is 'Managing The Decline Of America,'" February 22, 2010, http://blog.faithandfreedom.us/2010/02/president-obama-is-managing-decline-of.html#.UryuV7RzY-qM (accessed December 26, 2013).

Famous Quotes, http://www.larrywillis.com/quotes.html (accessed December 18, 2013).

_____, Alexander Fraser Tyler, http://www.famousquotessite.com/famous-quotes-6934-alexander-fraser-tyler-cycle-of-democracy-1770.html (accessed July 27, 2014).

Farmelant, Scott, Philadelphia City Paper, "Dead Men Can Vote," http://archives.citypaper.net/articles/101295/article009.shtml (accessed December 24, 2013).

Farrell, Paul B., Market watch, "The Real Crash is dead ahead as 2008 is forgotten," http://www.marketwatch.com/story/the-real-crash-is-dead-ahead-as-2008-is-forgotten-2012-07-31 (accessed December 23, 2013).

Federalist No. 62, James Madison, http://www.constitution.org/fed/federa62.htm (accessed December 23, 2013).

FederalReserveEducation.org, "The History of the Federal Reserve," http://www.federalreserveeducation.org/about-the-fed/history/ (accessed December 21, 2013).

Fedrico, P. J., Heinonline, "Colonial Monopolies and Patents," http://heinonline.org/HOL/LandingPage?collection=journals&handle=hein.journals/jpatos11&div=76&id=&page (accessed December 22, 2013).

Fenhoz, Tim, National Journal, "CBO Says Budget Deal Will Cut Spending by Only $352 Million This Year," April 13, 2011, http://www.nationaljournal.com/budget/cbo-says-budget-deal-will-cut-spending-by-only-352-million-this-year-20110413 (accessed January 15, 2014).

Ferrara, Peter, Forbes, "A Budget Cutting Deal That Boosts Federal Spending," August 4, 2011, http://www.forbes.com/sites/peterferrara/2011/08/04/a-budget-cutting-deal-that-boosts-federal-spending/ (accessed December 27, 2013).

Final Vote Results for Roll Call 887, November, 7, 2009, http://clerk.house.gov/evs/2009/roll887.xml (accessed December 27, 2013).

Find Law, second Amendment, http://constitution.findlaw.com/amendment2/amendment.html (accessed December 18, 2013).

Franc, Michael, The heritage Foundation, "Beyond The $800 Hammer," http://www.heritage.org/research/commentary/2001/06/beyond-the-800-hammer (accessed December 18, 2013).

Finger, Richard, Forbes, "Homeland Security Secretary: 11 Million llegals Have «Earned The Right To Be Citizens». Oh Really?," http://www.forbes.com/sites/richardfinger/2014/01/28/3302/ (accessed July 30, 2014).

Five Colleges Archives& Manuscript Collections, "Frances Fox Piven," http://asteria.fivecolleges.edu/findaids/sophiasmith/mnsss52_bioghist.html (accessed December 27, 2013).

Folger, Janet, "24 Years of Abortion on Demand Based on Lies," http://www.pregnantpause.org/abort/lies.htm (accessed December 23, 2013).

Fordham University, "French Revolution," http://www.fordham.edu/halsall/mod/modsbook13.asp (accessed January 15, 2014).

Fox Nation, "Biden Flashback: Launching an Attack Without Congressional Approval Is an Impeachable Offense," http://nation.foxnews.com/libya/2011/03/23/biden-flashback-launching-attack-without-congressional-approval-impeachable-offense (accessed February 14, 2014).

_____, "Obama Jokes at Jobs Council: 'Shovel-Ready Was Not as Shovel-Ready as We Expected,'" http://nation.foxnews.com/president-obama/2011/06/13/obama-jokes-jobs-council-shovel-ready-was-not-shovel-ready-we-expected (accessed December 24, 2013).

Fox News.com, "A Brief Look at Candidate Obama's 2008 Campaign Promises," http://www.foxnews.com/politics/2011/04/05/brief-look-at-candidate-obama-2008-campaign-promises/ (accessed December 31, 2013).

_____, « Administration Warns of 'Command-and-Control' Regulation Over Emissions», http://www.foxnews.com/politics/2009/12/09/administration-warns-command-control-regulation-emissions/ (accessed December 9, 2014).

_____, "Do Kids Count? Insurers Stop Selling Child-Only Policies Ahead of ObamaCare Provisions", http://www.foxnews.com/politics/2010/09/22/major-insurers-stop-selling-child-policies-ahead-new-obamacare-provisions/ (accessed December 21, 2013).

_____, "Justice Department sues Florida over effort to purge voter rolls of non-citizens," http://www.foxnews.com/politics/2012/06/12/justice-department-sues-florida-over-purging-voter-rolls-as-expected/ (accessed December 24, 2013).

_____, "New Numbers: 4.2M Americans Dropped From Health Plans," http://foxnewsinsider.com/2013/11/07/how-many-americans-have-lost-their-health-insurance-under-obamacare (accessed July 30, 2014).

_____, "Social Security Plan Cutoff to Be 55," http://www.foxnews.com/story/2005/02/02/social-security-plan-cutoff-to-be-55/ (accessed December 20, 2013).

_____, "U.S. Offers Foreign Aid to Countries Holding Billions in Treasury Securities," June 3, 2011, http://www.foxnews.com/politics/2011/06/02/us-offers-foreign-aid-to-countries-holding-billions-in-treasury-securities/ (accessed December 23, 2013).

Fraser, Alison Acosta, The Foundry, "Chairman Ryan's Budget Resolution Changes America's Course," April 5, 2011, http://blog.heritage.org/2011/04/05/morning-bell-chairman-ryans-budget-resolution-changes-americas-course/ (accessed January 15, 2014).

Free Republic, "THE LORD ACTON - GENERAL LEE CORRESPONDENCE," http://www.freerepublic.com/focus/news/828843/posts (accessed January 2, 2014

Freeman, Colin, Nick Meo in Benghazi and Patrick Hennessy, The Telegraph, "Libya: Arab League calls for United Nations no-fly zone," http://www.telegraph.co.uk/news/worldnews/africaandindianocean/libya/8378392/Libya-Arab-League-calls-for-United-Nations-no-fly-zone.html (accessed February 14, 2014).

From the Roman Republic to the Roman Empire, http://www.international-relations.com/History/RepublictoEmpire.htm (accessed December 31, 2013).

FrontLine, http://www.pbs.org/wgbh/pages/frontline/shows/kosovo/etc/press.html (accessed February 14, 2014).

Fund, John, Real Clear Politics, "Obama's Affinity for Saul Alinsky." March 29, 2012, http://www.realclearpolitics.com/2012/03/29/obama039s_affinity_for_saul_alinsky_276330.html (accessed December 27, 2013).

Funny Quotes from Famous People, http://cmgm.stanford.edu/~lkozar/Famous_Quotes.html (accessed January 15, 2014).

Gabbay, Tiffany, The Blaze, "Indoctrination and Data Mining in Common Core: Here's Why America's Schools May Be in More Trouble Than You Think," http://www.theblaze.com/stories/2013/03/27/indoctrination-and-data-mining-in-common-core-heres-why-americas-schools-may-be-in-more-trouble-than-you-think/ (accessed December 2, 2014).

Galloway, Lana, "Obama's Libya Briefing to Congress: 'Involvement to Be a Matter of Days, Not Weeks,'" http://www.obamashitlist.com/2011/03/19/obama%E2%80%99s-libya-briefing-to-congress-%E2%80%9Cinvolvement-to-be-a-matter-of-days-not-weeks%E2%80%9D/ (accessed February 14, 2014).

Gallup, Americans believe in God, http://www.gallup.com/poll/147887/americans-continue-believe-god.aspx (accessed December 18, 2013).

Gandel, Joe, The Moderate Voice, "Obama Weekly Video Address: Tax Breaks for Millionaires and Billionaires Must Be On the Table in Debt Ceiling Talks," July 2, 2011, http://themoderatevoice.com/115208/obama-weekly-video-address-tax-breaks-for-millionaires-and-billionaires-must-be-on-the-table-in-debt-ceiling-talks/ (accessed February 18, 2014).

Garrett, Garet, Ludwig von Misis Institute, "The Revolution Was," January 26, 2008, http://mises.org/daily/2726 (accessed January 2, 2014).

Gary North's Specific Answers, The Bible mandates free market capitalism. It is anti-socialist, http://www.garynorth.com/public/department57.cfm (accessed December 18, 2013).

Gensert, William L., American Thinker, "The Transformational Tyrant," January 17, 2012, http://www.americanthinker.com/2012/01/the_transformational_tyrant.html (accessed December 26, 2013).

Geraghty, Jim, National Review Online, "The Alinsky Administration," May 14, 2009, http://www.nationalreview.com/articles/227500/alinsky-administration/jim-geraghty (accessed December 29, 2013).

Get a Quote a Day, Lenin Quotes, "The Capitalists will sell us the rope with which we will hang them," http://quotes.liberty-tree.ca/quotes_by/vladimir+ilyich+lenin (accessed December 23, 2013).

Ghei, Nita, The Washington Times, "The crony-capitalist triumph," July 20, 2011, http://www.washingtontimes.com/news/2011/jul/20/the-crony-capitalist-triumph/ (accessed December 2, 2014).

Gibson, Dave, Examiner.com, "Obama refuses to secure border, sues states for trying to protect themselves," August 4, 2011, http://www.examiner.com/article/obama-refuses-to-secure-border-sues-states-for-trying-to-protect-themselves (accessed January 11, 2014).

Gilani, Shah, Money Morning, "Federal Reserve Has Destroyed the Meaning of Saving," December, 15, 2012, http://moneymorning.com/2012/12/15/the-federal-reserves-magic-act-is-destroying-america/ (accessed January 11, 2014).

Gill, Kathy, AboutNews.com, "Oaths of Office for federal Officials," http://uspolitics.about.com/od/usgovernment/a/oaths_of_office_4.htm (accessed December 11, 2014).

Gill, N. S., About.com, "End of the Roman Republic," http://ancienthistory.about.com/od/romerepublic/p/endRepublic.htm (accessed December 23, 2013).

_____, "Octavius Becomes the First Roman Emperor Augustus Caesar," http://ancienthistory.about.com/od/augustusbio/a/aa092397Augustu.htm (accessed January 11, 2014).

GGA Quotes, "Constitution," http://giga-usa.com/quotes/topics/constitution_t001.htm (accessed December 21, 2013).

Glenn Beck, "List of Obama's Czars," August 21, 2009, http://www.glennbeck.com/content/articles/article/198/29391/ (accessed December 29, 2013).

_____, "Obama says if it's not fixed in 3 years I'm done," http://www.glennbeck.com/2012/02/02/flashback-obama-says-if-its-not-fixed-in-3-years-im-done/ (accessed December 31, 2013).

Global Research, "Who Owns the Federal Reserve?," http://www.globalresearch.ca/who-owns-the-federal-reserve/10489 (accessed December 21, 2013).

Global Security.org: Military, "Where are the Legions? [SPQR]Global Deployments of US Forces," http://www.globalsecurity.org/military/ops/global-deployments.htm (accessed December 23, 2013).

Goldberg, Jonah, National Review Online, "Wait, Is Malaise French for "Soft"?," September, 29, 2011, http://www.nationalreview.com/corner/278769/wait-malaise-french-soft-jonah-goldberg (accessed December 26, 2013).

Good Reads, "Alexis de Tocqueville quotes," http://www.goodreads.com/author/quotes/465.Alexis_de_Tocqueville (accessed December 26, 2013).

_____, "Ayn Rand Quotes," https://www.goodreads.com/author/quotes/432.Ayn_Rand (accessed November 2, -2014).

_____, "James Madison Quotes," http://www.goodreads.com/quotes/23893-the-powers-delegated-by-the-proposed-constitution-to-the-federal (accessed Documents 9, 2014).

_____, "Leon Trotsky Quotes," http://www.goodreads.com/quotes/319203-in-a-country-where-the-sole-employer-is-the-state (accessed December 10, 2014).

_____, "Margaret Thatcher Quotes," http://www.goodreads.com/author/quotes/198468.Margaret_Thatcher (accessed January 2. 2014).

_____, "Winston Churchill Quotes," http://www.goodreads.com/quotes/106588-if-you-will-not-fight-for-right-when-you-can (accessed December 9, 2014).

Google, GM is alive and Bin Laden is Dead, https://www.google.com/search?q=GM+is+alive+and+Bin+Laden+is+dead&client=firefox-a&hs=zaX&rls=org.mozilla:en-US:official&tbm=isch&tbo=u&source=univ&sa=X&ei=CRXYUonHI4-osASVi4G4BQ&ved=0CDUQsAQ&biw=1787&bih=813&dpr=0.9 (accessed July 30, 2014).

GOP.gov, "The Federal Reserve Pumps More Money," http://www.gop.gov/policy-news/12/09/13/the-federal-reserve-pumps-more (accessed January 2, 2014).

Gordon, David, Ludwig von Mises Institute, "Nazi Economic Policy," January 2, 2009, http://mises.org/daily/3274 (accessed December 27, 2013).

Graham, Peter, PBS News Hour, "Are Banks Borrowing from the Fed at Low Interest and Making Money Buying U.S. Treasuries?," http://www.pbs.org/newshour/businessdesk/2010/05/are-banks-borrowing-from-the-f.html (accessed December 22, 2013).

Great Seal, http://greatseal.com/mottoes/unum.html (accessed February 7, 2014).

Greenstein, Tracey, Forbes, "The Fed's $16 Trillion Bailouts Under-Reported," September 20, 2011, http://www.forbes.com/sites/traceygreenstein/2011/09/20/the-feds-16-trillion-bailouts-under-reported/ (accessed December 12, 2011)

Greszler, Rachel and Romina Boccia, The Heritage Foundation, "Social Security Trustees Report: Unfunded Liability Increased $1.1 Trillion and Projected Insolvency in 2033," August 4, 2014, http://www.heritage.org/research/reports/2014/08/social-security-trustees-report-unfunded-liability-increased-11-trillion-and-projected-insolvency-in-2033 (accessed December 3, 2014).

Grove, Andy, Bloomberg Business Week Magazine, "How America can Create Jobs," July 1, 2010, http://www.businessweek.com/magazine/content/10_28/b4186048358596.htm (accessed December 22, 2013).

Guido, Jessica, NBC 5 Chicago, "Controversial Professor Bill Ayers Speaks With Occupy Chicago Protesters," November 17, 2011, http://www.nbcchicago.com/news/local/Controversial-Professor-Bill-Ayers-Speaks-With-Occupy-Chicago-Protestors--134045388.html?dr (accessed December 26, 2013).

Hahn, Michael, Lexis Nexis, "The Conflict in Kosovo: A Constitutional War?" https://litigation-essentials.lexisnexis.com/webcd/app?action=DocumentDisplay&crawlid=1&doctype=cite&docid=89+Geo.+L.J.+2351&srctype=smi&srcid=3B15&key=05e43c2b719ed5f4902c926ae18bd620 (accessed February 14, 2014).

Hall, Mike, AFL-CIO, "Union Movement Opens 'Arms and Hearts' to Occupy Wall Street Activists," October 9, 2011, http://www.aflcio.org/Blog/Corporate-Greed/Union-Movement-Opens-Arms-and-Hearts-to-Occupy-Wall-Street-Activists (accessed December 27, 2013).

Halper, Daniel, The Weekly Standard, "U.S. Spent $3.7 Trillion on Welfare Over Last 5 Years," October 23, 2013, http://www.weeklystandard.com/blogs/report-us-spent-37-trillion-welfare-over-last-5-years_764582.html (accessed December 4, 2014).

Hamilton, Alexander, "ARGUMENTS FOR THE CREATION OF A NATIONAL BANK," http://american_almanac.tripod.com/forbank.htm (accessed December 21, 2013).

——————————, "Second Report to Congress," http://american_almanac.tripod.com/hambank.htm (accessed December 21, 2013).

Hawkins, Awr, Brietbart, "Stimulus Money: A Slush Fund for Unions and Democrats," http://www.breitbart.com/Big-Government/2012/05/04/stimulus-money-a-slush-fund-for-unions-and-democrats (accessed December 31, 2013).

Hawkins, John, Town Hall.com, "The 40 Greatest Quotes From Winston Churchill," http://townhall.com/columnists/johnhawkins/2013/01/19/the-40-greatest-quotes-from-winston-churchill-n1492794/page/full (accessed December 2, 2014).

Hayek, F. A., The Constitution of Liberty, "True Coercion," http://books.google.com/books?id=nh_ZYYZJj8C&pg=PA79&lpg=PA79&dq=hayek+True+coercion+occurs+when+armed+bands+of+conquerors&source=bl&ots=KmFVhd2bjk&sig=GIZEZTjVF7D8SC8oToCWF08wN0I&hl=en&sa=X&ei=TCkPU-NG6fl2QW434GoAQ&ved=0CC4Q6AEwAg#v=onepage&q=hayek%20True%20coercion%20occurs%20when%20armed%20bands%20of%20conquerors&f=false (accessed December 10, 2014).

Hays, Don, The Hill, "THERE ARE NO CUTS! – The fallacy of baseline budgeting," http://thehill.com/blogs/congress-blog/economy-a-budget/195099-there-are-no-cuts-the-fallacy-of-baseline-budgeting (accessed December 27, 2013).

Hedgecock, Roger, U-T San Diego, "Suppressing the Military Vote," July 24, 2012, http://www.utsandiego.com/news/2012/jul/24/suppressing-the-military-vote/ (accessed December 24, 2013).

Helderman, Rosalind S., The Washington Post, "Democratic, Republican payroll tax cut extension plans both blocked by Senate," December 8, 2011, http://www.washingtonpost.com/blogs/2chambers/post/democratic-republican-payroll-tax-cut-extension-plans-both-blocked-by-senate/2011/12/08/gIQAmRzvfO_blog.html (accessed December 26, 2013).

HelpMe.com, "Upton Sinclair's The Jungle as Socialist Propaganda," http://www.123helpme.com/view.asp?id=16385 (accessed December 20, 2013).

Heritage Guide to the Constitution, "Guarantee Clause," http://www.heritage.org/constitution/#!/articles/4/essays/128/guarantee-clause (accessed January 11, 2014).

_____, "Origination Clause," http://www.heritage.org/constitution/#!/articles/1/essays/30/origination-clause (accessed December 27, 2013).

Hester, Wesley P., Times Dispatch, "Romney camp asks Va. to probe voter forms," July 25, 2012, http://www.timesdispatch.com/news/update-romney-camp-asks-va-to-probe-voter-forms/article_46e1b142-4c67-569a-b9c6-4ff2edca7d27.html (accessed December 24, 2013).

Higgs, Robert, The Independent Institute, "How War Amplified Federal Power in the Twentieth Century," July 1, 1999, http://www.independent.org/publications/article.asp?id=113 (accessed December 22, 2013).

Hillyer, Quinn, The American Spectator, "Alinsky to Obama to Occupiers," October 21, 2011, http://spectator.org/articles/36719/alinsky-obama-occupiers (accessed January 15, 2014).

History.com, "The Nuremberg Trials," http://www.history.com/topics/world-war-ii/nuremberg-trials (accessed July 30, 2014).

History.com: This Day in History, "Andrew Jackson shuts down Second Bank of the U.S.," http://www.history.com/this-day-in-history/andrew-jackson-shuts-down-second-bank-of-the-us (accessed December 24, 2013).

————————————————————, Calvin Coolidge, http://www.history.com/topics/calvin-coolidge (accessed December 22, 2013).

————————————————————, "Truman delivers his Fair Deal speech," http://www.history.com/this-day-in-history/truman-delivers-his-fair-deal-speech (accessed December 22, 2013).

History Central.com, "Indian Removal Act," http://www.historycentral.com/Indians/RemovalAct.html (accessed December 22, 2013).

History Learning Place, "Voting Patterns in America," http://www.historylearningsite.co.uk/voting_patterns_in_america.htm (accessed July 27, 2014).

History Matters, "Making the World "Safe for Democracy": Woodrow Wilson Asks for War," http://historymatters.gmu.edu/d/4943/ (accessed December 23, 2013).

History Net.com, "Indian Removal Act," http://www.historynet.com/indian-removal-act (accessed December 22, 2013).

History News Network: Quotes about History, http://hnn.us/article/1328 (accessed January 6, 2014).

History of the Taliban, http://www-pub.naz.edu/~aamghar6/History%20of%20the%20Taliban.htm (accessed December 27, 2013).

History Wired, "Not worth a Continental," http://historywired.si.edu/object.cfm?ID=437 (accessed December 24, 2013).

History Wiz, "Napoleon as First Consul," http://www.historywiz.com/consul.htm (accessed November 24, 2014).

Hoft, Jim, Gateway Pundit, "CBO Finds Obama Stimulus May Have Cost As Much as $4.1 Million Per Job," June 5, 2012, http://www.thegatewaypundit.com/2012/06/cbo-finds-obama-stimulus-may-have-cost-as-much-as-4-1-million-per-job/ (accessed December 24, 2013).

Holan, Angie Drobnic, Politifact, "Lie of the Year: 'If you like your health care plan, you can keep it,'" December 12, 2013, http://www.politifact.com/truth-o-meter/article/2013/dec/12/lie-year-if-you-like-your-health-care-plan-keep-it/ (accessed January 2, 2014).

Hook, Janet and Kristina Peterson, The wall Street journal, "Congress Passes Debt, Budget Deal," October 18, 2013, http://online.wsj.com/news/articles/SB10001424052702303680404579139212598765046 (accessed February 4, 2014).

Horney, James R., Center for Budget and Policy Priorities, "Republican Proposal To Pay For Payroll Tax Extension Would Increase Already Severe Cuts In Discretionary Programs," December 2, 2011, http://www.cbpp.org/cms/?fa=view&id=3633 (accessed December 26, 2013).

Horowitz, Carl, National Legal and Policy Center, "HUD Still Funds ACORN Affiliate Despite Ban" July 19, 2011, http://nlpc.org/stories/2011/07/19/hud-still-funds-acorn-housing-affiliate-despite-ban (accessed February 18, 2014).

Hot Air, "Obama's answer on experience: But I'm such a great campaigner!," September 2, 2008, http://hotair.com/archives/2008/09/02/obamas-answer-on-experience-but-im-such-a-great-campaigner/ (accessed December 9, 2014).

How Stuff Works, "Alien and Sedition Act," http://history.howstuffworks.com/revolutionary-war/alien-and-sedition-act.htm (accessed December 22, 2013).

Howley, Patrick, The daily caller, "Justice Department facilitated anti-Zimmerman protests," July 10, 2013, http://dailycaller.com/2013/07/10/doj-provided-security-for-anti-zimmerman-protests/ (accessed January 11, 2014).

Huffington Post, "Masoud Jazayeri, Iran General, Calls Wall Street Protest American Spring," http://www.huffingtonpost.com/2011/10/09/masoud-jazayeri-wall-street_n_1002598.html (accessed December 27, 2013).

_____, "NSA Admits Listening To U.S. Phone Calls Without Warrants," June 15, 2013, http://www.huffingtonpost.com/2013/06/15/nsa-phone-calls-warrants_n_3448075.html (accessed January 11, 2014).

Hughes, Brian, Washington Examiner, "Fight brewing over Social Security benefits for illegal immigrants," November 29, 2014, http://www.washingtonexaminer.com/fight-brewing-over-social-security-and-medicare-for-illegal-immigrants/article/2556750 (accessed December 3, 2014).

Human Events, "Obama Sues Arizona, Gives Sanctuary to Law Breakers," July 26, 2010, http://www.humanevents.com/2010/07/26/obama-sues-arizona-gives-sanctuary-to-lawbreakers/ (accessed December 29, 2013).

Humorous Quotes, Bill Clinton, "Character doesn't matter," http://gopcapital-ist.tripod.com/stupidquotes.html#character (accessed February 12, 2014).

Huston, Warner Todd, Publius Forum, "East St. Louis: More Voters Registered Than Citizens That Live There," March 28, 2011, http://www.chica-gonow.com/publius-forum/2011/04/east-st-louis-more-voters-registered-than-citizens-that-live-there/ (accessed December 24, 2013).

_____, News Busters, "Indiana: More Registered to Vote Than Eligible, Media Misses Story," http://newsbusters.org/blogs/warner-todd-huston/2008/10/09/indiana-more-registered-vote-eligible-media-misses-story (accessed December 24, 2013).

Hyak, F. A., "What distinguishes the Soviet system from all other despotic governments" http://books.google.com/books?id=ENQjPm-S7U EC&pg=PA351&lpg=PA351&dq=hyak+What+distinguishes+the+Sovi et+system+from+all+other+despotic+governments&source=bl&ots=l GrbneJkdO&sig=Cb9sT56UrYk6IA13Y8UgCBI8LrA&hl=en&sa=X&e i=1PUzVNnKE4P6yATu9ILQCA&ved=0CCAQ6AEwAA#v=onepage &q=hyak%20What%20distinguishes%20the%20Soviet%20system%20 from%20all%20other%20despotic%20governments&f=false (accessed December 2, 2014).

HyperHistpory.com, "Louis XIV," http://www.hyperhistory.com/online_n2/ people_n2/persons6_n2/louis.html (accessed December 23, 2013).

Imbriale, Kenneth S., "A Brief Examination of the Legality of Secession in the United States," http://www.historyvortex.org/LegalitySecession.html (accessed December 22, 2013).

InfoPlease, "John F. Kennedy's Inaugural Address," http://www.infoplease. com/ipa/A0878607.html (accessed December 18, 2013).

_____, "The Persian Gulf War. http://www.infoplease.com/ipa/ A0001293.html (accessed February 14, 2014).

I Go Pogo, "I have met the enemy and he is us," http://www.igopogo.com/ we_have_met.htm (accessed December 20, 2013).

Info Please.com, "Fabian Society," http://www.infoplease.com/encyclopedia/ history/fabian-society.html (accessed December 9, 2014).

International Business Times, "Fistful of Dollars: How the Federal Reserve destroyed America," May 1, 2011, http://www.ibtimes.com/fist-ful-dollars-how-federal-reserve-destroyed-america-211927 (accessed January 11, 2014).

_____, "Justice Dept. Tells Pa. Its Voter ID Law Is Under Investigation," July 23-2012, http://www.ibtimes.com/justice-dept-tells-pa-its-voter-id-law-under-investigation-730237 (accessed December 24, 2013).

Internet Encyclopedia of Philosophy, "Social Contract theory," http://www.iep.utm.edu/soc-cont/ (accessed December 18, 2013).

_____, "Virtue Ethics," http://www.iep.utm.edu/virtue/ (accessed February 4, 2014).

Investopedia, "Business Cycle," http://www.investopedia.com/terms/b/businesscycle.asp#axzz1ZLhdVkIq (accessed December 21, 2013).

_____, "Definition of 'Invisible Hand,'" http://www.investopedia.com/terms/i/invisiblehand.asp (accessed January 2, 2014).

_____, "Dirty Float," http://www.investopedia.com/terms/d/dirty-float.asp (accessed December 18, 2013).

_____, "Mixed Economic System," http://www.investopedia.com/terms/m/mixed-economic-system.asp (accessed December 18, 2013).

_____, "Quantitative Easing," http://www.investopedia.com/terms/q/quantitative-easing.asp#axzz1xlltQbSk (accessed December 24, 2013).

_____, "Smithsonian Agreement," http://www.investopedia.com/terms/s/smithsonian-agreement.asp (accessed December 18, 2013).

_____, The Federal Reserve: Introduction, February 25, 2009, http://www.investopedia.com/university/thefed/#axzz1XM8i0e4c (accessed December 26, 2013).

_____, "Troubled Asset Relief Program – TARP," http://www.investopedia.com/terms/t/troubled-asset-relief-program-tarp.asp#axzz1mYhRb3H0 (accessed December 31, 2013).

Investors.com, "Arpaio Unjustly in Justice Department Crosshairs," December 16, 2011, http://news.investors.com/ibd-editorials/121611-595048-arpaio-arizona-immigration-border-sb1070-panthers-.htm (accessed December 29, 2013).

_____, "Justice Department Encourages Voter Fraud The Chicago Way," http://news.investors.com/ibd-editorials/060112-613434-justice-department-promotes-voter-fraud-in-florida.htm?p=full (accessed December 24, 2013).

_____, "Wasted Stimulus," August 16, 2011, http://news.investors.com/ibd-editorials/081611-581654-wasted-stimulus.htm (accessed January 2, 2013).

Investor's Insights.com, "Government Takeover Revisited," http://www.investorsinsight.com/blogs/forecasts_trends/archive/2010/07/27/financial-reform-or-government-takeover-revisited.aspx (accessed December 22, 2013).

Jackson, Brooks, USA Today, "Obama's Supreme Court remarks," April 5, 2012, http://usatoday30.usatoday.com/news/washington/story/2012-04-04/fact-check-obama-court-unprecedented/54004040/1 (accessed December 27, 2013).

Jackson, David, The Oval, "Biden: Bin Laden is dead, General Motors is alive," April 26, 2012, http://content.usatoday.com/communities/theoval/post/2012/04/biden-bin-laden-dead-gm-is-alive/1#.UsWrr7RzYqN (accessed January 2, 2014).

_____, "Obama Still Thinks 9/11 Suspects Should be Tried in New York," April 17, 2011, http://content.usatoday.com/communities/theoval/post/2011/04/obama-still-thinks-911-suspects-should-be-tried-in-federal-court/1#.UsBCjLRzYqM (accessed December 29, 2013).

Jackson, Henry C., Washington Times, "Texas, Justice Department square off over voter ID law," http://www.washingtontimes.com/news/2012/jul/9/texas-justice-square-off-over-voter-id-law/ (accessed December 24, 2013).

Jayson, Sharon, USA Today, "More Kids Born out of Wedlock," http://usatoday30.usatoday.com/NEWS/usaedition/2012-04-12-Cohabiting---with-kids---_ST_U.htm (accessed February 4, 2014).

Jeffrey, Terence P., CNS News.com, "49% of Americans Get Gov't Benefits; 82M in Households on Medicaid," October 23, 2013, http://cnsnews.com/news/article/terence-p-jeffrey/census-49-americans-get-gov-t-benefits-82m-households-medicaid (accessed February 4, 2014).

_____, "Obama Has Now Increased Debt More than All Presidents from George Washington Through George H.W. Bush Combined," October 5, 2011, http://cnsnews.com/news/article/obama-has-now-increased-debt-more-all-presidents-george-washington-through-george-hw (accessed December 31, 2013).

JFK Experience, "Favorite JFK Quotes," http://www.jfkexperience.com/jfk-resources/favorite-jfk-quotes/ (accessed December 20, 2013).

Jakarta Globe, "Hu Jintao's Visit Ends Any Dreams of the US and China Sharing the World Stage," January 25, 2011, http://www.thejakartaglobe.com/archive/hu-jintaos-visit-ends-any-dreams-of-the-us-and-china-sharing-the-world-stage/418948/ (accessed January 9, 2014).

Joe Clarke.net, Al Sharpton, May 15, 2012, http://www.joeclarke.net/2010/05/al-sharpton-demands-that-everything.html (accessed December 18, 2013).

John Petrie's Collection of Winston Churchill Quotes, http://jpetrie.myweb. uga.edu/bulldog.html (accessed December 18, 2013).

Johnson, Haynes, Washington Post, "Carter Is Sworn In as President, Asks 'Fresh Faith in Old Dream," January 21, 1977, http://www.washingtonpost. com/wp-srv/national/longterm/inaug/history/stories/carter77.htm (accessed December 22, 2013).

Joyce, Helen, Plus Magazine, "Adam Smith and the invisible hand," http://plus.maths. org/content/adam-smith-and-invisible-hand (accessed December 21, 2013).

Judicial Watch, "New Documents Show IRS HQ Control of Tea Party Targeting" May 14, 2014, http://www.judicialwatch.org/press-room/press-releases/judicial-watch-new-documents-show-irs-hq-control-tea-party-targeting/ (accessed July 30, 2014).

_____, "Uncovers Documents from DHS Detailing Obama Plan to Impose DREAM Act by Suspending Illegal Alien Deportations," http:// www.judicialwatch.org/press-room/press-releases/jw-uncovers-documents-dhs-detailing-obama-plan-impose-dream-act-suspending-illegal-ali/ (accessed December 2, 2014).

Jutia Group, "Banks Biggest Buyers of U.S. Treasury Securities: Bank of America "«(NYSE: BAC), JPMorgan Chase (NYSE: JPM), Citigroup (NYSE: C), Wells Fargo (NYSE: WFC)," November 3, 2009, http://jutiagroup.com/20091103-banks-biggest-buyers-of-u-s-treasury-securities-bank-of-america-nyse-bac-jpmorgan-chase-nyse-jpm-citigroup-nyse-c-wells-fargo-nyse-wfc/ (accessed December 22, 2013).

Kakutani, Michiko, New York Time: Books, "The Evolution of Al Qaeda and the Intertwining Paths Leading to 9/11," http://www.nytimes.com/2006/08/01/books/01kaku.html?pagewanted=all&_r=0&gwh=BF4D89E00EE004B8C7C7E58E5A38F7AA&gwt=pay (accessed December 23, 2013).

Kelly, Martin, About.com "Jefferson and the Louisiana Purchase," http:// americanhistory.about.com/od/thomasjefferson/a/tj_lapurchase.htm (accessed December 22, 2013).

_____, About.com, "Lincoln Suspended the Writ of Habeas Corpus," http://americanhistory.about.com/b/2010/10/23/lincoln-suspended-the-writ-of-habeas-corpus.htm (accessed December 21, 2013).

_____, About.com, "Marbury v. Madison," http://americanhistory. about.com/od/judicialbranch/p/marbury.htm (accessed December 4, 2014).

_____, About.com, "Separation of Powers," http://americanhistory.about. com/od/usconstitution/g/sep_of_powers.htm (accessed January 29, 2014).

Kennedy and the New frontier, http://countrystudies.us/united-states/history-120.htm (accessed December 18, 2013).

Kenny, Thomas, About.com, "What is the Fiscal Cliff?," http://bonds.about.com/od/Issues-in-the-News/a/What-Is-The-Fiscal-Cliff.htm (accessed December 20, 2013).

Kerpen, Phil, the daily Caller, "Obama's illegal NLRB appointments are even more outrageous than his appointment of Cordray," January 6, 2012, http://dailycaller.com/2012/01/06/obama-illegal-nlrb-appointments-even-more-outrageous-than-cordray-appointment/ (accessed December 29, 2013).

Kessler, Glenn, The Washington Post, "Obama's royal flip-flop on using executive action on illegal immigration," http://www.washingtonpost.com/blogs/fact-checker/wp/2014/11/18/obamas-flip-flop-on-using-executive-action-on-illegal-immigration/ (accessed December 8, 2014).

Klein, Ezra, The Washington Post, "For some conservatives, even Ryan does not go far enough," March 22, 2012, http://www.washingtonpost.com/blogs/wonk-blog/post/wonkbook-for-some-conservatives-even-ryan-does-not-go-far-enough/2012/03/22/gIQAMIuSTS_blog.html (accessed December 23, 2013).

Klein, Peter G., Ludwig von Misses Institute, "Biography of F. A. Hyek 1899-1992," http://mises.org/page/1454/Biography-of-F-A-Hayek-18991992 (accessed December 22, 2013).

Klein, Rick, ABC News, "Democrats Seek to Own 'Occupy Wall Street' Movement," October 10, 2011, http://abcnews.go.com/Politics/democrats-seek-occupy-wall-street-movement/story?id=14701337 (accessed December 27, 2013).

Kline, Malcolm A., Accuracy in Media, "Progressive Segregation," http://www.aim.org/briefing/progressive-segregation/ (accessed December 21, 2013).

Klingebiel, Jacqueline, ABC News, "Obama: Mandate is Not a Tax," September 2, 2009, http://abcnews.go.com/blogs/politics/2009/09/obama-mandate-is-not-a-tax/ (accessed December 4, 2014).

Knickerbocker, Brad, The Christian Science Monitor, "US leads 'Odyssey Dawn' initial attack on Libya," http://www.csmonitor.com/USA/Military/2011/0319/US-leads-Odyssey-Dawn-initial-attack-on-Libya (accessed February 14, 2014).

Knowledgerush, "William McKinley," http://www.knowledgerush.com/kr/encyclopedia/William_McKinley/ (accessed December 23, 2013).

Koffler, Keith, The Whitehouse Dossier, "Obama Imposes Partial Dream Act by Fiat," June 15, 2012, http://www.whitehousedossier.com/2012/06/15/obama-imposes-dream-act-fiat/ (accessed February 4, 2014).

Korean War Casualty Statistics, http://www.zzwave.com/cmfweb/history/krwarcost.html (accessed February 14, 2014).

Krauthammer, Charles, Real Clear Politics, "Obama's Plan to Transform America," December 12, 2008, http://www.realclearpolitics.com/articles/2008/12/obamas_plan_to_transform_ameri.html (accessed December 11, 2014).

KRUGMAN, PAUL, New York Times, "Green Shoots and Glimmers," April 16, 2009, http://www.nytimes.com/2009/04/17/opinion/17krugman.html?_r=1& (accessed December 20, 2013).

Kudlow, Larry, Real Clear Markets, "Unleash the Great American Energy Industry," march 31, 2011, http://www.realclearmarkets.com/articles/2011/03/31/unleash_the_great_american_energy_industry_98939.html (accessed December 26, 2013).

Kuligowski, Monte, American Thinker, "A Clear Danger: Obama, a 'Living Constitution,' and 'Positive Rights,'" http://www.americanthinker.com/2010/10/a_clear_danger_obama_a_living.html (accessed December 29, 2013).

Kumar, Anita, McClatchy DC: Watching Washington and the World, "Obama turning to executive power to get what he wants," March 19, 2013, http://www.mcclatchydc.com/2013/03/19/186309/obama-turning-to-executive-power.html (accessed December 2313).

Kurzweil Technologies, "A Brief Career Summary of Ray Kurzweil," http://www.kurzweiltech.com/aboutray.html (accessed December 9, 2014).

Laffer, Arthur, The Heritage Foundation, "The Laffer Curve: Past, Present, and Future," June 1, 2004, http://www.heritage.org/research/reports/2004/06/the-laffer-curve-past-present-and-future (accessed December 23, 2013).

Lamb, Henry, WND, "Defining 'social democracy,'" http://www.wnd.com/2002/03/13255/ (accessed December 20, 2013).

Landay, Jonathan S. and Marisa Taylor, McClatchy DC, 'Obama's plan to predict future leakers unproven, unlikely to work,' July 9, 2013, http://www.mcclatchydc.com/2013/07/09/196211/linchpin-for-obamas-plan-to-predict.html#.Ud3pIW0UoXU (accessed January 11, 2014).

Lawnix, Wickard v. Filbum, http://www.lawnix.com/cases/wickard-filburn.html (accessed December 4, 2014).

Leach, Andrew, Alberta Oil, "The fine line between a subsidy and a tax credit," June 1, 2011, http://www.albertaoilmagazine.com/2011/07/insights-do-targeted-tax-incentives-work/ (accessed December 23, 2013).

Legal Theory Lexicon, "Strict Construction and Judicial Activism," http://lso-lum.typepad.com/legal_theory_lexicon/2004/05/legal_theory_le_3.html (accessed December 21, 2013).

LaHaye, Laura, Library of Economic Liberty, The Concise Encyclopedia of Economics, "Mercantilism," http://www.econlib.org/library/Enc/Mercan-tilism.html (accessed December 22, 2013).

Lapidos, Juliet, Explainer, "Is the Fed Private or Public?," http://www.slate.com/articles/news_and_politics/explainer/2008/09/is_the_fed_private_or_public.html (accessed December 24, 2013).

Ledderman, Josh, The Hill, "Schumer: Democrats will pay for payroll tax-cut with millionaire's tax," November 27, 2011, http://thehill.com/video/senate/195527-schumer-democrats-will-pay-for-payroll-tax-cut-extension-with-millionaires-tax (accessed December 26, 2013).

Letter From the Capitol, "Libya: Will Sarko Save the Day?" March 24, 2011 http://www.letterfromthecapitol.com/letterfromthecapitol/2011/03/libyan-update.html (accessed February 14, 2014).

Leonhardt, David, New York Times, "Challenge to Health Bill: Selling Re-form," July 21, 2009, http://www.nytimes.com/2009/07/22/business/economy/22leonhardt.html?_r=1& (accessed February 4, 2014).

LeVine, Steve and Theo Francis, Bloomberg Business Week, "Now, Obama 'Owns' General Motors," April 1, 2009, http://www.businessweek.com/bwdaily/dn-flash/content/apr2009/db2009041_951044.htm (accessed January 15, 2014).

Levy, Robert A., Cato Institute, "The Taxing Power of Obamacare," April 20, 2010, http://www.cato.org/publications/commentary/taxing-power-obam-acare (accessed December 27, 2013).

Lewis, Laura dawn, Government Structures 101, http://www.couplescompa-ny.com/features/politics/structure1.htm (accessed January 29, 2014).

Liberty News, "Justice Department 'Stonewalling' Congressional Investigators?," February 2, 2012, http://www.libertynews.com/2012/02/justice-department-stonewalling-congressional-investigators/ (accessed December 29, 2013).

Library of Congress, The Articles of Confederation, http://www.loc.gov/rr/program/bib/ourdocs/articles.html (accessed December 23, 2013).

Library of Economic Liberty, The Concise Encyclopedia of Economics, "Adam Smith," http://www.econlib.org/library/Enc/bios/Smith.html (accessed December 22, 2013)

_____, The Concise Encyclopedia of Economics, "Milton Friedman," http://www.econlib.org/library/Enc/bios/Friedman.html (accessed December 22, 2013).

Limbaugh, Rush, Liberty New Online, "BASELINE BUDGETING MAKES REAL FEDERAL BUDGET CUTS IMPOSSIBLE," August 2, 2011, http://www.libertynewsonline.com/article_301_30876.php (accessed December 26, 2013).

Liptak, Adam, The New York Times, "Justices to Hear Case on Obama's Recess Appointments," June 24, 2013, http://www.nytimes.com/2013/06/25/us/justices-agree-to-hear-case-on-presidents-recess-appointments.html?_r=2& (accessed January 11, 2014).

Live Leak, "More Democratic Voter Fraud Found in Chicago IL," http://www.liveleak.com/view?i=331_1288233022 (accessed December 24, 2013).

_____, "Bush: 'I've Abandoned Free Market Principles To Save The Free Market System,'" http://www.liveleak.com/view?i=4a2_1229470578 (accessed December 24, 2013).

Lind, Bill, Accuracy in Academia, "The Origins of Political Correctness," http://www.academia.org/the-origins-of-political-correctness/ (accessed January 9, 2014).

Locke, John, Constitution Society, "The Second Treatise of Civil Government," http://www.constitution.org/jl/2ndtreat.htm (accessed December 10, 2014).

Longley, Robert, About.com, "Lincoln Issues Proclamation Suspending Habeas Corpus Rights," http://usgovinfo.about.com/od/historicdocuments/a/lincolnhabeas.htm (accessed December 22, 2013).

Lowery, Annie, The New York Times, "Raising Minimum Wage Would Ease Income Gap but Carries Political Risks," February 13, 13, http://www.nytimes.com/2013/02/13/us/politics/obama-pushes-for-increase-in-federal-minimum-wage.html?pagewanted=all&_r=2& (accessed July 30, 2014).

Lucidcafe': Library, "Jean-Jacques Rousseau." http://www.lucidcafe.com/library/96jun/rousseau.html (accessed January 15, 2014).

Luhby, Tami, CNN Money, "Government Assistance Expands," February 7, 2012, http://money.cnn.com/2012/02/07/news/economy/government_assistance/index.htm (accessed December 18, 2013).

LyricsFreak, http://www.lyricsfreak.com/p/paul+simon/sounds+of+silence_20559740.html (accessed December 18, 2013).

Macke, Jeff, Breakout, "Bernanke: There Is No Inflation (and If There Were, We Could Stop It)," April 5, 2011, http://finance.yahoo.com/blogs/breakout/bernanke-no-inflation-were-could-stop-20110405-093226-104.html (accessed December 24, 2013).

MailOnline.com, "U.S. gives billions of dollars in foreign aid to world's richest countries - then asks to borrow it back," June 3, 2011, http://www.dailymail. co.uk/news/article-1393960/US-gives-billions-foreign-aid-worlds-richest-countries-asks-borrow-back.html (accessed December 23, 2013).

_____, "The shuttle as you've never seen it before: Space Station astronauts capture Atlantis re-entering the atmosphere from above ...hours before it is wheeled into hangar for the last time," http://www.dailymail.co.uk/sciencetech/article-2017122/Space-Shuttle-Atlantis-makes-historic-final-landing-Nasas-30-yr-programme-ends.html (accessed December 23, 2013).

Making Cities Livable, "Tahrir Square and the birth of Democracy?" http://www.livablecities.org/articles/tahrir-square-and-birth-democracy (accessed July 27, 2014).

Martin, Adam, The Wire, "Obama's New Immigration Policy Looks a Lot Like the DREAM Act," June 15, 2012, http://www.thewire.com/politics/2012/06/obamas-new-immigration-policy-looks-lot-dream-act/53600/ (accessed December 23, 2013).

Martosko, David, Mail Online, "Federal judge suddenly green-lights lawsuit that could stop Obamacare in its tracks," October 22, 2013, http://www.daily-mail.co.uk/news/article-2471978/Bombshell-Federal-judge-suddenly-green-lights-lawsuit-stop-Obamacare-tracks.html (accessed February 4, 2014).

Marx and Lenin, http://www.chsbs.cmich.edu/fattah/courses/modern-thought/marx.htm (accessed December 9, 2014).

Masch, Vladimir A., Bloomberg Business Week, "U.S. Trade Policy Needs Revamping," http://www.businessweek.com/debateroom/archives/2007/02/us_trade_policy_needs_revamping.html (accessed January 9, 2014).

Matthews, Terry, "The Convenient Sin," http://www.liberalslikechrist.org/about/slavery&southernchurches.html (accessed January 2, 2014).

McAuliff, Michael, Huffington Post, "Obama Tells Congress He's Keeping His Czars," April 15, 2011, http://www.huffingtonpost.com/2011/04/15/obama-czars-signing-statement_n_849963.html (accessed December 29, 2013).

McCarthy, Andrew C. National Review Online, "Obamacare's Unconstitutional Origins," October 5, 2013, http://www.nationalreview.com/article/360460/obamacares-unconstitutional-origins-andrew-c-mccarthy (accessed December 27, 2013).

_____, National Review Online, "Obama Gives Islamists a Walk," April 20, 2011, http://www.nationalreview.com/articles/265206/obama-gives-islamists-walk-andrew-c-mccarthy (accessed December 29, 2013).

McCormack, John, The Weekly Standard, "Millions of Americans Are Losing Their Health Plans Because of Obamacare," October 23, 2013, http://www. weeklystandard.com/blogs/millions-americans-are-losing-their-health-plans-because-obamacare_764602.html (accessed February 4, 2014).

McCormack, Richard, The American Prospect, "The Plight of American Manufacturing," December 21, 2009, http://prospect.org/article/plight-american-manufacturing (accessed December 22, 2013).

McGee, Matt, Search Engine land, "Ray Kurzweil's Job At Google: Beat IBM's Watson At Natural Language Search," http://searchengineland.com/ray-kurzweils-job-google-beat-ibms-watson-natural-language-search-185149 (accessed December 9, 2014).

McIntyre, Douglas A. and Brian Zajac, NBC News: Business, "Retirement plan: The corporate boards that love ex-politicians," July 13, 2012, http:// www.nbcnews.com/business/retirement-plan-corporate-boards-love-ex-politicians-826388 (accessed December 22, 2013).

McLaughlin, Seth, The Washington Times, "Obamacare's troubles a sign of things to come," October 23, 2013, http://www.washingtontimes.com/blog/ inside-politics/2013/oct/23/gop-rep-obamacares-troubles-sign-things-come/ (accessed February 4, 2014).

McNamara, Robert, About.com: 19th Century History, "Albert Gallatin's Report on Roads, Canals, Harbors, and Rivers," http://history1800s.about. com/od/canals/a/gallatinreport.htm (accessed December 22, 2013).

_____, About.com: 19th Century History, "American System (Economic Ideas Advanced by Henry Clay)," http://history1800s.about.com/ od/1800sglossary/g/americansysdef.htm (accessed December 26, 2013).

_____, About.com, "The Election of 1824 Was Decided in the House of Representatives: The Controversial Election was Denounced as 'The Corrupt Bargain,'" http://history1800s.about.com/od/leaders/a/elec-tionof1824.htm (accessed December 28, 2013).

Melchior, Jullian Kay, National Review Online, "Me and My Obamaphone," August 1, 2013, http://www.nationalreview.com/article/354867/me-and-my-obamaphones-jillian-kay-melchior (accessed December 18, 2013).

Meyers, Jim and Dan Weil, Newsmax, "Dems Rip Obama on Libya, Bring Up 'Impeachable Offense'!," March 22, 2011, http://www.newsmax.com/ Headline/obama-kucinich-randpaul-libya/2011/03/22/id/390339 (accessed February 14, 2014).

Military Industrial Complex, http://www.militaryindustrialcomplex.com/what-is-the-military-industrial-complex.asp (accessed December 22, 2013).

Miller, Emily, Human Events, "Senate Dems' New Proposal To Weaken Filibuster," January 2, 2011, http://www.humanevents.com/2011/01/03/senate-dems-new-proposal-to-weaken-filibuster/ (accessed December 22, 2013).

Mills, David G., Information Clearing House, "It's the Corporate State, Stupid," http://www.informationclearinghouse.info/article7260.htm (accessed December 27, 2013).

Minster, Christopher, About.com, "The Mexican Revolution," http://latina-mericanhistory.about.com/od/thehistoryofmexico/a/mexicanrevo.htm (accessed January 15, 2014).

Minter, Frank, Forbes, "Is The Obama Administration The Cause Of Gun Ammunition Shortages?," http://www.forbes.com/sites/frank-miniter/2013/10/20/is-the-obama-administration-the-cause-of-gun-ammunition-shortages/ (accessed December 2, 2014).

Modern History Project, "On July 19, 1962, Khrushchev said: «The United States will eventually fly the Communist red flag" http://modernhistoryproject.org/mhp?Article=FinalWarning&C=7.8 (accessed December 20, 2013).

Moran, Terry, ABC News, "State of the Union: The Slam, the Scowl and the Separation of Powers," January 28, 2010, http://abcnews.go.com/Politics/State_of_the_Union/state-of-the-union-president-obama-justice-alito-political-theater/story?id=9688639 (accessed December 27, 2013).

Morley, Robert, The Trumpet.com, "The Death of American Manufacturing," February 2006, http://www.thetrumpet.com/article/2061.904.80.0/economy/the-death-of-american-manufacturing (accessed December 22, 2013).

Morrissey, Ed, Free Republic, "Democrats catching impeachment fever? Obama's actions in Libya Unconstitutional," March 20, 2011, http://www.freerepublic.com/focus/f-news/2691955/posts (accessed February 14, 2014).

_____, Hot Air, "Dodd-Frank costs US financial sector 24 million man-hours per year for compliance," April 17, 2012, http://hotair.com/archives/2012/04/17/dodd-frank-costs-us-financial-sector-24-million-man-hours-per-year-for-compliance/ (accessed February 4, 2014).

MSNBC, "Obama says stimulus spending must pick up," http://www.nbcnews.com/id/31508658/ns/business-stocks_and_economy/ (accessed December 20, 2013).

MR. Conservative "Obama Rants That The Constitution Is A 'Charter of Negative Liberties,'" http://www.mrconservative.com/2013/06/18984-obama-rants-that-the-constitution-is-a-charter-of-negative-liberties/ (accessed December 26, 2013).

MRCTV, "Obama Says Americans «Lazy," http://www.mrctv.org/videos/obama-says-americans-lazy (accessed December 26, 2013).

NASW Foundation, "Richard A. Cloward (1926 - 2005)," http://www.naswfoundation.org/pioneers/c/cloward.htm (accessed December 27, 2013).

National Park Service, Historic Jamestowne, "The Virginia Company of London," http://www.nps.gov/jame/historyculture/the-virginia-company-of-london.htm (accessed December 22, 2013).

National Priorities Project, "Borrowing and the National debt," http://nationalpriorities.org/budget-basics/federal-budget-101/borrowing-and-federal-debt/ (accessed December 23, 2013).

National Register, "The Constitutional Amendment Process," http://www.archives.gov/federal-register/constitution/ (accessed July 30, 2014).

National Report, "Obama Issues Executive Order Granting Amnesty to Illegals who Enroll in Obamacare," http://nationalreport.net/obama-issues-executive-order-granting-amnesty-illegals-enroll-obamacare/ (accessed December 2, 2014).

National Socialist Party of Germany (NAZI) Quotes, http://quotes.liberty-tree.ca/quotes_by/national+socialist+party+of+germany+%28nazi%29 (accessed December 10, 2014).

Naval History and Heritage, "The Great White Fleet," http://www.history.navy.mil/faqs/faq42-1.htm (accessed December 23, 2013).

NBC News, "Court Rules Against Arizona Immigration Law," http://www.nbcnews.com/id/42537304/ns/politics-more_politics/t/court-rules-against-arizona-immigration-law/#.Ur2yubRzYqM (accessed December 27, 2013).

_____, "Hey! Who turned out the lights? Incandescent bulb ban just one of new year's new laws" December 30, 2013 http://usnews.nbcnews.com/_news/2013/12/30/22114574-hey-who-turned-out-the-lights-incandescent-bulb-ban-just-one-of-new-years-new-laws?lite (accessed December 2, 2014).

NBC Politics, "Obama health care promise named 'Lie of the Year,'" http://nbcpolitics.nbcnews.com/_news/2013/12/12/21880402-obama-health-care-promise-named-lie-of-the-year (accessed December 21, 2013).

Nerd Wallet Finance, "American Household Credit Card Debt Statistics: 2013," http://www.nerdwallet.com/blog/credit-card-data/average-credit-card-debt-household/ (accessed December 23, 2013).

Newman, Andy, The New York Times, "Rangel's Ethics Violations," November `16, 2010, http://cityroom.blogs.nytimes.com/2010/11/16/rangel-found-to-have-violated-multiple-ethics-rules/?_php=true&_type=blogs&_r=0 (accessed July 30, 2014).

NewsAlert, "The Political Corruption Behind Barack Obama and Chicago," January, 6, 2008, http://nalert.blogspot.com/2008/01/political-corruption-behind-barack_06.html (accessed December 26, 2013).

News Talk WCHB, "700 Arrested In Brooklyn Bridge "Occupy Wall St." Protest," October 3, 2011, http://wchbnewsdetroit.com/2347942/700-arrested-in-brookyln-bridge-occupy-wall-st-protest/ (accessed December 27, 2013).

New York Post, "OBAMA TASK FORCE TO 'LEVEL PLAYING FIELD,'" January 30, 2009, http://nypost.com/2009/01/30/obama-task-force-to-level-playing-field/ (accessed February 18, 2014).

New York Times, "A LETTER FROM PRESIDENT LINCOLN.; Reply to Horace Greeley. Slavery and the Union The Restoration of the Union the Paramount Object," August 24, 1862, http://www.nytimes.com/1862/08/24/news/letter-president-lincoln-reply-horace-greeley-slavery-union-restoration-union.html (accessed January 2, 2014).

Nimmo, Kurt, InfoWars.com, "EPA Threatens 'Command-and-Control' Economy to Push Climate Change Agenda," December 9, 2009, http://www.infowars.com/epa-threatens-command-and-control-economy-to-push-climate-change-agenda/ (accessed December 9, 2014).

Noah Webster Quotes, http://www.seekfind.net/NoahWebster.html (accessed December 31, 2013).

Nordquist, Richard, About Education, "Sophistry," http://grammar.about.com/od/rs/g/Sophistry.htm (accessed December 4, 2014).

Norman Thomas Quotes, http://quotes.liberty-tree.ca/quote_blog/Norman.Thomas.Quote.FFB1 (accessed January 2, 2014).

Norris, Chuck, Republic-Main Street, "Public Education: Progressive Indoctrination Camps," March 8, 2011, https://republicmainstreet.wordpress.com/2011/03/08/chuck-norris-public-education-progressive-indoctrination-camps/ (accessed December 27, 2013).

Noyes, Rich, News Busters, "Today's Push for ObamaCare Matches Media Spin for HillaryCare in 1990s," September 9, 2009, http://newsbusters.org/blogs/rich-noyes/2009/09/09/todays-push-obamacare-matches-media-spin-hillarycare-1990s (accessed December 22, 2013).

NPR, "President Bush's Second Inaugural Address," http://www.npr.org/templates/story/story.php?storyId=4460172 (accessed July 27, 2014).

O'Connor, Jerome, Real Clear History, "FDR's Undeclared Atlantic War," http://www.realclearhistory.com/2012/09/04/fdr039s_undeclared_atlantic_war_3306.html (accessed December 23, 2013).

Odom, Thomas H., Federal Constitutional Law: Introduction to Interpretive Methods ..., Volume 1 / Google Books, http://books.google.com/books?id =9PbXK83ru00C&pg=PT75&lpg=PT75&dq=There+is+no+power+above +them+to+control+any+of+their+decisions&source=bl&ots=hNx_LHsn FG&sig=haX8zMXm0RGeqge52D71saFRx1w&hl=en&sa=X&ei=rW2AV Lz8CteBygTus4GwBg&ved=0CCAQ6AEwAA#v=onepage&q=There%20 is%20no%20power%20above%20them%20to%20control%20any%20of%20 their%20decisions&f=false (accessed December 4, 2014).

On the Issues, "Richard Nixon on the Budget and the Economy," http://www. ontheissues.org/celeb/Richard_Nixon_Budget_+_Economy.htm (accessed December 22, 2013).

Orwell, George, Animal Farm, Sparks Notes, http://www.sparknotes.com/lit/ animalfarm/section10.rhtml (accessed December 10, 2014).

Our Documents, 17th Amendment, http://www.ourdocuments.gov/doc. php?flash=true&doc=58 (accessed December 22, 2014).

_____, "Marbury v. Madison," http://www.ourdocuments.gov/ doc.php?flash=true&doc=19 (accessed December 23, 2013).

Overby, Peter, NPR, "How Fannie, Freddie Became Kings Of The Hill," July 15, 2008, http://www.npr.org/templates/story/story.php?storyId=92540620 (accessed December 22, 2013).

Owens, Robert R. The Constitution Failed, http://www.amazon.com/Consti- tution-Failed-PH-D-Robert-Owens/dp/1609579615/ref=sr_1_1?ie=UTF8& qid=1350471788&sr=8-1&keywords=the+constitution+failed+owens (ac- cessed November 24, 2014).

OWR, "General Essay on Shi'a Islam," http://www.philtar.ac.uk/encyclope- dia/islam/shia/ (accessed December 23, 2013).

Patrick J. Buchanan Official Website, http://buchanan.org/blog/ (accessed December 22, 2013).

_____, "Let the People Rule," http://buchan- an.org/blog/let-the-people-rule-169 (accessed December 27, 2013).

Patton, David A.. Newsmax, "Obama: Constitution is 'Deeply Flawed,'" http://www.newsmax.com/InsideCover/obama-constitution/2008/10/27/ id/326165 (accessed December 29, 2013).

Paul, Rand, The Washington Times, "Obama's unconstitutional Libyan war," June 15, 2011, http://www.washingtontimes.com/news/2011/jun/15/obam- as-unconstitutional-libyan-war/ (accessed December 23, 2013).

Paul, Ron, "The Fed and the Debt," http://archive.lewrockwell.com/paul/paul740.html (accessed December 23, 2013).

Pavlich, Katie, Townhall.com, "NAACP Requires Photo I.D. to See Holder Speak in State Being Sued Over Voter ID," July 3, 2012, http://townhall.com/tipsheet/katiepavlich/2012/07/10/naacp_requires_photo_id_to_see_holder_speak (accessed December 24, 2013).

PBS: American Experience, "Durant's Big Scam," http://www.pbs.org/wgbh/americanexperience/features/general-article/tcrr-scam/ (accessed December 22, 2013).

_____, "Presidential Politics," http://www.pbs.org/wgbh/americanexperience/features/general-article/fdr-presidential/ (accessed December 27, 2013).

_____: Judgment Day, "Indian Removal," http://www.pbs.org/wgbh/aia/part4/4p2959.html (accessed December 27, 2013).

_____: New Perspectives on the West, "Worcester v. Georgia," http://www.pbs.org/weta/thewest/resources/archives/two/worcestr.htm (accessed December 27, 2013).

_____: Woodrow Wilson, "League of Nations," http://www.pbs.org/wgbh/amex/wilson/portrait/wp_league.html (accessed December 23, 2013).

PBS: Constitution USA with Peter Sagal, "Federalism," http://www.pbs.org/tpt/constitution-usa-peter-sagal/federalism/#.UsXhOrRzYqM (accessed January 2, 2014).

Perry, Mark J., A E Ideas, "Manufacturing's Death Greatly Exaggerated," December, 23, 2009, http://www.aei-ideas.org/2009/12/manufacturings-death-greatly-exaggerated/ (accessed December 22, 2013).

Peterson, Paul E., The Hoover Institute, "The Decline and Fall of American Education," January 30, 2003, http://www.hoover.org/publications/hoover-digest/article/6325 (accessed December 22, 2013).

Pew Research, Religion & Public Life Project, Religious Landscape Survey, http://religions.pewforum.org/reports (accessed December 18, 2013).

Picht, Jim, The Washington Times, "The debt ceiling agreement: a fiscal band-aid on mortal wounds," http://communities.washingtontimes.com/neighborhood/stimulus/2011/aug/4/debt-ceiling-agreement-fiscal-band-aid-mortal-woun/ (accessed December 9, 2014).

Picket, Kerry, The Washington Times, "EPA imposes Obama's cap and trade regs- energy prices 'skyrocket,'" August 20, 2011, http://www.washingtontimes.com/blog/watercooler/2011/aug/20/picket-obama-08-energy-prices-will-skyrocket-under/ (accessed December 23, 2013).

Pirates in America: Tripolitan War, http://nefertiti67.tripod.com/pirates/id1.html (accessed December 28, 2013).

PJ Media, "Occupy L.A. Speaker: Violence will be Necessary to Achieve Our Goals," October 11, 2011, http://pjmedia.com/tatler/2011/10/11/occupy-l-a-speaker-violence-will-be-necessary-to-achieve-our-goals/ (accessed December 27, 2013).

Pleuger, Gilbert , New Perspective Vol 9, No 1, "Totalitarianism," http://www.history-ontheweb.co.uk/concepts/totalitarianism.htm (accessed December 18, 2013).

Pluralism, http://www.udel.edu/htr/American/Texts/pluralism.html (accessed December 18, 2013).

Poe, Richard, DiscovertheNetworks.org, The Cloward-Piven Strategy," 2005, http://www.discoverthenetworks.org/Articles/theclowardpivenstrategy-poe.html (accessed December 10, 2014).

Political Culture of the United States, http://academic.regis.edu/jriley/421elazar.htm (accessed December 9, 2014).

Political Punch, http://abcnews.go.com/blogs/politics/2009/02/obamas-budget-a/ (accessed December 18, 2013).

Politifact, "Chris Smith says more than 54 million abortions have been performed since U.S. Supreme Court decided Roe v. Wade," http://www.politifact.com/new-jersey/statements/2012/mar/18/chris-smith/chris-smith-says-more-54-million-abortions-have-be/ (accessed December 23, 2013).

_____, "John Cornyn says 51 percent of American households pay no income tax," http://www.politifact.com/truth-o-meter/statements/2011/jul/08/john-cornyn/john-cornyn-says-51-percent-american-households-pa/ (accessed December 27, 2013).

_____, "Pat Toomey says U.S. has highest corporate tax rates in the world," http://www.politifact.com/truth-o-meter/statements/2011/jan/03/pat-toomey/pat-toomey-says-us-has-highest-corporate-tax-rates/ (accessed December 26, 2013).

_____, "The U.S. military «'s in 130 countries. We have 900 bases around the world,'" http://www.politifact.com/truth-o-meter/statements/2011/sep/14/ron-paul/ron-paul-says-us-has-military-personnel-130-nation/ (accessed December 26, 2013).

Political Vel Craft, "Personal Income Tax Violates U.S. Supreme Court Ruling ~ Privately Owned Federal Reserve Violates U.S. Constitution & President Kennedy's Executive Orders," http://politicalvelcraft.org/2011/09/08/u-s-supreme-court-struck-down-personal-income-tax-president-kennedy-struck-down-federal-reserve-both-not-enforced/ (accessed December 26, 2013).

Pollard, Jerry, Defeat Communism, "Useful Idiots," May 26, 2013, http://defeatcommunism.com/profiles/blogs/5467818:BlogPost:61704 (accessed January 2, 2014).

Pollak, Joel B., Breitbart, "Sorry, Jesse Jackson: South Africa Has Photo ID Voting," December 6, 2013, http://www.breitbart.com/Big-Government/2013/12/06/Sorry-Jesse-Jackson-South-Africa-Has-Photo-ID-Voting (accessed December 24, 2013).

PopMarket, http://www.azlyrics.com/lyrics/bobdylan/gottaservesomebody.html (accessed December 18, 2013).

Porter, George, The U. S. Federal Reserve System, http://www.converge.org.nz/pirm/fr_paul.htm (accessed December 26, 2013).

Portnoy, Howard, Hotair, "Occupy L.A.: We will need violence (and socialism!) to attain our goals," October 12, 2011, http://hotair.com/greenroom/archives/2011/10/12/occupy-l-a-we-will-need-violence-and-socialism-to-attain-our-goals/ (accessed December 27, 2013).

Presidential Campaign Slogans, Wilson, http://www.presidentsusa.net/1916slogan.html (accessed December 22, 2013).

Property and Socialism, http://www.punkerslut.com/propertyessays.html (accessed December 10, 2014).

Proverbia, Liberty, Norman Vincent Peal, http://en.proverbia.net/citastema.asp?tematica=704 (accessed December 2, 2014).

PsyBlog, Propaganda Techniques in Michael Moore's Fahrenheit 9/11, http://www.spring.org.uk/2007/11/9-propaganda-techniques-in-michael.php (accessed December 20, 2013).

QB, "It's the economy stupid," http://quotationsbook.com/quote/5097/#sthash.m1vGWCde.dpbs (accessed December 20, 2013).

___, "The enemy advances, we retreat; the enemy camps, we harass; the enemy tires, we attack; the enemy retreats, we pursue," http://quotationsbook.com/quote/44984/#sthash.xmCTFsaK.dpbs (accessed December 23, 2013).

Quizlet, Constitutional Amendments 1-27, http://quizlet.com/5149242/constitutional-amendments-1-27-flash-cards/ (accessed July 30, 2014).

Quora, Bernanke Quotes, "The U.S. government has a technology, called a printing press," http://www.quora.com/What-are-some-iconic-Ben-Bernanke-quotes (accessed December 24, 2013).

Quotation Collection, "Ronald Reagan," http://www.quotationcollection.com/author/Ronald-Wilson-Reagan/quotes (accessed December 9, 2014).

_____, "Will Rogers," http://www.quotationcollection.com/quotation/23/quote (accessed December 23, 2013).

Quote DB, Mark Twain Quote, «History doesn't repeat itself, but it does rhyme,» http://www.quotedb.com/quotes/3038 (accessed December 22, 2013).

_____, Winston Churchill, "«If you will not fight for the right when you can easily win without bloodshed … ," http://www.quotedb.com/quotes/2531 Accessed December 2, 2014).

Quote World, Benjamin Franklin, «We must hang together, gentlemen...else, we shall most assuredly hang separately.» http://www.quoteworld.org/quotes/4954 (accessed December 2, 2014).

Quotes of the Founding Fathers: The Importance of a Moral Society: http://www.free2pray.info/5founderquotes.html (accessed December 31, 2013).

Quotes on Liberty and Virtue, Douglas McArthur, http://www.liberty1.org/virtue.htm (accessed December 31, 2013).

_____, John Adams, http://www.liberty1.org/virtue.htm (accessed February 4, 2014).

_____, Patrick Henry, http://www.liberty1.org/virtue.htm (accessed February 4, 2014).

_____, Samuel Adams, http://www.liberty1.org/virtue.htm December 31, 2013).

_____, Theodore Roosevelt, http://www.liberty1.org/virtue.htm (accessed December 31, 2013).

_____, Thomas Jefferson, http://www.liberty1.org/virtue.htm (accessed December 31, 2013).

Raasch, Chuck, USA Today, "Obama aspires to a transformational presidency," April 16, 2009, http://usatoday30.usatoday.com/news/opinion/columnist/raasch/2009-04-16-raasch-column-04162009_N.htm (accessed December 29, 2013).

Rainey, James, Los Angeles Times, "On the Media: Tea party, Occupy Wall Street share a moment," October 12, 2011, http://articles.latimes.com/2011/oct/12/entertainment/la-et-onthemedia-20111012 (accessed December 27, 2013).

Rappleye, Hannah, New York Post, "OWS protesters cause mayhem across the city, 275 arrested," November 17, 2011, http://nypost.com/2011/11/17/ows-protesters-cause-mayhem-across-the-city-275-arrested/ (accessed December 26, 2013).

Real Clear Politics, "History of IRS Abuse," May 15, 2013, http://www.real-clearpolitics.com/lists/irs-scandal/ (accessed December 2, 2014).

Red Flag, "Carney Dismisses 14 Million Losing Their Health Insurance Because of Obamacare As A "Small Sliver" of The Population...," http://www.redflagnews.com/headlines/carney-dismisses-14-million-losing-their-health-insurance-because-of-obamacare-as-a-small-sliver-of-the-population (accessed July 30, 2014).

Reeves, Richard, Washington Post, "Missile Gaps and Other Broken Promises," February 10, 2009, http://100days.blogs.nytimes.com/2009/02/10/missile-gaps-and-other-broken-promises/?_r=0 (accessed December 22, 2013).

Reich, Robert, The American Prospect, "It's the Economy, Stupid -- But Not Just the Current Slowdown," December 5, 2007, http://prospect.org/article/its-economy-stupid-not-just-current-slowdown (accessed December 20, 2013).

Related Information: Patrick Henry, http://www.ushistory.org/declaration/related/henry.htm (accessed December 27, 2013).

Republic Magazine, "John Roberts, Constitutional Traitor: Chief Justice Approves Obamacare Tax Mandate," June 28, 2012, http://www.republicmagazine.com/news/john-roberts-constitutional-traitor-chief-justice-approves-obamacare-tax-mandate.html (accessed December 27, 2013).

Reuters, "General Petraeus hangs up uniform, warns on budget," http://www.reuters.com/article/2011/08/31/us-usa-petraeus-idUSTRE77U5HU20110831 (accessed December 27, 2013).

_____, "Obama: U.S. in worst crisis since Depression," October 7, 2008, http://www.reuters.com/article/2008/10/08/usa-politics-debate-economy-idUSN0749084220081008 (accessed December 20, 2013).

_____, "U.S. House approves $649 billion for defense in 2012," July 8, 2011, http://www.reuters.com/article/2011/07/08/usa-budget-defense-idUSN1E7670UA20110708 (accessed December 23, 2013).

Revolutionary War and Beyond, James Madison Quotes, http://www.revolutionary-war-and-beyond.com/james-madison-quotes-5.html (accessed December 9, 2014).

Reynolds, Alan, Townhall.com, "What 'Guns and Butter' Means," December 18, 2003, http://townhall.com/columnists/alanreynolds/2003/12/18/what_guns_and_butter_means/page/full (accessed December 18, 2013).

Right Edition, "Got a wet yard? EPA will take control," October 23, 2013 http://rightedition.com/2013/10/23/got-wet-yard-epa-will-take-control/ (accessed December 2, 2014).

Riley, Charles, CNN Money, "Occupy Wall Street... mansions," October 12, 2011, http://money.cnn.com/2011/10/10/news/economy/occupy_wall_street_protest/index.htm (accessed December 27, 2013).

Rise and Fall of Athenian Greatness, http://www.augie.edu/dept/history/athe.htm (accessed December 24, 2013).

Roife, Rebecca, The Washington Post, "American on Food Stamps," July 11, 2013, http://www.washingtonpost.com/wp-srv/special/politics/food-stamps/ (accessed December 18, 2013).

Rosenberg, Matt, About.com, "Pacific Rim and Economic Tigers," http://geography.about.com/od/urbaneconomicgeography/a/econtigers.htm (accessed December 22, 2013).

Rosenberg, M. J., The American Conservative, "Who Elected Hamas," http://www.theamericanconservative.com/articles/who-elected-hamas/ (accessed July 27, 2014).

Rosenzweig, Paul, The Heritage Foundation, "Is the Government Reading Your E-Mail?," March 21, 2013, http://blog.heritage.org/2013/03/21/is-the-government-reading-your-e-mail/ (accessed January 2, 2014).

Rothbard, Murray N.. Lew Rockwell.com, "Herbert Hoover's Depression," http://archive.lewrockwell.com/rothbard/rothbard184.html (accessed December 22, 2013).

_____, Ludwig von Mises Institute, "Origins of the Federal Reserve," November 13, 2009, http://mises.org/daily/3823 (accessed December 24, 2013).

Roy, Avik, Forbes, "Sen. Harry Reid: Obamacare 'Absolutely' A Step Toward A Single-Payer System," August 10, 2013, http://www.forbes.com/sites/theapothecary/2013/08/10/sen-harry-reid-obamacare-absolutely-a-step-toward-a-single-payer-system/ (accessed February 4, 2014).

Rubin, Barry, PJ Media, "It's Official: Obama Administration Promotes Islamist Regimes; Insists They are Moderate," November 8, 2011, http://pjmedia.com/barryrubin/2011/11/08/it%E2%80%99s-official-obama-administration-promotes-islamist-regimes-insists-they-are-moderate/ (accessed January 11, 2014).

Rutten, Tim, Los Angeles Times, "Paul Ryan's budget blueprint would push the aged into poverty," April 9, 2011, http://articles.latimes.com/2011/apr/09/opinion/la-oe-rutten-ryan-budget-20110409 (accessed January 15, 2014).

Sahadi, Jeanne, CNN Money, "Debt ceiling FAQs: What you need to know," May, 18, 2011, http://money.cnn.com/2011/01/03/news/economy/debt_ceiling_faqs/index.htm (accessed January 15, 2014).

_____, CNN Money, "Why the U.S. can't inflate its way out of debt," March 23, 2010, http://money.cnn.com/2010/03/10/news/economy/inflation_debt/index.htm (accessed 12-20-13).

Said What?, Churchill Quote, "Those that fail to learn from history, are doomed to repeat it," http://www.saidwhat.co.uk/quotes/political/winston_churchill/those_that_fail_to_learn_from_2804 (accessed December 22, 2013).

Samuelson, Robert J., Newsweek, "Social Security Is Middle-Class Welfare," March 6, 2011, http://www.newsweek.com/social-security-middle-class-welfare-66119 (accessed December 26, 2013).

Savage, Charlie, The caucus, "Justice Memo Upholds Libya Strikes," http://thecaucus.blogs.nytimes.com/2011/04/07/justice-memo-upholds-libya-strikes/ (accessed February 14, 2014).

Schmidt, Marcus, Times Dispatch, "Thousands of Virginia Voters on the Rolls in Other States," http://www.timesdispatch.com/news/state-regional/government-politics/thousands-of-va-voters-on-the-rolls-in-other-states/article_3ce0c700-9ac9-53c1-8bfa-54619d917feb.html (accessed December 22, 2013).

Snopes, http://www.snopes.com/politics/soapbox/borderpatrol.as (accessed December 18, 2013).

Schoen, Douglas, U.S. news, "'Occupy'-ers Seek Dissolution of Democracy, End of Capitalism," October 19, 2011, http://www.usnews.com/debate-club/is-occupy-wall-street-the-next-tea-party-movement/occupy-ers-seek-dissolution-of-democracy-end-of-capitalism-occupy-ers-seek-dissolution-of-democracy (accessed December 26, 2013).

Scott, Robert E., Economic Policy Institute, "The high price of 'free' trade," http://www.epi.org/publication/briefingpapers_bp147/ (accessed January 9, 2014).

Search Quotes, Tullius Cicero quotes, "We are in bondage to the law so that we might be free," http://www.searchquotes.com/quotation/We_are_in_bondage_to_the_law_so_that_we_might_be_free/32084/ (accessed December 23, 2013).

Seelye, Katherine D., New York Times, "DOLE IS IMPLORING VOTERS TO 'RISE UP' AGAINST THE PRESS," October 26, 1996, http://www.nytimes.com/1996/10/26/us/dole-is-imploring-voters-to-rise-up-against-the-press.html (accessed February 12, 2014).

Shear, Michael D., The Caucus, "Obama Defends 'Limited' Role in Libya," http://thecaucus.blogs.nytimes.com/2011/03/28/obama-defends-limited-role-in-libya/?_php=true&_type=blogs&_php=true&_type=blogs&_r=1 (accessed February 14, 2014).

Shmoop, "The Korean War," http://www.shmoop.com/korean-war/politics.html (accessed February 14, 2014).

Simendinger, Alexis, Real Clear Politics, "Obama's «We Can't Wait» Juggling Act," January 20, 2012, http://www.realclearpolitics.com/articles/2012/01/20/obamas_we_cant_wait_juggling_act.html (accessed December 31, 2013).

Slack, Kevin, The New Your Times, "Arguing That Health Mandate Is Not a Tax, Except When It Is," March 26, 2012, http://www.nytimes.com/2012/03/27/health/policy/arguing-that-health-mandate-is-not-a-tax-except-when-it-is.html?_r=1& (accessed December 4, 2014).

Sledge, Matt, The Huffington Post, "NSA Phone Records Collection Can't Be Challenged By The Callers, Government Argues," October 2, 2013, http://www.huffingtonpost.com/2013/10/02/nsa-phone-records-collection_n_4032985.html (accessed January 2, 2014).

Smith, Emily, CBS 2 New York, "OWS Protesters Chant 'Follow Those Kids!' As Small Children Try To Go To School On Wall Street: Tiny Tots, Some As Young As 4, Overwhelmed By Hostility, Crush Of Humanity," November 17, 2011, http://newyork.cbslocal.com/2011/11/17/ows-protesters-chant-follow-those-kids-as-small-children-try-to-go-to-school-on-wall-street/ (accessed December 26, 2013).

Snopes. "Border Patrol" http://www.snopes.com/politics/soapbox/borderpatrol.asp (accessed December 9, 2014).

Snyder, Michael, Info Wars, "19 Shocking Examples Of How Political Correctness Is Destroying America," http://www.infowars.com/19-shocking-examples-of-how-political-correctness-is-destroying-america/ (accessed December 2, 2014).

Snyder, Neil, The American Thinker, "Enough with Affirmative Action Presidents," October 10, 2012, http://www.americanthinker.com/articles/2012/10/enough_with_affirmative_action_presidents.html (accessed November 24, 2014).

Somin, Ilya, The Volokh Conspiracy, "Number of States Challenging the Constitutionality of Obamacare Rises to 28," January 19, 2011, http://www.volokh.com/2011/01/19/number-of-states-challenging-the-constitutionality-of-obamacare-rises-to-28/ (accessed December 27, 2013).

Sowell, Thomas, Redding.com, "Obama casts U.S. allies aside," http://www. redding.com/news/2011/feb/09/thomas-sowell-obama-casts-us-allies-aside/?print=1 (accessed January 11, 2014).

Spakovsky, Hans von, The Heritage Network, "The New Black Panther Party Evidence on Voter Intimidation," July 21, 2010, http://blog.heritage. org/2010/07/21/the-new-black-panther-party-evidence-on-voter-intimidation/ (accessed December 24, 2013).

Spartacus Educational: Adolf Hitler, http://www.spartacus.schoolnet.co.uk/ GERhitler.htm (accessed December 31, 2013).

_____, Benito Mussolini, http://www.spartacus.schoolnet. co.uk/2WWmussolini.htm (accessed December 31, 2013).

_____, Nazi Party, http://www.spartacus.schoolnet.co.uk/ GERnazi.htm (accessed December 31, 2013).

Spellerberg, Shirley, Real Clear Conservatives, "IS A BALANCED BUDGET AMENDMENT A DANGEROUS GIMMICK?," March 3, 2011, http://realclearconservatives.com/2011/03/30/is-a-balanced-budget-amendment-a-dangerous-gimmick/ (accessed January 14, 2015).

Stanford Encyclopedia of Philosophy, Equality of Opportunity, http://plato.stanford.edu/entries/equal-opportunity/ (accessed December 18, 2013).

Stanley, Paul, The Christian Post, "John Boehner Tries to Rally Support for Debt Plan," July 27, 2011, http://www.christianpost.com/news/boehners-plan-had-soft-support-with-gop-prospects-improving-quickly-52932/ (accessed December 28, 2013).

Starr, Penny, CNSNEWS.com, "6,125 Proposed Regulations and Notifications Posted in Last 90 Days--Average 68 per Day," November 9, 2012, http:// cnsnews.com/news/article/6125-proposed-regulations-and-notifications-posted-last-90-days-average-68-day (accessed December 10, 2014).

Stephey, M. J., Time Magazine, "The Bretton Woods System," October 21, 2008, http://content.time.com/time/business/article/0,8599,1852254,00. html (accessed December 18, 2013).

Stuchka, Peter, Distinguish between law and administrative regulation, http:// books.google.com/books?id=ENQjPm-S7UEC&pg=PA351&lpg=PA351&d q=peter+stuchka+distinguish+between+law+and+administrative+regulat ion&source=bl&ots=lGrbneJgfT&sig=jIy-7RXIDdvWmWJpPbEs&hl=en& sa=X&ei=XfQzVLaECoakyATU5IKgCg&ved=0CCMQ6AEwAA#v=onep age&q=peter%20stuchka%20distinguish%20between%20law%20and%20 administrative%20regulation&f=false (accessed December 2, 2014).

Spartacus Educational, "The Black Shirts," http://www.spartacus.schoolnet. co.uk/SPblack.htm (accessed December 27, 2013).

——————————, "Yalta Conference," http://www.spartacus.schoolnet. co.uk/2WWyalta.htm (accessed December 27, 2013).

SubtleTea.com, "The Wit and Wisdom of Thomas Paine," http://www.subtle-tea.com/thomaspainequotes.htm (accessed December 21, 2013).

SunServer.com, "Presidential Oath of Office," http://www.sonserver.com/america/oath01.htm (accessed December 29, 2013).

Sunstein, Cass, Bloomberg View, "Obama, FDR and the Second Bill of Rights," http://www.bloombergview.com/articles/2013-01-28/obama-fdr-and-the-second-bill-of-rights (accessed December 9, 2014).

Sweetness and Light, "Obama: Constitution is Living Document," http://sweetness-light.com/archive/obama-constitution-is-living-document#.Us-A6UrRzYqM (accessed December 29, 2013).

Tame, Chris R., "THE REVOLUTION OF REASON: PETER GAY, THE EN-LIGHTENMENT, AND THE AMBIGUITIES OF CLASSICAL LIBERAL-ISM," http://mises.org/journals/jls/1_3/1_3_7.pdf (accessed February 4, 2014).

Tampa Bay Times, PoliticFact.com, "Obama: 'If you like your health care plan, you'll be able to keep your health care plan," http://www.politifact.com/obama-like-health-care-keep/ (accessed December 9, 2014).

Tanner, Michael, National Review Online, "Democrats: The Constitution is 'Weird'," http://www.nationalreview.com/articles/248102/democrats-con-stitution-weird-michael-tanner (accessed December 10, 2014).

TAU, BYRON, Politico, "Intelligence community: U.S. out as sole superpower by 2030," December 12, 2012, http://www.politico.com/politico44/2012/12/intelligence-community-us-out-as-sole-superpower-by-151519.html (accessed December 20, 2013).

Tavakoli, Janet, Business Insider, "IMMINENT THREAT: Foreign Borrow-ings Will Lead To The Destruction Of The US Financial System," October 30, 2011, http://www.businessinsider.com/clear-and-present-danger-for-eign-borrowing-poses-an-imminent-threat-to-the-us-dollar-and-us-finan-cial-system-2011-10 (accessed December 23, 2013).

Tax Policy Center, "Taxes and the Budget: What does it mean for a government program to be 'off-budget'?," http://www.taxpolicycenter.org/briefing-book/background/taxes-budget/off-budget.cfm (accessed December 27, 2013).

T. B. Rickert's Call, "More Americans joining disability than finding jobs," July 18, 2012, http://tbrickert.wordpress.com/2012/07/18/more-americans-joining-disability-than-finding-jobs/ (accessed December 23, 2013).

Tea Party.org, "Harry Reid calls Tea Party 'Fanatics', 'Anarchists'," September 23, 2013, http://www.teaparty.org/harry-reid-calls-tea-party-fanatics-anar-chists-28626/ (accessed January 2, 2014).

Tenth Amendment Center, "About the Tenth Amendment," http://tenthamendment-center.com/about/about-the-tenth-amendment/ (accessed December 22, 2013).

_____, "A Constitutional Coup d'etat," http://tenth-amendmentcenter.com/2009/08/31/rob-natelson-a-constitutional-coup-detat/ (accessed December 11, 2014).

Terrell, Ellen, Library of Congress: Business Reference services, "History of the US Income Tax," February 2004, http://www.loc.gov/rr/business/hot-topic/irs_history.html (accessed December 26, 2013).

The Blaze, "Cass Sunstein's New Presidential Appointment Is Almost Hard to Believe...Especially Considering a Paper He Once Wrote," August 26, 2013, http://www.theblaze.com/stories/2013/08/26/cass-sunsteins-new-presiden-tial-appointment-is-almost-hard-to-believe-especially-considering-a-pa-per-he-once-wrote/ (accessed December 27, 2013).

_____, "Words Matter 2012 Presents: Clips From Obama's 'Apology Tour,'" October 23, 2012, http://www.theblaze.com/stories/2012/10/23/words-matter-2012-presents-clips-from-obamas-apology-tour/ (accessed January 11, 2014).

The Center for Media and Democracy, "Congressional Action on the Iraq War," http://www.sourcewatch.org/index.php?title=Congressional_ac-tions_on_the_Iraq_War (accessed February 14, 2014).

The Center for Public Integrity, "Obama rewards big bundlers with jobs, com-missions, stimulus money, government contracts, and more," June 15, 2011, http://www.publicintegrity.org/2011/06/15/4880/obama-rewards-big-bun-dlers-jobs-commissions-stimulus-money-government-contracts-and (ac-cessed January 2, 2014).

The Cold War Museum, The Fall of the Soviet Union, http://www.coldwar.org/articles/90s/fall_of_the_soviet_union.asp (accessed December 18, 2013).

The Constitution, http://constitutionus.com/ (accessed December 18, 2013).

The Declaratory Act, http://www.ushistory.org/declaration/related/declara-tory.htm (accessed December 9, 2014).

The Economist, "America's border troubles, north and south," January 25, 2005, http://www.economist.com/node/4318265 (accessed December 18, 2013).

The Econ Review, "President Nixon Imposes Wage and Price Controls," http://www.econreview.com/events/wageprice1971b.htm (accessed December 22, 2013).

The Federal Reserve Board, Remarks by Governor Ben S. Bernanke, "Deflation: Making Sure 'It' Doesn't Happen Here," November 21, 2002, http://www.federalreserve.gov/BOARDDOCS/SPEECHES/2002/20021121/default.htm (accessed December 24, 2013).

The Founder's Constitution, Article 1, Section 8, Clause 2, "Alexander Hamilton: Report on Public Credit," http://press-pubs.uchicago.edu/founders/documents/a1_8_2s5.html (accessed February 5, 2014).

_____, "Article 1, Section 9, Clause 8," http://press-pubs.uchicago.edu/founders/tocs/a1_9_8.html (accessed December 18, 2013).

_____, "Article 1, Section 8, Clause 18," The Necessary and Proper Clause, http://press-pubs.uchicago.edu/founders/print_documents/a1_8_18s5.html (accessed December 23, 2013).

_____, "Constitutional Government," http://press-pubs.uchicago.edu/founders/documents/v1ch17s9.html (accessed December 21, 2013).

_____, Patrick Henry, Virginia Ratifying Convention, http://press-pubs.uchicago.edu/founders/documents/preambles14.html (accessed December 9, 2014)

_____, Republican Government, "Hamilton's Report on Manufactures," http://press-pubs.uchicago.edu/founders/documents/v1ch4s31.html (accessed December 22, 2013).

The Frankfurt School, http://www.marxists.org/subject/frankfurt-school/ (accessed December 22, 2013).

The Free Dictionary, George Armstrong Custer, http://encyclopedia2.thefreedictionary.com/Custer%2c+George+Armstrong (accessed December 27, 2013).

_____, "Federalism," http://www.thefreedictionary.com/federal (accessed January 29, 2014).

_____, "Legal Positivism," http://legal-dictionary.thefreedictionary.com/Legal+Positivism (accessed July 30, 2014).

_____, "Necessary and Proper Clause," http://legal-dictionary.thefreedictionary.com/Necessary+and+Proper+Clause (accessed December 10, 2014).

_____, "Separation of Powers," http://legal-dictionary.thefree-dictionary.com/Balance+of+powers (accessed December 9, 2014).

_____, "Social Democracy," http://www.thefreedictionary.com/social+democracy (accessed December 22, 2013).

_____, "State's Rights," http://legal-dictionary.thefreediction-ary.com/States%27+Rights (accessed January 2, 2014).

The Guardian, "It means Yoweri Museveni wants to be Uganda's president for life," http://www.theguardian.com/world/2011/feb/16/uganda-election-yoweri-museveni-kizza-besigye (accessed July 27, 2014)

_____, "Wall Street protesters: over-educated, under-employed and angry," http://www.theguardian.com/world/2011/sep/19/wall-street-pro-testers-angry (accessed December 26, 2013).

The Heritage Foundation, FDR's Second Bill of Rights, http://www.heritage.org/initiatives/first-principles/primary-sources/fdrs-second-bill-of-rights (accessed December 9, 2014).

The History Place: Impeachment Proceedings, "Andrew Johnson," http://www.historyplace.com/unitedstates/impeachments/johnson.htm (accessed December 29, 2013).

_____, "Bill Clinton," http://www.historyplace.com/unitedstates/impeachments/clinton.htm (accessed December 29, 2013).

_____, "The Triumph of Hitler," http://www.his-toryplace.com/worldwar2/triumph/tr-fuehrer.htm (accessed July 27, 2014).

_____, World War Two In Europe, "Hitler's Enabling Act," http://www.historyplace.com/worldwar2/timeline/enabling.htm (accessed December 2, 2014).

The Library of Congress, "Alexander Hamilton: A Resource Guide," http://www.loc.gov/rr/program/bib/hamilton/memory.html (accessed February 5, 2014).

The Literature Network, http://www.online-literature.com/orwell/ani-malfarm/10/ (accessed December 18, 2013).

The New York Times, "Articles about Blackwater Worldwide," http://topics.nytimes.com/top/news/business/companies/blackwater_usa/index.html (accessed December 27, 2013).

The Obama File, "Cloward-Piven Strategy," http://www.theobamafile.com/_opinion/Cloward-Piven.html (accessed December 24, 2013).

The Oval, "Obama: Rich should pay 'fair share' of debt reduction," July 25, 2011, http://content.usatoday.com/communities/theoval/post/2011/07/obama-opposes-short-term-debt-deal-from-boehner/1#.UwPh0IVfTKk (accessed February 18, 2014).

The Quotation Collect, Ronald Wilson Reagan http://www.quotationcollection.com/author/Ronald-Wilson-Reagan/quotes (accessed December 18, 2013).

_____, http://www.quotationcollection.com/author/Ronald-Wilson-Reagan/quotes (accessed December 18, 2013).

The Quotation Page, Alexander Hamilton, http://www.quotationspage.com/quote/27458.html (accessed July 27, 2014).

_____, John Adams, "But a Constitution of Government once changed from Freedom, can never be restored. Liberty, once lost, is lost forever," http://www.quotationspage.com/quote/34444.html (accessed January 2, 2014).

_____, John Quincy Adams, http://www.quotationspage.com/quote/32145.html (accessed December 26, 2014).

_____, Karl Marx http://www.quotationspage.com/quote/36121.html (accessed December 18, 2013).

_____, Voltaire, http://www.quotationspage.com/quotes/Voltaire (accessed January 6, 2014).

The Ronald Reagan Presidential Foundation and Library, "The Second American Revolution: Reaganomics," https://www.reaganfoundation.org/economic-policy.aspx (accessed December 26, 2013).

The Sovereign Investor Daily, "Have You Read the U.S. Constitution?," http://thesovereigninvestor.com/diversified-investments/have-you-read-the-u-s-constitution/ (accessed December 10, 2014).

The TSA Blog, "Texas House of Representatives Seeking to Ban Current TSA Pat-Down," http://blog.tsa.gov/2011/05/texas-house-of-representatives-seeking.html (accessed December 27, 2013).

The U.S. Constitution, "The First Bank of the United States," http://www.nps.gov/history/history/online_books/butowsky2/constitution5.htm (accessed December 21, 2013).

The United States Constitution, http://constitutionus.com/ (accessed December 23, 2013).

The Virginia Declaration of Rights, Constitution Society, http://www.constitution.org/bcp/virg_dor.htm (accessed December 10, 2014).

The Washington Post, "House Democrats pass historical health-care legislation," http://www.washingtonpost.com/wp-srv/special/politics/votes/house/finalhealthcare/ (accessed December 27, 2013).

_____, "McDonald's may get its way with health-care law," http://voices.washingtonpost.com/blog-post/2010/10/mcdonalds_may_get_its_way_with.html (accessed December 21, 2013).

The War of 1812, http://www.gatewayno.com/history/war1812.html (accessed December 22, 2013).

The Washington Times, "Obama spending hits new records," March 8, 2011, http://www.washingtontimes.com/news/2011/mar/8/obama-spending-hits-new-records/ (accessed January 15, 2014).

The Weekly Standard, "Obama's Regulatory Rampage," January 28, 2013, http://www.weeklystandard.com/articles/obama-s-regulatory-rampage_696381.html (accessed January 2, 2014).

The White House, "Andrew Johnson," http://www.whitehouse.gov/about/presidents/andrewjohnson (accessed December 29, 2013).

_____, "Theodore Roosevelt," http://www.whitehouse.gov/about/presidents/theodoreroosevelt (accessed December 23, 2013).

_____, "We can't wait," http://www.whitehouse.gov/economy/jobs/we-cant-wait (accessed December 23, 2013).

_____, "Woodrow Wilson," http://www.whitehouse.gov/about/presidents/woodrowwilson/ (accessed December 23, 2013).

Think Exist.com, Albert Einstein Quotes, http://thinkexist.com/quotation/insanity-doing_the_same_thing_over_and_over_again/15511.html (accessed December 2, 2014).

_____, Benjamin Franklin Quotes, "Those who desire to give up freedom in order to gain security will not have, nor do they deserve, either one," http://thinkexist.com/quotation/those_who_desire_to_give_up_freedom_in_order_to/12888.html (accessed January 2, 2014).

Thinking Catholic Strategic Center, Obama Quote, "But the Supreme Court never ventured into the issues of redistribution of wealth, and more basic issues such as political and economic justice in society," http://www.thinking-catholic-strategic-center.com/anti-american-quotes.html (accessed January 2, 2014).

_____, Obama Quote, "In America, we have this strong bias toward individual action," http://www.thinking-catholic-strategic-center.com/anti-american-quotes.html (accessed January 2, 2014).

This Nation.com, "The Constitutional Convention," http://thisnation.com/textbook/constitution-convention.html (accessed February 5, 2014).

_____, "What is an Executive Order," http://thisnation.com/question/040.html (accessed December 21, 2013).

Thomas, Andrew, American Thinker, "Beware the Counterrevolution," August 16, 2009, http://www.americanthinker.com/articles/2009/08/beware_the_counterrevolution.html (accessed December 10, 2014).

Thompson, Loren, Forbes, "How To Waste $100 Billion: Weapons That Didn't Work Out," December 19, 2011, http://www.forbes.com/sites/lorenthompson/2011/12/19/how-to-waste-100-billion-weapons-that-didnt-work-out/ (accessed December 23, 2013).

Tiberius Gracchus, http://www.roman-empire.net/republic/tib-gracchus.html (accessed December 31, 2013).

Time Magazine, Clinton V. Congress: The Race is set, http://content.time.com/time/magazine/article/0,9171,983003,00.html (accessed December 18, 2013).

Trottman, Melanie, Jess Bravin and Michael R. Crittenden, The Wall Street journal, "Court Throws Out Recess Picks," January 25, 2013, http://online.wsj.com/news/articles/SB10001424127887324039504578263772492524536 (accessed December 18, 2013).

Trumbore, Brian, Buy And Hold, "William Duer and the Crash of 1792," http://www.buyandhold.com/bh/en/education/history/2000/8699.html (accessed December 21, 2013).

Two Documents on Indian Removal (1830s), http://www.pinzler.com/ushistory/indremsupp.html (accessed December 27, 2013).

United States History, "No Taxation Without Representation," http://www.u-s-history.com/pages/h640.html (accessed December 10, 2014).

United States Senate, "H.R. 3590 (Patient Protection and Affordable Care Act)," http://www.senate.gov/legislative/LIS/roll_call_lists/roll_call_vote_cfm.cfm?congress=111&session=1&vote=00396 (accessed December 27, 2013).

U.S. Constitution Online, Amendment 10, http://www.usconstitution.net/xconst_Am10.html (accessed December 9, 2014).

_____, "Amendment 14," http://www.usconstitution.net/xconst_Am14.html (accessed February 5, 2014).

_____, "Article 1 Section 7," http://www.usconstitution.net/xconst_A1Sec7.html (accessed December 4, 2014).

_____, "Article 1 Section 8," http://www.usconstitution. net/xconst_A1Sec8.html (accessed December 26, 2013).

_____, "Articles of Confederation," http://www.usconstitution.net/consttop_arti.html (accessed January 28, 2014).

_____, «Checks and Balances,» http://www.usconstitution.net/consttop_cnb.html (accessed January 29, 2014).

_____, Constitutional Amendments, The Amendment process, http://www.usconstitution.net/constam.html#process (accessed December 18, 2013).

_____, "Debts, Supremacy Oaths," http://www.usconstitution.net/xconst_A6.html (accessed February 5, 2014).

_____, "Rhode Island's Ratification," http://www.usconstitution.net/rat_ri.html (accessed January 2, 2014).

_____, "The I Have a Dream Speech," http://www.usconstitution.net/dream.html (accessed January 9, 2014).

_____, "The Tenth Amendment," http://www.usconstitution.net/xconst_Am10.html (accessed December 18, 2013).

U.S. Debt Clock.org, http://www.usdebtclock.org/ (accessed December 18, 2013).

U.S. Department of Defense, http://www.defense.gov/news/newsarticle.aspx?id=65432 (accessed December 18, 2013).

U.S. Government: The Balance of Power, http://library.thinkquest.org/J0110221/USGovernment.html (accessed December 21, 2013).

U.S. Government Spending, http://www.usgovernmentspending.com/debt_deficit_history (accessed December 21, 2013).

U.S. History, "Alexander Hamilton," http://www.u-s-history.com/pages/h367.html (accessed February 5, 2014).

_____, "Alien and Sedition Act," http://www.ushistory.org/us/19e.asp (accessed December 22, 2013).

_____, "Federalist Party,' http://www.u-s-history.com/pages/h445.html (accessed December 28, 2013).

_____, "Henry Kissinger," http://www.u-s-history.com/pages/h1966.html (accessed January 9, 2014).

_____, "Lyndon Johnson's Great Society," http://www.ushistory.org/us/56e.asp (accessed December 18, 2013).

_____, "Massachusetts Bay Colony," http://www.u-s-history.com/pages/h572.html (accessed December 22, 2013).

_____, "Report on Public Credit," http://www.u-s-history.com/pages/h441.html (accessed December 24, 2013).

_____, "Remember the Maine!" http://www.ushistory.org/us/44c.asp (accessed December 28, 2013).

_____, "Second Bank of the United States," http://www.u-s-history.com/pages/h256.html (accessed December 21, 2013).

_____, "Spanish-American War," http://www.u-s-history.com/pages/h3617.html (accessed December 22, 2013).

_____, "Spoils System," http://www.u-s-history.com/pages/h326.html (accessed December 22, 2013).

_____, "The Constitutional Convention," http://www.u-s-history.com/pages/h368.html (accessed February 5, 2014).

_____, "The Peculiar Institution," http://www.ushistory.org/us/27.asp (accessed January 2, 2014).

_____, "The Quartering Act of 1765," http://www.ushistory.org/declaration/related/quartering.htm (accessed December 23, 2013).

_____, "The Stamp Act," http://www.ushistory.org/declaration/related/stampact.htm (accessed December 23, 2013).

_____, "The New Deal", http://www.u-s-history.com/pages/h1851.html (accessed December 22, 2013).

_____, "The Trail of Tears — The Indian Removals," http://www.ushistory.org/us/24f.asp (accessed December 27, 2013).

_____, "The Trust Buster," http://www.ushistory.org/us/43b.asp (accessed December 22, 2013).

_____, "Truman Defeats Dewey," http://www.u-s-history.com/pages/h898.html (accessed December 18, 2013).

USHistory.org, Benjamin Franklin Quotes, http://www.ushistory.org/franklin/quotable/singlehtml.htm (accessed January 4, 2015).

_____, "The First bank of the United States," http://www.ushistory.org/tour/first-bank.htm (accessed December 22, 2013).

USLegal: Definitions, "Enumerated Power Law & Legal Definition," http://definitions.uslegal.com/e/enumerated-power/ (accessed December 21, 2013).

USLegal: Definitions, "Implied Power Law & Legal Definition," http://definitions.uslegal.com/i/implied-power/ (accessed December 21, 2013).

U.S. Mexican War, http://www.pbs.org/kera/usmexicanwar/war/ (accessed December 22, 2013).

Vadum, Matthew, Frontpage Mag, "Amnesty and Attack on American Workers," http://www.frontpagemag.com/2013/matthew-vadum/amnesty-and-the-attack-on-american-workers/ (accessed December 2, 2014).

Vance, Laurence M., Lew Rockwell.com, "Jeffersonian principles," http://archive.lewrockwell.com/vance/vance17.html (accessed December 23, 2013).

Vincent, Isabel, New York Post, "The case against Charlie Rangle," http://nypost.com/2009/10/04/the-case-against-charlie-rangel/ (accessed July 30, 2014).

Wallison, Peter J. & Edward J. Pinto, Forbes, "A Government-Mandated Housing Bubble," February 16. 2009, http://www.forbes.com/2009/02/13/housing-bubble-subprime-opinions-contributors_0216_peter_wallison_edward_pinto.html (accessed December 26, 2013).

Wander, Andrew, The Guardian/The Observer, "A history of terror: Al-Qaeda 1988-2008," July 12, 2008, http://www.theguardian.com/world/2008/jul/13/history.alqaida (accessed December 27, 2013).

Washington Times 8-4-11 http://communities.washingtontimes.com/neighborhood/stimulus/2011/aug/4/debt-ceiling-agreement-fiscal-band-aid-mortal-woun/ (accessed December 18, 2013).

Wassener, Bettina and Matthew Saltmarsh, New York Times, "China Urges U.S. to Protect Creditors by Raising Debt," July 14, 2011, http://www.nytimes.com/2011/07/15/business/global/china-urges-us-to-take-responsible-action-on-debt.html?_r=0 (accessed January 9, 2014).

Watergate.info, "Articles of Impeachment," http://watergate.info/impeachment/articles-of-impeachment (accessed July 30, 2014).

Waters, Richard, The Big Read, "Technology: Rise of the replicants," http://www.ft.com/intl/cms/s/2/dc895d54-a2bf-11e3-9685-00144feab7de.html#axzz2vnXoaFPR (accessed December 9, 2014).

Watson, Paul Joseph, Infowars.com, "10 Ways In Which China Humiliates The United States," http://www.prisonplanet.com/10-ways-in-which-china-humiliates-the-united-states.html (accessed January 9, 2014).

_____, "Ron Paul Likens Obama to "Dicta-tor" Over 'Recess Appointments,'" January 6, 2012, http://www.infowars.com/ron-paul-likens-obama-to-dictator-over-recess-appointments/ (accessed December 29, 2013).

Web Guide, Primary Documents in American History, The Articles of Con-federation, http://www.loc.gov/rr/program/bib/ourdocs/articles.html (accessed December 18, 2013).

Wells, H. G., A Short History of the World, Bartleby.com, "The French Revo-lution and the Restoration of Monarchy in France," http://www.bartleby.com/86/55.html (accessed November 24, 2014).

Wheeler, Winslow, Breaking Defense, "The Military Imbalance: How The U.S. Outspends The World," March, 16, 2012, http://breakingdefense.com/2012/03/the-military-imbalance-how-the-u-s-outspends-the-world/ (accessed December 23, 2013).

White House, Warren Harding, http://www.whitehouse.gov/about/presi-dents/warrenharding (accessed December 22, 2013).

Wilde, Robert, About.com , "French Revolution 101," http://europeanhistory.about.com/od/thefrenchrevolution/p/ovfrenchrev.htm (accessed November 24, 2014).

_____, "The Terror," http://europeanhistory.about.com/od/thefrenchrevolution/a/hfr7.htm (accessed January 7, 2014).

Williams, Nathan, History News Network, "How Did the United States Defeat the Barbary Pirates?," http://hnn.us/article/287 (accessed December 22, 2013).

Wilson, Scott, with Colum Lynch and Karen DeYoung, The Washington Post, "Obama administration seeks more U.N. authority to intervene in Libya," http://www.washingtonpost.com/politics/as-gaddafi-gains-wests-window-closes/2011/03/16/ABlGYNh_story.html (accessed February 14, 2014).

Wolverton, Joe, New American, "Obama Signs 2013 NDAA: May Still Arrest, Detain Citizens Without Charge," January 5, 2013 http://www.thenewamer-ican.com/usnews/constitution/item/14120-obama-signs-2013-ndaa-may-still-arrest-detain-citizens-without-charge (accessed January 2, 2013).

Wright, C. Edmund, American Thinker, "Why Geithner and Rangel Mat-ter," January 16, 2009, http://www.americanthinker.com/2009/01/why_geithner_and_rangel_matter.html (accessed July 30, 2014).

Yahoo News, Obama to Dems: I'll act with or without Congress, http://news. yahoo.com/obama-dems-39-ll-act-without-congress-004736977--politics. html (accessed July 30, 2014).

Yale Law School: The Avalon Project, Declaration of the Rights of Man – 1789, http:// avalon.law.yale.edu/18th_century/rightsof.asp (accessed November 24, 2014).

————————————————————, "Ratification of the Constitution by the State of New York; July 26, 1788," http://avalon.law.yale.edu/18th_century/ratny.asp (accessed January 2, 2014).

————————————————————, "Ratification of the Constitution by the State of Virginia; June 26, 1788," http://avalon.law.yale.edu/18th_century/ratva.asp (accessed January 2, 2014).

————————————————————, "The Tonkin Gulf Incident," http:// avalon.law.yale.edu/20th_century/tonkin-g.asp (accessed February 14, 2014).

————————————————————, "U.S. Constitution Section 1," http:// avalon.law.yale.edu/18th_century/art1.asp (accessed Dec ember 18, 2013).

————————————————————, "Washington's farewell Address 1796," http://avalon.law.yale.edu/18th_century/washing.asp (accessed December 23, 2013).

————————————————————, "War Powers Resolution," http://avalon.law.yale.edu/20th_century/warpower.asp (accessed February 14, 2014).

Yogi Berra Quotes, http://www.mindspring.com/~hsstern/maewest/y_berra. htm (ccessed December 18, 2013).

You Tube, "2001 Obama WBEZ Interview," https://www.youtube.com/ watch?v=OkpdNtTgQNM (accessed July 30, 2014).

————————, "America's Shame: Obama Calls U.S. «Arrogant» & «Dismissive» in Speech in France," http://www.youtube.com/watch?v=OLZer0P9l1M (accessed December 26, 2013).

————————, "Apology Tours," http://www.youtube.com/ watch?v=DAXA0WVwxiE (accessed December 18, 2013).

————————, Bush: «I've abandoned free market principles to save the free market system,» http://www.youtube.com/watch?v=Tmi8cJG0BJo (accessed January 6, 2014).

————————, "Congressman says 'I don't worry about the Constitution'," https:// www.youtube.com/watch?v=lgh-q4t0kzM (accessed December 10, 2014).

_____, "Fundamentally Transform America" http://www.youtube.com/watch?v=_cqN4NIEtOY (accessed December 18, 2013).

_____, "Fundamentally Transform America," http://www.youtube.com/watch?v=KrefKCaV8m4 (accessed December 18, 2013).

_____, "Income Tax Cut, JFK Hopes To Spur Economy 1962/8/13," http://www.youtube.com/watch?v=aEdXrfIMdiU (accessed December 22, 2013).

_____, "Michael Savage Explains the Mental Disorder of Liberalism," http://www.youtube.com/watch?v=AEwVcsHnf3o (accessed December 20, 2013).

_____, "Not a Christian country," http://www.youtube.com/watch?v=tmC3IevZiik (accessed December 18, 2013).

_____, "Obama: Constitution Flawed - Missing Redistribution of Wealth," http://www.youtube.com/watch?v=sMJS4CP3OC0 (accessed December 26, 2013).

_____, "Obama if you like your plan you can keep your plan," https://www.youtube.com/watch?v=wfl55GgHr5E (accessed December 10, 2014).

_____, "Obama small town guns and religion comments," http://www.youtube.com/watch?v=DTxXUufI3jA (accessed January 7, 2014).

_____, "Obama: If You've Got A Business, You Didn't Build That," http://www.youtube.com/watch?v=YKjPI6no5ng (accessed January 2, 2014).

_____, "Obama on single payer health insurance," http://www.youtube.com/watch?v=fpAyan1fXCE (accessed February 4, 2014).

_____, "Obama's Millionaires and Billionaires," http://www.youtube.com/watch?v=Koi_5o9mTsU (accessed December 31, 2013).

_____, "Obama Spreading the wealth around," https://www.youtube.com/watch?v=OoqI5PSRcXM (accessed December 9, 2014).

_____, "Obama Supports Occupy Wall Street," http://www.youtube.com/watch?v=aH99q2CRNZg (accessed January 15, 2014).

_____, "PETE STARK: - The Federal Government can do most anything in this country," https://www.youtube.com/watch?v=W1-eBz8hyoE (accessed 12-2-14).

_____, "Ron Paul, Dennis Kucinich on «Freedom Watch» talk Obama's Illegal, Unconstitutional Attack on Libya," http://www.youtube.com/watch?v=Se_YPdp5T1Q (accessed December 29, 2013).

_____, «Security» patrols stationed at polling places in Philly, http://www.youtube.com/watch?v=neGbKHyGuHU (accessed December 24, 2013).

_____, "Spread the Wealth Around," http://www.youtube.com/watch?v=RZcEHLr4gBg (accessed December 18-13

Your Dictionary, "Equality Before the Law," http://www.yourdictionary.com/equality-before-the-law#law (accessed December 18, 2013)

_____, "Republic," http://www.yourdictionary.com/republic (accessed January 29, 2014).

Zallman, Amy, About.com, "War in Afghanistan -- the History behind the U.S. War in Afghanistan," http://terrorism.about.com/od/warinafghanistan/ss/AfghanistanWar_3.htm (accessed December 27, 2013).

Zibel, Eve, Fox News, "Biden: 'We Misread How Bad the Economy Was,'" July 5, 2009, http://www.foxnews.com/politics/2009/07/05/biden-misread-bad-economy/ (accessed December 20, 2013).